lonely planet

Jamaica

Christopher P Baker

LONELY PLANET PUBLICATIONS
Melbourne • Oakland • London • Paris

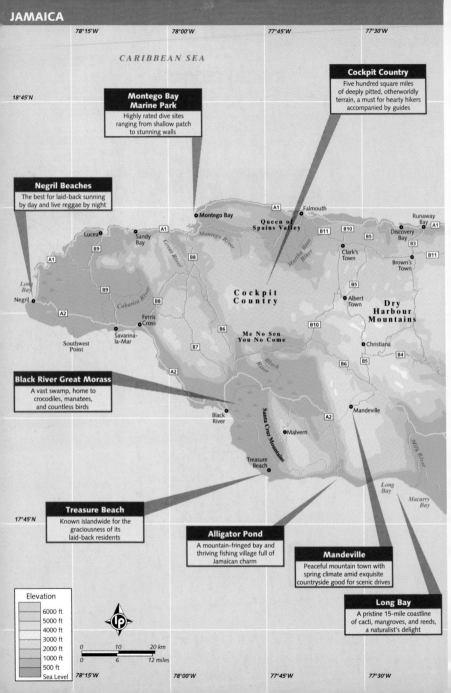

JAMAICA

CARIBBEAN SEA

Montego Bay Marine Park
Highly rated dive sites ranging from shallow patch to stunning walls

Cockpit Country
Five hundred square miles of deeply pitted, otherworldly terrain, a must for hearty hikers accompanied by guides

Negril Beaches
The best for laid-back sunning by day and live reggae by night

Black River Great Morass
A vast swamp, home to crocodiles, manatees, and countless birds

Treasure Beach
Known islandwide for the graciousness of its laid-back residents

Alligator Pond
A mountain-fringed bay and thriving fishing village full of Jamaican charm

Mandeville
Peaceful mountain town with spring climate amid exquisite countryside good for scenic drives

Long Bay
A pristine 15-mile coastline of cacti, mangroves, and reeds, a naturalist's delight

18°45'N
17°45'N
78°15'W
78°00'W
77°45'W
77°30'W

Montego Bay
Falmouth
Runaway Bay
Lucea
Sandy Bay
Discovery Bay
Brown's Town
Clark's Town
Queen of Spains Valley
Negril
Long Bay
Ferris Cross
Savanna-la-Mar
Southwest Point
Albert Town
Christiana
Cockpit Country
Dry Harbour Mountains
Me No Sen You No Come
Black River
Mandeville
Malvern
Treasure Beach
Santa Cruz Mountains
Long Bay
Macarry Bay

Montego River
Great River
Cabarita River
Martha Brae River
Black River
Milk River

A1, B11, B10, B5, B3, B9, B8, B7, B6, B4, A2

Elevation
6000 ft
5000 ft
4000 ft
3000 ft
2000 ft
1000 ft
500 ft
Sea Level

0   10   20 km
0   6   12 miles

Contents

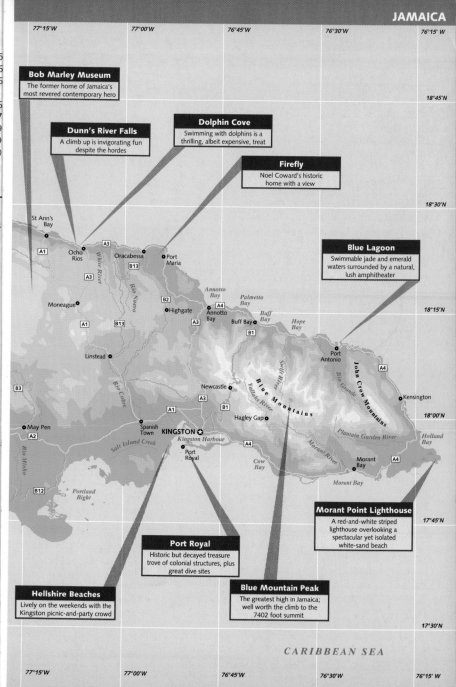

Bob Marley Museum
The former home of Jamaica's most revered contemporary hero

Dunn's River Falls
A climb up is invigorating fun despite the hordes

Dolphin Cove
Swimming with dolphins is a thrilling, albeit expensive, treat

Firefly
Noel Coward's historic home with a view

Blue Lagoon
Swimmable jade and emerald waters surrounded by a natural, lush amphitheater

Morant Point Lighthouse
A red-and-white striped lighthouse overlooking a spectacular yet isolated white-sand beach

Port Royal
Historic but decayed treasure trove of colonial structures, plus great dive sites

Hellshire Beaches
Lively on the weekends with the Kingston picnic-and-party crowd

Blue Mountain Peak
The greatest high in Jamaica; well worth the climb to the 7402 foot summit

CARIBBEAN SEA

Jamaica
3rd edition – January 2003
First published – August 1996

Published by
Lonely Planet Publications Pty Ltd ABN 36 005 607 983
90 Maribyrnong St, Footscray, Victoria 3011, Australia

Lonely Planet Offices
Australia Locked Bag 1, Footscray, Victoria 3011
USA 150 Linden St, Oakland, CA 94607
UK 10a Spring Place, London NW5 3BH
France 1 rue du Dahomey, 75011 Paris

Photographs
Many of the images in this guide are available for licensing from Lonely Planet Images.
W www.lonelyplanetimages.com

Front cover photograph
Beach along Negril strip (Greg Johnston)

ISBN 1 74059 161 5

Although the authors and Lonely Planet try to make the information as accurate as possible, we accept no responsibility for any loss, injury or inconvenience sustained by anyone using this book.

Contents

INTRODUCTION

FACTS ABOUT JAMAICA

REGGAE 'N' RIDDIMS

FACTS FOR THE VISITOR

GETTING THERE & AWAY

GETTING AROUND

MONTEGO BAY & NORTHWEST COAST

SOUTH COAST & CENTRAL HIGHLANDS   247

KINGSTON & SOUTHERN PLAINS   277

BLUE MOUNTAINS & SOUTHEAST COAST 326

LANGUAGE 340

JAMAICA MAP INDEX

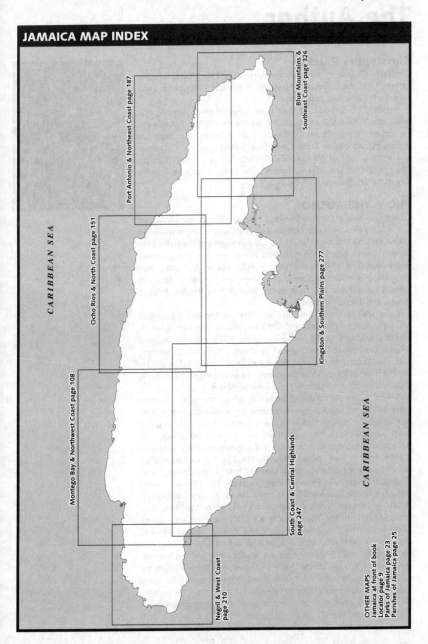

CARIBBEAN SEA

CARIBBEAN SEA

Port Antonio & Northeast Coast page 187

Blue Mountains & Southeast Coast page 326

Ocho Rios & North Coast page 151

Kingston & Southern Plains page 277

Montego Bay & Northwest Coast page 108

South Coast & Central Highlands page 247

Negril & West Coast page 210

OTHER MAPS
Jamaica at front of book
Locator page 9
Parks of Jamaica page 23
Parishes of Jamaica page 25

The Author

Christopher P Baker

Christopher is from Yorkshire, England. He earned his BA (Honours) in geography at the University of London, plus Masters' degrees in Latin American Studies and education.

In 1980 Chris settled in California and has since made his living as a travel and natural sciences writer for leading publications worldwide. He authored Lonely Planet's *Bahamas, Turks & Caicos* guidebook; has written guidebooks on Cuba, Costa Rica, Puerto Rico, and California; and is the author of *Mi Moto Fidel: Motorcycling Through Castro's Cuba*. Chris's many awards include the 1998 Caribbean Tourism Organization's 'Journalist of the Year.'

FROM THE AUTHOR

I'd like to express my sincere thanks to the many friends, acquaintances, and industry personnel who facilitated my research and helped make this edition possible. Above all, thanks to Fay Pickersgill and the staff of the Jamaica Tourist Board; and to Roland Alonzi, my dear friend Andrea Hutchinson, and all the other staff of Peter Martin Associates. Also deserving of special thanks are Michael Campbell and Dulcie Moody of Island Car Rentals; and Gordon 'Butch' Stewart, Amy Brindley, Baldwin Powell, and the staff of Sandals.

I also wish to thank Chris Blackwell, Brad Packer, and the staff of Island Outpost; Lyla Naseem and Cindy Tanenbaum of Patrice Tanaka & Co Public Relations; Cheryl Andrews of Cheryl Andrews Public Relations; Roberta Garzaroli and Kim Draganchuk of Jensen Boga Public Relations; Marcella Martinez of Martinez Public Relations; Darlene Salzer of Blue Sky Public Relations; and Shantini Ramakrishnan of Spring O'Brien Public Relations, all of whom provided invaluable assistance.

Several friends demonstrated the best of Jamaican hospitality, notably Vernon Chin of Seashell Inn, who selflessly shepherded me around Montego Bay and lodged me in his apartment; my dear friend Kerry-Ann Baker, who lodged me in Kingston and turned me on to Carnival; and, last but not least, a coterie of friends and acquaintances who each contributed in their own special ways: Shireen Aga and Barbara Walker, Nancy Beckham, Frederick Caesar, Doreen Clarke, Ginny Craven, Judith Donaldson, Yoshabelle Emanuel, Ziggy Garrison, Elena Gervan, Daniel and Sylvie Grizzle, Jason and Sally Henzell, Eleanor Hussey, Gail Jackson, Robert & Terri Lee, Barbara Lulich, Ann Lyons, Peter McIntosh, Tony Moncrieffe, Terri-Ann Morgan, Derrick O'Connor, Andreas Oberli, Michelle Palomino, Sharon Powell, Roma Pringle, Veronica Probst, Annabella & Peter Proudlock, Maggie Rivera, Paul Salmon, Greer-Ann Saulter, Gary Sewell, Prudence Simpson, Jenn Sparrow, Michael Stephenson, Melanie Wernig, Sherryl White-McDowell, and Rebekah Williams.

Thanks, too, to many other readers and fellow travelers who shared insights and experiences along the way, and to my many other wonderful Jamaican friends, each of whom brightened my time in Jamaica in their own special ways.

This book is dedicated with love to Sheri.

This Book

Christopher P Baker researched and updated this 3rd edition of Lonely Planet's *Jamaica*. He also authored the book's 1st and 2nd editions.

FROM THE PUBLISHER

Maria Donohoe commissioned this edition of *Jamaica* and oversaw its development. David Zingarelli coordinated the US production effort. Text was edited with keen eyes and deft hands by Jeff Campbell and impeccably proofed by Paul Sheridan. Tammy Fortin pitched in with map proofing. In-house production was an all-hands-on-deck affair thanks to the help of Susan Rimerman, Maria Donohoe, Michele Posner, Wendy Smith, Graham Neale, Erin Corrigan, Elaine Merrill and Vivek Waglé.

Cartographic kudos go to Sean Brandt, Alison Lyall, Annette Olson, Bart Wright, Kat Smith and Graham Neale.

The book was skillfully designed by Candice Jacobus, who also crafted the color pages. Andreas Schueller provided production support. Margaret Livingston designed the cover and Ruth Askevold handled its production. Susan Rimerman graciously provided guidance during the layout process. Illustrations were created by Justin Marler, Hugh D'Andrade, Hayden Foell, Shelley Firth and Jim Swanson.

Foreword

ABOUT LONELY PLANET GUIDEBOOKS

The story begins with a classic travel adventure: Tony and Maureen Wheeler's 1972 journey across Europe and Asia to Australia. There was no useful information about the overland trail then, so Tony and Maureen published the first Lonely Planet guidebook to meet a growing need.

From a kitchen table, Lonely Planet has grown to become the largest independent travel publisher in the world, with offices in Melbourne (Australia), Oakland (USA), London (UK) and Paris (France).

Today Lonely Planet guidebooks cover the globe. There is an ever-growing list of books and information in a variety of media. Some things haven't changed. The main aim is still to make it possible for adventurous travelers to get out there – to explore and better understand the world.

At Lonely Planet we believe travelers can make a positive contribution to the countries they visit – if they respect their host communities and spend their money wisely. Since 1986 a percentage of the income from each book has been donated to aid projects and human rights campaigns, and, more recently, to wildlife conservation.

> Although inclusion in a guidebook usually implies a recommendation, we cannot list every good place. Exclusion does not necessarily imply criticism. In fact, there are a number of reasons why we might exclude a place – sometimes it is simply inappropriate to encourage an influx of travelers.

UPDATES & READER FEEDBACK

Things change – prices go up, schedules change, good places go bad and bad places go bankrupt. Nothing stays the same. So, if you find things better or worse, recently opened or long-since closed, please tell us and help make the next edition even more accurate and useful.

Lonely Planet thoroughly updates each guidebook as often as possible – usually every two years, although for some destinations the gap can be longer. Between editions, up-to-date information is available in our free, quarterly *Planet Talk* newsletter and monthly email bulletin *Comet*. The *Upgrades* section of our website (**W** www.lonelyplanet.com) is also regularly updated by Lonely Planet authors, and the site's *Scoop* section covers news and current affairs relevant to travelers. Lastly, the *Thorn Tree* bulletin board and *Postcards* section carry unverified, but fascinating, reports from travelers.

Tell us about it! We genuinely value your feedback. A well-traveled team at Lonely Planet reads and acknowledges every email and letter we receive and ensures that every morsel of information finds its way to the relevant authors, editors and cartographers.

Everyone who writes to us will find their name listed in the next edition of the appropriate guidebook and will receive the latest issue of *Comet* or *Planet Talk*. The very best contributions will be rewarded with a free guidebook.

We may edit, reproduce and incorporate your comments in Lonely Planet products such as guidebooks, websites and digital products, so let us know if you don't want your comments reproduced or your name acknowledged.

How to contact Lonely Planet:
Online: **e** talk2us@lonelyplanet.com.au, **W** www.lonelyplanet.com
Australia: Locked Bag 1, Footscray, Victoria 3011
UK: 10a Spring Place, London NW5 3BH
USA: 150 Linden St, Oakland, CA 94607

Introduction

Jamaica enjoyed a reputation for exoticism long before Harry Belafonte lauded it as the 'Island in the Sun.' Swashbuckling movie hero Errol Flynn and his Hollywood pals cavorted here in the 1930s and 1940s, and England's equivalents – Noel Coward, Lawrence Olivier, and Sean Connery – had a penchant for this vibrant and colorful Caribbean island. Their interest attracted others, but even before the turn of the 19th century, visitors flocked to its shimmering beaches, ethereal mountains, and tropical climate.

Why choose Jamaica when there are more than 30 other Caribbean islands? Well, Jamaica still has a diversity and an allure that few other islands can claim.

Many islands have lovelier beaches (and more of them), but Jamaica has its fair share of stunners fringed by coral reefs. It also has the widest range of accommodations in the Caribbean, with something for every taste and budget. You can camp atop a coral cliff, choose a private villa with your own private beach, laugh your vacation away at a party-hearty, all-inclusive resort, or pursue a genteel lifestyle at a secluded retreat.

Water sports are well developed. So, too, are horseback riding, sport fishing, golf, and lazy river runs by bamboo raft. There are ample opportunities for birding, hiking, and many other offbeat adventures. You'll find colonial-era estates and work-a-day plantations to explore, along with centuries-old botanical gardens, forts, and other historical sites. And the bustling markets are a whirligig of color and motion.

Stray from the north coast resorts, and you'll discover radically different environments and terrain – perfect for exploring when you burn out on the beach.

The Jamaican experience arises from its complex culture, which aspires to be African in defiance of both the island's location and colonial heritage. Jamaica's evocative and somber history is rooted in the island's sugar-plantation economy: the slave era weighs heavy still in the national psyche.

To many people, Jamaica means reggae and Rastafarianism, both full of expressions

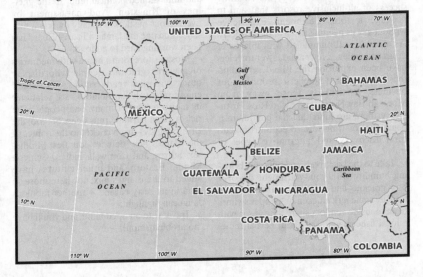

of hope, love, anger, and social discontent. Behind the Jamaica Tourist Board's clichés lies a country beset with widespread poverty and angst. Jamaica is a densely populated island struggling to escape dependency and debt. Colorful music and religion are opiates during hot nights, when Jamaicans move with a sensual ease, and everyone – dreadlocked local and clean-cut visitor alike – finds their nirvana in various combinations of reggae, reefers, and rum.

If you don't like reggae music (you can't escape it!), can't cope with poverty or power outages, and hate being hustled, then Jamaica is definitely not for you. To savor Jamaica properly, to appreciate what it is that makes people passionate about the place, it pays to be idiosyncratic. To rest content here you have to 'get' Jamaica, to take the punches in stride. If you can handle that, if you like travel with a raw edge, you'll love it.

Unfortunately, the 'real' Jamaica often battles to be seen amid the glare of the stereotypical image of big-spending commercial marketers: a sanitized playground of cocktails and water sports and pampered indulgence where everything is on the house and life is 'no problem, mon.' The trend has fueled (and been fueled by) the runaway success of all-inclusive resorts that aim to package a total Caribbean experience without guests needing to leave the property. As a result, and pummeled with images of drugs and violence, fewer and fewer travelers have been exploring the island serendipitously. Many small hoteliers are hurting for business, particularly those away from Montego Bay, Negril, and Ocho Rios. Fortunately, there are hints that the pendulum is beginning to swing toward ecotourism, cultural discovery, and 'alternative' types of travel.

Take to the backroads and hills and, bringing humility with you, you might discover how gracious and hospitable Jamaicans can be. Buy some jerk chicken or 'pepper swimp' from roadside vendors, share time at sea with a local fisherman, learn about herbal reme- dies from a 'market mammie' or a guide in 'de bush.' These are a few of the experiences that will give you a greater appreciation of the island and its flavorful, hard-pressed people.

Most of Jamaica is rugged and mountainous, reaching 7200 feet in the Blue Mountains, where the world's most sought-after coffee is grown. Pockets of wild, mysterious, thickly jungled terrain are so forbidding that during the 17th and 18th centuries bands of fiercely independent runaway slaves – the Maroons – survived here. Swampy wetlands harbor endangered crocodiles and manatees. Parched cactus-covered savannas line the south coast, where traditional fisherfolk draw their pirogues and nets up on otherwise lonesome dark-brown beaches. And visitors familiar with sleepy Caribbean capitals are surprised to find bustling Kingston a cornucopia of cosmopolitan culture that belies Jamaica's justly earned reputation for laidback, parochial ease.

Much has been written about crime and safety. True, Jamaica has its raw side, good for danger junkies. Yes, it's a volatile society, but violence rarely intrudes on the foreign visitor. It is mostly restricted to drug wars and impassioned political feuds in the ghettoes of Kingston. And harassment by overzealous hustlers is usually merely a nuisance, and one the Jamaica Tourist Board has been working hard to address.

Most visitors return home with memories of a warm, gracious people who display quick wits and ready smiles. The island enjoys relatively harmonious race relations: its motto is 'Out of many, one people.' The rich African heritage runs deep. So, too, the British legacy – from cricket to the names of the island's now defunct counties: Middlesex, Surrey, and Cornwall. Indian, Chinese, Middle Eastern, and other cultures have added to the island's mix, nowhere more so than in its zesty cuisine – another fabulous Jamaican highlight.

Travel with an open mind, and you'll have 'no problem, mon!'

Facts about Jamaica

HISTORY

Jamaica has a colorful and painful history marred by an undercurrent of violence and tyranny since European settlement in the early 1500s.

The Arawaks

Around AD 700 to 800, an Amerindian group, the Arawaks, arrived and settled the island. Experts say the Arawaks had originated in the Guianas of South America perhaps two thousand years earlier. After developing seafaring skills, they gradually moved northward through the Caribbean island chain.

The Arawaks were a short, slightly built race who lived in conical thatched shelters. Their communal villages were made up of several family clans, which were headed by a *cacique.*

The women gathered food, while the men hunted, fished, and tilled the fields. Jamaica's fertile soils yielded yams, maize, beans, spices, and cassava, which the Arawaks leached of poison and baked into cakes and fermented into beer.

The Arawaks had neither the wheel nor a written language, and they used neither beasts of burden nor metals (except for crude gold ornamentation). They evolved skills as potters, carvers, weavers, and boat builders. (Columbus was impressed with the scale of their massive canoes hewn from silk cotton trees.) The Arawaks were particularly adept at spinning and weaving cotton into clothing and hammocks – an Amerindian invention.

The Indians got fired up with maize alcohol, smoked dried leaves, and snorted a powdered drug through a meter-long tube called a *tabaco.*

They worshipped various gods who were thought to control rain, sun, wind, and hurricanes, and who were represented by *zemes,* idols of humans or animals. The Arawaks believed in a glorious afterlife in an idyllic place called *coyaba.*

Columbus & Spanish Settlement

When, on his second of four voyages to the New World, Columbus 'discovered' Jamaica on May 5, 1494, perhaps as many as 100,000 Arawaks inhabited the island they called Xaymaca ('Land of Wood and Water').

After anchoring for the night offshore in Bahía Santa Gloria (today's St Ann's Bay), Columbus sailed down the coast to a horse-shoe-shaped cove (today's Discovery Bay), where he had his men fire crossbows on a hostile group of Arawaks. He also set a fierce dog – the first the Arawaks had ever seen – on the Indians, thus establishing the vicious tone of future colonial occupation. Columbus took possession of the island for Spain and christened it Santo Jago. The Arawaks soon reappeared with peace offerings and feasted the strange newcomers throughout their brief stay.

On May 9, Columbus sailed on to El Golfo de Buen Tiempo (the Gulf of Good Weather; today's Montego Bay) and then on to Cuba. He returned later that year and explored the west and south coasts before again departing.

Columbus came back nine years later on his fourth and final voyage, still seeking a passage to Asia. Unfortunately, his worm-eaten ships were falling apart. He abandoned one, the *Gallega,* off Panama. Another sank off Hispaniola. Later, as he headed back to Hispaniola, storms forced him to seek shelter in Jamaica, and he barely made it to Bahía Santa Gloria. The two remaining vessels were so worm-riddled that Columbus and his 120 crewmen were forced to abandon ship and watch both vessels sink.

The luckless explorers spent almost a year marooned, and suffered desperately from disease and malnutrition. Finally, two officers paddled a canoe 150 miles to Hispaniola, where they chartered a ship to rescue the now broken explorer and his men. On June 29, 1504, Columbus sailed away, never again to return to Jamaica or the New World.

Nonetheless, Jamaica became Columbus' personal property. When he died in 1506, the title passed to his son Diego, whose descendants to this day carry the honorary title of Marquis of Jamaica. Diego appointed as governor one of his father's lieutenants, Don Juan de Esquivel. In 1510, Esquivel established a capital called Nueva Sevilla (New Seville) near present-day St Ann's Bay.

From their arrival, the Spaniards had exacted tribute from the Arawaks, whom they enslaved and killed off through hard labor and ill-treatment. European diseases decimated the Amerindians, too, for they had no resistance to the common cold, influenza, and more deadly ailments. By Esquivel's time, the Indian population had been virtually wiped out, and the Spaniards began importing slaves to Jamaica, the first arriving in 1517.

In 1534, the Spanish uprooted and created a new settlement on the south coast, Villa de la Vega (today's Spanish Town). However, the Spaniards never developed their Jamaican colony, and it languished as a post for provisioning ships en route between Spain and Central America.

The English Invasion

In 1654, Oliver Cromwell, Lord Protector of England, devised his ill-fated 'Grand Western Design' to destroy the Spanish trade monopoly and accrue English holdings in the Caribbean. He amassed a fleet, jointly led by Admiral William Penn and General Robert Venables, to conquer the Spanish-held Caribbean islands. The ill-equipped expedition was repulsed in April 1655 by Spanish forces on Hispaniola.

Penn and Venables then sailed to weakly defended Jamaica. On May 10, 1655, this expeditionary force of 38 ships landed 8000 troops near Villa de la Vega. The Spaniards retreated north over the mountains, from where they set sail to Cuba.

Before leaving, the Spanish freed their slaves and encouraged them to harass the English, who promptly destroyed the Spanish capital. These *cimarrones* ('wild' runaways) took to the hills, where they mastered guerrilla warfare and fiercely defended their freedom. A small band of Spanish loyalists under General Cristobal Ysassi also fought a guerrilla war against the English. The decisive battle at Rio Bueno was won by the English under Colonel Edward D'Oyley.

In December 1656, some 1600 English arrived to settle the area around Port Morant near the eastern tip of Jamaica. The region proved too swampy: within one year, three-quarters of the settlers had succumbed to disease. Other settlers fared better and a viable economy began to evolve.

By 1662, 4000 colonists had arrived, including felons exiled to Jamaica and impoverished Scots and Welshmen who arrived as indentured laborers. Settlement hastened as profits began to accrue from cocoa, coffee, and sugarcane production.

Rise of the Buccaneers

During the 17th century, Britain was constantly at war with France or Spain. The English Crown sponsored individual captains – privateers – to capture enemy vessels and plunder enemy cities.

The privateers, or buccaneers (from *boucan*, a French word for smoked meat, which the privateers often sold), evolved as a motley band of seafaring miscreants, political refugees, and escaped criminals who formed the Confederacy of the Brethren of the Coast, committed to a life of piracy. Gradually they replaced their motley vessels with captured ships and grew into a powerful and ruthless force, feared throughout the Antilles.

Initially, the newly appointed governor of Jamaica, Sir Thomas Modyford, joined with the Spanish in attempts to suppress the buccaneers. But the outbreak of the Second Dutch War against Holland and Spain in March 1664 caused England to rethink its policy. Modyford contrived for the Brethren to defend Jamaica. Port Royal and Kingston Harbour became their base. Their numbers swelled astronomically, and within a decade Port Royal was Jamaica's largest city – a prosperous den of iniquity.

A ruthless young Welshman, Henry Morgan, established his supremacy and guided the buccaneers and Port Royal to their pinnacle. Morgan pillaged Spanish towns throughout the Americas before crowning an illustrious career by sacking Panama City. Eventually Morgan became governor of Jamaica and charged with suppressing privateering. Even so, he caroused in Port Royal, where he succumbed to dropsy (edema) and was entombed at Port Royal in 1688.

With England at peace with Spain, buccaneers were now regarded merely as pirates. Mother Nature lent a hand in their suppression when a massive earthquake struck Port Royal on June 7, 1692, toppling much of the city into the sea. More than 2000 people – one-third of Port Royal's population – perished.

The Slave Trade

Meanwhile, Jamaica's English planters grew immensely wealthy from sugar, and English merchants from the sordid market in West African slaves. Most slaves landed in Jamaica were from the Ashanti, Cormorante, Mandingo, and Yoruba tribes.

The grueling 'middle passage' across the Atlantic lasted anywhere from six to 12 weeks. The captives were kept chained below, where many died of disease in the festering holds. The captives who were still alive were fattened up as the boat reached port, and oiled to make them appear healthy before being auctioned. (Their prices varied between £25 and £75 for unskilled slaves; slaves who had been trained as carpenters and blacksmiths fetched a premium – often £300 or more. The most wretched had a worth of no more than a shilling.)

Kingston served as the main distribution point for delivery to other islands. Of the tens of thousands of slaves shipped to Jamaica every year, the vast majority were re-exported. The slave ships then returned to England carrying cargoes of sugar, molasses, and rum.

The First Maroon War

By the end of the 17th century, Jamaica was also under siege from within. The first major slave rebellion occurred in 1690 in Clarendon parish, where many slaves escaped and joined the descendants of slaves who had been freed by the Spanish in 1655 and had eventually coalesced into two powerful bands (called Maroons, from the Spanish word *cimarrón*): one in the remote Blue Mountains and one in the Cockpit Country of southern Trelawny, from where they raided plantations and attracted runaway slaves. (The eastern community became known as the Windward Maroons; those farther west were called Leeward Maroons.)

Pesky Pirates

Even after they were forced out of Port Royal following the 1692 earthquake, pirates added to the colony's problems, plundering ships of all nations and coming ashore to raid the sugar plantations that were sprouting all over Jamaica. Several pirates rose to infamy for their cruelty, daring, and occasionally, their flamboyant ways.

Every English schoolchild has heard of 'Blackbeard,' whose real name was Edward Teach. This brutal giant of a man terrorized his victims by wearing flaming fuses in his matted beard and hair. And 'Calico Jack' Rackham, although equally ruthless, became known for his fondness for calico underwear. Like many pirates, Rackham was captured and executed, his body hung on an iron frame on a small cay off Port Royal (the cay is still called Rackham's Cay).

Blackbeard

In 1729 the English launched the First Maroon War offensive to eradicate the Maroons. The thickly jungled mountains, however, were ill-suited to English-style open warfare, and the Maroons had perfected ambush-style guerrilla fighting. Nonetheless, after a decade of costly campaigning, the English gained the upper hand.

On March 1, 1739, Colonel Guthrie and Cudjoe, the leader of the Maroons of Cockpit Country, signed a peace treaty granting the Maroons autonomy and 1500 acres of land. In return, the Maroons agreed to chase down runaway slaves and to assist the English in quelling rebellions.

The Maroons of the Blue Mountains, under a leader named Quao, signed a similar treaty one year later.

King Sugar

During the course of the 18th century, Jamaica became the largest sugar producer in the world (Jamaican sugar production eventually peaked in 1814 at 34 million pounds). Jamaica was jointly ruled by a governor appointed by the monarch and an elected assembly of planters. The island was divided into 13 parishes (their boundaries remain today). The Crown's interests at the parish level were looked after by an appointed custos (the Crown's local representatives).

The planters built sturdy 'great houses' in Georgian fashion high above their cane fields. Many planters were absentee landlords who lived most of the year in England, where they formed a powerful political lobby. In Jamaica, the planters lived a life of indolence, with retinues of black servants. Many overindulged in drink and sexual relations with slave mistresses, frequently siring mulatto children (known as 'free coloreds,' they were accorded special rights).

The economic and political life of the times was an exclusively male arena. The planters' wives spent much of their time playing cards, arranging balls, and otherwise socializing, while the daily care of their children was given to wet nurses and female slaves.

The Heyday of Slavery

Slavery came to dominate Jamaican life. By 1700 there were perhaps 7000 English in Jamaica and 40,000 slaves. One century later, the number of whites had tripled, and they ruled over 300,000 slaves. Tens of thousands were worked to death. Many were put to work building factories, houses, and roads. Others were domestic servants, cooks, footmen, butlers, and grooms.

During their few free hours, slaves cultivated their own tiny plots. Sunday was a rest day, and slaves gathered to sell yams and other produce at the bustling markets. If fortunate, a slave might save enough money to buy his freedom, which a master could also grant as he wished.

The planters ran their estates as vicious fiefdoms under the authority of an overseer (the 'busha'), who enjoyed relatively free reign. Some planters showed kindness and nurtured their slaves, but most resorted to violence to terrorize the slave population into obedience. The extreme treatment was eventually regulated by slave codes, but plantation society remained tied to the rule of the whip.

Rebellions & Revolutions

Naturally, the slaves despised their 'massas' (masters) and struggled against the tyranny imposed on them. Insurrections were put down with the utmost severity.

Tacky's Rebellion, the first major uprising (named after the slave leader), erupted on Easter Monday in 1760 in Port Maria in St Mary parish. The rebellion rippled through the western parishes as slaves joined the uprising. The flames of rebellion flickered for months before finally being extinguished. White society enacted a swift and violent retribution.

The spirit of independence fomenting abroad also affected Jamaica. During the American War of Independence, which began in 1775, Britain reacted by blockading North America's eastern seaboard, cutting it off from trade with Jamaica, which relied on food imports from North America. As many as 15,000 slaves may have died of starvation from the food shortages, which prompted the introduction of breadfruit from the South Seas as a staple for slaves.

Meanwhile, France and Spain took advantage of Britain's preoccupation with its North American colonies to recapture Britain's Caribbean islands. France and Spain, now in alliance, attempted to invade Jamaica in April 1782. Admiral George Rodney set sail from Port Royal with a naval fleet and soundly defeated the enemy fleet in the Battle of the Saints.

A Second Maroon War broke out in 1795 after two Trelawny Maroons were sentenced to flogging for stealing pigs. The slaves who inflicted the punishment had been runaways that the Maroons had captured and returned to the British authorities. The proud Maroons were incensed at the insult, and simmering tensions boiled over into full-scale war.

Eventually, colonial authorities brought in trained bloodhounds to hunt down the Maroons, who surrendered on a pledge that they could retain their land. In a betrayal of good faith, the governor, the Earl of Balcarres, banished the Maroons to Nova Scotia, from which they were eventually sent to Sierra Leone, becoming the first New World Africans ever repatriated to Africa. An English barracks was erected in Trelawny Town, forever ending the Maroon threat.

The Demise of Slavery

The beginning of the 19th century saw growing antislavery sentiment, spurred by the arrival of nonconformist missionaries and the emergence of the evangelical clergy within the established Church of England, which up to then had supported slavery and was the sole denomination in Jamaica.

The last and largest of the slave revolts in Jamaica erupted in 1831. The Christmas Rebellion was inspired by 'Daddy' Sam Sharpe, an educated slave and lay preacher who used his prayer meetings to incite passive resistance.

Though Sharpe had hoped for a peaceful uprising, the rebellion turned violent. As many as 20,000 slaves joined the revolt, which spread throughout the island, leaving in its wake enormous destruction. Once again, martial law was declared and troops were employed with vicious force. The governor persuaded the slaves to surrender on a promise of full pardon. Once the slaves had lain down their arms, more than 400 were hanged; hundreds more were whipped.

The accounts of retribution fostered a wave of revulsion in England and helped the abolitionist cause. Parliament finally abolished slavery throughout the empire on August 1, 1834; it had banned the slave trade in 1807. (See 'Preaching Resistance' in the Montego Bay & Northwest Coast chapter.)

The Era of Emancipation

Before permitting freedom, Parliament decided that slaves should serve a six-year unpaid 'apprenticeship' for their previous masters, but this proved untenable. Slaves simply left the estates. The apprenticeship system was soon abandoned, and the slaves were set free unconditionally in 1838. The plantocracy attempted to sustain the crippled estates by importing indentured laborers.

Blacks, though free, had no political voice. White magistrates continued to mete out harsh 'justice' to a free but marginalized peasantry relegated to the least fertile lands.

Jamaica's mulattos, however, had been enfranchised in 1830 and granted full rights equal to English citizens. Many received a good education and rose into the middle classes. Most looked up to the white society of their fathers. Others, understandably, sided with the oppressed, whose cause was taken up vociferously in the 1860s by mulatto lawyer and liberal assemblyman George William Gordon.

Jamaica's economy, already weakened by emancipation, degenerated further during the American Civil War (1861-65), when naval blockades cut off vital supplies. Desperation finally boiled over in 1865. A demonstration in Morant Bay, led by a black Baptist deacon named Paul Bogle, descended on the town courthouse. The militia fired into the crowd, killing dozens of people, and a violent rebellion ensued.

Governor Edward Eyre and his followers used the Morant Bay Rebellion as a pretext to get rid of Gordon. He was arrested, swiftly tried by a kangaroo court, and promptly hanged alongside Paul Bogle. More than 430 other rebels were executed, countless scores were flogged, and thousands of homes razed in retribution.

The brutal repression provoked an outcry in Britain. The Jamaican Assembly was forced to vote its own dissolution and the island's internal affairs reverted to Parliament's control as a Crown colony, marking the beginning of a more enlightened era.

Banana Boom & Bust

In 1866 a Yankee skipper, George Busch, arrived in Jamaica and loaded several hundred stems of bananas, which he transported to Boston and sold at a handsome profit. He quickly returned to Port Antonio, where he encouraged production and soon had himself a thriving export business. Captain Lorenzo Dow Baker followed suit in the west, with his base at Montego Bay. Within a decade the banana trade was booming. Production peaked in 1927, when 21 million stems were exported.

To help pay the passage south to Jamaica, banana traders promoted the island's virtues and took on passengers. Thus, the banana-export trade gave rise to the tourism industry.

Birth of Modern Politics

A great earthquake toppled much of Kingston on January 14, 1907, killing more than 800 people. Hurricanes devastated the island in 1915, 1916, and 1917, adding to the hardships suffered during WWI through demise of trade. And in the 1930s, sugar and banana sales plummeted. The vast majority of Jamaicans were unemployed and destitute. Strikes and riots erupted, spilling over in 1938 when a demonstration at the West Indies Sugar Company factory at Frome, in Westmoreland, got out of hand. A battle between police and the unemployed seeking work left several people dead. The situation was defused when a locally born,

rabble-rousing labor leader, Alexander Bustamante, mediated the dispute.

Amid the clamor, the charismatic Bustamante (the son of an Irish woman and a mulatto man), formed the Bustamante Industrial Trade Union (BITU). That same year, Bustamante's dissimilar cousin, Norman Manley, formed the People's National Party, or PNP, the first political party in the colony (Bustamante would form his own party – the Jamaica Labour Party, or JLP – in 1943). Separately they campaigned for economic and political reforms. Say writers Philip Sherlock and Barbara Preston, 'Bustamante swept the Jamaican working class into the mainstream of Jamaican political life and Norman Manley secured the constitutional changes that put political power in their hands.'

Adult suffrage for all Jamaicans and a new constitution, which provided for an elected government, were introduced in 1944 (Bustamante's JLP won Jamaica's first election). In 1947 virtual autonomy was granted, though Jamaica remained a British colony under the jurisdiction of Parliament and the Crown – a prelude to full independence.

On August 6, 1962, Jamaica gained its independence (though it would remain part of the British Commonwealth). At midnight, the union jack came down, replaced by Jamaica's new flag with three new colors: black (for the people), green (for the land), and gold (for the sun).

Turbulent Years

Immediate post-independence politics were dominated by Bustamante and Manley, whose parties grew more ideologically apart. The JLP – back in power – tilted toward the USA and free-market policies while the PNP leaned left. Buoyed by the rapid growth of the bauxite industry, Jamaica experienced a decade of relative prosperity and growth.

Nonetheless, the buoyant mood of the early 1960s swiftly passed as the hopes of Jamaica's poor majority went unanswered. A growing radicalism was brewing. In 1965, Kingston erupted in riots. And Haile Selassie's April 1966 visit to Jamaica was an event of long-term significance that fueled a growing interest in Rastafarianism among the Jamaican poor, helping produce a more positive self-image and providing a radical outlet for the expression of discontent.

Following Manley's death in 1969, the PNP espoused increasingly radical social policies under the leadership of Manley's son, Michael, who attempted to make Jamaica a 'democratic socialist' nation. He initiated greater state control over the economy, resulting in a greater share of revenues for the island. Manley introduced a statutory minimum wage and legislation favoring workers' rights. A literacy campaign, socialist health care, and other liberal economic and social reforms proved popular with the masses.

Unfortunately, the move toward socialism caused a capital flight at a time when Jamaica was reeling from the shock of the world's oil crisis and worldwide depression. Inflation roared above 50%, foreign investors pulled out, unemployment skyrocketed, Jamaican society became increasingly polarized, and an antiwhite climate prevailed.

Outbreaks of violence boiled over into full-fledged warfare during the campaigns preceding the 1976 election. Heavily armed gangs of JLP and PNP supporters began killing each other in the partisan slums of Kingston (see Government & Politics later in this chapter). Still, the PNP won the election by a wide margin, which Manley took as a mandate supporting his socialist agenda.

The economy went into precipitous decline as skilled Jamaican workers and professionals fled the island en masse. Scores of businesses went bankrupt. Severe scarcities of even the most basic consumer items became common.

The US government was also concerned over the socialist path Manley was taking. He particularly antagonized the US by developing close ties with Cuba: Manley declared that he would go 'all the way to the mountaintop with Fidel.' Manley even began recruiting a 'home guard' outside the regular police and army, trained by Cuban advisers. When a Suppression of Crime Act was enacted, giving special powers to the security forces, Jamaica's middle class feared the worst.

Armed police and soldiers patrolled the streets, and army helicopters whirred overhead as gun battles raged throughout Kingston. A small right-wing clique of the Jamaica Defense Force even attempted an unsuccessful coup d'etat. Jamaica stood at the verge of civil war.

With the economy in free fall and society in dangerous disarray, Manley stepped back from the brink of disaster and began to reverse his policies.

About Face

In 1980, the voters decided it was time for a change, but not before witnessing the most violent year since the dramatic 1865 Morant Bay Rebellion.

Under Boston-born, Harvard-educated Edward Seaga (a cynical gangster-politician who bears responsibility for arming the vicious posses and introducing Haitian-style thuggery to Jamaican politics), the JLP inherited a country on the verge of bankruptcy and mired in domestic unrest. Seaga's efforts to restructure the economy included an austerity program and a painful devaluation of the dollar that created further hardships. Seaga also severed diplomatic relations with Cuba and nurtured strong ties with the Reagan administration.

When Jamaica joined the US invasion of Grenada in the autumn of 1983, Seaga called a sudden election to take advantage of a surprise boost in popularity and the absence of Manley, who was touring abroad. The PNP boycotted the snap election and thus the JLP 'won' all 60 seats.

For the next six years (1983-89), Jamaica had a corrupt one-party parliament. It was also a one-man show: Seaga held the position of Prime Minister, as well as the head of the ministries of finance, planning, information, culture, and defense. The cult of personality, government corruption, and growing poverty and unemployment in the midst of an economic revival turned the electorate against him.

In September 1988, Hurricane Gilbert tore across the island, causing US$300 million of damage and leaving one-quarter of Jamaica's population homeless.

Meanwhile, Manley had undergone a political reformation. In 1989, voters gave him a second term, during which he took a leaf from Seaga's book, further deregulating the economy, reducing the scope of state involvement, pursuing liberal-conservative economic policies, and initiating an antidrug program.

Manley retired from politics in 1992 due to ill health, handing the reins to his deputy, Percival James Patterson. In the March 1993 election, the PNP won by a landslide against an ailing JLP.

Recent Years

By 1997, however, Jamaica was again in the midst of a financial crisis even as voters delivered the PNP an unprecedented third term. Then, for three days in spring 1999, Jamaica erupted in nationwide riots over a government-proposed 30% gas tax hike. The riots left nine people dead, and the government rescinded the tax.

In 2001, Jamaica began building up to new elections in late 2002, and violence in West Kingston soared to new heights as criminal posses battled to control electoral turf and profit from the largesse that victory at the polls in Jamaica brings. Rival political gangs turned the area into a war zone, forcing residents to flee, and schools, businesses, and even Kingston Public Hospital to close.

As Queen Elizabeth and the Duke of Edinburgh visited Jamaica in February 2002 for the 40th anniversary of independence, Prime Minister PJ Patterson was pushing to make Jamaica a Republic, shedding the British monarch as head of state and severing ties with the Commonwealth. The election occurred after this book went to press.

GEOGRAPHY & GEOLOGY

At 4411 sq miles (11,425 sq km), about equal to the US state of Connecticut, or one-twentieth the size of Great Britain, Jamaica is the third largest island in the Caribbean and the largest of the English-speaking islands. It is one of the Greater Antilles, which make up the westernmost of the Caribbean islands.

Jamaica lies 90 miles south of Cuba, 100 miles west of Haiti, and 600 miles south of Miami. It is within the tropics, 18° north of the equator between latitudes 17° 43' and 18° 32' north and longitudes 76° 11' and 78° 23' west.

The Greater Antilles were first formed by a great volcanic welling about 140 million years ago, and Jamaica is still rising, in places as much as one foot every thousand years. Frequent quakes shake the island, often with devastating effect.

The island measures 146 miles east to west; widths vary between 22 and 51 miles.

Jamaica is rimmed by a narrow coastal plain except in the south, where broad flatlands cover extensive areas. Mountains run through the island's center, rising gradually from the west and culminating in the tortuous Blue Mountains in the east, which are capped by Blue Mountain Peak at 7402 feet. The island is cut by about 120 rivers, many of which are bone dry for much of the year but become raging torrents after heavy rains, causing great flooding.

Two-thirds of the island's surface is composed of soft, porous limestone (the compressed skeletons of coral, clams, and other sea life), in places several miles thick and covered by thick red-clay soils rich in bauxite (the principal source of aluminum). The interior, dramatically sculpted with deep vales and steep ridges, is highlighted by the 500-sq-mile Cockpit Country, a virtually impenetrable tract full of irregular limestone hummocks, vast sinkholes, underground caves, and flat valley bottoms.

CLIMATE

One of Jamaica's greatest allures is its idyllic tropical maritime climate. (English playwright and entertainer, Noel Coward, called his adopted home 'Dr Jamaica.')

There are two weather hotlines visitors can call in Jamaica: **north coast weather information** (☎ 924-0760) and **south coast weather information** (☎ 924-8055).

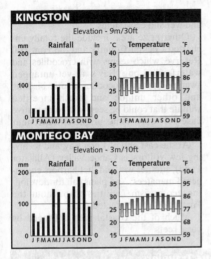

Coastal temperatures average a near-constant 80° to 86°F year-round. Temperatures fall steadily with increasing altitude but even in the Blue Mountains average 65°F or more. Down by the shore, days are cooled by warm trade winds – known as 'doctor breeze.' A less noticeable nocturnal offshore breeze is known locally as 'the undertaker.' Cool 'northers' can also blow December to March, when cold fronts that bring freezing conditions to Florida can affect Jamaica.

Annual rainfall averages 78 inches, but there are considerable variations nationwide, with the eastern (or windward) coast receiving considerably more rain than elsewhere on the island. Parts of the John Crow and Blue Mountains receive an average of 300 inches a year. By contrast, the south coast sees little rain and in places is semibarren.

A 'rainy season' begins in May or June and extends through November or December, with the heaviest rains in September and October. Rain can fall at any time of year, however, and normally comes in short, heavy showers, often followed by sun.

Although Jamaica lies in the Caribbean 'hurricane belt,' relatively few hurricanes touch it. Officially the hurricane season lasts from June 1 to November 30; August and September are peak months. The **Office of Disaster Preparedness** (☎ 972-9941; 12 Camp Rd, Kingston 5) offers advisories and advice.

ECOLOGY & ENVIRONMENT

Coastal mangrove and wetland preserves, montane cloud forests, and other wild places are strewn across Jamaica. Most travelers stick to beach resorts, however. Those who do get close to nature are as yet poorly served by wildlife reserves.

Ecologically, Jamaica is in dire straits. The island has been losing its forest cover at a rate of more than 5% per year, making Jamaica's rate of deforestation the highest of any country in the world, according to the Rainforest Trust (☎ 305-669-8955, fax 305-665-0691; ℮ rft@rainforesttrust.com; 6001 SW 63rd Ave, Miami, FL 33143, USA). Many of Jamaica's endemic (unique to the island) wildlife species are endangered or gone forever. According to the World Conservation Union, Jamaica ranks among the top ten countries in the world for number of both endangered amphibians and endangered plant species.

Legislation has been largely ineffectual: authorities are under funded, and fines are absurdly low.

The National Resources Conservation Authority (NRCA, c/o Natural Environment & Planning Agency; ☎ 754-7546, fax 754-7595; ℮ publiced@nrca.org; 10 Caledonia Ave, Kingston 5) is entrusted with responsibility for promoting ecological consciousness among Jamaicans and management of the national parks and protected areas under the Protected Areas Resource Conservation Project (PARC).

The past few years have seen a stirring of eco-awareness.

Other information resources include:

Jamaica Conservation & Development Trust (☎ 960-2848, fax 960-2850; ℮ jcdt@kasnet.com) 95 Dumbarton Ave, Kingston 10

Jamaica Environment Trust (☎ 960-3693, fax 929-1074; ℮ jet@infochan.com) 58 Half Way Tree Rd, Kingston 10

Jamaica Sustainable Development Networking Programme (☎ 978-855; ℼ www.jsdnp.org.jm) 115 Hope Road, Kingston 6

National Environmental Societies Trust (☎ 960-3316, fax 968-5872; ⓔ nest@infochan.com) 95 Dumbarton Ave, Kingston 19

Ecological Treasures

Visitors to the island can forsake sandals for hiking boots and follow mountain trails, shower in remote waterfalls, and shoot birds through the lens of a camera. Several areas have been developed as ecotour destinations, most notably the Black River Great Morass, a swampland penetrated by boat.

The Rio Grande Valley is a premiere destination for hiking. The Blue and John Crow Mountains have been opened up in recent years, notably along trails that begin at Hollywell National Park, as well as on the climb up Blue Mountain Peak (7402 feet). And Negril's Great Morass is being developed as an eco-attraction protecting fabulous birdlife and wetland ecosystems.

Other prize areas include the totally uncharted Cockpit Country and the Font Hill Reserve, which teems with crocodiles and waterfowl. Long Bay's as-yet-untapped swamps harbor crocodiles, exotic birdlife, and other unique and much-imperiled wildlife that could be seen with comparative ease – if only some bright entrepreneur would cotton on.

At the east end of Long Bay, and receiving few visitors, is Canoe Valley (Alligator Pond), another wetland that harbors endangered manatees. And plans call for developing ecotourism facilities throughout the Portland Bight Protected Area.

Much of the coastal area is fringed by coral reefs.

Tips for Environmentally Conscious Travelers

Don't litter. Take only photographs, leave only footprints. If you see litter, pick it up. Support recycling programs.

Respect the property of others. Never take 'souvenirs' such as shells, plants, or artifacts from historical sites or natural areas. Treat shells, sea urchins, coral, and other marine life as sacred.

Don't buy products made from endangered species. By buying products made of tortoise shell, coral, or bird feathers, you are contributing to the decimation of wildlife. (See 'Shopping with a Conscience' in the Facts for the Visitor chapter.)

Keep to the footpaths. When hiking, always follow designated trails. Natural habitats are often quickly eroded, and animals and plants are disturbed by walkers who stray from the beaten path.

Don't touch or stand on coral. Coral is extremely sensitive and is easily killed by snorkelers and divers who make contact. Likewise, boaters should never anchor on coral – use mooring buoys. It's the law!

Sponsor environmental consciousness in others. Try to patronize hotels, tour companies, and merchants that act in an environmentally sound manner. Consider their impact on waste generation, noise levels, energy consumption, and the local culture.

Support community tourism. Many local communities derive little benefit from Jamaica's huge tourism revenues. Educate yourself on community tourism and ways you can participate (see the boxed text 'Community Tourism' in the Central Highlands chapter). Use local tour guides wherever possible.

Respect the community. Learn about the customs of the region and support local efforts to preserve the environment and traditional culture.

Tell others. Politely intervene when you observe other travelers behaving in an environmentally or socially detrimental manner. Educate them about the potential negative effects of their behavior.

Community Involvement

Jamaica's Community Tourism efforts urge visitors to take meals, outings, work-visits, and accommodations with local villagers in an effort to stimulate tourism that complements and supports local communities.

Rural communities are also being encouraged to partake in preserving their natural heritage and, by doing so, to benefit from the ecotourism boom (27% of the nation's populace derives an income from tourism). Nature-guide training and environmental and cultural awareness programs are growing.

FLORA

Jamaica boasts more than 3000 species of flowering plants (including 237 species of orchids), of which at least 827 are endemic. Jamaica also boasts some 60 bromeliad species and 550 species of ferns.

Anthuriums, heliconias, and gingers are all common, as is hibiscus and periwinkle. Impatiens color roadsides at cooler heights.

Exotics introduced from abroad include the bougainvillea, introduced from London's Kew Gardens in 1858. Ackee, the staple of Jamaican breakfasts, was brought from West Africa in 1778. The first mango tree arrived in 1782 from Mauritius. And Capt William Bligh arrived in Jamaica in 1779 bearing 700 breadfruit. But cocoa and cashew are natives of Central America and the West Indies, as is cassava. A native pineapple from Jamaica was the progenitor of Hawaii's pineapples (the fruit even appears on the Jamaican coat of arms).

Many visitors are surprised to find cacti flourishing in the parched south. Jamaica has several unique cactus species, including the Turk's Head cactus, resembling a fez.

Tree Species

The national flower is the dark blue bloom of the lignum vitae tree. Its timber is much in demand by carvers. The national tree is blue mahoe, which derives its name from the blue-green streaks in its beautiful wood. Another dramatically flowering tree is the vermilion 'flame of the forest' (also called the 'African tulip tree').

Meet the People

Two decades ago, the Jamaica Tourist Board (JTB) developed the Meet the People program, so that visitors to the island could interact with Jamaicans in their home environment and gain an appreciation for island life. Normally this involves being invited to an afternoon tea, dinner, or cocktail party; joining a family at a church service; sightseeing; or even a few hours of visiting the host's work environment.

JTB officials interview the families and inspect their premises to ensure that they meet the program's standards. Hence, almost all the host participants seem to be drawn from the middle-classes. The JTB tries to match ages, professions, and hobbies of host and visitor. There's no charge, but a small gift (or picking up at least a portion of any tab) is considered a common courtesy.

For more information, visit Ⓦ www.jamaicatravel.com/meetthepeople.

Logwood, introduced to the island in 1715, grows wild in dry areas and produces a dark blue dye, for which it was grown commercially during the 19th century. Native mahogany and ebony have been logged and decimated during the past two centuries. Other native trees include the massive silk cotton, said to be a favored habitat of *duppies* (ghosts).

Palms are everywhere, except at the highest reaches of the Blue Mountains. There are many species, including the stately royal palm (a Cuban import), which grows to over 100 feet.

Much of Jamaica's coast is fringed by mangroves.

FAUNA
Mammals

Jamaica has very few mammal species. Small numbers of wild hogs and feral goats still roam isolated wilderness areas. There are 23 species of bat, but not the vampire bat.

The only native land mammal is the endangered Jamaican hutia, or coney, a large brown rodent akin to a guinea pig. Habitat loss now restricts the highly social, nocturnal beast to remote areas of eastern Jamaica.

The mongoose is the animal you are most likely to see, usually scurrying across the road. This weasel-like mammal was introduced from India in the late 19th century to control rats, but it is now considered a destructive pest.

Amphibians & Reptiles

Jamaica harbors plenty of slithery and slimy things. The largest are crocodiles (incorrectly called 'alligators' in Jamaica), found along the south coast, but also in and around Negril's Great Morass and adjacent rivers. (See the boxed text 'What a Croc!' in the South Coast & Central Highlands chapter).

Jamaica has 24 species of lizards, including the Jamaican iguana, which hangs on to survival in the remote backwaters of the Hellshire Hills. Geckos can often be seen hanging on your ceiling by their suction-cup feet. Locals attribute a dark side to the harmless critter, from which Jamaicans superstitiously recoil.

Jamaica has five species of snakes, none poisonous. All are endangered thanks mostly to the ravages of the mongoose, which has entirely disposed of a sixth species – the black snake. The largest is the Jamaican boa, or yellow snake – a boa constrictor (called *nanka* locally) that can grow to 8 feet in length.

The island also harbors 17 species of frogs and one toad. Uniquely, none of Jamaica's 14 species of endemic frogs undergoes a tadpole stage; instead, tiny frogs emerge in adult form directly from eggs.

Insects

There are mosquitoes and bees and wasps, but most bugs are harmless. For example, a brown scarab beetle, called the 'newsbug,' flies seemingly without control, and when it flies into people, locals consider it a harbinger of important news. Diamond-shaped 'stinky bugs' are exactly that, advertising their exotic nature with an offensive smell.

Jamaica has 120 butterfly species and countless moth species, of which 21 are endemic. The most spectacular butterfly is the giant swallowtail, *Papillio homerus*, with a 6-inch wingspan. It lives only at higher altitudes in the John Crow Mountains and the eastern extent of the Blue Mountains (and in the Cockpit Country in smaller numbers).

Fireflies (called *blinkies* and *peeny-wallies)* flash luminously in the dark.

Birds

The island has more than 255 bird species, of which 25 species and 21 subspecies are endemic. Many, such as the Jamaican blackbird and ring-tailed pigeon, are endangered.

Stilt-legged, snowy-white cattle egrets are ubiquitous, as are 'John crows,' or turkey vultures, which are feared in Jamaica and are a subject of several folk songs and proverbs.

That sneaky thief on your breakfast table is the cling-cling, or shiny black Greater Antillean grackle (also called a 'tingling'), with eyes like Spanish beads and a kleptomaniac's habits in hotel dining rooms.

Patoo (a West African word) is the Jamaican name for the owl, which many islanders superstitiously regard to be a harbinger of death. Jamaica has two species: the screech owl and the endemic brown owl. There are also four endemic species of flycatchers, a woodpecker, and many rare species of doves.

Birdwatchers can also spot herons, gallinules, and countless other waterfowl in the swamps. And pelicans can be seen diving for fish, while frigate birds soar high above.

Jamaica has four of the 16 Caribbean species of hummingbirds. The crown jewel of West Indian hummingbirds is the streamertail, the national bird, which is indigenous to Jamaica. This beauty boasts shimmering emerald feathers, a velvety black crown with purple crest, and long, slender, curved tail feathers. It is known locally as the 'doctorbird,' apparently for its long bill that resembles a 19th-century surgical lancet. The red-billed streamertail inhabits the west, while the black-billed lives in the east. It adorns Jamaican two-dollar bills and the logo of Air Jamaica.

Marine Life

Coral reefs lie along the north shore, where the reef is almost continuous and much of it is within a few hundred yards of shore.

Leaf-like orange gorgonians spread their fingers upward toward the light. There are contorted sheets of purple staghorn and lacy outcrops of tubipora resembling delicately woven Spanish *mantillas,* sinuous boulderlike brain corals, and soft-flowering corals that sway to the rhythms of the ocean currents.

Over 700 species of fish zip in and out of the exquisite reefs and swarm through the coral canyons: wrasses, parrotfish, snappers, bonito, kingfish, jewelfish, and scores of others. The smaller fry are ever-preyed upon by barracudas, giant groupers, and tarpon. Sharks, of course, are frequently seen, though most of these are harmless nurse sharks. Farther out, the cobalt deeps are run by sailfish, marlin, and manta rays.

Three species of endangered marine turtles – the green, hawksbill, and loggerhead – lay eggs at Jamaica's beaches.

About 100 endangered West Indian manatees – a shy, gentle creature once common around the island – survive in Jamaican waters, most numerously in the swamps of Long Bay on the south coast.

Dolphins are frequently seen, particularly off the south coast.

NATIONAL PARKS

Jamaica's embryonic park system comprises three national parks: Blue Mountains-John Crow National Park, Montego Bay Marine Park, and Negril Marine Park.

The 300-sq-mile Blue Mountains-John Crow National Park (Jamaica's largest) includes the forest reserves of the Blue and John Crow mountain ranges. Both marine parks are situated around resort areas and were developed to preserve and manage coral reefs, mangroves, and offshore marine resources.

There are also a fistful of other wilderness areas granted varying degrees of protection, such as the Portland Bight Protected Area.

Additional national parks are being conceptualized and have been touted for years. (See the Parks of Jamaica map for proposed sites.)

The **Nature Conservancy** (☎ 703-841-4878, 800-628-6860; 4245 N Fairfax Dr, Arlington, VA 222203, USA) is working in partnership

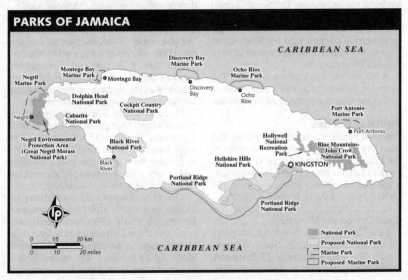

PARKS OF JAMAICA

CARIBBEAN SEA

Negril Marine Park

Montego Bay Marine Park — Montego Bay

Discovery Bay Marine Park

Ocho Rios Marine Park

Dolphin Head National Park

Discovery Bay

Ocho Rios

Negril

Cabarita National Park

Cockpit Country National Park

Port Antonio Marine Park

Port Antonio

Negril Environmental Protection Area (Great Negril Morass National Park)

Black River National Park

Black River

Hollywell National Recreation Park

Blue Mountains-John Crow National Park

KINGSTON

Hellshire Hills National Park

Portland Ridge National Park

Portland Ridge National Park

0   15   30 km
0   10   20 miles

CARIBBEAN SEA

National Park
Proposed National Park
Marine Park
Proposed Marine Park

with the Jamaica Conservation & Development Trust and other national agencies to develop protected "spinal corridors" linking vital forest habitats.

GOVERNMENT & POLITICS

Jamaica inherits its political institutions from Britain. It is a stable parliamentary democracy within the Commonwealth.

Although Jamaica is independent, its titular head of state is Queen Elizabeth II of England. She is represented by a Jamaican-born governor general (often referred to as 'GG' by islanders), who is appointed on the advice of the prime minister and a six-member Privy Council. The governor's duties are largely ceremonial and include appointing the prime minister, who is always the leader of the majority party after each national election.

Executive power resides with a cabinet appointed and led by the prime minister, and which is responsible to Jamaica's Parliament. Parliament consists of a bicameral legislature – a 60-member elected House of Representatives and a nominated 21-seat Senate, of which 13 members are appointed by the prime minister and eight by the leader of the opposition. The Senate's main function is to review legislation sent forward by the elected House. The House may override a Senate veto, but a two-thirds vote in both houses is required to change Jamaica's constitution.

A full parliamentary term is five years. The governor, however, may call a national election at any time the prime minister requests.

Political Parties

Post-independence Jamaican politics has been largely a struggle between two parties: the People's National Party (PNP) and the Jamaica Labour Party (JLP). There are also a handful of minor parties, including the United People's Party, formed in 2001 as a third party alternative to the ineffectual National Democratic Movement.

The PNP is a social-democratic party closely affiliated to the National Worker's Union. The PNP's leader is PJ Patterson, the current prime minister, whose political philosophy blends free-market economics with a large dose of government largesse.

Despite its name, the JLP is a conservative party with ties to the Bustamante Industrial Trade Union. It is currently led by ex-prime minister Edward Seaga, an autocratic, cynical, bullying self-promoter instrumental in the creation of murder-ridden one-party enclaves (called 'garrisons'); he is commonly accused of fostering the cocaine trade for political ends, and at last visit was facing charges of massive tax fraud.

Local Government

Jamaica is divided into three counties (Cornwall, Middlesex, and Surrey) and subdivided into 12 parishes – Clarendon, Hanover, Manchester, Portland, St Ann, St Catherine, St Elizabeth, St James, St Mary, St Thomas, Trelawny, and Westmoreland – plus two contiguous corporate areas, Kingston and St Andrew. (See the Parishes of Jamaica map.)

Local government is administered by parish and municipal councils.

Corruption & 'Garrison' Politics

The one thing the PNP and JLP have in common is a flair for corruption and pandering – what Jamaicans call 'politricks.'

Graft is a way of life in Jamaican politics, cronyism is entrenched in the system, and the government's so-called social and economic support program is a gravy train for contractors with political connections. Leading officials are usually political appointees eager to cash in for themselves before the next change of government.

Election time in Jamaica is often an explosive affair, though things have calmed down since the late 1970s and early 1980s, when hundreds of Jamaicans lost their lives in partisan killings in 'garrison constituencies,' zones where political parties maintain their dominance through thuggery.

Violent retribution and intimidation (performed by gangster affiliates) are common. During the heady 1970s, individual politicians developed strangleholds over low-income areas in Kingston by pandering to 'dons' (gang leaders) who would deliver blocks of votes in exchange for government

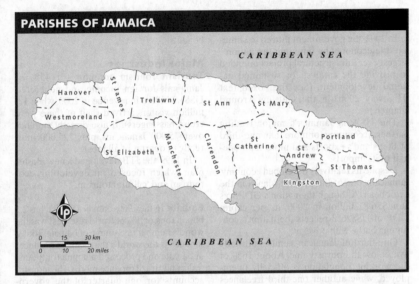

PARISHES OF JAMAICA

CARIBBEAN SEA

Hanover
St James
Trelawny
St Ann
St Mary
Westmoreland
St Elizabeth
Manchester
Clarendon
St Catherine
St Andrew
Portland
St Thomas
Kingston

0   15   30 km
0   10   20 miles

CARIBBEAN SEA

contracts and other largesse such as jobs and housing. Political discipline was enforced by the barrels of Armalite and M16 rifles. Tivoli Gardens, for example, is a JLP stronghold, while neighboring Arnett Gardens is a PNP garrison.

The Military

Jamaica has no army, navy, or air force. However, the Jamaica Defense Force, comprising 2500 members, is a well-armed and highly efficient military unit with its own Coast Guard and Air Wing. It works closely with the US Drug Enforcement Agency in drug interdiction.

Police

The average policeman or policewoman on the street is exemplary: civil, courteous, and dedicated to upholding the law. Yet the force is beset with corruption. Branches of the police have a reputation for execution-style killings and other criminal misconduct. In 2001, an Amnesty International report identified Jamaica as having more people, proportionate to the population, killed by police than any other nation.

The force boasts a well-armed, militaristic component that does duty in a vigorous battle against drug lords and syndicated crime figures. Most police carry guns, and it is not unusual to see heavily armed patrols (usually during drug searches) bearing fearsome weaponry.

Officers of the Resort Patrol Services patrol the major resorts to guard the welfare of tourists.

ECONOMY

Jamaica's economy is highly developed compared to the economies of most Caribbean islands. It has a vital financial sector with many international banks, a large skilled workforce, and a relatively broad-based economy. The economy, however, is dependent on imported consumer goods and raw materials, which have exceeded earnings from tourism and bauxite (which account for three-quarters of Jamaica's foreign exchange earnings), plus sugar and bananas, all of which are susceptible to erratic worldwide demand. The island has had to confront an acute balance-of-payments crisis and is beleaguered by a massive foreign debt (US$4.7 billion). Jamaica also suffers from high inflation (7.3% in 2000) and persistent unemployment.

In 2002, the government moved to stimulate the economy by initiating the nation's largest ever infrastructural project intended to provide the catalyst for sustained national development. (See the boxed text 'Highway 2000' in the Getting Around chapter.)

The USA is Jamaica's major trading partner, accounting for more than one-third of the island's exports and more than one-half of its imports.

Despite its relatively developed economy, Jamaica is one of the poorest islands in the Caribbean. Although the nation's GDP was at US$6.82 billion in 2000, its per capita GDP of US$2653 reflects the nation's continuing battle with poverty.

One-third of Jamaican families officially live below the poverty line. About 16% of the working population is officially unemployed, while another one-third freelances in what is called the 'informal sector' –

prostitution, higgling (bargaining), and hustling. Jamaica has no general unemployment benefits.

Major Industries

Tourism Tourism accounts for 45% of Jamaica's foreign income and generated US$1.3 billion in revenue in 2000, when 1.8 million visitors arrived (half of these were cruise passengers). It also directly employs over 75,000 Jamaicans, plus 225,000 indirectly (a quarter of all jobs).

In 1999, the JTB developed a new master plan, which focused on developing ecotourism and 'cultural tourism.'

Bauxite In the 1960s, Jamaica (which has 2.5 billion tons, or 7% of world reserves) was the world's number one source of bauxite. Today, Jamaica is the world's third largest producer of bauxite and processed alumina (only Australia and Brazil produce more). The industry accounts for one-quarter of the government's income.

Hallowed Grounds

Since coffee grows best on well-watered, well-drained slopes in cooler yet tropical climates, it is no surprise that it thrives in Jamaica's Blue Mountains.

In 1728, governor Sir Nicholas Lawes introduced coffee to Jamaica at Temple Hall Estate, and other planters followed suit, prompted by the growing demand in Europe. During the peak years, from 1800 to 1840, production rose to 17,000 tons a year and Jamaica was the world's largest exporter.

Emancipation in 1838 doomed the plantations. Many slaves left the estates and planted their own coffee. As steeper slopes were planted, coffee quality began to decline. The end of Britain's preferential tariffs for Jamaican coffee further damaged the industry at a time when high-quality coffee from Brazil was beginning to sap Jamaica's market share. A series of hurricanes during the past century did further inestimable damage. By the close of WWII, Jamaica's coffee industry was on its last legs.

There has been a resurgence in the popularity of Blue Mountain coffee in recent years under Japanese stimulus and aided by the Jamaican Coffee Industry Board (CIB; ☎ 758-1259; e coffee board@jamaicancoffee.gov.jm). Blue Mountain coffee is a treasured commodity in Japan, where the beans sell for US$60 or more per pound. To stimulate production, Japanese companies offered growers development loans at 4% and 5% interest. They also bought the Carighton Estate plantation. In doing so they have cornered the market. More than 90% of Blue Mountain coffee is sold to Japan at a preferential rate of about US$9 a pound (of which farmers get only US$5 a pound). A pound produces 100 cups of coffee, each of which sells for US$15 in Japan.

The region's distinctly flavored coffee is acclaimed by many connoisseurs as the best in the world. To be designated 'Blue Mountain,' it must be grown – and roasted – in a prescribed area

Agriculture Agriculture is an important source of employment (accounting for 21% of the labor force), despite its relatively low contribution to the GDP (about 7.5%). The fertile plains are the domain of large holdings producing sugar and other crops for export. The rocky hillsides and mountains are the domain of the peasant smallhold farmer.

The vast majority of Jamaica's 160,000 farmers cultivate less than 5 acres (the average holding is 1½ acres). Owning one's 'own likkle piece of rockstone' is still the ideal in a nation where 55% of the land – almost exclusively the most fertile flatlands – is owned by 5% of the population.

In the late 1800s, Jamaica was the world's largest banana producer. Though the industry gradually declined during the 20th century to a low of 28,000 tons annually in the 1980s, it has recently seen a recovery: Jamaica exported 42,500 tons of bananas in 2000.

Almost one-third of Jamaica's agricultural land (203 sq miles) is planted with sugar. The sugar economy remains the largest employer in Jamaica. Formerly the engine of the Jamaican economy, the industry has declined steadily since 1965, when production peaked at 501,000 tons. Production in 2000 amounted to 216,000 tons.

Increasing attention is being given to allspice (pimento), citrus, coffee, ginger, cocoa, rum, ornamental flowers, and cattle. Citrus projects, in particular, have expanded rapidly in the past 20 years.

And then there's ganja! In the 1970s and '80s, ganja was 'king' in Jamaica and a major contributor to the country's economic development. Thanks to a committed antinarcotics drive by the Patterson government, many farmers who once relied on the crop now struggle to make a living. Still, the trade continues. (For more on ganja, see the boxed text 'Holy Smoke!' later in this chapter.)

Manufacturing & Service Industries Manufacturing contributed 35.2% of the GDP in 2001 and employs about 19%

Hallowed Grounds

within the parishes of St Thomas, St Andrew, and Portland between 2000 and 5000 feet above sea level. Coffee grown elsewhere is called 'High Mountain' or 'Jamaica Prime.' About 12,000 acres of Jamaica's 30,000 acres under coffee cultivation lie within the designated Blue Mountain zone.

Blue Mountain coffee is lighter and sweeter than other coffees and yet more robust, with a unique woody flavor. It also has less caffeine. However, not all Blue Mountain coffee lives up to its reputation or its astronomical price, much of which is due to marketing hype.

Although the CIB purports to maintain strict standards and regulates the use of the name 'Blue Mountain coffee,' the policy is questionable. The board oversees four processing plants in the region and acts as the sole exporter of 'Blue Mountain coffee.' The factories are supplied by scores of small-scale farmers who are required by law to sell to them at whatever price the coffee board chooses to pay, regardless of the world market value. Only beans processed at the four plants may be sold as 'Blue Mountain coffee.'

The four factories blend the high-quality beans with lesser-quality Lowland and Mountain beans. Many independent producers complain that their superior beans are thus degraded and even poor beans end up being sold as 'Blue Mountain coffee.' Hence, many smallholders refuse to sell to the central processors and cure and roast their own beans (often over a smoky wood fire), which they sell privately (and illegally) at bargain prices. Only in 1997, after a protracted battle, was a license granted to an independent roaster – the Old Tavern Estate, run by the Twyman family – to roast, package, and sell its own coffee as 'Blue Mountain' coffee (see Section in the Blue Mountains & Southeast Coast chapter).

of the active workforce. Investment incentives have resulted in the growth of sizable processed-goods and textile industries.

Kingston is one of the Caribbean's leading financial centers. Jamaica has dozens of banks and financial institutions, plus an important stock market.

The broader service industry employed 41% of the working population and comprised 57.4% by value of Jamaica's GDP in 2000.

POPULATION & PEOPLE

Jamaica's population is currently estimated at 2.665 million, of which about 800,000 live in Kingston. At least another two million Jamaicans live abroad. Emigration has served as an escape valve to help balance the high birthrate of 20 per 1000 (down from 25.2 per 1000 in 1990). One-third of the population is under 14 years of age. Life expectancy was over 75 years in 2001, when the infant mortality rate was 14 deaths per 1000 live births.

A Diverse People

The nation's motto – 'Out of Many, One People' – reflects Jamaica's diverse heritage. Tens of thousands of West Africans, plus large numbers of Irish, Germans, and Welsh arrived throughout the colonial period, along with Hispanic and Portuguese Jews and those whom Jamaicans call 'Syrians' (a term for all those of Levantine extraction). Following emancipation in 1838, Chinese and Indians arrived as indentured laborers from Hong Kong and Panama. A new wave of Hong Kong Chinese has settled in recent years, bringing new vitality to retail trade.

Some 91% of the population is classified as being of pure African descent; 7.3% are of Afro-European descent; the remainder are white (0.2%), East Indian and Middle Eastern (1.3%), and Afro-Chinese and Chinese (0.2%).

Jamaica proclaims itself a melting pot of racial harmony. Still, insecurities of identity *have* been carried down from the plantation era. Class divisions in Jamaica are still related to color, and there is much lingering

resentment – as well as prejudice – against whites, particularly among the poorer segment of society.

Whites are divided into 'white Jamaicans' (immigrants from Europe, mostly England) and island-born 'Jamaican whites,' most of whom are really 'off-whites' who contain at least a trace of black blood. You'll also come across many brown-skinned, green-eyed, blond-haired mulattos (so-called 'red' people, a pejorative term), notably around Treasure Beach in St Elizabeth.

The Black Color Scale

Color in Jamaica is the ultimate status symbol in a society that exhibits great admiration for status symbols. This is a legacy of the plantation era, when plantocracy developed a scale of 'whiteness.' The lexicon passed into general parlance and expressed the percent of black blood: 'sambo' (three-quarters), mulatto (half), 'quadroon' (one-quarter), 'octaroon' (one-eighth), and 'musteefino' (one-sixteenth). Jamaicans still have a name for every nuance of shade. A partial list includes white, 'off-white,' 'high yellow,' 'coolie-royal,' 'chinee-royal,' 'red,' 'brown,' 'high brown,' and black. 'She black, black, black, so 'til' means she's very dark indeed.

Today, the lighter one's shade of skin, the more skilled and prosperous one is assumed to be. Jamaican politics and businesses have always been dominated by whites and light-skinned 'browns.' The very poorest of Jamaicans are usually very dark. Even many of the most successful black Jamaicans are not comfortable with their blackness. Many darker Jamaicans still attempt to 'lift' their color by marrying a lighter-skinned person, and it's not uncommon for newspapers and magazines to attempt to slander or flatter public figures by darkening or lightening their photographs. It's a standing joke in Jamaica, which prides itself on the beauty of its women, that the safest bet at the Miss Jamaica contest is the contestant with the lightest skin.

EDUCATION

During the late 19th century, the British established in Jamaica the foundations of an admirable education system. Jamaica still boasts some of the finest schools in the Americas. Case in point: Jamaica produced the winner of the 1998 US National Spelling Bee championship.

However, per-student spending has steadily fallen during the past few decades. Low salaries fail to attract quality teachers. Although primary education is free and compulsory to the age of 15, about 60% of Jamaican schoolchildren (mostly in rural areas) drop out early. Children in rural areas must often walk many miles to reach school. And in Kingston's ghettoes, a huge population of children remain illiterate because it is too dangerous for them to venture through what is literally a war zone.

ARTS

Jamaica has evolved a powerful artistic and cultural expression rooted in African traditions, while quintessentially Jamaican styles have evolved across the spectrum of arts. In addition, Jamaica's crafts industry supports tens of thousands of artisans, who offer a cornucopia of leatherwork, ceramics, shell art, beadwork, and basket-weaving.

Dance & Theater

Jamaica has a rich heritage of dance and theater.

The country shuns classical Shakespearean theater, preferring farces and homilies that draw on local traditions. They're often bawdy and tend to portray the trials of the poor. Theater productions are often performed in *patois* (Jamaica's local dialect).

Kingston's scene is vibrant enough to sustain half a dozen or more concurrent productions, including the internationally acclaimed Little Theater Movement, the Jamaica Folk Singers, the National Chorale, the University Players, and above all the National Dance Theater Company (NDC), which is based in Kingston's Little Theater. The NDC's dancers, musicians, and singers explore African themes and forms, often in vividly imaginative costumes, through performances based on Jamaican history and daily life.

Pantomime This stage show is a musical comedy – a blend of lively song, dance, and words that lampoon Jamaican foibles, historic events, and well-known figures in Jamaican life. During performances, the audience gets drawn in, volubly so.

The National Pantomime – a monument of folk theater and irreverent family entertainment – is staged by the Little Theater Movement and is traditionally held in Kingston's Ward Theater.

The pantomime has its roots in the British tradition, in which performances are based on childhood fairy tales and stories such as 'Cinderella' and 'Jack and the Beanstalk.' But over the years, folkloric characters such as Anancy and Tacooma (both originated in West Africa) began to appear on stage, as did adapted versions of Jamaican folktales.

Music

From hotel beach parties to the raw 'soundsystem' discos of the working-class suburbs, Jamaica reverberates to the soul-riveting sounds of calypso, soca, and above all, reggae. Music is everywhere. And loud!

Reggae may have put Jamaica on the musical map, but the nation's musical heritage runs much deeper. Inspired by the country's rich African folk heritage, music spans mento (a folk calypso), ska, rocksteady, 'roots' music, and contemporary dancehall and raga. Kingston is the 'Nashville of the Third World,' with recording studios pumping out dozens of new titles each month See the Reggae 'n' Riddims special section for an in-depth description.

Jamaica also has a strong heritage in military bands, notably the Jamaica Military Band, which dates back to England's first West India Regiment in 1795 and still uses its unique Zouave (light infantry of North African origin) uniform.

Pottery & Sculpture

Jamaican ceramists have been making a name for themselves of late, led by Cecil Baugh, an octogenarian potter who uses

Egyptian motifs. Munchi is an outstanding fourth-generation Afro-Caribbean potter who chooses as her creative ground the shady earth beneath the same mango tree that her mother, Ma Lou, used for inspiration. Wassi Art, in Ocho Rios, has a stable of young artists being trained to self-expression at the highest caliber. And a Montegonian, David Pinto, is another ceramist of note, working from his base at Good Hope, Falmouth.

Jamaica's foremost sculptor this century is undoubtedly Edna Manley, the multitalented wife of ex-prime minister Norman Manley. Her works in wood, metal, and stone are displayed in a magnificent collection in the National Gallery in Kingston. In addition to fine artists, thousands of self-taught woodcarvers hew intuitive carvings.

Literature

Jamaica has its literati, most of whom are haunted by the ghosts of Jamaica's slave history and the ambiguities of Jamaica's relationship to Mother England. Novels tend to focus on survival in a grim colonial landscape and escape to Africa, which often proves more grim.

The classic *White Witch of Rose Hall* by Herbert de Lisser has as its setting the plantation era and tells the tale – now an established part of Jamaican lore – of Annie Palmer, the wicked mistress of Rose Hall who supposedly murdered three husbands and several slave lovers.

Children of Sisyphus by Orlando Patterson was one of the first novels ever to treat Rastafarianism fairly. It is set in Kingston's ghettoes and tells of a young prostitute's efforts to elevate herself from life on the edge.

Perry Henzell's *Power Game* is a tale of power politics based on real events in the 1970s, told by the director of the movie *The Harder They Come* (see Film later). The poignant novel of that name, written by Michael Thewell, tells the story of a country boy who comes to Kingston, turns into a 'rude boy,' and becomes fatally enmeshed in the savage drug culture. Victor Headley's *Off Duty* tells of a Jamaican lawman playing by ghetto rules.

In recent years, a number of Jamaican women have gained notice: Christine Craig *(Mint Tea)*, Patricia Powell *(Me Dying Trial)*, Michelle Cliff *(Abeng, Land of Look Behind)*, and Vanessa Spence *(Roads Are Down)*, among others. Coping is still the main theme, and the oppressors are the men within the characters' lives.

Also see Books in the Facts for the Visitor chapter.

Architecture

Most colonial-era plantation 'great houses' and government buildings built of local sandstone and limestone still stand foursquare, as do the former homes of wealthy merchants. The stones were fixed and finished by mortar and plaster containing lime produced by burning conch shells. Being thick, these massive walls became temperature sinks, keeping the building relatively cool, aided by wide jalousied windows and doorways.

Many fine clapboard houses still stand, too, graced by gingerbread fretwork in a classic Caribbean vernacular style that has enjoyed a recent renaissance, sponsored by Jamaican architect Ann Hodges.

Film

Jamaica has produced some excellent films (pronounced 'flims' in Jamaica). Native-born singer Jimmy Cliff rocketed to fame in *The Harder They Come* (1973), in which he starred as a 'rude boy' (armed thug) in Kingston's ghettoes. The brilliant cult movie was produced by Kingstonian Perry Henzel, who in 2001 began production of a sequel, *The Harder They Come II*.

The most emotionally engaging – and successful – movie in years is *Dancehall Queen,* a powerful tale of redemption for a struggling, middle-aged street vendor who finds a novel way of escaping the harrowing, violence-prone mean streets of Kingston through the erotic intoxication of dancehall. The movie is one of a crop of powerful Jamaican productions coming from Chris Blackwell's Palm Pictures studio, which also produced *Third World Cop,* a tale of corrupt police. Also see Films in the Facts for the Visitor chapter.

Painting

Jamaican art has its origins in the 18th and 19th centuries, when itinerant artists roamed the plantations, recording life in a Eurocentric romanticized light that totally ignored the African heritage. Satirist William Hogarth was one of few artists to portray the hypocrisy and savagery of plantation life.

In the 1920s, artists of the so-called Jamaica School began to develop their own expressions shaped by realities of Jamaican life. The Jamaican School evolved two main groups: painters who were schooled abroad and island-themed primitives, or 'intuitives' – self-taught artists such as Bishop Mallica 'Kapo' Reynolds (1911-89) and John Dunkley (1891-1947).

'Kapo' Reynolds, a leading Revivalist cult leader (see Religion later in this chapter), is the most renowned of the intuitive artists. He painted mystical landscapes and visions. Dunkley was a Kingston barber who painted his entire shop in tangled vines, flowers, and abstract symbols. Dunkley later turned to canvas. Bars, shops, restaurants, and rum shops islandwide copy Dunkley's Jungian style (usually with vines crawling along a black wall) or display whimsical alfresco trompe l'oeil cartoons dramatizing Jamaican life. Colloquially, the pop-style wall murals are known as 'yard art,' after the 'yards' of Kingston ghettoes, where powerful politically inspired murals are painted in big, bold colors that can be absorbed at a glance. Others are cheery, adding color and humor to otherwise depressing environments.

The Jamaican School's more international group includes contemporary Jamaican artists such as Gloria Escoffrey, Michael Escoffrey, Carl Abrahams, Ken Abendana Spencer, Barrington Watson, Osmond Watson, and Christopher Gonzalez, all of whom have earned world renown for their museum pieces. Many of these artists studied abroad in the 1960s and 1970s and returned to the island inspired by new ideas that they wedded to their nationalist spirits.

Rastafarians are common subjects, as are market higglers, animals, and religious symbols merged with the myths of Africa. The intuitive works of Everald Brown (a priest in the Ethiopian Coptic Church) and Albert Artwell especially concentrate on Rastafarian symbolism.

Jamaica has a comparatively large crop of female artists, many of them expatriates. Judy Macmillan is renowned for a Rembrandt-like use of light in her portraits. The works of Roberta Stoddart, an Australian, are pervasive with satirical humor. Elizabeth Roberts is known for her tropical murals.

Englishman Graham Davis is perhaps the best known and most influential of foreign-born male artists now resident in Jamaica.

SOCIETY & CONDUCT
Traditional Culture

Few traces remain of the original Jamaican people, the Arawaks, though many Arawak words have been passed down into common parlance, including the island's Arawak name: Xaymaca. Jamaica's strongest legacy comes from the African slaves.

Anancy This devious spider is Jamaica's unlikely leading folk hero. The folktales originated with the Ashanti tribe of Ghana but have become localized through the centuries. Many of Jamaica's traditional folk songs derive from Anancy stories. Like Brer Rabbit, Bredda (brother) Anancy survives against the odds in a harsh world by his quick wit, sharp intelligence, cunning, and ingenuity. Anancy, his wife, Crooky, and his son, Tacooma, frequently appear in the annual Christmas pantomime.

Folk Healing Traditional folk healing is still very much alive. Healers, called 'balmists,' rely on native herbs mixed into concoctions – bush medicines – the recipes for which span many generations. Colored flags (usually red) and other talismans hang outside their 'balmyards' to chase away evil spirits. Some are associated with obeah cults and are involved in witchcraft ('high science'), both good and bad, to foil duppies, or ghosts, or perhaps to win back an errant lover by dispensing 'Oil of Come Back'.

Day Work Jamaicans also still participate in 'day work,' in which villagers perform a common task such as building a house or planting a field. The tradition is translated on Labour Day into community effort when everyone pitches in to paint road markings or pick up litter.

Nine Nights Many Jamaican elders still observe nine nights, a 'wake' held on the ninth night after someone's death to ensure that the spirit of the deceased departs to heaven. If such a ceremony is not performed, the person's spirit will hang around to haunt the living.

Modern Culture
Jamaica has a complex and challenging culture, with layer upon layer of complexity shaped by an agonized past. From strutting 'rude boys' and Rastafarians clutching their 'cutchie' ganja pipes to besuited city sophis-

ticates driving BMWs and Mitsubishi 4WDs, from cheery market 'mammies' to dancehall queens in 'batty rider' shorts and high-heeled secretaries in designer fashions – Jamaica is a complex potpourri. In many ways it is a culture in crisis.

The Jamaican People Jamaicans are an intriguing contrast. Much of the population comprises the most gracious people you'll ever meet: hard-working, happy-go-lucky, helpful, courteous, genteel, and full of humility. The majority of Jamaicans are lovely people. If you show them kindness, they will give it back in return.

Often, poorer Jamaicans are very slow to warm to strangers, however, and trying to get a smile can be like pulling teeth. It can take a long time to earn their trust; they give a piece one day, another the next. Jamaican children are usually well behaved and extremely polite, as are the senior citizens.

Dealing with Duppies

Many Jamaicans believe in duppies, the ghosts or spirits of the dead that appear only at night. The term is derived from the Twi tribal word dupon (from Africa) for the roots of a tree. The superstition is based on an African belief that humans have two souls. One goes to heaven for judgment; the other lingers on earth, where it lives in trees and sends shivers down the spines of superstitious Jamaicans.

Duppies are a force of either good or evil, and can be captured and used to either help, as in myal, or harm, as in obeah. Talismans are used to manipulate them. For example, many Jamaicans still place a crossed knife and fork and a Bible near young babies at night to keep away an evil, blood-sucking, witchlike duppy called Ol' Hige, who casts aside her skin at night before setting out on her wicked forays. If you want to be rid of her for good, you have to find her skin and douse it with salt and pepper. Like vampires, evil duppies are also terrified when folks 'cutten' (make the sign of the cross).

You may even come across rural Jamaicans carrying a handful of matches or stones that they drop on the road if they think they're being followed by a duppy. Duppies are incurably curious and will stop to see what has been dropped; since they can't count beyond three, local folklore says that they'll count the first three objects and then have to start at the beginning again.

Many rural Jamaicans remain terrified of another duppy – the Whistling Cowboy, whose breath can kill. He rides a three-legged horse, so be careful if you hear 'itty-itty-hop-itty-itty-hop.'

Otaheite apples for sale

Pineapple ready for the picking

Ackee, a tree-grown fruit native to Africa

Harvesting young coconut meat, or 'jelly'

Red ginger flower

Somerset Falls, hidden in a deep gorge overhung with thick foliage

A game of volleyball in Montego Bay

The Caribbean's clear, turquoise waters are a snorkeler's dream.

Unfortunately, a significant minority of the population (notable among poorer, uneducated males) is composed of the most sullen, boastful, cantankerous, confrontational, and aggressively self-righteous people you could ever wish not to meet. Foreign visitors are often shocked at the surliness and bluster they so often encounter.

Charged memories of slavery and racism have continued to bring out the spirit of anarchy latent in an ex-slave society divided into rich and poor. Jamaicans struggling hard against poverty are disdainful of talk about a 'tropical paradise.' There is fire in the Jamaican soul. A seething mistrust runs through society like an undercurrent.

Much of Jamaica's contemporary cultural malaise is fueled by a competitive spirit in a dog-eat-dog world. Jamaicans are assertive (they dislike cowering behavior in a person), not least in their driving behavior and propensity for vulgar ostentation (ghetto youth will starve to dress in gold 'cow-rope' chains and gaudy designer clothes, called 'trash 'n' ready'). Jamaican culture also owes much to the role model of their Machiavellian folk hero, Anancy. Guileful, cheating, double-dealing, and subtle theft are how a large segment of the underprivileged get by. If someone can get away with it, he earns respect among peers.

Jamaicans love to debate, or 'reason.' You'll not meet many Jamaicans without strong opinions, and they tend to express themselves forcefully, turning differences of opinion into voluble arguments with some confounding elliptical twists, stream-of-consciousness associations, and what writer/journalist Chris Salewicz calls 'Barthslike [or Bart Simpson-like] word de- and reconstructions.' Private differences don't stay that way for long – part of the national psyche is an instinct to get involved in others' 'bisniss.' There is little reserve. When Jamaicans are not pleased, they tell you in no uncertain terms.

Jamaicans make light of their own foibles, which are a source of humor in theater and pantomimes. But Jamaicans love their island (the success of the Reggae Boyz, Jamaica's national soccer team, in reaching the 1998 World Cup, for example, united Jamaica in a massive outpouring of national pride). Countless Jamaicans have accomplished great things. But Jamaican society as a whole is deeply insecure, and self-esteem is low among the uneducated classes.

Young males, in particular, are severely challenged and often mask their lack of self-esteem by putting on a hard-nosed face or bravura mask. Sensitivity is rarely displayed for fear of being regarded as 'sissy.' Heroic models are drawn from a musical world that belts out a message exhorting misogyny, violence, and profit from rip-offs or laziness. Unemployment exacerbates the problem, and for every hardworking youth there now seems to be another wanting to be paid for doing nothing.

Wit & Humor Jamaicans' sarcastic and sardonic wit is legendary. The deprecating humor has evolved as an escape valve that hides their true feelings. The saying that 'everyt'ing irie' is 'black' humor, because life *is* a problem.

Often Jamaican wit is laced with sexual undertones. Jamaicans like to make fun of others, often in the most subtle yet no-punches-pulled way, but they accept being the source of similar humor in good grace. Individual faults and physical abnormalities inspire many a knee-slapping jibe.

The lusty humor will sometimes be directed at you. Take it in good humor. You'll be an instant hit if you give as good as you get, but the key is subtlety, not malice.

Sex & Family Life Many Jamaicans are sexually active at an early age. Noncommittal sexual relationships are the norm, especially among the poorer classes. It is still common for a poor couple to marry only late in life, if at all. Typically, a Jamaican woman will have a limited number of men in her life to whom she is loyal – one at a time. She may return to each briefly, with long hiatuses between involvements with a particular man. It is not unusual for women to have children by several men and for men to sire families with several women. Approximately 80% of children are born out of wedlock. Middle-class

Jamaicans, in general, display more spousal loyalty. Nonetheless, it is common for most married males to have a girlfriend or a 'baby-mother,' and the local lexicon is full of terms related to the theme ('jacket,' for example, refers to a child fathered by someone other than a woman's husband).

Though true-blue Christians are conservative, Jamaicans as a whole are at ease with their bodies and comfortable with – and direct about – sex ('night food,' in local parlance). At weddings or other respectable social occasions, for example, even the most prim-and-proper females, regardless of age, will gleefully 'wine' (to make overt sexual motions with a member of the opposite gender) on a dance floor, to roars of approval.

Women in Jamaica Jamaica is a macho society, and in general, life for women is extremely challenging. It is also a matriarchal society in the African (and slave plantation) tradition. The sexes lead independent lives, at least among the lower classes. In the slave system, men were commonly sold and separated from their lovers and children. Even women slaves were sold, never to see their children again. When that happened, the grandmother, aunt, or another family member would care for the child – termed a 'keeper family.' The tradition continues. It is common for a woman to leave her children in the care of a relative for months or even years at a time while she takes up with another man, or for reasons of employment or hardship.

Jamaican women are strong and independent (in 40% of households, a woman is the sole provider). This independent spirit translates into a self-assured striving. Jamaican women attain far higher grades in school and have higher literacy rates, and middle-class women have attained levels of respect and performance commensurate with their counterparts in North America and Europe. Women comprise about 46% of Jamaica's labor force, although the majority are in extremely low paying jobs. Some 13% of the women in the labor force have reached senior management and professional level, compared to only 8% of male workers, and more than three-quarters

of University of the West Indies students are women. They also do the cooking, the housework, and the child-rearing. Among the poorer classes, men traditionally factor little in a child's upbringing, and a common sight is to see adolescent girls and women struggling with buckets of water while young men laze around on the roadside.

Jamaican women complain that many males feel threatened, especially by educated women, whom they regard as too independent.

Work & Living Conditions The majority of Jamaicans live in the hills, out of sight of tourists: many get by quite adequately, living in aged wooden homes in Caribbean style or concrete cinder block in Western style; others eke out a marginal existence in ramshackle villages and rural shacks, sometimes in pockets of extreme poverty, as in Kingston's ghettoes and shanties. Many low-income Jamaicans have been unable to find a way out of poverty, so they hustle. They hang out on the streets waiting for an opportunity to present itself. A general malaise prevalent among a large segment of the male underclass is fired by a belief that a subtle apartheid force is purposely holding them back.

In contrast, Jamaica has a significant middle class, who live a lifestyle familiar to its counterpart in Europe and North America. They are, as a whole, well educated; they have vivacious and well-honed intellects, are entrepreneurial and contemporary looking, and exhibit a preference for shopping trips to Miami or New York. However, many live with a surprising lack of contact with the harsh reality in which the majority of Jamaicans live, and they seem to muster little empathy. Not infrequently you'll hear defensive denials that poverty even exists in Jamaica.

Dos & Don'ts

Do be firm and direct. Jamaicans prefer it. If you beat around the bush, not only will they fail to get your point, but they may take advantage of you.

Don't expect Jamaicans to honor commitments. Jamaicans don't always tell it as it is, and often fail to show for appointments or dates…a notorious trait among Jamaican women. Take such promises with a grain of salt.

Do relax. Tropical time happens at a slower pace. 'Soon come' is a favorite expression often translated at face value by foreigners but that really means 'it'll happen when it happens.'

Do be empathetic. Try to understand the hardships that the majority of Jamaicans face. Don't try to take advantage of an individual's plight.

Don't call Jamaicans 'natives.' Jamaicans may be natives of the island, but the term is laden with racial connotations and can be taken as a slur. 'Islanders' or simply 'Jamaicans' is more appropriate.

Do be formal with strangers. Jamaicans are more formal than many foreigners, particularly North Americans used to quickly reaching a first-name basis. To show respect, address people you meet with 'Mr' or 'Miss,' or even 'Sir' or 'Lady.' Using a first name can be taken as treating someone as inferior.

Do ask before snapping a photo. Many Jamaicans enjoy being photographed, sometimes for a small fee, but others prefer not to pose for tourists and can respond angrily. Always respect the privacy of others.

RELIGION

Jamaica professes to have the greatest number of churches per square mile in the world, with virtually every imaginable denomination represented. More than 80% of Jamaicans identify as Christians.

Jamaicans are inordinately superstitious and firm believers in ghosts and evil spirits. Many islanders, for example, still recoil from harmless lizards as if they were ferocious dragons.

Christianity

On any day of the week, but notably on weekends, it's common to see adults and children walking along country roads, holding Bibles, and dressed in their finest outfits – the girls in white, the men and boys in somber suits, and the women in heels, hats, and bright satins. On Sundays every church in the country seems to overflow with the righteous, and the old fire-and-brimstone school of sermonizing is still the preferred mode. Bible-waving congregations sway to and fro, roll their heads, and wail and shriek 'Hallelujah!' and 'Amen, sweet Jesus!' while guitars, drums, and tambourines help work the crowds into a frenzy.

The most popular denomination, the Anglican Church of Jamaica, accounts for 43% of the population. About 5% of the population today is Catholic. Fundamentalists have made serious inroads in recent years because of aggressive proselytizing.

Revivalist Cults

Jamaica has several quasi-Christian, quasi-animist sects that are generically named Revivalist cults after the post-emancipation Great Revival, during which many blacks converted to Christianity. Revivalism is popular among the poorest classes, but is looked down on by most educated Jamaicans.

The cults are derived from West African animist beliefs (animism has nothing to do with animal spirits; the name is derived from the Latin word *anima,* for soul) based on the tenet that the spiritual and temporal worlds are a unified whole. A core belief is that spirits live independently of the human or animal body and can inhabit inanimate objects and communicate themselves to humans; how humans call them determines whether they will be a force of good or evil.

Many Jamaicans commonly consult practitioners – 'balmists' – who claim to be able to invoke the assistance of spirits and duppies for black magic (called obeah, an Ashanti word from West Africa) for medicinal purposes or for ensuring a successful romance on behalf of a supplicant, for example. When used for good, obeah is called myal.

Pocomania The most important Revivalist cult is Pocomania, mixing European and African religious heritages. The cult is organized into hierarchical bands, which hold meetings at consecrated 'mission grounds' (or 'seals') and are overseen by a 'leader' or 'shepherd' (or 'mother' if female).

The ritual meetings are frenzied affairs involving prayers, dances, and rhythmic drumming. Adherents often go into a trance, frequently aided by rum and ganja. Then a worshipper sometimes becomes 'possessed' by a spirit who becomes his or her guardian.

Kumina This is the most African of the Jamaican religious cults and is strongest in St Thomas parish. Based on the worship of ancestor spirit-deities, Kumina focuses on appeasing wandering spirits of dead people who did not receive proper rites and are a menace to society. Kumina ceremonies are performed for all sorts of social occasions. Goats are frequently sacrificed. Drums are particularly powerful during Kumina ceremonies, which use a ritual Bantu language from the Congo, where the cult originated.

Rastafarianism
Rastafarians, with their uncut, uncombed hair grown into long sun-bleached tangles known as 'dreadlocks' or 'dreads,' are synonymous with the island in the sun. There are perhaps as many as 100,000 Rastafarians in Jamaica. They adhere to an unorganized religion – a faith, not a church – that has no official doctrine or dogmatic hierarchy and is composed of a core of social and spiritual tenets that are open to interpretation. Not all Rastafarians wear dreads, for example, and others do not smoke ganja. All adherents, however, accept that Africa is the black race's spiritual home to which they are destined to return.

Garveyism Rastafarianism evolved as an expression of poor black Jamaicans seeking fulfillment during the 1930s, a period of growing nationalism and economic and political upheaval. It was boosted by the 'back to Africa' zeal of Jamaican Marcus Garvey's Universal Negro Improvement Association, founded in 1914 (see the boxed text 'One God, One Aim, One Destiny' in the Ocho Rios & North Coast chapter). Rastafarians regard Garvey as a prophet. The nationalist predicted that a black man – a 'Redeemer' – would be crowned king in Africa. Haile Selassie's crowning as emperor of Abyssinia (now Ethiopia) on November 2, 1930, fulfilled Garvey's prophecy and established a fascination with Ethiopia that lies at the core of Rastafarianism.

Many Garvey supporters saw their Redeemer in Selassie, and they quoted biblical references in support of Selassie's claim to be the 225th descendant from King David. He traced his family tree back to King Solomon and the Queen of Sheba, and took the title 'King of Kings, Lord of Lords, Conquering Lion of the Tribe of Judah.' These Garveyites believed Selassie was God incarnate. They adopted his precoronation name, Ras Tafari: Ras (prince) and Tafari (to be feared).

One charismatic leader, Leonard Percival Howell, developed the tenets of Rastafarianism and began a proselytizing tour. In 1940, Howell established the first Rastafarian community – the Pinnacle – at Sligoville, northwest of Kingston. His followers adopted the 'dreadlocked' hairstyle of several East African tribes – an allegory of the mane of the Lion of Judah.

Howell's commune endured numerous police raids, and in 1954 was broken up by police. Many of the members settled West Kingston and the still-extant commune at Bull Bay, east of Kingston. By the end of the decade there were perhaps 15,000 Rastafarians in Kingston's Back-A-Wall district. As their militancy increased, leftist political activists and criminals penetrated their ranks. The deaths of two British soldiers in ensuing skirmishes did much to demonize Rastafarianism, although a subsequent report characterized the movement, correctly, as pacifist. At least 15 different sects had emerged by the 1960s, when Rastafarianism evolved a firm philosophy and solid foundation.

Disillusionment helped turn ghetto youth toward the social and spiritual salvation implicit in Rastafarianism, which came of age with Bob Marley's ascendancy to international fame and acceptance.

Rastafarian Tenets Howell's document 'Twenty-One Points' defined the Rastafarian philosophy and creed. One tenet was that the African race was one of God's chosen races, one of the Twelve Tribes of Israel descended from the Hebrews and displaced. Jamaica is

Babylon (after the place where the Israelites were enslaved), and their lot is in exile in a land that cannot be reformed. A second tenet states that God, whom they call *Jah*, will one day lead them from Babylon – any place that 'downpresses' the masses – to Zion (the 'Promised Land,' or Ethiopia). A third addresses Selassie's status as the Redeemer chosen to lead Africans back to Africa.

Rastafarians have also adapted traditional Christian tenets to fit their philosophical mold or 'reasoning,' the term used to cover their distinctive discourse. They believe that the Bible originally told the history of the African peoples, but was stolen and rewritten by whites to suppress and dominate blacks. This interpretation underpins the Rastafari-

ans' mistrust of white society. Rastafarians believe that heaven is on earth in the present. Though Selassie died in 1975, a commonly held belief is that he still lives among them unidentified in a new guise.

Rastafarian leaders continue to petition Queen Elizabeth II to repatriate them to Africa. Meanwhile they wait for redemption.

Ganja & Good Living Rastafarians believe that ganja provides a line of communication with God. Again, they look to the Bible, specifically Psalm 146:8, which says,

> Who covereth the heaven with clouds, and prepareth rain for the earth. Who maketh grass to grow on the mountains, and herbs for the service of men.

Holy Smoke!

Ganja (marijuana) is an omnipresent fact of a Jamaican vacation. The weed, which grows throughout the island, has been cultivated for its narcotic effect since 1845, when indentured Indian laborers brought the first seeds from Asia. Its use spread rapidly among the plantation workers. Since it induced indolence and reduced productivity, it was outlawed. Nonetheless, islanders have used it ever since. Today, an estimated 20% to 40% of Jamaicans smoke it on a regular basis. As such, in 2001 a government commission recommended that marijuana be legalized for private use and possession.

Ganja use crosses all social strata; it is no less common for friends of the highest income levels to offer guests an after-dinner 'tote' than it is for the urban poor, who often smoke spliffs the size of bazookas. Many Jamaicans don't see ganja as a drug but as a medicinal and religious herb. To Rastafarians it is a source of wisdom.

For Jamaica's impoverished farmers, growing 'poor man's friend' is one of the few sure ways of earning money. The remote interior provides ideal conditions; the five-lobed plant thrives in Jamaica's rich red soil. And the main export market – the USA – is nearby.

First the seedlings are meticulously raised under protective cover and then transplanted into fields (guano, or bat dung, used as a fertilizer supposedly produces the most prolific plants). There they mature in five or six months, reaching heights as great as 10 feet. Ganja is planted between other crops by small-scale farmers, and in larger plots by more serious entrepreneurs. Once harvested, the plants are pressed to extract hash oil, and the leaves are then dried. Distributors collect the dried and baled ganja, which they transport to lonesome boat docks and remote airstrips for rapid shipment to the USA. Legitimate businesses sometimes act as covers (many respected businesspeople in Jamaica reportedly got their start in drug trafficking).

During the 1980s heyday, the annual wholesale value of Jamaica's ganja crop exceeded US$1.5 billion, and the trade had tacit approval at the government level. Nonetheless, since 1986 the Jamaican government has cracked down on drug trading at the behest of the US Drug Enforcement Agency (DEA). The DEA claims that Jamaica's ganja production has fallen by 80%, and that exports have fallen by two-thirds.

The strongest varieties are Burr, Cotton, and Lamb's Breath, which are marketed in the USA as sinsi (short for sinsemilla, Spanish for seedless).

Most but not all adherents smoke ganja copiously from cigar-size spliffs (reefers) and the 'holy chalice,' a bamboo pipe made of a goat's horn. Through it they claim to gain wisdom and inner divinity through the ability to 'reason' more clearly. The search for truth – 'reasoning' – is integral to the faith and is meant to see through the corrupting influences of 'Babylon.'

In recent years, Rastafarianism has concerned itself less with redemption than with resolution of the problems of the poor and dispossessed. Despite its militant consciousness, the religion preaches love and nonviolence, and adherents live by strict biblical codes that advocate a way of life in harmony with Old Testament traditions. They are vegetarians and teetotalers who also shun tobacco and the staples of western consumption. Those who copy Rastafarian style but bring ill-repute are referred to as 'wolves.'

Rastafarian Sects Adherents are grouped into regional sects. The Bobo Ashantis, who live above Bull Bay, follow a strictly ascetic and reclusive life, shunning interactions with Babylon, hoping intently for the day of repatriation, and relegating women to a subservient role. A sect known as the Twelve Tribes of Israel (Bob Marley was a member) is composed primarily of more accomplished, well-to-do Jamaicans who have managed a greater accommodation with Babylon and honor women, if not quite as equals, then almost.

Rasta 'yards' or communes are distinguished by the presence of flags and a figure of a lion representing Haile Selassie. Here they hold their *nyahbinghis,* organized gatherings also known as 'groundations.'

A Unique Lexicon One of the 21 tenets of Rastafarianism is the belief that God exists in each person, and that the two are the same. Thus the creed unifies divinity and individuality through the use of personal pronouns that reflect the 'I and I.' ('One blood. Everybody same, mon!') 'I' becomes the id

or true measure of inner divinity, which places everyone on the same plane. Thus 'I and I' can mean 'we,' 'him and her,' 'you and them.' (The personal pronoun 'me' is seen as a sign of subservience, of acceptance of the self as an 'object.')

Rastafarians have evolved a whole lexicon that has profoundly influenced 'Jamaica talk' (see the Language chapter) and is laced with cryptic intent and meaning. This revisionist 'English' is inspired by Rastafarian reasoning that sees the English language as a tool in the service of Babylon designed to 'downpress' the black man. In short, they believe the language is biased. Every word is analyzed, and in this frame even the most insignificant word can seem tainted. The well-meant greeting 'Hello!' may elicit the response: 'Dis not 'ell and I not low!'

LANGUAGE

Officially, English is the spoken language. In reality, Jamaica is a bilingual country, and English is far more widely understood than spoken. The unofficial lingo, the main spoken language of poor Jamaicans, is patois (PA-twah) – a musical dialect with a staccato rhythm and cadence, laced with salty idioms and wonderfully and wittily compressed proverbs.

Patois evolved from Creole English and a twisted alchemy of the mother tongue peppered with African, Portuguese, and Spanish terms and, in this century, Rastafarian slang. Linguists agree that it is more than simplified pidgin English, and it has its own identifiable syntax.

Patois is deepest in rural areas, where many people do not know much standard English. Although it is mostly the lingua franca of the poor, all sectors of Jamaica understand patois, and even polite, educated Jamaicans lapse into patois at unguarded moments. Most Jamaicans vary the degree of their patois according to whom they're speaking.

See the Language chapter for vocabulary and phrases.

REGGAE 'N' RIDDIMS

Whether you've been inspired by Bob Marley's lyrics or scandalized by Lady Saw's, skanked the night away at a ganja-smoke-filled rum shop, or wined groin-to-groin at a steamy dancehall, you can't help but feel the punchy pulse of Jamaican music, hitting you in the gut like a shot of overproof rum.

Jamaican music is associated above all with reggae…synonymous with one man: Robert Nesta Marley. Marley laid the foundation, beginning with the Wailers. But reggae is actually only one of several distinctly Jamaican sounds, which have evolved through six clear stages, each defined by a specific beat: ska (about 1960–66), rock-steady (1966–68), early and 'rebel' reggae (1969–74), 'roots' reggae (1975–79), dancehall (1979–85), and more recently, ragga. The varying musical forms have reflected the changing mood of the Jamaican people.

The scene is impressively fecund: Jamaica has spawned more than 100,000 records, and Kingston has dozens of recording studios. About 500

45s pour out of Kingston pressing plants monthly (the 7-inch 45rpm vinyl remains the dominant format in Jamaica).

The sheer creativity and productivity has produced a profound effect around the world. International stars such as Eric Clapton, the Rolling Stones, and Paul Simon incorporated reggae tunes into albums in the 1970s. In the early 1980s UK reggae bands such as Steel Pulse often shared concert billing with the Clash and other punk bands, exemplifying their commonality in uncompromising lyrical assaults on the 'shit-stem.' And the contemporary rap, rave, and hip-hop cultures owe much to Jamaica's sound-system-based dancehall culture.

African Roots

Jamaican music draws on its rich heritage of folk music introduced by African slaves, influenced through contact with white culture.

Although slave owners attempted to suffocate African culture, traditional music survived and evolved its own forms. Particularly important were the *burru* ('talking drums'), which were used to pass information, and folk songs derived from the cane fields, which were most often based on 'call-and-response' singing.

Over generations, European elements such as the French quadrille introduced by planters were assimilated, creating a uniquely Caribbean style that slave communities made their own.

The violin joined the hourglass-shaped African drum to give island music its distinctive form.

Mento

The earliest original Jamaican musical form was mento, a simple folk calypso that emerged at the turn of the 20th century as an accompaniment to a dance derived from the French quadrille and English-inspired maypole dances.

Mento fused burru-based calypso with Cuban influences – guitar, banjo, shakers, and rumba box – introduced by Jamaican migrant workers, with melodies played on banjo and violin accompanied by small accordions, kettledrums, gourds, and calabashes. Mento was slow and rhythmic, perfectly suited to the undulating groin-to-groin 'dubbing' of the African-derived dance styles. Most songs were underwritten by a wry, raunchy humor that dealt with the material discomforts of everyday life.

Mento developed a faster pace during the 1940s and 1950s and became as popular throughout Jamaica as reggae is today. By the late 1950s, however, the music was fading under a wave of popular North American music, particularly early boogie-woogie and R&B brought back to Jamaica by seasonal workers or carried on radio signals from New Orleans and Miami.

As North America shifted to rock 'n' roll in the 1950s, producers began to bring Jamaican performers into local studios to record the shuffling sounds their listeners wanted to hear.

Though still driven by shuffle boogies, the Jamaican R&B musicians lent the rhythm guitar on the offbeat more prominence and charged the third beat with an emphatic bass-drum kick that created a 'more Jamaican' sound. Gradually, the emphasis switched to the after-beat that would become the hallmark of Jamaican syncopation, conjuring ska out of American-influenced R&B by late 1961.

Ska

The Ska movement, though short-lived, was the first distinctive style of Jamaican music. Ska's fast, upbeat, enigmatic tempo was uniquely inventive; it blended mento's folk derivatives with elements from jazz, merengue, the Kumina religion, and nyahbinghi rhythms. It was mostly horn-driven, with a danceable double-time beat provided by the guitar and piano, lending the form its onomatopoeic name from the skat, skat, skat sound of the guitar.

The music's own unique bobbing dance style (also called ska, or skanking) became an overnight sensation, with shuffling feet seemingly moving like crankshafts and arms pumping like pistons.

'Prince' Buster was the most prolific ska producer and personified the 'one-man record company' that remains a staple of the Jamaican record production scene. He produced soulful singer Derrick Morgan and had ska's biggest hit in the early years with Eric Morris' 'Humpty Dumpty,' an insinuating nursery rhyme lyric that set off a brief trend.

Sound System Rivalry

Sound systems evolved in the mid-1940s and were concentrated in central Kingston in an area known as 'Beat Street.' The systems were set up at outdoor fenced-in plots (called 'lawns' or dance-halls), usually next to bars or liquor stores, whose owners were the main promoters.

During the 1950s and '60s, four promoters – 'Coxsone' Dodd, 'Duke' Reid (a former policeman who favored a sequined leather outfit and carried two pistols), 'King' Edwards, and 'Prince' Buster – dominated the scene. Their rivalry is legendary and generated fierce, and often violent, loyalty among their fans. Rival sound systems would often set up on opposite sides of the street and attempt to poach each other's fans through exclusive music pumped out over a more powerful bass. 'Enforcers' often attacked opponents' dances, and even destroyed their sound systems.

The greatest battles of all occurred at prearranged 'sound clashes' when DJs and sound systems vied to see who could 'flop' the oppo-nent and earn the sound-system crown. DJs still square off in fierce battles in deafening arenas where freshly pressed 'dub plates' become lethal weapons for DJs seeking the ultimate 'burial tune.'

Toots & the Maytals and the Skatalites hit big. Although they were together formally for only two years, the Skatalites (who were at one time managed by current Jamaican prime minister PJ Patterson), led by trombonist Don Drummond, produced hundreds of 45s, and their in-fluence on the island music scene was inestimable.

The Skatalites were also the backing group for the Wailing Rude Boys (later the Wailers), a youthful band led by Bob Marley and named for the lawless youths – 'rude boys' – of Kingston's ghettoes. In the early days many performers looked north, and the Wailers modeled them-selves on Curtis Mayfield and the Impressions.

Radio stations spread ska to North America and Europe, and per-formers such as Toots & the Maytals and Byron Lee & the Dragonaires became household names. In England, ska found a strong following among Jamaican immigrants and gained prominence with Millie Small's 1964 hit 'My Boy Lollypop.'

Rock-Steady

Ska had a therapeutic effect on a nation still in its infancy. But as socio-economic pressures mounted, discontent set in, and musicians began to address a younger, more militant ghetto audience, charging their music with angrier lyrics that reflected the changing times.

Sounds increasingly glamorized the 'rudies.' However, the Wailers also were in tune with the rising influence of Rastafarianism and recorded several more positive numbers. Tosh's 'Rasta Shook Them Up,' which celebrated Haile Selassie's visit in 1966, combined the pumping piano riffs of rude-boy music with a traditional Rasta chant, presaging the move toward 'reality,' or social-consciousness songs of the forthcoming decade. These songs would find their greatest expression through the voice of Bob Marley, Black Uhuru, and Burning Spear and become known as 'rebel' or 'roots' music.

Gradually the drums and bass came to prominence, slowing ska down still further to half speed so that it became a more syncopated, melodic, and slick music. The dance style was more languid, with minimal movements that gave the new 'ska' its own name: rock-steady, typified by Jimmy Cliff's 'You Can Get It If You Really Want' and Marcia Griffiths' 'Young, Gifted, and Black.'

Rock-steady helped shift Jamaica's music away from the dominant big sound-system bosses, and almost overnight it became *the* sound of the all-important dancehall.

Reggae

Reggae is the heartbeat of Jamaica, and it is as strongly identified with the island as R&B is with Detroit or jazz with New Orleans.

To Jamaicans, reggae has two distinct meanings: first, it is a generic term for all popular Jamaican music, and more particularly, it refers to a specific beat and style popular from about 1969 to 1983.

Reggae evolved from romantic-themed rock-steady but was fired in a crucible of tensions and social protest simmering violently in the late 1960s and early 1970s. Jamaicans will tell you that reggae means 'comin' from de people,' a phrase coined (as was the name *reggae* itself) by Frederick 'Toots' Hibbert of Toots & the Maytals in the single 'Do The Reggay' in 1968. The music expresses a yearning for respect, self-identity, and affirmation.

Early reggae was experimental and ranged widely, incorporating the jerky instrumentals of session bands and the sweet harmonies of established vocal groups, while inventing new types of rhythms.

Rebel Music & Roots Reggae

Rastafarians came to dominate the scene by the mid-1970s with their 'rebel music.' Rebel singers such as Max Romeo, the anguished Junior Byles, and Winston 'Niney' Holness forcefully imbued their recordings with traditional Rasta chants. Instrumental to their success was the influence of radical producer Lee 'Scratch' Perry, who tinged their music with a slow, edgy mood of 'dread,' a foreboding style suggestive of impending violence that resonated among the island populace.

Perhaps the most profound rebel entrée was the eye-popping debut, in 1969, of Burning Spear (Winston Rodney), who attained international status in the mid-1970s when his epochal Marcus Garvey album established him as the quintessential rebel singer.

Meanwhile, all three of the Wailers had become Rastafarians and now sported dreadlocks. As disillusion with Manley's PNP government deepened, Rastafarianism gained ground among the general populace. In 1970, Perry began to coach Bob Marley toward a new voice that led to an outpouring of relatively unknown recordings that musicologists acclaim as representing the Wailers at their peak. By the mid-1970s nyahbinghi drumming and Rasta chants were common rhythm elements, played in an updated, in-vogue version of the rocksteady rhythm, known as 'rockers.'

The genre had also earned a new moniker – 'roots reggae' – and was

poised for international acclaim (see the boxed text, 'Bob Marley – Reggae Royalty'). Ironically, Marley's songs initially received relatively little airplay in Jamaica, where the music – redolent with menacing social protest – was anti-establishment. (Reggae was actually banned from the airwaves.)

Jamaica's only other self-contained reggae band to reach stardom was Third World (Burning Spear was essentially a solo performer), who also signed to Island Records, as did Black Uhuru, who proved perhaps the most dynamic – and militant – reggae act of the late 1970s and early 1980s.

The era was dominated by male performers, although the I-Threes – Rita Marley, Judy Mowatt, and above all, Marcia Griffiths – had solo hits.

By the early 1980s, local audiences were tiring of the socially conscious lyrics that were an integral part of roots reggae, often made for an international audience. Jamaican music was taking a new direction more in tune with the changing focus of ghetto youth.

Non-Roots Reggae

Although the Rastafarian influence dominated the reggae scene in the latter 1970s, many artists recorded more mainstream sounds focusing on the vocal harmonies of the 1960s. Gregory Isaacs, Freddie McGregor, and Dennis Brown ('Crown Prince of Reggae') crafted beautifully melodic, romanticized reggae – called 'lovers rock.' McGregor came closer than any other Jamaican performer of the era in approaching US-style soul-pop.

Dancehall

The term 'dancehall,' although used to mean a sound-system venue, is also used specifically to refer to the musical genre dominant from 1979 to 1985. Dancehall is a kind of Caribbean rap music that focuses on earthly themes dear to the heart of young male Jamaicans, principally 'gal business,' gunplay, and ganja. This is hardcore music, named for the loosely defined, outdoor venues at which outlandishly named 'toasters' (rapper DJs) set up mobile discos with

Bob Marley – Reggae Royalty

Robert Nesta Marley was born on February 6, 1945, in the tiny village of Nine Mile in St Ann parish. His 17-year-old mother, Cedella, was a Jamaican, and it was she who raised him after his 51-year-old father, Norval Marley – a white, English-born, former army captain – deserted the family while Bob was still a youngster.

In his teens, Marley moved to Trench Town, a poverty-ridden ghetto in Kingston that would be his home for most of his life and which reverberated with the experimental sounds of young kids with musical aspirations.

Marley had begun singing in informal sessions on Third St in Trench Town, where he was mentored by a musician called Joe Higgs. Here, in 1960, he met Bunny 'Wailer' Livingston, Peter Tosh, and Junior Braithwaite. In 1961 they formed the Teenagers, and the following year Marley cut three solo records – 'Judge Not,' 'One Cup of Coffee,' and 'Terror' – released under the name Bob Martell. They flopped.

Lyricists had by now begun marrying music to social protest, and Marley and his cohorts renamed themselves the Wailing Rude Boys, later shortening it to the Wailers. In mid-1963, the group auditioned for Coxsone Dodd and had their first modest hit with 'Simmer Down,' which urged the rude boys to cool their heels during a period of rising tensions in Kingston.

In February 1966, Marley left for Wilmington, Delaware, USA, where he lived with his mother and found work in a car factory. Later that year, Marley married Rita Anderson. In 1967 Marley returned to his home parish, where he tried farming. During the heyday of ska, Marley had established himself as an early leading influence, with his creative style and unique stage presence. Texan rock-steady singer Johnny Nash, who had seen Marley perform on Jamaican TV, set out to find the reclusive singer. Nash signed Marley to his JAD label and, unsuccessfully aiming at the US market, began producing Marley's ground-breaking melodies that the world now knows as reggae.

In 1972, the Wailers came under the wing of promoter Chris Blackwell, whose Island Records was the UK's top independent label. Blackwell was keen to promote reggae and that year had released Jimmy Cliff's soundtrack to the movie *The Harder They Come*, a cult classic that helped thrust reggae onto the world stage. Island produced the Wailers' *Catch a Fire* (1972) as the first reggae album aimed at the album-buying rock audience, followed by a UK tour in the manner of a rock band. *Catch A Fire* and a second album, *Burnin'* (1973), rocketed to the top of the world charts and put reggae – and the Wailers – on the map.

The group's two Island albums set the stage for Marley's solo career, which was boosted in 1974 when Eric Clapton had a hit with a remake of 'I Shot the Sheriff,' a Marley song on the *Burnin'* album. Marley followed the Wailers' success with solo blockbuster albums, including *Exodus*, which spent 56 weeks in the Top 10 of the UK album chart.

There was just too much energy and individual ability to be contained in one outfit. Fellow Wailer Peter Tosh – the outspoken rebel – and Bunny Wailer – the soulful, dedicated Rasta – were jealous that Blackwell was focused on promoting Marley, who seemed more marketable than his musical partners. And Tosh's egotistical ways and simmering rage clashed with Marley's gentler character. By 1974 the group had separated, ending an 11-year musical partnership.

Marley took the band's name and performed with a new group as Bob Marley & the Wailers, and a trio of female back-up singers, the I-Threes, comprising his wife, Rita, Judy Mowatt, and Marcia Griffiths, who each continue to perform as soloists two decades later. The women added a more 'acceptable' sound to rock audiences and lent a softer visual note when touring – all part of Blackwell's vision for crossover market success.

Bob Marley – Reggae Royalty

Marley was now a member of the liberal Rastafarian Twelve Tribes of Israel sect, which gave him the name 'Joseph.' He was instantly recognizable with his thick dreads, but not afraid to be photographed haloed in clouds of ganja. And his womanizing was well known: although he and Rita remained man and wife until his death 15 years later, he is known to have fathered at least 11 children by other women, including Junior Gong, his son by former Miss Jamaica and Miss World Cindy Brakespeare.

Marley's stature was such that he was courted by politicians at times when Jamaica was seething with violence and animosities. In 1976, the election campaign spilled over into a mayhem of murder, and Prime Minister Michael Manley declared a state of national emergency and staged a Smile Jamaica concert intended to calm the situation. Marley – now nicknamed the Tuff Gong – was headlined, but on the eve of the concert he and Rita were nearly killed when gunmen burst into his home in Kingston. Two days later, a bandaged Marley went on stage and induced political archrivals Edward Seaga and Michael Manley to link arms (unenthusiastically) with him in a plea to stop the sectarian violence.

After recuperating at Strawberry Hill, Chris Blackwell's home in the Blue Mountains, Marley left Jamaica and spent two years recording and performing in Europe and North America, where reggae lovers greeted him as a demigod. By 1978, when he returned to Jamaica, multimillionaire Marley had attained superstardom.

Despite his revered stature, Marley never forsook his roots. He remained intensely spiritual. A consistent voice against racism, oppression, and injustice, Marley became the musical conscience of the world. Throughout the Third World, he was received as a messiah, with his crowning moment on April 17, 1980, when he led a triumphant concert to celebrate Independence Day at the transformation of colonial Rhodesia into Zimbabwe.

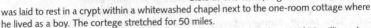

While touring the USA in 1980, Marley was diagnosed as having brain cancer. On the eve of his death, he was awarded the Order of Merit, Jamaica's highest honor. The Honorable Robert Nesta Marley, OM, died at the age of 36 on May 11, 1981, at Miami's Cedars of Lebanon Hospital. Dressed in a blue denim suit and a tam of red, green, and gold, his body lay in state at Kingston's National Arena, a Bible in one hand, a guitar in the other. He was laid to rest in a crypt within a whitewashed chapel next to the one-room cottage where he lived as a boy. The cortege stretched for 50 miles.

Marley died without making a will. His fortune – estimated at about US$50 million – has been the source of ongoing legal battles between family members.

Two decades after his death, Bob Marley continues to be reggae's biggest seller (his *Legend* album is nearing 10 million sales).

Marley's wife, Rita, and four of their children (performing as the Melody Makers) have continued to hold aloft the family flame.

For more information in Jamaica, contact the Bob Marley Foundation (☎ 927-9152; e marleyfoundation@cwjamaica.com; 56 Hope Road, Kingston 8).

enormous speakers, and singers and jive-talking DJs pumped-up with braggadocio perform live over instrumental rhythm tracks.

The form harks back to the 1950s when DJs traveled about the island with their sound systems and chatted over the music they played. During the 1960s, DJs were still largely confined to the dancehalls and worked to promote the sound systems that employed them; they encouraged the dancers by compliments or 'toasts,' with lyrics interjected emcee-style over songs and instrumentals.

By the close of the 1970s, producers had begun adopting computerized effects such as echo and reverb machines, producing 'dub' music and dancehall 'version' tracks (established rhythms remixed into infinite variations) that proved popular, permitting DJs to move to center stage.

Sexually explicit lyrics had been a popular staple of dancehall for many years, but during the 1980s songs gradually became mired in lewd lyrics, called 'slack,' epitomized by Yellowman (Winston Foster), who rose against all odds to become the undisputed king of slack. The talented albino became the best-selling DJ of all time and was also the first Jamaican DJ signed by a major US label (CBS). Although he has lost his prominence, he remains a staple of the island's music scene.

Other artists countered slackness with socially conscious lyrics known as 'dub poetry.'

The dancehall genre was so dominant (during the mid-1980s few hits sported an original rhythm track) that the only singers who could compete with DJs were those such as Junior Reidand and Barrington Levy, who had risen through the DJ sound-system ranks.

Ragga & the Digital Revolution

The dancehall craze spawned scores of new sound-system operators and producers, who remixed favorite tunes in true Jamaican manner, without heed for any copyright concerns.

The crown was seized by a producer called Prince Jammy (later renamed King Jammy). Many of Jammy's successful numbers featured backing rhythms by the High Times Band, whose sound overlaid a brash modern dancehall beat of classic rock-steady rhythms culled from decades before. Their hegemony was challenged by the irrepressibly experimental duo of Sly Dunbar and Robbie Shakespeare (today, still the most sought-after producers and rhythm-makers in Jamaica), whose own Taxi label put out scores of hits by songsters as diverse as Gregory Isaacs, Sugar Minott, Barrington Levy, and Freddie McGregor.

Sly & Robbie's experimentation with electronic 'robotic' rhythms in the mid-1980s was a signal of the radical new direction that dancehall was about to take as sound engineers switched from analog to digital recording formats.

The revolution in digital music technology fostered experimentation with original soundtracks that resulted in a blossoming of producers and labels. It also assured the demise of traditional session bands; computerization permitted just one or two musicians to make a 'band.' The new synthetic beat mood was captured in 1985 in Junior

Dancehall Divas

Jamaican women have had to work doubly hard to break into the island's musical scene. They have traditionally been relegated to the role of back-up singers or are employed just to moan on 'slack' numbers.

Dancehall has provided a vital venue, however, for a few talented female DJs, such as Lady Saw and Lady G. Lady Saw is the island's top female DJ chatter, with massive stage presence. She is renowned for her aggressive sexual overtures and slack lyrics offered from a woman's perspective, as in 'Condom,' advising safe sex. But she can run with the most obscene of male DJs, as in 'Stab Out the Meat,' and her proclamations of her own sexual prowess are often aimed as put-downs of boastful men.

Lady G has also made a name for herself at the top of the charts as a cultural DJ with incisive ghetto reality lyrics, notably with 'Nuff Respect,' which aimed barbs at misogynist male DJs and became an anthem for Jamaican women.

Others, such as super-talented Chevelle Franklyn, got their first taste of music in a church choir.

But other than the inimitable Marcia Griffiths, whose long pedigree (dating from the 1960s) assured her success with several ragga hits, no female ragga singer has yet made a mark on the crossover market, and relatively few vinyls by women singers have appeared.

Delgado's 'Ragamuffin Year.' The word – an identification with ghetto youth – was shorted to 'ragga' and adopted as the generic term for the new dancehall music.

Ragga is the ever-evolving, techno-driven, in-vogue music of the current dancehall generation – an often angry, in-your-face musical form echoing the restlessness of Jamaican youth. The music reflects a technological rather than aesthetic leap (to the lay-listener, ragga is associated most strongly with egotistical DJs spouting crass lyrics over a usually monotonous yet always fast-paced, compulsive, computerized, two-chord beat).

The ever-astute King Jammy herded the best talent of his day into his studio and became the 'don' of early ragga. Jammy produced most of the well-known leading vocalists, such as Delroy Wilson, Alton Ellis, Dennis Brown, and Gregory Isaacs.

Jammy's chief engineer, Bobby Digital, set out alone with his Digital B label, immediately providing a friend and relatively unknown, gravel-voice DJ called Shabba Ranks his first break with 'Peanie Peanie' and other numbers that launched Shabba to ragga stardom. Digital's reputation helped launch other stellar DJs, including Ninjaman, Beenie Man, Bounty Killer, and a sharp storyteller named Lieutenant Stitchie.

Bad Boys

Shabba started as a slack DJ whose favorite topic was his own sexual prowess, typified by 'Hard and Stiff.' Shabba's endorsement of Buju Banton's homophobic 'Boom Bye Bye' in 1992 sealed his image as a bad boy DJ, although he has matured in ensuing years, veering from slackness, exposing a greater creativity and even humor, and making a huge crossover leap to success under the major US label Epic with the hit 'Mr Loverman.'

Shabba's move to Epic permitted Ninjaman and Buju Banton to fill his shoes. Ninjaman established for himself a unique style that propelled him to the front in 1990. Rather than harnessing the rhythm track in the normal manner, he pitted himself against it in a stuttering, conversational style, as if he were 'reasoning' aloud. His favored topic has been a veneration of gun violence including his own outlaw past. The outspoken, gold-toothed DJ has more recently swum with the current, attempting to clean up his image with claims to be a born-again Christian called Brother Desmond.

Buju Banton also made girls and guns his dancehall staples. His star briefly faded in 1992 after his antigay 'Boom Bye Bye' exploded in his face, but he rebounded in 1993. Now a Rastafarian and powerfully 'conscious' rapper, Buju remains a leading force in the new ragga.

Roots Resurgence

In the early 1990s Jamaica began to witness a resurgence in the Rastafarian influence and with it a rebirth in the socially conscious focus that was the lifeblood of early reggae. Roots music is again the lick. Spearheading the renaissance was a group called Christian Souljahs, a trio comprising DJ-dubber Tony Rebel, a dub-poet Yasus Afri, and the soulful singer Garnett Silk, hailed at the time as an 'heir apparent' to Marley.

Silk's 'doctrine-steeped music' caught the national conscience and wrested the musical initiative from boastful dancehall 'dons' such as Beenie Man. Although Silk tragically died during a shoot-out in December 1994, the Rastafarian influence survived, inspiring a return to the days when Jamaican music was ruled by live horns, drums, and bass. To prove Buju Banton (and reggae) had come full circle, his song 'Untold Stories' won Jamaica's award for 'Song of the Year' in 1995 and is often compared to Bob Marley's 'Redemption Song.'

Shabba Ranks has also adopted 'cultural' ragga that even incorporates nyahbinghi drumming ('Kettle Drum') and a remake of Bob Marley's 'Heathen.' Similarly, Capleton – the slackest of all DJs in the early 1990s – discovered Rastafarianism and has incorporated nyahbinghi drumming in his cultural lyrics for the dancehall.

The Xterminator label, owned by Phillip 'Fatis' Burrell, is at the forefront of 'roots ragga' and has been instrumental in the leap to fame of the deeply religious, multitalented Luciano, who is edging toward superstardom with culturally conscious reggae evoking a universal message of spiritual hope.

Tony Rebel is considered the 'father' of the cultural revolution that began in earnest in 1995 and is still sweeping the dancehalls, inspiring a revisit to the protest chamber where reggae began.

An Explosion of Sounds

Some Jamaicans' experiments have also yielded intriguing hybrids. In 1996, the Taxi Gang's 'Western Farm' utilized country and western (even Lady Saw has blended country into dancehall ragga). Buccaneer's outrageous 'Sketel Concerto' brought opera into ragga. Reggae artist Gibby discovered heavy metal. The venerable Wailing Soul invoked a psychedelic tinge. And Sly & Robbie have created 'Latin reggae,' melding Cuban influences into the music scene.

Jazz has also begun to influence reggae in a big way, beginning in 1995 when jazz-propelled recordings were released by leading artists such as Spragga Benz, Papa San, and Beenie Man. And ska has had an enduring albeit malleable renaissance and, more recently, has been melded with jazz into a style called 'skazz,' a free-form hip-hop/ska/jazz combo, and even Christian ska bands, ska/punk (called 'ska-core'), and a fusion of ska with Latin sounds called 'salska.'

Ziggy Marley & the Melody Makers are the most commercially successful of all Jamaican musical acts, with a crossover audience that even Ziggy's dad would be proud of. Ziggy etched his own sound – albeit heavily influenced by his father – aimed at the international market, with little regard for ragga or other evolutions in the dancehall market. He experimented with acoustic reggae in the 1999 album *Spirit of Music*.

Resources

Online Resources The best online resource is the Jammin Reggae Archives site at W www.niceup.com, with links to reggae record companies and plenty of sound samples. Other good resources include W www.reggaesource.com and W www.reggaeweb.com.

Publications The definitive book on the topic is Rough Guide's *Rough Guide to Reggae* by Steve Barrow and Peter Dalton.

Reggae Routes by Wayne Chen and Kevin O'Brien Chang is required reading. This copious, lavishly illustrated volume is an insider's guide to reggae and popular Jamaican music in general, demystifying the music and correcting many misconceptions.

For books on Bob Marley, see Books in the Facts for the Visitor chapter.

Facts for the Visitor

HIGHLIGHTS

The Jamaica Tourist Board (JTB) has divided the island into seven 'resort' areas: Kingston, Mandeville, Montego Bay, Negril, Ocho Rios, Port Antonio, and Runaway Bay.

Beach Resorts

Montego Bay Also called 'MoBay,' this is the principal gateway to Jamaica and the main tourist center, with several public beaches and a good choice of hotels and all-inclusive resorts. A fistful of interesting historic sites lie close at hand, as do bamboo raft trips and, for hardy hikers, Cockpit Country.

Ocho Rios 'Ochi' is the main destination for cruise ships. The town itself is unappealing despite its two beaches, but there are plenty of historic sites, botanical gardens, and other attractions within a few minutes' drive.

Negril Jamaica's liveliest resort, Negril also boasts the longest (and one of the most stunning) beaches on the island. Live reggae shows, spectacular sunsets, and a let-your-hair-down attitude make this a favorite of budget and college-age travelers. Negril is also renowned for scuba diving and water sports.

Runaway Bay This small, secluded resort, midway between MoBay and Ocho Rios, is famous for its coral reefs and polo facilities. It has nice beaches, but the one-street town itself has no appeal whatsoever, and tourist infrastructure is minimal (nightlife is a bomb).

Port Antonio Secluded at the lush northeastern tip of Jamaica, offbeat Port Antonio is a center for bamboo raft trips and hiking in the Rio Grande Valley. Its highlights are its fully staffed, upscale villas and deluxe resorts tucked into coves east of town.

South Coast Most of the beaches along the south coast are long gray-sand beaches, appealing for their isolation and a lifestyle that still revolves around fishing. The best selection is around Treasure Beach, an in-vogue spot for travelers seeking an offbeat experience. Near at hand lie the Great Morass (a swamp area good for crocodile-spotting safaris), the YS waterfalls, Appleton rum estate, and Lover's Leap.

Other Escapes

Kingston The nation's bustling capital is more of a business locale than a tourism center. However, it *is* the center of island culture, with museums, art galleries, and important historic buildings, plus the Hellshire beaches are popular with Kingstonians on weekends.

Blue Mountains These mountains rise east of Kingston and offer an idyllic escape from the package-tour syndrome. The Blue Mountains-John Crow National Park has well-developed hiking trails.

Mandeville This historic agricultural and residential town lies in the cool upland interior, appealing to visitors who shun the beach resorts in favor of birding, scenic mountain drives, hiking, and interactions with local families.

PLANNING
When to Go

Jamaica is a year-round destination, though there are seasonal differences to consider. Weather-wise, temperature isn't an important factor: winter is usually warm by day and mild to cool by night; summer months are hot. The rainy season extends from May to November, with peaks in May and June and in October and November. Rain usually falls for short periods (normally in the late afternoon), and it's quite possible to enjoy sunshine for most of your visit during these months. In Portland parish, however, it can rain for days on end.

Tourism's high, or 'winter,' season runs from mid-December to mid-April, when hotel prices are highest. Many hotels charge 'peak season' rates during Christmas and Easter.

What Kind of Trip

Most visitors opt to laze on a beach, sip rum cocktails, and get a tan. The island's home-grown 'all-inclusive' resorts provide particularly appealing options for escapism. The downside is that your contact with the *real* Jamaica is at a minimum.

Meeting Rastafarians, playing dominoes in a rum shop, exploring off the beaten track, visiting a Kingston dancehall, etc, allow you to get to know and appreciate the colorful Jamaican character.

Travelers wishing to pursue special-interest activities are offered plenty of choices (see Activities later this chapter).

Maps

The Jamaican Tourist Board (JTB) publishes a *Discover Jamaica* road map (1:350,000) in association with Esso. No topographical details are shown. Similar road maps are published by Shell and Texaco and show topographical detail and greater road details. All include separate street maps (1:34,000) of Kingston and major towns. You can pick these maps up at the respective gas stations or at any JTB office.

The best maps are Hildebrandt's Jamaica map (1:300,000) and ITMB Publishing's maps (1:250,000), available at travel bookstores.

The most accurate maps are the Jamaica Ordnance Survey maps published by the **Survey Dept** (☎ 922-6630; 231½ Charles St, PO Box 493, Kingston 10; open 9am-1pm & 2pm-3pm Mon-Thur).

You can order individual Ordnance Survey sheets (plus the Hildebrandt and ITMB maps) from:

Australia The Map Shop (☎ 08-231-2033), 16a Peel St, Adelaide, SA 5000

Canada ITMB Publishing (☎ 604-879-3621; W www.itmb.com), 530 West Broadway, Vancouver BC V5Z 1E9

New Zealand Speciality Maps (☎ 9-307-2217), 58 Albert St, Auckland

UK Stanfords (☎ 020-7836-1321, fax 7836-0189; W www.stanfords.co.uk), 12-14 Long Acre, London WC2E 9LP

USA Omni Resources (☎ 800-742-2677, fax 336-227-3748; W www.omnimap.com), PO Box 2096, Burlington, NC 27216
Treaty Oak (☎ 512-326-4141, fax 443-0973; W www.treatyoak.com), PO Box 50295, Austin, TX 78763

For information about maritime maps and charts, see Sea in the Getting There & Away chapter.

What to Bring

Make sure your luggage is padlocked before parting with it, and don't leave anything of value in external pockets, as theft from baggage at the Montego Bay airport is frequent.

Clothing Travel light! Loose-fitting, lightweight cotton clothing is best because it allows air flow in the hot humid climate. Tight clothing tends to make you sweat more, as will synthetics like nylon. T-shirts and tank tops are the perfect wear for outdoors and are best worn untucked, allowing air to circulate.

A light sweater might prove handy at night and in upland areas.

Shorts are acceptable daywear. A long-sleeved shirt and long pants (trousers) are useful to guard against sunburn. You'll also need long pants for the more upscale discos and restaurants. Several ritzier hotel restaurants require jackets for men and elegant dresses for women.

You'll get by with a pair of sneakers, sandals, or flip-flops (thongs), and a pair of lightweight casual shoes for evening wear. Elastic canvas and rubber 'reef-walking' shoes are ideal for wading.

Pack a windproof jacket and a sweater and lightweight rain jacket if you plan on hiking.

Toiletries & Supplies At a minimum, your basic kit should include toothpaste, toothbrush, dental floss, deodorant, shampoo, skin creams, make-up, tampons, contraceptives, and a basic medical kit (see Health later in this chapter).

Few hotels in Jamaica provide complimentary toiletries, and many don't provide washcloths or beach towels, which you can buy in Jamaica.

Don't forget a spare pair of glasses or contact lenses, and any medicines you may require.

A flashlight (torch) is useful in the event of an electrical blackout (very common).

RESPONSIBLE TOURISM

Visitors are often tempted to buy souvenirs made from endangered wildlife – such as swallowtail butterflies, stuffed baby crocodiles, and black coral jewelry – without realizing the devastating impact this has on local ecology. (See Ecology & Environment in the Facts about Jamaica chapter.)

Getting Married in Jamaica

Jamaica is a popular destination for honeymooners, many of whom tie the knot on the island. Jamaican law allows couples to marry after only 24 hours on the island.

In addition to proof of citizenship (such as a certified copy of a birth certificate that includes the father's name), you'll need certified copies of appropriate divorce or death certificates, if one or both of you is divorced or widowed, and written parental consent if either partner is under 21 years of age. These documents must be notarized.

Most major hotels and tour operators will make arrangements; you'll usually need to send notarized copies of required documents in advance. Major resorts have wedding packages. If you prefer a religious ceremony, advance planning with a member of the clergy is required.

The JTB can make arrangements (see Tourist Offices, later). Alternately, you can apply in person at the **Registrar Office** (☎ 971-8556; 20 Market St, Montego Bay) or the **Registrar General's Office** (☎ 984-3041; W www.rgd.gov.jm) at Twickenham Park, St Catherine. A license costs US$54.

Buying ganja or cocaine not only is illegal but also helps foster drug trafficking and its concomitant handmaiden, crime.

Prostitution is tolerated and exists quite openly in tourist resorts. However, some females choosing to engage in sex with tourists are underage (16 is the legal age of sexual consent in Jamaica). Sexual activity with a minor carries heavy penalties, as well as being morally reprehensible. (See Prostitution in the Dangers & Annoyances section later in this chapter.)

The **Center for Responsible Tourism** (e CRTourism@aol.com; 1765-D LeRoy Ave, Berkeley, CA 94709, USA) publishes guidelines for tourists.

TOURIST OFFICES

The **Jamaica Tourist Board** (JTB; e jamaicatrv@aol.com) has offices in key cities around the world. You can request maps and literature, including hotel brochures, but they do not serve as reservation agencies. The website (W www.jamaicatravel.com) features a 'J-Mail Dispatch,' which automatically updates you via email about new events and happenings in Jamaica.

The **Caribbean Tourism Organization** (☎ 212-635-9530; W www.doitcaribbean.com; 80 Broad St, 32nd Floor, New York, NY 10004) can also supply information.

Local Tourist Offices

The **JTB headquarters** (☎ 929-9200, fax 929-9375; 64 Knutsford Blvd, PO Box 360, Kingston 5) is poorly stocked with literature. In addition, you'll find JTB offices in Montego Bay, Negril, Ocho Rios, Port Antonio, and Black River (see the regional chapters).

The JTB has a toll-free **Tourism Information Helpline** (☎ 881-991-4400) and a hotline (☎ 888-991-9999) for emergency assistance.

Roadside information booths exist in major resorts.

Tourist Offices Abroad

There are a number of JTB offices worldwide, including the following:

Canada (☎ 416-482-7850, fax 482-1730) 1 Eglinton Ave E No 616, Toronto

France (☎ 01-45-63-42-01, fax 01-42-25-66-40) c/o Target International, 32 rue de Ponthieu, 75008 Paris

Germany (☎ 6184-99-0044, fax 6184-99-0046) c/o Postfach 90 04 37, 60444 Frankfurt/Main 1

Italy (☎ 6-687-5693, fax 6-687-3644) c/o Sergat Italia, Via Monte Dei Cenci 20 7/A, 01186, Rome

Japan (☎ 3-3591-3841, fax 3-3591-3845) 3 Mori Building, 1-4-10 Nishi-Shinbashi Minato-ku, Tokyo 108

UK (☎ 020-7224-0505, fax 020-7224-0551) 1-2 Prince Consort Rd, London SW7 2BZ

USA Chicago (☎ 312-527-1296, fax 527-1472) 500 N Michigan Ave No 1030, Chicago, IL 60611

Miami (☎ 305-666-0557, fax 666-7239) Doral Executive Office Park, 3785 NW 82nd Ave Suite 403, Coral Gables, FL 33166

Los Angeles (☎ 213-384-1123, fax 384-1780) 3440 Wilshire Blvd No 1207, Los Angeles, CA 90010

New York (☎ 212-856-9727, 800-233-4582, fax 212-856-9730) 801 Second Ave, New York, NY 10017

VISAS & DOCUMENTS
Passports
US and Canadian citizens do not need passports for visits up to six months. However, they *do* need two pieces of identification, including proof of citizenship or permanent residency, such as a passport, birth certificate, or driver's license with photo ID.

All other visitors must arrive with a passport. British citizens need passports that will still be valid six months from their date of arrival.

Visas
No visas are required for entry to Jamaica for citizens of European Union countries, the USA, Canada, Mexico, Australia, New Zealand, Japan, or Israel.

Nationals of the UK, Ireland, USA, and Canada may stay for six months. Nationals of Austria, Belgium, Denmark, Finland, Germany, Iceland, Israel, Italy, Luxembourg, Mexico, the Netherlands, Norway, Sweden, Switzerland, Turkey, and Commonwealth countries (except Sri Lanka and

Pakistan) may stay for three months. Nationals of Argentina, Brazil, Chile, Costa Rica, Ecuador, France, Greece, Japan, Portugal, and Spain may stay for 30 days.

All other nationals require visas (nationals of most countries can obtain a visa on arrival, provided they are holding valid onward or return tickets and evidence of sufficient funds).

Immigration formalities require every person to show a return or ongoing airline ticket when arriving in Jamaica.

Travel Insurance
However you're traveling, it's worth taking out travel insurance. Everyone should be covered for the worst possible case: an accident, for example, that requires hospital treatment and a flight home.

A travel insurance policy that covers theft, loss of baggage, and medical treatment is a good idea. You might also consider trip-cancellation insurance if you have booked a prepaid package with cancellation penalty clauses. Any travel agent can recommend an appropriate package.

When purchasing medical insurance, consider a policy that pays for medical services immediately and directly. Otherwise you may have to pay on the spot, then claim for reimbursement once you return home. Check if the policy covers ambulances or an emergency flight. Also check if there are exclusions for any 'hazardous activities' you may be contemplating, such as renting motorcycles or scuba diving.

In the USA, the following companies are leading travel insurance suppliers:

American Express (☎ 800-234-0375; W www.americanexpress.com)

Travelers (☎ 800-243-3174; W www.travelers.com)

TravelGuard International (☎ 800-826-4919; W www.travelguard.com)

The **Council on International Education Exchange** (CIEE; W www.ciee.org) offers low-cost, short-term insurance policies called 'Trip Safe' to holders of the International Student Identification Card (ISIC), International Youth Card (IYC), or International Teachers Identification Card (ITIC).

In the UK, contact **Endsleigh Insurance** (☎ 020-7436-4451; W www.endsleigh.co.uk) or **STA Travel** (☎ 020-7361-6262; W www.sta.com).

In Australia, contact **AFTA** (☎ 02-9956-4800; W www.afta.com.au) or take a look at the info provided by **Travel Insurance on the Net** (W www.travelinsurance.com.au).

Driver's License & Permits

To drive in Jamaica, you must have a valid International Driver's License (IDL) or a current license for your home country or state, valid for up to six months. You can obtain an IDL by applying with your current license to any Automobile Association office.

A North American driver's license is valid for up to three months per visit from the date of entry; a UK license is valid for up to one year; and a Japanese license is valid for one month.

Hostel Card

Jamaica has no youth hostel system. Unless you plan on combining your visit to Jamaica with other destinations that have youth hostels, leave your IYHF and other discount cards at home.

Copies

All important documents (passport data page and visa page, credit cards, travel insurance policy, air/bus/train tickets, driving license etc) should be photocopied before you leave home. Leave one copy with someone at home and keep another with you, separate from the originals.

EMBASSIES & CONSULATES

It's important to realize what your own embassy – the embassy of the country of which you are a citizen – can and can't do to help you if you get into trouble. Generally speaking, it won't be much help in emergencies if the trouble you're in is remotely your own fault. Remember that you are bound by the laws of the country you are in. Your embassy will not be sympathetic if you end up in jail after committing a crime locally, even if such actions are legal in your own country.

In genuine emergencies, you might get some assistance from your embassy, but only if other channels have been exhausted. If you need to get home urgently, a free ticket home is exceedingly unlikely – the embassy would expect you to have travel insurance. If you find yourself in the unfortunate situation where all your money and documents are stolen, your embassy might assist you with getting a new passport, but a loan for onward travel is definitely out of the question.

Some embassies used to keep letters for travelers or have a small reading room with home newspapers, but these days most of the mail-holding services have been stopped and even newspapers tend to be out of date.

Jamaican Embassies & High Commissions

Unless otherwise noted, the details here are for embassies.

Canada *High Commission:* (☎ 613-233-9311, fax 233-0611; e jhcott@sympatico.ca) Standard Life Bldg, 275 Slater St Suite 402, Ottawa, Ontario K1P 5H9

Consulate General: (☎ 416-598-3008, fax 598-4928; e jcgtoronto@attcanada.net) 214 King St W Suite 402, Toronto, Ontario M5H 1KA

UK *High Commission:* (☎ 020-7823-9911, fax 7589-5154; e jhc@btinternet.uk) 1-2 Prince Consort Rd, London SW7 2BZ

USA (☎ 202-452-0660, fax 452-0081; e emjam@sysnet.net) 1520 New Hampshire Ave NW, Washington, DC

Consulate Generals: (☎ 212-935-9000, fax 935-7507) 767 Third Ave, New York, NY 10017 (☎ 305-374-8431, fax 577-4970) 842 Ingraham Bldg 25, SE Second Ave, Miami, FL 33131

Embassies & Consulates in Jamaica

At press time, more than 40 countries had official representation in Jamaica. Except for a couple of Montego Bay consulates, all are located in Kingston. If your country isn't represented in this list, check 'Embassies & High Commissions' in the yellow pages of the Greater Kingston telephone directory.

Australia *High Commission:* (☎ 926-3550, 926-3551) 64 Knutsford Blvd, Kingston 5

Austria *Consulate:* (☎ 929-5259) 2 Ardenne Rd, Kingston 10

Canada *High Commission:* (☎ 926-1500) 3 West Kings House Rd, Kingston 10
Consulate: (☎ 952-6198) 29 Gloucester Ave, Montego Bay

France (☎ 978-0210) 13 Hillcrest Ave, Kingston 6

Germany (☎ 926-6728) 10 Waterloo Rd, Kingston 10

Italy (☎ 978-1273) 10 Rovan Drive, Kingston 6

Japan (☎ 929-7534) 1 Kensington Crescent, Kingston 5

Mexico (☎ 926-6891) 36 Trafalgar Rd, Kingston 10

Netherlands (☎ 926-2026) 53 Knutsford Blvd, Kingston 5

Russia (☎ 924-1048) 22 Norbrook Drive, Kingston 8

Spain (☎ 929-6710) 25 Dominica Drive, Kingston 5

Sweden *Consulate:* (☎ 941-3761) Unit 3, 69 Constant Spring Rd, Kingston 10

Switzerland *Consulate:* (☎ 978-7857) 22 Trafalgar Rd, Kingston 10

Venezuela (☎ 926-5510) 36 Trafalgar Rd, Kingston 10

UK *High Commission:* (☎ 510-0700, 926-9050; ✉ bhckingston@cwjamaica.com) 28 Trafalgar Rd, Kingston 10
Consulate: (☎ 912-6859) Montego Bay

USA (☎ 929-4850, 926-6440 after hours, fax 935-6018; ✉ kingstonacs@state.gov) Life of Jamaica Bldg, 16 Oxford St, Kingston 2
Consulate: (☎ 952-0160, 952-5050; ✉ uscons agency.mobay@cwjamaica.com) St James Plaza, 2nd Floor, Gloucester Ave, Montego Bay

CUSTOMS
Entering Jamaica

You are allowed to import the following items duty-free: 25 cigars, 200 cigarettes, one pint of liquor (except rum), 1lb of tobacco, and one quart of wine. The following items are restricted: firearms, drugs (except prescription medicines), flowers and plants, honey, fruits, coffee, and meats and vegetables (unless canned).

You may need to show proof that laptop computers and other expensive items (especially electronics) are for personal use; otherwise you may be charged import duty.

Leaving Jamaica

US citizens can purchase up to US$600 duty-free per person, provided they have not used the allowance within the last 30 days. In addition, you may import 200 cigarettes, 100 cigars (except Cuban cigars, which are *not* permitted to be taken into the USA), plus 1L of liquor or wine.

Canadian citizens are allowed an annual allowance of C$500, plus 200 cigarettes, 50 cigars, 2lb of loose tobacco, and 40oz of liquor. In addition, you can mail unsolicited gifts valued up to C$40 per day.

British citizens may import goods worth up to £200 in addition to 200 cigarettes, 50 cigars or 250g of loose tobacco, and 2L of wine plus 1L of spirits (depending on alcohol proof).

Australian citizens are permitted to bring back A$400 of gifts and souvenirs, plus 250 cigarettes or 250g of tobacco, and 1125ml of alcohol.

New Zealand citizens may bring back NZ$700 worth of souvenirs, plus 200 cigarettes or 50 cigars, and 4.5L of beer or wine and 1125ml of spirits.

MONEY
Currency

The unit of currency is the Jamaican dollar, the 'jay,' which uses the same symbol as the US dollar ($).

Jamaican currency is issued in bank notes of J$10, J$20, J$50, J$100, and J$200. Coins are issued for 10 cents, 25 cents, J$1, and J$5. The symbol used for cents (¢) is also the same as in the United States.

Prices for hotels and valuable items are usually quoted in US dollars, which are widely accepted. It's always wise to check whether a quoted price is in Jamaican or US dollars, particularly when using taxis. (Duty-free goods must be purchased with foreign currency.)

Exchange Rates

The official rate of exchange fluctuates daily, and as of April 2002 it was about J$47 to US$1, and J$67 to £1. Long-term, the Jamaica dollar has been in gradual and steady decline against the US dollar.

Exchanging Money

It's a wise idea to always have some 'jay' on hand throughout your island visit. However, US dollars are accepted everywhere (you'll receive change in Jamaican dollars; usually at rates 5% to 10% lower than the official exchange rate), and almost any commercial entity will change dollars for you.

Cash Commercial banks have branches throughout the island. Those in major towns maintain a foreign exchange booth. Bank hours are generally 9am to 2pm Monday to Thursday, and 9am to 4pm Friday. Some banks close at 2pm and reopen from 3pm to 5pm Friday. A few local banks also open 9am to noon Saturday.

Traveler's Checks Traveler's checks are widely accepted in Jamaica, although some hotels, restaurants, and exchange bureaus charge a hefty fee for cashing them.

Immediately report lost traveler's checks: American Express (☎ 800-221-7282); Thomas Cook (☎ 800-223-7373).

ATMs Most city bank branches throughout Jamaica now have 24-hour automated teller machines (ATMs), which dispense incidental cash using a credit or debit card. Many, but not all, are linked to international networks such as Cirrus or Plus.

Credit & Debit Cards Major credit cards are widely accepted throughout the island.

You can use your credit card to get cash advances at most commercial banks for a small transaction fee. You'll usually lose out as much as 5% to 10% in the conversion from 'jay' to US dollars. Credit-card purchases are subject to a government sales tax that might not otherwise apply.

To report lost or stolen credit cards, call: American Express (☎ 800-528-4800); MasterCard (☎ 800-826-2181); Visa (☎ 800-336-8472).

International Transfers If you need emergency cash, you can arrange a telegraph or mail transfer from your account in your home country, or from a friend or family member.

Western Union (☎ 926-2454, 888-991-2056; W www.westernunion.com; 7 Hillview Ave, Kingston 5) has offices islandwide.

Black Market Young Jamaican men are eager to change Jamaican dollars in street transactions. It's strictly illegal, however, and not worth it: the black market rate is rarely more than 5% lower than the official exchange rate, and many black-marketeers are scam artists.

Money Changers Virtually every town and village has at least one licensed money-changer, known as 'cambios' or 'FX-Trader.' They offer rates slightly lower than banks and charge a processing fee that is between 2% and 5% of the transaction. All kinds of outlets operate as 'cambios,' including supermarkets and general stores.

Security

Carry as little cash as needed when away from your hotel. Keep the rest in a hotel safe. You can rely on credit cards and traveler's checks for most of your purchases. However, you'll need cash for most transactions in rural areas and at gas stations.

Don't carry your cash where it can be seen, and never in a back pocket. Stash your money in a money belt or pouch worn inside your clothing. Set a small sum aside for emergencies in case you get ripped off.

Costs

How much you spend depends on your sense of style. Even hard-core budget travelers will need at least US$25 a day. Roadside stalls and budget restaurants sell patties for US$0.50 and jerk pork and other local meals for as little as US$2. A hand of bananas or half a dozen mangoes will cost about US$0.50. More touristy restaurants, however, can be expensive, as many of the ingredients they use are imported: expect to pay at least US$8 per person, and for the finest restaurants, as much as US$50.

Car rentals begin at about US$45 a day for the smallest vehicle. Public transport is inordinately cheap (see the Getting Around chapter), although tourist taxis are expensive (usually US$7 minimum for even the shortest journey).

Budget accommodations charge US$20 or more, even for spartan conditions. Midrange hotels range from about US$40 to US$100, while luxury resorts can charge US$300 or more. All-inclusive hotels can offer tremendous bargains, as everything you consume or participate in is included in room rates.

Discounts To save money, visit in 'summer,' or low season (mid-April to mid-December), when hotel prices plummet and airfares are often reduced.

See Reservations in the Accommodations section later in this chapter.

Tipping & Bargaining
A 10% tip is normal in hotels and restaurants. Some restaurants automatically add a 10% to 15% service charge to your bill. Check your bill carefully, as often the charge is hidden. Some all-inclusive resorts have a strictly enforced no-tipping policy. Bellhops expect a tip (US$0.50 per bag is plenty).

Bargaining – *higgling* – is a staple of market life in Jamaica, though most prices in shops are fixed.

Taxes
The government charges a General Consumption Tax (GCT) of 15% on restaurant bills and most purchases in stores. The GCT charge varies according to type of hotel, from 6.25% to 15%.

POST & COMMUNICATIONS
Postal Rates
Every town has a post office and most villages have postal agencies.

Post offices are open 8am to 5pm Monday to Friday. Postal agencies are usually open Monday, Wednesday, and Friday mornings only, although times vary.

Postcards cost J$10 to anywhere in the world. Airmail letters worldwide cost J$40 for the first 30 grams, and J$90 for 30-110 grams. Domestic letters cost J$15 for up to 110 grams.

The Jamaica Post website, W www.jamaica post.gov.jm, lists rates.

Sending Mail
Postal service is *sloooow!* Airmail to North America usually takes about 10 days to two weeks, and a few days longer to Europe. Surface mail can take forever…well, almost.

Postal theft is common. Never mail cash or valuables. Use an express mail service for any valuable documents.

When sending mail to Jamaica always include the addressee's name, address or post office box, town, and parish, plus 'Jamaica, West Indies.'

Many individuals, hotels, etc, have no street addresses or PO Box, but pick up their mail at the nearest post office; this would be written, for example, as 'Maggotty PO, St Elizabeth.'

Express Mail Services Express mail services are listed in the yellow pages and include UPS (☎ 923-0371 in Kingston) and Federal Express (☎ 952-0411, 888-991-9081 in Montego Bay, ☎ 960-9192 in Kingston).

Receiving Mail
You can have mail addressed to you marked 'Poste Restante' care of a major central post office. Thus, you should have a letter or package addressed with '(your name), Poste Restante, General Post Office,' then the town and parish, plus 'Jamaica, West Indies.'

Telephone
Jamaica has a fully automated, digital telephone system operated by **Cable & Wireless Jamaica** (☎ 888-225-5295; W www.cwjamaica .com), which has offices islandwide (see regional chapters).

You can make direct calls at Cable & Wireless Jamaica offices or at privately run 'call-direct centres,' where an operator places a call on your behalf and you're directed to the appropriate phone booth. You will be charged 'time and charge,' in which the operator will advise you of the cost upon completion of your call.

Public Telephones You'll find public telephones at Cable & Wireless Jamaica offices. Even remote villages are served by public telephones, which often serve the entire community.

To use a public phone, pick up the receiver and wait for the clicking tone before dialing. You deposit your coins *after* a connection, after which you can begin talking.

Cable & Wireless Jamaica phone cards – CardPhone – have replaced coin-operated public call boxes. The plastic cards are available from Cable & Wireless Jamaica offices, retail stores, hotels, banks, and other outlets displaying the 'Phone Cards on Sale' sign. There's always an outlet close by the phone, even in the boondocks. The card is paid for in advance in denominations of J$20 to J$500. When calls are made, the telephone shows the balance remaining on a digital screen, and deducts the charges from the value of your card.

To make a call using the CardPhone, simply lift the receiver and insert the card (picture-side up) into the special slot. Then dial ☎ 113; when you hear the tone, press the # button, then dial your number. Wait for the other party to start talking before pressing the 'Press to Talk' button.

Domestic Calls Jamaican numbers all have seven digits, which you dial for calls within the same parish. For calls to other parishes, dial '1' then the seven-digit number.

Toll-free numbers begin with ☎ 800 or 888 and should be preceded by '1.'

International Calls Major hotels have direct-dial calling; elsewhere you may need to go through the hotel operator, or call from the front desk. Hotels add a 15% government tax, plus a service charge, often at sticker-shock rates.

Outside major hotels, direct dial requires that you call ☎ 113, wait for a tone, then press the # button, wait for a tone, and finally dial your desired number.

You can save money by using a 'home-direct' service such as AT&T USADirect, MCI CallUSA, or Sprint Express. Dial an access number from any telephone to reach a US operator who links your call. You can bill your home phone, phone card, or call collect. Scams are frequent; *never* give your calling-card number to anyone other than the operator.

To place collect or calling-card calls from Jamaica, simply dial the appropriate code below:

country/service	code
USA	
AT&T USADirect	☎ 872 or 800-872-2881
MCI CallUSA	☎ 873 or 800-674-7000
Sprint Express	☎ 875 or 800-877-8000
Canada	
Canada Direct	☎ 876 or 800-222-0016
UK	
BT Direct	☎ 874 or 800-364-5263

Note that MCI no longer permits calling card calls from Jamaica due to a large volume of fraud cases.

You can also buy WORLD*TaLK calling cards (issued by Cable & Wireless) in Jamaica, good for use on any telephone, including public call boxes and cellular phones. To use, dial the access number (☎ 958-2273), wait for a tone, then enter the card account number, wait for a tone, then dial the number you are calling.

You can make international collect calls (reverse charges) using WORLD*TaLK cards. However, the process for connecting to 'home-direct' service is different.

country	service	code
USA	AT&T USADirect	☎ #1
	MCI CallUSA	☎ #2
	Sprint Express	☎ #3
Canada	Canada Direct	☎ #4
UK	BT Direct	☎ #5

For countries that cannot be dialed direct, call the **international operator** (☎ 113 toll-free).

Calling Jamaica from Abroad If you wish to call Jamaica from abroad, dial your country's international dialing code, then

☎ 876 (Jamaica's country code), and the seven-digit local number.

Cellular Phones You can bring your own cellular phone into Jamaica, but you'll be charged a customs fee upon entry (this is refunded when you leave). You can also rent cellular phones from **Cable & Wireless Jamaica** (☎ 888-865-2355), which also offers roaming service if you bring your own phone.

Fax

Many towns have private fax services, which are listed in regional chapters. You can send faxes from hotels, major post offices, and Cable & Wireless Jamaica centers, which send telegrams, too.

Email & Internet Access

Many upscale hotels provide in-room, dial-up access for laptop computers. Others offer guests email and Internet access through business centers.

Cable & Wireless Jamaica offers Internet access via its **Voyageur Internet Service** (☎ 888-225-5295).

Most town libraries now have Internet access (J$50 for 30 minutes). Most towns also have at least one commercial entity where you can access the Internet. See regional chapters for details.

DIGITAL RESOURCES

The World Wide Web is a rich resource for travelers. You can research your trip, hunt down bargain airfares, book hotels, check on weather conditions and chat with locals and other travelers about the best places to visit (or avoid!).

There's no better place to start your Web explorations than the Lonely Planet Web site (ⓦ www.lonelyplanet.com). Here you'll find succinct summaries on traveling to most places on earth, postcards from other travelers and the Thorn Tree bulletin board, where you can ask questions before you go or dispense advice when you get back. You can also find travel news and updates for many of our most popular guidebooks, and the subWWWay section links you to the most useful travel resources elsewhere on the Web.

BOOKS

Most books are published in different editions by different publishers in different countries. As a result, a book might be a hardcover rarity in one country but readily available in paperback in another. Fortunately, bookstores and libraries can search by title or author, so your local bookstore or library is best placed to advise you on the availability of the following recommendations.

Macmillan Caribbean (☎ 0256-29242 in the UK; ⓦ www.macmillan-caribbean.com), a division of Macmillan Press, publishes a wide range of books about the Caribbean.

Information on bookshops throughout Jamaica can be found in the regional chapters.

Guidebooks

Lonely Planet's *Eastern Caribbean* is an invaluable guidebook to the region if you're planning to do some island hopping.

Tour Jamaica by Margaret Morris is an excellent guide for anyone exploring the island by car. The book has 19 recommended tours.

Lonely Planet's *Diving & Snorkeling Jamaica* by Hannie & Theo Smitt is the most comprehensive guide for underwater enthusiasts, with lavishly illustrated regional sections and maps complementing an introductory overview.

Travel

Swashbuckling Hollywood hero Errol Flynn, who lived in Jamaica for many years, recalls his colorful experiences in his autobiography *My Wicked, Wicked Ways*.

Anthony Winckler's *Going Home to Teach* tells of the novelist's time in Jamaica as a teacher during an epoch of anti-white sentiment in the tension-filled late 1970s.

Internet Resources

The explosion in recent years of communications in cyberspace has fostered dozens of travel sites on the Internet. Addresses (URLs) for hotels, tour companies, and the like are listed throughout the book. Meanwhile, here are good starting points for general information about Jamaica or travel:

Lonely Planet
W www.lonelyplanet.com
Especially good for practical tips on preparing for your trip

Great Outdoor Recreation Page
W www.gorp.com
If you plan on hiking, mountain biking, or the like, try this site with extensive listings on maps, gear, and outfitters.

Specific to Jamaica

There are dozens of Jamaica-specific sites. Your starting point should be the JTB's website.

Jamaica Tourist Board
W www.jamaicatravel.com
Covers most of the bases for travelers and has numerous links

Go Jamaica
W www.go-jamaica.com
Generic site with links covering news, sports, travel, communities, etc

Jamaica Attractions
W www.attractions-jamaica.com
Listings of great houses, plantations, and other sites

Jamaica Observer
W www.jamaicaobserver.com
Jamaica's leading newspaper's site with current day's paper online, plus archives

Jamaica Travel Net
W www.jamaica-tours.com
The website of tour company Changes in L'attitudes provides listings of attractions, hotel reviews, flight information, and booking services.

Jamaicans.com
W www.jamaicans.com
Information and links regarding culture, tourism, business, and news

Jamweb
W www.jamweb.com
This site has pages serving news, environment, music, society and culture, economy and business, politics, sports, arts, and vacations, all with links to related sites.

Jamaica! Yellow Pages
W www.yellowpagesjamaica.com
Has a listing of all businesses in Jamaica

National Library of Jamaica
W www.nlj.org.jm
The largest online directory of Jamaican websites

Netsearch Jamaica
W www.netsearchjamaica.com
Broad-based Web directory covering arts, business, culture, entertainment, travel, etc

Top 5 Jamaica
W www.top5jamaica.com
Comprehensive links spanning arts to travel

Villa Jamaica
W www.villa-jamaica.com
Large volume of well-organized links to Jamaica-related sites

Kingston: A Cultural & Literary Companion by David Howard charts a course through the city, with the eyes of literati as guides.

History & Politics

Mavis Campbell's *The Maroons of Jamaica* is a serious study of the origins of the Maroons and their evolution as a culture through to the end of the last century.

Tony Sewall's *Garvey's Children: The Legacy of Marcus Garvey* provides a look at the rise of black nationalism inspired by national hero Marcus Garvey.

Alexander Bustamante and Modern Jamaica by George Eaton follows the rise of nationalism to its logical conclusion: independence and the birth of a nation under the fostership of national hero Alexander Bustamante.

The biography of Jamaica's most controversial prime minister is traced in Darrell E Levi's *Michael Manley: The Making of a Leader.*

Laurie Gunst's *Born Fi Dead* is a chilling account of Jamaica's ruthless street gangs and the politicians' role in creating them. I consider this essential reading.

General

Flora & Fauna *Flowering Plants of Jamaica* by C Dennis Adams has detailed descriptions of individual species, accompanied by illustrations.

Lepidopterists should refer to *An Annotated List of Butterflies of Jamaica* by A Avinoff and N Shoumatoff.

Birders should turn to the authoritative *Birds of Jamaica: A Photographic Field Guide* by Audrey Downer and Robert Sutton.

James Bond's classic *Birds of the West Indies* is another reference for serious birdwatchers. It was recently republished as *Peterson Field Guide to Birds of the West Indies*.

If you're into snorkeling or diving, refer to Eugene Kaplan's *Peterson Field Guide to Coral Reefs: Caribbean and Florida.*

Culture & Society *Rude Boy* by Chris Salewicz is an engaging and incisive personal journey recalling the author's twenty years among Jamaica's music giants and underclass. In similar vein is *Jamaican Warriors,* Stephen Foehr's narrative on Rastafarian and reggae culture.

Reggae Explosion by Chris Salewicz and Adrian Boot is a large-format photo-essay book tracing the history of reggae.

The definitive and engaging *Catch a Fire: The Life of Bob Marley* by Timothy White analyzes the forces that shaped Marley's political and spiritual evolution.

Rough Guide to Reggae by Steve Barrow and Peter Dalton is the definitive guide to reggae music. Also see *Reggae Routes* by Kevin O'Brien Chang and Wayne Chen.

Jamaica In Focus: A Guide to the People, Politics & Culture by Marcel Bayer provides an accurate and concise account of Jamaican society and contexts.

The sympathetic *Dread: The Rastafarians of Jamaica* by Joseph Owens and *Rastafari: For the Healing of the Nation* by Dennis Forsythe are noteworthy books on Jamaica's most talked-about creed.

The Jamaican Woman: A Celebration by Joanne Simpson provides biographies on 200 women who have made major contributions to Jamaican society.

Cuisine Galloping gourmands should refer to *Classic Jamaican Cooking* by Caroline Sullivan.

Two other good books are *Real Taste of Jamaica* by Enid Donaldson and *Traveling Jamaica with Knife, Fork & Spoon: A Righteous Guide to Jamaican Cooking* by Robb Walshand and Jay McCarthy.

Vegetarians should seek out *The Rasta Cookbook* by Laura Osbourne, a gourmand's guide to I-tal cooking.

Art & Architecture *Jamaica Art* by Kim Robinson and Petrine Archer Straw is a well-illustrated treatise on the evolution of the island's art scene. Likewise, *Modern Jamaican Art* by David Boxer and Veerle Poupeye provides an illustrated overview of the works of 82 Jamaican painters and sculptors.

Jamaican Houses: A Vanishing Legacy by Geoffrey de Sota Pinto has descriptions and black-and-white prints of Jamaica's most important historic houses.

Language *Understanding Jamaican Patois* by Emilie Adams provides an understanding of English as spoken in Jamaica.

Cassidy and RB LePage's *Dictionary of Jamaican English* is the definitive lexicon on patois.

Literature Terry McMillan tells a semi-autobiographical tale of holiday romance in *How Stella Got Her Groove Back,* the story of a mature black woman and her unexpected relationship with a much younger man. Russell Banks' *Book of Jamaica* also revolves around a Jamaica vacation, in which a college professor is seduced by marijuana and the local lifestyle.

For a list of books by Jamaican authors, see Literature in the Arts section of the Facts about Jamaica chapter.

FILMS

Jamaica has had strong links to James Bond movies ever since novelist Ian Fleming concocted the suave, macho spy 007 at his home near Oracabessa. The Bond movies *Dr No* and *Live and Let Die* were both shot on location along Jamaica's north coast.

Portions of *20,000 Leagues Under the Sea* were filmed in Jamaica, as were scenes from *Papillon, Lord of the Flies, Flipper, Prelude to a Kiss, Search for Tomorrow, Clara's Heart, Hammerhead, Club Paradise, Cool Runnings, Cocktail, Mighty Quinn, Blue Lagoon, Treasure Island, Wide Sargasso Sea,* and *How Stella Got Her Groove Back.*

Also see Film in the Arts section of the Facts about Jamaica chapter.

NEWSPAPERS & MAGAZINES
Foreign Publications

Leading international newspapers and magazines are sold throughout Jamaica, at two to three times the cost at home.

Before you go, take a look at some magazines about Jamaica and the Caribbean. *Caribbean Travel & Life* is a beautiful, full-color, bimonthly magazine; *Caribbean World,* published quarterly in the UK, profiles the lifestyles of the rich and famous. *Caribbean Beat,* published in Trinidad, is the quality in-flight magazine of BWIA airlines. *Caribbean Week* is a high-quality, biweekly news magazine that covers the region.

Jamaican Publications

The *Gleaner* is a high-standard, conservative daily that gives both national and international events reasonable coverage. The *Gleaner's* rival is the *Jamaica Observer.*

The *Star* is a trashy tabloid. The *X-News* is another gutter tabloid, heavy on sports, entertainment, and flesh, as are the *Sunday Punch* and *Hardcore.* The dregs of the sewer is *ExS* – consider the anagram.

The *Jamaica Tourist Guide,* a 16-page newspaper geared to international visitors, is distributed free in hotel lobbies, as is *Focus on Jamaica,* a slick little tourist magazine.

Domestic magazines are few. One of the finest is *Sky Writings,* the bimonthly in-flight magazine of Air Jamaica. *Reggae Times* is a slick magazine for music lovers.

RADIO & TV
Radio

In 2002 there were some 23 radio stations. Call-in talk shows are popular, and there is considerable political debate on the air. As the island is so small and parochial, radio serves as a kind of community service grapevine. Deaths, for example, are announced with somber details (and muted morguelike music behind) followed by a long roll call of relatives and friends requested to attend the funeral.

Radio Jamaica Rediffusion (RJR; 91.1 FM) is a 24-hour public broadcast station that mixes talk shows, political analysis, and cricket coverage with reggae and popular music. RJR also broadcasts FAME FM (91.5/98.1 FM), a popular music station.

Reggae lovers should tune in to IRIE FM (105.5/107.7 FM) or Love FM (101.1 FM), while KLAS (89.5 FM), Power 106 (106.5 FM), and Radio Waves (102.9 FM) are alternatives.

Television

There are seven Jamaican TV stations. News coverage follows the BBC style, with broad international coverage.

Most hotels offer satellite or cable TV with international programming. Others receive only local stations, which broadcast only at certain hours.

PHOTOGRAPHY & VIDEO
Film & Equipment
The major resort towns have duty-free stores selling cameras (including video cameras) and lenses at prices similar to North America and Europe.

Film is expensive, so ensure you bring enough to last your entire trip. Print film is widely available, but slide (transparency) film is extremely rare.

Many places leave film sitting in the sun; avoid this like the plague, as heat and humidity deteriorate film. Don't forget to check the expiration date, too. Once you've finished a roll of film, try to keep it cool and have it developed as soon as possible. Consider having your film developed on the island, or mailing it home for development (you can purchase prepaid mailers for this purpose).

Carry silica gel packages in your camera bag to soak up moisture.

Photographing People
Most Jamaicans delight in having their photographs taken. However, some Jamaicans object to having their picture taken, and can get quite volatile if you persist. Depending on the circumstances, you should honor their wishes with good grace. You have every right to take a photo over their objections if, for example, the person happens to be part of a broader subject of interest.

Expect to be asked to pay a small 'donation' to take photographs.

Airport Security
In today's security-conscious environment, requests to have your film hand-checked are rarely honored. Fortunately, most modern X-ray machines will not 'fog' low-speed film (400ASA and below).

TIME
In autumn and winter, Jamaican time is five hours behind Greenwich Mean Time, and the same time as in New York (Eastern Standard Time). Jamaica does not adjust for daylight saving time. Hence, from April to October, Jamaica is six hours behind London and one hour behind New York.

ELECTRICITY
Most hotels operate on 110 volts, the same as in the USA and Canada. A few outlets operate on 220 volts, as in the UK (these are usually marked).

Sockets throughout Jamaica are usually two or three-pin – the US standard. Occasionally, particularly in older establishments, you may find three-square-pin sockets.

WEIGHTS & MEASURES
Distances are still shown on some maps in miles and inches, although Jamaica officially uses the metric system (road signs, for example, give speed limits and distances in kilometers).

The antiquated English 'chain' is still a commonly used measure of distance in Jamaican parlance. It equals 22 yards, but few Jamaicans have the foggiest notion of that. 'Jus' a couple o' chains' can mean anywhere from exactly that to a couple of miles or more.

Liquids and weights are measured in metric, although many Jamaicans still refer to pints, quarts, and (Imperial) gallons, as well as to ounces and pounds.

There is a conversion chart at the back of this book.

LAUNDRY
Self-service, coin-operated laundries are few. Drop-off laundries are available in major resort towns.

Most hotels can arrange next-day or two-day laundry. For more modest establishments, expect your laundry to be washed in a river and beaten over rocks (don't expect your clothes to be ironed).

Many establishments that advertise 'dry cleaning' don't use a chemical treatment. Often this means that your garment will be hand-washed in cold water.

TOILETS
There are very few public toilets. Those that do exist are places to avoid.

HEALTH

Jamaica poses few health risks. The water is chlorinated and potable (though it's still wise to drink purified water), and food hygiene standards are generally high. The greatest threats are usually dehydration and an excess of sun and booze.

If you require a particular medication, take an adequate supply, as it may not be available locally. Take the prescription with you to show that you legally use the medication.

Travel Health Guides

A worthwhile book on travel health is *Travel with Children*, by Cathy Lanigan (Lonely Planet Publications). It includes basic advice on travel health for younger children.

Predeparture Preparations

Health Insurance An insurance policy to cover theft, loss, and medical problems is a wise idea. For more details about health insurance, see Travel Insurance in the Visas & Documents section earlier in this chapter.

Immunizations No vaccinations are required to enter Jamaica unless you have visited the following locations within the previous six weeks: Asia, Africa, Central and South America, Dominican Republic, Haiti, and Trinidad & Tobago. Check with the JTB or your travel agent before departure to see what current regulations may be. Yellow fever is not a threat in Jamaica, but immunization may be required of travelers arriving from infected areas, chiefly in Africa and South America.

Tetanus and diptheria, typhoid, and infectious hepatitis are vaccinations you may want to look into receiving. Your doctor may still recommend booster shots against measles or polio.

It is recommended you seek medical advice at least six weeks prior to travel.

Basic Rules

Taking care in what you eat and drink is the most important health rule; stomach upsets are the most likely travel health problem. Don't become paranoid; trying the local food is part of the experience of travel.

Water Water is generally safe to drink from faucets throughout the island, although it is recommended that you stick with bottled water. The same is true for ice, particularly ice sold at street stands as 'bellywash,' 'sno-

Medical Kit Checklist

A small, straightforward medical kit is a wise thing to carry. A possible list of kit supplies includes:

- ❏ **Aspirin** or **Panadol** - for pain or fever
- ❏ **Antihistamine** (such as Benadryl) - useful as a decongestant for colds, allergies, to ease the itch from insect bites or stings, and to help prevent motion sickness
- ❏ **Antibiotics** - carry the prescription with you.
- ❏ **Kaolin preparation (Pepto-Bismol), Imodium,** or **Lomotil** - for stomach upset
- ❏ **Rehydration mixture** - for treatment of severe diarrhea. This is particularly important if traveling with children.
- ❏ **Antiseptic** (such as Betadine) - for cuts and grazes
- ❏ **Calamine lotion** - to ease irritation from bites or stings
- ❏ **Bandages** and **Band-Aids**
- ❏ **Scissors, tweezers,** and a **thermometer** (note that mercury thermometers are prohibited by airlines)
- ❏ **Throat lozenges** and **cold and flu tablets** - pseudoephedrine hydrochloride (Sudafed) may be useful if flying with a cold, to avoid ear damage.
- ❏ **Insect repellent, sunscreen, lip balm,** and **water purification tablets**
- ❏ **Multivitamins** - consider for long trips, when dietary vitamin intake may be inadequate.

Extracting juice from sugar cane

Roasting coffee in the Blue Mountains

Preparing gumbo for a picnic, Bluefields

To market in Montego Bay

Roasted corn on offer at a Kingston market

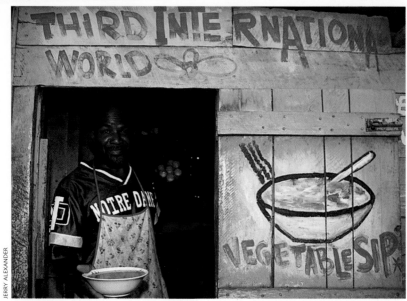

Kingston-area roadside stall specializing in peanut soup

Profile of a Rastafarian

Ice cream and its biggest fans, Montego Bay

cones,' or 'skyjuice,' shaved-ice cones sweetened with fruit juice.

Milk should be treated with suspicion, as it is often unpasteurized. Boiled milk is fine if it is kept hygienically, and yogurt is always good. Tea or coffee should also be OK, since the water should have been boiled.

If you're camping or using hovel-like budget accommodations and are unsure of your water supply, then purify it. The simplest way is to boil it vigorously for five minutes.

If you cannot boil water, it should be treated chemically. Chlorine tablets will kill many but not all pathogens, including giardia and amoebic cysts. Iodine is very effective in purifying water and is available in tablet form, but follow the directions carefully, as too much iodine can be harmful.

Food Salads and fruit should be washed with purified water or peeled where possible. Ice cream is usually OK, but beware of street vendors selling ice cream that has melted and been refrozen. Thoroughly cooked food is safest, but not if it has been left to cool or if it has been reheated. Shellfish such as oysters and clams should be avoided as well as undercooked meat, particularly in the form of mince. Steaming does not make shellfish safe for eating.

Everyday Health In Jamaica's backwaters, clean your teeth with purified water rather than tap water. Wash your hands before eating. Avoid overexposure to extremes: keep out of the sun at its peak. Avoid potential diseases by dressing sensibly; for example, you can get worm infections from walking barefoot.

Climatic &
Geographical Considerations
Sunburn Don't underestimate the power of the tropical sun, no matter how dark your skin color. You can get sunburned surprisingly quickly, even on cloudy days. Use a sunscreen with a protective factor of 15 or more. Build up your exposure to the sun gradually. A hat provides added protection,

and you should also use a barrier cream for your nose and lips. If you do get burnt, calamine lotion and aloe vera will provide soothing relief.

Prickly Heat Prickly heat is an itchy rash caused by excessive perspiration trapped under the skin. It usually strikes people who have just arrived in a hot climate and whose pores have not yet opened sufficiently to cope with increased sweating. To alleviate symptoms, keep cool and bathe often, use a mild talcum powder, or resort to air-con.

Dehydration & Heat Exhaustion You'll sweat profusely in Jamaica. Drink lots of water – don't rely on feeling thirsty to indicate when you should drink. Not needing to urinate, or very dark yellow urine, is a danger sign. You'll lose quite a bit of salt through sweating. Salt deficiency is characterized by fatigue, lethargy, headaches, giddiness, and muscle cramps, and in this case salt tablets may help. Vomiting or diarrhea can also deplete your liquid and salt levels. Anhydrotic heat exhaustion, caused by an inability to sweat, is quite rare. Unlike other forms of heat exhaustion, it is likely to strike people who have been in Jamaica's hot climate for some time, rather than newcomers.

Avoid booze by day, as your body uses water to process alcohol. Drink water, or drink coconut water straight from the husk.

Heat Stroke Long, continuous periods of exposure to high temperatures can leave you vulnerable to heat stroke, a sometimes fatal condition that occurs if the body's heat-regulating mechanism breaks down and the body temperature rises to dangerous levels.

The symptoms are feeling unwell, not sweating very much (or at all), and a high body temperature. Where sweating has ceased, the skin becomes flushed and red. Severe, throbbing headaches and lack of co-ordination will also occur, and the sufferer may be confused or aggressive. Eventually the victim will become delirious or convulse. Hospitalization is essential, but meanwhile get victims out of the sun, remove their clothing, cover them with a wet sheet or towel, and fan them continually.

Fungal Infections Hot weather fungal infections are most likely to occur on the scalp, between the toes or fingers (athlete's foot), in the groin (jock itch or crotch rot), and on the body (ringworm). You get ringworm (which is a fungal infection, not a worm) from infected animals or by walking on damp areas, such as shower floors.

To prevent fungal infections, wear loose, comfortable clothes, avoid artificial fibers, wash frequently, and dry carefully. If you get an infection, wash the infected area daily with a disinfectant or medicated soap and water, then rinse and dry well. Apply an antifungal powder. Try to expose the infected area to air or sunlight as much as possible, and wash all towels and underwear in hot water (as well as changing them often).

Motion Sickness Eating lightly before and during a trip will reduce the chances of motion sickness. Find a place that minimizes disturbance – near the wing on aircraft, close to midship on boats, near the center on buses. Fresh air usually helps. Commercial anti–motion-sickness preparations, which can cause drowsiness, have to be taken before the trip commences; when you're feeling sick, it's too late. Ginger is a natural preventative.

Jet Lag To minimize the impact of jet lag:

- Rest for a couple of days prior to departure; try to avoid late nights and last-minute dashes.
- Try to select flight schedules that minimize sleep deprivation; arriving late in the day means you can go to sleep soon after you arrive. For very long flights, try to organize a stopover.

- Avoid excessive eating and alcohol during the flight. Instead, drink plenty of water.
- Make yourself comfortable by wearing loose-fitting clothes. Bring an eye mask and ear plugs to help you sleep.

Diseases of Poor Sanitation

Diarrhea A change of water, food, or climate can all cause the runs. Despite precautions, you may still have a bout of mild travelers' diarrhea; a few rushed trips to the toilet with no other symptoms is not indicative of a serious problem. Dehydration is the main danger with any diarrhea, particularly for children. Fluid replacement remains the mainstay of management. For severe diarrhea, a rehydrating solution is necessary to replace minerals and salts. Stick to a bland diet as you recover.

Lomotil or Imodium can be used to bring relief from the symptoms, although they do not actually cure the problem. Only use these drugs if absolutely necessary – if you *must* travel. For children, Imodium is preferable. Do not use these drugs if diarrhea is accompanied with a high fever or severe dehydration.

Giardiasis The parasite causing this intestinal disorder is present in contaminated water. The symptoms are stomach cramps, nausea, a bloated stomach, watery, foul-smelling diarrhea, and frequent gas. Giardiasis can appear several weeks after you have been exposed to the parasite. The symptoms may disappear for a few days and then return; this can go on for several weeks.

Tinidazole, known as Fasigyn, or metronidazole (Flagyl) are the recommended drugs for treatment. Antibiotics are of no use for giardiasis.

Dysentery This is caused by contaminated food or water and is characterized by severe diarrhea, often with blood or mucus in the stool. There are two kinds of dysentery: bacillary, characterized by a high fever and rapidly onset headache, vomiting, and stomach pains; and amoebic, which is often more gradual in the onset of symptoms, with cramping abdominal pain and vomiting less likely, and fever may not be present. A stool test is necessary to diagnose which kind of dysentery you have, so you should quickly seek medical help.

Flagyl or Fasigyn can be used as presumptive treatment in an emergency.

Viral Gastroenteritis This is characterized by stomach cramps, diarrhea, and sometimes by vomiting or a slight fever. All you can do is rest and drink lots of fluids.

Hepatitis Hepatitis A is a very common problem among travelers to areas with poor sanitation. Protection is offered by the vaccine Havrix or the short-lasting antibody gamma globulin.

The disease is spread by contaminated food or water. The symptoms are fever, chills, headache, fatigue, feelings of weakness, and aches and pains, followed by loss of appetite, nausea, vomiting, abdominal pain, dark urine, light-colored feces, jaundiced skin, and the whites of the eyes may turn yellow. You should seek medical advice, but in general there is not much you can do apart from rest, drink lots of fluids, eat lightly, and avoid fatty foods. People who have had hepatitis must forego alcohol for six months after the illness.

Hepatitis B is spread through contact with infected blood, blood products, or bodily fluids. The symptoms of type B are much the same as type A except that they are more severe.

Although there is no treatment for hepatitis B, an effective prophylactic vaccine is readily available in most countries.

Hepatitis Non-A and Non-B is a blanket term formerly used for several different strains of hepatitis, which have now been separately identified. They are fairly rare.

Typhoid Contaminated water and food are responsible. Vaccination against typhoid is not totally effective, and it is one of the most dangerous infections, so medical help must be sought.

In its early stages typhoid resembles many other illnesses: sufferers may feel like they have a bad cold or flu on the way, as early symptoms are a headache, a sore throat, and a fever that rises a little each day until it is around 104°F or more. The victim's pulse is often slow relative to the degree of fever present – unlike a normal fever when the pulse increases – and gets slower as the fever rises. There may also be vomiting, diarrhea, or constipation.

In the second week, the high fever and slow pulse continue and pink spots may appear on the body; trembling, delirium, weakness, weight loss, and dehydration are other symptoms. If there are no further complications, the fever and other symptoms will slowly fade during the third week. But you must get medical help before this because pneumonia (acute infection of the lungs) and peritonitis (perforated bowel) are common complications, and because typhoid is very infectious.

Worms These parasites are common in rural, tropical areas. They can be present on unwashed vegetables or in undercooked meat, and you can pick them up through your skin by walking barefoot. If left untreated, they can cause severe health problems.

Diseases Spread by People & Animals

Tetanus This potentially fatal disease is present in Jamaica as in other undeveloped tropical areas. It is difficult to treat, but is preventable with immunization. Tetanus (lockjaw) occurs when a wound becomes infected by a germ that lives in the feces of animals or people; clean all cuts, punctures, or animal bites. The first symptom may be discomfort in swallowing, or stiffening of the jaw and neck, followed by painful convulsions of the jaw and whole body.

Sexually Transmitted Diseases There's a high prevalence of venereal diseases in Jamaica. Gonorrhea and syphilis are the most common; sores, blisters, or rashes around the genitals, and discharges or pain when urinating are common symptoms. Symptoms for women may be less marked or not observed. Syphilis symptoms eventually disappear, but the disease continues and can cause severe problems – even death – in later years. The treatment of gonorrhea and syphilis is by antibiotics.

While sexual abstinence is the only certain preventative, using condoms is also effective.

HIV & AIDS The Human Immunodeficiency Virus (HIV) may develop into Acquired Immune Deficiency Syndrome (AIDS). Any exposure to infected blood or bodily fluids puts the individual at risk. Apart from abstinence, the most effective preventative is always to practice safe sex using condoms. It is impossible to detect the HIV-positive status of an otherwise healthy-looking person without a blood test.

HIV can also be spread through infected blood transfusions; Jamaica cannot afford to screen blood for transfusions. The virus can also be spread by dirty needles – vaccinations, acupuncture, tattooing, and ear or body piercing can potentially be as dangerous as intravenous drug use if the equipment is not clean. If you do need an injection, ask to see the syringe unwrapped in front of you, or better still, take a needle and syringe pack with you when you go overseas.

Jamaica has a toll-free **AIDS/STD Helpline** (☎ 888-991-4444; 10am-10pm Mon-Fri).

Jamaica AIDS Support (JAS; ☎ 929-9408; ⓔ jas@colis.com; 78 Half Way Tree Rd, Kingston 10) operates a hospice and provides assistance for anyone infected with HIV.

The **National AIDS Committee** (☎ 967-1100, fax 967-1280; ⓔ info@nacjamaica.com; 2-4 King St, 4th Floor, Oceana Bldg, Kingston) is an invaluable resource.

Insect-Borne Diseases
Fortunately malaria isn't present in Jamaica. Among Caribbean islands it is relegated to the island of Hispaniola (Haiti and the Dominican Republic).

Dengue Fever Although extremely rare, dengue fever is present in Jamaica, notably in Portland parish and around Kingston. There is no prophylactic available for this mosquito-spread disease. A sudden onset of

fever, headaches, and severe joint and muscle pains (hence its colloquial name, 'broken bone disease') are the first signs. Later a rash starts on the trunk of the body and spreads to the limbs and face. After another few days, the fever will subside and recovery will begin.

To avoid mosquitoes, especially at night, wear light-colored clothing, long pants, and long-sleeved shirts; use mosquito repellents containing the compound Deet (diethylmetatoluamide); avoid highly scented perfumes or aftershave; and use a mosquito net and coil.

Chagas' Disease In rural areas this parasitic disease is transmitted by a bug that hides in crevices, palm fronds, and often the thatched roofs of huts. It comes out to feed at night. A hard, violet-colored swelling appears at the site of the bite in about a week. Usually the body overcomes the disease unaided, but sometimes it continues and can eventually lead to death years later. Chagas' disease can be treated in its early stages, but it is best to avoid thatched-roof huts, sleep under a mosquito net, and use insecticides and insect repellents.

Typhus Typhus is spread by ticks, mites, or lice. It begins as a bad cold, followed by a fever, chills, headache, muscle pains, and a body rash. Often a large painful sore appears at the site of the bite, and nearby lymph nodes can become swollen and painful. A strong insect repellent can help you avoid getting bitten.

Cuts & Scratches
Skin punctures can easily become infected in hot climates and may be difficult to heal. Treat any cut with an antiseptic. Where possible, avoid bandages and Band-Aids, which can keep wounds wet. Coral cuts are notoriously slow to heal, as the coral injects a weak venom into the wound. Clean any cut thoroughly with sodium peroxide if available.

Bites & Stings
Bee and wasp stings are usually more painful than dangerous. Calamine lotion

will give relief, and ice packs will reduce the pain and swelling.

Various fish and other sea creatures can sting or bite dangerously. Jamaica has no venomous snakes.

No-See-'Ums These well-named irritants are almost microscopically small fleas that hang out on beaches and appear around dusk (especially after rain) with a voracious appetite. Their bite is out of all proportion to their size. Most insect repellents don't faze them. A better bet is a liberal application of Avon's Skin So Soft, a cosmetic that even the US Army swears by.

Jellyfish Local advice on where to swim is the best way to avoid contact with these sea creatures with their stinging tentacles. If you get stung, dousing with vinegar will deactivate any stingers that have not 'fired.' In addition to calamine lotion, antihistamines and analgesics may reduce the reaction and relieve the pain.

Bedbugs, Lice & Scabies Often, microscopic bedbugs live in dirty mattresses and bedding. Spots of blood on bedclothes or on the wall around the bed can be read as a suggestion to find another hotel.

Lice, which are larger and easy to see, cause itching and discomfort. They make themselves at home in your hair (head lice), your clothing (body lice), or in your pubic hair (crabs). You catch lice through direct contact with infected people or by sharing combs, clothing, and the like. Powder or shampoo treatment will kill the lice.

Likewise, scabies – an infestation of microscopic mites – is acquired through sexual contact, bed linen, towels, or clothing. The first signs – severe itching caused by infestation of eggs and feces under the skin – usually appear three to four weeks after exposure (as soon as 24 hours for a second exposure) and is worse at night. Infestation appears as tiny welts and pimples, often in a dotted line, most commonly around the groin and lower abdomen, between the fingers, on the elbows, and under the armpits. Treatment is by pesticidal lotions.

At the same time as using the treatment, you must wash *all* your clothing and bedding in hot water.

Women's Health

Poor diet, lowered resistance due to the use of antibiotics, and even contraceptive pills can lead to vaginal infections. Wearing skirts or loose-fitting trousers and cotton underwear will help to prevent infections while traveling in hot climates.

Yeast infections, characterized by a rash, itch, and discharge, can be treated with a vinegar or even lemon-juice douche, or with yogurt. Nystatin suppositories are the usual medical prescription.

Trichomoniasis is a more serious infection; symptoms are a discharge and a burning sensation when urinating. Sexual partners must also be treated, and if a vinegar-water douche is not effective, medical attention should be sought. Metronidazole (Flagyl) is the prescribed drug.

If you are pregnant, note that most miscarriages occur during the first three months of pregnancy, so this is the most risky time to travel.

Health Facilities

Jamaica has 23 general hospitals, seven specialist hospitals, and about 350 regional clinics. There are also several private hospitals. Most maintain 24-hour emergency wards. If it's within your budget, private medical clinics and hospitals are to be preferred. For serious ailments, the best advice is to go home.

Most large hotels have resident nurses, plus doctors on call.

See regional chapters for hospital listings.

Ambulances

The emergency number for public ambulances is ☎ 011.

A free ambulance service is provided by **St John's ambulance brigade** (☎ 926-7654 in Kingston, 994-1126 in Ocho Rios).

Wings Jamaica provides a local and overseas 24-hour **air ambulance service** (☎ 923-6573, 923-5416), as does **Karvinair Air Ambulance** (☎ 978-8405).

Medical Assistance Organizations

Many companies offer a range of medical assistance for travelers, including emergency evacuation, medical attention, and payment of on-site medical treatment. Most maintain 24-hour emergency hotline centers that connect travelers to professional medical staff worldwide.

Such organizations include:

International SOS Assistance (☎ 215-244-1500, 800-523-8662 in the USA, 215-245-4707 alarm center; ☎ 020-8762-8000 in the UK, 020-8762-8008 alarm center; ⓦ www.internationalsos.com)

Traveler's Emergency Network (☎ 800-275-4836; ⓦ www.tenweb.com)

WOMEN TRAVELERS
Attitudes Toward Women

'Political correctness' hasn't yet filtered down from the educated Jamaican middle class to the male masses. Many Jamaican men display behavior and attitudes that might shock visiting women, often expressing disdain for the notion of female equality or women's rights. Rape is common in Jamaica, and occasionally involves female tourists (one reader claims to have been raped by security staff at an all-inclusive resort).

If you're single, it will be assumed that you're on the island seeking a 'likkle love beneat' de palms.' Any remonstration to the contrary will likely be met with wearying attempts to get you to change your mind. Black women can expect to hear a 'roots' trip.

If you go along with the flirting, don't expect a Jamaican man to understand if you've no intent of going all the way. Your innocent acceptance will be taken as a sign of acquiescence. The Jamaican male has a fragile ego and is likely to react strongly to feeling like a fool. Don't beat about the bush for fear of hurting the man's feelings.

Many foreign women welcome these advances, as evidenced by the proliferation of 'rent-a-Rastas' – semiprofessional good-time guys, or gigolos – on the arms of North American and European women. Most often, the man is excited more by your economic clout than your looks – a foreign catch brings status and the possibility for wheedling some cash. You'll be the moneybags in any romantic encounter.

Many younger, poorer Jamaican women also hold a stereotypical image of foreign females and resent what they see as poaching of their men. A clear exception is in Kingston, where thousands of educated professional women live a cosmopolitan lifestyle and are less tethered by the hardships of raising children in dire economic circumstances. Such women range more freely throughout society and more fully engage with foreigners as equals.

Also see Women in Jamaica in the Society & Conduct section in the Facts about Jamaica chapter.

Safety Precautions

Women traveling alone can reduce unwanted attention by dressing modestly when away from the beach. You should avoid walking alone at night and otherwise traveling alone in remote areas.

Women travelers should *not* hitchhike. And, if driving, be extremely cautious about whom you choose to pick up roadside.

Organizations & Resources

Women's organizations in Jamaica include:

Association of Women's Organizations (☎ 968-8260) 9 Westminster Rd, Kingston 10

Jamaica Federation of Women (☎ 926-7726) 74 Arnold Rd, Kingston 5

Woman's Center of Jamaica (☎/fax 926-5768) 42 Trafalgar Rd, Kingston 5

Good resources abroad include the **International Federation of Women's Travel Organizations** (☎ 334-393-4431 in the USA; ☎ 95-205-7060 in Spain; ⓔ ifwto@ifwto.org; PO Box 466, 29620 Torremolinos, Spain).

Jamaica Journeys (☎ 508-432-3114; ⓔ majamaica@hotmail.com) specializes in special-interest programs for women.

Travelers' Tales: Gutsy Women, Travel Tips & Wisdom from the Road by Mary Beth Bond is replete with handy tips and practicalities.

GAY & LESBIAN TRAVELERS

Jamaica is an adamantly homophobic nation. Homosexual intercourse between men is illegal, and antigay hysteria is a staple of musical lyrics. Homosexuality is a subject that evokes extreme reactions among Jamaicans, and it is difficult to hold a serious discussion on the topic.

Most Jamaican gays are still in the closet. Nonetheless, many hoteliers are gay or gay-tolerant, and you should not be put off from visiting the island. Just don't expect to be able to display your sexuality openly without an adverse reaction.

Organizations & Resources

The only gay and lesbian support group I'm aware of in Jamaica is **F-flag** (☎ 978-1954, fax 978-7876; W www.jflag.org).

The following organizations can provide assistance in planning a trip:

International Gay & Lesbian Association (☎ 212-620-7310, 800-421-1220; e info@gay center.org), 208 West 13th St, New York, NY 10011, USA

International Gay & Lesbian Travel Association (☎ 954-776-2626, 800-448-8550, fax 776-3303; e iglta@iglta.org), 4431 N Federal Hwy No 304, Ft Lauderdale, FL 33308, USA

Odysseus Publishing & Travel (☎ 516-944-5330, 800-257-5344, fax 944-7540; e odyusa@ odyusa.com), PO Box 1548, Port Washington, New York, NY 11050, USA

Two good travel guides for gays and lesbians are the *Spartacus International Gay Guide* (☎ 602-863-2408, 800-962-2912, fax 439-3952; e ferrari@q-net.com; PO Box 37887, Phoenix, AZ 85069, USA), and *Odysseus: The International Gay Travel Planner*.

DISABLED TRAVELERS

Few allowances have been made in Jamaica for disabled travelers, though things are improving, partly as a result of lobbying by Derrick Palmer, director of **Disabled Peoples International** (☎ 931-6155; 9 Tunbridge Terrace, Kingston 19). Another useful resource is the **Disabled Peoples' Organization of the Caribbean** (☎ 967-9439; 1F North St, Kingston 5).

Two other organizations are the **Jamaica Association for Mentally Handicapped Children** (☎ 927-2054; 7 Golding Ave, Kingston 7) and the **Jamaica Association for the Deaf** (☎ 926-7709; 9 Marescaux Rd, Kingston 5).

The JTB or Derrick Palmer can provide a list of hotels with wheelchair ramps. Buses for the disabled operate in Kingston.

Organizations & Resources

Contact the following for more information:

Society for the Advancement of Travel for the Handicapped (☎ 212-447-7284, fax 725-8253; W www.sath.org), 347 Fifth Ave No 610, New York, NY 10016, USA

American Foundation for the Blind (☎ 212-502-7600, 800-232-5463; e afbinfo@afb.org), 11 Penn Plaza No 300, New York, NY 10001, USA

Flying Wheels Travel (☎ 507-451-5005, 800-535-6790, fax 507-451-1685; W www.flyingwheels travel.com), 143 W Bridge St, Owatonna, MN 55060, USA

SENIOR TRAVELERS

Most airlines offer senior discount programs for travelers 62 or over. Some car-rental companies also extend discounts, as does Air Jamaica Express.

Otherwise, Jamaica is virtually devoid of seniors' discounts.

The **American Association of Retired Persons** (AARP; ☎ 800-424-3410; W www .aarp.org; 601 E St NW, Washington, DC 20049) offers travel discounts and trips.

TRAVEL WITH CHILDREN

All-inclusive resorts such as FDR Resort (Runaway Bay), FDR Pebbles (Falmouth), Beaches (Boscobel, Negril, and Whitehouse), and Starfish (Trelawny) cater specifically to families and have an impressive range of amenities for children. Most hotels also offer free accommodations or reduced rates for children staying in their parents' room. Many hotels provide a babysitter or nanny by advance request.

It's a good idea to prearrange necessities such as cribs, babysitters, cots, and baby food at hotels other than family resorts.

Rascals in Paradise (☎ 415-921-7000, 800-872-7225 in the USA; ☒ www.rascalsinparadise.com; 2107 Van Ness Ave Suite 403, San Francisco, CA 94109, USA) arranges family vacations.

Lonely Planet's *Travel with Children,* by Cathy Lanigan gives you the low-down on preparing for family travel.

USEFUL ORGANIZATIONS

The **Jamaica Information Service** (☎ 926-3740, 888-991-2327, fax 926-6715; 58a Half Way Tree Rd, Kingston 10) dispenses information geared to domestic issues.

The **Institute of Jamaica** (☎ 922-0620; 12 East St, Kingston) has reading rooms. The **Jamaica National Heritage Trust** (☎ 922-1287, fax 967-1703; ☒ www.jnht.com; Headquarters House, 79 Duke St, PO Box 8934, Kingston), a branch of the Institute, maintains the **Jamaica Archives** (☎ 984-2581) in Spanish Town.

DANGERS & ANNOYANCES

The JTB publishes a pocket-size pamphlet, 'Helpful Hints for Your Vacation,' containing concise tips for safer travel. Use the **JTB hotline** (☎ 888-991-9999) for emergency assistance.

The **US State Dept** (☎ 202-647-5225; ☒ www.travel.state.gov/jamaica.html) publishes travel advisories that advise US citizens of trouble spots, as does the **British Foreign & Commonwealth Office** (☎ 020-7008-0232; ☒ www.fco.gov.uk/travel/default.asp; Travel Advice Unit, Consular Division, Foreign & Commonwealth Office, 1 Palace St, London SW1E 5HE).

Cockroaches This being the tropics, cockroaches are everywhere. Many are veritable giants! However, they're not a problem, except in restaurants, where they can contaminate food.

Crime The island's pervasive poverty and a malaise among young Jamaican males has fostered a pandemic of crime. Jamaica, and in particular Kingston, has the worst reputation in the Caribbean for violent crime (the nation had a record 1,138 murders in

Hope For Jamaica's Youth

Jamaica's youth are severely challenged by problems that arise from abuse, abandonment, and deprivation. Among the organizations that work to provide hope and respect are:

Area Youth Foundation (ⓔ esslo@hotmail .com), based at St Andrew's Scots Kirk United Church, provides an avenue for Kingston's inner-city youth to perform theatrically and find outlets for creative expression.

Hope For Children (☎ 923-3594, fax 757-3909; 74 Spanish Town Rd, Kingston 11) provides skills training, educational assistance, after-school programs, daycare centers, and community advocacy.

Jamaica Children's Project (☎/fax 510-763-6666; ⓔ gh8899@aol.com; 311 Lester Ave No 8, Oakland, CA 94606, USA) works to support youth programs and provide for the needs of street children.

Negril Youth Initiative (☎ 617-731-8999; ⓔ nealsmagic@aol.com; PO Box 180664, Boston, MA 02118, USA) offers Jamaican (and other) kids scholarships to attend Med-o-Lark, an international camp where teenagers build self-esteem and learn personal responsibility.

Uplifting Adolescents Program (☒ www .jamaica-kidz.com) is a joint project of the Jamaican government and the United States Agency for International Development (USAID), which works for the betterment of at-risk youth.

Youth Educational Support System (☎ 924-9434, fax 922-0054; Duke St, Kingston) has a school, clinic, library, and photography lab for inner-city youth.

2001). Although most violent crime occurs in ghettoes far from tourist centers, many readers continue to report being robbed, mugged, or scammed, despite government claims that crime against visitors has dropped. Several tourists have been murdered, a fact highlighted by the disappearance (and presumed murder) of a female travel writer while staying at an all-inclusive resort in Negril in 2000.

Many among Jamaica's underclass seem permanently 'pissed off' and – as one reader reported – 'at war' with foreigners, whom they are often intent to rip off.

Most crime against travelers is petty and opportunistic. Take sensible precautions with your valuables (see Money earlier in this chapter). Steer clear of ghettoes, where you are very likely to get into serious trouble. Try to avoid walking at night, but if you do, stick close to main thoroughfares. The US State Dept and British Foreign & Commonwealth Office travel advisories also warn against taking public transport and visiting downtown Kingston unless absolutely necessary.

Several readers report being robbed at gunpoint ('stick-ups') in their cars or hotel rooms. Keep hotel doors and windows securely locked at night, and lock car doors from the inside while driving. Don't open your hotel door to anyone who cannot prove his or her identity. If you're renting an out-of-the-way private villa or cottage, check in advance with the rental agency to establish whether security is provided. And don't assume you're entirely safe at all-inclusive resorts. Readers report issues of security even here.

It is *very* unsafe to camp in the wild, especially alone or in small groups.

Be cautious if invited to see the 'real Jamaica' by a stranger. And be constantly wary of young Jamaican males with whom you may strike up a seeming friendship; many readers have written to tell of being assaulted and robbed by locals whom they'd come to trust.

Women need to be doubly cautious, as rape is common.

Many local police are members of the communities they serve and cannot always be trusted to be impartial.

Critics to Beware Of Sea urchins cluster on the seabed and on coral walls. If you step on one, the 'quills' will pierce your skin and break off. They're agonizingly painful, as is the bristleworm: one touch and you're impaled by tiny needles that detach as keepsakes. Fire coral is named for the severe burning sensation it causes when brushed up against. Two-thirds of coral species are poisonous – another reason to remember, *hands off!*

Many a diver who has reached out to pet moray eels has been bitten.

The scorpion fish sits on the seabed and resembles the rocks and corals around it, thus is difficult to spot. Its raised spines inflict venom that can be fatal to humans. Likewise, stingrays often lie buried in sand; if you tread on one, its tail may slash you with a venomous spike. When wading in sandy shallows, *slide* your feet along the sea bed to avoid stepping on the otherwise harmless rays.

Poisonous jellyfish also pulse in Jamaica's waters in late summer.

Swimming is usually no problem in the presence of sharks – mostly wary and harmless nurse sharks. Still, they'll attack in self-defense if provoked or cornered. Give them plenty of room.

Jamaica's crocodiles are generally fish-eaters, not human-killers, although a woman was killed in 2001. Use caution if swimming near river estuaries.

Driving Hazards Driving in Jamaica can be dangerous. Be on the lookout for people alongside the roads or animals that might dash in front of you. Pedestrians should take heed of many drivers who would as soon hit you as slow down.

Roadblocks used by residents to draw attention to particular issues and street dances that draw large crowds can block traffic without warning; they require extreme caution by drivers, as Jamaican crowds can be volatile.

For tips on driving conditions, see the Getting Around chapter.

Drug Trade Ganja (marijuana) is everywhere in Jamaica, and you're almost certain to be approached by hustlers selling drugs. Cocaine is also widely available. The street sale of drugs is a sad pandemic that has corroded society and led to frightening levels of violence.

Possession and use of drugs in Jamaica is strictly illegal and penalties are severe. Roadblocks and random searches of cars are common, undertaken by squads of well-armed police in combat gear (professionalism is never guaranteed, and 'dash' – extortion – is often extracted to boost weekly wages). If you *do* buy drugs in Jamaica, don't be stupid enough to try to take any out of the country. If you get caught in possession, you will *not* be getting on your plane home, however small the amount. A night (or a lengthy sentence) in a crowded-to-bursting Jamaican lock-up is dangerous to your health!

Smoking a Jamaican spliff or *chillum* will pack an almighty punch. Many Jamaicans are used to smoking cigar-sized joints with their first breath of air every morning without noticeable side effects. You can't. It's not unknown, too, to find cocaine is actually Ajax.

Women should be aware that so-called 'date rape' drugs have become common at clubs and private parties.

If you plan on hiking off the beaten path, it's wise to do so with a local guide. Many areas in the hinterland are centers for ganja production. Strangers (especially white travelers) are often suspected of being undercover US Drug Enforcement Agency agents. If you accidentally stumble across a large ganja plantation, you could put your life in jeopardy.

Fearsome Flora The manchineel tree, which grows along the Jamaican shoreline, produces small applelike green fruits. Don't eat them – they're highly poisonous. Don't sit beneath the tree either, as the raindrops running off the leaves onto your skin can cause blisters.

Garbage The Jamaican countryside is terribly polluted by garbage. Very few among the Jamaican masses seems bothered about fouling their own yards. There is no more appalling site than a Jamaican produce market, where offal, spoiled produce, and other trash lies rotting underfoot in huge piles that attract flies, cockroaches, and rodents.

Harassment Usually, the traveler's biggest problem is the vast army of hustlers (mostly male) who harass visitors, notably in and around major tourist centers. A hustler is someone who makes a living by seizing opportunities, and the biggest opportunity in Jamaica is *you!*

Hustlers walk the streets looking for potential buyers of crafts, jewelry, or drugs, or to wash cars, give aloe vera massages, or offer any of a thousand varieties of services. A sibilant 'sssssst!' to catch your attention is the first indication that hustlers have their eyes on you. If you as much as glance in their direction, they'll attempt to reel you in like a flounder.

Aggressive persistence is key to their success and shaking them off can be a wearying process. Hustlers often persist in the hope that you'll pay just to be rid of them. A sale for many Jamaicans is a matter of economic survival; the ideal victory is to achieve a 'rip-off.'

Don't underestimate the hustlers' understanding of the human mind. They're experts in consumer psychology and have an instant answer for any excuse you might throw.

Alas, many wily Jamaicans professing to aid you or proffering friendship are really intent on getting some of your money. You stop, say, to admire a beauty spot or swim in a refreshing pool and almost magically a self-appointed attendant will emerge with suggestions for an even better spot to enjoy or looking to become your buddy. The service is rarely free. In resort areas *any* unsolicited approach by a stranger is suspect. The goal is most frequently to make you feel indebted as a prelude to importuning. Anything other than saying 'no' will lead by default into a commitment. Fortunately, there *is* always the possibility that a genuine friendship might emerge; at the very least you'll learn the ropes.

A good defensive gambit is to play like a savvy local: 'Cho mon, doan't harass de touris'!' If harassment continues, seek the assistance of a tourist police officer.

In Kingston, hustlers tend to gravitate to captive audiences, such as at traffic lights, where a couple of young men will feverishly wash your car at a red light, even if you adamantly say 'No!' Keep your window closed and doors locked.

If you hire a guide, don't expect him to do more than keep you from getting lost or keep other hustlers at bay. Establish parameters up front, such as what he'll provide and for how much.

A good resource is *The How to be Jamaican Handbook* by Trevor Fearnon, Kim Robinson, and Harclyde Walcott, available islandwide.

Hurricanes Public warnings will be issued if a hurricane is due to come ashore, in which case seek shelter in the sturdiest structure you can find, and stay sober. You'll need your wits about you both during and after the storm.

The **Office of Disaster Preparedness** (☎ 928-5111) issues guidelines for what to do if a hurricane strikes.

For current weather information, contact **Weather.com** (W www.weather.com) or the **National Weather Service** (W www.nws .noaa.gov).

Prostitution Sex work is rife among the young female underclass, and the 'rent-a-Rasta' trade – Jamaican gigolos for foreign females – was given a boost in 1998 by the hit movie *How Stella Got Her Groove Back*. Negril, in particular, attracts large numbers of Jamaicans eager to attach themselves to foreigners. Single foreigners (male and female) are likely to be approached at some stage in not-too-subtle terms. Go-go dancers usually double as prostitutes, and most clubs have private rooms to facilitate this. Resist any temptations, as AIDS and other STDs are noted risks, and many street-walkers are crack addicts. Many dancers also live in relatively unsanitary, sometimes scabies-ridden conditions.

Soon Come! In Jamaica things happen when they happen, and if you can't handle slow (and occasionally surly) service, you're in the wrong place. A phrase you'll hear often is 'Soon come!,' which really means:

'Hey, relax...what's the rush?' 'Soon come!' could be one minute or a darn long time.

Sometimes this is mixed with a shockingly lackadaisical attitude toward you, the client. Jamaican-born photographer Cookie Kincaid told me a story that exemplifies Jamaicans' lackadaisical approach to life:

A tourist arrived at Kingston airport and went to a car rental company to pick up a car he'd reserved through his travel agency. There was no record of his reservation, and no cars were available. The receptionist was no help: 'Me know not'n' about it, mon!' she said, brushing him off disdainfully. Eventually he persuaded her to call her head office. She sat with the phone to her ear for an eternity. He watched, exasperated, as she filed her nails with the phone all the while tucked in the crease of her neck. Eventually he asked her if anyone had answered yet. 'No, mon,' she replied. 'De phone line is busy.'

Undertows Some beaches have dangerous undertows, particularly along the east and south coasts, where you should never swim alone off isolated beaches. Long Bay is especially dangerous. Seek local advice about conditions before swimming.

DISCRIMINATION

Jamaica is overwhelmingly a black society and one that prides itself on an apparent ease of relationships between the black majority, the white minority, and all the shades in between. Overt displays of racial discrimination are not tolerated, and foreign visitors who attempt to treat black Jamaicans as subservient will usually meet a forthright remonstration.

Everywhere, white visitors will find themselves a tiny minority. This can be unnerving if theirs is the only white face for miles around and Jamaican children and even adult men begin calling out 'Whitey!' or 'Jake!' Such epithets are common in more remote areas, but the individuals usually mean no offense. It's usually a matter-of-fact statement of surprise, not a term of abuse. Nonetheless, a small yet not insignificant percentage of Jamaicans display open or barely hidden hostility toward whites.

Black visitors to Jamaica are easily and rapidly identified as tourists and are treated just like white tourists.

LEGAL MATTERS

Jamaica's drug and drunk-driving laws are strictly enforced. Don't expect leniency because you're a foreigner. Jamaican jails are Dickensian hellholes!

If you are arrested, insist on your rights to call your embassy in Kingston to request its assistance.

BUSINESS HOURS

Most business offices are open 8:30am to 4:30pm Monday through Friday. Very few offices are open Saturday.

Most stores open at either 8am or 9am and close at 5pm, except Saturday, when they are open until noon. Generally shops are closed on Sunday, except pharmacies, which are open every day.

PUBLIC HOLIDAYS & SPECIAL EVENTS
Public Holidays

Public holidays are the following:

January New Year's Day (January 1)

February Bob Marley Day (February 6), Ash Wednesday

March-April Good Friday, Easter Monday

August Emancipation Day (August 1), Independence Day (August 6)

September Labour Day

October National Heroes' Day (October 19)

December Christmas Day (December 25), Boxing Day (December 26)

Special Events

The JTB publishes an annual 'Calendar of Events,' available from its offices worldwide.

The three biggest events are Ocho Rios' Reggae Sunsplash, which is held in February; Montego Bay's 'Reggae Sumfest' in August; and Kingston's Carnival, in April. (See the regional chapters for more on these concerts.)

Most of the events below follow a predictable schedule, although for some events the specific month may vary year to year.

The JTB can provide phone numbers and dates for specific events (see Tourist Offices earlier in this chapter), of which the following are the most important:

January

Accompong Maroon Festival, Accompong, St Elizabeth (January 6)

High Mountain 10K Road Race, Williamsfield, Manchester

Negril Sprint Triathlon, Negril

Red Stripe Cup Cricket Competition, Kingston

February

Carib Cement International Marathon, Kingston

Pineapple Cup Yacht Race, Miami to Montego Bay

Bob Marley Birthday Bash – Reggae Sunsplash, Ocho Rios

UWI Carnival, University of West Indies campus, Kingston

March

Gospel Spring Festival, Ocho Rios

Jamaica Orchid Society Spring Show, University of West Indies campus, Kingston

Miss Jamaica Universe Beauty Pageant, Kingston

Negril Music Festival

April

Montego Bay Yacht Club Easter Regatta

Harmony Hall Easter Crafts Fair, Ocho Rios

Devon House Easter Craft Fair, Kingston

Carnival, Kingston

Jake's Triathlon, Treasure Beach

Cable & Wireless Test Cricket, Kingston

Jamaica Beachfest, Negril

May

Calabash Literary Festival, Treasure Beach

Manchester Horticultural Society Show, Mandeville

Red Bones Blues Festival, Kingston

June

All-Jamaica Tennis Championships, Kingston (late May through mid-July)

Ocho Rios Jazz Festival

July

National Dance Theater Company's Season of Dance, Little Theater, Kingston

Reggae Sumfest, Montego Bay

August

Independence Day Parade, Kingston (August 6)

Caribbean Fashion Week, Kingston

Hi-Pro Family Polo Tournament & International Horse Show, Mammee Bay

Portland Jamboree, Port Antonio

Sashi Festival, Oracabessa

September

Miss Jamaica World Beauty Pageant, Kingston

Panasonic Golf Championship, Ocho Rios

Montego Bay Marlin Tournament

Ocho Rios International Marlin Tournament

October

Jamaica Open Pro Am Golf Tournament, Montego Bay

Great Jamaican Canoe Race and Hook 'n' Line Fishing Tournament, Treasure Beach

Shell/Sandals Cricket Competition, Kingston and Montego Bay

All That Heritage & Jazz Festival, Montego Bay

Port Antonio International Marlin Tournament

Caribbean Heritagefest, Portmore, near Kingston

November

Air Jamaica Jazz & Blues Festival

Harmony Hall Anniversary Crafts Fair, Ocho Rios (mid-November)

Holland Bamboo Run, Bamboo Avenue, St Elizabeth

Caribbean Music Expo, Ocho Rios

Jamaica Film & Music Festival, Kingston

December

Jam-Am Yacht Race, Montego Bay

Best of Harmony Hall, Ocho Rios

Devon House Christmas Fair, Kingston

Johnnie Walker World Golf Championship, Tryall Estate

LTM National Pantomime, Kingston (December 26 through April)

ACTIVITIES
Hiking

Jamaica's embryonic organized trail system is relegated to the Blue Mountains-John Crow National Park, where a Blue Mountain Ridge Trail, akin to the Appalachian Trail of the eastern USA, is being developed. The most popular trail leads to the summit of Blue Mountain Peak.

The most developed area is the Rio Grande Valley in Portland parish, where local tour guides offer one- to three-day hikes, including into the Blue and John Crow Mountains.

Elsewhere, rough and narrow bridle tracks span remote areas, such as the rugged and dramatic Cockpit Country and Hellshire Hills, where a trail system is finally being developed.

Most trails are hilly, rugged, and often overgrown by bush. Oppressive heat and humidity can turn what seems like an easy stroll into a grueling trudge, and distances can appear deceptively short on a map.

Travel light. Always carry plenty of water, insect repellent, and a small first-aid kit. And carry a windbreaker and a sweater or jacket in hilly or mountainous areas, as weather conditions can change quickly, such as when sudden torrential downpours turn hiking trails into mud. Long pants are best for hiking through bush, as they protect against thorns. Invest in lightweight canvas hiking boots for handling the sharp limestone of the Cockpit Country and Hellshire Hills.

Always stay on established trails: Jamaica's mountainous terrain is too treacherous to go wandering off the track, as thick vegetation hides sinkholes and crevasses. Seek advice from locals about trail conditions before setting out.

Resources Maya Lodge & Hiking Center (☎ 702-0314, 702-0112, 800-532-2271; PO Box 216, Kingston 7), at Jack's Hill, north of Kingston, is a good source of information on hiking.

Grand Valley Tours (☎/fax 993-4116; e grandvalleytoursja@hotmail.com; PO Box 203, Port Antonio PA) specializes in hiking trips in the Rio Grande Valley.

Strawberry Hill (☎ 944-8400, fax 944-8408; e lyndaleeburks@yahoo.com) offers hiking trips in the Blue Mountains; see Irish Town in the Blue Mountains chapter.

Sun Venture Tours (☎ 960-6685, fax 920-8348; w www.sunventuretours.com; 30

Balmoral Ave, Kingston 10) specializes in guided tours of the Blue Mountains and Cockpit Country.

See Specialty Tours in the Getting There & Away chapter for international companies specializing in hiking in Jamaica.

Scuba Diving

Jamaica offers fabulous scuba diving, especially along the north coast where the treasures range from shallow reefs, caverns, and trenches to walls and drop-offs just a few hundred yards offshore. Other sites to explore include ship wrecks (plus aircraft and even cars), especially around the rarely dived Hellshire cays (near Kingston) and Port Royal, which boasts a sunken pirate city (currently off limits).

Jamaica's waters offer exceptional visibility and water temperatures above 80°F year-round. Wet suits are not required for warmth, though a body wet suit is recommended and a full wet suit comes in handy to prevent scrapes on coral.

See the regional chapters for more suggested diving sites, prices, and diving course information. An excellent resource for divers is Lonely Planet's *Diving & Snorkeling Jamaica* by Hannie and Theo Smitt.

As for safety, remember that dives are restricted in Jamaica to 100 feet. See Dangers & Annoyances earlier in this chapter for information on hazardous marine life. The only decompression chamber is at the

University of West Indies Marine Laboratory (☎ 973-3274 24 hours, 973-2241; ⓔ nquinn@ uwimona.edu.jm; open 9am-5pm daily) in Discovery Bay.

Organizations The following dive organizations are good to know:

Divers Alert Network (DAN; ☎ 919-684-2948, 800-446-2671, 919-684-8111 24-hour emergency line; ⓦ www.diversalertnetwork.org), 6 West Colony Place, Durham, NC 27705, USA. Offers divers' health insurance, covering evacuations and treatment in emergencies

National Association of Underwater Instructors (NAUI; ☎ 813-628-6284, fax 628-8253; ⓦ www .naui.org), 9942 Currie Davis Drive Suite H, Tampa, FL 33619-2667, USA

Professional Association of Diving Instructors (PADI; ☎ 949-858-7234, 800-729-7234, fax 949-858-7264; ⓦ www.padi.com), 30151 Tomas St, Rancho Santa Margarita, CA 92688-2125, USA

Operators By law, all dives in Jamaican waters must be guided. Dozens of licensed dive operators offer rental equipment and group dives led by qualified dive masters. Many hotels also have dive facilities. Most dive operators belong to the **Jamaica Association of Dive Operators** (JADO; ☎ 974-6900). See the regional chapters for listings of local operators.

'Resort courses' for beginners (also called 'Discover Scuba' or 'Intro to Scuba') are offered at most major resorts (about US$50), which also offer PADI or NAUI certification courses (US$350-375) and advanced courses.

Certified divers should be sure to bring their dive cards.

Many dive packages are available from specialist dive-tour operators in North America or Europe. Reputable companies in the USA include the following:

Caribbean Adventures (☎ 954-467-0821, 800-934-3483, fax 954-467-3335; ⓦ www.pngexpeditions.com), 1525 S Andrews Ave Suite 227, Ft Lauderdale, FL 33316

Tropical Adventures Travel (☎ 206-441-3483, 800-348-9778, fax 206-441-5431; ⓦ www.divetropical.com), 111 Second N, Seattle, WA 98109

Sharks & Dolphins It's common to see sharks in the waters and reefs around Jamaica. Don't worry! Mostly these are harmless nurse sharks. Wary of humans, they usually give divers a wide berth.

Dolphins are far more approachable. Remember that they're unpredictable wild creatures, despite their cute smiles. Do not swim or chase after dolphins, and never touch them.

Dolphin Cove, in Ocho Rios, is a commercial operation that permits swimming with dolphins (see the Ocho Rios & North Coast chapter).

Golf

Jamaica has 12 championship courses, more than any other Caribbean island.

All courses rent out clubs and have carts. Most require that you hire a caddy – a wise investment, as they know the lay out of the course intimately.

For more information, contact the **Jamaica Golf Association** (☎ 926-4546; ℮ jamgolf@n5.com.jm).

For details on individual courses, see regional chapters. For information on golf tournaments, see Special Events earlier in this chapter.

Bird Watching

Jamaica is a birder's haven (see Fauna in the Facts about Jamaica chapter). The Blue Mountains, the Cockpit Country, the Black River Great Morass, the Negril Great Morass, and the Rio Grande Valley are good spots. All you need in the field is a good pair of binoculars and a guide to the birds of the island (see Books earlier in this chapter).

Birdlife Jamaica (☎/fax 927-1864; ℮ birdlifeja@yahoo.com; 2 Starlight Ave, Kingston 6), formerly Gosse Bird Club, offers field trips and educational programs and is the best overall birding resource in Jamaica.

Strawberry Hill (☎ 944-8400, fax 944-8408; ℮ lyndaleeburks@yahoo.com) runs birding trips in the Blue Mountains.

Grand Valley Tours (see Hiking earlier in this chapter) offers birding trips in the Rio Grande Valley.

Sun Venture Tours (see Hiking earlier in this chapter) offers birding trips into Cockpit Country.

For personalized birding tours, contact Robert Sutton (☎ 904-5454) in Mandeville; Fritz (☎ 952-2009; J$2,000 for three hours) at Rocklands, near Montego Bay; or Dwight Pryce (☎ 960-2848, fax 960-2850; ℮ www .greenjamaica.org), c/o Jamaica Conservation & Development Trust, at Hardwar Gap in the Blue Mountains.

Also see Birding & Ecological Tours in the Getting There & Away chapter.

Sailing

Most beachside resorts provide small sailboats called Sunfish, either as part of the hotel package rate or for a small hourly rental fee.

Marinas islandwide rent out charter yachts or motorboats, either with a crew or 'bareboat.' See regional chapters for details on rental opportunities.

See the Charter Yachts section in the Getting There & Away chapter for information on maps and charts.

Sport Fishing

Jamaica's waters are a pelagic playpen for schools of blue and white marlin, dolphin fish, wahoo, tuna, and dozens of other species. Deepwater game fish run year-round through the deep Cayman Trench that begins just 2 miles from shore.

Though present all year, sailfish and marlin are usually caught in late summer and autumn, off the north coast.

Almost a dozen fishing tournaments are held annually (see Special Events earlier in this chapter). Contact the JTB (see Tourist Offices earlier in this chapter) for a complete current listing.

You can charter sport-fishing boats at most marinas. Rates range from US$350 to US$400 for half a day to US$600 or more for a full day, with bait and tackle provided. You usually provide your own food and drinks. Most charter boats require a 50% deposit. Some boats keep half the catch, so discuss terms with the skipper prior to setting out.

For a more 'rootsy' experience, local fishermen will take you out in 'canoes' (long, narrow longboats with outboards) using hand lines.

Rafting

Raft trips are a staple of the Jamaican tourist menu, offering a calming trip aboard rafts made of sturdy bamboo poles lashed together. You sit on a raised seat with padded cushions while a 'captain' poles you through the washboard shallows and small cataracts.

It's a marvelous experience, and grants you a sample of outback Jamaica. Take a hat and sunscreen to guard against the sun.

Trips are offered on the Great River, Martha Brae, Rio Grande, and White Rivers (single companies hold a monopoly at each). See the regional chapters for details.

Spelunking

Jamaica is honeycombed with limestone caves and caverns, most of which boast fine stalagmites and stalactites, underground streams, and even waterfalls.

Use extreme caution. Many rivers and streams disappear underground and flow through the cave systems. During heavy rains the water level can rise rapidly, trapping and drowning unwary spelunkers.

Many people succumb to pulmonary histoplasmosis, a fungal disease resulting from infection with the organism *Histoplasma capsulatum*, which is common in Jamaican caves. It causes flu-like symptoms and, in severe cases, requires hospitalization.

Take powerful flashlights and spare bulbs and batteries. An indispensable guidebook is *Jamaica Underground* by Alan Fincham.

A Belgian cave-explorer, Guy Van Rentergem (e guy.van.rentergem@sky net.be), provides downloadable maps and information of Jamaican caves. For further information, contact the **Jamaica Caving Club** (☎ 927-2778; e nmartin@infochan.com; c/o Geological Society of Jamaica, University of West Indies, Mona, Kingston).

Some caves are tourist attractions, with guided tours. These include Green Grotto near Runaway Bay, Roaring River near Savanna-la-Mar, and Nonsuch Caves near Port Antonio. Lesser-known caves include Ghourie Caves, Coffee River Cave, Ipswich Caves, Windsor Caves, and Oxford Caves.

Cycling

Mountain bikes and 'beach cruisers' can be rented at most major resorts.

For serious touring, bring your own mountain or multipurpose bike (you'll need sturdy wheels to handle the potholed roads). Bicycles can travel by air. You can pack a bike in pieces in a bike bag or box, and check it on airlines as a piece of baggage. Check requirements with the airline well in advance, preferably before you pay for your ticket.

Carry an adequate repair kit plus plenty of spare parts, such as inner tubes. Bicycle stores are few and far between.

Travel as light as possible. Carry plenty of water (a Camelback is ideal; these plastic water containers strap to your back and allow you to sip through a tube as you cycle). And wear a helmet! Conditions are hazardous.

Cycling trips that range from a half day to three days are offered by touring companies at major resorts. See regional chapters for information.

Manfred's Jamaican Mountain Bike Tours (☎ 705-745-8210 in Canada; e manfreds@ peterboro.net) offers bicycling tours of the south coast. The **Jamaica Mountain Bike Association** (JAMBA; ☎ 957-0155; PO Box 104, Negril) is a good information source.

Surfing

The east coast draws surfers to ride waves coming in from the Atlantic. Boston Beach, 9 miles east of Port Antonio, is the best spot. Also good are Long Bay and tiny Christmas Beach, about 4 miles farther south. The southeast coast, including the Palisadoes peninsula, also gets good surf.

The **Surfing Association of Jamaica/Jamnesia Surf Club** (☎ 750-0103; e jasurfas@ hotmail.com; PO Box 167, Kingston 2) can help you plan a surfing vacation.

Other Activities

Most large beach hotels provide water sports, often free of charge for guests. Independent concessions provide water sports on major beaches, from jet-skiing and waterskiing to windsurfing and banana-boat rides.

Most upscale hotels have tennis courts, and stables providing organized horseback rides are located in most resort areas. See regional chapters for additional details.

WORK

Visitors are admitted to Jamaica on the condition that they 'not engage in any form of employment on the island or solicit or accept any order for goods or services, for or on behalf of any persons, firm or company not carrying on business with the island.' Professionals can obtain work permits if sponsored by a Jamaican company, but casual work is very difficult to obtain.

The **Peace Corps** (☎ 800-424-8580; W www.peacecorps.gov) accepts volunteers for work in Jamaica, with assignments in environmental education and community development, including projects to guide youth at risk.

In the UK, **British North America Universities Club** (BUNAC; W www.bunac.org) accepts university graduates for teaching posts in Jamaican schools.

ACCOMMODATIONS

Jamaica offers accommodations for meeting every budget and style. There are some splendid bargains at all price levels, from cozy budget guesthouses for US$20 nightly to ritzy, US$500-a-night, all-inclusive resorts. However, far too many hotels in Jamaica are overpriced or soulless.

The JTB publishes a guide and rate sheet to 140 or so hotels and 300 guest houses that have been inspected and are 'JTB approved.'

Caribbean Vacation Network (☎ 800-423-4095; W www.caribbeanmagic.com) has a 40-page catalog showing dozens of properties.

Note that Jamaica has no youth hostel association, and there are no hostels on the island.

Rates & Seasons

Throughout this book and unless otherwise stated, prices (given in US dollars) are for double rooms in low season and refer to

European Plan (EP), or room only. Some hotels quote rates as Continental Plan (CP; room and breakfast), Modified American Plan (MAP; room plus breakfast and dinner), or American Plan (AP; room plus three meals daily). Don't forget to check if the quoted rate includes tax and service charge; if not, the compulsory 6.25% to 15% GCT (and possibly a 10% to 15% service charge) may be added to your bill.

Low season (summer) is usually mid-April to mid-December; high season (winter) is the remainder of the year, when hotel prices increase by 40% or more and popular hotels are often booked solid. Some hotels have even higher rates for 'peak' season: usually at Christmas and Easter. A few hotels have year-round rates. Some offer discounts for stays of a week or more. All-inclusive packages can be a great bargain; they're usually based on three-day minimum stays.

Most hotels accept payment by credit card or traveler's check.

Reservations

You can make reservations directly with hotels. Reserving by mail is best avoided, as it can take several weeks. Instead send an email, phone, fax, or use a travel agent, hotel representative, or online reservation service. Online reservation services to consider include **Travelocity** (W www.travelocity.com) and **Expedia** (W www.expedia.com).

It is advisable to book several months in advance.

The **Ring of Confidence** (W www.in-site.com/ring) is a group of family-style Jamaican hotels that work together to help visitors plan the next stage of their trip by 'handing' guests on to another property within the ring. You reserve your first night's accommodations in advance, then pay a 10% deposit for bookings – handled by your current host – which is deducted from the bill of each subsequent property.

Camping

Jamaica is not developed for campers. Negril is the only resort area with facilities. A few isolated campsites are also scattered elsewhere. Many budget properties will let you pitch a tent on their lawns for a small fee. Some even rent tents and have shower, toilet, and laundry facilities.

It is unsafe to camp anywhere in the wild in Jamaica.

Guesthouses

Guesthouses are the lodgings of choice for Jamaicans when traveling. Most are no-frills properties with a live-in owner who provides breakfast and sometimes dinner. They're an inexpensive option, and they're good places to mix with locals.

Some are no more than a couple of dingy rooms with shared bathrooms (most guesthouses have shared bath). Others are self-contained apartments. Still others are indistinguishable from hotels or faceless motels.

The JTB publishes an 18-page *Inns of Jamaica* catalog.

B&Bs

A B&B ('bed and breakfast') usually is a lodging where the owner plays live-in host and provides breakfast in the quoted room rate. In Jamaica the term is often misused, and true B&Bs are few and far between.

Hotels

Jamaican hotels run the gamut. Terms such as 'deluxe' or 'first-class' have been so abused that it is unwise to rely on a hotel's brochure.

Jamaica is particularly noted for its unbeatably stylish hotels, many attracting a who's who of Hollywood and royalty. Some – Jamaica Inn (outside Ocho Rios) comes to mind – exude an old world charm, with butlers and white-gloved waiters who call you 'm'lady,' though they're not all so stuffy.

Jamaica offers quintessentially Caribbean, avant-garde boutique hotels that evoke the finest in unpretentious and gracious living, epitomized by the **Island Outpost properties** (☎ 305-672-5254, 800-688-7678, fax 305-672-6288; ☎ 020 7440 4360 in the UK; **W** www.islandoutpost.com; 1330 Ocean Drive, Miami Beach, FL 33139, USA).

All-Inclusive Resorts All-inclusive resorts are cash-free, self-contained resorts: you pay a set price and (theoretically) pay nothing more once you set foot inside the resort.

All-inclusives offer a pampered vacation, but shelter guests from mingling with locals and discovering the colorful, gritty, real Jamaica. Most resorts offer excursions, and you're free to explore on your own.

Sandals (**W** www.sandals.com) sets the standard that others attempt to reach, with varying degrees of success; check the Sandals website for ongoing discounts. **SuperClubs** (**W** www.superclubs.com) is the main competitor. Both specialize in honeymoon resorts (ie, heterosexual couples only), as does the **Couples** (**W** www.couples.com) chain. Sandals also operates four **Beaches** properties (**W** www.beaches.com) for families, couples, and singles, regardless of sexual orientation; SuperClubs competes with its Breezes and Starfish properties.

For more information on Sandals, contact:

Canada (☎ 416-223-0028, 800-545-8283, fax 416-223-3306)

UK (☎ 020-7581-9895, 0800-742742, fax 020-7823-8758)

USA Unique Vacations (☎ 305-284-1300, 800-726-3257, fax 305-687-8996)

For more information on SuperClubs, contact:

Canada (☎ 800-553-4320)

UK (☎ 01749-677200)

USA (☎ 954-925-0925, 800-467-8737, fax 954-925-0334)

Outside these chains, caution is needed when choosing an all-inclusive resort, as many properties have jumped onto the bandwagon for marketing purposes. Check carefully for hidden charges.

Homestays

You can also make your own arrangements to stay with individuals or families that do not rent rooms as a normal practice. Diane McIntyre-Pike arranges family stays through her community tourism program; see the boxed text 'Community Tourism' in the South Coast & Central Highlands chapter. Also see the boxed text 'Meet the People' in the Facts about Jamaica chapter.

Villa Rentals

Jamaica boasts hundreds of private houses for rent, from modest cottages to lavish beachfront estates. They're very cost-effective if you're traveling with family or a group of friends. Many include a cook and maid, and often a veritable army of staff.

Two good starting points are the **Caribbean Villas Owners Association** (☎ 877-248-2862), and the **Jamaican Association of Villas & Apartments** (JAVA; ☎ 974-2508, fax 974-2967; W www.villasinjamaica.com; PO Box 298, Ocho Rios). JAVA's other offices include:

UK The Caribbean Centre (☎ 020-8940-3399, fax 020-8940-7424; e jan@caribbean.itsnet.co.uk), 3 The Green, Richmond, Surrey, TW9 1PL

USA (☎ 305-673-6688, 800-845-5276, fax 305-673-5666; e javavillas@aol.com), 1680 Meridian Suite 504, Miami Beach, FL 33139

Other villa-rental companies include:

Sun Villas (☎ 888-625-6007; W www.sunvillas.com), 3400 Irving Avenue S, Minneapolis, MN 55408

Villas by Linda Smith (☎ 301-229-4300, fax 301-320-6963; W www.jamaicavillas.com)

Villascaribe (☎ 800-645-7498; W www.villascaribe.com)

Rates start as low as US$100 per week for budget units with minimal facilities. More upscale villas begin at about US$750 weekly and can run US$10,000 or more for a sumptuous multibedroom estates. Rates fall as much as 30% in summer. A large deposit (usually 25% or more) is required.

FOOD

Jamaica's homegrown cuisine is a fusion of many ethnic traditions and influences. The Arawaks brought callaloo, cassava, corn, sweet potatoes, and several tropical fruits to the island. The Spanish adopted native spices, later enhanced by spices brought by slaves from their African homelands. Immigrants from India brought hot and flavorful curries, often served with locally made mango chutney. *Roti,* a bread of Indian origin, is also popular served with a dollop of curried goat or chicken in the middle and eaten folded. Middle Eastern dishes and Chinese influences have also become part of the national menu. And basic roasts and stews followed the flag during three centuries of British rule, as did Yorkshire pudding, meat pies, and hot cross buns.

The Jamaicans have melded all these influences into dishes with playful names, such as 'solomon grundy.'

A fair amount of Jamaican cuisine is an adventure in tongue-lashing. A key ingredient is pimento (allspice), which is indigenous to Jamaica. The main condiment is savory, piquant Pickapeppa sauce, the recipe for which is a closely guarded secret.

Two cultural events celebrate Jamaican cuisine: the weeklong Terra Nova Heritage Food Festival, in Kingston each October; and the two-day Jamaica Spice, in Ocho Rios each July.

Out to Eat

Dining in Jamaica ranges from wildly expensive restaurants to humble roadside stands where you can eat simple Jamaican fare for as little as US$1. Don't be put off by their basic appearance (unless they're overtly unhygienic). Most serve at least one vegetarian meal, which is often called 'I-tal,' a Rastafarian inspiration for 'pure' or health food.

Most hotels incorporate Jamaican dishes in their menus.

Food bought at grocery stores is usually expensive, as many of the canned and packaged goods are imported. Dirt-cheap fresh fruits, vegetables, and spices sell at markets and roadside stalls islandwide. Wash all produce thoroughly!

Likewise, you can usually buy fish (and lobster, in season) from local fishermen.

Virtually every town has fast-food joints such as McDonald's, Burger King, and Kentucky Fried Chicken. The local equivalents are Mother's, King Burger, and Juici-Beef Patties.

Snacks

The staple and most popular snack is a patty – a thin, tender yet crisp crust filled with highly spiced, well-seasoned beef or vegetables. 'Stamp and go' are saltfish cakes eaten as appetizers.

Main Dishes

Jamaicans typically forsake corn flakes for more savory fare at breakfast: ackee and saltfish is typical. The average Jamaican eats a light lunch. Other dishes could be pepper pot stew, fried fish, or 'jerk' pork, or another national dish using island ingredients simmered in coconut milk and spices.

Many meals are accompanied by starchy vegetables – 'breadkinds' – such as plantains and yam, or other bread substitutes such as pancake-shaped cassava bread (or *bammy*) and 'johnny cakes' (delicious fried dumplings, an original Jamaican fast-food).

The island staple is rice and 'peas' (red beans), most often served with pork, the staple meat. Goat, another staple, is usually served curried, chopped into small bits with

Ackee & Saltfish

A typical Jamaican 'plantation breakfast' is ackee and saltfish, the national dish. Ackee is a tree-grown fruit (native to Africa), the golden flesh of which bears an uncanny resemblance to scrambled eggs when cooked. Served with 'johnny cakes,' callaloo (a leafy vegetable), and flaked escovietched fish, it makes a fantastic breakfast.

The fruit is highly toxic when unripe (known as 'Jamaica poisoning'), and it can be eaten only after the pods have fully opened to reveal the canary yellow arils within.

meat on the bone. It is also the main ingredient of 'mannish water,' a soup made from goat offal. Jamaican soups are thick, more like stews, and loaded with vegetables and 'breadkind.' 'Dip and fall back' is a salty stew served with bananas and dumplings.

Jamaica's most popular dish is jerk, a term that describes the process of cooking meats smothered in tongue-searing marinade. Chicken, pork, or fish are first washed with vinegar or lime juice, then marinated in a hot sauce of island-grown spices (including volatile Scotch bonnet pepper), and barbecued slowly in an outdoor pit – usually an oil drum cut in half – over a fire of pimento wood, which gives the meat its distinctive flavor. Jerk is best served hot off the coals wrapped in paper. You normally order by the pound (US$2 should fill you up).

Jamaican steaks are generally tough and meant for stewing.

Naturally, there's a strong emphasis on seafood. Snapper and parrot fish are two of the more popular species. Kingfish, grouper, and marlin are also common. A favorite is *escoveitched* fish, pickled in vinegar then fried and simmered with peppers and onions. Bammy and 'festival' are popular accompaniments.

Pickled herring bears the improbable name of 'solomon grundy.' 'Rundown' is mackerel that's cooked in coconut milk; it's usually eaten at breakfast.

Nouvelle Jamaican Cuisine

Recent years have witnessed the beginnings of an evolution in Jamaican nouvelle cuisine, also called Caribbean fusion. A new generation of local chefs is reinterpreting traditional dishes and creating new ones that fuse traditional Jamaican ingredients and techniques to international concepts.

Here are the top trend-setting restaurants (see the regional chapters for details):

Bloomfield Great House, Mandeville

Café Aubergine, Moneague, near Ocho Rios

Culloden Café, near Whitehouse

Evita's, Ocho Rios

Mille Fluers, Drapers, East of Port Antonio

Houseboat Grill, Montego Bay

Norma's on the Terrace, Kingston

Red Bones Blues Café, Kingston

Strawberry Hill, Irish Town (Blue Mountains)

Toscanini, Harmony Hall, Ocho Rios

Vineyard Restaurant, Coyaba Beach Resort, Ironshore

The term 'lobster' is also used for the local clawless freshwater crayfish, usually served grilled with butter and garlic, or curried, for as little as US$5 at stalls. Likewise, freshly caught and highly spiced 'shrimp' (called 'pepper swimp,' though actually *janga* or crayfish) is a favorite in the Black River area.

Vegetables

Yams are the island staple, along with carrots and scallions. Pumpkin is another staple side dish served boiled and mashed with butter.

You may also come across breadfruit in various guises. This starchy vegetable grows wild throughout the island. The round 'fruits' weigh up to 4lb. Young or immature fruit is eaten as a staple – either added to soups or served as an accompaniment to the main dish. The mature (but not yet ripe) vegetable is roasted or deep-fried.

Callaloo is a spinachlike vegetable, usually served shredded and steamed or lightly boiled. It also finds its way into spicy pepper pot stew. Local lore says pepper pot can be

Fruits

Jamaica is a tropical Eden ripe with native fruits such as the peachlike naseberry, banana, pineapple, coconut, star apple, soursop, ugli, and the ortanique (a citrus crossbred from oranges and tangerines). Tiny roadside shacks also proffer fresh papayas, mangoes, and young or unripe bananas.

The starchy, rather bland-tasting plantain, closely related to the banana, cannot be eaten in its raw state, but must be cooked. It is usually fried or baked and served as an accompaniment to a main dish. In its unripe form it is used to make delicious chips. Jamaica's fruits include:

Guava is a small ovoid or rounded fruit with an intense, musky sweet aroma. It has a pinkish, granular flesh studded with regular rows of tiny seeds. It is most commonly used in nectars and punches, syrups, jams, chutney, and even ice cream.

Guinep is a small green fruit (pronounced GI-nep) that grows in clusters, like grapes, and can be bought July through November. Each 'grape' bears pink flesh that you plop into your mouth whole. It's kind of rubbery and juicy, and tastes like a cross between a fig and a strawberry. Watch for the big pit in the middle.

Mango is a lush fruit that comes in an assortment of sizes and colors, from yellow to black. Massage the glove-leather skin to soften the pulp, which can be sucked or spooned like custard. Select your mango by its perfume.

Papaya has cloaks of many colors (from yellow to rose) that hide a melon-smooth flesh that likewise runs from citron to vermilion. The central cavity is a trove of edible black seeds. Tenderness and sweet scent are key to buying papayas. They are commonly served with breakfast plates, in fruit salads, as jams and ice cream, and baked in desserts.

Soursop is an ungainly, irregularly shaped fruit with cottony pulp that is invitingly fragrant yet acidic. Its taste hints at guava and pineapple. It's most commonly used for pudding, ice cream, syrup, and canned drinks.

Star apple is a leathery, dark-purple, tennis-ball–size, gelatinous fruit of banded colors (white, pink, lavender, purple). Its glistening seeds form a star in the center. The fruit is mildly sweet and understated. Immature fruits are gummy and unappetizing: feel for some give when buying.

Sugar apple is a strange name for a fruit that resembles a giant pine cone, with bractlike sections that separate when the fruit is ripe. The gray, juicy flesh is sweet and custardlike and shot with watermelonlike seeds.

Ugli is a fruit that is well named. It is ugly on the vine – like a deformed grapefruit with warty, mottled green or orange skin. But the golden pulp is delicious: acid-sweet and gushingly juicy.

generations old, as the pot is reheated each day with fresh ingredients added.

Cho-cho (also known as *christophine)* is a pulpy squashlike gourd served in soups and as an accompaniment to meats; it is also used for making hot pickles.

Desserts

Jamaicans have evolved their own desserts, too, such as *matrimony,* a salad of pulped orange and star apple (and sometimes other fruits) with cream; and *duckunoo* (or 'blue drawers'), a pudding made of cornmeal, green bananas, and coconut and enlivened with sugar and spices.

'Chocolate tea ball' is made from a chocolate paste rolled into a hard ball with a touch of nutmeg and cinnamon (they're now rare, but you'll find them around Port Antonio, where they're still made by the Fairy Hill's Long Road Co-operative).

DRINKS

Jamaica has a variety of refreshing drinks – both alcoholic and nonalcoholic. Tap water is generally safe, except in some backcountry areas. To avoid doubt, order bottled water (see also Water in the Health section earlier in this chapter).

Nonalcoholic Drinks

Coffee Jamaican Blue Mountain coffee is considered among the most exotic coffees in the world. It's also the most expensive (see the boxed text 'Hallowed Grounds' in the Facts about Jamaica chapter).

The coffee is relatively mild, light-bodied, and has a musty, almost woody flavor, and its own unmistakable aroma.

Most upscale hotels and restaurants serve it as a matter of course. Unfortunately, the majority of lesser hotels serve lesser coffees from other parts of the country or – sacrilege! – powdered instant coffee. Be careful if you ask for white coffee (with milk), which Jamaicans interpret to mean 50% hot milk and 50% coffee.

Tea Coffee is not Jamaica's drink of choice. Locals prefer herbal teas such as 'fevergrass,' said to bring down a fever, or soursop leaves for calming the nerves. 'Tea' is a generic Jamaican term for any usually hot, nonalcoholic drink, commonly referring to popular herbal 'teas' used by locals as medicines and aphrodisiacs.

Jamaicans will make teas of anything: Irish moss is often mixed with rum, milk, and spices. Ginger, mint, ganja, and even fish are brewed into teas. Be careful if innocently tempted by 'mushroom tea,'; the fungus in question is hallucinogenic, and unless you're in search of an LSD-like buzz, steer clear.

Cold Drinks A Jamaican favorite for cooling off is 'skyjuice': a shaved-ice cone flavored with sugary fruit syrup and lime juice, and sold at streetside stalls, usually in a small plastic bag with a straw. Sanitation is sometimes questionable. The same is true of 'snocones' and 'bellywash,' the local name for limeade.

The best way to quench a thirst is to drink coconut water straight from the nut. They're for sale for about US$0.50 from streetside vendors, who will lop off the top and provide a straw.

Another refreshing and nutritious drink is a fruit punch of blended ripe fruits or ginger beer, which isn't a beer at all, but a delicious, slightly spicy soda – a perfect tonic for hot days. And watch for *sorrel,* traditionally a bright red Christmas drink made from flower petals.

Ting, a bottled grapefruit soda, is Jamaica's own soft drink.

Alcoholic Drinks

Red Stripe is the beer of Jamaica. Crisp and sweet, it's perfectly light and refreshing. It's also the only known antidote to hot spicy jerk meats. If you hear locals calling for 'policemen,' don't panic: the beer is named for the 'natty trim' – a conspicuous red seam – on the trouser legs of the uniform of the Jamaican police force.

Real Rock is a slightly heavier, tastier local lager.

Heineken is also brewed in Jamaica. Malty Dragon Stout is also popular, and is a favorite of Jamaican women, as is bottled Guinness, brewed under license locally.

Rum ranges from dark rums to a mind-bogglingly powerful white (clear) rum, the libation of choice for poorer Jamaicans.

Jamaica produces many liqueurs, mostly of rum, but also of coffee beans and fruits. The original coffee liqueur is Tía Maria.

ENTERTAINMENT

Jamaica has plenty to keep you amused, from ear-shattering 'stageshows' for the masses to ballet for the social elite. Most of the high culture, including theater, and the best discos and upscale bars are to be found in Kingston. Elsewhere the key word is reggae (see the Reggae 'n'

Riddims special section), although jazz is growing in popularity. The various elements of Jamaican society each has its own genre.

Few outlets cater specifically to women or seniors, and there are few clubs and formal organizations.

If all you want is a film, most large cities have at least one cinema showing top-run Hollywood movies. Anticipate a lot of booing and screams and other audience interruptions.

Secure Any Tickets (☎ 967-2213; 25 Sutton St, Kingston 10) is a ticket office for entertainment and sporting events.

The Story of Rum

Jamaican sugar has been turned into alcohol since Spanish times, when *meleza* (cane molasses) was fermented to make a liquor called *aguardiente*. The British introduced distillation to produce a cane liquor called *saccharum*, from which the term 'rum' is derived.

Making rum involves three stages: fermentation, distillation, and aging. The traditional distillation process used copper pots and produced a heavily flavored rum containing 85% alcohol and 15% water. The distilled liquor was then poured into charred-oak barrels and matured from three to 20 years. Rum derived its distinct flavor and color from the barrel. A small percentage was lost every year to evaporation: the 'angel's share.'

Very little rum is produced in this manner today. The modern, continuous-still method produces a more lightly flavored rum of higher alcohol content. Most modern rum is aged in stainless steel vats for no more than three years, and since all rums are clear after distillation, the color and flavor are 'manufactured' with caramel and other additives.

'White overproof' is the rum of the poor Jamaican, and it's an integral part of island culture. Overproof rum from homemade stills is virtually pure alcohol (legally overproof rum is 151 proof, but bootleg liquor can be a brain-melting, throat-searing 170 proof). It is used as a remedy for all sorts of maladies, from toothaches to colds (it was originally called 'Kill Devil'). It's also used to clean newborn babies and to baptize them. Of course, it drowns sorrows and is imbibed liberally at wakes to chase away duppies. White rum is also supposedly good for a man's libido (a popular version is the 'Front End Loader').

Rum Shops

Rum shops are the staple of island entertainment and can be found on virtually any street and in every village. They are funky bars and clubs catering to poorer Jamaicans. Rum shops are patronized pretty much exclusively by men, and de rigueur decor includes Christmas lights and girlie pinups.

Go-Go Clubs

Go-go clubs are another staple of Jamaican nightlife. Almost every village has at least one. Usually it's simply a bar with a mirrored stage where young women dance – in lingerie, string bikinis, topless, or even naked – and perform often quite raunchy contortions. Most have private rooms for one-on-one 'private dances.' They're generally nonthreatening places, but see Prostitution in the Dangers & Annoyances section, earlier in this chapter, for warnings.

Stageshows

Concerts – 'stageshows' – are usually held at open-air venues and draw big crowds, catered to with itinerant vendors selling beer and rum. The distinct smell of ganja drifts through the air, amidst the deafening noise from banks of speakers the size of double-decker buses. The billing often includes top-name performers, such as Third World, Buju Banton, Gregory Isaacs, and Lady Saw. However, *caveat emptor!* The billed artists often don't appear; sometimes they're not even booked!

'Sound-system parties' or 'jump-ups' are smaller, impromptu concerts that are ubiquitous on weekends throughout the island, often at improvised 'lawns' in remote locations where the music can be cranked up until the earth trembles (literally!) and noise restrictions are not likely to be enforced. Often, rival DJs vie against each other at 'clashes.' Sound-system parties are popular with a young, often unruly male crowd and violence is always a possibility. Security guards usually frisk for weapons, but often someone will sneak in fireworks to throw, or even a gun to letoff as a bravado demonstration of appreciation.

Discos & Nightclubs

Kingston has more than a dozen discos ranging from earthy dancehall venues frequented mostly by the urban poor to upscale discos playing US and European chart-toppers plus soca for the middle classes. The leading resort towns each have a choice of two or three discos. Many hotels also have their own discos.

Thursday is traditionally 'ladies nite,' offering either free entry or free drinks to women. Sunday is traditionally oldies night, with a selection of R&B, old-time reggae, and ska.

Many clubs get jam-packed and are sweaty, horribly smoky affairs with the music cranked up full-bore, beer bottles (often broken) littering the floor, and the omnipresent gigolos and salacious females ever-ready to hit up on foreign tourists.

Theater

Although small-scale theater can be found in all the major towns, Kingston is where the real action is. Jamaica's most beloved theater company is the National Dance Theater Company, which performs at the Little Theater. The company tours the island, along with smaller repertoire companies catering to a local audience. Also see Arts in the Facts about Jamaica chapter.

Gambling

There are no casinos in Jamaica. However, several larger hotels have video slot-machines (one-arm bandits), and at last visit several dedicated 'gaming rooms' had opened. The largest is the Coral Cliffs Gaming Room in Montego Bay, with a hundred gaming machines.

Betting on horse racing is permitted at Caymanas Park, Portmore, and at betting shops ('off-track') nationwide.

SPECTATOR SPORTS

Horse racing often draws large, enthusiastic crowds to Caymanas Park. Polo is played at St Ann Polo Club and at Chukka Cove Farm, both in St Ann parish, and at Knolford Polo & Tennis Ranch, near Linstead, in St Catherine.

The Dover Raceway, south of Runaway Bay, hosts the Motor Sports Championship

Series of car and motorcycle racing, held from April to December.

Cricket

Cricket, played virtually year-round, is as much a part of Jamaica's cultural landscape as is reggae. You'll come across small fields in even the most remote backwaters, where boys with makeshift bats practice the bowls and swings that may one day take them from rural obscurity to fortune and fame. Games between leading regional and international teams are played frequently at Sabina Park in Kingston.

Jamaica has no national team. Instead, the best players from the cricketing nations of the Caribbean form the West Indies team, which has dominated world cricket for two decades. Regional competitions feature teams from individual islands.

See Special Events earlier in this chapter for a listing of cricket matches.

Soccer

Soccer is Jamaica's second sport and was given a huge boost by the success of the Reggae Boyz -Jamaica's national soccer team – in qualifying for the 1998 World Cup. Weekend games between village teams draw large crowds. International matches are played at the **National Stadium** (☎ 929-4970; Arthur Wint Drive) in Kingston.

Athletics

Jamaica is a leader on the international athletics scene, regularly producing track-and-field athletes of world-record caliber dating back to sprinter Arthur Wint, Jamaica's first Olympic gold medal winner (in 1948) through to the more recent successes of Merlene Ottey (gold medal winner in 1996). Major meets are hosted at Kingston's National Stadium.

SHOPPING

Jamaica has a wide range of arts, crafts, and duty-free items, plus food items and drinks such as Blue Mountain coffee, rum liqueurs, Pickapeppa sauce, and marinades such as Busha Brown's gourmet pickles, relishes, and other gourmet products.

Cigars

Most gift stores in upscale hotels sell premium Cuban cigars. (Technically it's illegal for US citizens to buy Cuban cigars in Jamaica.)

Fine handmade Jamaican cigars give Havana cigars a run for their money though. **Cifuentes y Cia Ltd** (☎ 925-1080; 45 Elma Cres, Kingston 20) has been operating in Jamaica for over 40 years. The company specializes in premium Macanudo cigars.

Duty-Free Goods

Resort towns feature a plethora of duty-free and in-bond shops, and most upscale hotels sell duty-free items – from name-brand colognes to Gucci watches and Colombian emeralds (at up to 30% below US or European retail prices). You can also buy island-made products such as rums, liqueurs, and cigars for 50% or greater savings. It pays to comparison shop.

Shopping with a Conscience

Many souvenirs sold in Jamaica are made from protected species of plants and animals that have been acquired illegally. By collecting or purchasing these items, you undermine wildlife conservation efforts.

Most sea turtle products, including 'tortoise shell' jewelry and combs, are made from the highly endangered hawksbill sea turtle. Other turtle species are killed for eggs, food products, taxidermy, leather, and oil for creams. And eggs are poached for baking and for downing raw in rum-shops as aphrodisiacs. All are prohibited, as are products made of endangered American crocodile, black and white coral products, and swallowtail butterflies, which are commonly offered for sale in and around the Blue Mountains. Many species of plants – especially orchids – are endemics and also protected by law.

Under US and international laws, violation of a foreign wildlife law is automatically a violation of domestic law.

By law you must pay for duty-free goods in foreign currency. In certain cases you may find that you cannot walk out with your purchase; instead, the goods will be delivered to your hotel or cruise ship.

Arts & Crafts

Tens of thousands of Jamaicans make a living as artists selling to the tourist trade. Much of the artwork is kitsch, paintings of and intuitive hardwood carvings of Bob Marley, glistening with oil, and fishes and animals, often painted in rainbow hues and touched with pointillist dots.

There's plenty of first-rate art, too, at galleries islandwide (see Arts in the Facts about Jamaica chapter). Good buys include colorful bead jewelry, baskets, and other straw goods, including straw hats. Look for 'jippi-jappa' hats (pronounced hippy-happa) from St Catherine parish, beautifully woven from fine strips of palm-leaf in the style of Panama hats.

Never pay the asking price. Higgle! It's expected. Expect to settle on a price at least 20% below the initial asking price.

Aggressive hustlers who accost you with crafty schemes – called 'runnings' – cannot in general be trusted.

Getting There & Away

AIR
Airports
Jamaica has international airports in Montego Bay and Kingston. For flight arrival and departure information at either one, call the airports, visit their websites, or call the airline directly.

Montego Bay The majority of visitors to Jamaica arrive at Donald Sangster International Airport (☎ 952-5530; W www.sangster-airport.com.jm), about 2 miles north of Montego Bay.

There's a **Jamaica Tourist Board** (JTB) information booth in the arrivals hall. A 24-hour money-exchange bureau is immediately beyond immigration. There's a transport information desk plus desks representing tour companies, hotels, and rental cars immediately as you exit customs. A police station (☎ 952-2241) is outside.

Ensure your luggage is locked and don't leave valuables in unlocked pockets.

An adjacent terminal serves domestic flights. The terminals are not linked by walkway and are a sweaty 10-minute walk apart. The charter airlines, including Air Jamaica Express, provide connecting shuttles.

Kingston Norman Manley International Airport (☎ 924-8452, 924-8024; W www.manley-airport.com.jm) is about 11 miles southeast from downtown.

There's a JTB information desk in the arrivals hall, a money-exchange bureau before customs, and a taxi information booth as you exit customs. Beyond customs there's a bank and Island Car Rentals. Straight ahead is the JUTA taxi office, a police station (☎ 924-8002), an ATM, a telephone office, and the Otahetis Café.

Airlines
The following major airlines have offices in Jamaica:

Air Canada (☎ 924-8211, 888-991-9063)
7 Trafalgar Rd, Kingston
(☎ 952-5160, 888-991-9063) Montego Bay

Air Jamaica (☎ 888-359-2475) islandwide

Air Jamaica Express (☎ 923-8680, 888-359-2475) Kingston
(☎ 952-5401) Montego Bay
(☎ 957-5251) Negril
(☎ 726-1344) Ocho Rios
(☎ 993-3692) Port Antonio

ALM Antillean (☎ 926-1762) 23 Dominica Drive, Kingston 5
(☎ 952-5530) Montego Bay

American Airlines (☎ 920-8887, 888-359-2247) 26 Trafalgar Rd, Kingston 10
(☎ 979-9334, 888-359-2247) Montego Bay

British Airways (☎ 929-9020) 25 Dominica Drive, Kingston 5
(☎ 952-3771) Montego Bay

BWIA International Airways (☎ 929-3770, 888-991-2210) 19 Dominica Drive, Kingston 5

Cayman Airways (☎ 926-1762) 23 Dominica Drive, Kingston 5

Warning

The information in this chapter is particularly vulnerable to change: Prices for international travel are volatile, routes are introduced and cancelled, schedules change, special deals come and go, and rules and visa requirements are amended. You should check directly with the airline or a travel agent to make sure you understand how a fare (and ticket you may buy) works, and be aware of the security requirements for international travel.

The upshot of this is that you should get opinions, quotes and advice from as many airlines and travel agents as possible before you part with your hard-earned cash. The details given in this chapter should be regarded as pointers and are not a substitute for your own careful, up-to-date research.

91

Continental Airlines (☎ 952-5530) 23 Dominica Drive, Kingston 5

COPA Airlines (☎ 926-1762) 23 Dominica Drive, Kingston 5
(☎ 952-5530) Montego Bay

Cubana (☎ 978-3410) 22 Trafalgar Rd, Kingston 10
(☎ 952-4706) Montego Bay

International AirLink (☎ 940-6660)

Northwest Airlines (☎ 952-9740, 800-225-2525) Montego Bay

US Airways (☎ 940-0172, 800-622-1015) Montego Bay

Buying Tickets

It usually pays to book as far in advance as possible. Some of the cheapest tickets have to be bought months in advance, and popular flights sell out early. Note any restrictions. If you discover that those impossibly cheap flights are 'fully booked,' keep phoning around. APEX, or 'advance purchase excursion,' fares are usually the cheapest.

You can research fares online. In North America, try W www.orbitz.com, W www.travelocity.com, or W www.expedia.com. In the UK, try W www.ebookers.com. Some discount online services are likely to quote rates offered to wholesalers and consolidators, for which special conditions and restrictions apply (see Discount & Last-Minute Tickets later in this chapter).

Higher fares normally apply in 'high season,' from mid-December through mid-April, with even higher fares for peak times such as Christmas and around the New Year. You can save 20% or more by traveling in low season; weekday flights offer savings, too.

In the UK or the USA, the cheapest flights are advertised by 'bucket shops' (called 'consolidators' in the USA), which act as clearinghouses for 'unsold' seats that an airline anticipates being unable to fill. Call the airline to see if it can match the consolidator's price with a promotional fare.

Travel agents usually can't match rock-bottom fares, but offer greater security. Firms such as STA Travel (☎ 800-781-4040 in the USA; W www.statravel.com) and Council Travel (☎ 888-268-6245 in the USA; W www.counciltravel.com) have offices worldwide and specialize in low fares for students, although no discount fares are available to Jamaica from North America.

If you plan on visiting additional Caribbean destinations, consider buying an airpass that permits any number of stopovers (see The Caribbean & South America later in this chapter).

Travelers with Special Needs

If you have special needs, inform the airline as soon as possible so that they can make arrangements accordingly. Remind them when you reconfirm your booking (at least 72 hours before departure) and again when you check in at the airport.

Most international airports will provide escorts from check-in through boarding, and there should be ramps, lifts, accessible toilets, and reachable phones.

Guide dogs for the blind will often have to travel in a specially pressurized baggage compartment with other animals, away from their owners, though smaller guide dogs are sometimes admitted to the cabin. Only animals born and raised in Britain are currently allowed into Jamaica.

Children under two years of age travel for 10% of the standard fare (or free, on some airlines), as long as they don't occupy a seat. 'Skycots' should be provided by the airline if requested in advance. Children between two and 12 years of age can usually occupy a seat for half to two-thirds of the full fare, and they get a baggage allowance.

Departure Tax

At last visit, Jamaica's departure tax was US$27, payable when you check in for your flight.

The USA

The most popular routings are via Miami (90 minutes) and New York (three hours, 20 minutes). Jamaica is also served by direct flights from about a dozen other cities.

The following US carriers fly to Jamaica (the toll-free airline information and reservation numbers are valid anywhere in the USA, Canada, Mexico, and the Caribbean):

Air Jamaica ☎ 800-523-5585;
Ⓦ www.airjamaica.com

American Airlines ☎ 800-433-7300;
Ⓦ www.aa.com

Delta Airlines ☎ 800-221-1212;
Ⓦ www.delta.com

Northwest/KLM ☎ 800-225-2525;
Ⓦ www.northwestairlines.com

TWA ☎ 800-892-4141;
Ⓦ www.twa.com

US Airways ☎ 800-428-4322;
Ⓦ www.usairways.com

Fares quoted around press time for roundtrip travel to Montego Bay originating on a weekend averaged about US$525 low season, US$675 high season from New York, and US$415 low season, US$475 high season from Miami. These fares should be considered only ballpark figures.

The big boy is Air Jamaica, which has code-sharing with Delta Airlines. Air Jamaica flies more people to the island than any other airline (about 45% of all arrivals), and from more USA gateways (13), with direct service from Atlanta, Baltimore/Washington, Boston, Chicago, Fort Lauderdale, Houston, Los Angeles, Miami, New York (Newark and JFK airports), Orlando, Phoenix, Philadelphia, and Washington, DC. Air Jamaica offers connecting flights through Montego Bay at no extra charge to destinations throughout the Caribbean.

Air Jamaica also promotes a 'Seventh Heaven Fly Free Program': If you buy seven roundtrip tickets in any two-year period, you get the seventh free (if three tickets were first class, then the free ticket is also first class). Air Jamaica trip credits can also be earned flying Delta or Virgin Atlantic and through Hertz car rentals.

Charter Flights These flights generally offer the lowest fares for confirmed reservations (as much as one-third lower than regular airline prices). You can sometimes also book one-way tickets with charter airlines for less than half the roundtrip fare. Often the charter price is for a package that includes the flight and accommodations. They are usually direct flights, without the hub-stop common on standard airlines. Few charters are listed in airline computer reservations systems, as they're operated by wholesale tour operators with whom you or your travel agent will have to deal directly.

Normally, you have to fix your departure and return dates well ahead of time; a substantial fee may apply for any changes or cancellations (you should consider cancellation insurance in the event of illness, etc). Planes are usually full, service isn't always up to par with scheduled airlines, and flights often depart at inconvenient hours. If the tour operator or airline defaults, you may have problems getting your money back. Also, processing at airline counters often is more confusing and time-consuming than with scheduled carriers.

Contact the JTB (Ⓦ www.jamaicatravel.com) for a comprehensive list of charter tour and package operators. Some of the key operators to Jamaica include:

Air Jamaica Vacations ☎ 800-508-3247;
Ⓦ www.airjamaicavacations.com

American Airlines Vacations ☎ 800-433-7300;
Ⓦ www.aavacations.com

Apple Vacations ☎ 800-727-3400 for east coast gateways, ☎ 800-365-2775 for west coast;
Ⓦ www.applevacations.com

Caribbean Vacation Network ☎ 800-423-4095;
Ⓦ www.caribbeanmagic.com

Changes in L'Attitudes ☎ 800-330-8272;
Ⓦ www.changes.com

Delta Dream Vacations ☎ 800-654-6559;
Ⓦ www.deltavacations.com

GoGo Worldwide Vacations Ⓦ www.gogoww.com;
works through travel agents only

Sunburst Holidays ☎ 800-786-2877;
Ⓦ www.sunburstholidays.com

Travel Impressions ☎ 800-284-0044;
Ⓦ www.travelimpressions.com

Vacation Express ☎ 800-309-4717;
Ⓦ www.vacationexpress.com

Courier Flights If you're willing to fly on short notice and travel light, courier flights are one of the cheapest ways to go – about half the standard fare or less. As a courier, you 'deliver' an item, such as a parcel or document, on behalf of a company. Usually the courier company takes care of pick-up and delivery; you merely act as its agent by occupying a seat. In exchange, you usually give up your baggage allowance, which the courier company uses for the item to be delivered.

A leading booking agency for courier companies is **Cheaptrips** (☎ 800-282-1202; W www.cheaptrips.com). You pay a one-time registration fee.

Discount & Last-Minute Tickets Several discount ticket agencies sell reduced-rate tickets to the Caribbean. Online, try **Airfares For Less** (☎ 954-565-8667; W www.airfares-for-less.com); **Cheapairlines** (☎ 800-852-2608; W www.cheapairlines.com); and **Discount Airfares** (W www.discount-airfares.com).

If you can fly on very short notice (usually within seven days of booking'), consider buying a ticket from a 'last-minute' ticket broker. These companies buy surplus seats from airlines at hugely discounted prices. Discounts can be as great as 40%.

Last Minute Club (☎ 416-449-5400, 877-970-3500; W www.lastminuteclub.com) specializes in air/hotel packages to the Caribbean. Also check out **Moment's Notice** (☎ 212-486-0500, 888-241-3366; W www.moments-notice.com).

Canada

Air Canada (☎ 800-247-2262; W www.aircanada.com) serves Montego Bay from Montreal, Halifax, and Winnipeg in winter, and Montego Bay and Kingston from Toronto daily year-round. **Air Jamaica** (☎ 416-229-6024, 800-523-5585; W www.airjamaica.com) flies nonstop from Toronto and Montreal.

Canadian Universities Travel Service (☎ 416-614-2887, 800-667-2887; W www.travelcuts.com) sells discount airfares. It has 25 offices throughout Canada.

The following companies offer charter flights and package tours to Jamaica (see Package Tours later in this chapter).

Air Transat ☎ 514-987-1616, fax 987-9750; W www.airtransat.com

Albatours ☎ 416-485-1700, 800-665-2522; W www.albatours.com

Conquest Tours ☎ 416-665-9255, fax 665-6811; W www.conquestvacations.com

Regent Holidays ☎ 905-673-3343, 800-263-8776

Signature Vacations ☎ 416-967-1510, fax 967-7154; W www.signaturevacations.com

Sunquest Vacations ☎ 416-485-1700, fax 485-9479; W www.sunquest.ca

Australia & New Zealand

Travelers from Australia or New Zealand must fly via the USA, where you can connect to flights to Jamaica.

Direct service between Australia, New Zealand, and California is provided by the following airlines:

Air New Zealand ☎ 02-9223-4666 in Sydney, ☎ 09-366-2400 in Auckland

Delta Airlines ☎ 02-9262-1777 in Sydney, ☎ 09-379-3370 in Auckland

Qantas ☎ 02-9957-0111 in Sydney, ☎ 09-357-8900 in Auckland

United Airlines ☎ 02-9237-8888 in Sydney, ☎ 09-307-9500 in Auckland

You can also fly via Santiago, Chile, or Buenos Aires, Argentina.

Fares from Australia to Los Angeles begin at about A$1600 for special fares, and about A$2300 for regular APEX fares. From New Zealand, fares begin at about NZ$2495.

A round-the-world (RTW) ticket offers the option of several additional stopovers at marginal cost. You can also save money by buying a Liat or **BWIA International Airways** (☎ 02-9223-7004) air-pass if you plan on exploring other islands of the Caribbean (see The Caribbean & South America later in this chapter).

In Australia, **STA Travel** (☎ 02-9212-1255, 800-637-444; W www.sta-travel.com) and **Flight Centre International** (☎ 133-133; W www.flightcentre.com.au) specialize in cheap airfares.

Three tour agencies that specialize in the Caribbean are **Caribbean Destinations** (☎ 800-816717; Level 4, 115 Pitt St, Sydney); **Caribbean Bound** (☎ 02-9267-2555; W www

.caribbean.com.au; Suite 102, 379 Pitt St, Sydney 2000, NSW); and **Contours** (☎ 03-9670-6900, fax 9670-7558; 84 William St, Melbourne, Victoria 3000).

In New Zealand, **Brisbane Discount Travel** (☎ 09-366-0061, 800-808040); **Flight Centre** (☎ 09-309-6171); and **STA Travel** (☎ 09-309-0458; W www.statravel.co.nz) specialize in cheap airfares.

Innovative Travel (☎ 03-365-3910, fax 365-5755; 247 Edgeware, Christchurch) is a tour operator specializing in the Caribbean.

The UK

At press time, **Air Jamaica** (☎ 020-8570-7999) was the only carrier offering direct service to Montego Bay and Kingston, with flights from Heathrow and Manchester. **British Airways** (☎ 020-8897-4000; W www.britishairways.co.uk) canceled its flights between Gatwick and Montego Bay in March 2002; it's worth checking to see if they've been reinstated.

You can buy an Air Jamaica, Liat, or **BWIA International Airways** (☎ 020-8577-1100, fax 8577-2112; e mail@bwee.com) airpass to combine a visit to Jamaica with explorations of other Caribbean islands; see The Caribbean & South America later in this chapter.

Typical APEX fares for 2002 average about £455 in low season, £750 in high season.

It may be cheaper to fly via the United States, changing aircraft in New York or Miami (return fares between London and Miami can be as low as £200 in low season). Airlines that fly to the USA from the UK include **American Airlines** (☎ 800-433-7300), British Airways (see above), **Delta Airlines** (☎ 800-221-1212), **United Airlines** (☎ 0845-844-4777; W www.unitedairlines.co.uk), and **Virgin Atlantic** (☎ 800-862-8621; W www.virgin.com).

For discount tickets, try the following travel agencies:

Trailfinders (☎ 020-7937-5400; W www.trailfinders.co.uk) 215 Kensington High St, London W8

STA Travel (☎ 08701-600-599; W www.statravel.co.uk) 86 Old Brompton Rd, London SW7

Council Travel (☎ 020-7437-7767) 29a Poland St, London W1V

London Flight Centre (☎ 020-7244-6411; W www.topdecktravel.co.uk) 125 Earls Court Rd, London SW5

For additional low-fare options, look in the magazine *Time Out* and the Sunday papers for ads.

The **Caribbean Centre** (☎ 08707-509885; W www.caribbeancentre.co.uk; 3 the Green, Richmond, Surrey TW9 1PL); **Caribbean Expressions** (☎ 020-7431-2131; W www.expressionsholidays.co.uk; 104 Belsize Lane, London NW3 5BB); and **Caribbean Travel** (☎ 020-8960-3226; 367 Portobello Rd, London W10) all specialise in travel to the Caribbean.

If you're flexible with dates and can travel last minute, try **Cheapflights** (W www.cheapflights.com).

Charter Flights Jamaica is a major charter destination from the UK. All charter flights are into Montego Bay. They are usually considerably cheaper than scheduled fares, although departure and arrival times are often inconveniently scheduled in the middle of the night. You should be able to find fares as low as £250 in low season, and £550 in high season.

Good resources include **Charter Flight Centre** (☎ 020-7854-8434; W www.charterflights.co.uk) and **Dial a Flight** (☎ 0870-566-6666; W www.dialaflight.co.uk).

Leading charter operators to Jamaica include:

British Airways Holidays ☎ 01293-617000; W www.british-airways.com/holidays

Caribbean Connection ☎ 01244-341131, fax 01244-310255

Caribtours ☎ 020-7581-3517; W www.caribtours.co.uk

Cosmos Holidays ☎ 0870-442-8601; W www.cosmos-holidays.co.uk

Thomas Cook Holidays ☎ 0870-510-1520; W www.tcholidays.com

Thomson Holidays ☎ 0870-165-0079; W www.thomson-holidays.com

In Northern Ireland, **Chieftain Tours** (☎ 028-9024-7795) offers charter flights from Belfast (and Dublin) year-round.

Continental Europe & Ireland

There are few direct flights to Jamaica from continental Europe. The following are your best bets:

Belgium

Neckerman (☎ 9241-1857) Operates charters to Montego Bay from Brussels

France

Alternative Travel (☎ 01-42-89-42-46, fax 42-89-80-73) 8 Ave de Messine, Paris 75008

Austral Voyages (☎ 02-97-21-14-70, fax 02-97-21-96-08) 53 Rue de Liége, Lorient 56100

Germany

LTA (☎ 800-888-0200; W www.ltu.de) Serves Montego Bay from Dusseldorf

Condor (☎ 01802-337135; W www.condor.de) Serves Montego Bay from Frankfurt

Ireland

Aeroflot (☎ 06-47-2299 in Eire, ☎ 020-7355-2233 in UK; e infres@aeroflot.co.uk), 70 Piccadilly, London W1V 9HH; weekly service from Shannon Airport in Eire

Italy

Ventaclub (☎ 39-2-467-541, fax 4675-4999) Via Dei Gracchi 35, Milano 20146 Operates its own charters

Viaggidea (☎ 39-2-895-29300, fax 895-00406; W www.viaggidea.it) Via Lampedusa 13, Milano 20141 Operates a weekly charter flight from Milan to Montego Bay year-round

Netherlands

Martinair (☎ 020-60-11-767; W www.martin air.com) Flies between Amsterdam and Montego Bay

The JTB (W www.jamaicatravel.com) provides a list of European companies with tour packages to Jamaica.

Asia & Africa

There are no direct flights; travelers fly via London or the USA.

From Asia, Hong Kong is the discount plane ticket capital. STA Travel (see the UK earlier in this chapter) has branches in Hong Kong, Tokyo, Singapore, Bangkok, and Kuala Lumpur.

In Japan, try **Alize Corporation** (☎ 03-3407-4272, fax 3407-8400; Aoyama Kyodo Bldg, No 803, 3-6-18 Kita Aoyama Minato-ku, Tokyo 107), or **Island International** (☎ 03-3401-4096, fax 3401-1629; 4-11-14-204 Jingumae, Shibuya-ku, Tokyo 15).

The Caribbean & South America

Air Jamaica (☎ 800-523-5585; W www.air jamaica.com) uses Montego Bay as a hub for connecting its US flights with Antigua, the Bahamas, Barbados, Bonaire, Cuba (you can reserve flights between Jamaica and Cuba in the USA, but you must purchase your ticket in Jamaica), Curacao, Dominican Republic, Grand Cayman, St Lucia, and Turks and Caicos. Passengers are permitted a stopover in Jamaica, or may continue to a second or third Caribbean destination at no extra cost.

Many flights are operated by Air Jamaica's domestic airline, **Air Jamaica Express** (☎ 923-8680, 888-359-2475 in Kingston, ☎ 952-5401 in Montego Bay; ☎ 800-523-5585 in the USA).

Jamaica is also linked by **BWIA International Airways** (☎ 924-8376, 800-538-2942 in Kingston; ☎ 800-538-2942 in North America; W www.bwee.com) to Antigua, Barbados, Haiti, and Trinidad. It also serves Puerto Rico, as does **ALM Antillean Airlines** (☎ 800-327-7230 in North America), which has flights to Aruba, Bonaire, Colombia, Panama, and St Martin. **Cayman Airlines** (☎ 800-422-9626 in North America) connects Jamaica with the Cayman Islands. **COPA** (☎ 952-5530 in Jamaica, ☎ 227-5000 in Panama) has service to and from Panama five times weekly. And **Sky King** (☎ 649-941-5353 in Providenciales) links Kingston with Turks and Caicos.

Liat (☎ 268-480-5600, fax 480-5625; W www.liatairline.com) offers a 21-day 'Explorer Pass' (US$300) permitting stops at any three of the 26 islands that it services, with purchase of a ticket from North America or other international gateway. A 30-day 'SuperExplorer' pass allows unlimited stopovers (US$575). An 'Air Pass' costs US$85 per island.

Trinidadian-based BWIA (see above) has a similar 30-day pass with unlimited stops (from US$399). And Air Jamaica offers a 30-day 'Caribbean Hopper' pass permitting up to five island stopovers at no extra cost (fares cost US$399 economy and travel must commence and end in the USA).

For charter flights, call **Tropical Airlines** (☎ 920-3770 in Kingston, ☎ 979-3565 in Montego Bay), which flies 19-seater Beechcraft charters from Jamaica to Varadero (Cuba) and Santiago de Cuba, and to Cancún, Mexico, and other Caribbean destinations.

SEA

Jamaica is a popular destination on the cruising roster, mainly for passenger liners but also for private yachters. Arrival by freight liner is even an option.

The USA

Cruise Ship If all you want is a one-day taste of Jamaica, then consider arriving by cruise ship. A cruise is a good way to get a feel for several Caribbean destinations, and it can help you select a site for a future land-based vacation. Port visits are usually one-day stopovers at either Ocho Rios or Montego Bay.

The **Cruise Line International Association** (☎ 212-921-0066, fax 921-0549; e info@cruising.org; 500 Fifth Ave No 1407, New York, NY 10110) can provide information on cruising and individual cruise lines.

The following featured Jamaica in their 2002 itineraries:

Carnival Cruise Lines	☎ 800-327-9501
Celebrity Cruises	☎ 800-437-3111
Commodore Cruise Lines	☎ 800-237-5361
Costa Cruise Lines	☎ 800-462-6782
Holland America Line	☎ 800-426-0327
Norwegian Cruise Line	☎ 800-327-7030
Royal Caribbean Cruise Line	☎ 800-327-6700
Sun Cruises	☎ 800-468-6400
World Explorer	☎ 800-854-3835

The *Valtur Prima* sails from Montego Bay every Friday on seven-night cruises to Grand Cayman, Calica (Mexico), and Havana. Contact **West Indies Cruises** (☎ 877-818-2822, fax 905-238-6177; e sales @westindiescruises.com).

Freighter Several freighters that ply between North America and Europe call in on Jamaica, and some take paying passengers. Most have plush cabins and passengers are well looked after by stewards. Book early!

Ford's Freighter Travel Guide (☎ 818-701-7414; 19448 Longelius St, Northridge, CA 91324) lists freight ships that take some passengers.

Two agencies specialize in freighter cruises: **Freighter World Cruises** (☎ 626-449-3106, 800-531-7774, fax 626-449-9573; W www.freighterworld.com; 180 S Lake Ave No 335, Pasadena, CA 91101), and **Maris USA** (☎ 203-222-1500, 800-996-2747, fax 203-222-9191; W www.freightercruises.com; 215 Main Street, Westport CT 06880).

Private Yacht Many yachters make the trip to Jamaica from North America. If you plan to travel in summer, keep fully abreast of weather reports; mid-to-late summer is hurricane season.

Upon arrival in Jamaica, you *must* clear customs and immigration at either Montego Bay (Montego Bay Yacht Club), Kingston (Royal Jamaican Yacht Club, Port Royal), Ocho Rios (St Ann's Bay), or West Harbour in Port Antonio. In addition, you'll need to clear customs at *each* port of call in Jamaica.

You'll need the regular documentation for foreign travel (see Visas & Documents in the Facts for the Visitor chapter). An invaluable resource is *Cruising Guide to the Leeward Islands,* published by Cruising Guides Publications.

Charter Yacht Both experienced sailors and novices can charter sailboats, yachts, and cruisers by the week in Florida and elsewhere for sailing in the Caribbean.

Two leading companies are **Florida Yacht Charters** (☎ 305-532-8600, 800-537-0050; W www.floridayacht.com; 1290 5th St, Miami Beach, FL 33199) and **Moorings** (☎ 813-535-1446, 800-535-7289, fax 813-530-9747; W www.moorings.com; 19345 US Hwy 19 N, Clearwater, FL 33764).

Maps & Charts For maps and charts of the Caribbean, contact **Bluewater Books &**

Charts (☎ 954-763-6533, 800-942-2583; W www.bluewaterweb.com; 1481 SE 17th St, Causeway, Fort Lauderdale, FL 33316). The **National Oceanic & Atmospheric Administration** (☎ 301-436-8301, fax 436-6829; W chart maker.ncd.noaa.gov) sells U.S. government charts.

Europe

Cruise Ship Several companies that operate summertime cruises in European waters reposition their vessels to the Caribbean in winter, and vice versa. Passengers can participate in weeklong repositioning cruises.

Freighter *Cap Blanco* sails from Hamburg to South America, calling at Kingston. Contact **Hamburg-Sud Reiseagentur** (☎ 0403-705-155, fax 7-052-420; Ost-West Strasse 59-61, 20457 Hamburg).

Harrison Line offers passenger service from England to the West Indies aboard the MV *Author,* which sails on 42-day roundtrip voyages from Felixstowe. And the **Geest Line** accepts passengers aboard its banana freight ships that ply between Southampton and the West Indies. Book well in advance through **Strand Cruise & Travel Centre** (☎ 020-7836-6363, fax 7497-0078; Charing Cross Shopping Concourse, the Strand, London WC2N 4HZ).

ORGANIZED TOURS
Package Tours

Dozens of tour companies offer sun-and-sand package tours to Jamaica, usually using charter airlines and featuring roundtrip airfare, airport transfers, hotel accommodations, breakfast, and certain other meals, all for a guaranteed price. Most offer a selection of hotels to choose from, with prices varying. Per-person rates are usually quoted based on double occupancy; an additional charge ('single supplement') applies to anyone wishing to room alone.

For listings of package tour operators, see the Charter Flights sections under the countries of origin earlier in this chapter.

Specialty Tours

Among the few companies offering specialty tours to Jamaica are **Ken's Jamaican Tours**

(☎ 202-258-3753; W www.kensjamaican tours.com; 1217 12th St NW, Washington, DC 20005, USA), and **Jamaica Journeys** (☎ 508-432-3114; e majamaica@hotmail .com), which specializes in special-interest programs for women. The 2002 itinerary included programs in writing, Shakespeare in Jamaica, birding, and hiking.

Unique Destinations (☎/fax 993-3881, ☎ 993-7267; W www.portantoniojamaica.com; PO Box 89, Port Antonio; ☎/fax 401-647-4730 in the USA; 127 Westcott Rd, North Scituate, RI 02857, USA) also specializes in eco-cultural tours, including hiking and birding.

An excellent resource is **Specialty Travel Index** (☎ 415-459-4900, 800-442-4922; W www.specialtytravel.com; 305 San Anselmo Ave, Suite 313, San Anselmo, CA 94960, USA).

Birding & Ecological Tours In the USA, **Field Guides** (☎ 512-263-7295, 800-728-4953, fax 512-263-0117; W www.fieldguides.com; 9433 Bee Cave Road, Bldg 1, Suite 150, Austin, TX 78733) offers birding trips in Jamaica, as does **Victor Emanuel Nature Tours** (☎ 512-328-5221, 800-328-8368, fax 512-328-2919; e info@ventbird.com; 2525 Wallingwood Drive, Suite 1003, Austin, TX 78746).

In the UK, **Discovery Initiatives** (☎ 020-7299-9881, fax 7229-9883; 68 Princess Square, London W2 4NY) offers birding and ecotours, as does **Birdtours** (W www.bird tours.co.uk).

Also see Unique Destinations, above.

Cultural & Music Tours Ecotours for Cures (☎ 203-598-0400, 800-829-0918; W www.naturalnurse.com; PO Box 525, Oyster Bay, NY 11771, USA) offers 10-day tours during which guests spend time with Rastafarians and Maroons, learning hands-on healing remedies.

The **Friends of Georgian Society of Jamaica** (W www.jamaica-georgian.org.uk) offers occasional tours to study architecture with an aim to supporting preservation efforts.

The JTB's **Insider Jamaica Program** (☎ 800-526-2422; W www.insidersjamaica

.com) features roundtrip airfare, five nights or longer accommodations, transfers, discounts at participating restaurants and attractions, and a meet-the-people experience.

Also consider **SERVAS** (☎ 212-267-0252; W www.servas.org; 11 John St, Suite 706, New York, NY 10038), an organization that acts as a clearinghouse for travelers wishing to engage with local communities through hosts in Jamaica.

Most package tour companies listed under the Charter Flights sections earlier in this chapter offer tours to the various music festivals.

Clothing-Optional Tours Many of the all-inclusive resorts welcome nudists, notably those of the Sandals, SuperClubs, and Couples chains, most of which have nude beaches (see regional chapters for details).

Companies catering to travelers seeking an all-over tan include **Bare Necessities** (☎ 512-499-0405, 800-743-0405; W www.bare-necessities.com; 904 West 29th St, Austin, TX 78705, USA) and **Travel Au Naturel** (☎ 800-728-0185, W www.travelaunaturel.com; PO Box 890, Land O' Lakes, FL 34639, USA).

Lifestyle Tours & Travel (☎ 714-821-9939, 800-359-9942, fax 714-821-1465; W www.playcouples-travel.com; 2641 W La Palma, Suite A, Anaheim, CA 92801, USA) offers tour packages for adults with a 'sex-positive' attitude.

Getting Around

AIR

Domestic Airports
There are four domestic airports: Tinson Pen in Kingston, Boscobel near Ocho Rios, Negril Aerodrome, and Ken Jones Aerodrome at Port Antonio.

Montego Bay's Donald Sangster International Airport has a domestic terminal adjacent to the international terminal. The terminals are not connected by a walkway, and it's a haul to walk. Air Jamaica Express provides a shuttle.

In Kingston, most domestic flights use Tinson Pen, 2 miles west of downtown, but it's a 40-minute ride from Norman Manley International Airport. (See the Kingston & Southern Plains chapter for details.)

Domestic Airlines
Air Jamaica Express (☎ 923-6664, 888-359-2475, 800-523-5585 in the USA; **W** www
.airjamaica.com) has daily service between Montego Bay, Kingston's Tinson Pen, Negril, Ocho Rios, and Port Antonio. See regional chapters for specific information.

Typical one-way fares (for purchase outside Jamaica) are:

Kingston-Montego Bay	US$60
Kingston-Negril	US$65
Kingston-Ocho Rios	US$47
Kingston-Port Antonio	US$47
Montego Bay-Negril	US$54
Montego Bay-Ocho Rios	US$51
Montego Bay-Port Antonio	US$60
Negril-Ocho Rios	US$56
Negril-Port Antonio	US$65
Ocho Rios-Port Antonio	US$47

Charter Flights
Jamaica Air Link (☎ 940-1574; 877-359-5465 in North America; **W** www.jamaicairlink
.com) connects MoBay with Kingston, Negril, Ocho Rios, and Port Antonio with nonscheduled charter service. The follow-ing also do this: **Air Negril** (☎ 940-7747, fax 940-6491 in Montego Bay; ☎ 957-5325, fax 957-5291 in Negril; **e** airnegril@cwjamai ca.com); **Aero Express** (☎ 952-5807 in Montego Bay; 937-5011 in Kingston; 957-9108 in Negril); and **International Air Link** (☎ 940-6660, 866-952-5807 in North America; **W** www.intlairlink.com).

Timair (☎ 952-2516 in Montego Bay, 957-5374 in Negril, fax 979-1113; **W** www.timair
.net) offers charter services aboard small aircraft islandwide.

Helicopter
You can charter a helicopter for transport to any airport or for personalized tours from **Helitours** (☎ 974-2265, fax 974-2183; ☎ 800-678-1300 in North America; **e** helitoursja@ infochan.com; 120 Main St, Ocho Rios). From Montego Bay, transfers are about US$400 to Negril, US$550 to Ocho Rios, US$750 to Kingston, and US$1200 to Port Antonio. Charter rates begin at US$500 per hour.

BUS & TAXI
Traveling by public transport could be the best – or worst! – adventure of your trip to Jamaica. The island's extensive transport network links virtually every village and comprises several options that range from standard public buses to private taxis, with 'coasters,' 'route taxis,' and 'robots' in between.

Public buses and coasters are regulated by the **Transport Authority** (☎ 926-5328; **e** transauth@infochan.org; 119 Maxfield Ave, Kingston 10).

Students, children, handicapped persons, and pensioners are charged half-price on public buses.

Public buses, coasters, and route taxis depart from and arrive at each town's trans-portation station, which is usually near the main market. Locals can direct you to the appropriate vehicle, which should have its destination marked above the front window (for buses) or on its side.

Public Buses
Jamaica's public bus system has long been the epitome of chaos. Fortunately, things have improved in recent years. Kingston now has 150 gleaming new Mercedes-Benz and Volvo buses. A metropolitan bus system has finally been introduced to the MoBay metropolitan area. The regional buses have been upgraded, too, although less-traveled routes still use antiquated Hungarian contraptions.

Kingston and MoBay buses manage, more or less, to keep to their schedules.

Bus stops are located at most road intersections along the routes, but you can usually flag down a bus anywhere except in major cities, where they're inclined to stop only at designated stops.

When you want to get off, shout, 'One stop!' The conductor will usually echo your request with, 'Let off!'

The following fares applied to public buses at last visit (new fares were about to be introduced):

Kingston metropolitan region	J$20-30
Montego Bay licensed area	J$20
Rural areas	J$10 flat rate, plus J$1.36 per km

Coasters
'Coasters,' or private minibuses, operate like buses but cost up to three times more. They have traditionally been the workhorses of Jamaica's regional public transport system. All major towns and virtually every village in the country are served. Coasters usually stop along their routes to drop off and pick up people.

Licensed minibuses display red license plates with the initials PPV (public passenger vehicle) or have a Jamaican Union of Travelers Association (JUTA) insignia. JUTA buses are exclusively for tourists.

They usually depart their point of origin when they're full, often literally overflowing, with people hanging from the open doors. Once the bus sets off, the driver usually manages to scare passengers to death with a hair-raising display of reckless driving.

You pay a conductor (or 'ductor'). Some 'ductors' inflate prices to foreign passengers. And you may be charged an extra seat if you put your baggage on the seat next to you. Guard your luggage carefully against theft.

Route Taxis
These communal taxis are a recent addition to the Jamaican scene and are today the most universal mode of public transport, reaching every part of the country. They operate like coasters (and cost about the same), picking up as many people as they can squeeze in along their specified routes. A 30-minute ride typically costs about US$2; a one-hour ride costs about US$3.

Most are white Toyota Corolla station wagons (estate cars). They should have 'Route Taxi' marked on the front door, and they are not to be confused with identical licensed taxis, which charge more.

Robots
'Robots' are communal taxis that are legally prohibited from picking up tourists, although many do.

Be sure to agree on a fare *before* getting in. Bargain hard! If you don't, you're most likely going to get ripped off. Determine if the driver means Jamaican or US dollars, and whether 'three bills' means three *hundred* Jamaican dollars.

Freelance taxis have a reputation for theft. Don't let yourself be talked into visiting specific shops, where the driver can expect to receive a commission on anything you purchase.

Licensed Taxis
Licensed taxis – called 'contract carriages' – have red PPV license plates (those without such plates are unlicensed). They're expensive, but are affordable if you share the cost with other passengers.

JUTA (☎ 979-0778 in Kingston, 952-0813 in Montego Bay, 957-9197 in Negril; @ juta@cwjamaica.com) operates islandwide and is geared almost exclusively to the tourist business. Other taxicab companies are listed in the yellow pages and in the regional chapters of this book.

The Transport Authority has established fixed rates according to distance (different rates apply for locals and tourists, who pay considerably more). Licensed cabs should have these posted inside. Taxis are also supposed to have meters, but many drivers don't use them.

Locals are charged an initial flat fee of J$100, plus J$20 for each kilometer thereafter. Tourists are charged higher rates, in US dollars.

The following were typical fares in 2002, based on up to four people per taxi:

Sangster International Airport to Montego Bay	US$8
Around Montego Bay	US$8 to $15
Montego Bay to Ocho Rios or Negril	US$70
Negril Aerodrome to Negril	US$8
Norman Manley airport to Kingston	US$15 to $21
Kingston to Ocho Rios	US$100 to $120
Kingston to Port Antonio	US$100 to $120

Many Jamaicans hire themselves out as licensed driver-guides. A reader recommends **Paul Bowen** (c/o Burke's Transport & Tours; ☎ 925-9448, fax 931-9450; [e] algen@cw jamaica.com) in Kingston.

Hotel Transfers

Many hotels include airport transfers in their room rates. Leading tour operators also offer minibus transfers. JUTA is the largest transfer provider. Major car-rental companies also offer private transfers (see Car Rental later in this chapter). The following are typical one-way fares from Montego Bay Airport to various destinations:

Downtown	US$8
Negril	US$24
Mandeville	US$28
Ocho Rios	US$26
Port Antonio	US$35
Kingston	US$35

TRAIN

Those railway tracks marked on maps don't mean very much. The railway system was

shut down in 1992. At press time, the government was in final negotiations to privatize the railway, with possible service to begin in 2003 between Kingston and Linstead, May Pen, and Williamsfield.

CAR

Exploring by rental car can be a joy. There are some fabulously scenic journeys, and with your own wheels you can get as off the beaten track as you wish, discovering the magic of Jamaican culture beyond the pale of the touristy areas.

A paved coastal highway circles the entire island (in the southern parishes it runs about 20 miles inland). Main roads cross the central mountain chains, north to south, linking all the main towns. A web of minor roads, country lanes, and dirt tracks provides access to more remote areas.

The main roads are usually in reasonable condition, despite numerous potholes, although conditions had deteriorated dramatically at last visit. Many secondary roads, or B-roads, are in appalling condition and best tackled with a 4WD vehicle. Most roads are narrow with frequent bends.

A new two-lane highway linking Montego Bay and Negril was nearing completion at last visit. And in 2002, work started on Hwy 2000, the nation's first toll highway (see the boxed text).

The following list indicates distances and approximate driving times between major destinations:

route	distance	duration
Montego Bay-Mandeville	70 miles	3 hours
Montego Bay-Negril	52 miles	2 hours
Montego Bay-Ocho Rios	67 miles	2½ hours
Montego Bay-Treasure Beach	64 miles	2½ hours
Ocho Rios-Port Antonio	66 miles	2½ hours
Ocho Rios-Kingston	55 miles	2 hours
Port Antonio-Kingston	61 miles	2½ hours
Treasure Beach-Kingston	87 miles	2½ hours

Road Rules

Always drive on the *left*. Remember: 'Keep left, and you'll always be right.' Here's

Highway 2000

Highway 2000 (H2K) – a multilane toll highway that will connect Kingston with Montego Bay and Ocho Rios – is the largest infrastructure project ever undertaken in the English-speaking Caribbean. Ground was broken for the first phase (a four-lane section between Kingston and Williamsfield) of the 145-mile (230km) highway in early 2002.

The estimated cost of US$390 million will be shared between the private sector and the Government of Jamaica. A French company (Bouygues) will be responsible for building and maintaining the highway for 35 years, after which it will revert to the nation.

It is estimated that the project will eventually create 120,000 new jobs and increase the national GDP by 3.7%.

Travel times between Kingston and Montego Bay will be reduced from four hours to 1.5 hours, and between Kingston and Ocho Rios from two hours to one hour.

A number of tourist attractions are to be built along the route, as well as a new township – Clarendon New Town – and a 2900-acre cargo airport and free-zone park.

another local saying worth memorizing: 'De left side is de right side; de right side is suicide!' The speed limit is 30mph in towns and 50mph on highways.

Jamaica has a compulsory seatbelt law. It is not compulsory to wear helmets when riding motorcycles.

Driving Conditions

Jamaican drivers rank among the world's rudest and most dangerous drivers. Cars race through towns and play hopscotch with one another, overtaking with daredevil folly, often passing long lines of cars even on blind curves with total disregard for road rules or the rights and safety of other vehicles.

Jamaica has the third highest auto fatality rate in the world – behind Ethiopia and India – with a staggering 343 fatalities per

100,000 cars (compared to 26 per 100,000 in the US, and 22 per 100,000 in the UK).

Use extreme caution and drive defensively, especially at night when you should be prepared to meet oncoming cars that are either without lights or blinding you with their high-beams.

Use your horn liberally, especially when approaching blind corners.

Warning! Lock your car doors from the inside while driving in towns, especially Kingston.

Directions

Signage on main roads is very good, but directional signs are few and far between as soon as you leave the main roads. Many B-roads are not shown on maps. And what may appear on a map to be a 30-minute journey may take several hours. (See Maps in the Facts for the Visitor chapter.)

Take directions given by locals with a grain of salt. Those Jamaicans who don't own cars tend to underestimate distance and are overly optimistic about road conditions. You may be blithely told that your destination is 'straight ahead,' for example, only to discover that the road peters out into a walking track. Believe any Jamaican, however, who tells you a road is bad.

Avoid asking, 'Is this the way to so-and-so?' A better question is, 'Where does this road go?' Often, too, whomever you're asking directions of will answer only your specific question. Thus, if you ask, 'Is this the way to so-and-so?' and it isn't, they may tell you 'No, mon!' without then pointing you in the right direction unless you specifically ask them to. Worse, they often tell you 'Yes, mon!' when they have no idea.

Jamaicans tend to say 'left' for both left *and* right when giving directions. Ask to have directions repeated with a hand signal ('Turn left a mile up de road' will often be accompanied by a hand signal to turn *right*). And anyone telling you to continue 'straight' – which usually means 'ahead' – is sure to have forgotten to point out the Y-fork just around the bend. Ask if there are any forks in the road…and then ask which direction you should take.

Gasoline

Many gas stations close after 7pm or so. In rural areas, stations usually close on Sunday. In 2002, gasoline cost about US$1.75 per gallon (about J$25 per liter). Cash only, please! Credit cards are not accepted.

Security

Always park in hotel (or other secure) car parks. Even 'secure' hotel parking lots are rarely fully secure. *Always* remove your belongings. At the very least, keep them locked in the trunk.

Women should consider not driving alone in remote areas. (See Women Travelers in the Facts for the Visitor chapter.)

The majority of Jamaicans – man, woman, and child – get around by standing at the side of the road and flagging down passing cars with a lackadaisical sweep of the outstretched hand. As a visitor with a car, you're a privileged person. Empty seats in your car will go a long way toward easing the burden of Jamaicans forced to rely on buses and passing cars. However, your rental policy may specifically forbid giving rides to strangers; check the fine print.

Use caution if offering rides to men.

Mechanical Problems

There is no national roadside service organization to phone when you have car trouble. Most car-rental agencies have a 24-hour service number in case of breakdowns and other emergencies. If you do break down, use a local mechanic only for minor work; otherwise the car-rental company may balk at reimbursing you for work it hasn't authorized. If you can't find a phone or repair service, seek police assistance. *Never* give your keys to strangers.

Accidents

If you 'mash up,' don't move the vehicles, and don't let anyone else do so, including the other driver. Have someone call the police, and remain at the scene until a police officer arrives. Get the name and address of anyone else involved in the accident, as well as their license number and details about their vehicle. Take photos of the scene if

possible, and get the names and addresses of any witnesses. Above all, don't be drawn into an argument. Jamaican emotions are volatile, so you should do your best to keep tempers calm. Call your rental company as soon as possible.

You'll be lucky to find any witnesses who'll admit to having seen the accident. Jamaicans are loath to get involved where the police are concerned. Unfortunately, there's a tendency, too, to point a finger at tourists. If you're the victim of an accident caused by someone else, be prepared to defend your position vigorously.

Car Rental

Several major international car-rental companies operate in Jamaica, along with dozens of local firms. Car-rental agencies are listed in the local yellow pages.

High-season rates begin at about US$50 per day and can run as high as US$125, depending on the vehicle. Cheaper rates apply in low season. Some companies include unlimited mileage, while others set a limit and charge a fee for excess miles driven. Most firms require a deposit of at least US$500, but will accept a credit card imprint. Keep copies of all your paperwork. Renters must be 21 years of age (some companies will rent only to those 25 years of age or older). For additional details, see the Driver's License & Permits section under Visas & Documents in the Facts for the Visitor chapter.

You can reserve a car upon arrival, but in high season consider making your reservation in advance. Reconfirm before your arrival.

Before signing, go over the vehicle with a fine-tooth comb to identify any dents and scratches. Make a note of each one before you drive away. You're likely to be charged for the slightest mark that wasn't noted before. Don't forget to check the cigarette lighter and interior switches, which are often missing.

Type of Vehicle Most companies utilize modern Japanese sedans. A big car can be a liability on Jamaica's narrow, winding roads.

Most companies also rent 4WD vehicles, which are recommended if you intend to do *any* driving away from main roads.

Stick shift is preferable because frequent and sudden gear changes are required when potholes and kamikaze chickens appear out of nowhere. Remember, though, that you'll be changing gears with your *left* hand. If this is new to you, you'll soon get the hang of it.

Insurance Check in advance to see whether your current insurance or credit card covers you for driving while abroad. All rental companies will recommend damage-waiver insurance, which limits your liability in the event of an accident or damage. It costs about US$12-15 per day and is a valuable investment. American Express' car rental loss-and-damage-waiver insurance is not valid in Jamaica.

Rental Companies Jamaica's largest and most reputable car-rental company is Island Car Rentals. Five categories of cars cost US$41 to $69 daily in low season, US$49 to $83 high season. You'll find information at W www.islandcarrentals.com or through the following offices:

Kingston
    Main office (☎ 926-8861, 926-5991, fax 929-6787), 17 Antigua Ave, Kingston 10
    Norman Manley International Airport (☎ 924-8075, fax 924-8389)
Montego Bay
    Sangster International Airport (☎/fax 952-5771)
Ocho Rios
    (☎/fax 974-2334)

You can also make arrangements from abroad at the following numbers:

Canada   ☎ 800-526-2422
USA   ☎ 800-892-4581

The major international companies are also represented by these offices in Jamaica:

Budget
    (☎ 924-8762) Norman Manley International Airport, Kingston
    (☎ 952-3838) Sangster International Airport, Montego Bay

Dollar
    (☎ 953-9100) Montego Bay
    (☎ 974-7000) Ocho Rios

Hertz
    (☎ 800-654-3131)
    (☎ 924-8028) Norman Manley International Airport, Kingston
    (☎ 979-0438) Sangster International Airport, Montego Bay

The following major car-rental companies have offices in Jamaica:

North America

Budget	☎ 877-825-2953
Dollar	☎ 800-421-6868
Hertz	☎ 800-654-3001
Island Car Rentals	☎ 800-892-4581

The UK & Ireland

Budget	☎ 0800-181181
Hertz	☎ 0990-996699

Australia & New Zealand

Budget	☎ 13-2727 in Australia, ☎ 9-375-2222 in New Zealand
Hertz	☎ 13-3039 in Australia, ☎ 9-309-0989 in New Zealand

Fly & Drive Packages A program called 'Fly-Drive Jamaica' is a prepurchased package combining car-rental and hotel vouchers. You simply arrive at the airport, pick up your car, and set off to roam the island armed with vouchers good at 72 participating hotels. The program is offered by **Caribbean Vacation Network** (☎ 305-673-8822, 800-892-4581 in Jamaica, ☎ 800-423-4095 in the USA, ☎ 800-526-2422 in Canada; W www.caribbeanmagic.com).

MOTORCYCLE

Dozens of companies rent motorcycles and scooters, available at any resort town. They're far more lax than car-rental companies; you may not even have to show your driver's license. If you're not an experienced motorcycle driver, rent a scooter, which is far easier to handle. Scooters cost about US$25 per day. Motorcycles cost about US$45 a day.

Road in Jamaica conditions are hazardous. If the rental agency has helmets available, *wear one!*

BICYCLE

Cycling is a cheap, convenient, healthy, environmentally sound, and above all, fun way of traveling. Conditions are hazardous, however, and Jamaican drivers are not very considerate to bicyclists.

See Cycling in the Facts for the Visitor chapter.

HITCHHIKING

Hitchhiking is never entirely safe in any country in the world, and we don't recommend it. Travelers who decide to hitch should understand that they are taking a small but potentially serious risk. People who do choose to hitch will be safer if they travel in pairs and let someone know where they are planning to go.

BOAT

A ferry service links Kingston to Port Royal. See Port Royal in the Kingston & Southern Plains chapter for details.

See Sea in the Getting There & Away chapter, and Sailing in the Facts for the Visitor chapter, for details on cruising in Jamaican waters.

ORGANIZED TOURS
General Interest

Scores of reputable Jamaican companies offer guided excursions and tours (see 'Sightseeing Tours' in the yellow pages). A good resource is the **Association of Jamaican Attractions** (☎ 940-0704, fax 979-7437; e ajal@jamaica-irie.com), which lists all the major attractions islandwide.

The following are among the leading tour companies (the addresses listed are the companies' headquarters):

Caribic Vacations (☎ 953-8343) 1310 Providence Drive, Ironshore Estate, Montego Bay

Galaxy Tours (☎ 925-1492) 75 Red Hills Rd, Kingston 20

Glamour Tours (☎ 979-8207) Montego Bay Shopping Centre, Montego Freeport

Infinity Tours (☎ 967-2399; e infinity@ infochan .com) 40 Duke St, Kingston 5

Jamaica Tours (☎ 953-2825; e jtladmin@info chan.com) Providence Drive, Ironshore

Jam Venture (☎ 952-4221; e jamventure@colis.com) 13 Market St Plaza, Montego Bay

JUTA Tours (☎ 952-0813; e juta@cwjamaica.com) 8 Claude Clarke Ave, Montego Bay

Tourwise (☎ 974-2323, 888-991-1009; e tourwise@ cwjamaica.com) 103 Main St, Ocho Rios

At the deluxe end, Island Car Rentals (see Car Rental earlier in this chapter) offers personally chauffeured tours.

Special Interest Tours

For activities such as cycling, hiking, and bird watching, see Activities in the Facts for the Visitor chapter.

Barrett Adventures (☎ 382-6384, fax 979-8845; w www.barrettadventures.com; Rose Hall, Little River PO), operated by husband-wife team Errol and Carolyn Barrett, offer customized tours, including eco- and special-interest adventures. This company is recommended.

Grand Valley Tours (☎/fax 934-3398, 401-647-4730 in the USA; w www.portantonio jamaica.com; c/o Unique Destinations, 127 Westcott Rd, North Scituate, RI 02857, USA) specializes in ecotours of Portland parish.

Safaris River safaris up the Black River in search of crocodiles and birdlife are popular. Three major outfitters operate excursions from the town of Black River. Tour companies also offer excursions from resort towns, often in combination with a visit to YS Falls. (See the South Coast & Central Highlands chapter.)

Safari Tours Jamaica (☎ 785-0482, fax 974-3382; e safari@cwjamaica.com; Arawak PO, Mammee Bay) offers separate daylong 'jeep safaris' of Orange Valley and the Blue Mountains using Land Rovers. It even has a two-day mule ride and trekking tour in the Blue Mountains.

Chukka Blue Adventure Tours (☎ 979-6599, fax 952-8302; e info@chukkablue.com; Blue Hole, Sandy Bay, Hanover) offers similar jeep safaris.

Helicopter Tours Helitours (☎ 974-2265, fax 974-2183; 800-678-1300 in North America; ℮ helitoursja@infochan.com; 120 Main St, Ocho Rios) offers sightseeing tours by Bell 206B Jetranger III helicopters. A 15-minute 'Fun Hop' around Ocho Rios costs US$50 per person. Longer journeys range from the hour-long 'Jamaican Showcase' (US$190), which whisks you across the island, including Kingston and the Blue Mountains, to a daylong 'Island Delight' (US$2500 for up to four people).

Montego Bay & Northwest Coast

Montego Bay is the second largest city on the island and Jamaica's most important tourist resort.

The region boasts a greater concentration of well-preserved colonial houses than any other, some of which are working plantations that offer guided tours. And several championship golf courses, horse stables, and the island's best shopping add to the region's appeal.

Falmouth, a town of intriguing historical interest, is gateway for rafting on the Martha Brae River, horseback riding at Good Hope, and hiking in the fascinating and rugged Cockpit Country.

Montego Bay

Montego Bay (population 92,000), capital of St James parish, is dependent on tourism. It's also a thriving port city, based on the container-shipping trade at Montego Freeport. The town, colloquially called 'MoBay' by locals (native-born Montegonians are called 'bawn-a-bays'), spreads tentacles of light industry west as far as Reading, 4 miles away. An equal distance to the east, Ironshore is now a burgeoning resort (see Ironshore later in this chapter).

MoBay's primary attractions are its golf courses, historic great houses, and the private beach resorts outside of town. Every kind of water sport is represented, and the snorkeling and scuba diving are world-class in the waters of the Montego Bay Marine Park. Admirable Georgian stone buildings still stand downtown. The duty-free shopping is excellent. And there are hotels for every taste, from budget to upscale all-inclusive resorts.

At Easter, crowds of rowdy spring break kids hit town.

HISTORY
Columbus anchored in Montego Bay in 1494 and called it Gulf of Good Weather. In 1655,

Highlights

- Reggae Sumfest, Jamaica's world-class midsummer reggae festival
- Belvedere Estate, for a firsthand glimpse of a working plantation
- Magnificently restored Rose Hall, embellished by an eerie legend
- Rocklands Bird Feeding Station, where you feed birds by hand
- Sunset sailing trips, perfect for the party crowd
- A hike in Cockpit Country – not for the faint-hearted

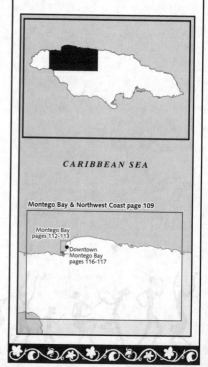

CARIBBEAN SEA

Montego Bay & Northwest Coast page 109

Montego Bay pages 112-113

Downtown Montego Bay pages 116-117

MONTEGO BAY & NORTHWEST COAST

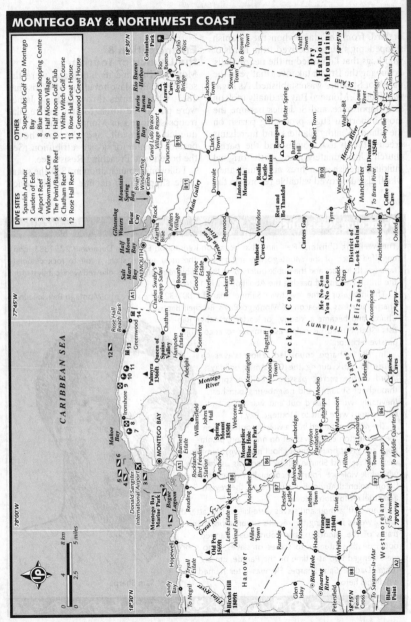

DIVE SITES
1 Spanish Anchor
2 Garden of Eels
3 Airport Reef
4 Widowmaker's Cave
5 The Point/Basket Reef
6 Chatham Reef
12 Rose Hall Reef

OTHER
7 SuperClubs Golf Club Montego Bay
8 Blue Diamond Shopping Centre
9 Half Moon Village
10 Half Moon Golf Club
11 White Witch Golf Course
13 Rose Hall Great House
14 Greenwood Great House

CARIBBEAN SEA

a settlement appeared on Spanish maps: Manterias, after the Spanish word *manteca*, or lard, from the days when the Spanish shipped 'pig's butter' derived from herds of wild hogs that flourished in the nearby hills. Following the British takeover that year, the parish of St James was established. As sugar was planted, Montego Bay gradually took on new importance, and St James became the most important sugar-producing parish on the island. Wealthy planters and merchants erected lavish townhouses and the parish church. Unfortunately, many of the original buildings perished in fires and hurricanes, which also destroyed valuable records in the western part of the island, obscuring this early history.

Emancipation & the Launch of Tourism

Montego Bay and its hinterland were the setting for the slave rebellion of Christmas 1831, when estates throughout St James were put to the torch. Militia and regular troops stationed in Montego Bay quickly quelled the revolt, and the courthouse became a center for savage retribution. (See the boxed text 'Preaching Resistance.')

Following emancipation in 1834, the sugar trade slipped into decline. The city once

---

Preaching Resistance

The weeklong Christmas Rebellion that began on Kensington Estate on December 27, 1831, and engulfed much of the Montego Bay region was the most serious slave revolt to rock colonial Jamaica. Its impact and the public outcry over the terrible retribution that followed were catalysts for the British Parliament passing the Abolition Bill in 1834.

The instigator of the revolt was Samuel Sharpe (1801-32), the slave of a Montego Bay solicitor. Sharpe acted as a deacon of Montego Bay's Burchell Baptist Church and became a 'daddy,' or leader, of native Baptists. Sharpe used his pulpit as a forum to encourage passive rebellion.

In 1831 Sharpe counseled fellow slaves to refuse to work during the Christmas holidays. Word of the secret, passive rebellion spread throughout St James and neighboring parishes. Inevitably, word leaked out and war ships and extra troops were sent to Montego Bay.

The rebellion turned into a violent conflict when the Kensington Estate was set on fire. Soon, plantations and great houses throughout northwest Jamaica were ablaze, and Sharpe's noble plan was usurped by wholesale violence. Fourteen colonialists were murdered before colonial authorities suppressed the revolt. Swift and cruel retribution followed.

More than a thousand slaves were killed. Day after day for six weeks following the revolt's suppression, magistrates of the Montego Bay Courthouse handed down death sentences to scores of slaves, who were hanged two at a time on the Parade, among them 'Daddy' Sam Sharpe. He was later named a national hero.

Sam Sharpe

again languished until revived by the development of the banana trade, and by the tourist trade that developed in the late 1880s when Dr Alexander G McCatty founded a sanitarium at what is today Doctor's Cave Beach. Rich Americans and Britons flocked on the banana boats to 'take the waters.' Many later bought homes here, adding luster to Montego Bay.

The Jet-Set Age

During WWII, the US Air Force built an airstrip east of town, which in the postwar years served to open up Montego Bay to tourism on a larger scale. Round Hill and Tryall Resorts were built west of town, cementing the town's chic reputation.

In the late 1960s the bay was dredged, and Montego Freeport was constructed (today the freeport is a center of light industry). Later, a separate cruise-ship terminal appeared, launching a new breed of visitor.

In the 1990s, the resort became somewhat jaded, but in recent years it has been revived and spruced up with a remarkable makeover. The opening of the Montego Bay Convention Center (to be located at Rose Hall) in 2003 should further boost the city's fortunes. So, too, the proposed expansion of Montego Bay harbor to permit mega-liners to berth.

ORIENTATION

The tourist quarter, north of the town center, arcs along Gloucester Ave, a narrow shoreline strip (christened the 'Hip Strip') lined with hotels, restaurants, and public beaches. Northward, Gloucester Ave becomes Kent Ave, which stretches for half a mile and ends at tiny Dead-End Beach. The airport is accessed from Sunset Blvd, which stretches east from the junction of Gloucester and Kent Aves and continues east, beyond the airport, as the A1 to Ironshore and the north coast.

Queen's Drive traverses steep Miranda Hill, which rises behind the tourist strip, linking the airport with the southern end of Gloucester Ave, forming a roundabout. The town center lies south of this junction and is

accessed by Fort St, a bustling thoroughfare that leads to Sam Sharpe Square, MoBay's vibrant heart.

The compact historic center is laid out as a rough grid of narrow, chaotically crowded streets. St James St, the bustling main street, runs south from Sam Sharpe Square and ends at Barnett St, which is one-way heading into town but becomes two-way after its intersection with Cottage Rd. Barnett St turns into the A1 heading west to Reading and Negril.

Howard Cooke Drive begins at the Gloucester Ave roundabout and runs south along the bayfront, linking the A1 with Montego Freeport.

The *Discover Jamaica* map published by the JTB includes a detailed map of Montego Bay. You can obtain a free copy at any JTB office (see below).

INFORMATION
Tourist Offices & Travel Agencies

The **JTB** (☎ 952-4425, fax 952-3587; PO Box 67; open 8:30am-4:30pm Mon-Fri, 9am-1pm Sat) has an office off Gloucester Ave, opposite the entrance to Cornwall Beach.

There's also a **JTB information booth** (cnr Market & Harbour Sts) in the downtown Craft Market, and another in the arrivals hall at the Donald Sangster International Airport (☎ 952-2462).

On the Internet, two good starting points are W www.montego-bay-jamaica.com and W www.go-montegobay.com.

Two of the more reputable travel agencies are **International Travel Services** (☎ 952-2485; 14B Market St) and **Stuart's Travel** (☎ 952-4350; 40 Market St).

Money

There's a 24-hour money exchange bureau in the arrival hall at Sangster International Airport. And **National Commercial Bank** (☎ 952-2354) has a branch at the airport.

You'll need local currency if you plan to take the bus into town. Taxis, though, accept US dollars.

Downtown, money exchange bureaus include **FX Trader** (☎ 952-3171; 37 Gloucester Ave; open 9am-5pm Mon-Sat) at the

MONTEGO BAY

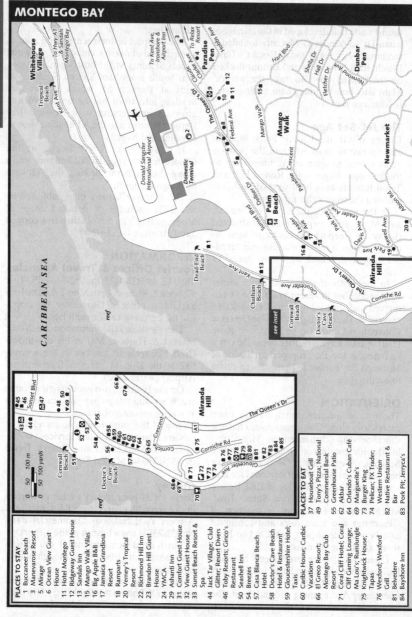

PLACES TO STAY
1 Buccaneer Beach Resort
3 Manevarose Resort
5 Mirage
6 Ocean View Guest House
11 Hotel Montego
12 Ridgeway Guest House
13 Sandals Inn
15 Mango Walk Villas
16 Big Apple B&B
17 Jamaica Grandiosa Resort
18 Ramparts
20 Verney's Tropical Resort
22 Richmond Hill Inn
23 Brandon Hill Guest House
24 YMCA
29 Ashanti Inn
31 Comfort Guest House
32 View Guest House
33 Sunset Beach Resort & Spa
44 Jack Tar Village; Club Glitter; Resort Divers
46 Toby Resorts; Ginco's Restaurant
50 Seashell Inn
54 Breezes
57 Casa Blanca Beach Hotel
58 Doctor's Cave Beach Hotel & Restaurant
59 Gloucestershire Hotel; Taxis
60 Caribic House; Caribic Vacations
66 El Greco Resort; Montego Bay Club
71 Coral Cliff Hotel; Coral Cliff Gaming Lounge; Ma Lou's; RumJungle
75 Knightwick House; Tapas
76 Wexford; Wexford Grill
81 Belvedere
84 Bayshore Inn

PLACES TO EAT
37 Houseboat Grill
49 Tony's Pizza; National Commercial Bank
55 Greenhouse Patio
62 Akbar
64 Orlando's Cuban Café
69 Burger King
73 Marguerite's
74 Pelican; FX Trader; Western Union
82 Native Restaurant & Bar
83 Pork Pit; Jerryca's

MONTEGO BAY

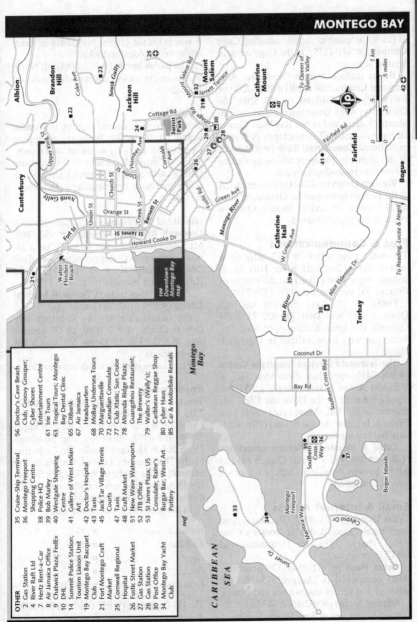

OTHER
2 Gas Station
4 River Raft Ltd
7 Hertz Rent-a-Car
8 Air Jamaica Office
9 Chatwick Plaza; FedEx
10 DHL
14 Summit Police Station;
   Tourism Liaison Unit
19 Montego Bay Racquet
   Club
21 Fort Montego Craft
   Market
25 Cornwall Regional
   Hospital
26 Fustic Street Market
27 Gas Station
28 Gas Station
30 Post Office
34 Montego Bay Yacht
   Club

35 Cruise-Ship Terminal
36 Montego Freeport
   Shopping Centre
38 Police HQ
39 Bob Marley
40 Westgate Shopping
   Centre
41 Gallery of West Indian
   Art
42 Doctor's Hospital
43 Taxis
45 Jack Tar Village Tennis
   Courts
47 Taxis
48 Craft Market
51 New Wave Watersports
52 JTB Office
53 St James Plaza; US
   Consulate; Rainie's
   Burgar Bar; Wassi Art
   Pottery

56 Doctor's Cave Beach
   Club; Groovy Grouper;
   Cyber Shores
   Entertainment Centre
61 Irie Tours
63 Tropical Tours; Montego
   Bay Dental Clinic
65 Citibank
67 Air Jamaica
   Headquarters
68 MoBay Undersea Tours
70 Marguerittaville
72 Canadian Consulate
77 Club Xtatic; Sun Cruise
78 Miranda Ridge Plaza;
   Guangzhou Restaurant;
   The Brewery
79 Walter's (Wally's);
   Caribbean Reggae Shop
80 Cyber Haus
85 Car & Motorbike Rentals

Pelican restaurant and in Overton Plaza. Several bureaus can be found on St James St (look for 'cambio' signs), including **Cage Cambio** (☎ 971-1135), in the Cage on Sam Sharpe Square.

Banks include two on Gloucester Ave: **National Commercial Bank** (☎ 952-6320; cnr Ewin Dr), and **Citibank** (☎ 971-5260; 166 Gloucester Ave). Downtown, banks on Sam Sharpe Square and in the Bay West Centre all have 24-hour ATM machines. A branch of **National Commercial Bank** (☎ 979-8060) in the Montego Freeport Shopping Centre serves the cruise-ship terminal.

Western Union (☎ 926-2454) has branches at the Pelican restaurant on Gloucester Ave; at 19 Church St; and in Shop 9, Overton Plaza, at the top of Dome St.

Post & Communications

The **main post office** (☎ 952-7016; open 9am-4:30pm Mon-Sat) is on Fort St. A second major post office is at the corner of Cottage Rd and Barnett St (☎ 952-7389).

FedEx (☎ 952-0411, 888-991-9081; 10 Queen's Dr) and **DHL** (☎ 922-7333; 34 Queen's Dr; open 8:30am-5pm Mon-Fri, 9am-1pm Sat) have offices in Chatwick Plaza.

The **Teleworld Services Telephone Centre** (☎ 940-7415; open 8am-10pm Mon-Sat), in Miranda Ridge Plaza, charges US$1 per minute for calls to the USA and US$2 per minute to the UK. Most cyber cafés (see Email & Internet Access below) offer international call service.

Cable & Wireless Telecommunications (C&W; ☎ 888-952-9700; 20 Church St) has public phones outside its offices on either side of Church St.

Email & Internet Access

Cyber Shores (☎ 971-8907; Gloucester Ave; open 8am-8:30pm daily), at Doctor's Cave Beach, charges US$2 for 15 minutes, and US$7.50 per hour.

Cyber Haus (☎ 971-9548; 37 Gloucester Ave) competes; it charges J$50 for 15 minutes and serves sandwiches and snacks.

Internet Access (☎ 952-1542; 34 Market St) is three blocks east of Sam Sharpe Square.

Bookstores & Libraries

Sangster's Bookshop (☎ 952-0319; 2 St James St) is the largest bookstore in town, albeit only modestly stocked.

The **parish library** (☎ 952-4185), off North St, has an impressive collection of books on Jamaica.

Laundry

The only coin-operated laundry is **Wonder Wash** (☎ 971-4739; Westgate Shopping Centre) on the A1, south of downtown. There's a drop-off laundry at the **Fabricare Centre** (☎ 952-6897; 4 Corner Lane), which offers one-hour dry cleaning plus laundry service.

Medical Services

Cornwall Regional Hospital (☎ 952-5100; Mt Salem Rd), the main hospital, has a 24-hour emergency department, as does **Doctor's Hospital** (☎ 952-1616; Fairfield Rd), a private hospital southeast of town.

Private clinics include **Cornwall Medical Centre** (☎ 979-6107; 19 Orange St).

For dental care, try the **Montego Bay Dental Clinic** (☎ 952-1080, 19 Gloucester Ave; ☎ 952-2338, 11 Dome St), which has two locations.

Pharmacies are a dime a dozen downtown.

Emergency

The town has four **police stations** (☎ 952-2333, 952-1557, 14 Barnett St; ☎ 940-3500, 49 Union St; ☎ 952-4396, 952-5310, 29 Church St; ☎ 952-4997, 953-6309, cnr Southern Cross Rd & Howard Cooke Dr, Catherine Hall). The Tourism Liaison Unit is in the **Summit Police Station** (☎ 952-1540; Sunset Blvd). At last visit, a new police station was due to open on Gloucester Ave.

In the case of an emergency call:

Air-Sea Rescue	☎ 119
Ambulance	☎ 011
Fire	☎ 110, 952-2311
Police	☎ 119
Rape Crisis Centre	☎ 952-5333

The **US Consulate** (☎ 952-0160, fax 952-5050; e usconsagency.mobay@cwjamaica.com) is in St James Plaza, 2nd Floor, Gloucester Avenue. The **Canadian Consulate** (☎ 952-6198; 29 Gloucester Ave) is in Maya's Plaza.

Dangers & Annoyances

Montego Bay has a reputation for tourist harassment by hustlers. Things have dramatically improved on Gloucester Ave in recent years, though harassment remains an annoyance. Visitors can expect to be approached in none-too-subtle terms by locals offering their services as gigolos and 'good-time girls.' And the barrage of young men selling drugs is a wearying constant.

Uniformed members of the Montego Bay Resort Patrol police the strip. Downtown is not patrolled, and you need to keep your wits about you. Avoid the dangerous Flankers area, across the highway from the Sangster International Airport.

At night, don't walk downtown or on any back streets, especially alone.

Beware traffic! Cars are often driven at a breakneck pace; don't expect the driver to give way. Use caution when crossing streets, and watch for deep gutters and potholes.

WALKING TOUR

Montego Bay's downtown is of historical interest and warrants a walking tour. Allow two hours.

Fort Montego to Downtown

Begin your tour at **Fort Montego**, on Fort St at the southern end of Gloucester Ave. Virtually nothing remains of the main fort, which once stood atop the hill. The sole remnant is a small battery with three brass cannons on rails.

Immediately south of the fort, beyond the roundabout, follow Fort St as it curls around to Union St, and turn left (east) for the **Georgian House** (☎ 952-0632; cnr Union St & Orange St). This venerable brick-and-stone house with its bow-shaped frontage is today the Georgian House Restaurant. There are two buildings: the original owner, a wealthy merchant, apparently housed his wife in one and his mistress in the other.

Retrace your steps to Fort St and continue one block south to arrive in the heart of Montego Bay.

Sam Sharpe Square

This bustling, cobbled square is centered on a small bronze fountain dedicated to Captain J Kerr, a pioneer in the banana trade.

The square, formerly called the Parade, is named for national hero the Right Excellent Samuel Sharpe (1801-32), leader of the 1831 Christmas Rebellion (see the boxed text 'Preaching Resistance' earlier in this chapter). At the square's northwest corner is the **National Heroes Monument**, an impressive bronze statue of Paul Bogle and Sam Sharpe, Bible in hand, speaking to three admiring listeners.

Also on the northwest corner is **the Cage**, a tiny cut-stone and brick building built in 1806 as a lockup. At this writing it serves as a cambio (currency exchange booth).

At the southwest corner is the copper-domed **Civic Centre**, a handsome colonial-style cut-stone building that opened in late 2001 (but was not furnished at last visit) on the site of the ruined colonial courthouse. It is slated to contain the **History Museum of Jamaica** (admission US$3), with relics and other exhibits tracing local history from Taino days to the recent past. An art gallery and 200-seat theater are also featured.

Market Street

From the square, head east along Market St. Two blocks east of Sam Sharpe Square, you pass **Burchell Memorial Baptist Church** (☎ 952-6351), a brick structure dating to 1835. Samuel Sharpe was a deacon here. The original church was founded in 1824 by Rev Thomas Burchell. An angry mob destroyed the church in reprisal for Burchell's support of the emancipation cause, but the missionary escaped to sea. Sam Sharpe's remains are buried in the vault. The concrete hulk across King St is **St Paul's Catholic Church** (☎ 952-2481).

Continue up Market St one block and turn south onto East St. This brings you to Church St. Turn left and follow it uphill one block to Dome St, and turn right.

DOWNTOWN MONTEGO BAY

PLACES TO STAY & EAT
4 KFC; Pizza Hut
10 Island Grill
12 Viennese Bakery
15 Lychee Gardens
18 Butterflake Pastries
21 Juici Patties
23 Georgian House Restaurant
35 Burger King
36 Town House
41 Linkage Guest House;
   Maroon Attraction Tours
45 Dragon Bay Restaurant
47 Hilton's Bakery; Western
   Union
60 Lyle's Intensified Inn

OTHER
1 Fort Montego
2 Aquasol Theme Park;
   Voyage Sports Bar & Grill
3 Klass Kraft
5 Parish Library
6 City Centre Building;
   Delicious Rot Restaurant
7 Photo Express
8 Post Office
9 Cornwall Medical Centre
11 Gas Station
13 Gas Station
14 Gully Market
16 National Commercial Bank
17 Bay West Centre; Devon
   House I-Scream
18 Taxi Stand
20 Fabricare Centre
22 National Commercial Bank
24 National Commercial Bank
25 International Travel Services
26 Ventura Photo Service
27 Stuart's Travel
28 Internet Access
29 Overton Plaza; Western
   Union; FX Trader
30 MoBay Shopping Centre
31 JTB Information Booth;
   Currency Exchange
32 The Cage; National Heroes
   Monument; Currency
   Exchange
33 Civic Centre
34 Mutual Security Bank;
   Scotiabank
37 C&W Telecommunications
38 Burchell Memorial
   Baptist Church
39 St Paul's Catholic Church
40 National Housing Trust
42 Tafara Products
43 Goldfingers Disco &
   Go-Go Club
44 Montego Bay Dental Clinic
46 Strand Theater
48 Western Union
49 St James Parish
   Church
50 C&W Telecommunications
51 Police Station
52 Dome House
53 Sharky's; Montego Bay
   Marine Park Trust
54 Creek Dome

55 Sangster's Bookshop
56 Transportation Station;
   Taxis
57 Police Station
58 Gas Station
59 Gas Station
61 Gas Station

To Donald Sangster
International Airport
& Falmouth

Walter
Fletcher Beach

Gloucester Ave

The Queen's Dr

Fort St

Howard Cooke Dr

Fort St

Orange St

Paradise Row

North St

Love Lane

Embassy Place

William St

St James St

Union St

N Corner

Market St

Sam Sharpe
Square

(ped mall)

Church St

Church Lane

St James St

Strand St

Harbour St

Craft
Market

Pier 1
Marina

Gun
Point Wharf

River
Bay

Orange St

Creek St

Barnett St

Fish Lane

Deans Lane

Railway Lane

Barnett Lane

Payne St

To Montego Freeport

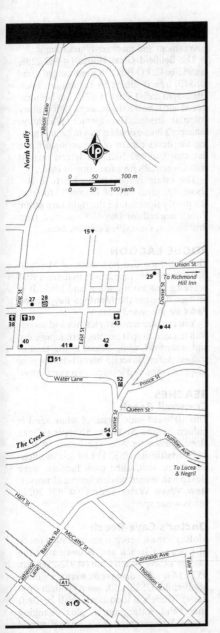

Dome Street

About 100 yards south, at the junction with Water Lane, is **Dome House**, a restored plantation home in cut stone, with large sash windows and an opulent interior. It's now a **dance and theater space** (☎ 952-2571).

A stone's throw south, at the corner of Dome and Creek Sts, is **Creek Dome**, built in 1837 above the underground spring that supplied the drinking water for Montego Bay. The structure is actually a hexagon with a crenellated castle turret in which the 'Keeper of the Creek' lived and collected a toll.

Retrace your steps along Dome St or Water Lane and walk west down Church St.

Church Street

Many of the most interesting buildings in town are clustered along Church St, the most picturesque street in MoBay. At the corner of Water Lane is a two-story, plantation-style octagonal structure that today houses a police station. Fifty yards west, at the corner of King St, is a red-brick Georgian building harboring the **National Housing Trust** (☎ 952-0063; 1 King St). Equally impressive is the three-story Georgian building at 25 Church St – headquarters of Cable & Wireless Jamaica.

The highlight, however, is **St James Parish Church** (☎ 952-2775; Church St), regarded as the finest church on the island. The current church was built between 1775 and 1782 in the shape of a Greek cross but was so damaged by the earthquake of March 1, 1957, that it had to be rebuilt.

With luck the tall church doors will be open and you can view the beautiful interior, which contains a stunning stained-glass window behind the altar. Note the marble monuments, including fine works by John Bacon, the foremost English sculptor of the late 18th century. One is a memorial to Rosa Palmer, whose virtuous life was upended in literature to create the legend of the White Witch of Rose Hall. Look carefully at her neck and you'll detect faint purple marks. Locals consider this proof of the fable that the 'witch' was strangled.

Facing the church is the **Town House** (☎ 952-2660; 16 Church St), with a handsome

Montego Bay Marine Park

In 1992, the Montego Bay Marine Park was established as the first national park in Jamaica with an aim to conserve and manage the coral reefs, seabed grasses, and shoreline mangroves.

The park extends from the eastern end of Sangster International Airport westward (almost 6 miles) to the Great River. It covers an area of some 15 sq miles and encompasses the mangroves of Bogue Lagoon.

Authority is vested in the Montego Bay Marine Park Trust (MBMPT; ☎ 971-8082; W www.montego-bay-jamaica.com/mbmp; Pier 1, off Howard Cooke Dr). MBMPT maintains a meager **Resource Centre** (open 8am-6pm daily), which has a library on the vital ecosystem. Presentations are offered in the evenings.

Fishing is banned within the marine park's perimeter; water sports are also limited to designated areas. Boats are required to use mooring buoys and can no longer anchor at will atop the coral. And collecting shells or coral or otherwise interfering with or molesting wildlife is prohibited.

red brick frontage buried under a cascade of bougainvillea and laburnum. It dates from 1765, when it was the home of a wealthy merchant. It has since served as a church manse and then, circa 1850, as a townhouse for the mistress of the Earl of Hereford, Governor of Jamaica. In the years that followed, it was used as a hotel, warehouse, Masonic lodge, lawyer's office, and synagogue. Today it houses an eponymous restaurant (see Places to Eat later in this chapter).

Two blocks west you will see the 1930s-era, art deco **Strand Theater** at 8 Strand St.

BARNETT ESTATE

The sea of sugarcane south of Montego Bay is part of Barnett Estate, a plantation owned and operated since 1755 by the Kerr-Jarretts, one of Jamaica's preeminent families; their holdings once included most of the Montego

Bay area. Today the family (now in its 11th generation) holds the land in trust for the government and manages it accordingly.

The **Bellfield Great House** (☎ 952-2382, fax 952-6342; PO Box 876; prearranged tours US$10, free if dining in restaurant; open 10am-5pm daily), built in 1735, has been restored and is now a showcase of 18th-century colonial living. The former plantation manager's house doubles as a museum charting the development of the area since the day that Colonel Nicholas Jarrett arrived with Cromwell's invasion army in 1655.

The estate is located on Fairfield Rd, about 800 yards east of Doctor's Hospital. It's poorly signed: take the right turn at the Y-fork marked for Day-O Plantation, then turn right at Granville Police Station.

BOGUE LAGOON

The island-studded bay south of Montego Bay is lined with mangroves that are a vital breeding ground for fishes and birds. It is protected within the **Montego Bay Marine Park** (see the boxed text).

You can hire canoes or kayaks and set out with a guide to spot herons, egrets, pelicans, and waterfowl, while below, in the tannin-stained waters, juvenile barracudas, tarpon, snapper, crabs, and lobsters swim and crawl.

BEACHES
Cornwall Beach

This 100-yard-wide swath of white sand is hidden behind St James Shopping Plaza along Gloucester Ave. The beach (☎ 952-4439; adult/child US$2/1) had lost its clientele at last visit, when most facilities were closed and verged on dereliction. However, **New Wave Water Sports** (☎ 991-2021) offers water sports.

Doctor's Cave Beach

MoBay's main beach is immediately south of Cornwall Beach and is owned by the Doctor's Cave Beach Club (☎ 952-2566, fax 952-1140; e drscave@cwjamaica.com; adult/child US$3/1.50; open 8:30am-6pm daily). There's a food court, grill bar, gift shop, and water sports, plus changing rooms. You can rent shade umbrellas and inflatable 'lilos' for US$5, and chairs rentals are US$4.

Walter Fletcher Beach

This long sliver of white sand, at the south end of Gloucester Ave, is now the venue for the **Aquasol Theme Park** (☎ 940-1344; e aquasol@cwjamaica.com; adult/child US$5/2; open 9am-10pm), with netball, volleyball, tennis courts, water sports, the MoBay 500 go-cart track, and Voyage Sports Bar & Grill (see Places to Eat later in this chapter). It rents lockers, beach mats, and chairs and umbrellas.

Swimming is not advisable after heavy rain, for the overflow of sewer pipes in the gully washes out to sea nearby – that's not brine you're smelling!

ACTIVITIES

Each of the beaches offers **water sports**, and the resort hotels have their own concessions.

For **rafting**, see the Great River and Martha Brae sections later in this chapter.

For **horseback riding**, see the Ironshore section later in this chapter.

If you want to **golf**, MoBay offers three championship courses east of town (see Ironshore later in this chapter). A fourth course, at Tryall, is a 30-minute journey west.

For **tennis**, there are courts at Walter Fletcher Beach, and most resort hotels have courts for guests. The **Jack Tar Village tennis courts** (☎ 940-5856; cnr Sunset Blvd & Kent Ave) cost US$5 per hour for nonguests. The **Montego Bay Racquet Club** (☎ 952-0200, fax 979-7210; cnr Sewell & Park Aves) charges US$10 per hour (US$20 at night).

Sport Fishing

The waters off Jamaica's north coast offer spectacular game fishing. Beyond the north-shore reefs, the ocean floor plummets for thousands of feet. Deep-water game fish use the abyss – known as 'Marlin Alley' – as a migratory freeway (June and August are peak months for marlin). The **Montego Bay Marlin Tournament** is held in late Septem-

ber; contact the Montego Bay Yacht Club (see Sailing & Cruising below).

Half- and full-day charters can be booked through hotels, at Pier 1 Marina, or from **Rhapsody Cruises** (☎ 979-0102; Shop 204, Chatwick Plaza).

Also see Ironshore later in this chapter and Sport Fishing in the Facts for the Visitor chapter.

Sailing & Cruising

Several yachts and cruise boats operate party cruises. Most companies charge US$35-50 for three-hour party cruises, and US$25-35 for sunset and dinner cruises. Most vessels sail from **Pier 1** (☎ 952-2452; e info@pieronejamaica.com).

Rhapsody Cruises (☎ 979-0102; Shop 204, Chatwick Plaza) offers a 'wet 'n' wild cruise party' at 10am and 3pm Monday to Saturday aboard *Tropical Dreamer*, a catamaran specially designed as a party boat.

Calico Sailing Cruises (☎ 952-5860; White Sands PO) operates *Calico*, a 55-foot ketch resembling an old pirate ship.

You can charter yachts for private group sailing trips from any of the above companies, or from the **Montego Bay Yacht Club** (☎ 979-8038, fax 979-8262; e mbyc@cwjamaica.com; PO Box 1133), at Montego Freeport.

The 'Undersea Semi-Submarine Tour' aboard a semi-submersible operates from Margueritaville. The vessel doesn't dive – you look at the marine life through bubble-dome windows beneath the boat. You can also snorkel and hand-feed fish. Contact **MoBay Undersea Tours** (☎ 940-4465; e undersea@montego-bay-jamaica.com; Gloucester Ave). Tours are 11am and 1:30pm Monday through Saturday, and the cost is US$30/15 for adults/children.

Sharky's (☎ 971-1049; Pier 1, Howard Cooke Dr) offers a sunset cruise with underwater viewing, with complimentary drinks. Tours depart Pier 1 at 4pm daily and cost US$25 including transfers.

Also see Ironshore later in this chapter.

Scuba Diving

MoBay offers first-rate dive sites. Most sites are close to shore and range from teeming patch reefs to awe-inspiring walls that begin in as little as 35 feet of water.

For advanced divers, **The Point**, north of the airport, is considered 'the ultimate wall dive,' due to the dense corals and fish, sharks, and rays that are fed by crystal-clear waters scoured by currents. The wall here starts at 70 feet and drops to at least 300 feet. The **Airport Reef**, off the southwestern edge of the airport, is considered by many to be the best site on the island, with masses of coral canyons, caves, and tunnels, and even a DC-3 wreck.

The large sponges at deeper sites such as **Basket Reef** are spectacular. **Widowmaker's Cave** is famous for being swarmed by wrasses, barracuda, and parrot fish.

Beginners explore the shallow reef close to shore off Doctor's Cave Beach, and also **Chatham Reef**, offshore from Sandals Montego Bay. Another great shallow dive is **Rose Hall Reef**, known for its walls and its tall columns of pillar coral.

Also see Scuba Diving in the Facts for the Visitor chapter, and see Montego Bay to Tryall Estate later in this chapter.

Organized Diving & Snorkeling The following operators offer dives and certification courses and rent equipment: **Resort Divers** (☎ 953-9699, 940-1183; ⒺDIV resdiv@ bigfoot.com), at the Jack Tar Village; **Reef Keeper Divers** (☎ 979-0104, fax 979-0101; Shop 204, Chatwick Plaza); and **Seaworld Resorts** (☎ 933-2180, fax 953-2550; PO Box 610). Most all-inclusive resorts have their own dive facilities for guests.

Lady Sharon (☎ 953-2021; Ⓔ coolaqua@ cwjamaica.com), based at Rose Hall Beach Park (see later in this chapter), offers two-hour snorkeling trips at 10am daily (US$45).

Most companies above also offer snorkeling trips.

Also see the Ironshore and Reading sections later in this chapter.

ORGANIZED TOURS

JUTA Tour Company (☎ 952-0813, fax 952-5355; Ⓔ juta@cwjamaica.com; PO Box 1155; Chatwick Plaza, Claude Clarke Ave) and **Tropical Tours** (☎ 952-0400; 19 Gloucester Ave) offers a guided tour of Montego Bay.

Caribic Vacations (☎ 979-6073, 953-2584, fax 953-9897; u www.caribicvacations.com; 69 Gloucester Ave) offers a wide range of tours islandwide, including the 'Appleton Estate Rum Tour' every Tuesday and Wednesday (US$65). It specializes in excursions to Cuba. Irie Tours (% 971-5886, fax 971-8073; c irietoursltd@cwjamaica.com), its affiliate in the same office, also has a broad range of island tours, including a jeep safari (US$75) and a Montego Bay highlight tour on Monday and Friday (US$35).

Tourwise (☎ 952-6096, Chatwick Plaza; ☎ 979-1027, Sangster International Airport) is the main rival of Caribic Vacations.

Barrett Adventures (☎ 382-6384, fax 979-8845; Ⓔ carolyn@barrettadventures.com; Rose Hall, Little River PO) offers customized tours by minivan.

Jamaica ATV Tours (☎ 953-9598; Ⓔ info@ atvtoursjamaica.com; Half Moon PO, St James), at Rose Hall, offers 4WD motorcycle tours into the hills.

Maroon Attraction Tours (☎ 952-4546, fax 979-0308; 32 Church St) offers a 'cultural, educational, and historic tour' to Accompong in Maroon Country (see the South Coast & Central Highlands chapter).

Other tour agencies post advertisements around town.

SPECIAL EVENTS
Reggae Sumfest

This internationally acclaimed reggae festival (☎ 940-6398, 953-3835, fax 979-7437; Ⓔ info@ reggaesumfest.com; PO Box 1178), held over five days each July or August, starts with a beach party on Walter Fletcher Beach, followed by four theme nights, including a 'street jam' on Gloucester Ave. The festival typically includes more than 50 world-class reggae artists and has recently taken place at three venues: the Rose Hall Beach Park, Pier 1, and the Bob Marley Entertainment Centre (also called the Catherine Hall Entertainment Centre; on Howard Cooke Drive).

At this writing, tickets cost US$15-30 per night. The street jam is free. Tickets go on sale in Jamaica about two weeks before the concert. Full-week bracelets that allow you to attend all events cost US$100-150.

Sumfest packages are offered from the USA by **Alken Tours** (☎ 718-856-7711, 800-221-6686; W www.alkentours.com; 1661 Nostrand Ave, Brooklyn, NY 11226); **Jamaica Travel Specialist** (☎ 510-489-9552, 800-544-5979; W www.jamaicantravel.com; 33576 Alvarado-niles Rd, Union City, CA 94587); and **Sunburst Holidays** (☎ 212-567-2900, 800-786-2877; W www.sunburstholidays.com; 4779 Broadway, New York, NY 10034).

Miami to Montego Bay Yacht Race

This annual 800-mile race, colloquially called the Pineapple Cup Yacht Race, takes place in mid-February and is an excuse for four days of partying. Contact the Montego Bay Yacht Club (see Sailing & Cruising earlier in this chapter), which also hosts an **Easter Regatta**, or Jamaica Sailing Week, each March or April. It also sponsors the **Jam-Am Yacht Race** (☎ 979-8262) in December.

Other Happenings

The **All That Heritage & Jazz Festival** (☎ 929-2498) is held in mid-October. It's followed by a 'Family Fun Fair.'

The annual five-day Montego Bay **International Marlin Tournament** is held in September. Contact the Montego Bay Yacht Club.

An **International Horse Show & Polo Match** is held each February at Rocky Point Stables (☎ 953-2286; Half Moon PO).

The **Montego Bay Marathon and Fun Run** (☎ 979-8240) is held in March.

PLACES TO STAY

Montego Bay boasts the largest number of guest rooms of any resort area in Jamaica. Most of the hotels are clustered along Gloucester Ave; deluxe resorts nestle on their own beaches east of town at Ironshore and Mahoe Bay.

If you arrive without reservations, the JTB information booth in the arrivals hall at Sangster International Airport can assist with reservations.

Places to Stay – Budget

Downtown Linkage Guest House (☎ 952-4546, 972-0308; 32 Church St; rooms with shared/private bath from US$18/20) has 14 rooms in an old wooden house. They're simple but clean and have fans, louvered windows, and hot water in the shared bathrooms. Discounts are offered for stays of a week or longer. Meals are served. The owners offer Maroon heritage tours to Accompong.

YMCA (☎ 952-5368, 832-8017; 28 Humber Ave; rooms US$15-28), on a cul-de-sac at the east end of Humber Ave, maintains a hostel on the south side of town. Its 15 basic rooms share bathrooms (cold water only) and have fans. There's a TV lounge, plus ping-pong.

Gloucester Avenue Caribic House (☎ 979-6073, fax 979-3421; 69 Gloucester Ave; singles US$39-51, doubles US$44-60 year-round) is a compact, no-frills option above the Caribic Vacations' office directly opposite Doctor's Cave Beach; it's a favorite of budget-minded Europeans. It has 17 basically furnished rooms with fans, TVs, and large bathrooms.

Farther Afield Ocean View Guest House (☎ 952-2662; 26 Sunset Blvd; singles/doubles US$30/38), the cheapest hotel near the airport, is a bargain at these rates, although rooms are no-frills. It has a TV lounge. Free airport transfers are available on request.

Comfort Guest House (☎ 952-1238, fax 979-1997; 55 Jarrett Terrace; rooms US$50), on the southeast edge of town, has Christian owners who offer home-cooked meals. Carpeted rooms are basically furnished and overpriced, but have cable TV. There's a shady patio.

View Guest House (☎ 952-3175, fax 979-1740; 56 Jarrett Terrace; rooms with fan/aircon US$28/34), across the road from the Comfort, also has home-cooked meals and has 14 marginally nicer, albeit basically furnished rooms. It has a swimming pool.

Ashanti Inn (☎ 952-6389; 50 Thompson St, cnr Cottage Rd; rooms with fan/air-con US$40/50-60), on the east side of town, is preferable, being well-kept and having tasteful albeit modest furnishings. It has 15 rooms with cable TV and phones, opening to shaded patios.

Brandon Hill Guest House (☎ 952-7054, fax 940-5609; e brandonhillja@hotmail.com;

28 Peter Pan Ave, PO Box 187; single/double standard US$36/40, superior U$40/50) is an attractive option, with 16 modestly furnished, well-lit rooms. A pool is inset in a patio and hillside garden with views.

Places to Stay – Mid-Range

Gloucester Ave **Toby Resorts** (☎ 952-4370, fax 952-6591; ⓔ reservations@tobyresorts.com; cnr Gloucester Ave & Sunset Blvd, PO Box 467; singles/doubles summer US$60/70, winter US$70/80) is my favorite in this price range. The 72 air-conditioned rooms are in two-story units surrounding a pool and sundeck with bar. Rooms are nicely furnished with faux-marble floors and pine-and-rattan furniture, plus phones. Most have small verandas. Facilities include a gameroom, Zoups Café, the pool bar, and an elevated bar with a lounge and large-screen TV. The hotel is popular with Europeans.

Seashell Inn (☎ 952-6590, fax 979-3821; ⓔ d.chin@cwjamaica.com; Mable Ewen Dr; singles/doubles summer US$75/85, winter US$85/135), off Gloucester Ave and opposite Cornwall Beach, has 28 spacious, though sparsely furnished, air-con rooms long overdue for renovation at last visit. Superior rooms (US$5 extra) have fridges, TVs, and four-poster beds. Apartment units were planned. There's a dining terrace beneath a huge fig tree next to a pool, but the bar and restaurant remain closed.

Bayshore Inn (☎ 952-1046; ⓔ khruma@yahoo.com; 27 Gloucester Ave; rooms per night/week US$50/280), attached to the Pork Pit and facing Walter Fletcher Beach, is a pleasant modern place with 15 modestly furnished rooms with fans and air-con. Most have cable TV.

Knightwick House (☎ 952-2988, fax 971-1921; ⓔ thegenie40@hotmail.com; Corniche Rd; rooms per person US$45), behind and above Coral Cliff, is a delightful B&B run by a charming couple, Jean and Stanley Magnus. The colonial structure – boasting terra-cotta floors, wrought-iron railings, and abundant artwork – has three modest yet appealingly furnished bedrooms that are well-lit and airy. Each has a balcony. Its restaurant is acclaimed. Rates include breakfast.

Seashore Inn (☎/fax 979-6874; 33 Gloucester Ave; singles or doubles US$55, with balcony US$57), formerly the Belvedere, near Walter Fletcher Beach, has 19 rooms with air-con, cable TV, telephones, and hot and cold water. They vary greatly. Some, upstairs, are fairly spacious and have balconies with views over the bay. Others are cellarlike – the bathrooms small, the furniture basic, and one reader thought the air-con sounded like a B-52. A dipping pool has a poolside bar.

Coral Cliff Hotel (☎ 952-4130, fax 952-6532; ⓦ www.coralcliffjamaica.com; PO Box 253; standard single/double summer US$70/80, winter US$90/100; superior single/double summer US$85/95, winter US$110/130; suites summer US$150, winter US$180) has been recently upgraded. The 21-room hotel, attached to the Coral Cliff Gaming Lounge, offers nine centenary rooms with a yesteryear charm, 10 modern rooms furbished with appealing tropical decor, and two suites in elegant plantation style with spacious balconies. All rooms have air-con, cable TV, and phones. There's a swimming pool, gym, library and TV lounge, and an atmospheric restaurant plus flamboyant video-slot lounge.

Buccaneer Beach (☎ 952-6489, fax 979-2580; ⓔ buccaneerbeach@hotmail.com; 7 Kent Ave; singles or doubles US$75) is a small, modest property with a homey feel. Its 51 air-con rooms have tile floors, phones, cable TVs, and safety boxes, plus large balconies. There's a plunge pool in each of the front and back courtyards, plus a piano bar with large-screen TV. Its reclusive location at the end of Kent Ave is a five-minute walk from Gloucester Ave.

Miranda Hill **Ramparts** (☎ 979-5258, fax 979-5259; 7 Ramparts Close; singles or doubles US$45), with 10 rooms boasting lots of dark timber and natural stone, is pleasantly atmospheric. Its intimate bar and the TV lounge, which serves as a dining room, are exquisitely Old World English. The small pool is a satisfying place to catch some rays.

Big Apple B&B (☎ 952-7240, fax 940-7516; ⓦ www.bigapples.com; 18 Queen's Dr;

doubles US$50-60, suites US$70), near Ramparts, is a hilltop B&B with 21 carpeted, air-con rooms, all with two double beds and views. Rooms vary. Furnishings are modest and bathrooms are small. Newer rooms are larger. Rates do *not* include breakfast. Meals can be prepared.

Verney's Tropical Resort (☎ 952-2875, fax 979-2944; 3 Leader Ave; doubles US$50-75) offers a secluded spot in the hills with views inland over the sugarcane fields. The 25 rooms are homey and clean and have air-con and cable TV. The open-air bar is pleasant, and there's a large pool and restaurant. Verney's is popular with Jamaican families.

Mirage (☎ 952-4637, fax 952-6980; 6 Queen's Dr; rooms summer/winter US$50/70) is a cozy hotel complex with 22 spacious, carpeted rooms with rattan furniture and satellite TV. The rooms overlook a small amoeba-shaped pool. Upper-floor rooms have skylights but get warm.

Farther Afield Manevarose Resort (☎ 979-9584, fax 940-3188; Ⓔ manevarose@insite.com; 17 Claude Clarke Ave; rooms US$40-50, suites US$65), in the hills east of town, is a modern complex with 20 rooms with fans, TV, refrigerator, and hot water. There's a swimming pool, plus a bar and restaurant upstairs.

Relax Resort (☎ 979-0656, fax 952-7218; ☎ 800-742-4276 in North America; Ⓦ www .fantasyisle.com/relax.htm; 26 Hobbs Ave; superior room summer US$72, winter US$94; 1-3–bedroom suite summer US$102-228, winter US$132-258) is a breeze-swept property. Its 47 rooms have ocean views, with floral prints, tile floors, spacious bathrooms, tiny TVs, and telephones. It has a sumptuous three-bedroom villa, plus four new studio apartments and two one-bedroom apartments. Tours are offered.

Ridgeway Guest House (☎ 952-2709, 940-0637, fax 940-0636; 34 Queen's Drive; rooms without/with air-con from US$45/60), directly opposite the airport, is popular with Europeans. The eight rooms are large and attractive and feature private baths with hot water. Rates include continental breakfast.

You can rent TVs. Free beach and airport shuttles are provided.

Hotel Montego (☎ 940-6009, 952-3286, fax 979-0351; Federal Ave, PO Box 74; singles or doubles/suites US$43/75) is convenient to the airport. Its 33 air-con rooms and suites have TV and telephone plus king-size beds, but the decor is frumpy. There's a breezy veranda pool, plus a bar and restaurant.

Places to Stay – Top End
Gloucester Ave Glousershire Hotel (☎ 952-4420, fax 952-8088; ☎ 877-574-8497 in North America; ☎ 0800-169-7103 in the UK; Ⓦ www.gloustershire.com; PO Box 86; singles summer US$100-115, winter US$105-120; doubles summer US$105-120, winter US$110-125; suites single/double summer US$120/125, winter US$125/130), formerly the Quality Inn, is a recently renovated 88-suite hotel across the street from Doctor's Cave Beach. Most rooms feature a balcony; all have air-con, direct-dial phones, room safes, satellite TV, and pleasant pastel decor. It offers a pool deck with Jacuzzi, and there's a restaurant and tour desk.

Doctor's Cave Beach Hotel (☎ 952-4355, fax 952-5204; Ⓔ info@doctorscave.com; PO Box 94; standard singles/doubles summer US$90/120, winter US$120/145; superior summer US$100/130, winter US$130/145; suite summer US$150, winter US$170; breakfast & dinner US$29) is a family-run option. Its labyrinthine corridors lead to 78 rooms and 12 suites. Rooms were recently refurbished in lively tropical decor. The lush gardens at the back are tight up against the cliff face, where there's a whirlpool. Other facilities include a small gym, a piano bar, and a splendid restaurant that opens onto a small swimming pool and has live entertainment…creating a noise concern.

Wexford (☎ 952-2854, fax 952-3679; Ⓦ www.wexfordhotel.com; 39 Gloucester Ave, PO Box 108; garden view single/double summer US$85/95, winter US$95/105; ocean view rooms add US$5; villas add US$15) is a run-of-the-mill option. The 61 recently-upgraded rooms are modestly furnished and have balconies, telephones, and TVs. One wing has one-bedroom apartments with kitchenettes. There's a pool, the Zee Bar, and Wexford Grill (see Places to Eat).

Casa Blanca Beach Hotel (☎ 952-0720, fax 952-1424; e casablanca@cwjamaica.com; PO Box 469; singles/doubles summer US$109/178), is an all-inclusive property that stands out for its position and relaxed mood. This low-rise property sits atop the coral shore south of Doctor's Cave Beach. It has its own pocket of sand where free water sports (sailing, surfing, and snorkeling) are offered. The 80 air-con oceanfront rooms have queen-size beds, private baths, and balconies. Suites have four-poster beds. Facilities include two pools, a gameroom, TV lounge, and seaside dining terrace. Rates include meals, drinks, etc.

Breezes (☎ 940-1150, fax 940-1160; 'cabin' US$210-250, 'deluxe' US$245-285, 'deluxe ocean view' US$285-325, suite US$325-370) towers over Doctor's Cave Beach, to which guests have free access. This soulless Super-Clubs all-inclusive has 124 graciously appointed but cramped rooms and suites around an L-shape pool that at night forms the foreground for a high-tech stage – a noise problem if you want to sleep. Rooms have satellite TVs, VCRs, and CD players, hair dryers, and in-room safes. Entertainment features theme nights. Facilities include two restaurants, beach grill, four bars, rooftop Jacuzzi, gameroom, water sports, beauty salon and massage, fitness center, and a nightclub. (For international contact information, see All-Inclusive Resorts in the Facts for the Visitor chapter.)

Jack Tar Village (☎ 952-4340, fax 940-5646; ☎ 800-858-2258, fax 305-262-5570 in North America; w www.allegroresorts.com; 2 Gloucester Ave, PO Box 144; standard singles/doubles summer US$169/232, winter US$177/248; superior summer US$183/258, winter US$191/274) is a favorite in the all-inclusive breed. It is a welcoming, low-rise, beachfront, adults-only resort with 128 rooms with lively tropical decor and its own private beach overlooked by an elegant restaurant. All rooms have ocean views and balconies. The hotel offers a full range of activities and water sports, plus complimentary massage.

Sandals Inn (☎ 952-4140, fax 952-6913; w www.sandals.com; Kent Ave, PO Box 412; rooms per person summer US$180-240, winter US$215-275) is a modest, 52-room couples-only resort, totally refurbished in 2001. It's run to exacting standards and offers a range of entertainment, water sports, and top-notch cuisine. Guests get privileges at the other Sandals resorts. The public beach, across the road, is much smaller than the hotel brochure suggests, but guests get free access to Sandals' other two MoBay properties. (For international contact information, see All-Inclusive Resorts in the Facts for the Visitor chapter.)

Miranda Hill Mango Walk Villas (☎ 952-1473, 940-3379, fax 979-3093; 5 Mango Walk Rd; studios winter US$45, 1-/2-bedroom units US$55/75) has attractive studios and one- and two-bedroom units. All are air-conditioned and furnished in rich fabrics, and all have kitchen, living room, and patio. The villa is centered on a deep pool and bar, and is in a reclusive hilltop district that's 10 minutes by car to the town and beaches.

Montego Bay Club Resort (☎ 952-4310; 212-840-6636, 800-223-9815 in the USA; Queen's Dr; singles/doubles summer from US$65/76, winter from US$94/112), also for self-caterers, is a 14-story high-rise apartment complex rising from the Queen's Drive. Apartments are clean, spacious, and clinically white, with kitchenettes and balconies with good views. There's a swimming pool and restaurant. An elevator provides direct access to Gloucester Ave.

El Greco Resort (☎ 940-6116, fax 940-6115; ☎ 888-354-7326 in the USA; ☎ 800-597-7326 in Canada; w www.elgrecojamaica.com; Queen's Dr, PO Box 1624; 1-/2-bedrooms US$99/126) shares its clifftop setting with Montego Bay Club Resort, and has 96 one- and two-bedroom air-con suites with kitchenettes, satellite TV, tile floors, rattan furniture, and floral prints. French doors open to balconies. There's a swimming pool, restaurant, and tennis courts.

Richmond Hill Inn (☎ 952-3859, fax 952-6106; w www.richmond-hill-inn.com; Union St, PO Box 362; singles/doubles summer

US$60/70, winter US$70/90; suites summer US$120-175, winter US$140-200), 500 feet above town, is a venerable hotel built of limestone and molasses, and is chock-full of antiques. Rooms have air-con, cable TV, and modest furnishings. It's noted for its restaurant, which has attracted many among the great and famous. There's also a six-person penthouse suite.

Farther Afield Sandals Montego Bay (☎ 952-5510, fax 952-0816; W www .sandals.com; N Kent Ave; all rates per person: rooms summer US$230-305, winter US$265-335, suites summer US$320-695, winter US$350-695) takes up 19 acres of splendid beachfront north of the airport, and is a superb all-inclusive, couples-only resort where you and the one you love can seek out that honeymoon sparkle, snorkeling, sailing, and sunning to your heart's content. It has 245 rooms in 10 categories, all with lively plantation-style furniture. There are four pools, four whirlpools, five restaurants, four bars, and top-notch entertainment. Every kind of water sport is available, including scuba. Check Sandals' website for discounts. (For international contact information, see All-Inclusive Resorts in the Facts for the Visitor chapter.)

Sunset Beach Resort & Spa (☎ 979-8800, 800-888-1199; W www.sunsetbeachjamaica .com; Sunset Dr; doubles summer US$230-290, winter US$250-310; suites summer/ winter $400/450), at the end of the Montego Freeport Peninsula, is a 420-room, twin high-rise, upscale all-inclusive resort with a vast lobby opening to a massive pool bar. Choose from five categories of rooms with ocean or bay view, all with one king-size or two double four-poster mahogany beds, air-con, hair dryer, telephone, cable TV, in-room safe, and private balcony. Twelve of 32 suites have Jacuzzis. It also has four restaurants, five bars, a disco, slot casino, nightly entertainment, plus four tennis courts, three pools, state-of-the-art gym and spa, cyber center, Sega center, a high-tech business center, and three beaches (with a nudist section) and water sports. A Kiddies Club caters to families.

Jamaica Grandiosa Resort (☎ 979-3205, fax 979-3203; e jamaicagrandiosa@hotmail.com; 3 Ramparts Close; singles or doubles US$65) is a newer hilltop property with 38 air-con rooms with modest furnishings, cable TVs, and grandiose views. The dining room has a lofty vista. It has a small breeze-swept pool and sundeck, plus a gameroom and an undistinguished bar.

PLACES TO EAT
Jamaican
Lyle's Intensified Inn (☎ 952-4980; 36 Barnett St), downtown, lets you fill up for under US$3. It sells pastries, patties, fried fish, and bammy.

Georgian House Food Court (☎ 952-0632; 2 Orange St; open 7am-11pm), in the courtyard of the Georgian House Restaurant, serves take-out local fare, such as curried chicken (US$4) and 'Rasta pasta' (US$5).

Butterflake Pastries (☎ 952-0070; 2 Union St) and nearby Juici Patties (☎ 979-3733; 36 St James St) are good for cheap meat and vegetable patties.

Pork Pit (☎ 952-1046; 27 Gloucester Ave; open 11am-11pm) is world famous. Here you eat at open-air picnic tables beneath a shade tree. Finger-lickin' jerk chicken and pork costs from US$3 with yams, 'festival,' and sweet potatoes extra.

Raine's Burger Bar (no ☎; St James Plaza; open 7am-6pm) is a popular breakfast spot. This small outdoor eatery offers breakfasts all day, including homemade muffins, omelettes, and ackee and saltfish (US$3-8).

Greenhouse Patio (☎ 952-7838; Gloucester Ave; open 7am-11pm) has bland food, but it's open early for breakfast. It can be ice-cold inside. Next door, the poolside restaurant at Doctor's Cave Beach Hotel, is much better. For breakfast, try the callaloo omelette (US$4.50). Its lunch and dinner menu ranges from fish-and-chips (US$7) to jerk pork chops (US$9.25).

Groovy Grouper (☎ 952-3680; open 9am-1:30am), at Doctor's Cave Beach Club, has a fabulous beachside location and serves snacks, Jamaica fare, and seafood from *escoveitched* fish (US$8) to lobster (US$21).

Pelican (☎ 952-3171; Gloucester Ave) is a steadfast good-value favorite of upscale locals. Its menu of Jamaican dishes includes stew peas with rice and stuffed conch with rice and peas (US$7), but it also serves sirloin steaks and seafood. Take a sweater.

Wexford Grill (☎ 952-2854; Gloucester Ave; open 7am-11pm), in the Wexford hotel, specializes in seafood and steak and ribs (including sweet-and-sour ribs and honey-garlic ribs) for US$17-22. Try the weekend brunch special.

Voyage Sport Bar & Grill (☎ 940-1344; Gloucester Ave; US$2-15), at Aquasol Theme Park on Walter Fletcher Beach, serves Jamaican fare such as jerk chicken wings, I-tal stew, and peppered shrimp, plus sandwiches, burgers, and seafood.

Orlando's Cuban Café (☎ 952-8554; 47 Gloucester Ave; 11am-2am) is a splendidly atmospheric place with Cuban art and music. The menu is mostly Jamaican, plus sandwiches, but Cuban dishes such as *croquetas* (US$7) are present.

Nouvelle Jamaican Tapas (☎ 952-2988; Corniche Rd; open 6:30pm-10pm), on the veranda of Chef Oliver Magnus' private home and behind Coral Cliff Gaming Lounge, bills itself as 'where the chefs eat.' The creative menu features mouthwatering dishes: corn crab bisque with ginger, carne asada in coffee-based sauce, and grilled scampi in honey-brandy sauce are typical (US$8 to US$15).

Ma Lou's (☎ 952-4130; 165 Gloucester Ave), in the Coral Cliff Casino, is one of the nicest places in town, with African-themed decor and exciting nouvelle Jamaican cuisine, such as roasted Peking chicken (US$15), curry with coconut and fried plantain (US$10), and specialty jerks (from US$9).

Marguerite's (☎ 952-4777; Gloucester Ave; US$8-33; open 6pm-10:30pm), adjoining Margueritaville, is a great place to watch the sunset over cocktails, followed by dinner on the elegant cliff-top patio. The pricey menu edges toward nouvelle Jamaican, but also includes sirloin steak and a seafood platter.

Continental

Ginco's (☎ 971-4370; 1 Kent Ave; US$4-15), at Toby Resorts, serves 'European-Caribbean fusion' and has a Friday night fish fry.

Georgian House (☎ 952-0632; 2 Orange St) features silverware, crystal, and gilt chandeliers. You can also dine alfresco at wrought-iron tables in a courtyard shaded by palms. Entrees (from US$20) include shrimp Creole, lobster Newburg, and tenderloin of pork.

Town House (☎ 952-2660, fax 952-3432; 16 Church St) offers a choice of dining in the brick-walled cellar or more elegantly upstairs in the Blue Room of this 18th-century structure. Choose from red snapper papillot (US$23) – cooked in a paper bag – or stuffed lobster (US$30) and the like.

Native Restaurant & Bar (☎ 979-2769; 29 Gloucester Ave) is modestly elegant and recommended for good food, pleasant ambience, and fair prices. It offers free hotel shuttle. The menu ranges from salads to 'goat in a boat' (curried goat in a pineapple half; US$9) and a 'seafood royale' (US$31).

Houseboat Grill (☎ 979-8845; e thehouseboatgrill@hotmail.com; Southern Cross Blvd; open 6pm-10pm Tues-Sun), anchored in Bogue Bay at Montego Bay Freeport, is now one of Jamaica's top-notch restaurants, offering eclectic Caribbean fusion cuisine such as roasted garlic caesar salad (US$6), spicy Jamaican snapper with callaloo and cream sauce (US$15), and homemade ice cream. It has a changing menu and a warm ambience. You can dine inside, or reclusively out on the sundeck. The bar draws the local middle-class and is open until the last guest goes home. Reservations are strongly recommended on weekends.

Asian

Guangzhou Restaurant (☎ 952-6200; 39 Gloucester Ave, Miranda Ridge Plaza; open noon-9:45pm Mon-Fri, 5pm-9:45pm Sat & Sun) serves a huge variety of Chinese dishes, but also has Thai and Mongolian dishes (US$5-20). Discounts are offered between noon and 4pm.

Lychee Gardens (☎ 952-9428; 18 East St; open noon-10pm daily) is an elegant downtown restaurant recommended for Szechuan cuisine (US$4-24).

Dragon Bay Restaurant (☎ 952-6494; 1 Church Lane), downtown, is the genuine article: it offers true Chinese fare (US$2-30) from the hands of a recent Chinese immigrant.

Delicious Roti Restaurant (☎ 940-6646; open 11am-10pm), upstairs in the City Centre Building, serves basic Indian fare (US$2.50-12).

Akbar (☎ 957-0113; 71 Gloucester Ave; open 11:30am-4pm & 6pm-11pm), opposite Doctor's Cave Beach, is recommended for superb Indian cuisine and tremendous atmosphere. It offers a reasonably priced and broad menu (US$8-18) that includes tandoori and vegetarian dishes.

Fast Food

There's a food court in the MoBay Shopping Centre.

Tony's Pizza (☎ 952-6365; Gloucester Ave; open 11am to 2am) is recommended for pizza (U$7-15).

Island Grill (cnr Embassy Place & Harbour St) is a fast-food option serving jerk fish and chicken, festival, pumpkin rice, and the like.

KFC and **Pizza Hut** (cnr of Howard Cook Dr & Harbour St) have outlets, as does **McDonald's** (Bay West Centre), one block east, and **Burger King** (Gloucester Ave).

Cafés, Ice Cream & Yogurt

Jerryca's Italian Ice Cream (Gloucester Ave) serves gelatos priced from J$50 (a little over US$1) for a tiny cup – expensive but delicious.

Devon House I-Scream (☎ 940-4060; Howard Cook Dr) has an outlet in the Bay West Centre.

Groceries

You can buy fresh produce downtown at the **Gully Market** (Orange St between Union and William Sts) and **Fustic Street Market** (Barnett St).

You'll find supermarkets downtown in the **MoBay Shopping Centre** (Howard Cooke Dr & Market St), and the **Westgate Shopping Centre** (Barnett St) on the A1 south of town.

For bakeries, try the **Viennese Bakery** (☎ 952-3711; 43 St James St) or **Hilton's Bakery** (☎ 979-3128; 5 Church St).

ENTERTAINMENT

Most upscale hotels have live bands and limbo and carnival-style floor shows, and if you're staying at an all-inclusive resort, you may never be tempted to prowl outside the compound at night.

Bars

Margueritaville (☎ 952-4777; Gloucester Ave; admission after 10pm US$5) is the king of the day-and-night entertainment scene, with four open-air bars, 15 big-screen TVs, and dance floors on decks overhanging the water. It even has a 110-foot waterslide and an outdoor hot tub. Monday is Red Stripe beer fest; Tuesday is 'Marguerita Madness'; a wet T-shirt and bikini contest is hosted on Wednesday; and Sunday is karaoke night.

Groovy Grouper Beach Bar & Grill (☎ 952-3680), at Doctor's Cave Beach Club, has big-screen TVs, plus board games, etc.

Voyage Sports Bar & Grill (Walter Fletcher Beach) is also popular and has 42 large-screen TVs. Other sports bars include **The Brewery** (☎ 979-3552; Miranda Ridge Plaza; open 10am-2am) and **Walter's** (☎ 952-9391; 39 Gloucester Ave), also known as Wally's.

Montego Bay Yacht Club (☎ 979-8038) attracts an eclectic crowd that includes crusty old sea-salts (nonmembers must be signed in as guests).

RumJungle (☎ 952-4130), in the Coral Cliff Gaming Lounge, is the most atmospheric bar…great, if you don't mind the constant background noise of slot machines. It offers a nightly cabaret. The African decor – like something from an Indiana Jones movie – is worth the visit alone.

The **poolside bar** at Doctor's Cave Beach Hotel has live music with theme parties nightly.

Beach Parties & Stageshows

Montego Bay is rightfully famous for *boonoonoonoos,* or 'beach parties,' where the DJs crank it up until you can feel the vibrations loosen your fillings. The crowds crush shoulder-to-sweaty-shoulder; the air is thick with ganja smoke; and the whole street is full of revelers *wining* ('dirty dancing') en masse. The location changes; check with the JTB (☎ 952-4425) for the latest venues. The JTB sponsors a weekly street carnival on Gloucester Ave, from 10pm until midnight on Monday. At last visit, however, it was being offered during Spring Break only.

Aquasol Theme Park (☎ 940-1344, e aquasol@cwjamaica.com), at Walter Fletcher Beach, hosts stage shows and theme beach parties, including impy-skimpy bikini and beauty contests, such as 'Miss Treasure Chest' (Tuesday nights). Thursday is oldies night ('60s and '70s music).

Reggae Sumfest in August is the big daddy of stage-shows (see Special Events earlier in this chapter). The main venue, the **Bob Marley Entertainment Centre** (Howard Cooke Dr), sometimes called the Catherine Hall Entertainment Centre, also occasionally hosts 'sound systems'; look for posters advertising forthcoming performances as well.

Discos

The disco in the **Sunset Beach Resort & Spa** at Montego Freeport is a hot spot, as is **The Voyage** (☎ 979-9447) nightclub at Aquasol Theme Park.

Club Glitter (cnr Kent & Gloucester Aves; admission US$5) is a no-frills disco with occasional live bands.

Pier 1 Disco, off Howard Cooke Drive, was demolished by Hurricane Michelle in 2001 and at last visit was scheduled to be rebuilt.

Go-Go Clubs

Club Xtatic (Gloucester Ave; admission US$2.50), above Miranda Ridge Plaza, has exotic go-go dancers.

Goldfingers Disco & Go-Go Club (☎ 952-1684; 51 Market St; admission US$5) is far earthier (don't walk; take a taxi). See the caveats in the section on Go-Go Clubs in Facts for the Visitor.

Other Venues

The only modern cinema is at Ironshore (see later in this chapter). **The Strand** (☎ 952-5391; 8 Strand St) is dingy and not in the best area for nighttime walking.

You can gamble at **Coral Cliff Gaming Lounge** (☎ 952-4130; Gloucester Ave; open 24 hrs), which has over 100 video slot machines, plus a big-screen TV and free drinks, with fashion shows, cabarets, and/or live jazz nightly.

Dance and theater performances are hosted at **Dome House** (☎ 952-2571; Dome St), and **Fairfield Theatre** (☎ 952-0182; Fairfield Rd), east of Doctor's Hospital, is where Montego Bay's Little Theatre Company performs.

SHOPPING

For film, try **Photo Express** (☎ 952-3120; 57 Fort St) or **Ventura Photo Service** (☎ 954-5864; 22 Market St), both downtown.

Arts & Crafts

MoBay's streets are spilling over with stalls selling wooden carvings, straw items, jewelry, ganja pipes, T-shirts, and other touristy items.

For the largest selection, head to the downtown **Craft Market** (Harbour St; open 7am-7pm daily) that extends for three blocks between Barnett and Market Sts, or the **Fort Montego Craft Market** (Gloucester Ave), behind the fort.

Wassi Art Pottery (☎ 952-6698; St James Plaza) sells magnificent handcrafted pottery.

Gallery of West Indian Art (☎ 952-4547; W www.galleryofwestindianart.com; 11 Fairfield Rd), in the Catherine Hall suburb, has quality arts and crafts from around the Caribbean, including Cuban canvases, hand-painted wooden animals, and handmade jewelry.

Tafara Products (☎ 952-3899; 36 Church St) is an African/Rastafarian cultural center selling books, arts and crafts, and natural foods.

Klass Kraft (☎ 952-5782; 44 Fort St) sells leather sandals (US$12-35).

Duty-Free Goods
The **City Centre Building** – a modern shopping plaza opposite the library on Fort St – has several duty-free shops, including **Bijoux** (☎ 952-2630), **Chulani** (☎ 952-2158), and **Casa de Oro** (☎ 952-3502), all selling jewelry, ceramics, etc. Most duty-free stores open at 10am.

Reggae Reminders
For the biggest selection of tapes, you should check out **Top Ranking Record Shop** (☎ 952-1216; Shop No 4) in the Westgate Shopping Centre, or the **Caribbean Reggae Shop** (☎ 971-6658; 39 Gloucester Ave). The shop is located just up the hill behind Wally's.

GETTING THERE & AWAY
Air
Air Jamaica Express (☎ 922-4661, 888-359-2475; ☎ 800-523-5585 in the USA; 9 Queen's Dr; open 9am-4:30pm Mon-Fri) operates scheduled flights between Montego Bay's Sangster International Airport and Kingston's Norman Manley International airport (14 flights daily; US$60 each way), Negril (eight daily; US$54), Ocho Rios (two daily; US$51), and Port Antonio (one daily; US$60).

See the Getting Around chapter for more details on domestic charter service. See the Getting There & Away chapter, earlier in this book, for information about international air service.

Public Transportation
Buses, coasters, and route taxis arrive and depart from the transportation station off Barnett St, at the south end of St James St (for a complete description of public transportation options, see Buses & Taxis in the Getting Around chapter). There's an **inspector's office** (open 7am-6pm) inside the gate, where you can ask the departure point of the bus you're seeking.

The following approximate fares apply for coasters and route taxis:

route	duration	cost
Duncans	1 hour	US$3
Falmouth	30 minutes	US$2
Frome	1 hour	US$3
Kingston	3½ hours	US$8
Little London	2 hours	US$5
Lucea	1¼ hours	US$3
Negril	1½ hours	US$4
Ocho Rios	2 hours	US$6

The **Montego Bay Metro Line** (☎ 952-5500; 19A Union St) bus service was introduced in 2001, linking MoBay with suburbs and outlying towns (a flat fare of J$20 applies).

Taxi
JUTA (☎ 952-0623, fax 952-5355, Claude Clarke Ave, PO Box 1155; ☎ 979-0778, 6 Queen's Dr) has taxi stands opposite Jack Tar Village and Doctor's Cave Beach on Gloucester Ave, downtown at the junction of Market and Strand Sts, and by the bus station. JUTA and **Caribic Vacations** (☎ 979-3421; 69 Gloucester Ave) offer transfers to other resorts.

Car
The following companies have offices at Sangster International Airport:

Bargain Rent-a-Car	☎ 952-0762
Budget	☎ 952-3838
Hertz	☎ 979-0438
Island Rental Car	☎ 952-5771

Companies with offices in Montego Bay include:

Budget (☎ 953-9765; e budget@jamweb.net)
Lot 125, Ironshore Industrial Estate
Caribbean Car Rental (☎ 952-0664)
19 Gloucester Ave
Dhana Car Rental (☎ 953-9555)
Holiday Village Shopping Centre
Sunbird Car Rentals (☎ 952-5536)
19 Gloucester Ave

Boat
Cruise ships berth at Montego Freeport, about 2 miles south of town. Taxis to downtown cost US$10. (See the Getting There &

Away chapter for details on cruise companies serving Montego Bay.)

Montego Bay Yacht Club (☎ 979-8038, fax 979-8262), at Montego Freeport, has hookups, gasoline, and diesel.

GETTING AROUND

You can walk between any place along Gloucester Ave and downtown (it's about 1½ miles from Kent Ave to Sam Sharpe Square). You'll need a vehicle for anywhere farther.

Or, get around in a horse-drawn carriage. **All Nations Carriage Tours** (☎ 979-2514) charges US$25 per hour, and tours begin at the fort at the south end of Gloucester Ave.

To/From the Airport

You'll find taxis outside the arrivals lounge at Sangster International Airport. An official taxi booth is immediately outside Customs. Your taxi driver will probably call for a porter…who'll expect a tip for taking your luggage the 10 yards to your car! A tourist taxi to Gloucester Ave costs US$8. You can catch a coaster or route taxi from the gas station at the entrance to the airport (J$30).

Public Transportation

There is no in-town bus service. Montego Bay Metro Line buses (see Getting There & Away) operate to the suburbs, as do coasters and route taxis. All depart and arrive at the transportation station near the junction of St James and Barnett Sts.

The following regulated fares applied at last visit:

Greenwood	J$50 bus,	J$60 coaster/taxi
Ironshore	J$40 bus,	J$40 coaster/taxi
Rose Hall	J$40 bus,	J$40 coaster/taxi

Taxi

Licensed taxis cruise Gloucester Ave (a steep US$8 minimum). Published fares from Gloucester Ave include the following:

Airport	US$8
Greenwood	US$20
Ironshore	US$10
Montego Freeport	US$10
Rose Hall	US$10

Unlicensed 'robots' (see the Getting Around chapter) cruise the town. Any ride in town should cost no more than US$1.

Motorcycle & Bicycle

Outlets along Gloucester Ave rent bicycles and motorbikes (from US$40 a day). Scooters (US$30) are recommended for inexperienced riders. Try **Sun Cruise** (☎ 979-0614; 32 Gloucester Ave), just west of Miranda Ridge Plaza.

The Coast: Montego Bay to Trelawny

East of Montego Bay, the A1 hugs the coast, which here is not particularly scenic, all the way to Falmouth, 23 miles away.

IRONSHORE

This residential suburb about 5 miles east of Montego Bay is a center for deluxe resorts and villas, several of which are at scintillating Mahoe Bay. The resorts line the shore; the residential area is in the hills, inland.

Along the highway east of Ironshore, the Half Moon Village shopping center has a **Scotiabank** and the **MoBay Hope Medical Center** (☎ 953-3549). Blue Diamond Shopping Centre, on the highway at Ironshore, also has a Scotiabank, as well as **Diamond Drugs Pharmacy** (☎ 953-9184) and **Express Laundromat** (☎ 953-8918).

Golf

Most noteworthy is **Half Moon Golf, Tennis & Beach Club** (☎ 953-2560, 953-3105), about 3 miles east of Ironshore; this is a 7115-yard, par-72, Robert Trent Jones–designed course (green fees cost US$130 year-round, plus US$35 for cart rental and US$15 for a caddy). The **David Leadbetter Golf Academy** (☎ 953-9767, fax 953-9369) is here.

SuperClubs Golf Club Montego Bay at Ironshore (☎ 953-2800) is a links-type course (6633 yards and par 72) known for its blind-shot holes. Green fees are US$52 in summer, US$58 in winter, plus US$29 for cart rental and US$13 for a caddy.

White Witch Golf Course (☎ 953-2800), at the Ritz-Carlton Rose Hall, is a 6718-yard, par-71 championship course, new for 2000. Green fees cost US$125, plus US$50 for club rental. A golf package with caddy and cart costs US$225.

Other Activities

Seaworld/Princess Cruises (☎ 953-2180, fax 953-2550; PO Box 610) offers deep-sea fishing from the Cariblue Beach Resort. It also offers cruises, scuba diving, and a 'snorkeling safari.' **Resort Divers** (☎ 953-9699, 940-1183; ℮ resdiv@bigfoot.com), at the Holiday Inn Sunspree, and **Jamaica Scuba Divers** (☎ 953-2266), at the Half Moon Golf, Tennis & Beach Club, offer dives, certification courses, and rent equipment. Most all-inclusive resorts have scuba facilities and snorkeling gear for guests.

For horseback trail rides, try the **Double A Ranch** (☎ 936-6106), opposite the Holiday Inn Sunspree. **Rocky Point Stables** (☎ 953-2286, fax 953-9489; ℮ r.delisser@cwjamaica.com; PO Box 35, Falmouth), just west of Half Moon Village, is a full-blown equestrian center. Rides include a 90-minute ride into the mountains (US$50). Lessons cost US$30 per half-hour.

Places to Stay

Guest Houses A no-frills place, **Cocomo's Guest House** (☎ 953-9437, 831-7584; ℮ cocomos1@aol.com; Coral Gardens PO; rooms US$22-33), on the A1, has seven rooms featuring air-con, cable TV, and dowdy, beat-up furniture. Some share a toilet and shower. There's also an apart-

ment. It has a pool with simple bar and grill, and meals are made on request.

Resorts On the A1, **Cariblue Beach Resort** (☎ 953-2022, fax 953-3580; ℮ infocb@caribluehotel.com; PO Box 610, Rose Hall; standard single/double summer US$60/70, winter US$65/75; deluxe summer US$80/90, winter US$90/110) offers 24 spacious though meagerly furnished air-con rooms with telephones and TVs. Most have a balcony. It has a restaurant, a pool, a dive shop, and a wide range of water sports, plus excursions aboard its 47-foot *Princess* motor-yacht.

Sandals Royal Caribbean (☎ 953-2231, fax 953-2788; PO Box 167, Montego Bay; all rates per person: rooms summer US$240-305, winter US$270-340; suites summer US$360-395, winter US$380-445) is a recently remodeled, upscale couples-only all-inclusive at Mahoe Bay. It offers 190 rooms in seven categories, all in Sandals' trademark plantation style. Its beach is relatively small, but water sports, land sports, entertainment, and cuisine are up to par. Highlights include Kokomo Island, with the Indonesian-style Bali-Hai Restaurant (one of four restaurants) and its own swimming pool and Jacuzzi. Check Sandals' website for discounts. (For international contact information, see All-Inclusive Resorts in the Facts for the Visitor chapter.)

Coyaba Beach Resort & Club (☎ 953-9150, 800-237-3237, fax 953-2244; ⓦ www.coyabajamaica.com; Little River PO; garden-view/ocean-view rooms summer US$190/220, winter US$290/340), at Mahoe Bay, is a tranquil family-run resort offering contemporary elegance. It has 50 recently refurbished luxurious rooms and junior suites furnished 'plantation style' with hand-carved beds, floral drapes, and rich mahogany reproduction antiques. Some rooms have direct beach access, but all feature in-room safe, telephone, and satellite TV/VCR. At last visit, bathrooms were being redone in marble. Water sports are offered, and there's a handsome pool and sundeck; children's activity center is slated to open.

The elegant Vineyard Restaurant offers splendid nouvelle Jamaican cuisine; there's an oceanside bar and grill; and there's a second bar with a warm clubby feel. The full-service **SpaSerenity** (open 9am-6pm Mon-Sat; Sun by appointment) is here.

Half Moon Golf, Tennis & Beach Club (☎ 953-2211, 800-626-0592, fax 953-2731; ☎ 800-424-5500 in the USA; W www.half moon-resort.com; Half Moon PO, Rose Hall; all rates summer/winter: superior US$120/195, deluxe US$145/245, junior suite US$175/295, suite US$195/345, villas US$480-1680/780-2730) is an exclusive colonial-style resort named for its private, mile-long crescent beach, behind which are 400 acres of beautifully landscaped gardens containing a 20-acre bird reserve. It has 42 rooms and 179 suites with Georgian plantation-era decor. All guest rooms have high-speed Internet access. Adjacent to the hotel are 20 super-deluxe five-, six-, and seven-bedroom villas with private pools. Each comes with its own cook, maid, gardener, and even its own rental car. Public areas boast gracious appointments. Facilities include gourmet restaurants, squash courts, 13 tennis courts, equestrian center, full-service spa, conference center, championship golf course, and the Half Moon Village.

Holiday Inn Sunspree (☎ 953-2485, fax 953-9480; ☎ 800-465-4329 in North America; PO Box 480, Rose Hall; all rates summer/winter: garden-view US$130/245, ocean-view US$150/265, oceanfront US$169/285, suite US$229/385) is an all-inclusive family resort with 516 tastefully appointed air-con rooms and 26 family suites in ungainly seven-story buildings around a handsome sundeck and vast free-form pool. It has special facilities for children. Mom and dad are also catered to with a fitness spa, tennis and volleyball courts, miniature golf, glass-bottom boats, disco, and four bars. Children 12 and under stay free.

Jamaica Rose Resort (☎ 953-3993; ☎ 205-836-2929, 800-358-3938, fax 205-836-2931 in the USA; 427 Ferguson Ave; doubles per person US$149), in the hills of Ironshore

Estate, offers 10 deluxe air-con rooms with TVs and private baths. There's a sundeck and private pool, plus two terrace bars. Guests can use the SuperClubs Golf Club Montego Bay. Breakfast and dinner are US$15 extra. Prices listed require a 3-night minimum stay.

Ritz-Carlton Rose Hall (☎ 953-2800, fax 953-8981; ☎ 800-241-3333 in North America; W www.ritzcarlton.com; 1 Ritz-Carlton Drive, Rose Hall; rooms summer US$205-500, winter US$365-695, peak US$475-845) is a deluxe addition that opened in 2000 with 1,500 feet of prime beachfront. Rich fabrics and mahogany abound. The 430 rooms and sumptuous suites are resplendent, decorated in fresh tropical colors, and boast cable TVs, three telephones apiece, safety deposit boxes, computer hook-ups, and ritzy marble bathrooms with terry robes. The 51 executive suites and 36 'club rooms' are regal indeed. Features include six restaurants and lounges, a tennis center, business center, championship golf course, full service spa and fitness center, full convention facilities, five restaurants, and two tennis courts.

Villas & Apartments There are dozens of upscale villas for rent. Companies to contact include **Exclusive Villa Resorts** (☎ 979-5037; Lot 217, Upper Deck, Sewell Ave, Montego Bay) and **Russell Villas of Rose Hall** (☎ 953-3707, 800-238-5289, fax 953-2732; e rrus sell@infochan.com).

See Villa Rentals in the Facts for the Visitor chapter for other companies and conditions.

Places to Eat

Most restaurants are at the resorts.

Vineyard Restaurant (☎ 953-9150; dinner from US$20; closed Wed), at Coyaba Beach Resort, is the place to head for nouvelle Jamaican cuisine with an international flavor. The menu is creative and the fare among the best on the island.

Sakura (☎ 953-9686; meals from US$20; open 11am-3pm and 6pm-11pm), in the Half Moon Village, specializes in teppanyaki cooked at hibachi-grill tables.

Sugar Mill Restaurant (☎ 953-2228; US$8-36; open 11am-11pm), at Half Moon Golf Club, serves Caribbean and international cuisine in an elegant setting.

Blue Mountain Coffee Shop, in the Half Moon Village, sells cappuccinos, espressos, pastries, and snacks.

Entertainment

The **Bob Marley Experience** (☎ 953-3449, fax 953-9725; w www.bobmarleyexperience.com; admission free), at the Half Moon Village, has daily showings of a documentary on Marley's life in a 68-seat theater.

Blue Diamond Cinema (☎ 953-9020) is in the Blue Diamond Shopping Centre.

Planet Xaymaka Disco (☎ 953-3840), in Half Moon Village, is open for special functions.

Tropigala Nightclub (☎ 953-2257, 952-8263; admission US$10), 400 yards inland of the A1, has cabaret stage shows, plus a skating rink.

Pleasure Dome (open 9pm-5am; entrance US$7), in the Blue Diamond Shopping Centre, offers exotic dancing.

Shopping

Images Art Gallery (☎ 953-9043), in the Half Moon Golf, Tennis & Beach Club, there are displays of antique collectibles, plus works by Jamaica's foremost artists. You will find that the A1 is lined with makeshift stalls selling wood carvings and crafts.

ROSE HALL TO GREENWOOD

East of Ironshore, the A1 dips and rises past coastal scrubland, residential estates, and several Colonial-era great houses.

Bob Marley School of Arts Institute

The Rastafarian owners of this still-to-be-developed college-cum-theme park (☎ 781-2416, 954-5252; e bobarts@jol.com.jm; PO Box 1823, Falmouth), 2 miles east of Greenwood, tout plans to create a center for up-and-coming musicians, with a beach club, amphitheater, and hotel. At last visit, the site

was little more than a bunch of semiderelict old huts.

Rose Hall Great House

This mansion (☎ 953-2323, fax 953-2160; e rosehall@cwjamaica.com; PO Box 186, Montego Bay; adult/child under 12 US$15/10; open 9am-6pm daily), with its commanding hilltop position 2 miles east of Ironshore, is the most famous great house in Jamaica.

The imposing house was built in the 1770s by John Palmer, a wealthy plantation owner. Palmer and his wife, Rose (after whom the house was named), hosted some of the most elaborate social gatherings on the island. Slaves destroyed the house in the Christmas Rebellion of 1831, and it was left in ruins for over a century. In 1966, the

---

The White Witch of Rose Hall

John Rose Palmer, grandnephew of John Palmer, who built Rose Hall, married Anne May Patterson in 1820. Although the young woman was half English and half Irish, legend has it that she was raised in Haiti, where she learned voodoo. Legend also says that Anne May was a murderous vixen. The lascivious lady allegedly practiced witchcraft, poisoned John Palmer, stabbed a second husband, and strangled her third. Her fourth husband escaped, leaving her to dispose of several slave lovers before she was strangled in her bed.

This famous legend is actually based on a series of distorted half-truths. The inspiration for the story, originally told in writing in 1868 by John Costello, editor of the *Falmouth Post*, was Rose Palmer, the initial lady of Rose Hall. She did have four husbands, the last being John Palmer, to whom she was happily wed for 23 years (she died before her husband, at age 72). Anne Palmer, wife to John Rose Palmer, died peacefully in 1846 after a long, loving marriage.

In 1929, novelist HG DeLisser developed the fable into a marvelous suspenseful romance, the *White Witch of Rose Hall*.

three-story building was restored to haughty grandeur.

Beyond the Palladian portico, the house is a bastion of 18th-century style, with a magnificent mahogany staircase and doors, and silk wall fabric that is an exact reproduction of the original designed for Marie Antoinette during the reign of Louis XVI. *Don't touch!* Many of the antiques are the works of leading English master carpenters of the day.

Part of the attraction is the legend of Annie Palmer, a multiple murderer said to haunt the house (see the boxed text 'The White Witch of Rose Hall'). Her bedroom upstairs is decorated in crimson silk brocades. The cellars now house an old-English-style pub and a well-stocked gift shop. There's also a snack bar.

Tours of the house commence every 15 minutes till 5:15pm.

Greenwood Great House

This estate (☎ 953-1077; ☒ www.green woodhouse-jamaica.com; PO Box 169, Montego Bay; admission US$12; open 9am-6pm daily) sits high on a hill 5 miles east of Rose Hall, and is a more intimate property. The two-story stone-and-timber structure was built about 1760 by the Honorable Richard Barrett, whose family arrived in Jamaica in the 1660s and amassed a fortune from its sugar plantations. (Barrett was a cousin of the famous English poet Elizabeth Barrett Browning.) Greenwood was intended primarily for entertaining guests, hence the large ballroom. Barrett was a member of the Jamaican Assembly. In an unusual move for his times, however, he educated his slaves, as the guides in period costume will tell you.

Unique among local plantation houses, Greenwood survived unscathed during the slave rebellion of Christmas 1831. The original library is still intact, as are oil paintings, Dresden china, a rare collection of musical instruments, a court jester's chair, and plentiful antiques...including a man-trap used for catching runaway slaves.

Buses traveling between Montego Bay and Falmouth will drop you off anywhere along the A1.

Rose Hall Beach Park

This private beach (☎ 953-2341; PO Box 186; admission adults/children US$6/3; open 9am-6pm daily), 2 miles east of the Wyndham Rose Hall Resort, is a peaceful place open to the public. It offers horseback riding and water sports, including banana-boat rides, jet-skiing, parasailing and scuba diving; a snorkel cruise runs at 10am and 5pm. There's a restaurant and bar.

Activities

Wyndham Rose Hall Resort & Country Club (☎ 953-2650) has a 6598-yard, par-72 golf course known for its superb coastal vistas. Green fees are US$50 in summer, US$60 in winter, plus US$33 for cart rental and US$15 for a caddy.

Cool Aqua Divers (☎ 953-2021; ☒ cool aqua@cwjamaica.com), at Rose Hall Beach, offers scuba diving.

White Witch Stables (☎ 953-2746) is located at Wyndham Rose Hall Resort & Country Club.

Special Events

The four-day **Jamerican Film & Music Festival** (☎ 323-692-9537 in the USA; ☒ www .jamericanfilmfest.com) is held in October and November at the Ritz-Carlton Rose Hall, and it features film screenings, writers' and actors' workshops, and special events.

Places to Stay

Wyndham Rose Hall Resort & Country Club (☎ 953-2650, fax 953-2617; ☎ 800-996-3426 in the USA; ☎ 020-8367-5175 in the UK; ☒ www.wyndham.com; PO Box 999, Montego Bay; all rates summer/winter: standard US$130/205, deluxe US$145/230, suite US$330/395) is a 488-room resort just west of Rose Hall Great House fronted by a beautiful 1000-foot-long beach. The twin-tower, seven-story hotel offers elegant furnishings in spacious rooms with king-size beds. Amenities include a choice of restaurants, video-game room, Cricketer's Pub, the Jonkanoo nightclub (which draws MoBay's middle class), and family facilities, plus an 18-hole golf course and six tennis courts. The entire property was recently upgraded and now boasts a major water complex – Sugar Mill Falls – with three terraced pools, a 280-foot waterslide, and meandering canals complete with waterfalls.

Dunn's Villa Resort Hotel (☎ 953-7459, fax 953-7456; ☎ 718-882-3917, fax 882-4879 in the USA; e glodunn@aol.com; Rose Hall, Little River PO, Montego Bay; single/double summer US$55/65, winter US$60/85) is in the hills, in the village of Cornwall, 2 miles inland (follow the signs from the highway). This well-kept, homey hotel has 11 air-con rooms with satellite TV and wide balconies, and rates include breakfast. The spacious public areas are minimally but attractively furnished. There's a pool and Jacuzzi on a raised sundeck. The gracious hosts offer a local tour by horse and buggy, rent mountain bikes (US$8), and offer lunch, dinner, and weekend brunch poolside.

Royal Reef Hotel & Restaurant (☎ 953-1700, fax 953-1705; w www.royal-reef.com; PO Box 10, Falmouth; rooms summer US$105-137, winter US$140-177), on the A1 at Greenwood, is a gracious, modern Mediterranean-style hotel with 19 rooms. Its decor includes classical wrought-iron furnishings as well as exquisite tropical murals. An elevated amoeba-shaped pool is inset in the terra-cotta terrace, which has an outside grill overlooking a tiny, unappealing beach overgrown by mangroves. The cuisine (served in three eateries, including a patio diner) is excellent.

Cameleon Sea Castles Hotel & Resort (☎ 953-3250, fax 953-3062; w www.airtransatholidays.com; PO Box 55, Montego Bay; rates upon request) was bought by Canada's Air Transat Holidays in early 2002, and at last visit was closed. It was expected to reopen as a 150-room all-inclusive, all-suite resort centered on a plantation-style great house at the heart of a 14-acre estate with private beach.

Places to Eat

White Witch's Hideaway Pub & Grill (☎ 953-2323; meals US$2-5), in Rose Hall Great House, serves typical Jamaican meals, plus fish-and-chips, sandwiches, etc.

The Coast: Falmouth to Rio Bueno

Much of Jamaica's history was written along this section of coast, and Falmouth provides a good education. Good beaches are few and far between. Inland, however, the scenery is terrific; see Cockpit Country (North) later in this chapter.

FALMOUTH

Few other towns in Jamaica have retained their original architecture to quite the same degree as Falmouth (population 8700), which has a faded Georgian splendor. The city, 23 miles east of Montego Bay, has been the capital of Trelawny parish since 1790. On weekends farmers come from miles around to sell their produce, recalling the days when Falmouth was Jamaica's major port for the export of rum, molasses, and sugar.

The town was used as a setting in *Papillon* and *Wide Sargasso Sea*.

There have been several plans to restore the town, but very little effort has been undertaken, and many historic buildings are now decrepit. However, several individuals have done fine restoration work, as has **The Georgian Society** (☎ 952-4089, fax 979-8013; PO Box 700, Montego Bay). Proposals to establish an open-air Slave Museum have not yet materialized.

The **Falmouth Yacht Club Fishing Tournament** (☎ 954-5934, fax 954-5881; e heatherw@cwjamaica.com) is held in early October.

Buses, coasters, and route taxis arrive and depart Water Square (Montego Bay, US$0.50; Ocho Rios, US$1).

History

Falmouth was laid out in 1790 and named for the English birthplace of Sir William Trelawny, then the island's governor. The streets were planned as a grid and patriotically named after members of the royal family and English heroes. Planters erected their townhouses using Georgian elements adapted to Jamaican conditions.

Advantageously positioned, Falmouth quickly grew into the busiest port on the north coast. Most of the outbound trade consisted of hogsheads (large casks) containing wet sugar and puncheons (casks) of rum, while slaves were off-loaded for sale in Falmouth's slave market.

The town's fortunes degenerated when the sugar industry went into decline during the 19th century, and it was dealt a further blow with the advent of steamships, which the harbor was incapable of handling. By 1890 the port was essentially dead. The city has struggled along ever since.

Orientation & Information

The A1 from Montego Bay runs along Duke St into Water Square, the town's node. The A1 then zigzags east, continuing to Ocho Rios. Market St, one block west of Water Square, runs south to Martha Brae and Good Hope.

National Commercial Bank (☎ 954-3232; Water Square) has a branch in town.

There's a **post office** (☎ 954-3050; cnr Cornwall & Market Sts). For telephone and fax services, go to the **Cable & Wireless office** (☎ 954-5910; 23 Market St; open 8am-4pm Mon-Fri), the **Call Direct Centre** (☎ 974-7942; 11 Market St), or the **Cornwall Communication Network** (☎ 954-4857; open 9am-6pm Mon-Fri, 10am-4pm Sat), in the forecourt of the Falmouth Resort.

The library (☎ 617-1404; Rodney St) offers Internet access (J$50 for 30 minutes).

Falmouth Hospital (☎ 954-3250; Rodney St) has emergency services. Dr Diane Glasgow runs a **clinic** (☎ 954-4580; 1 Trelawny St; open 8:30am-2:30pm Mon-Fri). Pharmacies include the **Orion Pharmacy** (☎ 954-3392; 26 Market St).

There are **police stations** (☎ 954-3222) on Rodney St and Market St.

Historic Downtown

Begin your walking tour at **Water Square**, at the east end of Duke St. Named for an old circular stone reservoir (dating to 1798), the square has a fountain topped by an old waterwheel. Today it forms a traffic roundabout.

The market, on the east side of Water Square, was built in 1894 and named for two of Queen Victoria's grandsons. Today, as the **Albert George Shopping & Historical Centre**, it still functions as a market with crafts stores, and contains an historic museum with a motley collection of colonial-era artifacts.

From here follow the main road east one block to peruse the **Phoenix Foundry**, a conical structure built in 1810 at the corner of Tharpe and Lower Harbour Sts. Behind the foundry, guarded by locked metal gates, is the **Central Wharf** where slaves were brought ashore, to be replaced in the holds by sugar, rum, and other victuals born of their back-breaking labor. The crumbling warehouses are on their last legs. Some 50 yards west is **Tharp House** (on Seaboard St), sagging from age yet still one of the best examples of elegant period townhouses. Today housing the tax office, it was formerly the residence of John Tharp, at one time the largest slaveholder in Jamaica.

Retrace your steps to Water Square and turn east for one block to Seaboard St. Here stands the grandiose Georgian **courthouse** in Palladian style, fronted by a double curling staircase and Doric columns, with cannons to the side. The current building, dating from 1926, is a replica of the original 1815 structure that was destroyed by fire. The town council presides here.

History buffs might follow Seaboard St west one block, then turn right onto Market St, which soon brings you to **Fort Balcarres** (on Charlotte St) – now a school. The remains are hidden by a high stone wall, and there's little to see.

By following the wall around you get to Rodney St, which runs west along the shore past the historic **police station**. It was constructed in 1814 as the Cornwall District Prison: a 'house of correction' for defiant slaves, with a separate cell for debtors. The prison once contained a 'treadmill,' a huge wooden cylinder with steps on the outside. Shackled above the mill, slaves had to keep treading the steps as the cylinder turned. If they faltered, the revolving steps battered their bodies and legs. The ancient lockups are still in use.

At the bottom of Market St is the **Methodist Manse**, a stone-and-wood building with wrought-iron balconies and Adam friezes above the doorways. A diversion along Trelawny St leads one block west to **Barrett House**, the handsome, restored former home of wealthy planter Edward Barrett.

One of the most stately edifices is the restored **Baptist Manse** (cnr Market & Cornwall Sts). It was formerly the residence of nonconformist Baptist preacher William Knibb, who was instrumental in lobbying for passage of the Abolition Bill that ended slavery. The porticoed **post office** is adjacent. Nearby is the **Knibb Memorial High School** (cnr Market & Trelawny Sts). Built in 1798, it was originally a Masonic hall.

On July 31, 1838, slaves gathered outside **Knibb Memorial Church** (cnr King & George Sts) for an all-night vigil, awaiting midnight and the dawn of full freedom, when slave shackles, a whip, and an iron collar were symbolically buried in a coffin. The scene is depicted in bas-relief on a marble panel above the baptismal trough inside the chapel.

The oldest extant building in town – **St Peter's Anglican Church** – built in 1785 and enlarged in 1842, lies four blocks west along Duke St. The graveyard tombstones are spookily sun-bleached like bones.

Charles Swaby's Swamp Safari

This crocodile breeding farm, nature reserve, and family park (☎ 954-3065, fax 965-2086; admission US$10; open 9am-5pm Mon-Fri) is a mile west of Falmouth. Crocs bask in the sun, eyeing you leeringly from behind wire fences. Other animals include mongooses and snakes, and there's a bird sanctuary and a kids' petting zoo. The scene in the movie *Live and Let Die* in which James Bond ran across the backs of crocodiles was filmed here. Tours are offered on the hour till 4pm.

You can take a short boat tour of the mangrove swamp behind the village. With luck you might even get to see Mr Swaby himself wrestling crocodiles, which through the years he has learned to manhandle and hog-tie with ease.

Windsurfing

Brian's Windsurfing (☎ 818-3952; ⓦ www .brianswindsurfing.com), based in Oregon, has its winter headquarters at Bounty Bay, a private beach outside Falmouth. A three-hour surf lesson costs US$60, and more advanced lessons are US$60-70; all are offered daily. Brian offers vacation packages with stays in a five-bedroom villa.

Places to Stay & Eat

Greenside Villa (☎ 954-3127; PO Box 119, Falmouth; studios with refrigerator/ kitchenette US$25/28, plus US$5 each additional person), 2 miles west of Falmouth, has studio apartments. The rooms are simple but spacious and clean and have private bath and ceiling fans. The units with kitchenettes have small gas stoves. Meals are cooked on request.

Falmouth Resort (☎ 954-3391; 22 Newton St; rooms US$40) is the only place in town. It has 12 modest rooms with private bath and hot water, and a popular restaurant.

Golden Pagoda (☎ 617-5486; 24 Duke St; open 11am-10pm) serves inexpensive Chinese, as does **A&A Exquisite Restaurant** (☎ 617-2590; Tharpe St; open 7am-7pm Mon-Thur, 7am-4pm Fri).

You can buy fresh baked breads, pastries, and spicy meat and vegetable patties at **Spicy Nice Bakery** (☎ 954-3197; Water Square).

Also see Glistening Waters later in this chapter.

MARTHA BRAE

This small village, 2 miles due south of Falmouth, sits astride the Martha Brae River, which rises at Windsor Caves in the Cockpit Country and spills into Glistening Waters, east of Falmouth.

From Martha Brae, a well-maintained road winds through the river gorge to Sherwood. Another, rougher road, leads southwest to Good Hope Estate and then links with a rough road that leads west from

Sherwood to the Queen of Spains Valley (see both sections, later in this chapter).

Buses regularly run to Martha Brae from Falmouth.

Rafting

The rafting trip down a 3-mile stretch of the Martha Brae River is exhilarating. The journey takes 90 minutes on long bamboo rafts poled by a skilled guide. The upper reaches tumble at a good pace before slowing farther downriver, where you stop at 'Tarzan's Corner' for a swing and swim in a calm pool. At the end, you'll be driven back to your car.

Trips begin from Rafters Village, about a mile south of Martha Brae. There you'll find a picnic area, bar, restaurant, swimming pool, bathrooms, changing rooms, and a secure parking lot.

A raft trip costs US$45 per raft (one or two people). Contact **River Raft Ltd** (☎ 952-0889, 940-6398, fax 979-7437; ☻ info@jamaicarafting.com; Chatwick Plaza, PO Box 1178, Montego Bay). Remember to tip your raft guide.

GLISTENING WATERS

At night Glistening Waters (also called Luminous Lagoon), a large bay at Rock, about a mile east of Falmouth, boasts a singular charm – it glows an eerie green when disturbed. The glow is due to the presence of microorganisms that produce photochemical reactions when disturbed. The concentrations are so thick that fish swimming by look like green lanterns.

Boat trips are offered from **Glistening Waters Marina** (☎ 954-3229, 888-991-9901, fax 954-4529; per person US$12) and **Time 'n Place** (US$20, including a beach bonfire and rum punch); see Places to Stay later.

Bear Cay & World Beach

A spit called Bear Cay hooks around the north side of the bay. World Beach, the lonesome white-sand beach on the north side, is good for snorkeling and sunbathing, and is popular with locals on weekends. You can access it at Time 'n Place (see Places to Stay later), or you can rent a boat at Glis-

tening Waters Marina and Fisherman's Inn; picnic meals are available.

Sport Fishing & Boating

The river mouth in Glistening Waters is one of the few places in Jamaica that still offers good fishing for tarpon, known as the 'silver bullet' for its feisty defense on a line. No license is required.

Glistening Waters Marina hires out sport-fishing boats. Also at the marina, the MV *Baltimore Patriot* III hosts sunset cruises (US$35) and dinner and party cruises (US$55).

At last visit, Time 'n Place (see below) was planning to offer boat rides.

Places to Stay

Time 'n Place (☎/fax 954-4371; ☻ timen place@cwjamaica.com; PO Box 93, Falmouth; cottages without/with air-con US$65/75), at the east end of Bear Cay, is for anyone seeking offbeat seclusion. Its delightful owner, Tony, has three quaint all-hardwood cottages (each housing up to three people) for rent right on deserted World Beach. The cottages have louvered windows, hot water, radios, and eclectic furniture. Four more rooms of bamboo and thatch were planned at last visit. The rustic beach bar and restaurant – popular for fashion shoots – is a great place to hang out. It was a setting in the movie *How Stella Got Her Groove Back*.

Fisherman's Inn (☎ 954-3427, fax 954-3078; singles/doubles US$75/100) is a nice hotel at Rock Wharf, 2 miles east of Falmouth. The 12 gleaming air-con rooms are spacious and pleasingly furnished, with big bathrooms and private patios. There's a pool and two restaurants (one outside). It's not really worth the rate asked, however, and the location has no great appeal.

Starfish Trelawny Beach & Fun Resort (☎ 954-2450, fax 954-2149; ☎ 800-659-5436 in North America; ☻ www.starfishresorts.com; PO Box 54, Falmouth; per person summer/winter US$175/220, children US$35), formerly Trelawny Beach Hotel, 4 miles east of town, is a twin-tower high-rise complex with 350 nicely decorated rooms, including 40 ground-level 'cottage rooms.' This attractive, budget all-inclusive resort, run by Super-Clubs, caters to singles, couples, and families, upon which it is heavily focused. Facilities include five restaurants, tennis courts, ice-skating rink, gym, rock-climbing wall, circus workshop, and a full range of water sports, including a dive operator. Kids' facilities include a castle with a moat for a pool.

FDR Pebbles (☎ 617-2500, 800-654-1337, fax 617-2512; ☎ 800-337-5437, fax 516-223-4815 in North America; ☎ 020-8795-1718, fax 8795-1728 in the UK; ℮ pebblesinfo@ fdrholidays.com; PO Box 1933, Falmouth; ocean-view rooms US$262-380, oceanfront US$252-350), at Glistening Waters, is a recently opened, all-inclusive family resort. The handsome property features all-cedarwood, two-story units with 96 junior suites with TV, telephone, minirefrigerator, and balcony. Facilities include an exquisite pool, full water sports, cyber café, fitness center, tennis, disco, and a panoply of facilities and activities for children. An on-staff nanny looks after the kiddies.

Places to Eat

Time 'n Place (see Places to Stay above) resembles a set from the Robin Williams movie *Popeye,* and indeed has been featured in movies and fashion shoots. The bamboo beachside hut has tables on the sand. There are swings and hammocks at the bar. Take your pick from burgers with fries (US$5) to an array of Jamaican dishes that includes coconut shrimp (US$12) and grilled garlic lobster (US$15.50). Thursday night is a music jam.

Fisherman's Inn (see Places to Stay above; entrees from US$10; open 7am-10pm) offers stylish dining indoors or on the terrace overlooking Glistening Waters. The menu ranges from salads, seafood, and steaks to Creole specialties such as brown stew.

Glistening Waters Marina Restaurant & Lounge (☎ 954-3229; open 8am-11pm) is a clean, modern place that offers Jamaican and continental fare, from onion rings (US$3.50) and steamed fish (US$10) to lobster (US$24) and pepper steak (US$11). It has killer cocktails in a tall sundae glass.

Country Club Restaurant, opposite the Starfish Trelawny Beach & Fun Resort, is most notable for its music nightly, which draws the local crowd. It serves seafood and the usual Jamaica fare (US$3-10).

Shopping

Bamboo Village, 200 yards west of the Starfish Trelawny Beach & Fun Resort, is an arts and crafts market.

Reggae to Wear (☎ 954-3552; Hague Industrial Estate; open 7am-5pm Mon-Thur, 7am-2:30pm Fri), at Hague, signed on the highway a mile inland from the A1, has a factory outlet selling hand-painted batik resort wear.

DUNCANS

This small town, on a hillside 7 miles east of Falmouth, is centered on an old stone clock tower in the middle of a three-way junction.

Kettering Baptist Church, built in 1893, commemorates William Knibb, a Baptist missionary and a leading abolitionist who founded an emancipation village for freed slaves here in 1840.

Three miles east of Duncans you'll pass a cleft in the roadside cliff face that opens into **Arawak Cave,** which has fruit bats, intriguing stalagmites and stalactites, and Arawak petroglyphs.

Silver Sands Villa Resort (☎ 954-2001, 888-745-7245, fax 954-2306; ⓦ www.silversands -jamaica.com; PO Box 1; one-bedroom cottage summer/winter from US$120/180, five-bedroom villa US$450/650), a mile west of Duncans, has more than 40 upscale one- to five-bedroom villas and cottages spread over 224 acres. The enclosed estate backs a private 1000-foot-long white-sand beach. Each unique villa is privately owned, individually decorated, and has a cook, housekeeper, and gardener. Most have TVs and their own pools. Weekly rates offer savings and include airport transfers. Facilities include a disco and bar-grill.

RIO BUENO

Rio Bueno is a tumbledown fishing village where fishermen still tend their nets and their lobster pots in front of ramshackle

Georgian cut-stone buildings. These are featured in the 1964 movie *A High Wind in Jamaica,* which was filmed here.

The town, 32 miles east of Montego Bay, is set on the west side of a deep, narrow bay that may be the site where Columbus first set foot in Jamaica on May 4, 1494, after anchoring his caravels, *Nina, San Juan,* and *Cardera.*

Sites of interest include the 18th-century ruins of **Fort Dundas**, an **Anglican church** dating to 1833, and a **Baptist church** erected in 1901 to replace another destroyed in antimissionary riots of the abolitionist era.

The stretch of coastal road from here to Discovery Bay (3 miles; see the Ocho Rios & North Coast chapter) is known as the Queen's Hwy.

Places to Stay

Hotel Rio Bueno (☎ 954-0046, fax 952-5911; e joejames@in-site.com; Main St; singles US$95, doubles US$100, suites US$225) has been converted from an old Georgian wharfside warehouse and has a pleasant decor and unique ambience. The hotel is a museum of Joe James's artwork (and includes a gallery of his naïve paintings and carvings). It has 20 rooms, most with French doors opening onto balconies that overlook the bay. The huge, atmospheric suite with hardwood floors, open-plan walls, and lots of light is recommended. Rates are rather hefty but include breakfast and tax.

Grand Lido Braco Village Resort (☎ 925-0925, fax 925-0334; ☎ 800-467-8737 in North America; ☎ 01749-677200 in the UK; w www .superclubs.com; all rates per person: gardenview US$375-420, ocean-view US$410-450, beachfront US$425-470, suites US$445-745), 2 miles west of Rio Bueno, is an all-inclusive, adults-only resort. It is designed as a time-warp village with a cobbled square and Georgian buildings of cut stone, red brick, and timber in Jamaican vernacular style, and populated with artisans, pushcart vendors, and country higglers dressed in period costume. It has 170 rooms and 52 suites in a medley of four plantation styles; decor is a tad insipid, but each has satellite TV, CD

player, in-room safe, and extras. It features a spectacular, jigsaw-piece–shape Olympic-size pool, a 2000-foot-long beach, a gym, spa, beauty shop, choice of restaurants and bars, plus water sports and even a soccer field. A nude section draws 'lifestyle' (swinger) groups.

Places to Eat

Lobster Bowl Restaurant (☎ 954-0046; Main St; open 7am-midnight Mon-Sat, from 9:30am Sun), in the Hotel Rio Bueno, serves seafood dishes (from US$15) and an Old Time Jamaican Sunday breakfast. The property also includes **Joe's Bar**, with tons of character, and hosts a 'Day of Jazz' on the first Sunday of each month.

Rio Brac Rest Stop (☎ 954-0269; Queens Hwy; open from 7am) is an upscale roadside restaurant about 400 yards east of Grand Lido Braco Village Resort. At the resort (see Places to Stay above), a day pass (10am to 6pm; US$75) or night pass (6pm to 2am; US$90) buys all you can eat plus access to all facilities, including entertainment and five restaurants.

Montego Bay to Tryall Estate

West from Montego Bay the A1 follows the coast, offering little in the way of nice beaches or attractions. Five miles west of town, the road crosses the mouth of the Great River, then sweeps past Round Hill Hotel & Villa and, farther along the A1, Tryall Estate and the world championship Tryall Golf Course.

READING

Reading, 4 miles west of Montego Bay, is a small hamlet at the junction of the A1 and B8, which leads south to Westmoreland and St Elizabeth parishes. Reading faces onto Bogue Lagoon. At the east end of Reading is the Desnoes & Geddes brewery where Red Stripe beer is brewed.

The **Great River**, at Unity Hall, 3 miles west of Reading, is popular for scenic bamboo raft trips (see Lethe later in this chapter).

Buses (US$0.10) and coasters and robots (US$0.20) ply between Montego Bay and Negril and Anchovy. A private taxi should cost US$14.

Scuba Diving & Fishing

Reading Reef just offshore from town offers good scuba diving. Spanish Anchor is known for its anchors, caverns, tunnels, and coral heads, where eagle rays hang out. Nearby, Garden of Eels is named for a species of conger eel that inhabits the seabed, but there's superb wall diving, too. For dive operators, see Scuba Diving under Montego Bay earlier in this chapter.

Charles Swaby (☎ 954-3065) offers fishing for tarpon and snook in the mouth of the Great River.

Places to Stay & Eat

Sahara de la Mer Resort (☎ 952-2366, fax 979-0847; ☎ 323-292-0731, fax 323-292-4803 in the USA; ℮ jamaica@saharahotels.com; PO Box 223, Reading; single summer/winter US$70/95, double US$85/115, suite US$130/140) is a modest two-story hotel 2 miles west of Reading. There are 24 spacious rooms with ho-hum furnishings, air-con and ceiling fans, hot water, satellite TV, telephone, and oodles of light. French doors open to a wide terrace; the suite has its own spacious balcony. There's also a beauty shop, restaurant, and Jacuzzi, and a swimming pool has been cut into the coral reef.

Reading Reef Club Hotel (☎ 952-5909, fax 952-7217; ☎ 402-398-3217, 800-315-0379 in the USA; ℮ rrc@n5.com.jm; PO Box 225, Reading; superior summer/winter US$85/115, deluxe US$110-125/135-150, suites US$220-270/265-325) is an upscale property tucked on its own small private beach. The recently renovated, intimate hotel has 37 elegant oceanfront rooms and two- and three-bedroom suites (some with king-size beds). All have verandas and louvered windows, air-con, fans, and telephone. There's a breezy terrace bar, a pool, a spa, and water sports.

Drambuie Estate (☎ 382-6384; ℮ drambuie@barrettadventures.com; Lion Hill; cottage nightly summer/winter US$150/170,

entire villa weekly US$5000/6000) is the former estate of Winston Churchill, and many mighty personages have passed through its doors. It is now a bed and breakfast in the hills overlooking Bogue Lagoon. It has three exquisitely albeit modestly decorated Cottage Suites with satellite TVs, plus a phenomenal Master Suite (available only when the entire villa is rented) with king-size antique four-poster bed and a marble bathtub with mirrored ceiling. Rates include breakfast.

Silent Waters (☎ 971-9119, fax 971-7568; 847-304-4700 in the USA; ⓦ www.jamaicavillas.net; 22 East Dundee Rd, Suite 21, Barrington, IL 60010, USA; suites weekly summer/winter $10,000/14,000, entire villa weekly US$14,000/18,000), a sumptuous, Thai-style villa complex in the hills at Unity Hall, near Great River, is for the insanely wealthy. Five suites, some with king-size beds, have marble flooring, Balinese furniture, oriental rugs, satellite TVs, air-con, ceiling fans, outdoor and indoor showers, and bathtubs with views over lavish grounds with fish ponds. There's a magnificent pool, and meals (not included in room rates) are served at a vast granite dining table.

Highland House (weekly summer/winter US$4900/7000), the former six-bedroom villa of Oscar Hammerstein, is rented out by Villas by Linda Smith (☎ 301-229-4300, fax 320-6963; ℮ linda@jamaicavillas.com; 8029 Riverside Drive, Cabin John, MD 20818, USA).

HOPEWELL

This small wayside village 5 miles west of Reading has a bustling daily market; on Saturday, the streets are cacophonous with the sounds of higglers from the hills.

Round Hill Hotel & Villas (☎ 956-7050, 800-972-2159, fax 956-7505; ℮ roundhill@cwjamaica.com; PO Box 64, Montego Bay; superior summer/winter US$260/420, deluxe US$310/510, suite US$370-550/600-850, villas weekly US$3500/7000) is a 98-acre resort, a mile east of Hopewell, with a roster of guests that says it all: from John F. Kennedy to Paul McCartney, plus a smattering of Hapsburgs and Borgheses. It's been said that this is where the haughty come to be naughty (owner John Pringle claims Kennedy made love to 'all my maids'). Pineapple House has 36 rooms exquisitely decorated with antique furniture and mahogany beds. The 28 privately owned two-, three-, and four-bedroom villas are furnished to their owner's tastes – Ralph Lauren owns one (he helped redecorate the resort's public areas). Many have private pools. Facilities include a gym, tennis courts, water sports (including scuba diving that's open to the public), a beauty salon, and a wellness center, which offers all manner of therapies, including reflexology at the hands of Professor Efrain Bernal, a Cuban-born whiz. Live jazz is offered thrice weekly. It has a family program.

Also at Round Hill, **Georgian Dining Pavilion & Almond Tree Terrace** (lunch from US$12; dinner from US$25) serves continental and Jamaican dishes. Dining on the terrace is a romantic indulgence, and worth the splurge for the setting. Afternoon tea is a bargain at US$3. Nonguests should call ahead.

Sports Club Restaurant & Bar, beside the entrance to Round Hill, offers Jamaican fare (US$3-6) served in modestly elegant surroundings.

TRYALL ESTATE

The **Tryall Water Wheel**, 3 miles west of Hopewell, stands amid the ruins of the old Tryall sugar plantation. Much of the estate, including the huge wheel (beside the A1) that drove the cane-crushing mill, was destroyed in the slave rebellion of Christmas 1831 (see the boxed text 'Preaching Resistance' earlier in this chapter). Restored to working condition in the late 1950s, the wheel is still turned by water carried by a 2-mile-long aqueduct from the Flint River.

The hilltop great house is today the hub of one of Jamaica's most exclusive resort properties: the Tryall Club (see Places to Stay & Eat later), built atop the remains of a small fort that is still guarded by cannons. The great house and 2200-acre resort complex are closed to nonguests.

Golf

The championship, 6920-yard, par-71 **Tryall Golf Course** (☎ 956-5681) is one of the world's finest courses. Green fees for guests cost US$40 in summer, US$80 in winter (nonguests pay US$150 year-round). Caddies cost US$15; cart rental costs US$27.

The course hosts the annual Johnny Walker World Championship, boasting the biggest purse in world golf. About 15,000 spectators gather daily in mid-December to watch the world's leading players compete for the coveted title.

Places to Stay & Eat

Tryall Club (☎ 956-5660, 800-238-5290, fax 956-5673; ☎ 800-336-4571 in North America; PO Box 1206, Montego Bay; ☑ reservations@tryallclub.com; 1-bedroom suites US$250-650, 2-bedroom suites US$300-975, 2-bedroom Estate Villas US$430-1115, 7-bedroom Estate Villas US$850-2190) is magnificently situated amid 2200 acres of lush hillside greenery. At its heart is the old hilltop great house with a bar and lounge where you can savor a traditional English afternoon tea while enjoying the views. Thirteen Great House Villa Suites are each fully staffed and include kitchen, living room, dining room, and oversized marble bathroom. A new wing includes 52 gracious, air-con Junior Suites. More than 55 privately owned, sumptuous one- to seven-bedroom Estate Villas are scattered throughout the estate. Each is uniquely decorated by individual owners and staffed with a cook, housekeeper, and gardener. There's a large pool, gourmet restaurant and bar, tennis, water sports, and golf. Rates depend on season.

BLUE HOLE ESTATE

This former great house is set amid pastures west of Sandy Bay, a hamlet immediately west of Tryall Estate. It was once the home of William DeLisser, former custos of Hanover parish. It is now the base for **Chukka Blue Adventures** (☎ 979-6599, fax 952-8302; ☑ info@chukkablue.com), which offers 2½-hour horseback rides, river tubing, and six-hour jeep safari tours.

Lollypop on the Beach (☎ 389-2911; rooms US$40), at Sandy Bay, has two small, basic but clean air-con rooms with cold water. They're overpriced and are directly above the stage and dance area, but there's no denying the place has offbeat atmosphere!

Lollypop is popular with locals for its mouth-searing jerk pork and chicken, and steam fish (US$7). It gets packed on weekends, when sound-systems are hosted.

Inland: South of Montego Bay

The hill country inland of MoBay offers working plantations, great houses, eco-resorts, and a village of poor white farmers that is one of Jamaica's strangest anomalies. Most points of interest are reached either via the B8, which winds south from Reading and crosses a broad upland plateau before dropping onto the plains of Westmoreland, or the B6, which leads southeast from Montpelier (6 miles south of Reading).

The southeast quarter of St James parish culminates in the wild Cockpit Country.

LETHE

This small village is the starting point for raft trips on the Great River. The turnoff for Lethe is 2 miles south of Reading off the B8; signs show the way. The graceful stone bridge spanning the Great River was built in 1828. The overgrown remains of an old sugar mill stand on the riverbank.

Driving west to Lethe, about 2 miles from the B8, you'll arrive at a Y-junction. The fork to the left leads to Lethe; that to the right leads to **Nature Village Farm** (☎ 912-0172; Eden, Lethe PO), a farm-turned-family-resort that offers fishing and other attractions.

Animal Farm

A perfect spot for the kids, Animal Farm (☎ 815-4104, fax 979-8466; e animalfarm@ lycos.com; PO Box 34, Reading; admission adult/child US$5/2.50; open 9am-5pm), at Copse, 2 miles west of Lethe, is dedicated to aviculture, with hundreds of birds. It also has a petting zoo, donkey rides, a playground, hiking, and birding. Guided tours are offered Wednesday to Sunday.

Rhea's World/Lethe Estate

Rhea's World (☎ 956-4920, fax 956-4927; e lethe@cwjamaica.com; c/o Great River Rafting & Plantation Tour Ltd, PO Box 23, Montego Bay), on the west bank of the river on the north side of Lethe, has a water garden and mini-botanical gardens where anthuriums are grown for export. Alas, they're not particularly appealing. A jitney tour leads into the adjacent banana plantation. Kids can take a donkey ride while adults laze in a hammock with a rum cocktail or coconut water. It's part of Lethe Estate, owned by Francis Tulloch, Minister of Tourism, and is the headquarters for Mountain Valley Rafting. A restaurant provides hot lunches for US$10.

More adventurous souls seeking an authentic bush experience can hire a guide (US$10) and hike into the hills.

Rafting

Mountain Valley Rafting (☎ 952-0527; 31 Gloucester Ave, Montego Bay; also see Rhea's World above) offers tranquil two-hour river trips from Lethe. You're punted 9 miles downstream to the mouth of the river aboard long, narrow bamboo rafts poled by an expert raftsman. Trips cost US$45 for two passengers (children under 12 are half-price), including lunch and transfers, or US$30 for the raft trip alone.

ROCKLANDS BIRD FEEDING STATION

Rocklands (☎ 952-2009; admission US$9; open 9am-5pm) is a favorite of birders, who have flocked here since 1958 when it was founded by Lisa Salmon, who tamed and trained over 20 bird species to come and feed from your hand (over 140 birds have been recorded here). A variety of birds show up reliably at 3:15pm: ground doves, orange quits, saffron finches, and hummingbirds, including the 'doctorbird.' Miss Salmon died in 2000, but her replacement, Fritz Beckford, is also an expert on birds.

Fritz, or another attendant, will pour birdseed into your hand or provide you with a sugar-water feeder with which to tempt birds. Guests sit in awe as hummingbirds streak in to hover like miniature helicopters before finally perching on their outstretched fingers.

The turnoff from the B8 is 200 yards south of the signed turnoff for Lethe. You can also take a bus from Montego Bay for Savanna-la-Mar or Black River.

MONTPELIER

Passing through Anchovy, you drop south into a broad valley planted in citrus, but formerly an important sugar estate. The great house of the old Montpelier sugar plantation burned down a few years back, but **St Mary's Anglican Church** still stands on a knoll overlooking the remains of the sugar factory.

The B8 splits at a gas station, a stone's throw south of the church. The main road continues southwest. The road to the southeast (the B6) leads toward Seaford Town.

Montpelier Blue Hole Nature Park

This 800-acre 'eco-park,' (☎ 909-9002; PO Box 26, Cambridge, St James; adult/child US$3/1; open 8:30am-5pm) is 3 miles south of Anchovy. A guided plantation tour is offered, as are horseback rides (US$10 per hour), through the groves of interspersed pineapple and citrus. There are botanical gardens and picnic groves, plus a 60-foot-wide circular swimming pool with cascades. A bird sanctuary includes peacocks.

The park owners permit camping (bring your own tent; US$7) and have toilets and cooking facilities.

Look for the signed turnoff 400 yards north of the gas station at Montpelier. You'll see St Mary's Church ahead; keep to the right and follow the potholed road steeply uphill for 2 miles.

About 400 yards beyond the park entrance is the Blue Hole – a jade-colored sinkhole measuring 164 feet deep. It's been tapped by the Water Commission, so iron fences have spoiled the setting. No swimming!

CAMBRIDGE

From Montpelier, the B6 follows the Great River Valley 5 miles to this little crossroads town centered on a railroad station in disuse. Cambridge (population 3000) is the center of a banana- and coffee-producing area. It has a bank and gas station.

Lou Lou's, half a mile south of Cambridge at Mount Faith, just beyond the crest of a hill, is a gaily painted little crafts shop and restaurant. Don't fail to stop! Lou Lou is a jovial, charismatic figure (and obeah practitioner) who cooks up fried chicken and fish, mutton, and pepperpot soup (US$2-6). You can also buy fresh coconuts to slake your thirst (US$0.70). 'We no rush people here. Leave de visitors to dem mind.' Her grandson, Fitzroy 'Tony' Dove, offers guiding locally.

CATADUPA

Twenty years ago, locals had a thriving trade selling crafts and making clothing to order for train passengers en route to the Appleton Rum Estate (you were measured for skirts or shirts en route to Appleton, and they were finished and ready for pick up on the way back). Today Catadupa, 2 miles east of the B6 from the hamlet of Marchmont, is a collection of aging buildings around the disused railroad station. Locals eke out a living growing coffee and bananas. The village is named for nearby cascades and reflects the Greek name for the Nile cataracts in Egypt.

Plans to privatize and restore the railway looked promising at last visit, hopefully giving Catadupa a second wind.

Croydon in the Mountains Plantation

This working plantation (☎ 979-8267; fax 979-8251; ☎ tlhenry20@hotmail.com), reached via a side road from Catadupa (1 mile), has 132 acres of hillside terraces planted in coffee, citrus, and pineapples. Honey is produced here; a hive under glass allows you to see what's buzzing in the bees' world. A 'see, hear, touch, and taste' tour is offered from 10:30am to 3pm Tuesday, Wednesday, and Friday; the fee is US$45, including lunch and transfers. Advance reservations are required.

Caribic Vacations (☎ 979-6073, 953-2584, fax 953-9897; 69 Gloucester Ave) offers a tour from Montego Bay.

HILTON

Overgrown with thumbergia, this beautiful hilltop plantation home (☎ 952-3343; e normads@n5.com.jm; PO Box 162, Reading, St James), at St Leonards 2 miles southwest of Marchmont, is the venue for the all-day 'Hilton High Day Tour,' which begins with a Jamaican breakfast in the house, where antiques abound. You then take a guided walk to Seaford Town (1 mile) and the village of St Leonards. The walk should create an appetite for a roast-suckling-pig luncheon prepared in a brick oven back at Hilton. The meal also features a choice of homemade lemonade, shandy (half lemonade, half beer), or rum punch. For the rest of the afternoon, you're free to relax or roam the 100-acre plantation on horseback (US$10 for 30 minutes).

Tours are offered on Tuesday, Wednesday, Friday, and Sunday (US$55 for call-in visitors; US$64 including transfers from Montego Bay).

SEAFORD TOWN

This sprawling hillside village of scattered tumbledown cottages has a singular history. It was settled between 1834 and 1838, when more than 1200 Germans arrived in Jamaica; an initial group of 251 settled Seaford. The land was donated by Lord Seaford (the Germans were promised that they would receive title after five years' labor; they toiled for 15 before the land became theirs). The initial community was a mix of Protestants and Catholics, but most were converted to Catholicism by Father Tauer, an energetic Austrian priest who settled here in the 1870s.

The farmland turned out to be a tangled wilderness. Few settlers were farmers; most were tradespeople or former soldiers. Fortunately, the immigrants received free rations for the first 18 months, but even before the rations ran out, the Germans had settled into a life of poverty. Tropical diseases and social isolation soon reduced the population, and only a fraction of the original settlers stayed.

Today, less than 200 Seaford inhabitants claim German ancestry, and white people are only 20% of Seaford's population. Still, despite 150 years, there are relatively few mulattos in evidence. Socially, Seaford remains segregated in key ways. Seaford's white residents remain practicing Catholics and still practice a few folk customs.

There's a gas station in the village.

The red, zinc-roofed, old stone **Church of the Sacred Heart** sits atop a rise overlooking Seaford. Its precursor was built by Father Tauer in the late 19th century but was totally demolished in the hurricane of 1912. Take time to browse the graveyard.

In front of the church is the tiny, somewhat dilapidated **Seaford Town Historical Mini-Museum** (☎ 995-9399; admission US$1), which tells the fascinating tale of Seaford's German origins. There are maps and photographs of the early settlement, plus artifacts spanning 150 years, including such curiosities as cricket bats made from the stems of coconut leaves.

The town priest, Friar Bobby Gilmore, keeps the key to the museum; he lives in the green-and-white house just opposite the museum. However, you should first seek out the caretaker, Spencer Gardner, who lives 100 yards beyond the museum.

BELVEDERE ESTATE

This estate (☎ 694-1004, fax 957-4097; PO Box 361, Montego Bay; admission US$15, with lunch US$30; open 10am-4pm Mon-Sat) is a family-owned working plantation raising cattle and tropical fruits.

The estate offers a fascinating perspective on modern estate life and a touristy re-creation of how things were centuries ago. You're welcomed by guides in Jamaican bandanna prints offering sugarloaf and pineapple and orange samplers, while a farmhand coaxes a donkey in circles to demonstrate the workings of an old sugar press. If you've arrived under your own steam, a guide accompanies you as you drive through groves of citrus and coconut palms and fields of Scotch bonnet peppers. There's also a botanical gardens and Post-Emancipation Village, featuring huts where a basket-weaver, baker, blacksmith, and coffee and cocoa grinder demonstrate traditional skills.

Trails lead to the Great River, which has a waterfall and pool.

The old great house (destroyed in the 1831 slave rebellion) still awaited restoration at last visit.

Belvedere is at Chester Castle, 3 miles southwest of Montpelier (take the B7, which splits from the B8). Belvedere is served from MoBay by coaster. Tour operators in Montego Bay offer excursions.

KNOCKALVA & AROUND

Following the B8 southwest from Montpelier leads to Knockalva, the center of an agricultural training farm and cattle breeding center.

The hills south of Knockalva are festooned with groves of bamboo. Five miles south of Knockalva you pass through the village of Whithorn. As you round a bend immediately beyond it, the sugarcane plains of Westmoreland are suddenly laid out below.

Moun Tambrin Retreat (☎ 918-4486, fax 918-4487; e jamountambrin@cwjamaica .com; PO Box 210, Savanna-la-Mar; per person US$130, 3-night minimum), at Darliston about 6 miles east of Whithorn, is an incredible mountain retreat where American artist Rus Gruhlke has created a fabulous garden and artists' retreat. Sculptures abound. It has six modestly furnished rooms (four with shared bath), plus a library-lounge. The property grants fabulous views over the southwest coast. Meals are served family-style. Rates include breakfast; a meal plan (US$189 nightly) is offered.

QUEEN OF SPAINS VALLEY

About 2 miles south of Montego Bay, the Montego River twists through a narrow, thickly wooded gorge that deposits you at **Adelphi**, 13 miles east of Montego Bay, at the head of the Queen of Spains Valley. The valley is as flat and green as a billiard table, with sugarcane rippling as far as the eye can see.

The valley runs east as far as Good Hope Estate. See Cockpit Country (North) later in this chapter.

A bus travels through the Queen of Spains Valley via Hampden from Montego Bay (US$0.20).

Hampden Estate

Hampden (☎ 912-9114, 954-6394; adult/child US$12/8; open by appointment 9am-4pm Mon-Fri), at Dumfries 3 miles east of Adelphi, is a working plantation with a rum distillery, sugar factory, and great house, one of the most impressive and beautiful buildings in Jamaica. The plantation house – a Teutonic structure with dark timbers and mansard roof – dates back to 1799 and is enclosed within dry-stone walls. The factory – built by Krupps, of Germany – processes 160,000 tons of sugar per year, and operates 24 hours a day, seven days a week, between January and July. It closes for renovations in the summer. The distillery operates February through October.

The factory is open for guided tours in sugar season only; admission includes a tasting tipple, but be warned that the overproof rum, called 'jancro batty,' is strong enough to burn a hole through armor plating. Ask for John Terry, the charming English manager.

If coming from Adelphi, turn left at the junction with an old steam engine sitting in a triangle. There are no signs. The smell of molasses and 'dunder' (the liquid waste from sugar-making) will guide you through the cane fields.

MONTEGO BAY TO MAROON TOWN

Few travelers venture into the hills southeast of Montego Bay, accessed by Fairfield Rd,

1½ miles south of town. The potholed road ascends to the western flanks of Cockpit Country.

The hamlet of **Kensington**, 13 miles southeast of Montego Bay, is famous as the site where, in 1831, slaves set fire to the ridge-top plantation and initiated the devastating 'Christmas Rebellion' (see the boxed text 'Preaching Resistance' earlier in this chapter). A roadside plaque commemorates the event.

Maroon Town, 3 miles southeast of Kensington, lies on the edge of the rugged Cockpit Country. Guides will tout themselves to lead you to nearby caves and supposed battle sites from the Maroon Wars, but there's little to see.

Organized Tours
Safari Tours Jamaica (☎/fax 972-2639; e Safari@cwjamaica.com; Arawak PO, Mammee Bay) offers daylong 'jeep safaris' into the Orange Valley.

Johns Hall Plantation (☎ 952-6944, e relax.resort@cwjamaica.com; 26 Hobbs Ave, White Sands Beach PO, Montego Bay; tour US$40; open 11am-2pm Mon, Wed & Sat), at Johns Hall about 6 miles southeast of Montego Bay, is open for the 'town and country tour' from Montego Bay.

Places to Stay & Eat
Orange River Ranch (☎ 919-1017; e WhitterGroup@mail.infochan.com; Johns Hall PO, Montego Bay; camping per tent US$5, dorm beds US$10, singles or doubles US$55, singles/doubles with breakfast US$64/70, with dinner US$84/106) is a gracious old plantation house, in the hills a mile north of Williamsfield (near Johns Hall), with views down a valley awash with bamboo. It focuses on holistic vacations. The lodge allows camping, has modest dormitory accommodations, and offers 24 simple, appealingly furnished rooms with half-poster beds, telephones, fans, and patios. A guided walking tour of the banana plantation is available, as is horseback riding (US$20 per hour), and there's a swimming pool and Jacuzzi. A beach shuttle runs twice

daily. The folks at the ranch host a family brunch each Sunday.

Cockpit Country (North)

Jamaica's most rugged quarter is a 500-sq-mile limestone plateau taking up the whole of southwest Trelawny, inland of Falmouth. The area of eroded limestone features is studded with thousands of conical hummocks divided by precipitous ravines.

The daunting region is overgrown with luxuriant greenery. Most remains unexplored and uninhabited. No roads penetrate the region (although a rough dirt road cuts across the eastern edge between Clark's Town and Albert Town) and only a few tracks make even half-hearted forays into its interior. The most dramatic way to see it is from above by plane or helicopter, from which you gain a sense of the Cockpits' scale and beauty.

Covered in dense vegetation, the reclusive region proved a perfect hideout for the Maroons, who through their ferocity maintained an uneasy sovereignty from the English colonialists. The southern section is known as 'District of Look Behind,' an allusion to the Maroon practice of ambushing English soldiers. Much of the vegetation around the perimeter has been cleared in recent years by charcoal burners. And a few valley bottoms are cultivated by small-hold farmers who grow bananas, yams, corn, manioc, and ganja. It's unwise for foreigners to explore here unless accompanied by someone known in the area. You could easily get lost or worse – if you stumble upon a major ganja plot, you're likely to be considered a DEA (Drug Enforcement Agency) agent, and the consequences could be serious (in 1994, a foreign journalist was murdered after such a transgression).

The area – a vital watershed and home to several endangered species – has been earmarked for national park status (it is currently a National Reserve).

The southern portion of Cockpit Country lies in St Elizabeth parish and is accessed from the south by side roads from the B6. See Nassau Mountains & Cockpit Country (South) in the South Coast & Central Highlands chapter.

Information

For information, contact **Southern Trelawny Environmental Agency** (☎ 610-0818, fax 954-4087; e stea@cwjamaica.com; 3 Grants Office Complex, Albert Town).

You'll find another good resource is the **Windsor Research Center** (☎ 997-3832; W www.cockpitcountry.com; Sherwood Content PO, Trelawny), at Windsor Great House (see Windsor later in this chapter).

Flora & Fauna

Most of the Cockpits are still clad in primary vegetation that in places includes rare cacti and other endemic species known only in that specific locale. Northern slopes typically are lusher. The hilltops are relatively sparsely vegetated due to soil erosion. The Cockpits themselves are generally covered in tall scrub, including brambles and scratchbush.

Most of Jamaica's 27 endemic bird species are found in the Cockpits, including black- and yellow-billed parrots, todies, and the endangered golden swallow. The Jamaican boa and giant swallowtail butterfly are among other rare species, which include 37 of Jamaica's 62 species of amphibians and reptiles.

Hiking

A few hunter's tracks lead into and even across the Cockpit Country. Most are faint tracks, often overgrown. Hiking away from these trails can be dangerous going. The rocks are razor-sharp, and sinkholes are everywhere, often covered by decayed vegetation and ready to crumble underfoot. Never travel alone. There is no one to hear your pleas for help should you break a leg or fall into a sinkhole. Take lots of water. There is no water to be had locally.

You'll need a machete and stout walking shoes plus rain gear and a powerful flashlight in the event of a delay past sunset. Take warm clothing if you plan on overnighting, as nights can get cold.

The easiest trail across the Cockpits connects Windsor (in the north) with Troy (in the south), about 10 miles as the crow flies. It's a full day's hike with a guide. It is a more difficult hike southbound, leading gradually uphill; an easier option is to begin in Troy and take the downhill route (see Troy in the South Coast & Central Highlands chapter).

In Windsor, you can hire either Martell or Franklyn Taylor as guides (from US$5, depending on distance).

Albert Town, on the east flank of the Cockpits, is evolving as a base for organized hikes (see Organized Tours below).

Spelunking

The Cockpits are laced with caves, most of them uncharted. Guides lead trips into the better-known caverns. Elsewhere, exploring is for experienced and properly outfitted spelunkers only. There is no rescue organization, and you enter the caves at your own risk.

Jamaica Underground by Alan Fincham is a rare but essential compendium providing the most thorough information available on the island's charted caves.

See Spelunking in the Facts for the Visitor chapter.

Organized Tours

Cockpit Country Adventure Tours (☎ 610-0818; W www.jamaica-adventure-tour.com; 3 Grants Office Complex, Albert Town, PO Trelawny), sponsored by the Southern Trelawny Environmental Agency, uses local guides to lead hiking and cave exploration adventures, from 'light adventures' to 'high adventures' into the rugged Freeman's Hall district.

Sun Venture Tours (☎ 960-6685 in Kingston, 920-8348 in Ocho Rios; e sun venture@hotmail.com; 30 Balmoral Ave, Kingston 10) offers guided hikes and birding trips into the Cockpits.

Also see Bird Watching in the Facts for the Visitor chapter and Organized Tours under Montego Bay earlier in this chapter.

GOOD HOPE ESTATE

This great house and working plantation is 8 miles south of Falmouth, at the western end of Queen of Spains Valley (see earlier in this chapter). The property is set on the northern edge of Cockpit Country, and the views have no rival.

The estate, which is called 'Bad Hope' by the locals because of its painful associations with slavery, was owned by John Tharp (1744-1804), who became the richest man in Jamaica. At one time he owned 10,000 acres and 3000 slaves in Trelawny and St James parishes. The house was built around 1755 atop a hillock. The estate office and slave hospital also still stand, as does the sugar works by the riverbank.

Good Hope stable offers rides through the plantation and along the banks of the Martha Brae River, 7:30am to 4:30pm (US$30 for 90 minutes; US$25 for hotel guests).

David Pinto, an acclaimed ceramist, has a **pottery studio** (☎ 954-4635) open to view; you can take pottery lessons. Workshops are offered through **Anderson Ranch Arts Center** (☎ 970-923-3181, fax 923-3871 in the USA; PO Box 5598, Snowmass Village, CO 81615, USA).

Good Hope Country House (☎/fax 610-5798, fax 979-8095; e goodhope1@cwjamaica.com; PO Box 50, Falmouth; weekly rates summer US$7900-12,400, winter US$9500-18,900; River Cottage summer US$2900, winter US$4400) is a great house that formerly operated as a stately 'country house hotel.' It now rents as a whole villa. You might recognize it from scenes in *How Stella Got Her Groove Back*. The architecture and mood are fabulous, and include high-raftered ceilings, Adam frieze, gleaming hardwood floors, and a two-story counting house with a basement once used as a lockup for defiant slaves. The house is fully furnished with period pieces that preserve the plantation-era atmosphere.

One of the four generously proportioned bedrooms in the main house has the original plantation owner's lead-and-tile-lined bathtub and a deep copper basin. The former coach house has an additional five rooms. A three-bedroom River Cottage can also be rented. There's a small swimming pool, plus tennis courts. Meals cost $35 per day.

WINDSOR

This narrow, 2-mile-long valley, southeast of Good Hope Estate, is surrounded by towering cliffs. It is most easily accessed from Sherwood at the north end. The paved road dead-ends at Windsor near the head of the valley, from whence you can hike across the Cockpits to Troy.

Windsor Great House was built in 1705 by John Tharp and today serves as a hostelry (see Places to Stay below) and scientific research center. Early evening is the best time to visit. Take insect repellent.

A bus and coasters and route taxis operate between Montego Bay and Brown's Town via Sherwood, from where you can walk or hitch the remaining 3 miles to Windsor.

Windsor Caves

These off-the-beaten-track caverns are fascinating. The entrance is a mile-long hike from the road ending with a clamber up a narrow rocky path. Beyond the narrow entrance, you'll pass into a large gallery full of stalactites and a huge chamber with a dramatically arched ceiling. In rainy season you can hear the roar of the Martha Brae River flowing deep underground.

About 50,000 bats inhabit the cave; their egress at dusk is an amazing sight!

You'll need a local guide, who can be hired at the Windsor Research Center (see Information in the Cockpit Country (North) section). **Martell and Franklyn 'Doc' Taylor** – two elderly and friendly Rastas – lead the way with flashlights. They charge US$5-10 per person (depending on group size) to visit Rat Bat Cave and a little more to the Royal Flat Chamber.

Also see Spelunking in the Facts for the Visitor chapter for warnings and general information.

Places to Stay

A Texan, Patrick Childres, offers two rooms for tourists to rent in a **two-story** house (no ☎; campsites US$10, rooms US$10) at Windsor. You can also camp by the river. The simple place has water from a spring, plus solar panels to power the radio and a battery for lighting. You can cook over a simple stove. Martell and Franklyn (see above) act as caretakers and will provide food and even cook lunch and dinner for US$5.

Budget travelers can also stay inexpensively at **Windsor Great House** (☎ 997-3832; ⓔ windsor@cwjamaica.com; first night US$30, subsequent nights US$25), a colonial mansion with two no-frills, cut-stone rooms with shared bathroom (cold water only; solar-heated water is to be added). Rates include breakfast. Lunch costs US$5-10; dinner costs US$10-15. Occasional four-course 'Meet the Biologist' dinners are offered (US$25); call for a schedule and reservations.

Miss Lily's (☎ 788-1022; Windsor PO; rooms US$30), in Cock's Heath, at the entrance to Windsor Valley, is a simple guest house run by a large, jovial lady. Two simply appointed rooms share a bath (cold water only) and have fans. There's a bar and grocery attached, and Miss Lily cooks meals.

ALBERT TOWN

This small market center lies high in the mountains about 15 miles inland of Rio Bueno. The B5 climbs through the Cockpits with dramatic views en route. Albert Town is a base for guided hikes into the Cockpit Country, immediately to the west (see Organized Tours earlier in this section).

The B5 rises southeast from Albert Town to the spine of Jamaica, with vistas of lush, rolling agricultural land interspersed with pine forest. You'll crest the mountains (and the boundary with Manchester parish) just south of Lorrimers, about 9 miles south of Albert Town. Christiana is about 2 miles farther south (see the South Coast & Central Highlands chapter).

West of Albert Town, the B10 climbs along the eastern edge of Cockpit Country and, beyond Warsop, drops dramatically to Troy (see the South Coast & Central Highlands chapter), a gateway to the Cockpits.

Every week before Easter, the **Trelawny Yam Festival** features such highlights as the yam-balancing races, best-dressed goat and donkey, and crowning of the Yam King and Queen.

The **Southern Trelawny Environmental Agency** (☎ 610-0818, fax 954-4087; ⓔ stea@cwjamaica.com; 3 Grants Office Complex, Albert Town) is on the west side of the town square. If you're looking for lodging, its staff can recommend **local B&Bs**.

Global Telefax (☎ 610-1853; open 8:30am-8pm Mon-Sat, 2pm-8pm Sun) is on the south side of the square.

You can appease your appetite at **TJ's Snacks & Pastries** at the north end of town, 50 yards north of the post office, or at **Ataurus Restaurant & Bar**, also in the town center.

Buses and minibuses operate between Albert Town and Falmouth, Mandeville, Kingston, and Spaldings. There's a gas station in town (closed Sun).

Ocho Rios & North Coast

NORTH COAST

Highlights

- Climbing Dunn's River Falls, invigorating and fun despite the crowds
- Scuba diving or snorkeling amid coral reefs
- Swimming with dolphins at Dolphin Cove
- Visiting Firefly, Noel Coward's former home
- Horseback riding through the ocean at Chukka Cove
- Paying homage at the Bob Marley Museum at Nine Mile

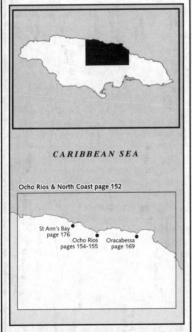

CARIBBEAN SEA

Ocho Rios & North Coast page 152

St Ann's Bay
page 176
Ocho Rios   Oracabessa
pages 154-155   page 169

Jamaica's north central coast – spanning St Ann and St Mary parishes – is replete with attractions. Dunn's River Falls, botanical gardens, working plantations, and a spot to swim with dolphins are within a few minutes' drive of Ocho Rios. Discovery Bay and Runaway Bay are lesser centers of resort development. East of Ocho Rios, cliffs edge up to the shore, making for increasingly dramatic scenery. Here you can escape the crowds and discover gems such as Firefly, Noel Coward's former home.

Hills rise south of the coast road (which is the A1 west of St Ann's Bay and the A3 to the east) and ascend into the scenic Dry Harbour Mountains.

Ocho Rios

Ocho Rios (population 9200), 67 miles east of Montego Bay, is an important resort backed by lushly vegetated hills and fronted by a reef-sheltered harbor. Offshore offers some excellent scuba diving with splendid coral formations slated to be protected within the as-yet-unrealized Ocho Rios Marine Park. Upscale hotels east of town have private beaches hidden in coves.

Ocho Rios is a popular stop for cruise ships. The town itself has little charm. The otherwise beautiful bay vista is marred by a bauxite-loading area beside the cruise port; there are few historic buildings of note; and when the cruise ships call in, the compact streets can be thronged. (Cruise ships rarely arrive on weekends; you would do well to plan your itinerary accordingly.)

HISTORY

Ocho Rios (Spanish for 'eight rivers') is an English corruption of *chorreras* ('waterfalls'), the name the Spaniards gave to the area.

Although plantations developed, Ocho Rios never evolved as a fruit-shipping port of any consequence. Things began to change when Reynolds Jamaica Mines built the

NORTH COAST

OCHO RIOS & NORTH COAST

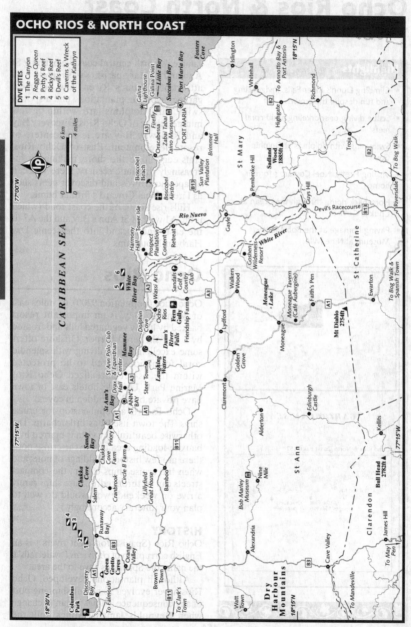

DIVE SITES
1 The Canyon
2 Reggae Queen
3 Ricky's Reef
4 Potty's Reef
5 Devil's Reef
6 Caverns & Wreck of the Kathryn

deep-water Reynolds Pier west of town in the 1940s. An overhead conveyor belt still carries bauxite ore 6.3 miles from the Reynolds open-cast mines at Lydford, in the hills south of town.

Nonetheless, Ocho Rios was still a quiet fishing village in the 1960s when the Jamaican government formed the St Ann Development Council, launching a systematic development. It dredged the harbor and built a small marina, reclaimed the shore, brought in sand for Turtle Beach, and built shopping complexes and housing schemes. By the early 1980s, Ocho Rios' character had been established: a meld of American-style fast-food franchises, nondescript shopping malls, an enclave of mediocre hotels in town, and more tasteful, upscale English-style hotels a discrete distance east.

Recent efforts to spruce up 'Ochi' include construction of a major shopping and entertainment complex (see the boxed text 'Island Village' later in this chapter).

ORIENTATION

Greater Ocho Rios extends for 4 miles between Dunn's River Falls, 2 miles to the west of the town center, and the White River, 2 miles to the east.

The main coast road, the A3, bypasses the town center via a two-lane highway. At its western end it becomes DaCosta Drive, which leads to a roundabout (traffic circle) and the A3 bypass, known officially as the Ocho Rios Redevelopment Rd; a trunk of the A3 (Milford Rd) leads south from the traffic circle to Fern Gully and eventually Kingston. The major thoroughfare downtown is Main St, which is lined with hotels and shops and runs in an S-curve along Turtle Bay. Main St and DaCosta Drive meet to the east at a clock tower that marks the center of town. Main St merges to its east and west ends with the A3, at Island Village and IRIE FM, respectively.

INFORMATION
Tourist Offices & Travel Agencies
The **JTB office** (☎ 974-2582, fax 974-2559; Main St) is upstairs at Shop 7 in Ocean Village Plaza. The JTB also maintains three information booths on Main St, near the Turtle Towers condominiums, across from Village Hotel, and at the east end of town at Pineapple Craft Village.

For information online, a good starting point is **W** www.go-ochorios.com.

International Travel Service (☎ 974-5108; Shop 2, cnr DaCosta Dr & Graham St) is a reputable travel agency.

Money
There are numerous banks, including **CIBC** (☎ 974-2824; 29 Main St), **National Commercial Bank** (☎ 974-2522; 40 Main St), and **Scotiabank** (☎ 974-2081; Main St). All have foreign exchange facilities and ATMs. There are also ATM booths next to Island Grill and Mother's bakery. You can arrange an urgent remittance of money via **Western Union** (☎ 926-2454; Shop 3, Pier View Plaza; open 9am-5pm Mon-Sat).

American Express (☎ 974-5482) is represented by Shop 11B, Taj Mahal Shopping Centre.

Post & Communications
The **post office** (Main St; open 8am-5pm Mon-Sat) is opposite the Ocho Rios Craft Park. You can send faxes and telegrams from there, and from the **Cable & Wireless office** (☎ 974-1574, 888-974-9700; Mutual Life Bldg, Graham St), **Call Direct Centre** (☎ 974-7594; 74 Main St), **Central Call Centre** (☎ 795-1387; 85 Main Stand), and **Towne Scribe** (☎ 974-5257, fax 974-6991; open 9am-5:30pm Mon-Sat), adjacent to Soni Plaza; all of which offer telephone service.

FedEx (☎ 795-3723; 17 Main St) has an office.

Email & Internet Access
ReggaeSun (☎ 795-1831; **e** production@ reggae.tv; 59 Main St), to the rear of the Little Pub, offers Internet service (US$3.50 for 15 minutes), as do the Central Call Centre (see above), and **Anngel.com** (☎ 795-2631; **e** admin@anngel.com.jm; 9 Pineapple Place).

The Ruins at the Falls (☎ 974-8888, fax 974-9098; **e** theruins@cwjamaica.com; 17

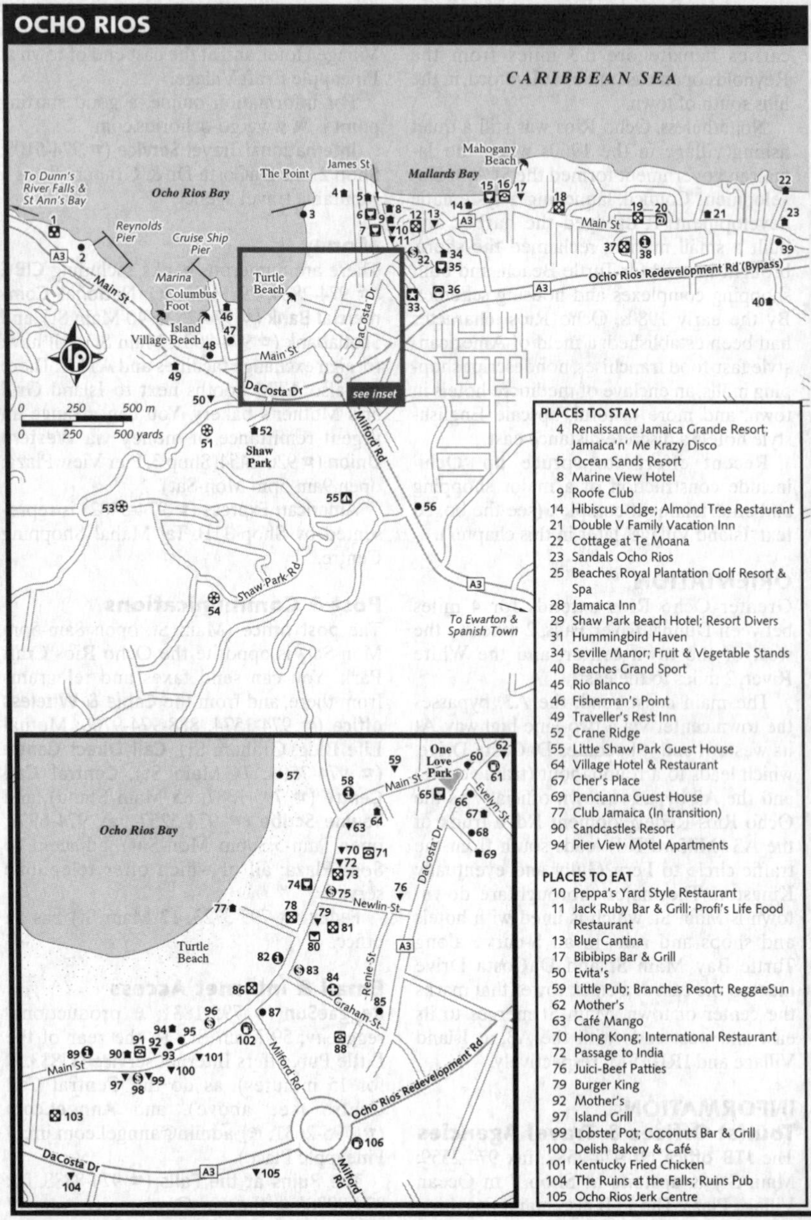
OCHO RIOS
CARIBBEAN SEA
To Dunn's River Falls & St Ann's Bay
Ocho Rios Bay
The Point
James St
Mahogany Beach
Mallards Bay
Reynolds Pier
Cruise Ship Pier
Marina
Columbus Foot
Island Village Beach
Turtle Beach
Main St
DaCosta Dr
see inset
Milford Rd
Shaw Park
Shaw Park Rd
Ocho Rios Redevelopment Rd (Bypass)
A3
To Ewarton & Spanish Town
0 250 500 m
0 250 500 yards
One Love Park
Evelyn St
Newlin St
Renie St
Graham St
Ocho Rios Redevelopment Rd
PLACES TO STAY
4 Renaissance Jamaica Grande Resort; Jamaica'n' Me Krazy Disco
5 Ocean Sands Resort
8 Marine View Hotel
9 Roofe Club
14 Hibiscus Lodge; Almond Tree Restaurant
21 Double V Family Vacation Inn
22 Cottage at Te Moana
23 Sandals Ocho Rios
25 Beaches Royal Plantation Golf Resort & Spa
28 Jamaica Inn
29 Shaw Park Beach Hotel; Resort Divers
31 Hummingbird Haven
34 Seville Manor; Fruit & Vegetable Stands
40 Beaches Grand Sport
45 Rio Blanco
46 Fisherman's Point
49 Traveller's Rest Inn
52 Crane Ridge
55 Little Shaw Park Guest House
64 Village Hotel & Restaurant
67 Cher's Place
69 Pencianna Guest House
77 Club Jamaica (In transition)
90 Sandcastles Resort
94 Pier View Motel Apartments
PLACES TO EAT
10 Peppa's Yard Style Restaurant
11 Jack Ruby Bar & Grill; Profi's Life Food Restaurant
13 Blue Cantina
17 Bibibips Bar & Grill
50 Evita's
59 Little Pub; Branches Resort; ReggaeSun
62 Mother's
63 Café Mango
70 Hong Kong; International Restaurant
72 Passage to India
76 Juici-Beef Patties
79 Burger King
92 Mother's
97 Island Grill
99 Lobster Pot; Coconuts Bar & Grill
100 Delish Bakery & Café
101 Kentucky Fried Chicken
104 The Ruins at the Falls; Ruins Pub
105 Ocho Rios Jerk Centre

NORTH COAST

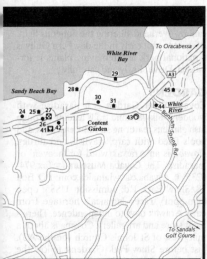

DaCosta Dr; open 8am-11pm) has an Internet café.

Internet Jungle, in Island Village, is a digital communication center scheduled to open soon at last visit.

Bookstores & Library

Bookland (☎ 974-8353; e novtraco@cwjamaica.com; Island Village) has the largest selection of books. Also try **Everybody's Bookshop** (☎ 974-2932; Shop 44 Ocean Village Plaza).

There is also a town **library** (☎ 974-2588; Milford Rd).

Laundry

Carib Laundromat (☎ 974-7631; Shop 6, Carib Arcade, Main St; load US$5; open 10am-7pm) offers a wash-and-dry service, as does **Express Laundromat** (☎ 795-0720; 18 Pineapple Place).

Medical Services

The nearest **hospital** (☎ 972-0150) is in St Ann's Bay, about 7 miles west of Ocho Rios. Your hotel's front desk can arrange a doctor's visit. Expect long lines at the public **Ocho Rios Health Clinic** (☎ 974-2691; Graham St; open 8am-4:30pm Mon-Thur, 8am-4pm Fri).

Medi-Rays (☎ 974-6251; Shop 10 Carib Arcade, Main St), has X-ray and ultrasound diagnostics; also here is the **Central Medical Lab** (☎ 974-2614; Shop 14, Carib Arcade) and **Dr Michael James' office** (☎ 974-5413; Shop 11 Carib Arcade).

The **Holistic Medical Centre** (☎ 974-6403) in Ocean Village Plaza offers 24-hour service plus a **24-hour ambulance** (☎ 999-7425).

Pharmacies include **Ocho Rios Pharmacy** (☎ 974-2398), at Shop 27 in Ocean Village Plaza, and **Pinegrove Pharmacy** (☎ 974-2023), in Pinegrove Plaza.

Emergency

The **police station** (☎ 974-2533) is off DaCosta Drive, just east of the clock tower.

Dangers & Annoyances

Ocho Rios' biggest annoyance is the persistent entreaties of hustlers (see Dangers &

Annoyances in the Facts for the Visitor chapter), who are especially thick around the clock tower and DaCosta Drive.

Avoid the area immediately behind the market south of the clock tower. Use caution at night anywhere, but particularly on James St, a poorly lit street with several nightspots and a hang-out strip of ill repute.

BEACHES

Ocho Rios' main beach is the long crescent of **Turtle Beach** (admission US$1; open 6am-6pm daily), stretching east from Turtle Towers condominiums to the Renaissance Jamaica Grande Resort. There are changing rooms, water-sport concessionaires, and palms for shade.

Island Village Beach, at the west end of Main St, is a peaceful, smaller beach with a complete range of water sports (see Activities later in this chapter) plus lockers (US$5), towels (US$5), and beach chairs and umbrellas (US$5 apiece).

Columbus Foot, immediately west of Island Village, is a tiny fisherman's beach with colorful pirogues (fishing boats) and nets festooning shade trees.

Mahogany Beach, half a mile east of the town center, is a small and charming beach.

REGGAE XPLOSION

This impressive museum (☎ 974-8353/4/5/6; admission US$10 Mon-Fri, US$5 Sat & Sun; open 9am-5pm), at Island Village, is billed as an 'interactive reggae experience' and dedicated to Jamaica's modern musical heritage. It is divided into mento, ska, reggae, dancehall, and other sections, including one commemorating Bob Marley. It features posters, photographs, and videos. Headphones let you listen to sounds of the era. There's even a makeshift artists recording studio with Lee 'Scratch' Perry's original sound gear.

The entrance fee includes a guided tour and full access to Island Village.

FERN GULLY

This lush gorge is one of Ocho Rios' prime attractions. Milford Rd (A3) zigzags uphill through the 3-mile canyon of an old water-course that was planted with hundreds of different fern species about 1880. Trees form a canopy overhead, filtering the aqueous light. It's best to visit early in the day. Fern Gully is a national park and removing plants is forbidden. Drive slowly and carefully.

GARDENS

Coyaba River Garden is a paradise with wooden walkways and trails leading through lush gardens featuring streams, cascades, and pools filled with carp, crayfish, and turtles. *Coyaba* is an Arawak word for 'heaven' or 'paradise.' The **Coyaba Museum** (☎/fax 974-6235; e coyaba.c@cwjamaica.com; PO Box 18, Shaw Park Rd; admission US$5; open 8am-5pm) traces Jamaica's heritage from early Arawak days to independence. There's a gift store and art gallery. Coyaba is about a mile west of St John's Church (on the A3), just before Shaw Park Gardens; follow the signs. Entrance includes a 30-minute guided tour.

The Enchanted Garden is a 20-acre Eden-like setting (☎ 974-1400; PO Box 284; Eden Bower Rd; US$5) that features a lush landscaped park with 14 waterfalls; huge pools; a fruit orchard; separate fern, spice, cactus, and lily gardens; and a walk-in aviary. Guided tours are offered 9am-4pm daily. In the past, Enchanted Garden has also offered accommodations, but these were closed and for sale at last visit (embroiled in JLP party leader Edward Seaga's tax-fraud problems).

Shaw Park Gardens (☎ 974-2723, fax 974-5042; e shawparkbchhtl@cwjamaica.com; PO Box 17, Shaw Park Rd; admission US$4; open 8am-5pm daily) is a tropical fantasia of ferns and bromeliads, palms, and exotic shrubs, spread out over 25 acres centered on an 18th-century great house. Trails and wooden steps lead past waterfalls that tumble in terraces down the hillside. A viewing platform offers a bird's-eye vantage over Ocho Rios. There's a bar and restaurant. The gardens are signed from opposite the public library on the A3.

DUNN'S RIVER FALLS & PARK

To visit Jamaica and not climb Dunn's River Falls (☎ 974-5944, 974-2857, fax 974-5197;

w www.dunnsriverja.com; climb falls adult/
child US$6/3; park open 8:30am-5pm), on
the A3, 2 miles west of town, is like touring
France without seeing the Eiffel Tower. Join
hands in a daisy chain at the bottom and
clamber up the tiers of limestone that
stairstep 600 feet down to the beach in a
series of cascades and pools. The water is refreshingly cool and the falls are shaded by a
tall rain forest.

You must buy a ticket, then follow the
stairs down to the beach. The powerful
current can sweep your feet from the slippery rocks, but your sure-footed guide (a tip
is expected) will hold you by the hand and
carry your camera. You climb at your own
risk – yes, occasionally people hurt themselves. There's a first-aid station supervised
by St John's Ambulance Brigade. You can
always exit to the side at a convenient point
if your nerves give out. Rubber sandals rent
for US$5.

It's a 30-minute climb. Swimwear is essential. There are changing rooms and
lockers (US$5) on the beach. However, it's
best to leave any valuables in your hotel
safe, as the lockers are reputed to not be
secure.

The recently remodeled facility now includes a mento yard (for live music), an
orchid garden, children's playground, a
crafts market, jerk stalls, snack bars, and a
restaurant.

Get there before 10am, when the tour
buses arrive, or plan your visit for when the
cruise ships aren't in town (weekends are
best). Avoid Easter.

DOLPHIN COVE
This new facility (☎ 974-5335, fax 974-9420;
w www.dolphincovejamaica.com; PO Box
21; admission US$15, 'touch encounter'
US$35, 'swim with dolphins' US$79-145;
open 9am-5pm), adjacent to Dunn's River
Falls along the A3, lets you swim with
bottlenose dolphins. Three packages are
offered, including 'Swim with Dolphins,'
which grants you 30 minutes in the dolphin
lagoon. Professional trainers direct the dolphins. Dolphin shows are offered at 9:30am,
11:30am, 1:30pm, and 3:30pm.

The site also has an aquarium and pools
with tropical fish, sharks, stingrays, and eels,
as well as a minizoo with exotic species to
be experienced on a 'Jungle Trail.'

Reservations are advisable in winter.
Bring a towel.

WASSI ART
This pottery studio (☎ 974-5044, fax 974-
8096; w www.wassiart.com; PO Box 781,
Bougainvillea Dr; open 9am-5pm Mon-Sat),
in the Great Pond District, is signed from
Milford Rd (the A3), from where it's a convoluted (but signed) drive. Visitors see more
than 50 employees at work, including up-
and-coming masters such as Homer Brown,
a ceramist with a reputation for his erotic
works. The pottery is named for the 'wassi'
wasp, or potter wasp, which makes a mud
pot for each of her eggs and stuffs it with a
caterpillar for food for her hatchlings. Free
tours are offered. A store sells work (US$4-
4000). The owners will ship.

PROSPECT PLANTATION
Prospect (☎ 994-1058, fax 953-2197; e jtlad
min@infochan.com), on the A3, 4 miles east
of town, grows pimento and limes commercially. The old hilltop great house is not
open to the public. The estate includes the
Prospect Cadet Training Centre, founded to
educate the youth of indigent families and
prepare them for the police force and
Jamaica Defense Force. The youngsters also
act as tour guides.

A tour by tractor-powered jitney offers incredible views and includes a visit to the
nondenominational college chapel, a sturdy
stone structure with a timbered roof. Tours
depart at 10:30am, 2pm, and 3:30pm Monday
to Saturday, and 11am, 1:30pm, and 3pm
Sunday (US$12). Three horseback tours are
also offered (US$20-50).

There's also bicycle rides (US$12) and
minigolf (adults/children US$5/2.50).

OTHER THINGS TO SEE & DO
A beautiful great house, **Harmony Hall**
(☎ 974-2870, fax 974-2651; e harmony@cw
jamaica.com; PO Box 192; open 10am-6pm
daily, closed Christmas, Good Friday, &

Sept), on the A3 about 4 miles east of town, dates to 1886 when it was a Methodist manse adjoining a pimento estate. The restored structure is made of cut stone, with a wooden upper story trimmed with gingerbread fretwork and a green shingled roof topped by a spire. It has been reborn as an arts-and-crafts showcase. Shows are held in the Front Gallery throughout the year; an exhibition season runs mid-November to Easter. The Back Gallery features fine arts and crafts.

A recreational estate, **White River Valley** (☎ 929-9403, fax 968-2977; Bonham Spring Rd), 7 miles southeast of Ocho Rios, has hiking trails through the forest, tube-rafting on the White River, horseback riding, mountain bike rides, an orchid house, plus picnic areas.

The English built the pocket-size **Ocho Rios Fort**, on the A3 west of town, in the late 17th century. The fortress later did duty as a slaughterhouse before being restored in the 1970s and fitted with cannons. It is not open to visitors.

ACTIVITIES

Virtually the entire shoreline east of Ocho Rios to Galina Point is fringed by a reef, and it's great for **snorkeling** and **scuba diving**. One of the best sections is **Devil's Reef**, a pinnacle that drops more than 200 feet. Nurse sharks are abundant at **Caverns**, a shallow reef about a mile east of the White River estuary; it has many tunnels plus an ex-minesweeper, the *Kathryn*. You can arrange dives and snorkeling at the **Garfield Diving Station** (☎ 818-3369, 373-5412; e resdiv@bigfoot.com; 50 Main St), on Turtle Beach, and **Resort Divers** (☎ 974-5338, 974-2552, fax 974-5042; Shop 2, Island Plaza, Shaw Park Beach Hotel). Most resorts have their own scuba facilities.

Sport fishing boats are available for charters from the marina, and from Resort Divers (see above).

Water-sport concessionaires on Turtle Beach offer jet-skiing, windsurfing, and paddleboating. Upscale hotels also offer water sports. **Beach World** (☎ 974-8353), at Island Village Beach, has kayaks (US$5-8),

floats (US$5), snorkeling gear (US$5 per hour), pedal bikes (US$5 for 30 minutes), windsurfing (US$40 for 30 minutes), and Hobie-cats (US$30 for 30 minutes).

Hyatt's Parasailing (☎ 972-9742) has outlets at Mahogany Beach, Carib Arcade, and Pineapple Place.

For **golf,** head to **Sandals Ocho Rios Golf & Country Club** (☎ 975-0119, fax 975-0180; Bonham Spring Rd; open 7:30am-5pm), in the hills, 4 miles southeast of town and signed off the A3. This is a 6600-yard, par-71 course with a driving range, putting green, and clubhouse. Greens fees are US$80 (US$50 for nine holes; complimentary to guests at Sandals resorts). Caddies are mandatory and cost US$15 (US$12 for nine holes), and cart rental is US$30. Club rental is US$18. Lessons are offered.

Prospect Plantation (see earlier in this chapter) offers guided **horseback tours** that range from one hour to 2½ hours (US$20-35).

ORGANIZED TOURS

JUTA Tour Company (☎ 974-2292; PO Box 160) offers an 'Ocho Rios Highlight Tour' and day excursions near and far, as do **Tourwise** (☎ 974-2323; 103 Main St) and **Ocho Rios Tours** (☎ 975-5279; e ionie@ocho-rios.com; PO Box 42, Tower Isle). Tourwise also lets you act the part of a pirate on the *Jolly Roger,* a brigantine that hosts parties and sunset cruises.

Safari Tours (☎ 785-0482, fax 974-3382; e safari@cwjamaica.com; Arawak PO, Mammee Bay) specializes in 4WD safaris, and also has bicycling and horseback riding trips.

Wilderness Tours (☎ 969-6653; e info@wildernessatvtours.com), at Reynold's Pier, offers all-terrain vehicle tours into the mountains and through the forest (US$59).

Blue Mountain Bicycle Tours (☎ 974-7075, fax 974-0635; e bmbike@cwjamaica.com; 121 Main St) has an 18-mile downhill bicycling tour in the Blue Mountains for US$85, including transfers, breakfast, and lunch.

Resort Divers (☎ 974-5338), at Shaw Park Beach Hotel; **Heave-Ho Charters** (☎ 974-

5367, fax 974-5461; e heave-ho@cwjamaica.com; 180 Main St); and **Red Stripe Cruises** (☎ 974-2446; e redstripecruises@cwjamaica.com) offer snorkeling, private charters and party-hearty sunset cruises. Most cruises leave from wharves at the north and south end of Turtle Beach.

Helitours (☎ 974-2265, fax 974-2183; e helitoursja@infochan.com; 120 Main St) offers three aerial tours on four-passenger Bell Jetranger helicopters. You can also charter a chopper. See the Getting Around chapter for details.

Calypso Rafting (☎ 974-2527; PO Box 54) offers a lazy journey by bamboo raft on the White River (US$45 per person). A reader complains that they spent very little time rafting. Every Tuesday, Wednesday, and Thursday, Calypso Rafting also features a 'Jungle Bachanaal' (US$40 per person) that includes a buffet on the riverbank.

SPECIAL EVENTS
Reggae Sunsplash
This four-night annual reggae extravaganza features performances (US$15-25) by leading artists spanning reggae, rock, gospel, and 'roots.' The event is normally staged at White River Reggae Park on February 6, coinciding with Bob Marley's birthday, but the venue can vary.

Formerly – and famously – the music didn't begin until late at night and would continue until dawn. These days, the six-hour shows begin at 8pm weekday nights and Saturday, and 7pm Sunday.

For information, call **Reggae Sunsplash International** (☎ 960-1904, fax 960-1906; W www.reggaesunsplash.com).

In the US, **Sunburst Holidays** (☎ 800-786-2877; W www.sunburstholidays.com) and **Alken Tours** (☎ 718-856-7711, 800-221-6686; W www.alkentours.com; 1661 Nostrand Ave, Brooklyn, NY 11226) offer package tours.

Other Events
The weeklong **Ocho Rios Jazz Festival** (☎ 927-3544; e jazzfestl@cwjamaica.com) is held mid-June at venues around Ochi. The **Air Jamaica Jazz Festival** (Jazz Hotline; ☎/fax 927-3544) is held here in November.

Caribbean Music Expo (☎ 968-8334; W www.cme.co.jm), in March, features seminars and live concerts by leading artists performing everything from gospel to dancehall at various venues. **It's Your Tour** (☎ 323-857-5358, 888-637-8111; W www.ochoriosjazz.com); **ITS Tours** (W www.magicvacation.com); and Alken Tours (see above) offer package tours from North America.

PLACES TO STAY
The accommodations below extend westward to Dunn's River Falls and eastward to Tower Isle. For hotels farther away, see the West of Ocho Rios and East of Ocho Rios sections later in this chapter.

Branches Resort (☎ 974-2324, fax 974-5825; e littlepub@reggaesun.tv; 59 Main St) is a union of five small hotels permitting full use of facilities at each.

Budget
Camping Little Shaw Park Guest House (see Guest Houses below), near Shaw Park Gardens in the hills above town, lets you camp (2 people US$25, including tent rental). The owners cook meals on request.

Hummingbird Haven (see Guest Houses below), on the A3, about 2 miles east of town, offers camping amid a peaceful garden (per person US$5).

Guest Houses Hummingbird Haven (☎ 974-5188, fax 974-5202; e colibri_cove@hotmail.com; PO Box 95; camping US$5, cabins US$25) is a funky, rough-around-the-edges budget place run by live-in owner Audrey Barnett, who offers basic rooms and cabins with fans, flush toilets, and showers.

Happy Hut B&B (☎ 994-1223; PO Box 291; rooms with/without kitchenette US$30/25) is run by Aston Young, a former producer of *Sesame Street*. He rents three bedrooms in his homey bungalow above Rivermouth Beach, about 200 yards west of Grand Lido Sans Souci, on the A3 about 3 miles east of downtown. Each has a private entrance and bathroom; one has a kitchenette. At last visit, it had cold water only, but hot water was to be installed.

Pencianna Guest House (☎ 974-5472; 3 Short Lane; rooms US$30-35), downtown, reminded one reader of an Italian pension. The rooms are small yet immaculately kept, with shiny red tile floors and crisp linens. Some have shared baths. The owners will whip up tasty Jamaican meals for US$3 and up.

Little Shaw Park Guest House (☎ 974-2177, fax 974-8997; e LittleShaw Park_2000@yahoo.com; 21 Shaw Park Rd; rooms US$50, studio apartments US$65) is a trim place with 10 rooms amid beautifully tended lawns and bougainvillea with a gazebo and hammocks. There's a room in the owner's house, plus seven spacious (though dark) cabins boasting homey decor. Meals are available by request. The owners also offer well-lit studio apartments with nicer furnishings.

Hotels Downtown, **Cher's Place** (☎ 974-1959; 4 Evelyn St; rooms US$45-50) has nine rooms with fans, louvered windows, cable TV, telephone, kitchenette, and small bathroom. Some rooms have air-con. They're modestly furnished and have tile underfoot.

Traveller's Rest Inn (☎ 974-8436; Main St; US$36), at the west end of town, near the Columbus Foot fisherman's beach, is a budget hotel with 20 simply furnished rooms (some with air-con), plus a roadside seafood restaurant. Hookers hang out here and use it as a quick-time motel.

Mid-Range
City Center An attractive property, **Ocean Sands Resort** (☎ 974-2605, fax 974-2605; e oceansands@cwjamaica.com; 14 James St; single/double summer US$45/55, winter US$55/65) has an oceanfront setting and its own pocket-size beach, with coral, at your doorstep. A tiny restaurant sits at the end of a wooden wharf. The 35 pleasant rooms have French doors that open onto private balconies. There's a small pool. Rates include breakfast.

Double V Family Vacation Inn (☎ 974-0173; 109 Main St; small/large rooms US$35/60) is a compact, uninspired prop-

erty in lush grounds. Its 13 spacious, air-con rooms have large beds but gaudy red carpets and dowdy furnishings. It features a pool, restaurant, and TV lounge.

Marine View Hotel (☎ 974-5753, fax 974-6953; 9 James Ave; rooms with fan US$35, with air-con US$40, with air-con and TV US$50, with air-con, TV, and king-size bed US$55) has 25 basically furnished rooms, all with private bathrooms with hot water. Top-floor rooms offer a glimpse (barely) of the sea. There's a small pool and a restaurant.

Pier View Motel Apartments (☎ 974-2607, fax 974-1384; 19 Main St; studios/rooms/apartments/suites from US$50/65/70/85) offers studios and a range of modestly furnished rooms and efficiency apartments, all with fans, refrigerator, and cable TV; there are also air-con suites. It has a small pool.

Fisherman's Point (☎ 974-5317, fax 974-2894; e fishermanspoint@cwjamaica.com; PO Box 747; singles summer US$70-75, winter US$100-110; doubles summer US$100-110, winter US$120-130), by the cruise ship pier, has 60 elegant apartments with kitchenettes, bamboo furnishings, satellite TV, and tiny private balconies. The complex's amenities include a pool, bar, and seafood restaurant.

Sandcastles Resort (☎ 974-5626, 800-537-8483, fax 974-2247; e sandcastles@cwja maica.com; 120 Main St; studios summer/winter US$88/95, 1-bedroom suites US$107/114, 2-bedroom suites US$144/151) is a recently refurbished all-suite resort with studios and one- and two-bedroom suites in various configurations. All have air-con and cable TV, plus modern furnishings. It has a sports bar.

Hibiscus Lodge (☎ 974-2676, fax 974-1874; PO Box 52, Main St; standard/deluxe rooms summer US$103/114, winter US$114/126) is one of the best bargains. Its breezy clifftop setting, amid lush grounds close to the town center, overlooks a coral reef where the snorkeling is superb. The rooms are spacious and modestly furnished. There's a small clifftop pool, an atmospheric bar, plus a fine restaurant – the Almond Tree. The hotel offers good value, especially

The imposing Rose Hall Great House, near Montego Bay, was built in the 1770s.

The bustle of Montego Bay's open-air market

Tropical delights in a Montego Bay bar

Girls playing in MoBay's warm sands

Fronted by a reef-sheltered harbor, Ocho Rios is a popular stop for cruise ships.

Bamboo rafts near Ocho Rios

Climbing the 600 steps up Dunn's River Falls

its discounted off-peak rates, which include breakfast and taxes.

Seville Manor (☎ 795-2900, fax 974-4054; 84 Main St; rooms US$45, 1-bedroom apartment US$66) is a small charmer tucked off Main St. Its 28 rooms, all with cable TV and air-con, offer rich modern furnishings and a cozy ambience. It has a restaurant and bar.

Little Pub (☎ 974-2324, 795-1831, fax 974-5825; e production@reggaesun.tv; PO Box 256, 59 Main St; single/double summer US$55/66, winter US$66/70) has 25 rooms, all with air-con, cable TV, telephone, safety box, and modern furnishings. Some units have loft bedrooms that, though well-lit, can get hot.

Farther Afield Sea Palms (☎ 975-4400, fax 975-4017; w www.seapalms-jamaica.com; PO Box 70, 103 Main St; 1-/4-bedroom unit per week summer US$735/1785, winter US$1000/2800), east of town at Tower Isle, has handsomely appointed, air-con waterfront apartments with fully equipped kitchens and personal maid and cook service. The resort also rents **Oceanview Villa** (☎ 772-6815; w www.oceanvilla jamaica.com) here.

Rio Blanco (☎ 994-1880, fax 974-8395; e rioblanco@cwjamaica.com; PO Box 252; single/double/suite per person summer US$84/59/74, winter US$94/64/89), on the A3 near the mouth of the White River, is a new all-inclusive on the inland side of the highway. The modestly furnished rooms in three-story units have cable TV.

Top End

City Center A modern charmer, **Village Hotel & Restaurant** (☎ 974-9193, fax 974-5440, ☎ 800-830-4863 in the USA; e village htl@cwjamaica.com; 54 Main St; rooms US$81-100, suites US$100-140) has 34 air-con, carpeted rooms that feature contemporary decor, cable TVs, and telephones; deluxe rooms have hot tubs. It also has one- and three-bedroom suites with kitchenettes. A courtyard restaurant serves Jamaican dishes, and there's a pool.

Renaissance Jamaica Grande Resort (☎ 974-2201, fax 974-5378, ☎ 800-468-3571 in North America; w www.offshore resorts.com; PO Box 100; rooms summer US$160-200, winter US$200-240; all-inclusive rates: single summer US$240-280, winter US$290-330, double summer US$320-360, winter US$380-420) is a splendid resort lording over the north end of Turtle Beach. It's centered on a grandiose open-air lobby overlooking a massive 'fantasy pool' with swim-up bar, swim-through grotto, and a waterfall fashioned after Dunn's River Falls. There are 720 rooms and 24 suites in two towers; each has cable TV and phone with data port. Facilities include five restaurants, nine bars, the Jamaica'n Me Krazy disco, video slots, a fitness center, tennis courts, and Club Mongoose for kids. It gets a lot of convention traffic, and at last visit many fixtures were broken. Theme parties and live entertainment are offered nightly.

Beaches Royal Plantation Golf Resort & Spa (☎ 974-5601, fax 974-5912, ☎ 888-232-2437 in North America; w www.beaches.com; per person summer US$350-1150, winter US$400-1260), nestled above its own private bay, is a stunning remake of the erstwhile Plantation Inn. Now part of the Sandals chain, this all-inclusive for adults 16 years of age and over retains its graceful qualities in 80 spacious oceanfront suites in six categories, all with remote air-con, cable TV, CD player, mahogany four-poster bed, and Edwardian antique reproductions. Effusive grounds cascade down to two beaches. Three eateries include Le Papillon Restaurant, with an eight-course set menu. A full-service spa, tennis courts, and water sports are among the attractions. Check the website for discounts. (For international contact information, see All-Inclusive Resorts in the Facts for the Visitor chapter.)

The former Club Jamaica, on Turtle Beach, has been bought by the SuperClubs all-inclusive chain. At last visit, it was preparing to open as a *non*-all-inclusive family resort after a much-needed renovation to a previously soulless property.

Farther Afield Jamaica Inn (☎ 974-2514, 877-470-6975, fax 974-2449; PO Box 1; ☎ 804-

469-5009, 800-243-9420 in North America; e jaminn@cwjamaica.com; superior single/ double summer US$235/300, winter US$475/550, suite summer US$335-630, winter US$635-1400, villa summer US$500-900, winter US$1200-1800) is an exquisite family-run inn tucked in a private cove that exudes patrician refinement; Winston Churchill thought it his favorite hotel in the world. The 45 suites are a soothing combination of whites and Wedgewood blues, with mahogany beds, Edwardian furnishings, and colonial-theme prints. The West Wing veranda suites hang over the sea (East Wing rooms nudge up to the beach). There's a small pool, croquet lawn, gameroom, library, and bar with a warm clubby feel. Men are required to wear jackets for dinner (plus a tie in winter) and women's dress code is in accordance. It's hard to believe that Keith Richards is a frequent visitor (he has a house nearby)…perhaps explaining why no children under 14 are allowed. Water sports include scuba diving, and guests have access to the facilities at Shaw Park Beach Hotel. Rates include breakfast and dinner.

Sandals Ocho Rios Resort & Golf Club (☎ 974-5691, fax 974-5700; PO Box771; all rates per person: rooms summer US$225-285, winter US$260-325, suites summer US$315-525, winter US$355-525), at the east end of Main St, 2 miles east of downtown, is a popular upscale couples' honeymoon resort. The complex has 237 rooms in five categories, all with air-con, king-size beds, satellite TV, telephone, and in-room safe. Suites get concierge service. Facilities embrace four specialty restaurants, three pools, a beauty salon, gym, and disco. Every water sport imaginable is available, as are land activities from bocci ball to basketball. Nightlife spans karaoke to toga parties. All-inclusive rates include airport transfers and golf at Sandals Golf & Country Club (see Activities earlier in this chapter). Check the website for discounts. (For international contact information, see All-Inclusive Resorts in the Facts for the Visitor chapter.)

For information on Sandals Dunn's River Golf Resort & Spa, see West of Ocho Rios later in this chapter.

Beaches Grande Sport (☎ 974-1027, fax 974-5838; W www.beaches.com; all rates per person: rooms summer US$215-250, winter US$265-310, suites summer US$275-825, winter US$340-1020), formerly Ciboney, behind Sandals Ocho Rios, was recently bought by Sandals and at last visit was in the midst of a multiphase refurbishment intended to turn the jaded property into a deluxe all-inclusive resort for adults 16 years and older. It has 289 rooms and suites in seven categories – some in the great house, but most in one-, two-, and three-bedroom villas with private pools (90 with whirlpools). The resort has a nightclub, four restaurants, two large pools with Jacuzzi, tennis courts, squash courts, a rock-climbing wall, a full-service spa, complete water sports, and no shortage of entertainment. Rates include golf at Sandals Golf & Country Club (see Activities earlier in this chapter). Check the website for discounts. (For international contact information, see All-Inclusive Resorts in the Facts for the Visitor chapter.)

Grand Lido Sans Souci (☎ 994-1353, fax 994-1544; ☎ 800-467-8737, fax 954-925-0334 in North America; ☎ 01749-677200 in the UK; PO Box 103; W www.superclubs.com; suites per person: July-Dec US$420-770, Apr-June US$445-835, Jan-Mar US$470-885), on the A3, is a sophisticated resort with a sublime setting in a secluded cove backed by lime-green lawns. All 146 suites are deluxe and feature king-size beds, CD player, cable TV with adult viewing, direct-dial telephones, and 24-hour room service. Some have Jacuzzis. One of two beaches is for nude bathing. The resort has a volleyball court, jogging track, and fitness center plus full-service spa. Complete water sports are offered, as are tennis and activities from scuba lessons to reggae dance classes. A Cyber Center has been added. Rates vary with room type.

Shaw Park Beach Hotel (☎ 974-2552, 800-377-1126, fax 974-5042; ☎ 800-223-6510 in North America; W www.shawparkhotel .com; Cutlass Bay, PO Box 17; standard single/double summer US$123/137, winter US$168/182; superior summer US$138/155, winter US$185/200; suites from summer $205, winter US$250) is a popular mid-range option. Its thatch-roofed units are spread along a wide golden-sand beach in a private cove. Choose from 33 standard, 60 superior, and 13 two-bedroom suites, all with air-con, cable TV, and private ocean-front balcony or terrace (ask for a tiled room; they're cooler). Features include an oval pool and children's wading pool, two tennis courts, gameroom, kiddies club, and disco, plus water sports and floor shows. It was for sale at last visit.

Crane Ridge (☎ 974-8050, toll-free 866-277-6374, fax 974-8070; w www.crane ridge.net; 17 DaCosta Dr; standard suite US$100, deluxe 1-/2-bedroom US$140/160), formerly Comfort Suites, offers a breezy hilltop location on the west side of town. The modern, all-suite resort features 119 one- and two-bedroom suites in six three-story structures. Some rooms have loft bedrooms. An airy restaurant on stilts looms over a large pool. A shuttle service is offered to the hotel's private beach and to Shaw Park Gardens and Dunn's River Falls.

Villa Rio Chico (☎ 800-327-1991; w www.riochico.com; cottage per week US$3500, villa per week US$28,000), on the A3, next to Dunn's River Falls, is a stunning six-bedroom colonial-style house amid 14 acres, with a grandiose garden and large private beach. Opulent furnishings include mahogany four-poster beds. You can also rent a two-bedroom cottage.

The Cottage at Te Moana (☎ 974-2870, fax 974-2651; w www.harmonyhall.com; PO Box 192; cabin US$100), is off Main St and inset in a small clifftop garden overhanging a reef. It is recommended as an exquisite reclusive rental with an adorable, iconoclastic motif. The clifftop bedroom – reached via an external staircase – has a king-size bed and ceiling fan plus a magnificent artist's aesthetic. It has a fully equipped kitchen, separate living area, plus a veranda with hammock chairs. Steps lead down to a coral cove good for snorkeling. Guests get use of kayaks.

Other local villas of varying ranges of opulence are represented by **Sun Villas** (☎ 888-625-6007; w www.sunvillas.com); **VHR Worldwide** (☎ 201-767-9393, 800-633-3284, fax 201-767-5510; e vhrww@juno.com; 235 Kensington Ave, Norwood, NY 07648, USA); and **Elegant Resorts Villas** (☎ 953-9562, fax 953-9563, ☎ 800-337-3499 in North America; PO Box 80, Montego Bay).

Also see Accommodations in the Facts for the Visitor chapter for more rental villas and apartments.

PLACES TO EAT
Fast Food
Mother's (open 24 hours; Main St), with several outlets, and **Juici-Beef Patties** (1 Newlin St) are fast-food eateries serving patties and pastries (US$0.50).

Blue Cantina (☎ 974-2430, 81 Main St; open 9am-9pm) serves tacos (US$2.50), burgers, and native fare such as curried goat (US$6).

Island Grill (☎ 974-3160; Main St, Island Village; US$2-8; open 8am-11pm) is good for take-out jerk dishes.

Kentucky Fried Chicken and **Burger King** are both on Main St.

Jamaican
Veggie Kitchen & Health Food (☎ 974-5797; 11 Island Plaza; open 8am-6pm Mon-Sat) serves breakfasts such as plantain porridge (US$1-2), lunches such as brown stew with rice and peas (US$4), corn and veggie patties, ackee and gluten, and veggie burgers (US$2-4).

Jack Ruby Bar & Grill (☎ 974-1146; 1 James St; open 11am-midnight) is a whirligig of Caribbean colors, serving the usual Jamaican fare from oxtail soup to ackee and saltfish (US$4-7). Attached is **Profi's Life Food Restaurant**, good for vegetarian fare.

Peppa's Yard Style Restaurant (James St; US$1-6), next door and popular with locals, is a simple outdoor shack serving local fare such as bammy, curry goat, and fresh cane juice.

Coconuts Bar & Grill (☎ 795-0064; 10 Main St; open 8am-11pm) offers tasteful Mediterranean decor and a wide-ranging 'snack-food' menu featuring conch fritters (US$6), chicken quesadillas (US$6), sandwiches,

NORTH COAST

burgers, and chocolate fudge cake, plus cappuccinos and teas.

Jimmy Buffett's Margaritaville (☎ 795-4643; US$3-25; open 10am-10pm), opened in 2002 in Island Village, is a high-energy bar and grill where a tropical margarita (or two) and a delicious 'Cheeseburger in Paradise' is de rigueur. The menu includes caesar salad, pizzas, and sandwiches. Also see Entertainment later in this section.

Ocho Rios Jerk Centre (☎ 974-2549; DaCosta Dr) is good for sizzling jerk chicken and pork.

Seafood
Lobster Pot (☎ 974-1461; 14 Main St; entrées from US$5) is a homey seafood restaurant.

Glenn's Jazz Club (☎ 975-4360; breakfast US$7) is a swank place on the A3 at Tower Isle. It serves breakfast as well as lunch and dinner with an international menu that includes fish-and-chips (US$10).

Continental
Bibibips Bar & Grill (☎ 974-8759; 93 Main St; open 10am-midnight) is a breezy oceanfront bar and restaurant overlooking Mahogany Beach and serving chicken wings (US$6), crab, cajun fries (US$5.50), burgers, and the like.

Café Mango (☎ 974-7416; 12 Main St; open 9am-10pm) offers airy dining and a large menu that includes spicy hot chicken wings, other finger foods, burgers, and pizzas (US$5-15).

Almond Tree Restaurant (☎ 974-2813; 83 Main St; entrées US$8-25; open 7am-2:30pm & 6pm-9:30pm), in the Hibiscus Lodge, serves meals with a view; wooden dining pavilions stairstep down the cliff and candlelit dinners are served alfresco. The menu ranges from hamburgers and continental fare to steadfast Jamaican dishes.

Little Pub (☎ 795-1831; e production@ reggaesun.tv; 59 Main St; open 8am-midnight) is totally touristy, yet enjoyable, and serves good American breakfasts. An eclectic lunch and dinner menu is strong on steak and seafood at modest prices. It has an all-you-can-eat-and-drink buffet on Friday nights (US$20).

Asian
Hong Kong International Restaurant (☎ 974-0588; 50 Main St; US$2.50-15; open 10am-10pm Mon-Sat, 2pm-10pm Sun), in the heart of downtown, serves inexpensive Chinese staples.

Passage to India (☎ 795-3182; 50 Main St; US$3-20; open 11am-10pm Tues-Sat, 12:30pm-10pm Sun), nearby in Soni Plaza, offers airy rooftop dining and serves up superb Indian and Indo-Chinese fusion cuisine. It has a large vegetarian menu.

The Ruins at the Falls (☎ 974-8888, fax 974-9098; e theruins@cwjamaica.com; 17 DaCosta Dr; appetizers from US$5, entrées US$9-30; open 9am-3pm) is a more expensive favorite recently enhanced by a total renovation. The Jamaican-Chinese restaurant is set amid tropical gardens with a bridal-veil waterfall and pools. An all-inclusive lunchtime buffet (Mon-Sat; US$14) includes beverages, live entertainment, and garden tour. A roadside diner serves similar fare (US$5-10).

Italian
Toscanini (☎ 975-4785; pasta US$5-12; open noon-2:30pm & 7pm-10:30pm Wed-Mon), at Harmony Hall, offers perhaps Jamaica's most superlative fare (Chef Pierluidi Ricci was voted Jamaica's 'Chef of the Year 2000'). It has a wide-ranging daily menu running from roquefort salad (US$10) and appetizers like marinated marlin (US$8) to lobster pasta (US$22) and shrimp sautéed with garlic and hot pepper flambé with Appleton rum (US$18). Leave room for desserts such as strawberry tart or apple and plum strudel (US$7). Treat yourself!

Evita's (☎ 974-2333; e em@cwja maica.com; Eden Bower Rd; open 11am-11pm Tues-Sun), high above Ochi in a romantically decorated 1860s house, has an airy setting with views. The Italian-Jamaican menu includes jerk spaghetti, and the trademark 'Lasagna Rastafari.' Recommended are the exquisite roasted garlic appetizers (US$2), goat-cheese salad (US$6.50), and herb-crusted lamb chops (US$18). Half-orders are available.

Island Village

This self-contained themed entertainment park (☎ 974-8353/4/5/6; e info@island village.com; w www.islandjamaica.com; admission adults US$10 Mon-Fri, US$5 Sat & Sun, children and senior citizens US$5; open 8am-10pm), next to the cruise-ship pier at the junction of Main St and DaCosta Drive, made a splash when it opened in 2002, ostensibly as a quaint 'Jamaican coastal village' with a beach, upscale craft shops showcasing Jamaican culture (no tacky T-shirts here), a cinema, cyber center, Jimmy Buffett's Margaritaville (a bar and restaurant), a video-casino, a museum showcasing reggae superstars, and a village green and amphitheater for live performances. It was conceived by resort and media visionary Chris Blackwell.

The entrance includes a guided tour of the Reggae Xplosion museum, plus live shows and use of beach and facilities. Admission is free after 5pm.

Coffee & Ice Cream

Delish Bakery & Café (☎ 974-6410; 16 Main St; open 10am-7pm Mon-Sat) is a hip place offering a lively color scheme, plus a meld of international cuisines, cappuccinos, espressos, etc.

For ice cream, head to **Devon House I-Scream** at Island Village.

Groceries

There's a **supermarket** in Ocean Village Plaza and smaller grocery stores scattered along Main St. You can buy fresh produce at the **produce market** on the south side of DaCosta Drive near the clock tower.

ENTERTAINMENT

For the gamut of entertainment options in one spot, check out Island Village (see the boxed text).

Discos

Amnesia Disco (☎ 974-2633; 70 Main St; admission US$5), formerly Acropolis, on the

second floor of Mutual Security Mall, remains the happening scene. It has theme nights, including 'Oldies' on Sunday, and 'Ladies Night' on Thursday. A dress code is enforced.

Strawberry (James St; admission US$5) attempts to compete. It has video slots and a pool downstairs.

Club Memories (☎ 974-2667; cnr DaCosta Dr & Main St) is another contender. Thursday is 'Ladies Nite,' and Sunday is oldies night. Happy hour is from 7pm to 9pm Friday. There's a dress code.

Jamaica'n Me Krazy (☎ 974-2201; admission US$30), in the Renaissance Jamaica Grande Resort, is very popular. Done up in fluorescent, psychedelic decor, it is nonthreatening, has a pool table, dancing, and draws mostly hotel guests and conventioneers. Entrance includes all you can drink.

Roofe Club (☎ 974-1042; 7 James Ave; admission US$3) is a gritty rooftop disco that sends earth-shattering music across the roofs of town; it's the place to get down and dirty with the latest dancehall moves. It can get rough.

The **Exxotic Bar** (☎ 974-9206; Coconut Grove Shopping Village), at the east end of Main St, also has a disco on Saturday.

Many all-inclusive resorts sell night passes permitting full access to meals, drinks, and entertainment.

Bars

Little Pub (☎ 795-1831; 59 Main St) is a touristy favorite and also has sports TV and eclectic entertainment to amuse you while you sit at the bar. A resident band plays six nights. Live entertainment includes an Afro-Carib musical; Tuesday is karaoke night; and there's a cabaret on Friday. Saturday is Ladies Nite. A dress code applies.

James St is dubbed 'Reggae Strip' with several discos and 'entertainment centers.' Use caution at night. **Jack Ruby Bar & Grill** (☎ 795-0768; 1 Main St) has live bands in the rear courtyard. **Balcony Bar Games & Entertainment Centre** is a rooftop center with pool, video games, card games, and occasional live music.

Jimmy Buffett's Margaritaville (☎ 795-4643; Island Village; admission US$5), burst onto the scene in 2002 with three bars, including the Cuban-feel Havana Day Dreamin' bar, plus a rooftop whirlpool tub, and a 100-foot-long waterslide that soars over the main bar and plunges into a freshwater pool.

Mangy Dog Bar (☎ 974-4309), at Mahogany Beach east of Hibiscus Lodge, is a happenin' bar that has live jazz and theme-night entertainment. Movies are shown on a big screen.

Ruins Pub (☎ 974-9712; 17 DaCosta Dr) offers a classy, peaceful environment for enjoying a quiet drink.

Go-Go Clubs

Shadows (☎ 974-5371; 47 Main St; 8pm-4am Wed-Sun; admission US$5) is an intimate spot with exotic dancing.

Shades (☎ 974-4713; admission US$5) is a go-go club at Content Hills, just east of Coconut Grove Shopping Village. The entrance fee includes one drink.

Live Music

Glenn's Jazz Club (☎ 975-4360), on the A3 east of town near Tower Isle, has live jazz. **White River Reggae Park** (☎ 929-4089), on the A3 east of town, hosts sound systems. The **Village Green**, at Island Village, hosts two live shows Monday through Friday. Most top-end hotels also have limbo and cabaret shows. See also Little Pub under Bars, above.

SHOPPING

Ocho Rios Craft Park, on Main St, and **Dunn's River Craft Park**, at Dunn's River Falls, have dozens of craft stalls, as do **Pineapple Place**, on Main St east of town, and **Coconut Grove Shopping Village**, on Main St opposite Beaches Royal Plantation Golf Resort & Spa. **Fern Gully** is lined with stalls where artists sell paintings and carvings at prices marginally lower than elsewhere.

Soni Plaza and **Ocean Village Plaza**, both on Main St, host duty-free stores, including **Taj Mahal** (☎ 974-6455), which offers a vast array of watches and jewelry.

Island Village (cnr Main St & DaCosta Dr) also hosts more than a dozen stores, including several beachwear shops, duty-free

stores, plus **Tallawah Arts** and **Carouches** for quality paintings, carvings, and crafts; **Rum, Roast & Royal**, specializing in rums and coffees; **Tropic Lines Resort Wear**; and a **Fuji** outlet for film and photography needs.

For the best quality art, check out **Harmony Hall** (☎ 975-4222; e info@harmonyhall.com), at Harmony Hall, 4 miles east of town. Harmony Hall is renowned for its Christmas, Easter, and mid-November craft fairs.

Wassi Art (see Wassi Art earlier in this chapter) has fantastic ceramics; it has a showroom in the ceramics factory.

For music tapes and CDs, try **Dis N Dat Music** (☎ 795-2775), Island Plaza, and **Vibes Music Shack** in the Ocean Village Plaza. The latter has more obscure sounds.

You can buy Cuban cigars at **Cigar World** (☎ 974-6317; 25 Taj Mahal Shopping Centre).

GETTING THERE & AWAY
Air

Ocho Rios aerodrome (☎ 975-3101) is at Boscobel, about 10 miles east of town. No international service lands here.

Air Jamaica Express (☎ 726-1344 at Boscobel, 888-359-2475) serves Ocho Rios with scheduled flights from Montego Bay, with connecting service. See Domestic Airlines in the Getting Around chapter for fares.

Also see Charter Flights in the Getting Around chapter.

Public Transportation

Buses, coasters, and route taxis arrive and depart Ocho Rios from the transportation center on Evelyn St.

Buses operate throughout the day between Ocho Rios and Montego Bay, plus Port Antonio, and Kingston (about US$2) and smaller towns throughout the country. Coasters and route taxis are almost as cheap (US$3) and more comfortable. It's a two-hour ride from either Montego Bay or Kingston.

Taxi

A licensed taxi costs about US$20 per person between Montego Bay and Ocho

Rios, and about US$80 between Ocho Rios and Kingston (US$100 to the airport).

JUTA (☎ 974-2292) is the main taxi agency catering to tourists. You can also call a cab from the **Maxi-taxi Association** (☎ 974-2971; Pineapple Place).

Island Car Rentals (☎ 974-2666 in Ocho Rios, 888-991-4255; ☒ www.islandcar rentals.com; Shop 2 Carib Arcade), offers chauffeured transfers to and from Kingston or Montego Bay, as does **Caribic Vacations** (☎ 974-9106, 979-6073 in Montego Bay; 23 Coconut Grove Shopping Village).

GETTING AROUND

There is no shuttle service from Boscobel to downtown. Local buses (US$0.30) and coasters and route taxis (US$0.75) pass by. A tourist taxi will cost about US$15.

Ocho Rios has no bus service within town. Coasters and route taxis ply Main St and the coast road (US$0.50 for short hauls; US$1.25 to Boscobel or Mammee Bay).

Island Car Rentals (see Taxi above) is the most reputable company. Also try **Bargain Rent-a-Car** (☎ 974-8047; Shop 1A Pineapple Place) or **Caribbean Car Rentals** (☎ 974-2513; 99A Main St).

Bikes n Cycles Trading (☎ 974-8247; 6 James Ave) rent scooters and motorcycles.

Government-established taxi fares from downtown are as follows:

Dunn's River	US$22
Firefly	US$55
Prospect Plantation	US$22
Sandals Golf & Country Club	US$28
Shaw Park Gardens	US$22

Note that many taxi drivers don't like to take tourists to places that don't pay them a commission.

Blue Mountain Tours (☎ 974-7075, fax 974-0635; ☒ bmtours@infochan.com; 152 Main St) rents bicycles.

Heave-Ho Sea Taxi (☎ 974-5367; ☒ heave-ho@cwjamaica.com; 11A Pineapple Place) services points along the coast between Couples Ocho Rios and Sandals Dunn's River.

East of Ocho Rios

TOWER ISLE TO BOSCOBEL BEACH

East of Ocho Rios, habitations begin thinning out along the A3. Several beaches lie hidden below the cliffs. Notable among them is Tower Isle, 5 miles east of Ocho Rios.

Jamaica Beach, between Tower Isle and the Rio Nuevo, is renowned for its dive sites offshore.

Rio Nuevo

The Rio Nuevo meets the ocean 5 miles east of Ocho Rios. In 1658, the bluff west of the river's mouth was the site of the most important battle ever fought on the island. A plaque records the events:

On this ground on June 17, 1658, was fought the battle of Rio Nuevo to decide whether Jamaica would be Spanish or English. On one side were the Jamaicans of both black and white races, whose ancestors had come to Jamaica from Africa and Spain 150 years before. The Spanish forces lost the battle and the island. The Spanish whites fled to Cuba but the black people took to the mountains and fought a long and bloody guerrilla war against the English. This site is dedicated to them all.

Boscobel Beach

Boscobel Beach, 4 miles east of Rio Nuevo, is a hamlet dominated by Boscobel Beach Spa Resort & Golf Club. The Boscobel airstrip is here.

Tiny coves farther east harbor fishing hamlets nestled in turquoise lagoons protected by coral reefs.

Places to Stay

Mid-Range Skip's Place (☎ 975-7295; Boscobel PO; doubles US$25-75, three-bedroom flats US$100, up to six people US$150), at Stewart Town, half a mile west of Boscobel Beach, has 16 modest rooms of varying sizes, cooled by cross-ventilation and featuring basic furnishings. Owners Skip and Patricia Walters also rent a three-bedroom flat with kitchen, and offer scuba diving and fishing.

NORTH COAST

Island of Light Centre for Holistic Development (☎/fax 975-4268; ⓔ reggae@mind spring.com; PO Box 6, Retreat St Mary; camping US$15, rooms US$40) is an exquisite B&B in a tastefully converted colonial cottage in the hills. Boasting fine art and antique furnishings, it offers a two-bedroom and a three-bedroom cottage at bargain rates. There's a plunge pool and hammocks under palms; the grounds offer sweeping vistas. The American owner, Sally Sherman, hosts workshops in yoga and meditation, massage therapy, and bodywork. Vegetarian meals are US$12, and feature produce straight from the garden. You can also camp here. To get here, turn off the A3 for Retreat, then turn right (east) by the police station in Retreat.

Top End Beaches Boscobel Spa Resort & Golf Club (☎ 975-7331, fax 975-7370; ☎ 888-232-2437 in North America; ⓦ www.beaches .com; all rates per person: rooms summer US$255-280, suites summer US$305-495, winter rates to be announced, children US$80 supplement), formerly Boscobel Beach, on the A3, was bought by Sandals in 2002 and closed at last visit for a complete renovation. It was slated to reopen as an upscale 230-room all-inclusive resort for singles, couples, and families. The multitiered resort cascades to a beach lined by a boardwalk arcade with cafés, stores, and entertainment facilities. The rooms and suites in nine categories are done up in elegant plantation style and boast king-size or two double beds. Educational programs, a petting zoo, computer lab, video-game room, disco, nursery, kid's pool with waterslide, and 24-hour programs keep the kids amused. There are adults-only areas, plus five bars, four tennis courts, a gym, volleyball, water sports, and an Olympic-size pool, plus complimentary golf at Sandals Golf & Country Club. (For international contact information, see All-Inclusive Resorts in the Facts for the Visitor chapter.)

Couples Ocho Rios (☎ 975-4271, fax 975-4439; ☎ 305-668-0008, 800-268-7537, fax 305-668-0111 in North America; ☎ 020-8900-1913, fax 8795-1728 in the UK; ⓦ www.couples .com; PO Box 330, Ocho Rios; all rates year-round for 2 persons: rooms US$470-520, suites US$625), at Tower Isle, is an upscale all-inclusive resort for couples only. The palm-lined driveway to the porte cochere and the marble lobby hints at the tasteful decor within. The 212 air-con rooms were recently refurbished in chic contemporary vogue – classy! – and have four-poster king-size beds, satellite TV, CD players, and balconies (public corridors, however, still needed work). Suites feature oversize Jacuzzis. A complete array of sports and water sports are offered. There are four restaurants. A small island is reserved for nude bathing and weddings.

Places to Eat
Colette's Café, between Tower Isle and Rio Nuevo, is a twee little roadside shop where Colette and her mum serve simple Jamaican fare, patties, ice cream, and bottled coconut water (US$3).

Skip's Place (☎ 975-7295; dishes from US$5) enjoys a breezy clifftop setting half a mile west of Boscobel Beach. It serves seafood and Jamaican dishes, although the surroundings are a bit dour.

Cliff View (☎ 975-4417; Tower Isle; open 8am-10pm), just west of the Rio Nuevo, is a popular upscale restaurant serving seafood, continental, and Jamaican dishes.

Entertainment
Campbell's Lawn, by the shore at Rio Nuevo, is the setting for 'sound systems' on Saturday nights, drawing crowds.

ORACABESSA
This small town (population 10,000), which hangs on a hillside 13 miles east of Ocho Rios, takes its name from the Spanish *oro cabeza,* meaning 'golden head.' Its main street boasts lots of Caribbean vernacular architecture, with wooden houses trimmed with old-fashioned fretwork. An **Old Fort** with cannon is overgrown.

Below Oracabessa is the marina (formerly a banana-loading port), in the lee of a tombolo on whose western flank pirogues and fishing boats bob at anchor. **James Bond Beach** (☎ 975-3665, fax 975-3399; ⓔ jbb@islandjamaica.com; open

9:30am-6pm Tues-Sun; admission adult/ child US$5/3) is today the setting for concerts and special events. It has toilets, showers, and changing rooms, plus a grill, and water sports that include jet skis (US$55), glass-bottom boats, and banana-boat rides.

The **Oracabessa Foundation** (☎ 975-3393; PO Box 38, Oracabessa) serves as a catalyst for the sustainable development of the town. A plan to develop the waterfront as a major tourist attraction based on a 19th-century theme was on hold at last visit.

James Bond – alias 007 – was 'born' here; see Goldeneye under Places to Stay, later in this section.

A **Scotiabank** (☎ 975-3203; Main St) is in the town center, as is the **post office** (Main St). The private **Oracabessa Medical Centre** (☎ 975-3304; Vermont Ave; open 7:30am-2:30pm Mon-Tues, 7am-12:30pm Wed-Sat) is opposite the Esso gas station at the east end of town; and there's a **public health clinic** (☎ 726-1625; Main St) opposite the **police station**. The **Oracabessa Pharmacy** (☎ 975-3241; Main St) is in Edwards Plaza.

Buses, coasters, and route taxis pass through en route between Ocho Rios and Port Antonio, and between Ocho Rios and Kingston.

Sun Valley Plantation

Sun Valley Plantation (☎ 995-3075; PO Box 20, Oracabessa; closed public holidays) is a working plantation and botanical farm at Crescent on the B13, some 3 miles south of Oracabessa and about 5 miles west of Port Maria. Owners Lorna and Nolly Binns offers garden tours in a plantation setting beside the Crescent River. You can opt to visit the groves of coconuts and other tropical fruits and medicinal herbs (US$12 including snack). Tours are offered.

Special Events

James Bond Beach hosts music events, including **Sashi** (☎ 866-727-4452 in the USA; ⓦ www.sashiconcert.com), a five-day spectacular featuring performances by premier international music stars, a fashion show, and parties.

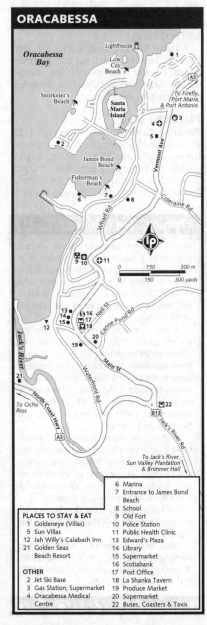

ORACABESSA

NORTH COAST

PLACES TO STAY & EAT	
1	Goldeneye (Villas)
5	Sun Villas
12	Jah Willy's Calabash Inn
21	Golden Seas Beach Resort

OTHER	
2	Jet Ski Base
3	Gas Station; Supermarket
4	Oracabessa Medical Centre
6	Marina
7	Entrance to James Bond Beach
8	School
9	Old Fort
10	Police Station
11	Public Health Clinic
13	Edward's Plaza
14	Library
15	Supermarket
16	Scotiabank
17	Post Office
18	La Shanka Tavern
19	Produce Market
20	Supermarket
22	Buses, Coasters & Taxis

The **James Bond Oracabessa Fishing Tournament** (☎ 975-3663, fax 975-3399) is held in October.

A **James Bond Festival**, first held in 1996, has since been cancelled but may be resurrected. For the latest information, contact the Ian Fleming Foundation (see the boxed text 'Fleming…Ian Fleming').

Places to Stay

Tamarind Great House (☎/fax 995-3252; e tamarind@go-jamaica.com; Crescent Estate, Oracabessa PO, St Mary; singles/doubles US$45/65) is a gem, and a bargain to boot. Nestled atop a hill 4 miles south of Oracabessa, this 'plantation guest house' is run by delightful English hosts Gillian and Barry Chambers. The setting is sublime, with lush valleys and mountains all around. The house boasts gleaming wood floors and reproduction antiques. The 10 cavernous bedrooms, reached by a wide staircase, each open to a vast veranda with Adirondack chairs. There's a TV lounge and an elegant dining room. It has a small swimming pool, and a fish pond stocked with tilapia to keep the kitchen supplied. Tamarind – which is also a working citrus plantation – is 1 mile south of Sun Valley Plantation (turn right at the first Y-fork, then right at the next fork).

Golden Seas Beach Resort (☎ 975-3251, fax 975-3243; w www.goldenseas.com; PO Box 1; singles summer US$83-110, winter US$94-121; doubles summer US$99-126, winter US$110-137; studio single/double summer US$125/141, winter US$136/152; suite summer US$149/165, winter US$160/175), on the A3 half a mile west of Oracabessa, is an attractive hotel of cut stone, with 79 comfortable if uninspired rooms with cable TVs, telephones, and patios overlooking a pool with swim-up bar. It offers water sports, tennis clinics, a spa and gym, cabaret shows, and a resident band.

Goldeneye (☎ 975-3354, fax 975-3620; ☎ 800-688-7678 in the USA; ☎ 020-7440-4360 in the UK; w www.islandoutpost.com; entire complex per night summer US$5000-8000, winter US$7500-10,000), on the A3 immediately east of Oracabessa, is *the* place to be if you're a group with deep pockets. Eight villas, including Ian Fleming's former home, sit on expansive grounds atop a quaint cove. The place attracts the international A-list, including supermodel Naomi Campbell and, appropriately, Pierce Brosnan…Bond himself! Fleming's three-bedroom house features spectacular decor, including Balinese fabrics. Additional clifftop cottages, built of wood and stone and painted autumnal colors, have ceiling fans, a kitchen, an entertainment/TV room, and pampering yet discreet stewards. The coup de grâce is a communal entertainment room where 007 movies are shown. Water sports and excursions are available. There's a tennis court and swimming pool. Cottages

Noel Coward's Peeny-Wally

Sir Noel Coward, the multitalented English actor, playwright, songwriter, and raconteur, first visited Jamaica in 1944 on a two-week holiday. He found peace of mind here and dubbed his dream-island 'Dr Jamaica.' Four years later he rented Ian Fleming's estate, Goldeneye, at Oracabessa, while he hunted for a site to build his own home. He found an incredible view over Little Bay near Galina, 'a magical spot' 4 miles east of Oracabessa.

In 1948 Coward bought the eight-acre estate and set to work building 'Coward's Folly,' a three-story villa with two guest cottages. He named his home Blue Harbour. He had a swimming pool built at the sea's edge and invited his many notable friends, a virtual Who's Who of the rich and famous. The swarm of visitors, however, eventually drove Coward to find another retreat.

While painting with his friend Graham Payne at a place called Lookout (so-named because the pirate Henry Morgan had a stone hut built atop the hill to keep an eye out for Spanish galleons), Coward was struck by the impressive solitude and incredible view. The duo lingered until nightfall, when fireflies appeared (or 'peeny-wallies' in the Jamaican dialect). Within two weeks Coward had bought the land, and eight years later he had a house built, big enough for only himself. He named it Firefly.

Coward lived a remarkably modest lifestyle in Jamaica; he set up the now-defunct Designs for Living shop in Port Maria, the profits from which went to train local schoolchildren in arts and crafts. Coward himself recorded his love of the island and islanders on canvas, in bright, splashy colors.

Coward had spent 30 'delightful years' in Jamaica when he suffered a heart attack at the age of 73. He is buried on the lawns of Firefly beneath a marble slab that reads simply: 'Sir Noel Coward/ Born 16 December 1899/Died 26 March 1973.'

can be rented individually (call for rates), or the complex can be rented as a whole. During November-April, reservations for individual cottages must be made within 90 days of arrival.

Sun Villas (☎ 888-625-6007; W www.sun villas.com) rents deluxe villas locally.

Places to Eat

Jah Willy's Calabash Inn (☎ 369-3617; open from noon), down by James Bond Beach, is a cool place to hang for a game of dominoes or volleyball with the locals. Willy serves seafood and jerk for US$2 and less.

Dor's Fish Pot (☎ 726-0372; Racecourse), on the A3 just over half a mile east of town, is a lively yet rustic jerk and seafood eatery atop the breezy cliffs.

Tamarind Great House is the place to head for a three-course gourmet meal (US$25) (see Places to Stay above).

La Shanka Tavern (Main St), opposite the market, is a lively rum shop, good for a spirited game of dominoes.

FIREFLY

A visit to Firefly (☎ 997-7201, 994-0920, fax 974-5830; PO Box 38, Port Maria, St Mary; admission nonresidents/Jamaican residents US$10/J$100; open 8:30am-5:30pm daily) is one of the most interesting excursions in Jamaica. The cottage, set amid wide lawns high atop a hill 3 miles southeast of Oracabessa and 3 miles west of Port Maria, was the home of Sir Noel Coward, the English playwright, songwriter, actor, and wit. When he died in 1973, Coward left the estate to his friend Graham Payne, who gifted it to the nation. Today the house is a museum, looking just as it did on Sunday, February 28, 1965, the day the Queen Mother visited.

Your guide will lead you first to Coward's art studio, where he was schooled in oil painting by Winston Churchill. The studio displays Coward's original paintings and photographs of the host and a coterie of famous friends. (A film about Coward's life had been discontinued at last visit, but may be shown again.) The upper lounge features a glassless window that

NORTH COAST

offers one of the most stunning coastal vistas in all Jamaica. Contrary to popular opinion, Coward didn't write his famous song 'A Room with a View' here; it was written in Hawaii in 1928. His bedroom features his mahogany four-poster bed and closets still stuffed with his Hawaiian shirts and silk PJs.

Coward lies buried beneath a plain white marble slab on the wide lawns where he entertained so many illustrious stars of stage and screen. A stone hut that once served as a lookout for the pirate Henry Morgan is now a gift store, bar, and restaurant. Musical and theatrical performances are hosted, and a Moonlick party (US$25 all-inclusive) with live jazz band is held on weekends closest to the full moon.

Firefly is well signed along three different routes from the A3.

GALINA POINT & LITTLE BAY

Three miles east of Oracabessa, the A3 winds around the promontory of Galina Point. A 40-foot-high concrete lighthouse marks the headland. South of Galina you'll pass Noel Coward's first house, Blue Harbour (see Places to Stay & Eat below) squatting atop 'the double bend,' where the road and shoreline take a 90 degree turn and open to a view of Cabarita Island. The road drops steeply from Blue Harbour to Cocomo Beach in Little Bay.

The beach is unappealing, despite being popular in the 1950s and 1960s with Coward and Co, but the snorkeling is good 50 yards out (check with locals about current swimming conditions).

The **Zabai Tabai Taino Museum** (☎ 994-9391; 12 Hudson St; free admission), on the main road, is an offbeat museum celebrating the Taino culture. Many of the artifacts were dug up on the owner's property, which has a cave with what are purportedly Taino paintings that glow translucent in winter. The museum has no set hours.

Places to Stay & Eat

Sea Lawn Coral Beach (☎/fax 994-9367; ⓦ www.sealawncoralbeach.com; camping US$10), tucked off a narrow lane from the A3 immediately east of Blue Harbour, is a back-to-basics place offering clifftop camping. You can rent a tent for US$5. You'll share an outside shower and toilet. Rooms with private bathrooms and hot water were being added at last visit, as was a communal kitchen. Meals are prepared to order (US$2-7). The owner offers bus tours. A trail leads to Cocomo Beach.

Belretiro Inn (☎ 994-0035; ⓦ www.1free space.com/belretiro; PO Box 151, Galina District PA, Port Maria; rooms US$25-40), signed off the A3, has 10 modestly furnished rooms with private baths and cold water. It has a seawater swimming pool and a bar.

Caribbean Pearl (☎ 725-0261, fax 725 0261; ⓔ caribbeanpearl@cwjamaica.com; PO Box 127, Port Maria; rooms summer/winter US$75/100), on the A3, is an attractive place that rests on a breezy hilltop at the southern end of Little Bay. It is run to excellent standards. This elegant and intimate villa-style hotel is centered on a pool, and has eight rooms furnished with hardwoods and white wicker, with mosquito nets over the beds. Wide windows open to shady verandas where you can relax on wicker hammocks. Rates include breakfast. It was for sale at last visit.

Hotel Casa Maria (☎ 725-0156; ☎ 509-547-7065, 800-222-6927, fax 509-547-1265 in North America; ⓔ nwas@cwt.com; PO Box 10, Port Maria; standard rooms US$40, superior US$50), next to the Caribbean Pearl, is an option if all else fails. The 20-room hotel has lost its panache since Noel Coward and his celebrated guests frequented the bar in the 1950s and 1960s. The rooms are pleasantly though modestly furnished. Cheaper rooms have garden views; superior rooms have private balconies with ocean views.

Tradewinds Resort (☎ 994-0420, fax 994-0423; ⓦ www.tradewinds-ja.com; Galina PO; downstairs/upstairs rooms US$55/65), farther along from Hotel Casa Maria, is a modern, motel-style resort, cascading down the windswept cliffs to a rocky shore. It has 14 modestly furnished rooms and a cottage suite, all with splendid views, white tiles, small TVs, phones, and remote air-con. There's a small lap pool and a restaurant. Rates include breakfast.

Blue Harbour (☎ 994-0289; ☎ 505-586-1244 in the USA; ⓔ blueharb@aol.com; PO Box 770, Questa, NM 87556, USA; rooms per person US$85), once owned by Noel Coward, is a rather offbeat and somewhat run-down hotel; famous guests once included Marlene Dietrich, Katherine Hepburn, Errol Flynn, and Winston Churchill. Villa Grande has four upstairs bedrooms with a combination of antiques and dowdy utility furniture, plus cable TV. Meals are served on a wide veranda with bay views. Villa Rose has four rooms with basic furnishings and decor. Villa Chica is smaller, very private, with more pleasing tropical decor. Blue Harbour comes fully staffed with cook and housekeeper, though some of the staff appear lackadaisical. Rates include three meals.

Bolt House (☎ 988-6102, fax 975-3620; ☎ 800-688-7678 in the USA; ☎ 0800-614790 in the UK; ⓦ www.islandoutpost.com; c/o Island Outpost, PO Box 118, Ocho Rios; rooms up to 6 people US$750) is set amid 50 cliffside acres across the road from Tradewinds. It has a marble-floored living room (with stupendous coastal views), three sunlit bedrooms, exquisite contemporary furnishings, and a pool overhanging the cliff top. Charlie Chaplin and Joan Sutherland are among an A-list of past guests in this erstwhile private home. It rents as a single unit and comes fully staffed. Rates include airport transfers and all meals.

PORT MARIA
Port Maria (population 8000) is the uninspiring capital of St Mary parish. It nestles in a deep turquoise and aquamarine bay with mountains rising behind.

Fishing pirogues are usually pulled up on **Pagee Beach**, lining the shore. You can hire a guide and boat to go fishing or to take you to Cabarita Island. The beach is safe for swimming. It is also the most westerly spot for surfing along the north coast, with long peelers. The rocks are sharp however; local surfers advise surfing in front of the point closest to town. The action is best in the morning before the trade winds kick in.

St Mary's Parish Church, at the extreme west end of town, was built in 1861 in quintessential English style. Facing it is the **old courthouse**, destroyed in 1988 by fire but since partially restored and today housing a **Civic Centre**. A monument in front commemorates 'Tacky of the Easter Rebellion.'

Remains of **Fort Haldane** can be seen on a bluff beside the A3, half a mile north of town.

Mango Tree Inn (☎ 994-2687; 49 Stennet St; rooms US$8), on the A3, is a very basic option about 800 yards south of the town center on the road to Port Antonio. The inn doubles as a rum shop and place of coital convenience. It has 13 rooms with bathtubs made of concrete, but with cold water only.

Juici Beef Patties (Stennet St), on the southeast side of the town square, sells beef and veggie patties (US$0.40). Wash them down with bottled coconut water.

You can catch buses or coasters to Port Maria from Ocho Rios (US$0.30 or US$2) and Kingston (US$1.50 or US$3.50).

BRIMMER HALL
This 2000-acre working plantation (☎ 974-2244, fax 974-2185; Port Maria PO; open 9am-4pm daily), near Bailey's Vale, 6 miles southwest of Port Maria, grows bananas, coconuts, sugarcane, pineapple, and citrus for export. It's centered on a wooden great house with an impressive interior furnished with oriental rugs and antique furniture, and even an original suit of armor. A one-hour plantation tour by canopied jitney costs US$15. It is signed from the A3. Tours are offered at 11:30am, 1:30pm, and 3pm.

South of Ocho Rios

The A3 winds through sweeping pastoral country on its way south. At Moneague, the road meets up with the A1 from St Ann's Bay, continues over Mt Diablo, and drops dramatically to Kingston.

WALKERS WOOD
This village, on the A3, in the cool hills of St Ann parish, has an active community life.

Bromley Great House sits atop a hill southeast of Walkers Wood. Tucked behind the great house is a small factory where a local cooperative called **Cottage Industries** (☎ 917-2318) makes world-renowned Walkers Wood sauces and spices. Neither Bromley nor the factory are open to the public, but if you call ahead, you can buy a box of sauce and such.

Murphy Hill (☎ 922-0440; Spring Mountain Rd; rooms US$30-40), in the hills near Lydford, 3 miles west of Walkers Wood, has a cozy guest house with clean rooms that boast genuine antiques. There's a small restaurant, but you can also use the kitchen. The grounds are also open to the public (admission US$3; open 10am-7pm daily), with horseback riding, trails for hiking, and a swimming pool popular with Jamaicans escaping the heat of the lowlands. It has fabulous views.

Art Beat (☎ 917-2154) is a craft shop owned by Nancy Burke, alias Inanci. She sells jewelry, carnival and *duppy* masks, painted rocks, and other intriguing creations.

GOSHEN WILDERNESS RESORT

This lakeside 'wilderness resort' (☎ 974-4613; Goshen PO; admission US$3; open 10am-5pm Tues-Sun), 4 miles east of Walkers Wood, happily proclaims: 'You catch it, we cook it.' Its prime attraction is 42 large ponds stocked with tilapia just waiting for you to yank them out of the water.

Attractions include an aviary, a petting zoo, volleyball, paddleboats and kayaks (US$1), nature trails, and horseback rides. A 30-minute 4WD tour of the plantation and nearby hills costs US$25. A fishing package (US$20) includes a drink, tackle, and a guide. The chef will prepare your fish with bammy and festival, but burgers, hot dogs, and jerk dishes are also available at the thatched restaurant and bar.

From Ocho Rios, take the turn-off from the A3 at the White River estuary. Eventually you'll reach a three-way road junction called Goshen. Turn east (left when coming from Ocho Rios) down the deteriorated road. The Wilderness Resort is half a mile beyond the gates for Goshen great house – marked 'Goshen.' If you don't have a car, you can take a minibus from Ocho Rios.

MONEAGUE

This small crossroads town, at the junction of the A3 and the A1, 12 miles south of Ochi, was favored during the 19th century as a hill resort, and before that as a staging post on the journey between Spanish Town and the north coast. The Moneague Training Camp of the Jamaica Defense Force is here, with two **Saracen armored cars** displayed at the gateway.

Café Aubergine (☎/fax 973-0527; Moneague PO; US$6-25; open 11:30am-9pm Tues-Sun), also called Moneague Tavern, is in a 250-year-old tavern half a mile south of town and has been voted 'Best North Coast Restaurant.' The place abounds in tasteful art, china, and real silverware. Jazz or New Age music plays. The menu, written on parchment, is Mediterranean-influenced Jamaican nouvelle cuisine, such as crayfish provençal, chicken in coconut curry sauce, and roast lamb in sauce provençal. Leave room for the chocolate gateau. It hosts an Oktoberfest Party with German fare.

FAITH'S PEN

South of Moneague, the A1 climbs steadily to Faith's Pen, 17 miles south of Ocho Rios. The roadside is lined with stalls selling citrus fruits and dozens of jerk stalls at **Faith Pen Vendor Centre**, where you can sample jerk and try oddities such as cow-cod soup, a concoction made of bull's testes – reputed to be an aphrodisiac – best washed down with 'roots' wine.

The road continues up the pine-forested slopes of Mt Diablo (2754 feet). At 2250 feet the A1 crests the mountain chain and begins its steep, winding descent to Ewarton and the lush Rosser Valley, beautiful from these heights. The summit marks the boundary between the parishes of St Ann to the north and St Catherine to the south.

West of Ocho Rios

The best of the many beaches along this stretch of coast have been snapped up by ritzy resorts. The Dry Harbour Mountains, rising steeply inland, offer recommended scenic drives.

MAMMEE BAY

A favorite with Jamaican beachgoers, Mammee Bay – 3½ miles west of Ocho Rios and 2½ miles east of St Ann – has several little beaches, some hidden away. Much of the beachfront is a private residential estate, but access is offered to the public beaches. Locals flock to **Fisherman's Beach**, where jet skis can be rented.

The St Ann Polo Club hosts the **Hi-Pro Family Polo Tournament & International Horse Show** in August.

Laughing Waters

These cascades – also called Roaring River – are half a mile west of Dunn's River Falls (and a mile east of Mammee Bay). A river appears from rocks amid a shallow ravine about 2 miles from the sea and spills to a charming little beach. This is where Ursula Andress famously appeared, dripping with brine, in the James Bond movie *Dr No* (the beach is known as 'James Bond Beach').

Look for the large fenced-in electrical power structure beside the A3. Follow the river to the beach. Public access to the falls is by foot.

Horseback Riding

The **St Ann Polo Club & Equestrian Centre** (☎ 972-2762; Mammee Bay) offers horseback lessons for US$15 per hour, as well as dressage instruction.

Safari Tours (see Organized Tours under Ocho Rios, earlier in this chapter) offers horseback trips.

Places to Stay

Rose Garden Hotel (☎/fax 972-2825; W www.rosegardenhotel.com; Mammee Bay PO; rooms summer/winter US$65/79, room for 4 people US$100, 600 yards east of Sandals (see below), has 24 air-con studio-suites with kitchenette, private bathroom with hot water, TV, and balcony. They're modestly furnished and uninspired, but clean, with

lots of light. There's a small pool and sundeck, plus a dining room. Rates include breakfast.

Cannon Villas & Silver Palms (☎ 927-1852, fax 977-6143; Mammee Bay PO; rooms summer/winter US$175/230) is at Old Fort Bay on the east side of Mammee Bay. Cannon offers six air-con cottages, each with a living and dining area, satellite TV, fully equipped kitchen, and patio. It also has modern three-bedroom townhouses (Silver Palms), plus one- and two-bedroom apartments fronting a pool and Jacuzzi. A housekeeper is provided.

Sandals Dunn's River Golf Resort & Spa (☎ 972-1610, fax 972-1611; PO Box 51, Ocho Rios; all rates per person: rooms summer US$250-335, winter US$280-365, suites summer US$365-615, winter US$395-645) is a popular, upscale, all-inclusive couples-only resort. A dramatic curving staircase and gleaming marble columns in the lobby recreate the opulence of an Italian palazzo, reflected in the ritzy Roman-style full-service spa. The 250 rooms come in eight categories, all in Sandals' quintessential plantation style. It boasts a huge swimming pool with a cascading waterfall, plus a second pool, three Jacuzzis (two big enough for 40 people each), a pitch-n-putt course, tour desk, four specialty restaurants, videogame room, billiards room, and a theater and disco. (For international contact information, see All-Inclusive Resorts in the Facts for the Visitor chapter.)

There are numerous villas for rent. Several are represented by **Sun Villas** (☎ 888-625-6007; e jamaica@sunvillas.com) and the **Jamaican Association of Villas & Apartments** (JAVA; ☎ 974-2508, fax 974-2967; W www.villasinjamaica.com; PO Box 298, Ocho Rios). Also see Villa Rentals in the Facts for the Visitor chapter.

ST ANN'S BAY

This small market town (population 11,800), 7 miles west of Ocho Rios, rises up the hillside above the bay that Columbus christened Santa Gloria. There are several interesting old buildings in Caribbean vernacular style, especially along Braco St.

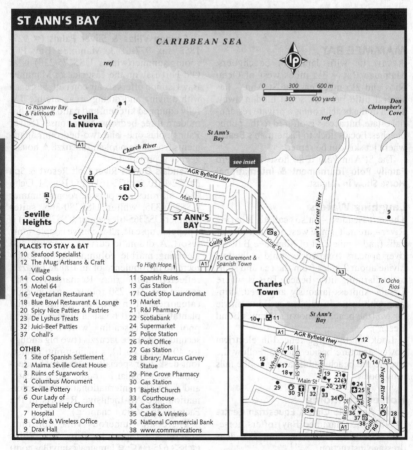

ST ANN'S BAY

CARIBBEAN SEA

reef

0   300   600 m
0   300   600 yards

Don Christopher's Cove

To Runaway Bay & Falmouth

Sevilla la Nueva

St Ann's Bay

reef

Church River

see inset

AGR Byfield Hwy

Main St

ST ANN'S BAY

Seville Heights

St Ann's Great River

Gully Rd

King St

Charles Town

To High Hope

To Claremont & Spanish Town

To Ocho Rios

PLACES TO STAY & EAT
10 Seafood Specialist
12 The Mug; Artisans & Craft Village
14 Cool Oasis
15 Motel 64
16 Vegetarian Restaurant
18 Blue Bowl Restaurant & Lounge
20 Spicy Nice Patties & Pastries
23 De Lyshus Treats
32 Juici-Beef Patties
37 Cohall's

OTHER
1 Site of Spanish Settlement
2 Maima Seville Great House
3 Ruins of Sugarworks
4 Columbus Monument
5 Seville Pottery
6 Our Lady of Perpetual Help Church
7 Hospital
8 Cable & Wireless Office
9 Drax Hall

11 Spanish Ruins
13 Gas Station
17 Quick Stop Laundromat
19 Market
21 R&J Pharmacy
22 Scotiabank
24 Supermarket
25 Police Station
26 Post Office
27 Gas Station
28 Library; Marcus Garvey Statue
29 Pine Grove Pharmacy
30 Gas Station
31 Baptist Church
33 Courthouse
34 Gas Station
35 Cable & Wireless
36 National Commercial Bank
38 www.communications

St Ann's Bay

AGR Byfield Hwy

Wharf St

Church St

Market St

Main St

Park Ave

Negro River

Gully Rd

St Ann's Bay figured prominently in the modern history of Jamaica. Christopher Columbus landed here in 1494 during his second voyage to the Americas. Santa Gloria must have seemed far from glorious in 1503, during his fateful fourth and final voyage, when the explorer had to abandon his worm-infested ships in the bay. Columbus and his crew were stranded for more than a year before finally being rescued (see History in the Facts about Jamaica chapter).

In 1509, the Spaniards built the first Spanish settlement on the island about 800 yards west of St Ann's, at Sevilla la Nueva.

The site was abandoned within four decades and later developed as a sugar estate by a British planter. Other planters established sugar estates nearby and a town grew and prospered as a bustling seaport with forts on opposite sides of the bay.

Marcus Garvey, founder of the Black Nationalist movement, was born here and is honored each August 17 with a parade.

Shoppers can browse the arts and crafts market, beside the A1 opposite Braco St.

Buses, coasters, and route taxis traveling between Montego Bay and Ocho Rios call at St Ann's.

Information

National Commercial Bank (☎ 972-0722; 19 Main St) and **Scotiabank** (☎ 972-2531; 18 Braco St) have branches with 24-hour ATMs.

The **post office** (☎ 972-2307; Main St) is just east of Braco St. You can make international calls and send faxes from the **Cable & Wireless office** (☎ 972-9701; 11 King St; open 8am-4pm Mon-Fri); and from **Www.com munications** (☎ 972-2737; Main St), which also offers Internet services.

The **parish library** (☎ 972-2660; 2 King St) is 100 yards east of Braco St. **Quick Stop Laundromat** is on Wharf St.

St Ann's Bay Public General Hospital (☎ 972-2272), at the far west end of Main St, has an emergency clinic. Several doctors' clinics are concentrated west of the town center on Main St. For pharmaceuticals, try **R&J Pharmacy** (☎ 972-2242; 16 Braco St) or **Pine Grove Pharmacy** (☎ 972-0334; 55 Main St).

The **police station** (☎ 972-2211) is at the corner of Main and Braco Sts.

Walking Tour

Begin outside the parish library (see above). Its grassy forecourt is dominated by the **Marcus Garvey Statue**, with the national hero portrayed larger than life in pewter-gray bronze (see the boxed text 'One God, One Aim, One Destiny').

Westward along Main St you'll pass the **Courthouse**, at the corner of Market St. It was erected in elegant cut limestone and red brick in 1866 with a pedimented porch bearing the scales of justice. Visitors are welcome to observe the court when it's in session. Across the way is the antique **market,** topped by a clock tower, and 100 yards farther west, quaint **St Ann's Bay Baptist Church** (☎ 972-0408).

Nearby, on Hospital Rd just off Main St, is the warehouse of **Seville Pottery** (☎ 972-9517), which makes superb ceramics, including exquisite blue-glazed bottles.

Continue west to the end of Main St, where stands the **Columbus Monument**, topped by a bronze figure of the explorer dressed as a Spanish grandee.

One hundred yards up the hill from the Columbus Monument is the exquisite church **Our Lady of Perpetual Help**, built in contemporary Spanish design by an Irish priest in 1939 of stones recovered from the

NORTH COAST

One God, One Aim, One Destiny

Marcus Garvey was born of working-class parents in St Ann's Bay on August 17, 1887. As a young man he traveled extensively throughout Costa Rica, Panama, and England. He returned well-educated and a firm believer in self-improvement. Inspired to raise the consciousness and well-being of blacks, he founded the United Negro Improvement Association (UNIA) in 1914 to unite 'all the Negro peoples of the world to establish a state exclusively their own.' In 1916 he traveled to the US, where he formed a branch of UNIA in New York (at its peak in the 1920s, UNIA had 5 million members). Garvey, a gifted orator, established a weekly newspaper, the *Negro World,* and built an enormous following under the slogan 'One God! One Aim! One Destiny!'

Garvey set up the Black Star Line, a steamship company, whose aim was to eventually repatriate blacks to Africa. The company, however, failed due to poor management.

The American and British governments considered Garvey a dangerous agitator. They conspired against him, and in 1922 they arrested him on mail-fraud charges. He served two years in Atlanta Federal Prison before being deported to Jamaica. Back in his homeland, the black nationalist founded the reformist People's Political Party. Universal franchise did not then exist in Jamaica, and he failed to gather enough support at the polls. In 1935 he departed for England, where he died in poverty in 1940.

His remains were repatriated to Jamaica in 1984 and interred with state honors in National Heroes Park.

ruins of Sevilla la Nueva. Inside, great beams support the organ loft.

Maima Seville Great House & Heritage Park

The modern history of Jamaica began in 1509, less than half a mile west of present-day St Ann's. The park marks the site of the first Spanish capital on the island – Sevilla la Nueva – and one of the first Spanish settlements in the New World. In 1982, Sevilla la Nueva was declared a Site of the Americas by the Organization of American States, which funds ongoing excavations that the Jamaica National Heritage Trust. This was also the site of an Arawak village.

Scant traces of the original buildings – accessed via a grassy track leading to the ocean from the A1 – can be seen.

When the English captured Jamaica from the Spanish, the land on which Sevilla la Nueva had been built was granted to Richard Hemming, an officer in Oliver Cromwell's invasion army. Over two centuries, Hemming's descendants developed the property as a sugar estate that is today owned by the Jamaica National Trust Commission and is dominated from on high by Seville Great House, built in 1745 by Hemming's grandson. You can explore the decrepit 'English Industrial Works' that include the ruins of a sugar mill, copra kiln, waterwheel, and boiling house, plus the Hemmings' tombs.

The original house, duly restored, contains a **museum** (☎ 972-0665; e seville@wtjam.net; admission US$4; open 8:30am-5pm) depicting the history of the site from Arawak times through slavery and the colonial period.

Horseback rides (US$60 including lunch) are offered. A nature tour allows you to learn about tropical fruits.

Additional ruins stand by the shore just east of the mouth of the Church River.

Activities

Hooves (☎ 972-0905, fax 972-9204; e hooves @cwjamaica.com; 61 Windsor Rd) offers horseback rides, with options for beach or mountain, plus a 'Mountain & River Walk.'

High Hope Adventures (☎ 972-2997, fax 972-1607; 16 Top Rd) offers bike trips in the hills.

Special Events

Jamaica Night, a festival of traditional music and dance, is held at Maima Seville Great House in April. An **emancipation celebration** is held on the grounds every July 29 to August 1, and a **National Mento Yard** celebrates the Jamaican heritage in October.

A **kite festival** (☎ 972-9607) is held each Easter Monday at Drax Hall, on the A3 immediately east of St Ann's Bay.

Places to Stay & Eat

Motel 64 (☎ 972-2308; Main St; rooms US$18) is very basic. Its 14 small rooms have minimal furnishings, but they are clean and have fans and private showers.

High Hope Estate (☎ 927-2277, fax 972-1607; e reservations@highhopeestate.com; PO Box 11; doubles US$85-155) is set amid 40 acres of manicured gardens, lawns, and woodland high in the hills above St Ann's Bay. This Italianate villa was built in 1961 as a private residence for a socialite couple who have welcomed illustrious guests from Charlie Chaplin to Adlai Stevenson. It has seven rooms decorated with priceless antiques. There's a well-stocked library. A lap pool is inset in a sundeck. Rates include breakfast and afternoon 'high tea.' You can rent the entire place fully staffed. To get there, take Market St south (uphill) three blocks from downtown St Ann's, turn right, then take the first left and continue uphill for a mile.

De Lyshus Treats (☎ 972-2317; Main St) is a clean, modern eatery serving inexpensive Jamaican fare, as does **Blue Bowl Restaurant & Lounge**, two blocks west on Main St.

Spicy Nice Patties & Pastries (22 Main St) sells patties for US$0.30.

Seafood Specialist (☎ 794-8870; cnr Jail Lane & A1; US$2-6), though rustic, serves wholesome local fare such as brown stew, plus excellent steamed or fried fish with yams and rice and peas, washed down with natural juices.

The Mug (☎ 972-1018), 300 yards east, beside the A1, serves seafood, including fish-and-chips, lobster, and conch. It has a popular barbecue on Wednesdays – 'Mug Night' – when it stays open until 1am.

Vegetarian Restaurant (☎ 794-8537; 18 Musgrave St; open 8am-9pm) is a health-food restaurant and store selling soups, patties, gluten, beans (US$4), and carrot juice and fruit drinks, etc.

Juici Beef Patties, on Main St, and **Cool Oasis** (☎ 972-2068), beside the A3 on the east side of town, are good for quick take-out snacks.

There's a **supermarket** on Braco St.

PRIORY & ENVIRONS
Priory, about a mile west of St Ann's Bay, has a small beach with water sports and several hotels.

You can turn inland and head into the hills for views down the coast. Here you'll find **Lillyfield Coffee Museum**, at Lillyfield Great House (see Places to Stay later in this section).

Chukka Cove Farm
Polo is the game of choice at Chukka Cove Farm (☎ 972-2506, fax 972-0814; ⓦ www .chukkacove.com; PO Box 160, Ocho Rios), an equestrian center a mile west of Priory. Polo was introduced to Jamaica by the British army in the late 19th century and has a fanatical following among the Jamaican elite.

Chukka Cove Farm also offers a three-hour 'Swim Your Horse Trek' along the sand, twice daily at 9am and 2pm (US$50). Other tours include a three-hour bicycling excursion, gliding and hiking trips, river tubing on the White River, and a 4WD tour to Bob Marley's birthplace (Sunday, Monday, Wednesday, and Saturday).

The farm also hosts a popular Easter Sunday carnival, when crowds flock from as far afield as Kingston.

Circle B Farm
This working plantation (☎ 913-4511; open 10am-5pm daily), at Lewis, near Richmond Hill, a mile south of the A1, has tours that demonstrate the raising of avocados,

bananas, coconuts, and vegetables (US$12; with lunch US$25). The farm is reached via a turnoff a half mile west of Sevilla la Nueva at Priory, 2 miles west of St Ann's Bay.

Cranbrook
This 130-acre botanical garden (☎ 995-3097, fax 770-8071; PO Box 8, Laughlands; adult/ child US$6/3; open 8am-5pm daily) is a treat, crafted in the lush valley that carves up into the hills south of Laughlands, about 3 miles immediately west of Priory; it's signed off the A1. The garden is built around a colonial-era building and includes theme gardens, a hothouse orchid display, pools, and lush lawns (with croquet) fringed by banks of anthuriums and other tropical flowers.

Guided nature walks (about 90 minutes) lead to the river, reflecting giant tree ferns, spectacular torch ginger, heliconia, and other exotic species. Pond fishing is available, as is volleyball, river tubing, and donkey rides.

Scuba Diving
The coral reef offshore of St Ann's Bay is impressive. You can rent equipment from the **Island Dive Shop** (☎ 972-2519) at Columbus Beach in Priory.

Places to Stay
Seacrest Beach Hotel (☎ 972-1594, fax 972-8973; ⓔ seacrestresort@cwjamaica.com; 12 Richmond Estate; rooms summer/winter US$70/90), formerly Jamel Jamaica, in Priory, is a compact property with a Mediterranean feel. Bougainvillea spills over white-washed walls onto a tiled sundeck. Each of the 33 air-con rooms has a TV, telephone, and private balcony overlooking the beach. It has a car-rental agency.

Lillyfield Great House (☎ 972-6045, 754-0997, fax 754-1021; PO Box 20, Bamboo; doubles US$100) is in the hills, about 5 miles east of Brown's Town and 2 miles west of Bamboo, 6½ miles uphill from the turnoff on the A1 at Priory. It is a graciously restored 18th-century, hilltop great house boasting elegant antique furnishings. The five rooms are festooned with modern art,

NORTH COAST

and rates include breakfast. Wooden floors, lofty beamed ceilings, and modern bathrooms add to the appeal. There's a lounge with large-screen TV, a bar and elegant dining room, and a recreation room and swimming pool. There are also four cottages.

RUNAWAY BAY

Runaway Bay (10 miles west of St Ann's) has a modicum of hotels and tourist facilities, though the place is far from sophisticated and of no particular appeal. This one-street village stretches along the A1 for 2 miles, merging with Salem to the east. Several small beaches are supposedly public, although most are the backyards for a few all-inclusive resorts.

Information

There's a Scotiabank **ATM** outlet on Main St in Salem.

A **post office** (☎ 973-2477) is on the main road in Runaway Bay. You can place international calls or send and receive faxes from the **Worldwide Communication Centre** (☎ 973-4830) in Salem Plaza, or nearby from **Telefax Communications** (☎ 973-6327, fax 973-7857; open 8am-11pm), which also offers Internet services.

Runaway Self-Service Launderette (☎ 973-6535; open 7am-10pm) is in Rose Plaza in Salem.

Dr Patrick Wheatle (☎ 973-7761; Main St) has a clinic next to **Johnny's Pharmacy** (☎ 973-6071) in Salem.

In an emergency, call the police (☎ 110 or 973-3433).

Scuba Diving & Water Sports

Runaway Bay has excellent diving. There's a wreck in shallow water in front of Club Ambiance, plus two cars and a plane offshore from Club Caribbean. A reef complex called **Ricky's Reef** is renowned for its sponges. More experienced divers might try the eponymously named **Canyon**. Here, too, is the *Reggae Queen*, a 100-foot tugboat. And **Potty Reef** will have you flush with excitement; divers can't resist having their photo taken sitting on, er, King Neptune's throne.

The following operators offer dives and certification programs: **Jamaqua** (☎ 973-4845, fax 973-4875; W www.jamaqua.com) at Club Caribbean; **Sundivers** at Club Ambiance (☎ 973-2066); and **Reef Divers** (☎/fax 973-4400; e reefdivers@pagescape.com; PO Box 137, Runaway Bay).

Reef Divers also rents snorkel gear (US$5 per hour, US$15 daily), has glass-bottom boat rides (US$12), waterskiing (US$20), banana-boat rides (US$10), and sailboat rentals (US$35 per hour).

Other Activities

SuperClubs Golf Club (☎ 973-7319; open 6:30am-9pm daily) is a par-72, 6884-yard course with several elevated tees and a putting green (US$40, or US$25 for nine holes). There's a pro shop and, upstairs, a classy restaurant and sports bar. Caddies are mandatory (US$15, or US$10 for nine holes).

Dover Raceway (☎ 975-2127), south of Runaway Bay, is the setting for auto and motorcycle races. Races are held once every other month, April to December.

Places to Stay

Budget **Whilby Resort Cottages** (☎ 973-6308; PO Box 111; camping US$10, rooms from US$45), on a hillside behind Runaway Bay HEART Hotel, lets you camp on the lawns. It's owned by the colorful Sister 'P' (Pat) Cassier. Facilities include water and toilets, and kitchen privileges are granted. Sister Cassier also rents eight simple yet cozy air-con rooms with kitchenettes and private bath and hot water.

Mid-Range **Salem Resort** (☎ 973-4256, fax 973-5017; PO Box 151; rooms with fan/air-con/kitchen US$44/49/55) is a family-run resort with 24 rooms, each modestly furnished, with air-con and satellite TVs. There's a bar and restaurant, plus a small pool.

Alamandra Inn (☎/fax 973-4030; PO Box 65; 1-bedroom apartments summer/winter US$50/60, 2-bedroom apartments US$80/90), in Salem, is modestly charismatic. Its 23 beautiful apartments are adorned with bougainvillea and feature air-con and TVs. Guests have use of Club Caribbean, nearby. No children are permitted.

Tamarind Tree Resort Hotel (☎ 973-2628, fax 973-5013; ✉ tamarindtree@cwjamaica.com; PO Box 235; rooms summer US$48-58, winter US$51-60; cottage summer US$133, winter US$144) is a 25-room hotel on the A1, 100 yards from the beach. All rooms have air-con, telephone, and cable TV, and are pleasantly furnished. The hotel also offers three three-bedroom cottages and boasts a disco.

Sunflower Villas (☎ 973-6171, fax 973-7381; PO Box 150; rooms per person US$67-102) has 80 units that range from one to five bedrooms; some have private dipping pools. Cooks and housekeepers are available. There are two pools, plus water sports on a rather scruffy beach. All-inclusive rates also include airport transfers.

Runaway Bay HEART Hotel (☎ 973-6671, fax 973-4704; ✉ runaway.heart@cwjamaica.com; PO Box 98; rooms summer/winter US$78/90) is a bargain. With a breezy hillside setting, this plantation-style manor has 56 spacious, pleasantly furnished, well-lit rooms with satellite TVs, air-con, and coastal vistas from balconies in an impressive new hillside block. Some guests report that the service is excellent, as well it should be: next door is the hotel training school. Others say the service is slow, which is also to be expected, since trainees are learning the ropes. In essence, you're a guinea pig. It overlooks the SuperClubs Golf Course, to which hotel guests have access. A shuttle runs to Cardiff Hall Beach. Amenities include a pool, fitness center, and an elegant restaurant. Room rates include tax & service charge.

Top End Club Ambiance (☎ 973-2066, fax 973-2067; ⓦ www.clubambiance.com; PO Box 20; standard single summer/winter US$125/135, double per person US$85/95, deluxe suite per person US$105/115) is a recently renovated all-inclusive popular with charter groups. It has two small beaches, plus a pool and sundeck. Its 80 air-con, oceanfront rooms and 15 junior suites have balconies and telephones. King-size beds or two queens are standard. It has a restaurant, three bars, and a disco, plus a dive facility.

Club Caribbean (☎ 973-3507, fax 973-3509; ☎ 212-545-8431, 800-223-9815 in North America; ⓦ www.clubcaribbean.com; PO Box 65, Runaway Bay; garden cottage single/double US$125/190, ocean-view cottage US$155/250, suite US$135/170), in Salem, is another favorite of European charter groups. This all-inclusive has 20 rooms, 130 conical, African-style thatched-roof cottages, and 20 one-bedroom suites behind a 1000-foot-wide beach (which also has a nude section). The rooms are spacious, with king-size beds and wooden ceilings. There's plenty of activity at the disco and three bars. Activities include a full range of water sports, a PADI dive center, and party cruises. Online bookings receive a 20% discount.

Breezes Runaway Bay Golf & Beach Resort (☎ 973-2436, fax 973-2352; ☎ 800-467-8737 in North America; ☎ 01749-677200 in the UK; PO Box 58, Runaway Bay; all rates per person: standard US$275-320, 'deluxe' US$300-335, 'premium' US$320-360, 'luxury' US$345-375, suites US$400-520) is a 234-room, 27-acre SuperClubs all-inclusive resort catering to couples and singles; it appeals to an unsophisticated crowd. It has a massive freeform swimming pool and fronts the best beachfront in Runaway Bay. A nude section has its own Jacuzzi (one of three on site). Facilities include scuba diving and a trapeze, plus well-stocked stores, a nightclub and disco, and a choice of restaurants. The price includes golf at the golf club.

Hedonism III (☎ 800-467-8737; ☎ 800-467-8737 in the USA; ☎ 01749-677200 in the UK; PO Box 250; ⓦ www.superclubs.com; all rates per person: pool view US$350-470, garden view US$385-470, oceanfront US$410-485, oceanfront 'au naturel' US$425-495, garden view 'au naturel' US$545-585, suites US$545-645) is SuperClubs' latest all-inclusive resort for uninhibited adults – even the female staff parade around in g-strings – and is billed, accurately, as 'wet and wild.' The 10-acre property offers 225 air-con rooms, including 'swim-up' rooms, with steps leading into a swimming pool. Rooms boast king-size beds, cable TVs (with adult viewing), lively tropical fabrics, and large Jacuzzi tubs. The two beaches, alas, are unimpressive. Activity centers on three pools, including a nude pool-and-Jacuzzi where XXX-rated antics occur. A see-through waterslide coils down from the Octopussy disco. Facilities include four restaurants, a piano bar, gym, tennis, volleyball, circus workshop, water sports, and complimentary golf. There are far more single men than women; a third female in a group stays free; and local hookers are permitted access to the resort.

Franklyn D Resort (☎ 973-4591, fax 973-4600; ☎ 800-337-5437, fax 516-223-4815 in North America; ☎ 020-8795-1718, fax 8795-1728 in the UK; ⓦ www.fdrholidays.com; PO Box 201; per person US$250-450 depending on season) is a Spanish-hacienda–style, all-inclusive, family resort with 67 newly redecorated suites, including some two- and three-bedroom apartments. Children are provided their own facilities. A 'Girl Friday' is assigned to each suite to look after the kids. The resort has three restaurants and five bars, plus a new oceanfront spa and waterslide, and a state-of-the-art computer/business center. Children under 16 stay free.

Piper's Cove Resort (☎ 973-7156, 800-258-6488, fax 973-7714; ⓔ info@piperscoveresort.com; PO Box 295; single/double US$70/80), next to Hedonism III, offers 14 spacious one-bedroom suites in Spanish-style villas with gracious plantation-style rattan furnishings, air-con, and cable TV. There's a bar and pool.

Siesta and **Bahia** (☎ 962-7130, fax 961-0549; ⓔ bloomfield.g.h@cwjamaica.com; PO Box 150, Mandeville; Siesta US$3400-4800, Bahia US$1000-1200), just east of the Shell gas station, are a fully-staffed five-bedroom beach house and adjoining honeymoon cottage sharing a lighted swimming pool with attached kiddies' pool. Siesta has a large lounge-cum-dining area with cable TV, VCR, and stereo; Bahia is cooled by fans and features a sleeping loft, lounge with TV, open kitchen, and observation deck. Guests get to use ocean kayaks.

The **Jamaica Association of Villas & Apartments** (JAVA; ☎ 974-2508, fax 974-

2967, ☎ 800-845-5276; ⓦ www.villasinjamaica.com; PO Box 298, Ocho Rios) offers beachside and hilltop villas, including **Osbourne Great House** (summer US$2000, winter US$2935), a restored gingerbread mansion dating from 1842, and **Bellaire Great House** (summer US$3200, winter US$4667), a centenary mansion that was once owned by English aristocracy.

Places to Eat

Seafood Giant (☎ 973-4801; US$3-16; open 7am-midnight), at the west end of Runaway Bay, serves such dishes as jackfish with spinach roasted in foil or fried with bammy, plantain, and rice and peas; or order curried, creole, or braised garlic shrimp. The filling meals are an excellent value. However, if you pick your own fish, you'll be charged 'according to size.'

Cardiff Hall Restaurant (☎ 973-2671; US$2-20; open 7am-10pm) is an elegant restaurant at Runaway Bay HEART Hotel, and offers a good bargain. Reservations are essential.

Nana Kofi Vegetarian Restaurant (☎ 973-4266; US$1-5; open 9am-7pm Mon-Sat), 100 yards west of the gas station, specializes in health food and vegetarian cuisine. Typical dishes include chick pea soup, vegetarian patties, and veggie burgers.

Rising Sun (☎ 973-7908; open noon-10pm, closed Mon), next to the gas station, is recommended for smoked marlin appetizer (US$5.50), pizzas (US$8-15), and curried shrimp (US$18).

In Salem, there's a **Devon House I-Scream** shop on the A3 and **L&M Grocery** (☎ 973-7292; Main St).

Entertainment

The usual charmless go-go clubs include the **19th Hole Club** (☎ 973-5766), in Salem Plaza, which also has pool and live music. Also here is **Club Encore**, one of the nicer bars among the less-than-inspiring scene, and **Slick's Tappa Top 8 Ball Sports Bar**, with pool tables.

For a more touristy experience, try the shows at **Club Caribbean** or the **Safari Disco** at Club Ambiance, which has special attractions on weekends. **Le Studio Dynamite** (☎ 973-2628; open 9pm-2am; admission US$5), a disco in the Tamarind Tree Resort Hotel, has a happy hour from 6pm to 8pm nightly; Friday is 'Ladies' Night.'

You can purchase a night pass to **Breezes** (US$45) granting unlimited booze, food, and entertainment.

Getting There & Around
Buses, coasters, and route taxis traveling the A1 between Montego Bay (1½ hours; US$1-2.50) and Ocho Rios (40 minutes; US$0.50-1.50) stop in Runaway Bay. Public transport arrives and departs from the square in front of Patty Place, catercorner to the post office.

Salem Car Rentals (☎ 973-4167, fax 973-5779; e salem.motors@cwjamaica.com; PO Box 207) and **Caribbean Car Rentals** (☎ 973-3539) are located on the main road in Salem.

Need a taxi? Try **Sir Win's Love Line Taxi Service** (☎ 973-4954).

DISCOVERY BAY
This wide flask-shaped bay, 5 miles west of Runaway Bay and 5 miles east of Rio Bueno, is a popular resort spot for locals drawn to its Puerto Seco Beach. The town itself has only marginal appeal.

The Kaiser Bauxite Company's Port Rhoades bauxite-loading facility dominates the town (it was used for Dr No's headquarters – Crab Cay – in the James Bond movie, *Dr No*). Large freighters are fed by conveyor belts from a huge storage dome. You can follow the road signed 'Port Rhoades' uphill half a mile to a lookout point offering fantastic views over the bay (there is a pair of high-power, pay-per-view binoculars). Note the metal likeness of Anansi, the folkloric spider, in the playground of the Kaiser's Sports Club, en route.

To the right of the loading dock is **Quadrant Wharf**, the meager remains of a fort built in 1777.

Locals consider this to be where Christopher Columbus first landed on Jamaican soil in 1494, though others say it was at Rio Bueno (see that town in the Montego Bay & Northwest Coast chapter).

The University of the West Indies has its **Marine Biology Laboratory** (☎ 973-3274), immediately west of Columbus Park (see below).

Information
There's a bank and supermarket at Columbus Plaza, on the A1, at the east end of town. The **Kaiser Medical Clinic** (☎ 973-3568; open 8am-4:30pm Mon-Fri) is just off the A1, immediately east of Port Rhoades Rd; its signed at the turnoff for Kaiser west of town. The **Discovery Bay Pharmacy** (☎ 973-9073; Main St) is on the A1 in the center of town.

You can make calls from **Fontana's Direct** (☎ 973-9431; open 8am-10pm Mon-Sat, till 4pm Sun), opposite Puerto Seco Beach.

Tumour Wash & Dry (☎ 973-3170; Main St; open 7am-8pm Mon-Sat) is in Columbus Plaza.

Puerto Seco Beach
The eastern side of the bay is rimmed with white-sand beaches. Puerto Seco Beach (☎ 973-2660; adult/child US$2/1; open 8am-5pm), in the center of town, is the main one. Open to the public, it has tennis courts, carousels, and a fun fair, plus rustic eateries and bars. On weekends and holidays locals flock from miles. You can also rent fishing boats here.

Columbus Park
This open-air roadside museum (admission free) sits atop the bluff on the west side of the bay. The eclectic historic memorabilia include anchors, cannons, nautical bells, sugar-boiling coppers, and an old waterwheel in working condition that creaks and clanks as it turns. There's also a diminutive locomotive formerly used to haul sugar at Innswood Estate.

Green Grotto Caves
This impressive system of caves and tunnels (☎ 973-2841; w www.greengrottocaves.com; adult/child US$20/10; open 9am-4pm), 2 miles east of Discovery Bay, extends for

about 10 miles. Steps lead down into the impressive chambers, where statuesque dripstone formations are illuminated by floodlights. Pre-Columbian Arawaks left their artwork on the walls. The highlight is Green Grotto, a glistening lake 120 feet down. The entrance fee includes fruit punch and a guided one-hour tour. Your guide will tap stalactites to produce eerie sounds. Children under age five get in free.

Special Events
A **Derby Day** sponsored by the Kaiser company is held each August and features live music, marching bands, dancing, and the Pushcart Derby, when dozens of youths representing parish teams compete in a downhill race on the wooden pushcarts that they normally use for transporting goods. Despite their miniature wheels, the carts have been clocked at 60 mph in the homestretch! Now you understand why the road, rising behind Port Rhodes, is marked with lanes like a racetrack and lined with tire barriers. The event is featured in the movie *Cool Runnings*.

Throughout the year, Kaiser sponsors occasional 'Family Days,' with push-cart racing, beauty contests, and 'sound systems.'

The **Discovery Bay Fishing Tournament** (☎ 925-0893, fax 931-5234; e discoverybay@ kasnet.com) is held every September or October.

Places to Stay & Eat
Villas of Discovery Bay (☎ 931-5234; w www.cariboutpost.com; summer from US$1000-5900, winter from US$1850-7200) are 19 private rental villas, many along the 'Fortlands Millionaires Row.'

Portside Villas (☎ 973-2007, 973-3135, fax 973-2720; PO Box 42; rooms/studios/one-bedroom suites/two-bedroom suites summer US$45/80/90/155, winter US$50/95/105/180, three-/five-bedroom villas weekly summer US$2000/3100, winter US$2100/3250) enjoys a splendid setting. Thirty of its rooms and apartments are set in pleasant grounds tight up against the shore; others are on the hillside across the road. There are also efficiency apartments with kitchenettes and two fully

staffed, three- and five-bedroom villas with their own pools. Facilities include water sports, fishing boat rentals, two pools, whirlpool spa, and a tennis court, plus a notable restaurant.

For a quick bite, try the cheap roadside stalls that line Main St and sell jerk chicken, bammy, etc.

Ultimate Jerk Centre (☎ 973-2054; US$2-8; open 11am-10pm), opposite Green Grotto Cave, serves jerk pork and chicken.

Sea Shanty Restaurant (☎ 973-2007; US$2-22; open 8am-10pm), in Portside Villas, offers a more formal albeit relaxed setting, and serves local dishes, sandwiches, burgers, seafood, plus continental favorites including steaks. It has a four-course dinner that varies nightly.

Classique Night Club (☎ 973-9224), on Main St, 200 yards east of Puerto Seco Beach, has exotic dancing, plus pool tables.

Getting There & Around
Buses, coasters, and route taxis ply the A1 between Montego Bay and Ocho Rios and stop in Discovery Bay, notably at the junction of the A1 and the road to Brown's Town. You can walk almost anywhere in town.

Dry Harbour Mountains

Paved roads lead south from Discovery Bay, Runaway Bay, and St Ann's Bay and ascend into the Dry Harbour Mountains. In this off-the-beaten-track area, the badly potholed roads twist and turn through scenic countryside as they rise to the island's backbone.

Only two main roads run east-west. The lower, the 'Great Interior Road' (the B11), parallels the coast about 7 miles inland. It begins at Rock, a mile east of Falmouth, and weaves east to Claremont.

BROWN'S TOWN
Brown's Town (population 8000) is a lively market town 7 miles south of Runaway Bay.

Many noble houses on the hillsides hint at its relative prosperity. The town is at its most bustling during market days (Wednesday, Friday, and Saturday), when the cast-iron **Victoria Market** (cnr Main St & Brown's Town Rd) overflows with higglers.

The town's Irish estate owner Hamilton Brown (1776-1843) financed the building of **St Mark's Anglican Church** (☎ 975-2641; cnr Main St & Brown's Town Rd) in Victorian Gothic style (allegedly, he also arranged for the Baptist church to be burned down so that blacks would have nowhere to worship). Also note the fine cut-stone **courthouse** (Brown's Town Rd) with neoclassical columned portico; and **St Hilda's School** (☎ 975-2218; St Christopher's Rd), a grand Teutonic Anglican-run structure on the hill immediately east of town; the girls wear lavender uniforms.

Most commercial businesses line the main road, called Main St north of the town center and Brown's Town Rd south of it. There's a **National Commercial Bank** (☎ 975-2242); **post office** (☎ 975-2216); **Direct Telecom** office (☎ 975-2926; Shop 4, Diedrick's Plaza) for international calls and faxes; the **DeCarteret Medical Centre** (☎ 975-2265), with a pharmacy nearby; and a historic **police station** (☎ 975-2233).

You can buy patties and pastries at **Spicy's Patties & Pastries** (☎ 975-2544; Top Rd), on the north side of the Victoria Market, which sells fresh produce at stalls that also spill along Main St. There are several modest restaurants along the commercial corridor selling hearty Jamaican fare for US$1-5.

Public transport arrives and departs from the east end of Top Rd, a block off Main St. Coasters and route taxis (US$3) operate between Brown's Town and Kingston, and more than a dozen ply the Ocho Rios route via Discovery Bay and Runaway Bay.

NINE MILE

In the middle of a poor farming district, this tiny mountain hamlet is 9 miles east of Alexandria, a small crossroads village that is 9 miles south of Brown's Town. Despite its totally out-of-the-way location, Nine Mile is

firmly on the tourist map for pilgrimages to Bob Marley's birth site and resting place, which the Bob Marley Foundation has turned into a commercial success.

The community where the 'King of Reggae' was born on February 6, 1945, is set dramatically in the midst of Cockpits. The road to Nine Mile continues to Claremont and the A1.

A memorial reggae concert is held here every February 6. For information, contact the **Bob Marley Foundation** (☎ 927-9152; e marleyfoundation@cwjamaica.com; 56 Hope Rd, Kingston).

Coasters and route taxis operate between Brown's Town, Alexandria, and Claremont, stopping in Nine Mile. **Caribic Vacations** (☎ 974-9106 in Ocho Rios, ☎ 979-6073, 953-8343 in Montego Bay) is among the tour companies that offer tours from Kingston, Montego Bay, and Ocho Rios.

Bob Marley Museum

This museum (☎ 999-7003; admission US$12; open 8am-5:30pm daily), containing the crypt of Bob Marley, is run by the Bob Marley Foundation, which ostensibly uses the proceeds to advance education, health, and social services in the local community (although the staff and guides – a mix of humble Rastafarians and others dolled up with gold chains – are hard-pressed to actually name any beneficiaries).

After paying your entrance fee, you are led by a Rastafarian guide up a steep path lined with international flags. Between puffs on a spliff of *ganja,* your guide will tell of Marley's childhood and simple lifestyle.

Marley was born in a house below the museum site. He moved into the hut on the hill – called Zion – when he was three months old. The hut, like virtually everything else, is painted yellow, green, and red, representing sunshine (yellow), nature (green), and blood (red). Inside there is merely a bed and walls covered with adoring graffiti and miscellany left by visitors. Behind the hut is the 'inspiration stone' (or 'Mt Zion Rock') on which Marley sat and learned to play the guitar.

Marley's body lies buried along with his guitar in an 8-foot-tall oblong marble

NORTH COAST

mausoleum inside a tiny church of traditional Ethiopian design.

The museum is a work-in-progress; a garden was being laid out at last visit.

No video camera or taping equipment is allowed.

The museum shop sells Marley paraphernalia of every description. The guides and abundant hangers-on have an annoying habit of hitting you up for extra money. Give them a J$100 (US$3) bill and you're likely to receive a contemptuous stare for being a skinflint! Don't be suckered. Some foreign women report having been pestered.

Places to Stay & Eat
Wailer's Villa (☎ 387-9742, 384-2157; Alexandria PA, St Ann; rooms US$22-45), opposite the museum, is a modern property with 14 basically furnished rooms with cool tile floors and attractive bathrooms; the upstairs rooms have lofty wooden ceilings plus balconies.

The **museum restaurant** (US$3-5) serves vegetarian I-tal dishes in a 'rootsy' bar.

Club Marcus, opposite the museum, is a lively little bar serving snacks.

CAVE VALLEY
This tiny village sits on the border of St Ann and Clarendon parishes, 8 miles south of Alexandria, at the north end of Vera Ma Hollis Savanna, a 7-mile-long valley. During the early years of the British occupation in the late 17th century, the region was a center for the Maroons. The British built a barracks here during the First Maroon War in the 1730s.

The Cave River rises in the mountains near Coleyville, 10 miles west of Cave Valley, where in the dry season you can see the **Cave River Sinks**, two holes into which the river disappears to reemerge 13 miles north near Stewart Town.

The road through the Cave River Valley eventually reaches Spaldings, Christiana, and Mandeville.

CLAREMONT & ENVIRONS
The A1 turns inland at St Ann's Bay and runs south 9 miles to Claremont (population 1500), a regional market town that prospered briefly during the 1960s and 1970s on the income generated by bauxite and cattle-ranching activities. The town has an attractive square centered on a handsome **clock tower**.

South of Claremont, the A1 climbs from sea level to 1500 feet in 5 miles and merges with the A3 at Moneague, rising beyond to Mt Diablo (2754 feet) on the border with St Catherine parish before dropping down to Spanish Town and Kingston.

Claremont is on the main bus route between the north coast and Kingston, and many coasters and route taxis from Kingston (US$4) and Ocho Rios (US$1) pass through.

Edinburgh Castle
One of Jamaica's more gory and fascinating stories surrounds the ruins of Edinburgh Castle, 8 miles southwest of Claremont, on the southern outskirts of Bensonton.

The two-story fortified house with towers was built by Lewis Hutchinson, a deranged Scot who settled in Jamaica in the mid-18th century. The 'castle' stood close by what was the main coach road between St Ann's Bay and Spanish Town. Hutchinson invited his victims into the house, where he wined and dined them before robbing and murdering them.

Eventually the maniac quarreled with a neighboring planter, whom he almost killed. A soldier was then sent to arrest him. He, too, was shot dead, but the game was up. Hutchinson was hanged on March 16, 1773.

Local lore says Hutchinson disposed of his victims in a deep sinkhole – the **Kenky Hole** – 400 yards south of the castle, where 43 watches belonging to his victims were discovered. Locals are frightened of the hole, which 'moans.'

Sun Seekers JA (☎/fax 973-7917; e sun seekersja@hotmail.com), in Runaway Bay, runs tours.

Port Antonio & Northeast Coast

The northeast coast is Jamaica's undiscovered quarter. The mountainous east coast parish of Portland (population 160,000)

Highlights

- Boston Bay for the best – and hottest – jerk in Jamaica
- The Rio Grande Valley for guided hiking
- Enchanting Blue Lagoon for swimming, a fine meal, and live jazz
- Exhilarating Reach Falls for cooling freshwater dips
- The Rio Grande for a soothing bamboo raft trip

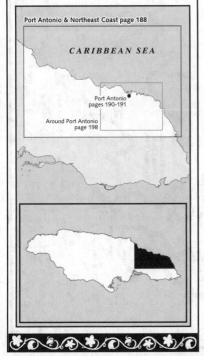

Port Antonio & Northeast Coast page 188

CARIBBEAN SEA

Port Antonio
pages 190-191

Around Port Antonio
page 198

receives far fewer tourists than rival resort areas.

This is the island's windward corner, where surf rolls ashore into perfect beach-lined coves, and waves chew at rocky headlands. Colonial-era edifices are relatively few, though beautiful pocket-size beaches line the shore. You'll also find several unspoiled fishing villages where budget travelers can ease into a laid-back local lifestyle. The only town of importance is Port Antonio, east of which a fistful of deluxe resort-hotels 'unfold like a board game of castles and palaces,' says writer Herb Hiller.

Portland is famed for its high rainfall. Year-round, moist northeast trade winds meet the John Crow and Blue Mountains, which force the saturated air to rise and cool until the moisture condenses and falls in torrents. Parts of upland Portland have sometimes recorded more than 300 inches of rain a year.

The vegetation is correspondingly lush. The forested mountains with their deep gorges and rushing rivers beckon invitingly to hardy hikers. The Rio Grande Valley and Blue Mountains-John Crow National Park – a last refuge for the guinea-pig–like Jamaican coney, and for the world's largest butterfly, the giant swallowtail – are being linked to the Port Antonio Marine Park by a 'conservation corridor.' Manatees are occasionally seen near the mouth of the Rio Grande. Fewer than one hundred of these extremely gentle creatures are thought to remain in the coastal waters of Jamaica. The slow-moving beasts cruise at 2 or 3mph, feeding on sea grasses in shallow waters and estuaries.

The Port Antonio Destination Marketing Program markets the region as 'Port Antonio *Naturally*' to an eco-conscious niche market. Contact Unique Destinations (see Organized Tours in the Getting There & Away chapter), which offers vacation and hotel packages, plus eco-excursions that include birding tours.

NORTHEAST COAST

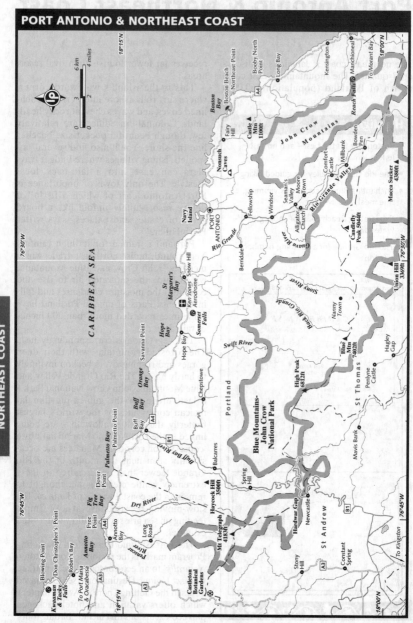

PORT ANTONIO & NORTHEAST COAST

Guest house owners are served by the **Port Antonio Guest House Association** (☎/fax 993-7118; Ⓦ www.go-jam.com).

Port Antonio

Port Antonio (population 14,400), 68 miles east of Ocho Rios, is the capital of Portland parish and is Jamaica's main banana port. The melancholic town still has the tropical lassitude of a maritime harbor, and there is little of the hustle of Montego Bay or Ocho Rios. Goats snoozing in the shade of verandas sum it all up.

But things are stirring. At last visit, the airport was being expanded. The arrival of Sandals resort chain in 2002 promises to lend marketing clout to the region. Navy Island is slated for redevelopment. The marina has been revitalized and was sched-uled to receive a boardwalk. And a super-yacht wharf was almost complete, aimed at attracting anew the international yachting crowd; for information, contact the Port Authority (☎ 922-290; Ⓦ www.themarina atportantonio.com; 15-17 Duke St).

All bananas exported from Jamaica depart from Port Antonio's dock. The loading of fruit is mechanized, so you'll no longer see the Tallyman tallying bananas or stevedores 'working all night on a drink of rum.'

HISTORY

The Spanish christened the bay 'Puerto Anton' in the late 16th century, but made no serious effort to settle. In 1723 the British laid out a rudimentary town on the peninsula and named it Titchfield; a fort was added in 1729. However, rampant fevers in the swampy coastlands and constant raids

Errol Flynn

Errol Flynn (1909-59), the infamous Hollywood idol, arrived in Portland parish in 1946 when his yacht *Zacca* washed ashore in bad weather. Flynn fell in love with the area and made Port Antonio his playground and home (his acting career was by then washed up). In his autobiography, *My Wicked, Wicked Ways*, he described Port Antonio as 'more beautiful than any woman I've ever seen.'

Flynn bought the Titchfield Hotel and Navy Island, where he threw wild, extravagant parties – locals tell exaggerated tales of Flynn's exploits: 'Remember de day 'im drove de Cadillac into de swimming pool?' Flynn's beguiling ways inevitably attracted the attention of other stars of stage and screen, like Clara Bow, Bette Davis, and Ginger Rogers.

With his third wife, Patrice Wymore, Flynn later established a cattle ranch at Boston Estate. He also planned a lavish home at Comfort Castle, and he had grandiose plans to develop Port Antonio into a tourist resort. But heavy drinking and a profligate lifestyle added to the toll of his ill-health. He died in 1959 before his plans could be brought to fruition. The wild parties are no more, but his legend lives on.

PORT ANTONIO

Navy Island

reef

trail

West Harbour

To Buff Bay & Kingston   A4

Boundbrook Crescent

Boundbrook Wharf

Ken Jones Pier

Port Antonio Marina

Boundbrook Rd

Rice Piece Rd

Annotto River

W Palm Ave

Little Annotto Rd

Hall's Ave

Nuttall Rd

E Baptist Ave

W Baptist Ave

E Baptist Ave

Portland Rd

Bonnie View Rd

Grossett Rd

Love Lane

0   50   100 m
0   50   100 yards

NORTHEAST COAST

PLACES TO STAY
- 3 Little Reef Guest House
- 4 Ocean Crest Guest House
- 5 Ivanhoe's
- 6 Scotia Guest House
- 7 DeMontevin Lodge
- 8 Brown's Caché Villa
- 9 Holiday Home
- 12 In & On Guest House
- 14 Shadows
- 18 Bonnie View Plantation Hotel
- 58 Triff's Inn

PLACES TO EAT
- 13 Blue Marlin Bar & Restaurant
- 25 Golden Happiness; Golden Cyber Centre
- 30 Huntress Marina Bar & Restaurant
- 33 Coronation Bakery
- 36 Three Star Lion Bakery
- 51 The Chicken Place
- 54 Juici Beef Patties

OTHER
- 1 Fort George Ruins
- 2 Titchfield School
- 10 Folly
- 11 Folly Oval Cricket Ground
- 15 Esso Gas Station
- 16 Port Antonio Hospital
- 17 New Craft Market
- 19 Port Antonio Yacht Marina
- 20 Village of St George; Ela Systems; Gallery Café; Club Extacy; Spencer Gallery
- 21 Shell Gas Station
- 22 Portland Parish Library
- 23 Craft Market
- 24 Eastern Communication, Ltd
- 26 Clock Tower
- 27 Public Telephones; Courthouse
- 28 Post Office
- 29 Jamaica Arcade
- 31 Huntress Marina & Charter Services; Bamboo Bike, Car & Jeep Rental
- 32 Gallery Art Ambokile
- 34 Grand Valley Tours
- 35 Musgrave Market
- 37 Roof Club
- 38 National Commercial Bank
- 39 Cenotaph; Port Antonio Square
- 40 A&E Pharmacy
- 41 Direct Telecom
- 42 CIBC Jamaica Banking Centre
- 43 JTB Office & City Centre Plaza
- 44 Police Station
- 45 Goebel Plaza; Travel Experts
- 46 Scotiabank
- 47 Transportation Station; Taxis
- 48 Cable & Wireless Office
- 49 Texaco Gas Station
- 50 Kamlyn's Supermarket
- 52 Eastern Rent-a-Car
- 53 RBTT Bank
- 55 Ever Brite Laundry
- 56 Agape Family Medical Clinic
- 57 Christ Church

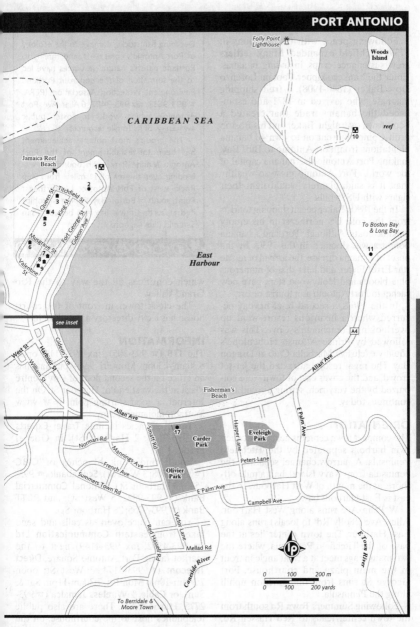

PORT ANTONIO

Folly Point
Lighthouse

Woods
Island

CARIBBEAN SEA

reef

Jamaica Reef
Beach

1

2

Titchfield St
3
4
5

Queen St
King St
Fort George St
Gideon Ave

To Boston Bay
& Long Bay

Musgrave St
6
7
8
9

Valentine
St

*East
Harbour*

10

11

see inset

West St
Harbour St
William St

Gideon Ave

Allan Ave

A4

Allan Ave

E Palm Ave

Fisherman's
Beach

Allan Ave

17

Smatt Rd
Mannings Ave

Norman Rd
French Ave
Summers Town Rd

Carder
Park

Harper Lane

Peters Lane

Olivier
Park

Eveleigh
Park

E Palm Ave

Campbell Ave

Victor Lane

Red Hassell Rd

Mellad Rd

Can側de River

E Town River

0   100   200 m
0   100   200 yards

To Berridale &
Moore Town

by marauding Maroons deterred all but a few settlers.

Following peace with the Maroons in 1739, Titchfield expanded. Many settlers grew sustenance crops, including bananas. Enter the Yankee skipper Captain Lorenzo Dow Baker (1840-1908), a fruit shipping magnate, who arrived in 1871 and established the banana trade that created a boomtown overnight. Baker and his Boston Fruit Company went on to own 40 banana plantations from Port Antonio to Buff Bay, making Port Antonio the 'banana capital of the world.' Port Antonio grew so wealthy that, it is said, planters would light their cigars with US$5 bills.

In the 1890s, Baker began shipping tourists from the cold US northeast in his empty banana boats. Although Portland's banana bonanza was doomed in the 1930s by the onset of Panama disease, the arrival of movie star Errol Flynn, and later that of numerous blue bloods and Hollywood stars, gave new cachet to Port Antonio as a tourist resort.

In the 1960s, a second brief heyday occurred when a luxurious resort went up overlooking Frenchman's Cove. This was followed by Prince Alfonso Hohenlohe's equally exclusive Marbella Club at Dragon Bay. The regal resorts attracted the jet-set crowd, and the coves east of town were colonized by the very rich, setting a trend that continues today.

ORIENTATION

The compact town center is nestled between twin harbors separated by the Titchfield Peninsula. A narrow channel separates the peninsula from Navy Island, half a mile offshore, at the mouth of West Harbour. To the east is East Harbour bay.

W Palm Ave runs along West Harbour. Allen Ave ('Folly Rd' to locals) runs along East Harbour. The town center lies at the base of the Titchfield Peninsula, where the two main drags meet at a right angle in front of the main plaza and courthouse. Fort George St runs from this junction uphill along the Peninsula.

Following Summers Town Rd south from the town center leads to Red Hassell Rd,

PEPA's Park Projects

Declining fish stocks, damage to the ecology of Port Antonio's coral reefs, and threats to Portland parish's natural resources have led to the formation of the nonprofit Portland Environment Protection Association (PEPA; ☎ 993-9632, fax 993-3407; 6 Allan Ave, Port Antonio), which works to foster public awareness of its fragile resources.

The group's most notable achievement has been the establishment of the Port Antonio Marine Park, with boundaries extending over an area of 11 miles, from Ship Rock, west of Port Antonio, to Northeast Point, south of Boston Bay. Fishing is prohibited at Turtle Crawle Bay and between San San and Blue Lagoon.

which continues all the way to the Rio Grand Valley.

The clock tower in front of the courthouse has a city directory painted on it.

INFORMATION

The **JTB** (☎ 993-3051, fax 993-2117; open 8:30am-4:30pm Mon-Fri, 9am-1pm Sat) has an office on the second floor of City Centre Plaza at the west end of Harbour St. On the Internet, a good starting point is ⓦ www .portantoniojamaica.com.

Travel agencies include **Travel Experts** (☎ 993-2645; 2 Harbour St), in Goebel Plaza.

You'll find bank branches of **CIBC** (☎ 993-2708; 3 West St), **Scotiabank** (☎ 993-2523; 3 Harbour St), **National Commercial Bank** (☎ 993-9822; 5 West St), and **RBTT Bank** (☎ 993-9755; 28 Harbour St).

You can place overseas calls and send faxes from **Eastern Communication Ltd** (☎ 993-4192, fax 993-4149) next to the market facing Port Antonio Square, **Direct Telecom** (☎ 993-3174; 3 West St; open 7:30am-10pm Mon-Fri, 7:30am-11pm Sat & Sun), or **Cable & Wireless Jamaica** (☎ 993-2775; Harbour St). There are also public telephones next to the courthouse, on the

NORTHEAST COAST

Sails catch the breeze near Port Antonio.

Cooking up jerked pork in Port Antonio

Tasty crabs up for grabs

Brooke Shields is long gone, but the Blue Lagoon still enchants with its jade and emerald waters.

Perched at Jamaica's westernmost tip, Negril provides a grandstand seat for spectacular sunsets.

Meat-filled, crusty 'patties,' Savanna-la-Mar

Strolling Negril's renowned 7-mile-long beach

STUART WASSERMAN

JERRY ALEXANDER

STUART WASSERMAN

town square. The **post office** (☎ 993-2651) is on the east side of the town square.

Ela Systems (☎ 715-3180; Shop 7, Village of St George; open 9am-5pm Mon-Sat) offers Internet services, as does **Golden Cyber Centre** (☎ 715-6615; 2 West St; open 10am-10pm).

The **Portland Parish Library** (☎ 993-2793; 1 Harbour St; open 9am-7pm Mon-Fri, 9am-1pm Sat) fronts the marina.

Ever Brite Laundry (☎ 715-1851; 20 Harbour St) offers drop-off laundry service.

The **Port Antonio Hospital** (☎ 993-2646; Nuttall Rd) is above town on Naylor's Hill, south of West Harbour. The **Agape Family Medical Clinic** (☎ 993-2338; 32 Harbour St; open 9am-4:30pm Mon-Sat) has emergency service. **A&E Pharmacy** (☎ 993-9348; 3 Market Square) is centrally located.

The **police station** (☎ 993-2527, 993-2546), on Harbour St, is also the base for the **Resort Patrol Services** (☎ 993-7482), which patrols to guard the welfare of tourists.

Note that many locals make a living from scamming tourists. Guard your valuables if browsing Musgrave Market, and stick to the main streets if walking at night.

WALKING TOUR

Port Antonio's heart is the **main square** at the junction of West St and Harbour St. It's centered on a clock tower and backed by a handsome red-brick Georgian courthouse topped by a cupola. From here walk 50 yards down West St to the junction of William St, where the smaller **Port Antonio Square** has a cenotaph honoring Jamaicans who gave their lives in the two world wars.

On the west side is the clamorous and colorful **Musgrave Market**, supported by thick limestone columns. Follow William St south to Harbour St and turn left to peek inside **Christ Church**, a red-brick Anglican building built in neo-Romanesque style around 1840 (much of the structure dates from 1903). The singular item of note is the brass lectern donated by Captain Lorenzo Dow Baker.

From here, follow Harbour St past the historic **police station** until you emerge back on the main square. You will be drawn to the north side by the imposing facade of the **Village of St George**, a beautiful three-story complex with an exquisitely frescoed exterior in Dutch style. Continue up Fort George St, along the **Titchfield Peninsula**. This hilly peninsula – known locally as 'the Hill' – supports several dozen Victorian-style gingerbread houses, notably **DeMontevin Lodge** (21 Fort George St), an ornate rust-red mansion. Many of the finest homes line King St, which runs down the center of the peninsula (parallel to Queen and Fort George Sts) and conjures up images of the American Deep South, with tall shade trees festooned with mosses known as old-man's-beard. The peninsula is now a National Heritage Trust Site and is slated to receive a restoration. *(Soon come!)*

Fort George and King Sts lead north to the remains of **Fort George** at the tip of the peninsula, dating from 1729. The parade ground and former barracks today house **Titchfield School**. Beyond the school, several George III-era cannons can still be seen mounted in their embrasures in 10-foot-thick walls.

Return to town via Gideon Avenue, which lines East Harbour and offers views.

NAVY ISLAND

The lushly vegetated, 60-acre island is popular with local day-trippers on weekends...or it was when the ferries ran.

In colonial days, the British Navy used it to careen ships for repair, and they built a small battery, plus jetties and warehouses. Nothing remains of their presence. In 1793, Captain William Bligh (of HMS *Bounty* fame) brought the first breadfruits to Jamaica from the South Seas. They were landed here before being sent to Bath Botanical Garden to be propagated and distributed throughout Jamaica.

In the 20th century, Errol Flynn bought the island. His former home became a hotel, which later sank into decay. In early 2002 the Urban Development Council and Port Authority jointly took over the island with a view to develop the jaded property as an upscale resort.

The water taxis that once departed from the wharf (opposite W Baptist Ave) on W Palm Ave were no longer operating at last visit.

FOLLY

This two-story, 60-room mansion, on the peninsula east of East Harbour, was built entirely of concrete in pseudo-Grecian style by a North American millionaire. It was in private use until 1936, when the roof collapsed. Sea water had been used in the construction, causing the iron reinforcing rods to rust.

Today the shell of the structure remains, held aloft by limestone columns. Despite being a popular spot for magazine photo shoots, there is little else here to recommend it.

Nearby stands the bright orange **Folly Point Lighthouse**, built in 1888.

ACTIVITIES

You can charter sport-fishing boats such as *La Nadine* (☎ 909-9552; e caribbecapt@aol.com) from the **Port Antonio Marina** (☎ 993-3209, fax 993-9745; w www.port antoniomarina.com), on W Palm Ave, and **Huntress Marina & Charter Services** (☎ 993-3318; West St).

Catamaran Sailing Cruises (☎ 817-8984) offers 90-minute sunset cruises (US$20), plus day charter (US$35 per person), departing the Port Antonio Marina.

ORGANIZED TOURS

Mocking Bird Tours (☎ 993-3370, fax 993-7133; e birdees@mail.infochan.com; PO Box 254, Port Antonio) specializes in putting visitors in touch with people in the local community.

Grand Valley Tours (☎/fax 993-4116; e grandvalleytoursja@hotmail.com; PO Box 203, Port Antonio PO), upstairs at 12 West St, offers guided hikes in the Rio Grande Valley (see Rio Grande Valley later in this chapter), plus horseback riding, birdwatching, and other trips.

Port Antonio Marina (☎ 933-3209), on W Palm Ave, offers a charter cruise to Frenchman's Cove (US$39 per person).

SPECIAL EVENTS

The weeklong **Portland Jamboree** is held mid-August, featuring a float parade, street dancing, food fair, and live music.

The weeklong **Port Antonio International Marlin Tournament** (☎ 927-0145, fax 977-6995; e rondq@mail.infochan.com) is held each October.

PLACES TO STAY
Budget

Scotia Guest House (☎ 993-2681; 15 Queen St; rooms with/without bath US$11/9) has 10 bare-bones rooms with fans and shared bath, as well as rooms with private bath. The Rasta owners can provide a less than welcoming reception.

Little Reef Guest House (☎ 993-9743; 1 Queen St; rooms US$7.50-10) is a comfy guest house with six small, basic rooms, some with private bathroom, that can accommodate up to four people. Meals are cooked to order, but guests can also use the kitchen.

Brown's Caché Villa (☎ 993-3112; 19 Fort George St; US$15), next to DeMontevin Lodge, is a clean albeit basic option with Old-World charm. The owner has seven rooms with kitchenettes and private baths with hot water.

Ivanhoe's (☎ 993-3043; 9 Queen St; rooms US$25-50) is a gracious property with 12 well-lit rooms with fans, louvered windows, and private bathrooms with hot water. It's well run, spotless, and quiet, and has a breezy patio and homey TV lounge. Breakfast costs US$5, and lunch and dinner are cooked to order.

Holiday Home (☎ 993-2425, 993-2882; 12 King St; PO Box 11; singles US$30, doubles US$35-40) is a charming hotel with nine rooms. They're basic and small, and some have shared bathrooms with cold water, but they're all spic-and-span. Breakfasts are cooked to order.

Ocean Crest Guest House B&B (☎ 993-4024; 7 Queen St; rooms US$30-35) is a ritzy modern facility furnished in somewhat Catholic tastes with antique reproduction furnishings. It has hardwood ceilings and gleaming tile floors. The lounge has a large-screen TV. Some of the seven rooms are gloomy.

In & On Guest House (☎ 993-3468, fax 993-3332; e npalmer@cwjamaica.com; 17A W Palm Ave; rooms US$45, cottages US$120) has six rooms, each with its own outside entrance and cable TV, radio, and hot water. Plus, there's a two-bedroom cottage with kitchen. Air-con was planned to be added at last visit.

Shadows (☎ 993-3823; 40 W Palm Ave; rooms US$30) offers five modern rooms with air-con, cable TV, and modest furnishings. There's a bar in the forecourt and a disco attached.

Mid-Range
DeMontevin Lodge (☎ 993-2604; 21 Fort George St; PO Box 85; rooms US$50-68) is a venerable Victorian guest house boasting a homey ambience and a blend of modern kitsch and antiques reminiscent of grannie's parlor. The 13 simple bedrooms (three with private bathrooms) are timeworn, but as clean as a whistle. New owners took over in 2001. Meals are no longer offered.

Triff's Inn (☎ 993-2162, fax 993-2062; e triffs@in-site.com; 1 Bridge St; singles/doubles/triples/quads US$45/55/75/95) is a well-run hotel that has 17 spacious and clean air-con rooms with telephones and private baths with hot water. Furnishings are minimalist. A lounge has cable TV.

Bonnie View Plantation Hotel (☎ 993-2862; 309-659-2358 in the USA; PO Box 82;) occupies an alluring spot 600 feet above town, and is surrounded by well-tended gardens and a plantation backed by the soaring Blue Mountains. The back garden contains a pool and, amazingly, a small beach. Alas, the new owner (a local politician) has let the place go to ruin, and it was closed at last visit, awaiting a second lease on life.

Top End
Jamaica Heights Hotel (☎ 993-2156, 993-3563 office, fax 993-3305; w www.jamaica heights.com; Spring Bank Rd; 1 Morris Ave; US$60-75), southwest of Boundbrook Crescent, is a splendid option. The exquisite hilltop plantation home is set amid lush gardens with a spectacular setting and incredible views. Columned verandas, white-washed walls, aged brick, dark hardwood floors, louvered windows, French doors, and a cool white-and-blue color scheme combine to provide a gracious environment. The six rooms and two studios are tastefully furnished with white wicker and antiques, plus four-poster beds with romantic netting. A two-bedroom cottage was being added. A spa offers massage and treatments, and there's a beautiful plunge pool plus a nature trail.

Evra Jam Villa Rentals (☎ 515-424-5447 in the USA; w www.jamaicatropics.com; 24 17th St SE, Mason City, IA 50401, USA) represents local villas. Also try the **Jamaican Association of Villas & Apartments** (JAVA; ☎ 974-2508, fax 974-2967; w www.villasinja maica.com; PO Box 298, Ocho Rios).

PLACES TO EAT
Dicky's Best Kept Secret (☎ 993-9591, 993-7570; US$15), an offbeat hut on the A4, half a mile west of town, offers the best bargain in town. 'Dicky' and Joy Butler serve five-course meals, with huge portions (especially of whipped potatoes) and attentive service. Typical dishes include garlic lobster. It has only two tables (reservations are essential; you need to order the same morning).

The Chicken Place (☎ 993-4984; 29 Harbour St; US$1-4) is good for fried chicken.

The Blue Marlin Bar & Restaurant (☎ 993-3209), at Port Antonio Marina, is a colorful waterfront eatery specializing in homemade pizza, and seafood from fish fingers (US$4) to garlic lobster (US$15).

Golden Happiness (☎ 993-4524; cnr Harbour & West Sts; dishes under US$5) has reasonable quality Chinese dishes – including a vast menu of chop sueys and sweet-and-sour dishes – and you can also request half orders.

Huntress Marina Bar & Restaurant (☎ 993-3053; US$2-15), at Huntress Marina, serves sandwiches, steamed fish, and other seafood.

Juici Beef Patties (William St) is a good spot for cheap patties. **Coronation Bakery**

(☎ 993-2710; 18 West St) is known for its doughnut-like pastries called 'holey bulla,' and other desserts. For fresh, oven-baked bread, try **Three Star Lion Bakery** (☎ 993-3007; 27 West St).

A cappuccino and bowl of delicious ice cream at the **Gallery Café** (☎ 715-5639; open 7:30am-11pm), upstairs in the Village of St George, is recommended.

If self-catering, you'll find a **supermarket** on Harbour St.

ENTERTAINMENT
Roof Club (☎ 993-3817; 11 West St) is Port Antonio's infamous hang-loose, rough-around-the-edges reggae bar. Young men and women move from partner to partner. You're fair game for any stranger who wants to 'wine' you. (Be prepared to withstand the incessant sponging of locals hitting on tourists to buy them drinks.) It's relatively dead midweek, when entry is free. But on weekends (US$3) it hops, especially on Thursday – 'Ladies Nite.'

Educated locals prefer the more upscale **Club Extasy** (admission US$3), a disco in the Village of St George. It has occasional go-go girls.

Shadows (☎ 993-3823; 40 W Palm Ave) is another option; it plays vintage music on Tuesday and Sunday, and has happy hour at 6pm Thursday and Friday.

Sister 'P' (☎ 715-3529; 10 Mathews Ave) and her daughter host nyahbinghi drum sessions. Maria Carla Gullotta of Draper's San Guest House arranges a 'Drumming Night' with traditional dancing.

You can watch cricket at the **Folly Oval** (Allan Ave) cricket ground, on the east side of East Harbour.

SHOPPING
Musgrave Market (West St) has a craft market on its north side, accessed off George St, as does **Jamaica Arcade**, immediately east of the courthouse. A new craft market was scheduled to open in Carder Park, Allan Ave.

Gallery Art Ambokile (☎ 993-3162, 931-5803; 22a West St) offers quality art, ceramics, and sculptures. Be sure to call in at

Gallery Carriacou in the Hotel Mocking Bird Hill (see East of Port Antonio later in this chapter).

Don't leave without checking out the **Spencer Gallery**, in the Village of St George, featuring works by local artist Ken Abendana Spencer.

GETTING THERE & AROUND
Air
Ken Jones Aerodrome (☎ 913-3173), 6 miles west of Port Antonio, was being expanded to accept jets and night flights at last visit. **Air Jamaica Express** (☎ 993-3692 at Ken Jones Aerodrome, 888-359-2475) operated once daily from MoBay at press time, with connecting flights from Kingston's Tinson Pen and Negril. See the Getting Around chapter for charter service.

Most upscale hotels offer free transfers to/from the Ken Jones Aerodrome for guests. There's no shuttle bus service, although you can flag down any coaster or route taxi passing along the A4. A tourist taxi will cost about US$10.

Public Transportation
A transportation center extends along the waterfront on Gideon Ave. Buses, coasters, and route taxis leave regularly for Annotto Bay, Port Maria (where you change for Ocho Rios), and Kingston.

Car & Motorcycle
Eastern Rent-a-Car (☎ 993-3624; 26 Harbour St) has an office in town.

Scooters and motorcycles are available from **Bamboo Bike, Car, & Jeep Rental** (☎ 993-3053), at Huntress Marina.

Taxi
JUTA (☎ 979-0778 in Kingston, 952-0813 in Montego Bay, 993-2684 in Port Antonio) offers taxi transfers from Montego Bay airport, and from Kingston airport, as does **Island Car Rentals** (☎ 926-8861 in Kingston, 924-8075 at Norman Manley International Airport, 952-5771 at Donald Sangster International Airport). Licensed taxis to Port Antonio cost about US$100 from Kingston, US$120 from Montego Bay.

For licensed taxis, call **JUTA/Port Antonio Cab Drivers' Co-op** (☎ 993-2684). Taxis hang out by hotels.

Boat
The **Port Antonio Marina** (☎ 993-3209, fax 993-9745; ✉ marina@portantoniomarina .com), on W Palm Ave, offers customs clearance for private vessels.

East of Port Antonio

PORT ANTONIO TO FAIRY HILL
Hugging Jamaica's northeastern coastline, the A4 winds around a series of deep bays and tiny coves with forested mountains hemming the shore.

Much of the mountain forest is threatened by developers, who have begun moving in. A nascent movement to protect the vital Williamsfield District watershed has been spearheaded by the owners of Hotel Mocking Bird Hill (see Places to Stay, later in this section).

The hamlet of Drapers has a small **post office** (open 8am-4pm Mon-Fri, 8am-noon Sat), and a **police station** (☎ 993-7315) half a mile east of Frenchman's Cove.

Turtle Crawle Bay
Two miles east of Port Antonio, the road circles around this deep bay, an important fish nursery that is protected as a part of the Port Antonio Marine Park.

Squatting atop the western headland is a magnificent gleaming-white castle built in the 1980s by Baroness Elisabeth Siglindy Stephan von Stephanie Thyssen. This is **Trident Castle**, part of the Trident Hotel & Villas resort. The architect, Earl Levy, eventually took over the property after a tiff with the Baroness. Scenes from *Clara's Heart* were filmed here, and Denzel Washington was seduced by hotel guest Mimi Rogers in the *Mighty Quinn*.

On the east shore of Turtle Crawle is the pseudo-Grecian **Jamaica Palace**; it was built by the Baroness in 1989. Thus the Baroness trumped the Earl; he has only a castle, but she has a palace. It, too, has appeared on screen: as the setting for *Playboy*'s 'Playmates in Paradise.'

Frenchman's Cove
This small cove, just east of Drapers, 5 miles from Port Antonio, boasts one of the prettiest beaches (entrance US$2.50) for miles. A stream winds lazily to a white-sand beach that shelves steeply into the water. Bring insect repellent. There's a snack bar and a secure parking lot; it's closed Tuesday.

San San Beach
San San Beach (open 10am-4pm daily; entrance US$7.50) is a private beach used by residents of the opulent villas on Alligator Head, and by guests of Goblin Hill, Fern Hill, and Jamaica Palace hotels. Passersby, however, can gain access. It has a bar and restaurant and snorkeling equipment.

Blue Lagoon
Yes, this *is* where 14-year-old Brooke Shields swam in the movie *Blue Lagoon.* Aptly named, it's embraced by a deep, natural amphitheater with forest-clad sides. The 180-foot-deep lagoon opens to the sea through a narrow funnel, but is fed by freshwater springs that come in at about 140 feet deep. Its color changes through every shade of jade and emerald during the day. At night, floodlights add to the romantic ambience.

Access is via Blue Lagoon Restaurant; you can rent snorkeling equipment and paddleboats (US$10).

Dragon Bay
This beautiful little cove, immediately east of Blue Lagoon, 7 miles east of Port Antonio, is where Tom Cruise set up his beach bar in the movie *Cocktail.* Formerly the private property of the Dragon Bay Resort, it has traditionally been open to the public for day use, but in 2002 the property was bought by the Sandals chain, renamed the Port Antonio Spa Village, and was closed at last visit.

NORTHEAST COAST

AROUND PORT ANTONIO

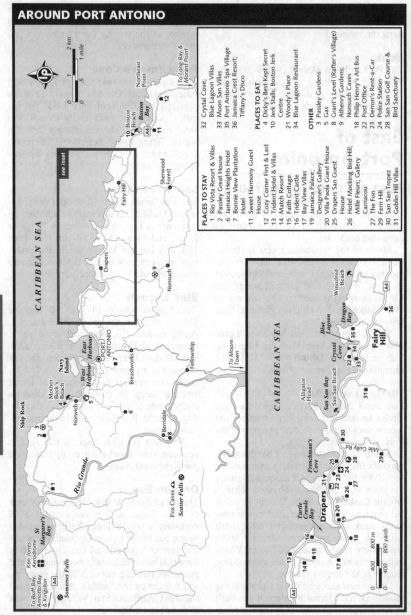

PLACES TO STAY

1 Rio Vista Resort & Villas
2 Passley Great House
6 Jamaica Heights Hotel
7 Bonnie View Plantation Hotel
11 Sweet Harmony Guest House
12 Cozy Corner First & Last
13 Trident Hotel & Villas
14 Match Resort
16 Trident Castle
17 Faith Cottage
19 Jamaica Palace; Designer's Gallery
20 Villa Paola Guest House
25 Drapers San Guest House
26 Hotel Mocking Bird Hill; Mille Fleurs; Gallery Carriacou
27 The Fon
29 Fern Hill
30 San San Tropez
31 Goblin Hill Villas

32 Crystal Cove; Blue Lagoon Villas
33 Moon San Villas
35 Port Antonio Spa Village
36 Jamaica Crest Resort; Tiffany's Disco

PLACES TO EAT

4 Dicky's Best Kept Secret
10 Jerk Stalls; Boston Jerk Centre
21 Woody's Place
34 Blue Lagoon Restaurant

OTHER

3 Passley Gardens
5 Gas
8 Grant's Level (Rafter's Village)
9 Athenry Gardens; Nonsuch Caves
18 Philip Henry's Art Bus
22 Post Office
23 Derron's Rent-a-Car
24 Police Station
28 San San Golf Course & Bird Sanctuary

Fairy Hill & Winnifred Beach

Fairy Hill, 8 miles east of Port Antonio, is a small clifftop hamlet. A dirt road leads steeply downhill to Winnifred Beach – a great place to hang with 'real' Jamaicans.

The beach was used as a setting for the Robin Williams movie *Club Paradise*. A coral reef offshore provides snorkeling, and horseback rides (US$2.50) for kids are offered on weekends. There are toilets and changing rooms.

The turnoff to the beach is opposite the Jamaica Crest Resort.

Activities

Good **scuba diving** abounds, as the shoreline east of Port Antonio boasts 8 miles of interconnected coral reefs and walls at an average of 100 to 300 yards offshore. **Alligator Head** is known for big sponge formations and black corals. Hammerhead sharks are common at **Fairy Hill Bank**.

Lady G'Diver (☎ 993-3281; PO Box 81, Port Antonio) is a full-service dive shop at Blue Lagoon Restaurant.

The **San San Golf Course & Bird Sanctuary** (☎ 993-7645, fax 993-7644; open 8am-5pm) is an 18-hole course laid out along valleys surrounded by rain forest. There's a clubhouse, a small pro shop, and bistro dining. A round costs US$50/70 (nine/18 holes). Caddies cost US$7/12, a pull-cart costs US$5, and golf club rental will set you back US$10/12. The bird sanctuary comprises primary forest and is not developed for tourism.

Places to Stay

Budget Drapers San Guest House (☎/fax 993-7118; ⓔ carla-51@cwjamaica.com; Drapers PO; doubles US$46) is a spic-and-span place above Frenchman's Cove and is run by a charming Italian woman, Maria Carla Gullotta. Her rambling little house comprises two cottages with five doubles and one single room (two share a bath), all with fans, louvered windows, and hot water. One unit is two-story, with a thick wooden staircase and a kitchen. A minimum two-night stay is required. It's all very family-oriented. Rates include breakfast.

Villa Paola Guest House (☎ 993-7525, fax 993-7524; Drapers PO; rooms US$50), next to the Jamaica Palace, is a genteel hilltop guest house with four rooms with ceiling fans and private baths with cold water. Rates include breakfast. The owners have fishing and cruise boats for rent, and they offer snorkeling (US$55 per hour, including boat).

The Fan (☎ 993-7915; ⓔ carla-51@cwjamaica.com; Drapers PO; villa US$80), in the hills behind Drapers, is a beautiful villa rental with gingerbread trim, a large living room, and a separate dining room in the guest apartment. Miss Rosie will cook for you. Reservations are made through the Port Antonio Guest House Association. Rates include breakfast.

Mid-Range Faith Cottage (☎ 993-3703; PO Box 50, Port Antonio; singles US$70, doubles US$85), inland of Trident Hotel & Villas at Turtle Crawle Bay, is a gracious, pink-painted hotel with turrets and gables. It has nine spacious rooms with small TVs, fans, and modern, modest decor – some even have columned bedrooms. There's a pool. Rates include breakfast.

Bay View Villas (☎/fax 993-3118; ⓦ www.caribicvacations.com; Caribic, 1310 Providence Dr, Ironshore Estate, Montego Bay; rooms US$56) offers three modestly furnished hillside villas overlooking Turtle Crawle Bay. One has six bedrooms; the others have two and three, respectively. There's a small bar, a restaurant, TV lounge, and a pool.

Frenchman's Cove (☎ 933-7270, fax 993-8211; ⓦ www.frenchmanscove.com; PO Box 101, Port Antonio; rooms US$70, suites US$80, 1-/2-/3-bedroom cottages US$80/110/140) has an old great house with 10 aircon rooms and two suites, plus 18 one-, two-, and three-bedroom stone cottages amid the broad greenswathe. Facilities are minimal.

Fern Hill (☎ 993-7374, fax 993-7373; ☎ 800-263-4354, fax 416-620-4843 in North America; PO Box 100, Port Antonio; standard rooms US$77, suites US$99, 1-/2-bedroom villas US$154/242) is on a breezy hilltop at San San, up Mile Gully Rd. The 16 spacious though slightly jaded twin-level units are spread across the hillside, and each has a balcony beyond French doors. There are also three villas. Suites have mezzanine bedrooms and their own hot tubs. When there's a full house, it offers a buffet and cabaret by the pool.

San San Tropez (☎ 993-7213, fax 993-7399; W www.sansantropez.com; San San Bay PO, Portland; single/double May-June US$70/94, July-Apr US$102/136) is an Italian-run hotel offering gracious, well-lit, cross-ventilated, air-con rooms and suites. The furnishings are modern and graced by bright tropical decor. There's a pool and sundeck. It gives passes to San San Beach.

Match Resort (☎ 993-9629, fax 993-2700; Lot 30, Dolphin Bay, Port Antonio; rooms US$65, villas US$75), about 200 yards inland of Trident Hotel & Villas, is a modern complex with a swimming pool. All 28 rooms and five villas are nicely furnished, with soft pastels, air-con, and cable TV.

Top End Moon San Villas (☎ 993-7600; e sansan1999@hotmail.com; Fairy Hill PO; rooms US$125), sitting above Blue Lagoon, is a tastefully decorated three-level house with a TV/VCR lounge, and four bedrooms, each with wide windows, fans, and its own utterly romantic decor. Two rooms have king-size beds. The bargain rates include a gourmet breakfast and two passes to both San San Beach and Blue Lagoon. French-inspired dinners cost US$16-20.

Goblin Hill Villas (☎ 993-7443, 800-472-1148, fax 993-7537; e hotelg@cwjamaica .com; 11 East Ave, Kingston 10; 1-bedroom villas summer/winter US$90/110, 2-bedroom villas US$145/185) is a 700-acre hilltop estate above San San Beach that's popular with families. Its 16 two-bedroom and 12 one-bedroom self-catering villas are surrounded by lawns and forest. Those closest to the sea have views down to San San Bay. A nature trail encircles the property. The air-con villas are huge and have massive open windows and wide verandas. Each comes with its own private maid and butler (optional), but have neither telephones nor TVs. The resort has a TV lounge and reading

room, a large pool, two tennis courts, and a Tree Bar built around a massive fig tree. The property's guest villas remain long overdue for renovation.

Trident Hotel & Villas (☎ 993-2602, fax 993-2590; ☎ 800-633-3284 in the USA; ☎ 020-7730-7144, fax 7938-7493 in the UK; e trident@infochan.com; PO Box 119, Port Antonio; single summer/winter US$160/365, double US$220/385, suites US$340/620, Trident Castle US$5500/7500) sits atop a cliff overlooking a tiny cove. Peacocks stroll about the croquet lawn. Stepping through the lofty mahogany front door is like entering a European mansion. It offers 26 deluxe rooms and villa suites, plus the luxurious Imperial Suite. The place – which has drawn clients from the international A-list – is a bit standoffish and snooty. Jackets for men (and ties during winter season) and 'cocktail attire' for women have traditionally been required in the restaurant. Rates include breakfast and dinner. The castle, immediately east of the hotel, is a medieval-style confection with eight rooms. It rents as a single unit and is fully-staffed. Rates are all-inclusive.

Hotel Mocking Bird Hill (☎ 993-7267, fax 993-7133; W www.hotelmockingbirdhill .com; PO Box 254, Port Antonio; garden view summer/winter US$125/180, superior US$160/230), a romantic, 'eco-chic,' 10-room property in the hills above French-man's Cove, is *the* place for relaxed, button-down ambience. This gem – the best hotel in Portland parish – is run with finesse by Shireen Aga and Barbara Walker. All rooms are lovingly appointed with well-chosen fabrics and modern art and appliances. Most boast ocean views from private balconies. Facilities include a small pool, a Caribbean-bright TV lounge, a bar, plus a variety of health and wellness services, including massage. The erudite and charming couple are also gourmands, and meals are sublime (see Places to Eat later in this section). Trails lead through the lush hillside gardens...fabulous for birding! The endangered black-billed streamertail is commonly seen from the dining terrace.

Jamaica Palace (☎ 993-7720, 800-472-1149, fax 993-7759; W www.jamaicapalace.com;

PO Box 277, Port Antonio; deluxe summer/winter US$100/120, superior US$120/140, junior suites US$140/180, 'Getaway Package' per person US$95) is a gracious if aloof neoclassical property overlooking Turtle Crawle Bay. The cavernous 24 rooms and 55 suites boast king-size beds, crystal chandeliers, period antiques, and Georgian bay windows. In the landscaped grounds is a 114-foot-long pool shaped like Jamaica. Rates include tax and service charge.

Blue Lagoon Villas (☎ 993-8748, 888-816-9714, fax 993-7792; ⓦ www.bluelagoonvillas.com; PO Box 2, Port Antonio; 1–4-bedroom villas summer US$4000-9000, winter US$5000-10,000), immediately west of Blue Lagoon, provides a stunning setting, with a fistful of luxurious waterfront villas made famous as a popular locale for fashion shoots. Each one- to four-bedroom villa is exquisitely furnished and staffed with a housekeeper-cook and houseman. Sea kayaks are provided. Rates are based on three-night minimum stay, including airport transfers.

Crystal Cove (☎ 925-8108, fax 925-6248; 11 East Ave, Kingston 10; summer: doubles US$265, 3-6 people US$305; winter: doubles US$305, 3-6 people US$390), adjacent to Blue Lagoon Villas, offers similar luxury. This villa has three bedrooms and three bathrooms. It comes fully staffed and requires a five-night minimum stay.

Jamaica Crest Resort (☎ 993-8400, fax 993-8432; ☎ 305-573-2006, 800-247-8718 in the USA; ⓔ reservations@jamaicacrest.com; PO Box 165, Fairy Hill, Port Antonio; 1-bedroom summer/winter US$95-105/110; 2-bedrooms summer/winter US$180/200), at Fairy Hill, has 46 air-con, red-tile–roof hillside rooms. Each has kitchenette, cable TV, telephone, and balcony (a housekeeper-cook is optional). The complex features an elevated sundeck and pool, plus an elegant, aloof restaurant, bar, disco, conference center, two tennis courts, and a gym. It specializes in Christian retreats.

Port Antonio Spa Village (ⓦ www.sandals.com), formerly Dragon Bay Resort, enjoys a beautiful 55-acre setting overlooking a flask-shaped cove and tiny beach. At last visit, the 90-room property had just been bought by Sandals Resorts International and was closed for a total remake aimed at turning it into a deluxe health-focused boutique resort (but it will not be all-inclusive, as is the Sandals norm). See All-Inclusive Resorts in the Facts for the Visitor chapter for Sandals contact information.

Elegant Resorts Villas (☎ 953-9562, fax 953-9563; ☎ 800-337-3499 in North America; PO Box 80, Montego Bay) is an agency renting three villas at San San Beach.

For a complete list of available villas, contact the **Jamaican Association of Villas & Apartments** (JAVA; see Villa Rentals in the Facts for the Visitor chapter).

Places to Eat

Woody's Place (☎ 993-7888; US$2.50-9; open 8am-11pm), beside the A4 in Drapers, serves tremendous hot dogs and burgers, grilled cheese, and Jamaican dinners to order. It hosts live reggae on the last Friday of every month.

Mille Fleurs (☎ 993-7267; 3-course dinner US$36; open 7am-10pm), in Hotel Mocking Bird Hill, offers superb gourmet nouvelle Jamaican specialties by candlelight. A set three-course dinner, including a vegetarian option, ends with a trolley of Sangster's liqueurs. The special Mille Fleurs continental breakfast costs US$12.50. Reservations required.

Blue Lagoon Restaurant (☎ 993-8491; ⓔ marz@cwjamaica.com; US$6-16, set lunch US$15, Sun dinner special US$20; open 10am-10pm), overhanging the lagoon, serves a creative, entirely jerk menu, including jerk crayfish, marinated jerk lamb chops, and jerk pork tenderloin. Freshwater lobster is available, and there's spicy honey-garlic conch. Try the potentially lethal Blue Lagoon cocktail (US$5), served in a half-pint glass, or the XXX-rated 'Sex in the Lagoon.' Lunch includes a to-die-for Tía Maria rum cake dessert. On Saturday nights, there is live jazz and reggae (US$25, including dinner).

The restaurant at **San San Tropez** (☎ 993-7399, 993-7213; entrées US$10-25; open 8am-10pm) is the place to head for Italian seafood and pizzas. The menu is vast, and there's a large wine list.

For a drink and dancing, **Tiffany's Disco** (☎ 993-8400; admission US$5), in the Jamaica Crest Resort, has theme nights. Thursday is 'Ladies Nite.'

Shopping

The best quality crafts are sold at **Designer's Gallery** (☎ 993-7332), in the Jamaica Palace, and at the **Gallery Carriacou** (☎ 993-7267, fax 993-7133; open 10am-5pm Thur-Tues), at Hotel Mocking Bird Hill in Frenchman's Cove. Carriacou boasts a fabulous array of paintings, ceramics, sculptures, and other quality works of fine art by local artists, and it also hosts workshops and cultural events.

En route, you might call in at **Philip Henry's Art Bus** (☎ 993-3162), roadside at Turtle Crawle Bay.

Getting There & Away

Infrequent buses run between Port Antonio and Boston Bay and points beyond. Coasters and route taxis (US$0.75-1.50) are more frequent.

Derron's Rent-a-Car (☎ 993-7111, fax 993-7253; ☎ 800-550-6288 ext 4040 in North America; e derrons@mail.infochan.com) has an outlet in Drapers.

BOSTON BEACH

Boston Beach, 1.5 miles east of Fairy Hill, is a pocket-size beach shelving into jewel-like turquoise waters. High surf rolls into the bay, and locals spend much of their time surfing (you can rent boards on the beach). Boston Beach is perhaps the best surfing spot in Jamaica.

Boston Beach is known for highly-spiced jerk chickens and pork sizzling away on smoky barbecue pits along the roadside.

Cozy Corner First & Last (☎ 993-8450; Boston PO; doubles US$25) has two simple but nicely appointed rooms with fans, TV, and hot water. It's half a mile south of Boston Beach, on the roadside about 200 yards from the shore. It has a small bar, but doesn't serve food.

Sweet Harmony Guest House (☎ 993-8779, fax 993-3178; Boston PO; rooms US$40, villas US$60) is run by a friendly French couple, Candida and Jean-Michel.

The place has three clean rooms with double beds with mosquito nets, wall fans, and shower-bath with cold water only. Rates include breakfast. The couple also has a two-story villa for five people. It's 400 yards inland from the A4.

There are plenty of simple open-air jerk stalls, but the most significant is **Boston Jerk Centre**, which is popular with tour groups as well as locals. Get there early, as food tends to be sold out by mid-afternoon. You'll pay about $4 for a half pound of chicken, washed down with a Red Stripe (US$1).

There are a few rum shops, including **Burn It Down**, about 2 miles south of Boston Beach; it has go-go dancing on Wednesday.

Boston Beach is 9 miles east of Port Antonio; buses (about US$0.50) and coasters and route taxis (US$1.50) will get you there and back. In Kingston, public transport operates from the Beckford St transportation center.

LONG BAY

This is one of the most dramatic settings in all of Jamaica – sunrises are spectacular! The mile-wide bay has rose-colored sand, deep turquoise waters, and breezes pushing the waves forcefully ashore. Canoes are drawn up on the beach, with fishing nets drying beside them. There's a dangerous undertow, so avoid swimming, but surfers love the waves.

Long Bay appeals to budget travelers, as well as surfers, and has drawn a large number of expats who have put down roots and opened guest houses. The lifestyle here is laid-back and rootsy, kind of like Negril felt 30 years ago.

Ken Abendana Spencer, a renowned modernist artist, has his studio here. His concrete home is a rambling, multistoried palace (reminiscent of a 3-D trompe l'oeil by M C Escher) as fanciful as some of his pricey works. Take the dirt road inland from the post office near the gas station; follow the track to the right until you reach a high stone wall and castlelike gates.

The coconut palms hereabouts had been totally decimated by blight at last visit, and the beach is horrendously littered.

Coasters and route taxis run between Port Antonio and Long Bay (US$1.75).

Dangers & Annoyances

Drugs are rife, and an aggressiveness toward foreign visitors has been sensed on past visits. Readers have also reported burglaries and instances of violent assault, even rape. Things seem to have improved of late, with tourism now firmly rooted. Still, campers should remain wary, and never camp 'wild.'

Places to Stay

To write to any of the following guest houses, address to Long Bay PO.

Fisherman's Park (camping about US$3; rooms US$18) has three simply furnished rooms with private bath and hot water, but no fans. It also allows you to camp beneath shade trees on wide lawns, with hammocks and outside toilets and showers.

Blue Heaven (☎ 913-7014; W www.blue heaven-jamaica.com; cottages/rooms/cabins US$12.50/20/40), at the north end of Long Bay, is owned by a rough-around-the-edges American, John. The place is perfect for escape artists who don't mind spartan. John has two basic bamboo cottages with kitchenette, ceiling fans, and cold water, plus two rooms with private toilets and showers, and a cabin with kitchen and sundeck. Alas, he has illegally bulldozed the coral shore to create a tiny man-made beach.

Long Bay Chalet (☎ 913-7126; rooms US$20) is a two-story beachfront house with two simply furnished rooms, both of which have fans and private bathrooms with hot water.

Villa Seascape (☎ 913-7762; ☎ 978-464-2949 in the USA; e vwaterhous@aol.com; downstairs US$40, upstairs US$50) is a well-maintained hotel offering two two-story buildings, each with three modest, nicely furnished rooms with fans. Two rooms share a bathroom. Upstairs rooms have private bathrooms with hot water. Meals are prepared to order.

Rolling Surf (☎ 913-7334; rooms US$13-25), at the southern end of the bay, has six rooms, each with two single beds plus ceiling fan and private bathroom. They're simply furnished and clean.

Seacliff Resort (☎ 926-2248, 929-1163; W www.kasnet.com/pscresorts; villa summer/ winter US$125/200) is considerably more upscale, atop the cliffs 2 miles south of Long Bay. A three-bedroom villa is set amid expansive lush lawns with a volleyball court and a beautiful stone-fringed swimming pool shaded by palms (that had all lost their fronds at last visit). The villa is nicely furnished and well kept, and the rate given here is 'negotiable.'

Places to Eat

Numerous rustic beachside shacks sell inexpensive Jamaican fare (US$2-6) and double as no-frills 'rum shops' with music at night.

Bamboo Lawn and **Cool Runnings Beach Bar & Grill** serve conch, shrimp, lobster, etc. The latter has sand volleyball.

Chill-Out, run by a Belgian-French couple, is another popular thatched beachfront eatery serving pizzas, seafood, and Jamaican fare. It has sound-system parties.

M&M's Pastry Centre sells cakes, patties, fudge, and ice cream.

Ocean View Supermarket, at the east end of Long Bay, sells groceries.

MANCHIONEAL

This sleepy fishing village, 7 miles south of Long Bay, is set in a deep, scalloped bay with calm turquoise waters and a wide, shallow beach where colorful pirogues are drawn up. It's a center for lobster fishing. And the surf is 'killer' – July is said to be the best month.

A family of manatees reappeared in the bay a few years back and have made this their home!

Heartical Roots Corner (☎ 993-6138; Manchioneal PA; camping US$15, rooms US$30), 2 miles north of Manchioneal, is run by unsmiling Jamaicans who have a thatched, family-size room for rent in an Arawak-style octagonal cabin. You can also camp on the riverbank. Bring mosquito repellent! The owners' pals – full of bravura – hang at a bar serving simple meals to order.

There are plenty of jerk stalls and rum shops. Try **Foxy Legs Inn** (☎ 993-6035),

NORTHEAST COAST

serving steamed fish, fish tea, roast conch, etc. It has a pool table and table football.

REACH FALLS

The below-the-falls sex scene in the movie *Cocktail* was filmed at this waterfall – a peaceful spot surrounded by virgin rain forest. A series of cascades tumble over limestone tiers from one hollowed, jade-colored pool to another. A half-mile hike upriver leads to **Mandingo Cave**, which has a whirlpool and is worth the hike. Beware of deep pools and strong currents, which can be dangerous.

Entrance costs US$4, and guides are available (their fee is 'negotiable'). There are changing rooms above the parking lot, where Rastafarians attempt to sell you woolen tams, jewelry, etc.

At last visit, there were rumors that the Urban Development Council was to take the place over and develop it.

Frank Clarke rents two basic **rooms** (☎ 993-6138; US$20) with barebones furnishings and private bath with cold water. He also has a basic restaurant – **Ranch Bar** – atop the falls; he cooks I-tal meals for US$1-5.

Zion Country (☎ 993-0435, fax 993-0551; e answers@cwjamaica.com; Muirton Pen PO, Long Road, Portland; camping US$12 per person, rooms single/double US$25/35), atop the shoreline cliffs about 1 mile south of the falls, is a better bet. It's run by Susanne and Frei (locally called 'Free-I'), who have four hillside log-and-bamboo cottages sharing two bathrooms, with hammocks on the veranda. There is also a bar and small restaurant set in a lush garden. Free-I provides transfers and will run you around in his car. You can camp; tent rental costs US$3.

You can catch any of the coasters and route taxis that run between Kingston and Port Antonio via Morant Bay; get off in Manchioneal, then walk or hitch 2 miles uphill to Reach Falls (the turnoff is signed, half a mile south of Manchioneal). A taxi from Port Antonio costs about US$50 roundtrip.

Rio Grande Valley

The Rio Grande rushes down from 3000 feet in the Blue Mountains and has carved a huge gorge that forms a deep, V-shaped wedge between the Blue Mountains to the west and the John Crow Mountains to the east.

Red Hassell Rd runs south from Port Antonio and enters the Rio Grande Valley at Fellowship.

Hiking

There are many narrow trails – many known only to farmers. Most link remote hamlets.

Popular hikes include those to White Valley, known for its large population of giant swallowtail butterflies; to Dry River Falls; and to Scatter Falls and Fox Caves (see below).

Other hikes are demanding, with muddy, overgrown trails and small rivers that require fording. Don't attempt to hike off the beaten path without a guide. The Corn Puss Gap trail is particularly difficult, as is the wild path from Windsor to the site of Nanny Town.

Organized Hikes Grand Valley Tours (see Organized Tours under Port Antonio earlier in this chapter) offers a series of guided hikes. Hikes range from simple walks (US$30-45), such as to Scatter Falls and Fox Caves, to challenging hikes, such as to Nanny Town (US$100), and overnight hikes. Prices depend on the number of people hiking. It also has horseback rides (US$50), and offers 'bush' camping.

Scatter Falls & Fox Caves A recommended easy hike takes you to Scatter Falls and Fox Caves, reached by crossing the Rio Grande on a bamboo raft at Berridale, then hiking 15 minutes through a series of hamlets. The falls tumble through a curtain of ferns. There are pools for refreshing dips, plus toilets and changing rooms, a campground, a bamboo-and-thatch bar, and a kitchen that serves hot lunch (which must be ordered in advance through Grand Valley Tours).

A steep, 15-minute hike from the waterfall leads to the caves, which have interesting formations that your guide will conjure into vivid imaginings: a lion's head, lovers in flagrante delicto, and another that resembles a bed and has caused more than one amorous couple to request that the guide depart for a few minutes ('...but please leave the lantern!'). The roof is pitted with hollows in which tiny bats dangle.

Nanny Town This former village stronghold of the Windward Maroons is on the brink of a precipitous spur on the northeastern flank of Blue Mountain Peak, about 10 miles southwest of Moore Town as the crow flies. It is named for an 18th-century Ashanti warrior priestess and Maroon leader and, today, a national hero. (See Moore Town, later in this chapter, for more about Nanny.) Eventually, in 1734, English troops captured and destroyed Nanny Town, which is said to be haunted.

It's a tough 10-mile hike from Windsor, 3 miles north of Moore Town. Grand Valley Tours has a three-day guided hike. There are numerous side trails, and it's easy to get lost if you attempt to hike on your own.

Rafting

Errol Flynn supposedly initiated rafting on the Rio Grande during the 1940s, when moonlight raft trips were considered the ultimate activity among the fashionable.

Today, paying passengers make the three-hour, 6-mile journey from Grant's Level or Rafter's Village, about a mile east of Berridale, to Rafter's Rest at St Margaret's Bay. En route, you'll pass through **Lovers Lane**, a moss-covered narrow stream where you're supposed to kiss and make a wish.

Rio Grande Tours Ltd (☎ 913-5434, 993-3778; PO Box 128, Port Antonio) offers trips 9am to 5pm (US$45 per raft, double for full-moon rides). You can buy tickets at Rafter's Village at Grant's Level if you don't have reservations.

Hotel pickups are offered, or you can have your car driven to Rafter's Rest to await your return (US$15). The drivers are insured, but make clear to your driver that you expect him to drive slowly and safely.

A coaster or route taxi from Port Antonio to Grant's Level costs about US$2. Taxis cost about US$17 roundtrip.

ATHENRY GARDENS & NONSUCH CAVES

Athenry Gardens, high in the hills southeast of Port Antonio, is a former coconut plantation and agricultural research center that today, as a lush garden, boasts many exotic and native species. The highlight is Nonsuch Caves (☎ 993-3740; admission US$5; open 9am-5pm), 14 separate chambers full of stalagmites and stalactites and marine fossils. Bats occupy the dank bowels.

The caves and garden are about 7 miles southeast of Port Antonio via Red Hassell Rd. After 2 miles along Red Hassell Rd there's a Y-fork at Breastworks. The right fork leads to Berridale and the Rio Grande; take the left for Nonsuch.

You can also reach Nonsuch Caves by a road that heads uphill via Nonsuch Village and Sherwood Forest from Fairy Hill.

MOORE TOWN

This one-street village, 10 miles south of Port Antonio, stretches uphill for several hundred yards along the Wildcane River. It looks like any other Jamaican village, but is important as the former base of the Windward Maroons. The village was founded in 1739 following the signing of a peace treaty granting the Maroons their independence. Moore Town is still run semi-autonomously by a council of 24 elected members headed by a 'colonel.' The locals attempt to keep alive their lore and legends, and still bring out their *abengs* (goat horns) and talking drums on occasion.

Trails lead from Moore Town, including one to **Nanny Falls**, about 45 minutes away.

Grande Valley Tours (see Organized Tours under Port Antonio earlier in this chapter) offers tours, including a 'Moonlight at Moore Town' community tour that connects visitors to the spirit of the Maroons.

Bump Grave

Moore Town's sole site of interest is Bump Grave, at the southern, uppermost end of town. A plaque on the oblong stone grave reads:

NANNY of the Maroons/National Hero of Jamaica/Beneath this place known as Bump Grave lies the body of Nanny, indomitable and skilled chieftainess of the Windward Maroons who founded this town.

The grave is topped by a flagpole flying the Maroon and Jamaican flags.

Faith Healing

On Monday, Mother Roberts, a local faith healer, performs in the Deliverance Centre. People gather from far and wide for revivalist music, dancing, and lots of hysteria – don't be surprised to see her pull a rusty nail from someone's head! On Wednesday, Mother Roberts holds private healings in a shack at the back of her house. You take a ticket and wait in line.

Getting There & Away

Moore Town is unmarked and lies in a hollow to the left of a Y-junction at Seaman's Valley; the road to the right continues through the Upper Rio Grande Valley. In Moore Town, the road dead-ends in the village.

Coasters and route taxis operate to Moore Town from Port Antonio (about US$1 each way). A bus from Port Antonio runs in early morning and again in early afternoon (US$0.40).

UPPER RIO GRANDE VALLEY

The road to the right of the Y-junction at Seaman's Valley leads via **Alligator Church** to Bowden Pen, 10 miles or so up the river valley. The paved road ends at Alligator Church. Beyond, the dirt road is extremely rough and narrow and you'll need a 4WD.

The Blue Mountains-John Crow National Park ranger station is at **Millbank**, 2 miles before Bowden Pen, near the summit ridge of the John Crow Mountains, which parallels

the valley like a great castle wall. A trail leads to the **White River Fall**, a series of seven cascades. It's a tough trek through the rain forest.

A short distance above **Bowden Pen**, the track begins rising more precipitously and the vegetation closes in. Don't push too far, for there is nowhere to turn your vehicle back. You can continue on foot across the Compass Gap.

Grande Valley Tours (see Organized Tours under Port Antonio earlier in this chapter) offers tours, as does **Sun Ventures** (☎ 960-6685; ⓦ www.sunventuretours.com; 30 Balmoral Ave, Kingston 10). Grand Valley Tours has a campsite just beyond Millbank. You must arrange with the company in advance.

Ambassabeth Cabins (☎ 938-5036, fax 977-8565; Millbank PO; camping US$5, cabins per person US$15) is near the valley head above Bowden Pen. It allows camping and has two very basic wooden cabins without running water or electricity, but with bamboo seats amid lawns and views toward Compass Gap. Meals cost US$5-10 extra. Bring mosquito repellent.

There's a tiny, well-stocked grocery store in Comfort Castle and another – **Lex Nightclub & Grocery** – at Millbank.

A bus from Port Antonio goes as far as Millbank, as do route taxis (US$1.75).

West of Port Antonio

PASSLEY GARDENS

Passley Botanical Gardens, 2 miles west of Port Antonio, is a 680-acre facility laid out around a well-preserved great house run as a hotel. In addition to well-tended gardens, the grounds include an experimental livestock farm and groves of tropical fruit trees.

Visitors are welcome and admission is free. Students lead **tours** (☎ 993-5490) by appointment only; you travel on a tractor-pulled jitney.

Passley Great House (☎ 993-5786, 993-5436; c/o College of Agriculture, Science & Education, PO Box 170, Passley Gardens;

doubles US$70) has five air-con bedrooms, each with private bathroom. They feature terra-cotta floors, lofty ceilings, and adequate furnishings. A living room has cable TV. Maid service is provided, and meals (US$26 per package) can be prepared for guests, or you can use the kitchen or take meals in the faculty cafeteria.

HOPE BAY & AROUND

There's nothing inspirational about Hope Bay, which has an ugly gray beach. A loop drive, however, can be made from here up the Swift River Valley, where plantations grow cacao.

Buses (US$0.50) and coasters and route taxis (US$1.50) pass Somerset Falls and Hope Bay between Annotto Bay and Port Antonio, and between Ocho Rios and Kingston.

Somerset Falls

These falls (☎ 913-0108; open 9am-5pm daily; adult/child US$4/2), on the A4, 9 miles west of Port Antonio, are hidden in a deep gorge about 2 miles east of Hope Bay. The Daniels River cascades down through a lush garden of ferns, heliconias, lilies, and crotons. You'll have to negotiate some steep, twisty steps.

The entrance fee includes a guided tour to the Hidden Fall that tumbles 33 feet into a jade-colored grotto.

Places to Stay & Eat

Content Farm (☎ 913-0690, 953-2387; Content, Hope Bay PO; camping US$5, rooms US$25), at Content, in the mountains above Hope Bay, affords an insight into the rural Jamaican lifestyle. Sister P (for Pauline) has five bamboo cabins with outhouse toilets, no electricity, and cold water from an outside barrel. You'll bathe in an invigorating mountain stream. The rates include all meals (I-tal food and natural juices). Content Farm is featured on the Lonely Planet video *Jamaica Experience*, though the school no longer functions. To get there, turn south at the police station in Hope Bay, turn right after 1 mile, then take the second left. 4WD is recommended.

Paradise Inn (☎ 993-5169, fax 993-5569; ☎ 020-7350-1009, fax 7228-3536 in the UK; Snow Hill PO; rooms US$45-88), on the A4 at Snow Hill, has modestly furnished, self-catering one-bedroom suites and studios, some with air-con and kitchenettes. It's a 20-minute walk to the beach.

Rio Vista Resort & Villas (☎/fax 993-5444; e riovistavillaja@jamweb.net; PO Box 4, St Margaret's Bay PO, Portland; 1-bedroom villas US$110, 2-bedroom villas US$140; honeymoon cottage US$120), atop a ridge near the turnoff for Rafter's Rest on the Rio Grande, 4 miles west of Port Antonio, is a superb option. This handsome modern home is built into the remains of an old plantation home and boasts an enviable setting high above the Rio Grande, with mountains behind. The main house has an atrium lounge. Antiques abound. Five genteel villas have lofty ceilings and polished wood floors; three have two bedrooms and kitchen plus TV lounge. The 'honeymoon' cottage was featured as a 'Room with a View' in *Condé Nast Traveler*. All units feature a kitchen, satellite TV, ceiling fans, and a housekeeper. Meals are made to order (try the seafood gumbo for US$18, or vegetable platter for US$10). Henry, your gracious host, offers airport transfers and represents Island Car Rentals.

Rafter's Rest (☎ 993-2778; open 8am-7pm daily), in a columned Georgian mansion, at the mouth of the Rio Grande 600 yards downhill from the A4, is the place to head for elegant dining. It was closed for renovation at last visit.

Sundial (☎/fax 913-0690; Main St), a colorful store in the center of Hope Bay, sells health products, including the 'Ashanti energy lifter,' and other tonics.

BUFF BAY

This small, neatly laid-out town, in the midst of a major banana producing area, has several colonial-era buildings of modest interest, centered on the Anglican church.

Fishdone Waterfalls is a beautiful spot on a private coffee plantation near Buff Bay. The falls are surrounded by rain forest, and there are trails for hiking.

The coast between Orange Bay and Annotto Bay is good for surfing.

The post office is 100 yards east of the church. Buff Bay also has a small **hospital** (☎ 996-1478), and the **police station** (☎ 996-1497) is at the east end of town.

Kildare Villa Great House (☎ 996-1240; Main St), at the east end of town, is a colonial structure operating a well-stocked gift store selling patties and desserts. The Jamaican seafood restaurant, upstairs, offers patio dining and serves such fare as ackee, saltfish, and brown stew chicken (US$5), and staples such as fried chicken and curried goat (US$5-12). There's a grocery store attached.

Pace Sitter Café (☎ 996-1240; 22 Victoria Rd) is the place to go for breakfast (about US$5). It's run by Earle and Pat Brown, who offer inexpensive meals, including curried goat, rice and peas, and delicious pastries and coffee.

BUFF BAY RIVER VALLEY

The B1 heads south from the town center and climbs 20 miles through the valley of the Buff Bay River to Hardwar Gap, at an elevation of 4500 feet, before dropping down to Kingston.

These slopes are an important coffee-producing area.

Blue Mountain Tours, based in Ocho Rios, offers a 'Blue Mountain Downhill Bicycle Tour' (US$85; see Ocho Rios in the Ocho Rios & North Coast chapter). The thrilling 18-mile descent begins at the company's handsome restaurant high up in the Blue Mountains at 5060 feet. Included are roundtrip transfers, breakfast and lunch, refreshments, and a guide.

ANNOTTO BAY

This erstwhile banana port – named for the annatto, a dye plant (*Bixa orellana*) that once was grown commercially here – is a downtrodden, one-street town that springs to life for Saturday market. Depressing shanties line the waterfront. At the town's center is an old courthouse that now houses the office of the collector of taxes. The paltry remains of **Fort George**, plus ginger-

bread colonial-era structures boasting columned walkways, stand on Main St. Most intriguing is the venerable yellow-and-red-brick **Baptist chapel,** built in 'village baroque' style in 1894, with cut-glass windows and curious biblical exhortations engraved at cornice height.

Two miles west of town is the junction of the A4 with the A3.

The town has a small **hospital** (☎ 996-2222). The **police station** (☎ 996-9169) and a **National Commercial Bank** (☎ 996-2213) are on Main St.

River Edge (☎ 944-2673, fax 944-9455; Annotto Bay PO; camping per person US$5, dorms US$20, apartments US$45) is nestled on the banks of the Penscar River, at Long Road, about 8 miles inland from Annotto Bay. It is a guest house with basically furnished dorm rooms and simple studio apartments with kitchenettes and private bathrooms with hot water. You can camp on the lawns (tents are rented). It has two swimming pools, and massage is offered, drawing locals on weekends for Sunday brunch (US$10).

You can buy grilled lobster, conch, saltfish, and peppered shrimp from roadside higglers who congregate immediately east of Annotto Bay. Wash them down with fruit juices or coconut milk.

ROBIN'S BAY

Midway from Port Maria from Annotto Bay, on the A3, you'll pass a turnoff to the north that hugs a lonesome shoreline with gray-sand beaches backed by lagoons. After 2½ miles, you emerge in **Mt Pleasant Heights**, a fishing village nestled atop **Don Christopher's Point**, named for the Spanish guerrilla leader, Don Cristobal Arnaldo de Ysassi, who led the resistance against the 1655 British invasion, culminating in the Battle of Rio Nuevo (see Rio Nuevo in the Ocho Rios & North Coast chapter).

The paved road ends at Robin's Bay (known as Strawberry Fields in the 1970s, when it was a free-love haven for American hippies). You can also reach Robin's Bay from Port Maria by a hiking trial that leads along one of the few stretches of Jamaican coastline that remains pristine. Locals can lead you to remote Black Sand Beach, and the **Kwaaman** and **Tacky Waterfalls**, where 100-foot falls plummet into deep pools surrounded by forest.

Ecotours for Cures (☎ 203-263-2970, 800-829-0918; ⓦ www.46.pair.com/ecotours; 413 Grassy Hill Rd, Woodbury, CT 06798-3129, USA) offers six-day guided tours that include hikes to Kwaaman Falls (US$1299 including roundtrip airfare from New York).

Places to Stay

Sonrise Beach Retreat (☎/fax 999-7169; ⓔ sonrise@cwjamaica.com; Sonrise, Robin's Bay PO, St Mary; camping per person US$7.50, huts US$25, cabins with/without bath US$85/60, deluxe cabin US$130, honeymoon suite US$120) is a nature and health retreat at Robin's Bay that nestles above a tiny cove with a pocket-size beach and great snorkeling. The serene spot is run by a charming couple, Kim and Robert Chase, and is popular with religious groups and families from Kingston on weekends, when it has a beach party. You can camp beneath the trees on 18 acres; there's a bath and shower complex, plus picnic tables and benches. Tents (US$5) and air mattresses (US$2) can be rented. Or stay in one of six standard dorm-style cabins; the two-bedroom deluxe cabins have a kitchenette and loft bedroom. A charming, two-bedroom 'honeymoon cottage' has its own beach, and a modern 'spa-suite' has a private patio with Jacuzzi

overlooking the cove. Health-conscious meals cost US$15 per day. Massages, eco-adventure tours, and horseback riding are offered, and jazz and spiritual music concerts are hosted. Day entry costs US$3.

The **River Lodge** (☎/fax 995-3003; ⓦ www.river-lodge.com; Robin's Bay PO, St Mary; ☎/fax 089-74 999 797 in Germany, Grünbauer Strasse 28, 81479 München; singles US$46, doubles US$74-80, cottage per person US$40), about 400 yards west of Sonrise, is an atmospheric mill house on a century-old estate, with white bleached-stone walls, blood-red floors, and five spacious bedrooms lit by skylights. The bathrooms (cold water only) are festooned with climbing ivy; the bathroom in the upstairs room is outside. The owner serves I-tal food in a small thatched restaurant, and offers massage, bush hikes, and boat trips. There's volleyball. Rates include breakfast and dinner.

An as-yet-unnamed **40-room hotel** was nearing completion at last visit, 1 mile east of Sonrise Beach Retreat.

Getting There & Away

Any of the public vehicles between Ocho Rios and Annotto Bay or Port Antonio will let you off at the junction to Robin's Bay on the A3. It's a 4-mile walk to Robin's Bay. With good timing, you can connect with bus No JR16A, which operates between Kingston and Robin's Bay, or with the few 'route taxis' that run to Robin's Bay from the A3.

NORTHEAST COAST

Negril & West Coast

The stub-nosed west coast comprises the parishes of Hanover (to the north) and Westmoreland (to the south). The area is virtually undeveloped for tourism, although there's an intriguing museum at Blenheim and the vintage port city of Lucea is a living heritage museum of disheveled colonial facades slated for eventual restoration. The A1 snakes past lime-green cattle pastures and sleepy fishing villages tucked teasingly into coves rimmed by mangroves, with nary a beach of much worth in sight. Until you arrive at Negril, which is Jamaica's hippest, most casual resort, with the island's longest beach and a buzzing nightlife. Negril nestles at the westernmost tip of Jamaica, providing a grandstand seat for sunsets. It also boasts superb coral reefs making for excellent scuba diving and a large swamp area – the Great Morass – that is an ecotour haven.

Negril

Negril (population 4500), 52 miles west of Montego Bay, is the vortex around which Jamaica's fun-in-the-sun vacation life whirls. Tourism is Negril's only industry. Despite phenomenal growth in recent years, Negril is still more laid-back than anywhere else in Jamaica, and you are more likely to interact with locals here than in other resort areas.

What a pleasure it was to arrive in Negril in the mid-1970s, before the world had discovered this then-remote, sensual Eden. Back then, Negril was an off-the-beaten-track haven: nirvana to the budget-minded, beach-loving crowd. It was a 'far-out' setting where you could drool over sunsets of hallucinogenic intensity that had nothing to do with the 'magic' mushrooms that still show up in omelettes and teas.

Negril's innocence is long gone. The red-eyed hippies have been joined by neatly groomed youths who whiz about on rented motor scooters, often with a local lass or dreadlocked 'Rent-a-Rasta' clinging tightly behind. Topless sunbathers lie semi-submerged on lounge chairs in the gentle

Highlights

- Negril, hands down the best spot for laid-back sunning by day and sinning by night
- Negril's reefs, for excellent scuba diving
- Peaceful Royal Palm Preserve and the Great Morass, full of wildlife
- Mayfield Falls, for refreshing dips beneath cooling cascades
- Roaring River, for atmosphere and natural beauty

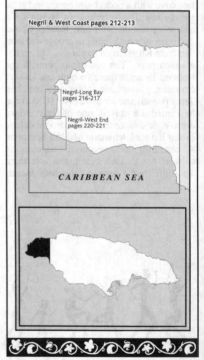

Negril & West Coast pages 212-213

Negril-Long Bay pages 216-217

Negril-West End pages 220-221

CARIBBEAN SEA

surf. And it's impossible to avoid the entreaties of drug-dealing locals: 'Hey, Tom Jones. A likkle smoke for you, mon?'

Compared to other resort towns, this is the 'real Jamaica,' permissive and unrestrained. Among the Negril devotees that flock from abroad are counterculture types colloquially called 'Jahmericans,' who put down ephemeral roots, mat their hair in dreadlocks, trade their accents for the local lexicon, exchange their T-shirts and jeans for a de rigueur uniform of string vest, tie-dyed shorts, and colored tam, and adopt their 'bredren's' barely disguised disdain for more uptight tourists.

You'll soon find yourself falling in love with Negril's insouciance and its scintillating 7-mile-long beach shelving gently into calm waters reflecting a palette of light blues and greens. Coral reefs lie just offshore. And you'll want your camera to record the consistently peach-colored sunsets that get more applause than the live reggae concerts for which Negril is equally famous.

HISTORY

The Spanish called the bay and adjacent headland Punta Negrilla, referring to the black conger eels that used to proliferate in the local rivers. During the colonial era, pirates favored Negril's two bays for safe anchorage for plundering forays. Later, British naval armadas used Bloody Bay as an assembly point, as in 1814, when it was the point of departure for the ill-fated expedition to storm New Orleans during the War of 1812 between England and the USA. Bloody Bay was also used by 19th-century whalers who butchered their catch here (hence the name).

Only in 1959 was a road cut to Negril, launching the development of what then was a tiny fishing village. Electricity and telephones came later. The sleepy beachfront village soon became a popular holiday spot for Jamaicans. About the same time, hippies and backpackers from abroad began to appear. They roomed with local families or slept on the beach, partook in ganja and magic mushrooms, and generally

---

'Calico' Jack

Negril's most touted and colorful piece of history was the capture of the pirate 'Calico' Jack Rackham (so named for his penchant for calico underwear). The amorous buccaneer was seized here in 1720 along with his two pirate mistresses, Mary Read and Anne Bonney, after dallying a bit too long on the beach.

Rackham was executed and his body suspended in an iron suit on what is now called Rackham Cay, at the harbor entrance at Port Royal, as an example to other pirates. The lives of Read and Bonney were spared because they claimed to be pregnant.

---

gave Negril its laid-back reputation. In 1977 the first major resort – Negril Beach Village (later renamed Hedonism II) – opened its doors to a relatively affluent crowd seeking an uninhibited Club Med–style vacation. Tales of Hedonism's toga parties and midnight nude volleyball games helped launch Negril to fame. By the mid-1980s, Negril was in the throes of a full-scale tourism boom that continues today. (The early days of tourism in Negril are regaled in *Banana Shout,* a humorous novel by local hotelier Mark Conklin.)

The let-it-all-hang-out tradition overflows still during the March-April spring break, when US college kids swarm for wet T-shirt contests, drinking competitions, and general party time.

Nonetheless, the resort has evolved an active, environmentally conscious spirit under the guidance of expat residents, resulting in the creation of the Negril Marine Park within the Negril Environmental Protection Area (see map). The park encompasses the shoreline, mangroves, offshore waters, and coral reefs, and is divided into eight recreational zones.

In 2001, the Chamber of Commerce adopted an environmental 'green' standard for hotels to adhere to. A hotel training

NEGRIL & WEST COAST

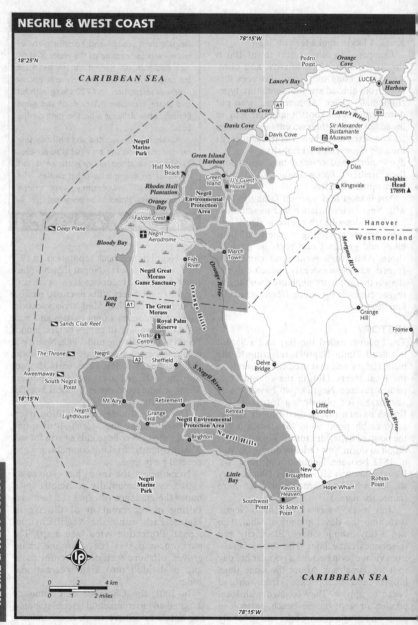

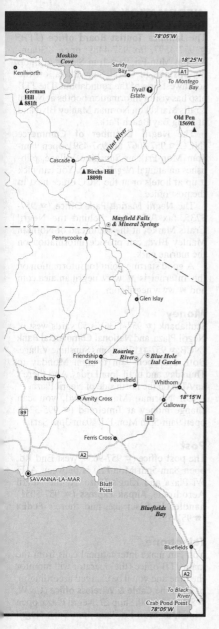

school recently opened, staffed by Cuban and French teachers.

ORIENTATION

Negril is divided in two by the South Negril River, with Long Bay to the north and West End to the south. The apex is Negril Village, which lies immediately south of the river and is centered on a small roundabout – called Negril Square – from which Norman Manley Blvd leads north, West End Rd leads south, and Sheffield Rd goes east and becomes the A2, which leads to Savanna-la-Mar, 19 miles away.

Long Bay

Long Bay and its blindingly white, 7-mile-long beach fringed by palms stretches north from the South Negril River. Long Bay is paralleled by Norman Manley Blvd, a two-lane highway about 100 yards inland of the beach. There are no sidewalks, so be careful when walking the road; traffic whips past pell-mell. The road is lined with hotels, restaurants, and food shacks for almost its entire length, except for a half-mile section toward its northern end that has been set aside as **Long Bay Beach Park** (☎ 957-9828), popular for nude bathing.

The beach draws gigolos and hustlers proffering everything from sex to aloe massages and, always, 'sensi.' 'Pssst! Bredda, you want ganja? Negril de place to get high, mon!' Tourist police now patrol the beach, but by law all Jamaican beaches must permit public access, so the hustlers are free to roam.

Water-sports concessions line the beach. By night this section is laden with the blast of reggae from disco bars.

In late 2001, Hurricane Michelle shaved about 10 yards from the beach, which was beginning to recover at last visit.

Bloody Bay

Long Bay is anchored to the north by the low rocky headland of Rutland Point. Beyond is a deeply scalloped cove, Bloody Bay, rimmed by a beautiful beach. Negril's upscale all-inclusive resorts are all located here or on the north end of Long Bay.

Negril Village

Negril Village, centered on the roundabout at the southern end of Norman Manley Blvd, consists of two shopping plazas and a handful of banks and other commercial ventures, plus a few score of houses and shacks dispersed among the forested hills known as Red Ground.

West End

A rocky limestone plateau rises south of the South Negril River and extends southward for several miles. The area is known as the West End or 'the Rock.' The coral cliff top is indented with coves good for swimming in crystal-clear azure waters, providing a dramatic setting for dozens of small hotels and restaurants built atop the rock face. It was the setting for scenes from *20,000 Leagues Under the Sea, Papillon,* and *Dr No.*

West End Rd snakes south along the cliff top (be careful walking – the road is narrow, with many blind corners and fast-moving vehicles). About a mile south, the road is renamed Lighthouse Rd, which leads past Negril Lighthouse, beyond which its name changes again to Ocean Drive. Ocean Drive runs through scrubland for 4 miles to the junction with William Hogg Blvd, which runs inland over the Negril Hills, meeting up with Whitehall Rd and then dropping down to Sheffield Rd.

Negril Hills

This range of low-lying hills rises inland of Negril's West End. The raised limestone upland is wild and smothered in brush. Tiny hamlets sprinkle the single road that provides access from Negril: Whitehall Rd leads south from Sheffield Rd to the hamlet of Grange Hill, swings east through the hills via the village of Retirement, and eventually links to the A2 for Savanna-la-Mar.

The only site of note is **Whitehall Great House**, in ruins following a fire in 1985. The surrounding plantation grounds provide a stage for horseback rides. Don't be fooled into paying US$5 for a tour by the locals who hang out and attempt to attach themselves as self-ascribed 'guides.'

INFORMATION
Tourist Offices

The **Jamaica Tourist Board office** (JTB; ☎ 957-4597, fax 957-4489; open 8:30am-4:30pm Mon-Fri, 9am-1pm Sat) is in Shop 20, upstairs in Coral Seas Plaza, on the southwest side of the roundabout. The JTB also has visitor information booths at Negril Crafts Market on Norman Manley Blvd and at Long Bay Beach Park.

The **Negril Chamber of Commerce** (NCC; ☎ 957-4067, fax 957-4591; open 9am-4pm Mon-Fri), in Sunshine Village, publishes an annual *Negril Guide.* You can pick it up at hotels or at the NCC office next to the post office.

The **Negril Marine Park Office** (☎ 957-3735, fax 957-4626), behind the Negril Crafts Market at the south end of Norman Manley Blvd, can provide information on the marine park.

A good starting point for information on the Internet is W www.negriljamaica.com and W www.negril.com.

Money

Scotiabank (☎ 957-4236) is 50 yards west of Negril Plaza, and **National Commercial Bank** (NCB; ☎ 957-4117) adjoins Sunshine Village. Both are open 9am to 2pm Monday to Thursday, and until 4pm Friday. And there's an **ATM** on the north side of Negril Plaza.

On Norman Manley Blvd, you can change money at **Timetrend** (☎ 995-3242; open 9am-5pm Mon-Fri, 10am-3pm Sat).

Post

The **post office** (☎ 957-9654; West End Rd; open 8am-5pm Mon-Fri) is between A Fi Wi Plaza and King's Plaza. At the Negril Aerodrome, **Airpak Express** (☎ 957-5051) handles UPS service, and there's **FedEx** (☎ 957-5533).

Telephone

You can make international calls from the main JTB office (the operator will monitor the time and you'll be charged accordingly), or from the **Cable & Wireless office** (C&W; ☎ 888-957-9700; Shop 27, Negril Plaza; open 8am-4pm Mon-Fri, 9am-4pm Sat); **Negril**

Calling Service (☎ 957-3212; Negril Plaza; open 9am-11pm daily); Café Taino (☎ 957-4380; e cafetaino@hotmail.com; Norman Manley Blvd; open 8:30am-11pm daily); and West End Calling Service (☎ 957-0724; West End Rd; open 10am-noon & 2pm-4pm Mon-Sat).

Email & Internet Access
Café Taino (see Telephone above), offers email and Internet service, as does Irie Vibes (☎ 957-3997; Norman Manley Blvd), across the road. Negril Cyber Café (☎ 957-9103; W www.negrilcybercafe.com), on the beach next to Sandi San Hotel, charges US$5 for 20 minutes. Negril Calling Service (see Telephone above) charges US$1.50 for the first 15 minutes and US$0.15 for each subsequent 5 minutes. In the West End, Mi Yard (☎ 957-4442; e info@miyard.com; West End Rd; open 24 hours) charges US$5 for 20 minutes. Nearby, Easy Rock Cyber Café (☎ 957-0671) offers a similar service.

Travel Agencies
Advanced Travel Service (☎ 957-4057), upstairs in Negril Plaza, is the only full-service travel agency. Caribic Vacations (☎ 957-3309, fax 957-3208; Norman Manley Blvd) can also make travel arrangements.

Bookstores & Libraries
Top Spot (☎ 957-4542), in Sunshine Village, is well stocked with international publications. Negril has a small library (☎ 957-4917; West End Rd; open 10am-6pm Mon-Wed, 1pm-5pm Thur, 10am-6pm Fri).

Laundry
You can have your dirties washed and ironed at West End Cleaners (☎ 957-0160), behind Scotiabank. Laundry costs $0.50 per pound. Pants cost US$5; a shirt costs US$3 for 'dry-cleaning' (which here means hand-washed in cold water).

Medical Services
The Negril Minor Emergency Clinic (☎ 957-4888, fax 957-4347; Norman Manley Blvd; open 24 hrs daily) has a laboratory (open 9:30am to 2pm Tues & Fri). The Omega

Medical Centre (☎ 957-9307) is in Negril Plaza. Dr Henry Blythe (☎ 957-4697) is on-call for hotel visits.

The government-operated Negril Health Centre (☎ 957-4926; open 9am-8pm Mon-Fri) is on Sheffield Rd.

The nearest hospitals are at Savanna-la-Mar and Lucea. A government ambulance (☎ 110) operates 24 hours a day from the Negril fire station.

There's a dental clinic (open noon-6pm Mon-Sat) in King's Plaza.

The Negril Pharmacy (☎ 957-4076; open 9am-7pm Mon-Sat, 10am-4pm Sun) is at Shop 14 in the Coral Seas Plaza. The Ocean View Pharmacy (☎ 957-9599) is in King's Plaza.

Dr Peggy Daugherty (☎ 957-0969; e peggy@manual-medicine.com; PO Box 2660) offers massages, including workshops.

Emergency
The police station (☎ 957-4268) is on Sheffield Rd. The fire brigade (☎ 110 or 957-4242) is on Red Ground Rd.

Dangers & Annoyances
There are no particular problems in Negril that can't be encountered elsewhere in Jamaica, although in Negril they are multiplied, and a few reminders are in order. For more information on any of the subjects below, turn to the Dangers & Annoyances section of the Facts for the Visitor chapter.

As anywhere on the island, sun, heat, and insects can be intense. Though mosquitoes are not usually the problem along the coast that they are inland in the Great Morass (which is the perfect breeding ground), 'no-see-ums' come alive just before dusk, when you'll be glad to leave the beach.

The peskiest annoyance is the persistent importuning by touts, and the most irritating is the pitching of ganja and cocaine ad nauseam. Though ganja is smoked in plain view in Negril, undercover police agents are present, and rarely a day goes by without one or more visitors being arrested.

Experiences of tourists suffering harmful side effects from ganja, especially from ganja cakes, have been reported. This is also

NEGRIL & WEST COAST

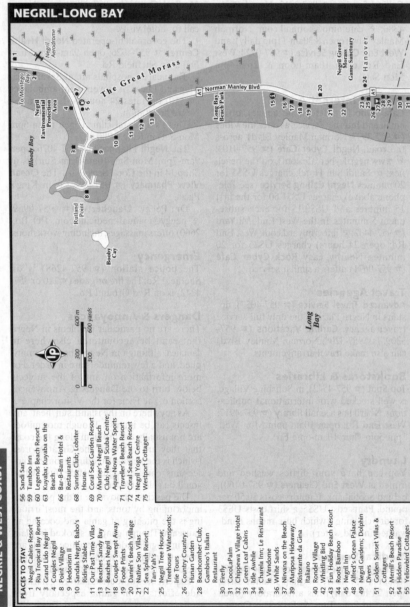

NEGRIL-LONG BAY

NEGRIL & WEST COAST

PLACES TO STAY

1 Negril Cabins Resort
2 Riu Tropical Bay Resort
3 Grand Lido Negril
4 Couples Negril
8 Point Village
9 Hedonism II
10 Sandals Negril; Babo's Riding Stables
11 Our Past Time Villas
13 Beaches Sandy Bay
17 Beaches Negril
18 Couples Swept Away
19 Foote Prints
20 Daniel's Beach Village
21 Native Son Villas
22 Sea Splash Resort; Tan-Yah's
25 Negril Tree House; Treehouse Watersports; Irie Tours
26 Country Country; Hunan Garden
28 Beachcomber Club; Gambino's Italian Restaurant
30 Firefly
31 CocoLaPalm
32 Chippewa Village Hotel
33 Green Leaf Cabins
34 Idle Awhile
35 Charela Inn; Le Restaurant le Vendome
36 White Sands
37 Nirvana on the Beach
39 Mariposa Hideaway; Ristorante da Gina Italiano
40 Rondel Village
42 Whistling Bird
43 Fun Holiday Beach Resort
44 Roots Bamboo
45 Negril Inn
48 Alfred's Ocean Palace
49 Negril Gardens; Dolphin Divers
51 Golden Sunset Villas & Cottages
52 Merrill's Beach Resort
54 Hidden Paradise
55 Yellowbird Cottages
56 Sandi San
59 Tamboo Inn
60 Legends Beach Resort
63 Kuyaba; Kuyaba on the Beach
66 Bar-B-Barn Hotel & Restaurants
68 Sunrise Club; Lobster House
69 Coral Seas Garden Resort
70 Mariner's Negril Beach Club; Negril Scuba Centre; Aqua-Nova Water Sports
71 Traveller's Beach Resort
72 Coral Seas Beach Resort
74 Negril Yoga Centre
75 Westport Cottages

NEGRIL-LONG BAY

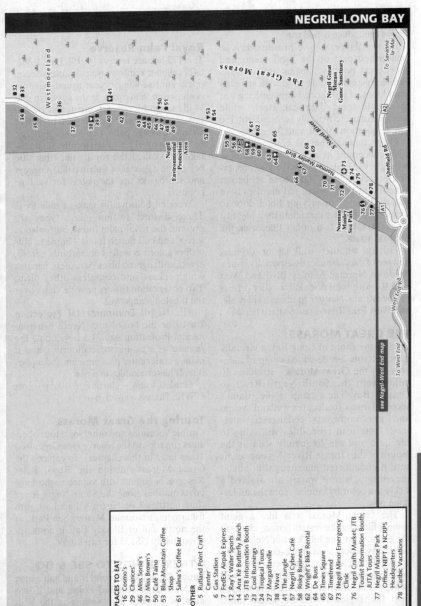

The Great Morass

Westmoreland

Negril Great Morass
Game Sanctuary

To Savanna-
la-Mar

■ 32
■ 33

■ 36

■ 41

□ 34
■ 35

■ 37

▼ 50
■ 51

■ 38
■ 39
■ 40
■ 42

■ 43
■ 44
■ 45
▶ 46
■ 47
■ 48
■ 49

▼ 53
■ 54

Negril
Environmental
Protection
Area

S Negril River

■ 52

▼ 61
■ 62

■ 65

■ 55
■ 56
□ 57
■ 58
■ 59
■ 60

■ 68
■ 69

Sheffield Rd

A2

Norman Manley Blvd

■ 64

■ 66

▓ 73
✚ 74
■ 75

A1

■ 70
■ 71

■ 72

Norman
Manley
Sea Park

■ 76
■ 77

■ 78

see Negril-West End map

To West End

NEGRIL & WEST COAST

PLACES TO EAT
16 Cosmo's
29 Chances'
46 Miss Sonia's
47 Miss Brown's
50 Café Taino
53 Blue Mountain Coffee
    Shop
61 Salina's Coffee Bar

OTHER
5   Rutland Point Craft
    Center
6   Gas Station
7   FedEx; Airpak Express
12 Ray's Water Sports
14 Ana Ké Butterfly Ranch
15 JTB Information Booth
23 Cool Runnings
24 Tropical Tours
27 Margaritaville
38 Wavz
41 The Jungle
57 Negril Cyber Café
58 Risky Business
62 Wright's Bike Rental
64 De Buss
65 Times Square
67 Timetrend
73 Negril Minor Emergency
    Clinic
76 Negril Crafts Market; JTB
    Tourist Information Booth;
    JUTA Tours
77 Negril Marine Park
    Office; NEPT & NCRPS
    Headquarters
78 Caribic Vacations

true of hallucinogenic wild mushrooms. Apparently, drinking alcohol while on mushrooms can induce a 'bad trip.'

As Negril is permissive, prostitution is an established part of the local scene, and short-term holiday liaisons are a staple. Female visitors should expect to hear a constant litany of well-honed lines enticing you to sample some 'Jamaican steel,' while foreign males are typically accosted with the simple question: 'So yu wan' fuk mi?'

Opportunistic theft is common, especially concerning items left on the beach, as is burglary in budget and mid-range properties. Several tourists have been robbed at gunpoint in their hotels, and murders have occurred; never open your hotel door to strangers without ascertaining their identity. At night, take a taxi rather than walk the dimly lit roads.

Finally, whether walking or driving, beware of cars! Jamaicans, especially males, fly down Norman Manley Blvd and West End Rd with total disdain for other drivers or pedestrians. Neither road has a sidewalk, and West End Rd has many sharp bends.

THE GREAT MORASS

Behind the shore of Long Bay, a virtually impenetrable 2-mile-wide swamp of mangroves – the Great Morass – stretches 10 miles from the South Negril River to Orange Bay. The swamp is the island's second-largest freshwater wetland system and forms a refuge for endangered waterfowl. American crocodiles still cling to life here and are frequently seen at the mouth of the Orange River. No one seems sure if endangered manatees still inhabit the swamp, whose waters are stained a sickly tea color by tannins from the underlying peat.

The Great Morass acts like a giant sponge filtering the waters flowing down to the ocean from the hills east of Negril, and is thereby a source of much-needed freshwater. Drainage channels cut into the swamp have lowered the water levels, and sewage and other pollutants have seeped into the region's shallow water table, making their way to sea where they have poisoned the coral reefs and depleted fish stocks.

Royal Palm Reserve

This 177-hectare reserve (☎ 957-3115, 1-382-6422 cellular; e info@royalpalmreserve.com; open sunrise-sunset year-round, visitors center open 9am-5pm), at the southern end of the Great Morass, was created in 1989 to protect the largest population of native 'swamp cabbage palm' (*Roystonea princeps*, or 'morass royal'), which is locally – and mistakenly – called the royal palm (that title belongs to a species of Cuban palm). Ospreys and sea hawks use the palms for vantage points.

Wooden boardwalks make a mile loop. Three distinct swamp forest types are present: the royal palm forest, buttonwood forest, and bull thatch forest – home to butterflies galore as well as doctorbirds, herons, egrets, endangered black parakeets, Jamaica woodpeckers, and countless other birds. Two observation towers provide views over the tangled mangroves.

The **Negril Environmental Protection Trust** (see the boxed text 'Negril Environmental Protection Area') is developing the reserve as a center for ecotourism, and it plans a craft center plus museum and aquarium. It has crocodiles in a pen.

Guided tours – starting at 10am – cost US$10. There's a snack bar.

Touring the Great Morass

Caribic Vacations and local tour operators run trips to the reserve (see Organized Tours later in this chapter). To explore the Great Morass outside the Royal Palm Reserve, negotiate with villagers who have boats moored along the South Negril River (just northeast of Negril Village), or with fishermen at Norman Manley Sea Park, at the north end of Bloody Bay. It costs approximately US$35 for two hours.

OTHER THINGS TO SEE & DO

Booby Cay is a small coral island half a mile offshore from Rutland Point, and it was used as a South Seas setting in the Walt Disney movie *20,000 Leagues Under the*

Negril Environmental Protection Area

This protected wilderness zone extends from Green Island on the north coast to St John's Point (south of Negril) and inland to the Fish River and Orange Hills. It also includes a marine park extending out to sea. The intention is to protect the entire Negril watershed (the area drained by the Orange, Fish, Newfound, North Negril, and South Negril Rivers), including the Great Morass swampland and all land areas that drain into the Caribbean between Green Island and St John's Point.

The Negril Environmental Protection Area (NEPA) was declared in November 1997, incorporating a Negril Marine Park and embracing uplands, morass, shoreline, offshore lagoon, and reefs. The NEPA plan establishes guidelines for tourism growth (future hotel construction will be controlled); moratoriums on further cutting or draining of mangrove or wetland areas; the establishment of 'fish management zones'; sewage systems for outlying communities; and the creation of tourism-related activities geared to the preservation ethic.

For information, contact **Negril Environmental Protection Trust** (NEPT; ☎ 957-3736, fax 957-3115; Ⓦ www.preservenegril.com), PO Box 2599, Negril, Westmoreland.

Sea. The island is named for the seabirds – 'boobies,' in local parlance – that nest here. Water-sports concessionaires can arrange boats for about US$20 roundtrip.

The **Ana Ké Butterfly Ranch & Rural Life Theme Park** (☎ 957-5228, fax 957-5947; Norman Manley Blvd; admission US$5), new in 2001, features a butterfly farm, aviary, minizoo, and a re-creation of a 'typical' Jamaica village. It also has a miniature train, go-kart track, and water park, plus fishing and boating.

The gleaming-white, 66-foot-tall **Negril Lighthouse** (3 miles south of Negril Village on West End Rd) illuminates the westernmost point of Jamaica, at 18° 15' north, 78° 23' west. The lighthouse, erected in 1894 with a prism made in Paris and originally powered by kerosene, is solar powered and flashes every two seconds. It's open 9am to sunset daily (no charge for entry). Wilson Johnson, the superintendent, will gladly lead the way up the 103 stairs for a bird's-eye view of the coast.

WATER SPORTS

The waters off Negril are usually mirror-calm – ideal for all kinds of water sports. Numerous concessions along the beach rent Jet Skis (about US$30 for 30 minutes),

plus sea kayaks, sailboards, and Sunfish (about US$15 per hour). They also offer waterskiing (US$25 for 30 minutes) and banana-boat rides (using an inflatable banana-shaped raft towed by a speedboat; US$15).

Negril Yacht Club (☎ 957-9224; West End Rd) charges US$20/30 half/full-day for kayaks.

Ray's Water Sports (☎ 957-4349), at the north end of Long Bay; **Aqua-Nova Water Sports** (☎ 957-4420, 957-4323; ⓔ gaynair@cwjamaica.com) at Mariner's Negril Beach Club; and **Treehouse Watersports** (☎ 957-4893; Norman Manley Blvd), at Negril Tree House, offer parasailing on Long Bay.

SCUBA DIVING

Negril's offers extensive offshore reefs and cliffs with grottos, with shallow reefs perfect for novice divers and mid-depth reefs right off the 7-mile-long main beach at Long Bay. Clusters of dwarf tube sponges are a noteworthy feature. The West End offers caves and tunnels; its overhangs are popular for night dives. Hawksbill turtles are common here.

Visibility often exceeds 100 feet, and seas are dependably calm. Most dives are in 35 to 75 feet of water. (For more general

NEGRIL & WEST COAST

NEGRIL-WEST END

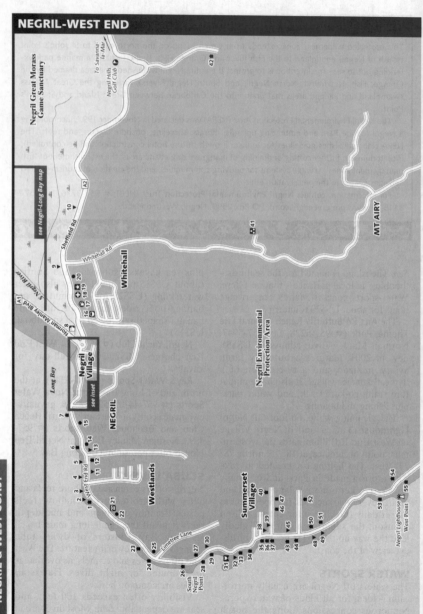

Negril Great Morass Game Sanctuary

Negril Hills Golf Club

To Savanna-la-Mar

see Negril-Long Bay map

Sheffield Rd

Whitehall Rd

MT AIRY

S Negril River

Norman Manley Blvd

Whitehall

Negril Environmental Protection Area

Long Bay

Negril Village

see inset

NEGRIL

Westlands

West End Rd

Limetree Lane

Summerset Village

South Negril Point

West Point

Negril Lighthouse

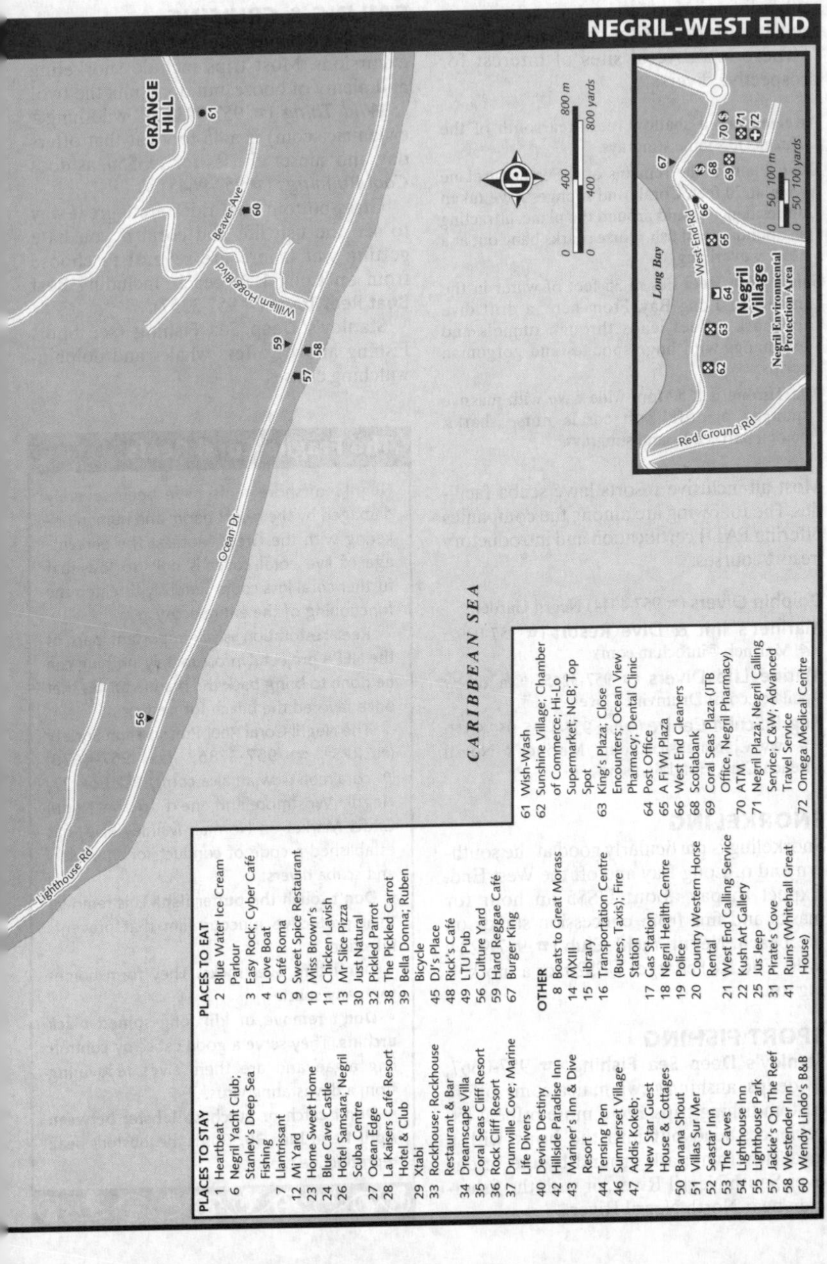

NEGRIL-WEST END
GRANGE HILL
Beaver Ave
William Hogg Blvd
Ocean Dr
Lighthouse Rd
CARIBBEAN SEA
Long Bay
West End Rd
Red Ground Rd
Negril Village
Negril Environmental Protection Area
0 400 800 m
0 400 800 yards
0 50 100 m
0 50 100 yards
PLACES TO STAY
1 Heartbeat
6 Negril Yacht Club; Stanley's Deep Sea Fishing
7 Llantrissant
12 Mi Yard
23 Home Sweet Home
24 Blue Cave Castle
26 Hotel Samsara; Negril Scuba Centre
27 Ocean Edge
28 La Kaisers Café Resort Hotel & Club
29 Xtabi
33 Rockhouse; Rockhouse Restaurant & Bar
34 Dreamscape Villa
35 Coral Seas Cliff Resort
36 Rock Cliff Resort
37 Drumville Cove; Marine Life Divers
40 Devine Destiny
42 Hillside Paradise Inn
43 Mariner's Inn & Dive Resort
44 Tensing Pen
46 Summerset Village
47 Addis Kokeb; New Star Guest House & Cottages
50 Banana Shout
51 Villas Sur Mer
52 Seastar Inn
53 The Caves
54 Lighthouse Inn
55 Lighthouse Park
57 Jackie's On The Reef
58 Westender Inn
60 Wendy Lindo's B&B
PLACES TO EAT
2 Blue Water Ice Cream Parlour
3 Easy Rock; Cyber Café
4 Love Boat
5 Café Roma
9 Sweet Spice Restaurant
10 Miss Brown's
11 Chicken Lavish
13 Mr Slice Pizza
30 Just Natural
32 Pickled Parrot
38 The Pickled Carrot
39 Bella Donna; Ruben Bicycle
45 DJ's Place
48 Rick's Café
49 LTU Pub
56 Culture Yard
59 Hard Reggae Café
67 Burger King
OTHER
8 Boats to Great Morass
14 MXIII
15 Library
16 Transportation Centre (Buses, Taxis); Fire Station
17 Gas Station
18 Negril Health Centre
19 Police
20 Country Western Horse Rental
21 West End Calling Service
22 Kush Art Gallery
25 Jus Jeep
31 Pirate's Cove
41 Ruins (Whitehall Great House)
61 Wish-Wash
62 Sunshine Village; Chamber of Commerce; Hi-Lo Supermarket; NCB; Top Spot
63 King's Plaza; Close Encounters; Ocean View Pharmacy; Dental Clinic
64 Post Office
65 A Fi Wi Plaza
66 West End Cleaners
68 Scotiabank
69 Coral Seas Plaza (UTB Office, Negril Pharmacy)
70 ATM
71 Negril Plaza; Negril Calling Service; C&W; Advanced Travel Service
72 Omega Medical Centre

scuba diving information, see Activities in the Facts for the Visitor chapter.)

There are several sites of interest for prospective divers:

Aweemaway, a shallow reef area south of the Throne, has tame stingrays.

Deep Plane is the remains of a Cessna airplane lying at 70 feet. Corals and sponges have taken up residence in and around the plane, attracting an abundance of fish. Nurse sharks hang out at a nearby overhang.

Sands Club Reef lies in 35 feet of water in the middle of Long Bay. From here, a drift dive to Shark's Reef leads through tunnels and overhangs with huge sponges and gorgonian corals.

The Throne is a 50-foot-wide cave with massive sponges, plentiful soft corals, nurse sharks, octopi, barracuda, and stingrays.

Most all-inclusive resorts have scuba facilities. The following are among the companies offering PADI certification and introductory 'resort courses:'

Dolphin Divers (☎ 957-4944) Negril Gardens

Mariner's Inn & Dive Resort (☎ 957-0392; e Mariners@infochan.com)

Marine Life Divers (☎ 957-3245; e mld@cwjamaica.com) Drumville Cove

Negril Scuba Centre (☎/fax 957-4425, 957-9641; w www.jamaica-irie.com) Mariner's Negril Beach Club, Hotel Samsara

SNORKELING

Snorkeling is particularly good at the southern end of Long Bay and off the West End. Expect to pay about US$5 an hour for masks and fins from concession stands on the beach. **Negril Yacht Club** (☎ 957-9224; West End Rd) charges US$20 for a snorkeling tour.

SPORT FISHING

Stanley's Deep Sea Fishing (☎ 957-0667; e deepseafishing@cwjamaica.com) offers custom fishing trips. For a more offbeat experience, head out into the briny with a local fisherman; ask around by the bridge over South Negril River, or with the fishermen near North Negril River.

SAILING & CRUISING

Several companies offer two and three-hour excursions. Most trips include snorkeling and plenty of booze, but don't mix the two!

Wild Thing (☎ 957-9930; e wildthing@cwjamaica.com) is a 45-foot cat that offers day and sunset cruises for US$50, as does *Cool Runnings* (☎ 957-9645).

Glass-bottom boat rides are a great way to see the fish life and coral if you hate getting wet. There are several to choose from on Long Bay beach, including **Best Boat Reef Tours** (☎ 957-3357).

Stanley's Deep Sea Fishing (see Sport Fishing above) offers whale- and dolphin-watching cruises.

The Fragile Coral Reefs

Negril's offshore reefs have been severely damaged by the resort boom and human tinkering with the Great Morass. The percentage of live coral cover is now so low that further coral loss could seriously threaten the functioning of the entire ecosystem.

Reef restoration is an important part of the NEPA project. Unfortunately, nothing can be done to bring back the marine turtles that once favored the beach for nesting.

The Negril Coral Reef Preservation Society (NCRPS; ☎ 957-3735, fax 957-4626; e coralreefs@cwjamaica.com), PO Box 27, Negril, Westmoreland, next to the Negril Crafts Market on Norman Manley Blvd, has established a code of conduct for snorkelers and scuba divers:

• **Don't touch the puffer fish!** This removes their protective mucous film that prevents infection.

• **Don't turn over rocks.** They form homes for many species.

• **Don't remove or kill long-spined black urchins.** They serve a good cause by controlling algae and are themselves recovering from a devastating virus.

• **Don't catch or purchase lobster between April 1 and June 30.** This is the lobster's peak reproductive time.

GOLF

The **Negril Hills Golf Club** (☎ 957-4638, fax 957-3890), on Sheffield Rd 3 miles east of Negril, is an 18-hole, par-72 course bordering the Great Morass. If you plop your ball in the water, forget it – the crocodiles will probably get to it first! There's a clubhouse, pro shop, and restaurant. The green fee is US$58. Golf carts are mandatory and cost US$35. Caddies cost US$14; club rentals are US$18.

HORSEBACK RIDING

Babo's Riding Stable (☎ 640-0989), near Sandals, offers lessons and two-hour rides for US$25. **Country Western Horse Rental** (☎ 957-3250; Sheffield Rd; open 8am-5pm), next to the police station, charges US$30 for rides. **Rhodes Hall Plantation** (☎ 957-6883; e rhodes@cwjamaica.com) has rather tame rides (US$40-60, including hotel transfers); see Green Island Harbour later in this chapter.

BICYCLING

Rusty's X-Cellent Adventures (☎ 957-0155, fax 957-4108; e rxadventures@cwjamaica .com; PO Box 104) offers guided bike tours into the Negril Hills. For rentals (about US$10 per day), try **Wrights** (☎ 957-4908), on Norman Manley Blvd, or **Ruben Bicycle** (☎ 830-5815), at Bella Donna restaurant in the West End.

ORGANIZED TOURS

Several tour operators offer a standard fare of excursions to the Black River Morass and Appleton Rum Estate (about US$75), Mayfield Falls (US$50), and Roaring River (US$54). These include **Caribic Vacations** (☎ 957-3309, fax 957-3208; Norman Manley Blvd; open 9am-6pm Mon-Fri, 10am-1pm Sat & Sun), the largest operator; **Tropical Tours** (☎ 957-4110; e tropical@cwjamaica .com; Norman Manley Blvd); **JUTA Tours** (☎ 957-9197), in the Negril Crafts Market; and **Irie Tours** (☎ 957-3806), at Negril Tree House.

Go-Bush Adventure Tours (☎ 957-3309, fax 953-9897; e gobuhjamaica@hotmail.com) has 4WD safaris Tuesday and Saturday.

SPECIAL EVENTS

The **Negril Spring Triathlon** (☎ 929-9200; e jamaicaevents@cwjamaica.com) is held each January at the Couples Swept Away resort's sports complex. The annual **Reggae Marathon & Half-Marathon** (☎ 948-5942) takes place in December.

The **Bob Marley Birthday Bash** is hosted each February 6, when top reggae stars perform at MXIII (☎ 957-0704; e mx3 negril@hotmail.com), a concert venue in the West End.

In mid-March, the three-night **Negril Music Festival** (☎ 968-9356) features leading Jamaican and international reggae stars, calypso artists, and other musicians.

The annual Spring Break **Jamaica Beachfest** – a four-day excuse to *paaarrty!* – is held each mid-April and features live music, plenty of booze, and wet T-shirt and bikini contests.

Rockwildaz Entertainment (w www.rock-wildaz.com/springbreak) hosts a similarly wet-and-wild party. In the same vein, the **Negril Carnival** (☎ 957-4220) is in May.

The weeklong **African Dance and Drum Retreat** is held in mid-October at Negril Tree House (see Places to Stay below).

PLACES TO STAY

Hotels given below are listed within each price range from roughly north to south beginning at Bloody Bay. Rates quoted are for summer (low season) unless otherwise noted. Winter (high season) rates can be 20% to 60% higher.

In general, beach properties are more expensive than hotels of equivalent standard in the West End. Unless otherwise noted, all 'Long Bay' beach hotels are on Norman Manley Blvd, and all 'West End' hotels are on the coast road, variously West End Rd, Lighthouse Rd, and Ocean Drive.

In the USA, **Vacation Hotline** (☎ 773-880-0030, 800-325-2485; e mdormanvh@ aol.com) acts as a reservation agent for over 50 properties in Negril.

Places to Stay – Budget

Camping Several budget hotels offer camping; for all, see Hotels below for contact information and full descriptions.

Along Long Bay beach, **Roots Bamboo** (summer single/double US$9/16, winter per person US$12) gets fairly busy. It has a communal shower block. Tent rental costs US$1 per person. **Westport Cottages** (camping US$6) lets you camp in the yard at these cottages and use the well-stocked kitchen.

Along West End, **Addis Kokeb** (per tent US$10) offers camping with communal shower and toilet. **Lighthouse Park** (doubles US$15, extra person US$5) has communal toilets and 'solar bag' showers plus a community kitchen. Meals can be cooked to order. No children are allowed.

Guest Houses – Negril Hills
Wendy Lindo's B&B (☎ 1-999-5793 cellular, fax 957-4591; e wendybbja@hotmail.com; Westcliff Gardens, Negril PO; doubles US$50, for 2 weeks US$650) is a quaint guest house on Beaver Ave, about 6 miles south of Negril, off William Hogg Blvd. Rates include breakfast and are a great bargain. Wendy, an expat from the Isles of Scilly, offers three rooms (two share a bath) in her charming house – a little piece of England built atop a coral outcrop with ocean views. Her cottage is full of antiques, cozy couches, and porcelain china. The clean, airy rooms have private patios, ceiling fan, screened windows, and hot water. Airport transfers are US$50 each way. Wendy's husband, John, offers a taxi service and island tours.

Hillside Paradise Inn (☎ 800-247-5554; w www.hspinn.com; Hessette Rd; single/double summer US$35/45, winter US$55/65) is a laid-back, reclusive, US-run retreat in the hills, 2 miles east of Negril. It has 10 modern, modestly appointed rooms surrounding a large pool, plus three rooms in a Colorado-style lodge. All have satellite TV, hand-carved wooden beds, and tile floors. A large bar evokes the Midwest US style, and stage-shows are hosted.

Hotels – Long Bay
Green Leaf Cabins (☎ 957-4677; cabins US$20-50, cottage US$140) offers 10 basic two-story cabins with patios (some with private bath) and a three-bedroom cottage with kitchen. A reader says they're not secure.

An Italian-run hotel, **Mariposa Hideaway** (☎ 957-4918, fax 957-3167; e mariposa@cwjamaica.com; Negril PO 3114; rooms per person summer/winter US$20/25, bungalows US$55/75, apartments US$110/145) is a twee place. In addition to rooms, it has bungalows with kitchenette, TV, and fans, as well as family-size apartments. It features the Ristorante da Gina Italiano.

Roots Bamboo (☎ 957-4479, fax 957-9191; e rootsbamboo@cwjamaica.com; c/o Ted Plummer, Negril PO, Westmoreland; single or double summer/winter US$22/36; double with porch & shower US$50/68, with air-con US$70/90) is another popular option. It has 32 soulless but well-kept cabins right on the beach. Some have showers; others share a communal shower block with campers. There's a small beachside bar and restaurant with pool tables.

Beachside, **Alfred's Ocean Palace** (☎ 957-4669, fax 957-9674; w www.alfreds.com; PO Box 3081; rooms US$40-50) has airy, well-lit, simply furnished rooms with hardwood floors. Alfred's famous bar is one of the liveliest around, with live concerts – a potential concern for early-to-bedders.

Yellowbird Cottages (☎ 412-343-1238 in the USA; w www.theyellowbird.com; rooms summer US$35-45, winter US$50-90; cottages summer US$50-100, winter US$100-200) has five two-bedroom cottages and five rooms. All are simply furnished, with wicker furniture, ceiling fans, and a refrigerator.

Golden Sunset Villas & Cottages (☎ 957-4241, 957-9703, fax 957-4761; w www.the goldensunset.com; PO Box 3021; economy room summer/winter US$39/45, standard US$55/68, superior US$65/85), formerly Arthur's Golden Sunset, is a longtime favorite of the budget crowd. It has 27 rustic cottages and 'economy' rooms with cold water only; 'standard' rooms with hot water; and 'superior' rooms with air-con and TV. All rooms share kitchenettes.

Travellers Beach Resort (☎ 957-3039, fax 957-9305; ☎ 718-251-9300 in the USA; e travellers@cwjamaica.com; cabins without/with kitchenettes summer US$40/45, winter US$50/55, rooms summer US$80/100, winter US$100/120) offers 14 basic cabins amid unkempt grounds, plus 16 rooms in a two-story beachfront block. All have fans and air-con plus private bath with hot water and enclosed verandas or patios. The rooms have telephones and cable TV; six have kitchenettes. There's a beachfront restaurant and bar.

Negril Yoga Centre (☎ 957-4397, 941-263-7322 in the USA; ⊞ www.negrilyoga.com; PO Box 48; rooms summer US$35-60, winter US$38-70) has eight rustic yet atmospheric rooms and cottages – most with fridges and fans – surrounding an open-air, wood-floored thatched yoga center set in a garden. Options range from a two-story, Thai-style wooden cabin to an adobe farmer's cottage; all are pleasingly if modestly furnished. The staff make their own yogurt, cheese, and sprouts and cook on request. Yoga classes are offered.

Westport Cottages (☎ 957-4736; doubles US$20) is an offbeat place popular with the laid-back backpacking crowd. A communal feel pervades the place, which owner Joseph Mathews says is approved for 'roach people.' Joseph has 15 very rustic huts with well-kept outside toilet and cold shower, plus mosquito nets and fans. Newer rooms to the rear are preferred. A well-stocked communal kitchen is available, and free bicycles and snorkeling equipment are provided.

Hotels – West End Negril Yacht Club (☎/fax 957-9224; ⓔ info@negrilyacht.com; PO Box 3034; rooms summer US$35-50, winter US$55-70) is an oceanfront hotel and a favorite of budget travelers. It has 16 no-frills rooms with fans, cable TV, refrigerator, and hot water in private bathrooms. The bar and restaurant is popular, and entertainment includes an acrobat and fire-dancer.

Mi Yard (☎ 957-4442; ⓔ info@miyard.com; rooms summer/winter US$40/50, cottages US$65/85) offers four simple, clean, albeit somewhat dark, tiled rooms (two with air-con) and two no-frills yet charming wooden Caribbean-style cottages with balconies. It has a popular little restaurant and offers Internet service.

Blue Cave Castle (☎/fax 957-4845; ⓔ info@bluecavecastle.com; PO Box 3066; tower

rooms single/double summer US$30/35, winter US$50/60; deluxe summer US$35/45, winter US$60/75; superior summer US$45/55, winter US$60/75) is an atmospheric, crenellated all-stone concoction, squat four-square atop the cliff. It has 14 bedrooms, each with ceiling fan and refrigerator; superior rooms also have air-con and cable TV. Stairs lead down to a sparkling grotto.

Addis Kokeb/New Star Guest House & Cottages (☎ 640-2312; ⓔ adddiskokebnewstar@yahoo.com; PO Box 78; doubles US$30, whole house US$100, cabins US$40), near Summerset Village off Lighthouse Rd, is a marvelous budget option in a 3-acre wilderness garden. Each of the four rooms in the rustic Colorado-style lodge have two double beds; guests share two bathrooms. There's a TV lounge, a small library boasting Persian throw rugs and deep-cushion sofas, an open mezzanine dining room, and kitchen with guest privileges. There are also three bare-bones cabins, each with stove, fridge, private bath, kitchen, and screened porch with hammocks. Cable TV was planned. Guests have access to a pool and beach shuttle.

Seastar Inn (☎ 957-0553; ⓔ reservations@seastarinn.com; PO Box 2653; rooms single/double summer US$44/54, winter US$59/69), off Lighthouse Rd, is a peaceful modern place run by a charming Canadian couple. It offers deluxe studio apartments with air-con, satellite TV, and safes. It has a pool plus restaurant and swim-up bar in the lush garden, plus free beach shuttle and bicycle use. Rates include breakfast.

Lighthouse Park (☎ 957-0252; ⓔ sef@cwjamaica.com; PO Box 3; cabins summer/winter US$50/75, cottages US$50/100, stone house US$75/150), south of the lighthouse, offers six rustic but charming and clean bamboo-and-thatch cabins, as well as A-frame cottages and a two-story, two-bedroom stone house with kitchenette. Breakfast is provided. Prices are 'negotiable.'

Lighthouse Inn (☎ 957-4052, fax 957-0460; PO Box 3108; cottages summer US$25-120, winter US$50-150) has four six-person cottages with solar-heated water, louvered windows, and wicker furniture. Rates depend on the number of people. It has a free beach shuttle, plus a restaurant offering candlelit dining.

Places to Stay – Mid-Range

Hotels – Long Bay Our Past Time Villas (☎ 957-5931, fax 957-5422; � www.ourpast timenegril.com; PO Box 45; rooms summer US$50-70, winter US$100-120; studios summer US$70-90, winter US$110-130; apartments summer US$130-150, winter US$210-240), near the north end, has 17 pleasant, modestly furnished rooms, studios, and two-bedroom apartments with satellite TV and patios. Some have air-con and kitchenettes. It has a bar and restaurant.

Foote Prints (☎ 957-4300, fax 957-4301; ⍷ info@foote-prints.com; PO Box 100; superior summer/winter US$60/85, deluxe US$95/145, studios US$115/165, apartments US$185/225) has 30 air-con rooms, studios (with kitchenettes), and two-bedroom apartments with TV, telephone, and safety box. Some have ceiling fans and most have balconies. There's an on-site restaurant and bar, plus Jacuzzi, tour desk, water sports, and excursions.

Daniel's Beach Village (☎ 957-4394, fax 957-4713; ⍷ danielbeach@cwjamaica.com; single/double summer US$50/75, winter US$55/85; apartments US$85-125) is a gleaming white 45-room property with studios and standard or deluxe apartments with kitchenette. Furniture, alas, is dowdy. It also has apartments with large kitchens and living areas. There's a large pool. It offers nature trips to a local farm (US$25).

Country Country (☎ 957-4273, fax 957-4342; � www.countrynegril.com; standard rooms summer/winter US$110/130, deluxe US$130/145) is a color-crazy charmer with 14 air-con wooden cottages with gingerbread trim and fretwork. Hot pastels dominate and lend a chic warmth. Some have king beds and separate sitting areas. All have in-room safes, minifridges, and balconies. There's a bar and grill, and Hunan Chinese restaurant.

Beachcomber Club (☎ 957-4170, 877-713-8784, fax 957-4097; ⍷ beachcomberclub@ cwjamaica.com; PO Box 98; rooms summer US$90-110, winter US$130-150; apartments

summer US$120-220, winter US$160-330) is a handsome 45-room hotel with an open-air beachside restaurant, Gambino's Italian restaurant, plus a nightly entertainment schedule, tennis, and water sports. All rooms are elegantly furnished, with air-con, ceiling fans, telephone, and satellite TV.

Firefly (☎ 957-4358, fax 925-5728; ☎ 800-477-9530 in the USA; ⍷ firefly@negril jamaica.com; PO Box 54; cottages US$154, studio US$134, suites US$160-186, apartments US$165-231) rents four handsome, all-hardwood cottages, plus one-bedroom studios, apartments, and penthouse suites. Each is different but all have kitchenettes and verandas. There's a Jacuzzi, and guests get free access to Couples Swept Away's facilities. It's popular with nudists.

Chippewa Village Hotel (☎ 957-4676; ⍷ chippewavillage@hotmail.com; cottage doubles US$55, 1-/2-/3-bedroom units US$100/120/140), owned by friendly Californian John Babcock, offers three octagonal studio units with screened porches and lofty ceilings and six one- to three-bedroom apartments. All are rustic, rough-hewn affairs oozing a warm ambience, epitomized by American Southwest decor, throw rugs, and tasteful fabrics. A small swimming pool under a shade canopy is inset in a wooden sundeck. There's a small restaurant and bar, with American home cooking (for guests only), plus a Jacuzzi, steam room, and viewing tower overlooking the Great Morass.

White Sands (☎ 957-4291, fax 957-4674; PO Box 60; ⍷ whitesands@cwjamaica.com; standard/deluxe/1-bedroom apartment/ villa summer US$54/75/92/240, winter US$61/89/123/340) is an attractive property where options range from simple yet elegant one-bedroom octagonal units to a four-bedroom, four-bath villa (sleeping 8 people) with its own pool. The tiled units sit in a well-maintained garden with a pool.

Rondel Village (☎ 957-4413, fax 957-4915; ⍷ rondel@cwjamaica.com; PO Box 96; rooms summer/winter US$75/100, 1-bedroom villas US$125/180, 2-bedroom villas US$190/250) has nicely appointed studios and beachfront rooms clustered around a small pool and Jacuzzi. You can also choose octagonal one- and two-bedroom villas that sleep up to six and feature air-con, marble floors, French doors, satellite TV, fully equipped kitchenettes, and Jacuzzi. It has a seafront café and snack bar.

Fun Holiday Beach Resort (☎ 957-3585, fax 957-4057; e karin@cwjamaica.com; rooms US$60-80), opposite the Jungle, was a work in progress at last visit and will have 40 rooms in two-story units. Each has air-con and cable TV, but meager furnishings. The bar and beach club hosts live bands and has water sports.

Hidden Paradise (☎ 957-3370, fax 957-9219; e jamaica@hidden-paradise.com; PO Box 9; single/double summer US$40/50, winter US$50/66; suites summer US$110/130, winter US$130/162) offers four twin-room cottages with air-con, fan, private verandas, and hot water. Two cottages have kitchenettes. It also features eight rooms in a house amid well-tended lawns. Rates include tax and service charges. A meal plan is offered. It has an elevated pool.

Sandi San Hotel (☎ 957-4487, fax 957-4234; w www.sandisannegril.com; PO Box 47; doubles summer US$75-105, winter US$120-180; cottages summer/winter US$115/190) is an intimate property; its seven studios, 15 rooms, and one suite all feature air-con with fans, hot water, and attractive decor, including hand-carved beds of native mahoe. It has its own beachside bar and open-air restaurant, plus beach volleyball. The noise from Risky Business, next door, might keep you awake into the wee hours. TVs and refrigerators rent for US$8 apiece.

Tamboo Inn (☎/fax 957-4282; PO Box 6; rooms summer US$46-70, winter US$70-93; 1-bedroom cottages summer US$58-87, winter US$87-110; 2-bedroom cottages summer US$105, winter US$175) has 13 rooms with balconies; two simple one-bedroom cottages; plus a one-bedroom cottage and two two-bedroom cottages with kitchenettes. All are modestly furnished hardwood structures. The beachside bar and restaurant is a bonus.

Legends Beach Resort (☎ 957-3834, fax 957-9783; w www.negrilhotels.com/legends; PO Box 23; rooms summer/winter/peak US$85/110/125) is a beachfront resort with 25 gleaming-white, air-con rooms. Their basic furnishings include ceiling fans, two double beds, and balconies. It has a lively and popular restaurant-cum-sports bar.

Kuyaba (☎ 957-4318, fax 957-9765; w www.kuyaba.com; PO Box 2365; cottages summer US$56-64, winter US$70-77; deluxe rooms summer/winter US$77/97; honeymoon suite US$85/106) is a tasteful and recommended family-run hotel. It offers six quaint though rustic wooden cabins with filigree trim, done up in bright Caribbean colors. There are also three deluxe rooms and a suite with king-size bed upstairs in a handsome stone-and-timber house tastefully decorated with terra-cotta floors. The eco-conscious owners are gourmands and run the splendid Kuyaba on the Beach restaurant, attached to the property (see Places to Eat later in this section). There's also a well-stocked gift store and live music 7pm to 9pm nightly. Rates include continental breakfast. The owners also have rooms across the street for US$77.

Bar-B-Barn Hotel & Restaurants (☎ 957-9619; e bar-b-barn@cwjamaica.com; single/double 'run of the house' (any room not occupied) summer US$48/55, winter US$58/60; standard/superior/deluxe single or double winter US$75/85/95) is a modern addition with 30 somewhat elegantly furnished air-con beachfront rooms with cable TV. Some are equipped for the disabled. It has a sports bar and pleasant open-air restaurant.

Mariner's Negril Beach Club (☎ 957-4220, fax 957-4364; w www.marinersnegril.com; PO Box 7; rooms single/double summer US$80/95, winter US$120/135; suites summer US$180/195, winter US$220/250) offers a smorgasbord of rooms that include 65 modest yet nicely furnished air-con rooms, plus studios and deluxe suites. Facilities include water sports, tennis courts, a pool, coffee shop, boutique, and health club, but the grounds are unkempt. Rates include tax.

Coral Seas Beach Resort (☎ 957-9226, fax 957-4724; ☎ 800-223-6510 in the USA; e coralseas@cwjamaica.com; PO Box 91; superior single/double summer US$80/85, winter US$90/120; studio summer US$90/95, winter US$100/125) is a sequestered beach-side place amid a garden of bamboo and hi-biscus. You can choose from rooms with verandas, fully equipped apartments, or two honeymoon suites. It has a pool with bar. There is also a one-bedroom unit with kitch-enette. **Coral Seas Garden Resort**, a sister property, is across the street from Coral Seas Beach Resort, and has rooms of a similar standard and price.

Sunrise Club (☎ 957-4293; e sunriseclub @yahoo.com; rooms summer US$40-60, winter US$55-75) is recommended. It has 15 rooms: older rooms to the rear are simply furnished but have neat bathrooms, while newer rooms are more tasteful, with blue mahoe furnishings. All have screened windows and fans. The Italian owner has infused a fine aesthetic, with earth colors, natural hardwoods, and creative architec-tural touches in American Southwest style. It has a hip bar and gourmet restaurant.

Hotels – West End Heartbeat (☎ 957-4329, fax 957-0069; e heartbeat@cwjamaica .com; PO Box 95; rooms US$49, studios US$85, duplex cottage US$55, pillar rooms US$100) is a peaceful and delightful option atop the cliffs, with thatched, all-hardwood octagonal cabins on pillars. You can also choose from self-sufficient studio apart-ments, a three-bedroom cottage, and a duplex cottage. They garner lots of light and have terraces and tile floors. Some of the units have kitchenettes.

Home Sweet Home (☎ 957-4478; ☎ 800-925-7418 in the USA; w www.homesweet homeresort.net; PO Box 2; rooms summer/winter US$74/110; suites summer US$150-175, winter US$180-250), formerly Reefcliff Resort, has 12 rooms plus two suites, all with private balconies, fans, and private showers. It features a cliff bar and restaurant, a small figure-eight pool, a Jacuzzi, and a boat pick up for fishing or snorkeling trips. Multi-tiered sundecks overhang teal-blue waters.

Hotel Samsara (☎ 957-4395, fax 957-4073; e samsara@cwjamaica.com; PO Box 23; rooms US$60-70, cottages US$55-65, pillar houses US$75; peak season rates are US$30-40 higher) offers 50 modestly fur-nished oceanfront rooms (some air-con) and cottages, plus it has charming thatched tree houses on stilts. Samsara boasts tennis and volleyball courts, a PADI scuba-diving center, a pool, a water slide into the ocean, and the Jah Beer Garden/Sports Café with satellite TV. It hosts a sunset happy hour and live concerts (fun, but consider the noise factor!) on the concrete sundeck.

Ocean Edge (☎ 957-4362, fax 957-0301; e oceanedge@cwjamaica.com; PO Box 71; garden-view/oceanside rooms summer US$45/55, winter US$55/60; suites summer/winter US$60/70), farther south, offers 30 rooms – some with air-con. It is poised on the cliffs, with 20 additional rooms in a block across the road. The hotel has a pool and Jacuzzi, plus glass-bottom boat tours and water sports. It suffers from loud music from the bar next door.

La Kaisers Café Resort Hotel & Club (☎ 957-0479, fax 957-0984; e kaiserscafe@ cwjamaica.com; PO Box 2936; garden-view rooms summer US$50-70, winter US$75-80, ocean-view rooms summer US$80-90, winter US$90-100) is a gaudy newcomer. The catholic architecture is remarkable for its excess of mismatched colored tiles, in-cluding inside the 38 air-con bedrooms, which feature red drapes and other gauche touches. It has a pool, bar, and restaurant, and hosts live concerts on the concrete clifftop courtyard.

Xtabi (☎ 957-0120, fax 957-0827; e xtabi resort@cwjamaica.com; PO Box 19; economy rooms summer/winter US$45/55, standard US$50/65, cottages US$110/160) is a good buttoned-down bargain. You can choose economy rooms, standard rooms, simple garden cottages, or quaint octagonal seafront bungalows perched atop the cliff. They're pleasingly appointed, if nothing fancy. The bar is lively and the restaurant appealing. It has sunning platforms built into the cliff. Massage is offered.

Rockhouse (☎ 957-4373, fax 957-0557; ☎ 708-823-5226 in the USA; e info@rock househotel.com; PO Box 24; standard summer/winter US$75/100, studio US$100/130, villa US$150/210) is another bargain with a stylish offbeat ambience. It boasts 13 thatched, hardwood rondavels (two are 'premium villas') of pine and stone, plus 15 studios dramatically clinging to the cliffside above a small cove. Decor is basic yet romantic, with mosquito-net–draped poster beds and strong Caribbean colors. Each cabin has a ceiling fan, hot plate, refrigerator, safe, minibar, alfresco shower, and wraparound verandas. Catwalks lead over the rocks to an open-sided, multilevel dining pavilion (with one of the best restaurants around; see Places to Eat later in this section) overhanging the ocean. A dramatically designed pool sits atop the cliffs; there's a spa; and at last visit the lounge was to receive a projection screen where 'Jamaica Movie Nights' will be offered.

Coral Seas Cliff Resort (☎ 957-3147, fax 957-0753; ☎ 800-223-6510 in the USA; e coralseas@cwjamaica.com; PO Box 91; standard summer/winter US$60/80, superior US$70/90, studio US$80/95), farther south, has elegant villas with nicely furnished rooms with cable TV. It has an impressive pool, airy restaurant, and bar in well-tended grounds.

Drumville Cove (☎ 957-4369, fax 978-4971; ☎ 800-423-4095 in the USA; ☎ 020-8940-3399 in the UK; e drumvillecove@hotmail.com; PO Box 72; rooms summer/winter US$65/75, cabins US$100) is a dramatically landscaped property. Its 19 rooms – some with air-con (add US$10) – are cramped but clean and romantic; deluxe rooms are larger. Another option is three cozy cabins with four beds (two in a loft) and a kitchenette. Drumville also boasts saltwater bathing and kiddie pools, a small restaurant, and a dive outlet.

Summerset Village (☎ 957-4409, fax 957-4078; PO Box 80; standard summer/winter US$55/75, superior US$65/85, 1-bedroom cottage US$70/90, 2-bedroom cottage US$110/125, Thatch House US$220/260) is about 300 yards inland on 7 acres of landscaped grounds centered on a large pool. In addition to standard rooms, there are 10 aircon 'superior' rooms in a condo-style unit; eight rooms in a 'chateau;' one- and two-bedroom octagonal cottages; and a five-bedroom 'Thatch House' with a suite and

kitchen that can also be rented by the room. Summerset offers a shuttle to the beach.

Devine Destiny (☎ 957-9184, 877-279-3625, fax 957-3846; e devine.destiny@cwjamaica.com; PO Box 117; rooms summer US$58-102, winter US$77-130; suites summer/winter US$125/180), near Summerset Village, offers a variety of rooms in pink brick-and-tile structures that are a strange blend of Teutonic and Caribbean design. Rooms have modest decor and all modern amenities. Facilities include a gameroom, TV room, and large free-form swimming pool. A beach shuttle operates daily.

Rock Cliff Resort (☎ 957-4331, fax 957-4108; e rockcliff@cwjamaica.com; PO Box 67; summer single US$80-92, double US$92-103; suite single or double summer/winter US$218/333) specializes in scuba packages, has a dive center on site, and is popular with European tour groups. It has 33 elegantly furnished, ocean-view rooms (standard and deluxe) with air-con and satellite TV. Facilities include water sports, volleyball, and a Jacuzzi.

Mariner's Inn & Dive Resort (☎ 957-0392, fax 947-0391; e/mail mariners@infochan.com; PO Box 16; summer: garden-view single/double US$55/65, ocean-view US$60/70, apartment US$80/90; winter: garden-view US$70/90, ocean-view US$80/100, apartment US$110/130) is also a scuba center. Its 52 rooms are appealing and represent a bargain, with rates including tax, tips, and an introductory scuba course. It also has apartments, and features a pool and elevated sundeck, Jacuzzi, bike rental, gift and grocery shop, tour desk, disco, gameroom, and two restaurants.

Tensing Pen (☎ 957-0387, fax 957-0161; e tensingpen@cwjamaica.com; PO Box 3013; rooms summer US$75-285, winter US$120-420) is among the more acclaimed places. This tranquil, reclusive option has 12 thatched cottages on 2 acres; most are 'pillar houses' perched atop the coral cliffs amid natural gardens. All have exquisite bamboo and hardwood details, though otherwise rooms differ markedly in decor. Facilities are minimal. Guests use a communal rock-walled kitchen. The bar serves only beer.

Banana Shout (☎/fax 957-0384; **w** www
.negril.com/bananashout; PO Box 4; cabins:
summer single US$35-50, double US$40-60;
winter single US$45-90, double US$50-100;
house summer/winter US$160/200) offers
seven cabins: three hidden among tropical
foliage and linked by interminably winding
paths, and four perched on the cliff face with
sundecks built into a cave with a freshwater
shower. They're offbeat, with loft bedrooms,
ceiling fan, hammocks, and kitchenettes.
There's also a house that accommodates
four people.

Villas Sur Mer (☎ 957-0342, fax 957-0177;
e villassurmer@NegrilJamaica.com; 1-/2-
bedroom US$165/220) is a handsome struc-
ture atop the cliffs, with tasteful appointments
in two one-bedroom and two two-bedroom
suites, each with air-con and a kitchen; a living
room and master bedroom open onto a
private balcony. Outside there's a small
amoeba-shape swimming pool and a can-
tilevered sundeck inset with whirlpool.

Westender Inn (☎/fax 957-4991; rooms
US$70, suite US$80), formerly Hog Heaven,
near the junction with William Hogg Blvd,
has been spruced up by new owners. It offers
13 clean, well-appointed self-catering units
set in handsome grounds that now feature a
small, clothing-optional beach. Rooms are
adequately appointed and have patios with
hammocks. A suite has a kitchenette, TV,
and Jacuzzi.

Places to Stay – Top End
Hotels – Long Bay Point Village (☎ 957-
5170, 957-5351; ☎ 877-704-6852 in North
America; ☎ 0800-328-7790 in the UK;
e pt.village@cwjamaica.com; PO Box 105;
studios single US$168-222, double US$248-
312; junior suites single US$198-252, double
US$268-370; suites single US$208-290,
double US$278-440; townhouse double
US$318-470, triple US$378-506) is an all-
inclusive hotel located at Rutland Point. It
has 175 recently refurbished one-, two-, and
three-bedroom suites with kitchens in
Mediterranean-style limestone villas scattered throughout 14 acres. The hotel's
wave-pounded shoreline holds pocket-size
beaches (one for nudes) and cooling pools

cut into the coral. Water sports, picnic trips
to Booby Cay, and guided bicycle rides are
included. Facilities include two restaurants,
a pool, tennis courts, barber and beauty
shop, boutique, beachside massage 'parlor,'
and nanny service.

Hedonism II (☎ 957-5200, fax 957-4289;
PO Box 25; garden-view US$350-425, ocean-
view US$385-470; garden-view 'au naturel'
US$385-470, ocean-view 'au naturel' US$425-
495) is an adults-only, all-inclusive resort
famous for its risqué attitude, which is highlighted by its weekly toga and lingerie parties
that are preludes to even more unrestrained
antics. Its 280 air-con rooms and suites have
mirrored ceilings but no telephones or TVs,
and at last visit the strange retro decor in
beige and sexual-flush was overdue for refurbishment. Two beaches (one nude), five bars,
tennis and squash courts, volleyball, basketball, rock-climbing wall, ice-skating rink,
cyber center, gameroom, disco (inset with
glass-bottomed Jacuzzi in the roof), full-
service spa, water slide, and a complete range
of water sports are among the attractions.
Swingers are drawn to the nude section – the
venue for XXX-rated activities. Guests
include many more single males than
females; a third female in a group stays free,
and local hookers are discreetly admitted.
For international contact information on this
SuperClubs property, see All-Inclusive
Resorts in the Facts for the Visitor chapter.

Sandals Negril (☎ 957-4216, fax 957-4338;
PO Box 12; all rates per person: rooms
summer US$270-335, winter US$300-365;
suites summer US$355-545, winter US$385-
575) is a tasteful all-inclusive, couples-only
resort. The 21-acre deluxe property sprawls
over wide lawns trimmed to perfection. At
its node is a huge pool with swim-up bar
abuzz with happy guests. There are 227
rooms in six categories, including exquisite
honeymoon suites in gracious cottages
replete with Edwardian decor, plus villa-
suites with loft bedrooms and marble bathrooms. Sandals features tennis, squash,
racquetball courts, a full-service spa, and a
medley of restaurants playing a calliope on
the international and Jamaican theme. For
international contact information and

website discounts, see All-Inclusive Resorts in the Facts for the Visitor chapter.

Beaches Sandy Bay (☎ 957-5100, fax 957-5229; all rates are per person: rooms summer US$230-260, winter US$255-315; suites summer US$285-430, winter US$330-485), formerly and briefly Beaches Inn (and, before that, Poinciana Beach Hotel), is a Sandals family resort. The recently renovated resort's 6 acres include 130 rooms in seven categories in three-story accommodations blocks and villas, which feature lively Caribbean decor. There are also suites and one-bedroom villas. Children and teens are offered a gameroom and organized activities, including beach volleyball. A three-day minimum stay is required. For international contact information, see All-Inclusive Resorts in the Facts for the Visitor chapter.

Beaches Negril (☎ 957-9270, fax 957-9269; all rates are per person, double occupancy: rooms summer US$275-345, winter US$315-400; suites summer US$370-845, winter US$425-965) is another impressive Sandals all-inclusive, this one catering to families, singles, and couples. It loosely resembles a castle, with thick limestone walls and patinated wrought-iron furniture and lanterns. It has 215 air-con rooms, including 39 junior suites, in nine categories in three-story units built in quasi–Spanish-hacienda style. All rooms boast a king-size bed, in-room safe, satellite TV, and a colonial feel. There's a 12,000-sq-foot pool, kiddie pool, five restaurants, huge theater, disco, several bars, pool room, 24-hour gym, sauna, and massage and beauty salon, plus a panoply of water sports. Facilities for children include a Sega Centre, a Kids Camp, and a 'funtrack' with electric bikes and cars. Guests get access to Sandals Negril. For international contact information and website discounts, see All-Inclusive Resorts in the Facts for the Visitor chapter.

Couples Swept Away Negril (☎ 957-4061, fax 957-4060; ☎ 800-268-7537, fax 305-668-0111 in North America; ⓦ www.couples .com; PO Box 3077; garden/atrium/beachfront suites per couple year-round US$510/550/640) is a magnificent all-inclusive, adults-only resort that boasts the island's most

replete sports and fitness facility. Pathways coil through a 20-acre botanical rush-hour of ferns and heliconias to the 134 suites, which are housed in 26 two-story villas and boast terra-cotta tile floors, deep-red hardwoods, and vast louvered windows. The gym, aerobics studio, 10 tennis courts, two squash courts, and two racquetball courts all come with professional instruction. You can recuperate in the spa and beauty parlor. The Feathers Restaurant is a gourmand's delight, and there's a 'Fruit and Veggie Bar,' plus cabaret and other entertainment. Free golf at Negril Hills Golf Club is included. Holistic programs and monthly 'health specials' are offered. A three-night minimum stay is required.

Native Son Villas (☎/fax 957-4376; ☎ 908-598-1158, fax 598-1151 in the USA; PO Box 120; villas summer US$130-210, winter US$175-275) offers four modern beachfront two-story duplex villas sleeping four to nine people. Modest furnishings are of rattan. It's a bargain for families or groups, with rates including a housekeeper/cook and a bottle of rum.

Sea Splash Resort (☎ 957-4041, 800-254-2786, fax 957-4049; ⓔ seasplashngl@cw jamaica.com; PO Box 123; garden-view single/double summer US$115/135, winter US$179/199; ocean-view summer US$109/119, winter US$199/219) is an elegant, recently refurbished resort with eight rooms and 15 spacious suites and junior suites. Rates include tax and transfers to and from Montego Bay. Tasteful decor highlights the suites, each with large balcony, fully equipped kitchenette, screened-off bedroom, air-con, satellite TV, and telephone. It has a handsome beach bar. Boardwalks lead through lush gardens.

Negril Tree House (☎ 957-4287, 957-4386; ☎ 412-231-4889, 800-634-7451, fax 412-231-5044 in North America; ⓦ www.negril-tree house.com; PO Box 29; rooms summer US$95-125, winter US$135-160; suites summer US$160-195, winter US$260-340) is another favorite. This unpretentious resort has 16 octagonal air-con bungalows and oceanfront villas nudging up to the beach. Each has a TV and a safe. More elegant one- and two-bedroom suites each feature kitchenette, king-size bed, and a Murphy bed in the lounge, which opens onto a wide veranda. The beachside bar is popular. Water sports are offered, and the resort has a tour desk, gift store, masseuse, and manicurist. Guests have day privileges at Couples Swept Away's sports complex (US$10 daily).

CocoLaPalm (☎ 957-4227, fax 957-3460; ☎ 612-493-5261, 800-320-8821 in the USA; ⓔ cocolap@cwjamaica.com; standard summer US$135-155, winter US$170-190; premium summer US$155-165, winter US$185-195; suite summer US$165-185, winter US$205-225) is a beachfront resort with 43 rooms in octagonal two-story units. Some have king beds; all have cable TV, telephone, safe, refrigerator, and coffeemaker. There's a beachside restaurant, a bar and grill, and a huge pool with Jacuzzi. It offers four types of rooms plus junior suites, all ocean-view or poolside. Guests receive privileges at Couples Swept Away.

Idle Awhile (☎ 957-9566, 877-243-5352, fax 957-9567; ⓔ info@idleawhile.com; deluxe rooms summer/winter US$125/170, junior suites US$160/225, suites US$190/275) is an exquisite newcomer with eight airy, delightfully appointed rooms and five suites with contemporary vogue and tropical decor. Guests are allowed free access to Couples Swept Away's sport complex. Snacks, seafood, and Jamaica dishes are served beachside beneath umbrellas. This resort is highly recommended.

Charela Inn (☎ 957-4277, fax 957-4414; ⓦ www.charela.com; PO Box 3033; garden-view single/double summer US$90/108, winter US$141/158; ocean-view summer US$102/123, winter US$158/180; deluxe summer US$138/148, winter US$190/210), run by a charming Jamaican-French couple, Daniel and Sylvie, is another good option. The 49 air-con rooms (19 deluxe; four family units) feature contemporary decor with lots of hardwoods, plus ceiling fans, hair-dryers, telephones, and balconies or patios. It resembles a Spanish hacienda and surrounds a courtyard with a large pool. Rates in summer include water sports, Sunfish and

sailboard instruction, and a sunset cruise. The restaurant uses only organic produce – leave room for the homemade ice cream! It hosts jazz on Monday nights, plus folkloric dance on Saturday. Children under 10 stay free, and a three-night minimum stay is required in summer.

Nirvana on the Beach (☎ 957-4314, fax 957-9196; ☎ 716-789-5955 in the USA; ⓦ www.nirvananegril.com; 3309 Morley Rd, Ashville, NY 14710, USA; double cottages US$165, oceanfront honeymoon suite US$210; extra person US$30) is the place to stay if you're seeking meditation, with three one-bedroom and five two- and three-bedroom cottages set in Zen-like tropical gardens. Each all-hardwood cabin has a king-size bed, dining room, kitchen, and screened wraparound windows.

Whistling Bird (☎ 957-4403; ☎ 303-442-0722 in the USA; ⓔ WhistlingBird@Negril Jamaica.com; summer/winter US$130/285) is similar to Nirvana, with 24 rooms in bungalows and cottages with classy contemporary decor. It's low-key and a great place to relax beneath shady bamboo. There's a restaurant and beach bar.

Negril Inn (☎ 957-4209, fax 957-4365; PO Box 59; singles/doubles summer US$110/180, winter US$140/220) is a 1960s Miami-style property that's divorced from the beach by an ugly wall. Its 46 rooms are nicely decorated, however, and facilities include an outdoor gym, massage, a pool, two Jacuzzis, floodlit tennis courts and basketball court, a TV lounge and billiards room, and a disco.

Negril Gardens (☎ 957-4408, fax 957-4374; ☎ 800-327-1991 in the USA; ☎ 0207-259-1840 in the UK; ⓔ negrilgardens@cwjamaica.com; PO Box 3058; garden-view rooms summer/winter US$120/145; beach-view US$150/175) is a better option than Negril Inn, with 65 nicely appointed air-con rooms in gaily-colored two-story villas with balconies. Garden-view rooms across the road overlook a pool.

Merrill's Beach Resort (☎ 957-4751, fax 957-3121; ⓦ www.merrilsbeach.com; PO Box 75; rooms summer/winter US$75/90, suites US$110/150), a short distance from Negril Gardens, is an attractive place with 28 air-con rooms in a two-story unit amid lush landscaped grounds. All rooms have verandas. It offers water sports and a beach bar, and is popular with European tour groups.

Hotels – Bloody Bay Negril Cabins Resort (☎ 957-4350, 957-4381; ☎ 800-382-3444 in North America; ℮ negrilcabins@cwjamaica.com; PO Box 118; standard summer/winter US$100/120, superior US$150/170, suite US$250/300) is an eco-conscious resort with heaps of jungly atmosphere. It has 86 all-hardwood, Thai-style cabins, including four split-level 'executive suites.' They're raised on stilts amid lush grounds full of croaking tree frogs. Interior decor features leather sofas and Chinese rugs. Air-con superior rooms have TV; all rooms have safes. Facilities include a fitness center and tennis court plus gameroom, Jacuzzi, a magnificent pool with swim-up bar, and romantic restaurant serving top-notch cuisine. A path leads to the beach. Rates include breakfast, tax, and service charge, and children under 16 stay free.

Couples Negril (☎ 957-5960, fax 957-5858; ☎ 305-668-0008, 800-268-7537, fax 305-668-0111 in the USA; ☎ 020-8900-1913, fax 8795-1728 in the UK; ⓦ www.couples.com; PO Box 35; all rates per couple per night: rooms summer US$470-560, winter US$510-600; suites summer US$620-695, winter US$660-735) boasts classy contemporary decor that the company terms 'Negril Chic.' The lobby opens over a wide pool at the heart of the 18-acre resort. The 216 rooms in nine blocks come in three classes: garden-view, ocean-view, and beachfront. They are also hip – appointed with blood-red fabrics, a canary-yellow duvet, iridescent curtains, dark bamboo, cobalt hints, and oh-so-chic furniture. All rooms have TV and CD player. The suites have a vast bathroom with Jacuzzi and 'his and her' sinks. Facilities include four tennis courts, a fitness center, gameroom, spa, beauty salon, and boutiques, plus a full range of water sports. Dining facilities include the Otaheite restaurant serving nouvelle Jamaican. A three-night minimum stay is required.

Grand Lido Negril (☎ 957-5010, fax 957-5517; PO Box 88; all rates per person: garden-

view junior suites US$310-420, ocean-view US$330-435, beachfront US$360-455; suites summer US$355-520, winter US$465-660), boasting a Mediterranean flair, is a flagship of the SuperClubs chain. The 210 spacious, tastefully furnished suites and split-level junior suites (some with whirlpool) with mezzanine bedrooms are spread through 22 acres of gardens, which feature nine bars, including three 24-hour bars with Jacuzzis. Dry cleaning, laundry, pedicures, 24-hour room service, and even wedding ceremonies are included in the price. Take your pick of several restaurants. There's a high-tech gym. A full range of water sports is offered, as are cruises aboard *M/Y Zien*, a 147-foot motor yacht that was a wedding gift from Aristotle Onassis to Prince Rainer and Grace Kelly. For international contact information, see All-Inclusive Resorts in the Facts for the Visitor chapter.

Riu Tropical Bay Resort (☎ 957-5900, fax 957-5727; ℮ hotel.tropicalbay@riu.com; all rates per person double occupancy: garden-view rooms US$190-210, ocean-view US$220-240, oceanfront US$270-290; suites US$320-340) opened in 2001 as a 396-room, all-inclusive resort for the budget-minded crowd. Room decor is tastefully contemporary and features Caribbean pastels. Rooms have satellite TV, in-room safes, and minibars. The resort features two swimming pools, a nude beach section, a full array of water sports, fitness center and spa, tennis courts, volleyball courts, disco, and a selection of restaurants and entertainment.

Breezes Negril, an all-inclusive resort for singles, couples, and families, was at last visit due to open on Bloody Bay in 2003. For contact information, see All-Inclusive Resorts in the Facts for the Visitor chapter.

Hotels – West End Llantrissant (☎ 957-4259; ☎ 305-321-7458, 800-331-6951 in the USA; ℮ info@beachcliff.com; PO Box 90; c/o Beachcliff Resorts, 5901 SW 87 St, South Miami, FL 33143, USA; 1-12 people weekly US$3200-6000), one of the more charming options, is a centenary two-story, four-bedroom home. The vintage house – simply yet exquisitely furnished, with ceiling fans and louvered windows – comes fully staffed and includes satellite TV, stereo, and fax and Internet access. Hammocks hang from shade trees. Snorkeling gear is included.

Dreamscape Villa (☎ 957-9188, 877-788-5680; e info@dreamscapevilla.com; PO Box 51; garden-view rooms US$150, ocean-view US$160; suite US$280) has five voluminous and very beautifully furnished rooms with kitchens, plus a two-bedroom suite, all with satellite TV and refrigerator. It has a pool, an outdoor Jacuzzi under a gazebo, and a private lawn with its own pleasant cove and sundeck. Rates include continental breakfast in your room.

The Caves (☎ 957-0270; ☎ 800-688-7678 in the USA; ☎ 0800-614-790 in the UK; e outpost800@aol.com; PO Box 15; 1-bedroom US$500, 1-bedroom suites US$600-675, 2-bedroom suites US$725-1100) is perhaps the finest boutique hotel in Jamaica, and one beloved of the Hollywood elite. It offers eight handcrafted, individually-styled one- and two-bedroom wood-and-thatch cottages amid lush gardens atop the cave-riddled cliffs. Rooms feature exquisite hand-carved furniture, batik fabrics, one-of-a-kind art, CD player with CDs, plus ceiling fans and mosquito nets over the king- or queen-size beds. Many have exquisite outside showers. Paths wind down to a free-form Jacuzzi studding the rock face, and thence to a cave with molded benches where you can recline and meditate to the reverberations of pounding waves. There's also a saltwater pool and a sauna, plus an Aveda spa offering full treatments. Yoga is also offered. Rates include all meals and self-service bar.

Jackie's on the Reef (☎ 957-4997; ☎ 718-469-2785 in the USA; w www.jackieson thereef.com; 512 Argyle Rd, New York, NY 11218, USA; rooms summer/winter US$125/150), 7 miles south of the Negril roundabout, just north of the intersection with William Hogg Blvd, is a more basic yet equally tranquil option. It operates as a New Age haven focusing on spiritual renewal. A natural stone cottage is divided into four rooms, each with two handmade wooden beds and an outdoor shower and bathroom enclosed within your own private backyard. Massages are given on a veranda, and meditation, tai

chi, and spa treatments are offered. There's a small cooling pool inset in the reef top. The facility is more rustic than the rates might suggest. Rates include breakfast, dinner, and exercise class. Day packages (lunch and massage) are offered to nonguests.

PLACES TO EAT

A plethora of rustic eateries along Long Bay (on Norman Manley Blvd) and on the coast road around West End offer budget snacks and meals. Some food stands have no access to running water – take all commonsense health precautions.

Local delicacies (besides mushroom omelettes) include crab pickled in red peppers.

A fully stocked grocery store in Negril Village is **Hi-Lo Supermarket** (☎ 057-4125), to the rear of Sunshine Village, which also has the fast-food stands **Shakey's Pizza** and **King Burger**. Small **grocery stalls** dot Norman Manley Blvd, and the best of several small groceries along West End Rd is **DJ's Place** (☎ 957-0943; open 8:30am-11:30pm).

Jerk on Wheels (☎ 952-5375; open 11am-midnight) delivers order-to-go jerk with rice 'n' peas, etc.

Jamaican

Long Bay Negril Yoga Centre (☎ 957-4397; US$5-10) is recommended for Jamaican health-food dinners such as Rasta pasta, chicken Jamaican style, and curried vegetables in coconut milk.

Tan-Yah's (☎ 957-4031), at the Sea Splash Resort, is recommended for its nouvelle Jamaican dishes.

Fun Holiday Beach Resort (☎ 957-3585) has a seafood restaurant with an all-you-can-eat buffet daily (US$8).

Miss Brown's, opposite Café Taino, is a simple shack serving magic-mushroom omelettes and teas. This shack is a smaller outlet to Miss Brown's famous restaurant (see below). In a similar vein, **Miss Sonia's** (5:30am until 'anytime'), adjacent, serves Miss Sonia's unique patties with fillings ranging from ackee and veggies to chicken and lobster.

Negril Village Miss Brown's (☎ 957-9217; Sheffield Rd; open 6:30am-midnight), a mile east of the roundabout, serves 'mushroom daiquiris,' mushroom omelettes (US$12-30), and mushroom tea (from US$10). Be warned – *they're hallucinogenic.*

Sheffield Rd contains several authentic Jamaican restaurants favored by locals. A favorite is **Sweet Spice Restaurant** (☎ 957-4621), with a menu that includes curried goat (US$5), conch steak (US$7), fish (US$5), and pepper steak (US$4).

A Fi Wi Plaza, on West End Rd west of the roundabout, has inexpensive snack bars to the rear serving real Jamaican fare.

West End Café Roma (☎ 957-0305; open 24 hrs) is a simple restaurant serving filling breakfasts and real mint tea. You can fill up on ackee and saltfish, etc, for around US$3.

Mi Yard (☎ 957-4442; US$1.50-7; open 24 hrs) also makes a great breakfast spot and serves omelettes, ackee and saltfish, fish-and-chips, and brown-stewed fish on its classic Jamaican menu. Dine in the garden or on a shady patio.

Easy Rock Cyber Café (☎ 957-0671), beachside, is another twee favorite with Jamaican fare, including breakfasts from 8am.

You can't go wrong at **Chicken Lavish** (☎ 957-4410; US$5-12), a bargain eatery with great atmosphere that serves curried chicken, pepper shrimp, and brown-stewed fish.

The Pickled Carrot (☎ 640-2171; open 7am-midnight), in a similar vein, is a gaily-colored favorite of local Rastas and serves roast yam and saltfish (US$2.50), curried lobster (US$13), and the like.

Rockhouse Restaurant & Bar (☎ 957-4373; US$5-18; open 7am-11pm daily), at the Rockhouse resort, is recommended for nouvelle Jamaican treats such as vegetable tempura with lime, ginger, and soy sauce, specialty pastas, and jambalaya. Lamplit at night, it's a romantic spot. It serves large and hearty breakfasts (average US$5), including muesli and pancakes.

Negril Hills Hillside Paradise Inn (☎ 800-247-5554; Hessette Rd) has a breeze-swept, open-air eatery in classic US-diner style

serving typical American breakfasts, plus curried conch, stewed peas with pigtail (US$4), and filet mignon (US$10).

I-tal & Vegetarian Food

West End Just Natural (US$1.50-4) serves veggie dishes and seafood, including tuna melts, veggie burgers, and burritos.

Culture Yard (☎ 957-0195; open 8am-10pm), beyond the lighthouse, is a pleasant spot serving I-tal foods such as hemp burgers made from marijuana plant seeds (US$2), jelly coconut, and red pea stew.

Hard Reggae Café (☎ 957-4991; US$2-14; open 7:30am-10:30pm), a simple place near the east end of Ocean Drive, has a large breakfast menu plus lunches that include daily I-tal specials.

Jackie's on the Reef (☎ 957-4997; breakfast/lunch/dinner US$6/8/18) specializes in health foods and herbal teas.

Seafood

Long Bay A steadfast beach favorite, **Cosmo's** (☎ 957-4330; US$5-14; open 9am-10pm) has three thatched bars and dining areas near Long Bay Beach Park. It specializes in conch soup, curried conch, and curried shrimp.

West End Love Boat (☎ 957-0958; open 11am-3pm & 4pm-11pm) is shaped like a ship's prow and garners heaps of light through huge porthole windows. The menu features baked and steamed fish, plus grilled lobster (US$18). It has a breezy open-air bar.

Lighthouse Inn (☎ 957-4052), also known as 'Busha's Place,' serves splendid appetizers, such as mozzarella with tomatoes, goat cheese and olives. Meals include an excellent seafood platter, lobster in curry, and red snapper stuffed with callaloo (US$8-20). The lively tropical decor is enhanced by candlelight.

Italian

Long Bay Gambino's Italian Restaurant (☎ 957-4170; US$4-25), a highly ranked restaurant in the Beachcomber Club, serves a wide range of pastas, lasagna, carbonara, and other Italian classics.

Lobster House (☎ 957-4293), at Sunrise Club, is a favorite spot. It serves genuine gourmet Italian fare such as octopus, beetroot and potato delight (US$5), pink gnocchi in parmesan cheese sauce (US$12), and lobster dishes (US$8-20).

Seeking pizza? Try **Chances** (☎ 957-3977), midway along Norman Manley Blvd.

West End A rustic eatery, **Bella Donna** (☎ 957-0628; entrées from US$10) serves Italian-Jamaican fare; its all-you-can-eat buffet (US$11) is offered on Wednesday. Live bands perform on Wednesday and Friday nights.

Hotel Samsara (☎ 957-4395; US$8-28) has an Italian restaurant, and **Summerset Village** (☎ 957-4409) hosts an Italian 'extravaganza' on Saturday nights (US$20).

Mr Slice Pizza (☎ 957-0584; slice US$3, pizza US$15) delivers.

Other Cuisines

Long Bay Salina's Coffee Bar (☎ 957-9519; 8am until late), makes a great breakfast spot serving callaloo and cheese omelettes, banana pancakes (US$7), killer smoothies, and hand-roasted coffee. The lunch menu features salads, burgers, satay chicken (US$7), and curried chicken in coconut cream (US$8).

Kuyaba on the Beach (☎ 957-4318), at the Kuyaba hotel, is a perennial beach favorite. This thatched, open-air restaurant has heaps of ambience. The lunch menu features burgers (US$7) and gourmet sandwiches, plus superb pepper shrimps (US$10). For dinner, check out a wide range of pasta dishes (US$11-20), a superb lobster bisque, or the Cuban crab and pumpkin cakes with papaya mustard (US$15). Live music is featured.

Tamboo Inn (☎ 957-4282), near Kuyaba, is a bamboo-and-thatch, two-story restaurant (lit by brass lanterns at night) with a varied menu that includes a breakfast of 'pigs in a blanket' (US$7), pancakes and sausage (US$6), and a fruit platter with ice cream (US$5). It also has snack foods such as deep-fried lobster niblets, plus sandwiches and pizzas (US$5-22).

Margaritaville (☎ 957-4467; open 9am-midnight) has a wide-ranging menu that includes quesadillas (US$7), curry (US$10), and pizza (from US$7). It has twice-daily shuttles between the club and West End.

Hunan Garden (☎ 957-4369; US$2.50-15; open 11am-10pm), at Country Country, is a romantic candelit option serving Chinese cuisine, such as sliced duck with ginger and scallion.

Le Restaurant le Vendome (☎ 957-4277; open 8am-10:30pm), at Charela Inn, serves French cuisine, including homemade patisseries, and a daily five-course gourmet dinner (about US$20).

Burger King (Negril Village), 50 yards west of Negril Square, serves fast-food junkies.

West End Rick's Café (☎ 957-0380; open 2pm-10pm), a sophisticated eatery lit by Tiffany lamps and graced by 1920s Hollywood posters, draws visitors lemminglike to watch the sunset. The eclectic menu includes pompano Jack fillet, conch steak, charbroiled fish platter, linguine bolognese, burgers (US$6), plus exotic desserts (US$3). Entrées begin at about US$10 and run to US$21 for curried shrimp. It has a two-for-one happy hour from 8pm onward.

LTU Pub (☎ 957-0382; open 11am-midnight), 100 yards south of Rick's Café, is a more homely option. This small cliffside, open-air bar has an eclectic menu with a wide range of specialty burgers (from US$6) and spaghetti dishes, fish-and-chips, and chicken with callaloo and cream, all for about US$8.

Xtabi (☎ 957-0120; US$4-24; open 8am-10pm) offers a marvelous cliff-face setting for enjoying a varied and reasonably priced menu mixing seafood, Jamaican, and continental dishes.

Cafés & Ice Cream Parlors

Salina's Coffee Bar (see Other Cuisines earlier) is recommended for cappuccino, espresso, and teas.

Blue Mountain Coffee Shop (☎ 957-3126; open 8am-10pm), 200 yards north on Norman Manly Blvd, serves cappuccino, espresso, and ice coffees, plus callaloo omelette (US$4) and burgers (US$3.50).

Frozen Yoghurt Hut, at Bar-B-Barn Hotel, charges $1.50 for a cone.

Blue Water Ice Cream Parlor, on West End Rd, has a shady patio over the water for enjoying gelatos, sundaes, and waffles.

ENTERTAINMENT
Stageshows
Negril's reggae concerts are legendary, with live performances every night in peak season, when there's sure to be some big talent in town. A handful of venues offer weekly jams, and they have a rotation system so they all get a piece of the action. Big-name acts usually perform at **MXIII** and **Hotel Samsara,** in the West End, plus **Wavz**, on Long Bay.

You'll also find sound-system jams where DJs ('selectors') play shatteringly loud music – usually dancehall with some Euro-disco – on speakers the size of railroad boxcars. The most popular jams are in the Negril Hills (see Little Bay & Vicinity later in this chapter).

You'll find information about upcoming events posted on streetside poles. The cover is normally about US$10 for most events.

Long Bay Risky Business (☎ 957-3912; @ riskybiz@cwjamaica.com) and **De Buss** (☎ 957-4405) host live bands on Monday, Thursday, and Saturday. Risky Business also has live jazz on Wednesday nights.

Alfred's Ocean Palace (☎ 967-4735; @ AlfredsOceanPalace@NegrilJamaica .com) plays host on Tuesday, Friday, and Sunday nights, when it's *the* place to be.

The hotel **Roots Bamboo** (☎ 957-4479) hosts live reggae concerts on Wednesday and Sunday.

Fun Holiday Beach Resort (☎ 957-3585) has live reggae on Saturday (with limbo and fire-dancers) and Monday (Ladies Nite, with free drinks all night for women), plus a Soca Beach Party with two-for-one rums at 8pm Thursday.

West End Negril Yacht Club (☎/fax 957-9224) hosts free live reggae on Friday and Saturday.

La Kaisers Café Resort Hotel & Club was preparing to host concerts again at last visit.

Bars
Negril has dozens of bars. The competition is fierce; many offer happy-hour incentives to lure you for sunset, notably along the West End, where the bars are lively in early evening before petering out as the beach bars take over.

Things really hop during rabble-rousing Spring Break.

Long Bay The liveliest spot, **Margaritaville** (☎ 957-4467; W www.margaritaville.com) boasts big-screen TVs, a basketball court, trampolines in the sea, volleyball, swing hammocks, and multiple bars with entertainment. It hosts wet T-shirt contests and the like, and has nightly specials, including karaoke on Sunday. A 'Prime-Time Pass' (11am-4pm; US$15) lets you drink all you can handle.

Alfred's Ocean Palace (☎ 967-4735), **Cosmo's** (☎ 957-4330), **Legends Beach Resort** (☎ 957-3834), and **Risky Business** (☎ 957-3918) compete with Margaritaville with satellite TVs, pool tables, and beach parties.

All the above fence off their beach sections at night and charge a cover for entry.

Sunrise Club, at the hotel of that name, has a cool bar if you want to escape the beach mayhem. It plays great music.

West End Atop the cliffs, **Rick's Café** (☎ 957-0382) is the prime gathering place to enjoy the sunsets. The happy hour at Rick's begins *after* sundown, when the crowd begins to drift away. Several bars have happy hours at about 5pm or 6pm, timed to steer you away from Rick's. A little down the road, the **LTU Pub** (☎ 957-0382) offers a less touristy alternative, and free dinner pick-up.

Pickled Parrot (☎ 957-4864) is similar and has a waterslide into the briny blue. It was closed, for sale, at last visit, when the slack had been picked up by **Pirate's Cove** (☎ 957-9528), adjacent.

Popular with Jamaicans, **Mi Yard** (☎ 957-4442; open 24 hrs) draws a late-night crowd into the wee hours, when you can swig shots of white rum and slap down dominoes with locals.

Discos

The Jungle (☎ 957-4005; Norman Manley Blvd; closed Mon) is a happening disco. Every night is theme night; Thursday in Ladies Night. A $10 cover includes a drink. It also has a pool table on an upstairs sundeck.

Nonguests can obtain passes for entry to the discos in the following upscale all-inclusive resorts: Sandals Negril, Hedonism II, Couples, Beaches, and Grand Lido. Once inside the gates you can booze and party to your heart's content without having to shell out another cent.

Go-Go Clubs

Close Encounters (☎ 957-0423; admission US$4), upstairs in King's Plaza, offers erotic stage acts until 4am. You can't miss it – between gigs, the dancers (often naked) hang out on the roadside balcony.

Wish-Wash, about 5 miles outside town on Whitehall Rd in the Negril Hills, also has go-go and draws the local masses (no cover).

SHOPPING

Locals hawk carvings, woven caps, hammocks, jewelry, macramé bikinis, T-shirts, and crafts on the beach and along West End Rd. Competition is fierce. Haggling is part of the fun. Don't be hustled into a purchase you don't want.

There are three main crafts centers: Rutland Point Craft Centre, opposite Couples Negril; the Negril Crafts Market, just north of Negril Plaza; and A Fi Wi Plaza in Negril Village, where painter and sculptor Lloyd Hoffstead has a studio (☎ 957-3903; e gallery hoffstead@hotmail.com) at Shop 34.

Times Square (☎ 957-9263; Norman Manley Blvd) and Negril Plaza, Coral Seas Plaza, and Sunshine Village have good souvenir shops. Times Square also has about a dozen duty-free and jewelry stores, including Tajmahal's (☎ 675-4579; open 9am-6pm Mon-Sat), and it has Cigar World and Cigar King, both selling Cuban cigars.

Kush Art Gallery (☎ 957-0728), on West End Rd, sells Wassi-Art pottery and other quality crafts, as does the Kuyaba arts-and-crafts boutique (☎ 957-4318).

Photo Prints (☎ 957-4828; West End Rd) has film and photo supplies.

GETTING THERE & AWAY

Negril Aerodrome is at Bloody Bay, about 7 miles north of Negril Village.

At press time Air Jamaica Express (☎ 957-5251 in Negril, 888-359-2475; 800-523-5585 in the USA) had one flight daily between Montego Bay and Negril (US$54 one-way), with connecting service.

See the Getting Around chapter for information on domestic charters.

Dozens of coasters and route taxis run between Negril and Montego Bay. The two-hour journey costs about US$4. You may need to change vehicles in Lucea. Be prepared for a hair-raising ride. Minibuses and route taxis also leave for Negril from Donald Sangster International Airport in Montego Bay (the price is negotiable, but expect to pay about US$10).

In Negril, buses bound for Montego Bay (US$2), Savanna-la-Mar (US$1), and Kingston (about four hours; US$8.50) depart from Sheffield Rd, just east of the roundabout.

Caribic Vacations (☎ 957-3309 in Negril) and Tropical Tours (☎ 957-4110 in Negril) offer minibus transfers between Montego Bay airport and Negril (about US$30 each way).

A licensed taxi between Montego Bay and Negril will cost about US$60. In MoBay, call the Jamaica Union of Travelers Association (JUTA; ☎ 979-0778).

GETTING AROUND

Negril stretches along more than 10 miles of shoreline, and it can be a withering walk. At some stage you'll most likely need transport. Upscale resorts at the north end of Long Bay have shuttles to Negril Village, and several hotels on the West End run shuttles to the beach.

There's no scheduled bus service between the airstrip and hotels. A taxi will cost a whopping US$8-12 for a journey between the airport and Negril Village or to any point in between. Even a half-mile journey to Rutland Point will cost US$8.

Coasters and route taxis cruise Norman Manley Blvd and West End Rd. You can flag them down anywhere. The fare between any two points should never be more than about US$1.

A free **Hi-Lo Shuttle** (2pm-8pm Fri-Sat; noon-5pm Sun) runs between Bloody Bay and the Hi-Lo Supermarket, in Sunshine Village, every 20 minutes.

Local car rental companies include **Jus Jeep** (☎ 957-0094, fax 957-0429), on West End Rd, and **Vernon's Car Rentals** (☎ 957-9724, 957-4354, fax 957-4057), at Fun Holiday Beach Resort and Shop 22, Negril Plaza.

More than a dozen places along Norman Manley Blvd and West End Rd rent motorcycles (US$40-65 per day), scooters (US$25-35), and bicycles (US$10). See Bicycling earlier in this chapter for a few bike rental places. Helmets are not mandatory and hardly anyone wears one, but you should. And use sunscreen!

Tourist taxis display a red license plate. Fares are regulated by the government (about US$2 per 2 miles), but few drivers use their meters. You can order taxis from **JUTA** (☎ 957-9197) or **Easy-Going Cabs** (☎ 957-3227). There are taxi stands at the Negril Crafts Market and in front of Coral Seas Plaza.

M Tours (☎ 957-0160, 1-819-9235 cellular, fax 957-0165; e mtour@cwjamaica.com) offers limousine service. Bertel Moore, the owner/driver, is extremely gracious.

Boats ply between Long Bay and the West End, with a base at Negril Yacht Club. They make regular calls at most hotels along the West End seeking business and charge US$5-15 per person, depending on length of journey. Fares are negotiable.

Negril to Tryall

Northeast from Negril, the A1 leads to Montego Bay, hugging the coast most of the way (an expressway was under construction at press time). It's a pleasing drive as the road wriggles past small fishing villages and winds in and out of tiny coves. The only town of note is Lucea.

GREEN ISLAND HARBOUR

Immediately north of Negril, the A1 swings around a wide expanse of swampland – the Great Morass – good for spotting crocodiles if you have the spirit to explore the mangroves. After 10 miles you pass the shores of a deep cove – Green Island Harbour – where pirogues line the thin, gray-sand shore.

Half Moon Beach (☎ 383-1844, 957-6467; e halfmoonbeach@cwjamaica.com; admission US$2.50; open 8am-10pm daily), is a recreational site with a beach and offshore islands (nudism is permitted). Snorkeling gear can be rented. The entrance fee is good toward purchase of a meal or drink.

Rhodes Hall Plantation (☎ 957-6334, fax 957-8333; PO Box 16), 2 miles west of Green Island Harbour, is a recreational site with several thatched bars and a restaurant backing a small but attractive beach where hot mineral springs bubble up. Follow the beach west and you may see crocodiles at the mouth of the river. Horseback riding is offered, and a beach party is hosted on Sunday night.

Places to Stay & Eat

Half Moon Beach (camping US$10, cabins US$30-50) lets you camp, and there are four simple but spacious wooden cabins with bare-bones furnishings. The thatched restaurant offers sandwiches, burgers, and simple Jamaican snacks.

JJ's Guest House (☎ 956-9159; Green Island PO, Hanover; single/double US$28/40; rooms with TV per person US$25), just east of Green Island Harbour, is a modest yet comfortable place atop a breezy hill with distant views of the ocean. There are eight rooms, each with two single beds, ceiling fans, and private bath with hot water. There's a bar and a plunge pool.

Rhodes Hall Plantation (☎ 957-6334, fax 957-8333; PO Box 16; 2-person & family cottage US$80 low season, US$100 high season) has two handsome air-con beach-front cottages with private bath with hot water, plus kitchen. One sleeps two; the second is family-size.

You can eat cheaply at the roadside **jerk stalls** at Green Island Harbour.

BLENHEIM

This tiny hamlet, 4 miles inland of Davis Cove, is important as the birthplace of national hero Alexander Bustamante, the island's first prime minister. The rustic three-room wooden shack where Bustamante was born has been reconstructed as the **Sir Alexander Bustamante Museum** (☎ 922-1287, fax 951-1703; c/o National Heritage Trust; open 9am-5pm daily; admission free). It includes memorabilia telling of the hero's life. It has public toilets and a picnic area to the rear.

A memorial ceremony is held in Blenheim in Busta's honor each August 6.

Coasters and route taxis run from Lucea. By automobile, the easiest route is from Davis Cove, 2 miles north of Green Island Harbour. Take the road that leads inland immediately east of the bridge over the Green River. After about 2 miles, you come to a hilltop T-junction; turn left and follow the narrow, winding lane downhill for about 800 yards, then turn sharp right (there are no other junctions). The road loops uphill 400 yards to the museum.

LANCE'S BAY

Lance's Bay, about 4 miles west of Lucea, offers a couple of small beaches, notably Gull Bay Beach, in a pocket-size cove. At Cousin's Cove, just west of Lance's Bay, a farmer named Ron has a cave – **Ron's Rat Bat Cave** (☎ 426-6315) – on his property, about 800 yards inland. He charges US$8 for a guided tour. The chambers contain stalagmites and stalactites, a mineral pool, and ancient petroglyphs.

LUCEA

'Lucy' (population 7500), as the town is commonly known, is built around a harbor ringed by hills on three sides. Twenty-five miles equidistant from Negril and Montego

Bay, Lucea is small enough for visitors to walk everywhere.

The town – once a bustling port – abounds in old limestone-and-timber structures in 'Caribbean vernacular' style, with gingerbread wood trim, clapboard frontages, and wide verandas. The oldest dates to the mid-1700s. Lucea has appeared in several movies, including *Cool Runnings* and *Wide Sargasso Sea*. The **Hanover Historical Society** (☎ 956-2584; Watson Taylor Dr, Lucea PO) is active in the town's preservation.

In town, the well-known artist Lloyd Hoffstead has a **gallery** (☎ 956-2241; Hanover St; open 9am-5pm Mon-Fri), 100 yards east of the Texaco gas station, which displays his paintings and sculptures.

Information

Scotiabank (☎ 956-2553) faces the roundabout in the center of town. **National Commercial Bank** (☎ 956-2348; Main St) also has a branch.

Cable & Wireless Jamaica (Shop 4, Uptown Shopping Centre) has a telephone exchange behind the courthouse.

Lucea Hospital (☎ 956-2233, 956-3836), on the headland behind Hanover Parish Church, has an emergency department. For other attention, try **Lucea Medical Centre** (☎ 956-2385; 31 Church St; open 8am-6pm Mon-Fri, until noon Sat).

The **police station** (☎ 956-2222; Watson Taylor Dr) is on Sir Alexander Bustamante Square.

Walking Tour

Begin your one-hour walking tour at **Sir Alexander Bustamante Square**, centered on a small fountain fronting the handsome courthouse. Note the vintage 1932 fire engine beside the courthouse.

The town's restored **courthouse** (☎ 956-2280; Watson Taylor Dr) has limestone balustrades and a clapboard upper story topped by a clock tower supported by Corinthian columns. The clock was sent to Lucea in 1817 by mistake – it was actually intended for the Caribbean island of St Lucia. It has supposedly worked without a hitch ever since, under the maintenance of the Williams family, who were given the responsibility for its running over 100 years ago. The tower resembles the helmet worn by the Prussian Imperial Guards.

On the east side of the square is bustling **Cleveland Stanhope market**. A walk north up the main frontage road curls past some of Lucea's finest historical houses, many in a near state of decrepitude, and deposits you atop the headland with a fine view east over Lucea Harbour. At the hillcrest is **Hanover Parish Church** (☎ 956-2253), established in 1725. It's architecturally uninspired but has several interesting monuments; a Jewish quarter within the walled cemetery recalls the days when Lucea had a lively Jewish community.

A side road that begins 200 yards west of the church leads to the **Hanover Museum** (☎ 956-2584; open 10:30am-4:30pm Mon-Fri, weekends by appointment; admission US$2), a tiny affair housed in an old police barracks. Exhibits include prisoners' stocks, wooden bathtub, and a miscellany of pots, lead weights, and measures. There's a tiny gift shop, toilets, and a snack bar.

On the headland beyond the church is **Rusea High School**, a venerable red-brick Georgian-style building constructed in 1843 as an army barracks. The overgrown remains of **Fort Charlotte** overlook the channel a short distance beyond Rusea High School. It's named after Queen Charlotte, wife of King George III of England. The octagonal fortress still boasts cannons in its embrasures.

Places to Stay & Eat
West Palm Hotel (☎ 956-2321; Ft Charlotte St; rooms without/with air-con U$20/26) is a musty old wooden building just behind Hanover Parish Church. It has 23 simple rooms with basic furnishings and private bath with hot water. The hotel is popular with businesspeople, and locals gather at the bar out back. It has a modest restaurant.

Global Villa Guest House (☎ 956-2916, fax 956-3109; e globalvilla_01@yahoo.com; PO Box 4719; rooms US$32-53) is a modern guest house, 5 miles west of town on the A1. It is clean with 10 nicely furnished rooms

with louvered windows and tile floors. Some have fans only; others have air-con and TV. It has a TV lounge, bar, and restaurant serving Jamaican fare, such as jerk dishes (US$3-10) and steam fish (US$5.50).

Sarducces Restaurant & Bar (☎ 956-2841; Moseley Dr; US$2-12; open 8am-10pm), on the hill next to the Baptist church, serves local dishes.

Tommy's Restaurant (☎ 956-3106; Main St; U$1.50-10; open 7:30am-10pm), on the A1, between the town square and Hanover Church, serves natural foods, including tofu dishes and steam fish, and natural juices.

Bruk-Up Fast Food (☎ 956-9926), beside the bus station, is the best of several food shacks serving simple Jamaican fare, plus natural juices.

Getting There & Away
Buses, coasters, and route taxis arrive and depart Lucea from the open ground opposite the market. Lucea is a midway terminus for public vehicles traveling between Montego Bay and Negril, and you may need to change vehicles here. A bus between Lucea and MoBay or Negril costs about US$1. A coaster or route taxi costs about US$3.50.

MAYFIELD FALLS
The Dolphin Head Mountains rise inland of Moskito Cove and are known for their cascades. The grandest of these are at Mayfield, near Pennycooke, about 10 miles south of Moskito Cove (4 miles east of Lucea). Here, a series of 21 falls and pools beckon you to take a refreshing dip in any of the delightful swimming holes, which are shaded by glades of bamboo. You can even swim through a cave.

Three entities compete for your business. **Original Mayfield Falls & Mineral Springs** (☎ 952-6634, ☎/fax 957-4729; admission US$12, with lunch US$20) is a working tropical farm and tour attraction. You'll cross a bamboo-and-log bridge, then follow the sun-dappled river course, clambering over river stones to reach the cascades. You can learn about ackee, breadfruits, and other Jamaican fruits, vegetables, and flowers, and even join in traditional African music and dance during show time (2:30pm Tues & Fri). There are hammocks beneath shade trees, plus volleyball.

Nearby, **Reality River Walk** (☎ 971-4814, 1-776-7305 cellular) and **Riverwalk at Mayfield Walks** (☎ 974-8000, 888-974-8000; ℮ bmwtours@cwjamaica.com) provide a similar experience.

Getting There & Away
From the A1, take the road inland from Moskito Cove via Cascade. The route is signed but there are several turnoffs; you should ask your way to be sure. You can also reach Mayfield Falls from Tryall or Hopewell via Pondside (see the Montego Bay & Northwest Coast chapter); or by turning north at Savanna-la-Mar and taking the Banbury or Amity Cross routes (about 15 miles) along a road that is deplorably potholed.

Caribic Vacations (☎ 979-6073, 953-2584 in Montego Bay, 957-3309 in Negril) offers excursions.

You can arrange a **'Mayfield Nature Pure Tour'** (☎ 957-3268, fax 957-3253) in advance at Shop 4, Negril Plaza (see Negril earlier in this chapter).

KENILWORTH
Just west of the Maggotty River east of Moskito Cove is the turnoff for the **Human Employment & Resource Training Trust** (HEART Trust; ☎ 953-5315; Kenilworth HEART Trust/NTA Academy Sandy Bay PO, Hanover), about a mile along a dirt road at Kenilworth. The HEART Trust is a residential academy providing vocational and personal development training to young Jamaicans. It occupies a 17th-century sugar plantation acclaimed as the best example of old industrial architecture in Jamaica. Tourists are welcome. The guard at the gate will let you in (no charge).

Most prominent among the ruins are the sugar boiling house and distillery and the long rectangular sugar mill with oval Palladian windows. There's a graveyard, 400 yards farther up the hill.

As yet unfulfilled plans call for the ruins to be restored.

Negril to Savanna-la-Mar

Tourism has been slow to develop along the southern shore of Westmoreland, a parish dependent on the sugar industry, with dismal Savanna-la-Mar the only town of any import.

Roads fan out from Savanna-la-Mar through the Westmoreland Plains. This flat, mountain-rimmed area, planted almost entirely in sugarcane, is drained by the Cabarita River, which feeds swamplands at its lower reaches. The fishing is good, and a few crocodiles may still live in more secluded swampy areas, alongside an endemic fish – the 'God-a-me' – that can live out of water in moist, shady spots. The river is navigable by small boat for 12 miles.

Several beaches with active fishing communities provide a slice of Jamaican life.

LITTLE BAY & VICINITY
Southeast of Retirement, a badly eroded side road loops down to **Homers Cove** ('Brighton Beach' to locals) and, immediately east, Little Bay, with handsome beaches and peaceful bathing. Little Bay is imbued with the kind of laid-back feel that pervaded Negril before the onset of commercialization. It's a great place to commune with Rastas and other Jamaicans who live by a carefree axiom in ramshackle homes, dependent on fishing and their entrepreneurial wits. The area is popular for reggae and dancehall sound systems that lure the local crowd from miles around.

Bob Marley used to hang out here in the 1970s. **Bob Marley's House** still stands beside **Bob Marley's Spring**, where he bathed; it's now a private guest house.

A mangrove swamp extends east of Little Bay, beyond which lies the fishing community of **Hope Wharf** and a long sliver of white sand called **Lost Beach**. Crocodiles and marine turtles can be found here. Dolphins and humpback whales frequent the waters offshore year-round.

You can hire a fisherman to take you fishing in a pirogue. Lost Beach Resort charges US$50 per person for sport fishing, and US$30 per hour for horseback riding.

The annual **Uncle Sam's Donkey Derby** is held on Little Bay beach the first Sunday in February.

Places to Stay & Eat

Garden Park (☎ 842-9029; per tent US$10, cabins US$20), also known as **Uncle Sam's**, on the cliffs of Little Bay, permits camping amid shady almond trees. This little budget heaven also has rustic cabins, and communal showers and toilets. It's atmospheric eatery – a gaily decorated bamboo bar festooned with girlie posters, dead crabs, and other miscellany – serves conch or 'dapper' soup and other simple fisherfolk fare (US$2-12). Uncle Sam's also puts on 'bashments' (parties), and full-moon parties are held in the **Bat Cave**, when a cavern is lit up with hundreds of candles, the reggae is cranked up, and everyone parties down.

Kevin's Heaven (☎ 383-6222; PO Box 70, Little London; cabins per person US$50 with 3 meals), at St John's Point, 5 miles east of Little Bay, is a fantastic, palm-shaded budget haven right on the sands at the end of a rough dirt road. The place offers simply furnished, all-wood cabins with large screened windows, bare-bones furnishings, and solar power. Kevin – a friendly, bearded sexagenarian – raises endangered Jamaican boas.

Romie's Ocean View (☎ 918-7130; e info@RomiesOceanView.com; Homer Bay, Little Bay PO; cottages US$30) has simple yet charming wooden cottages with verandas, plus shared bathrooms with solar-heated water. Bicycle and snorkel-gear rentals are offered, as are guided excursions. Jamaican meals are served (US$3-5).

Coconut Cottages by the Sea (☎/fax 920-731-9391; 800-962-5548 in the USA; e co conuts@execpc.com; PO Box 136, Presque Isle, Wisconsin 54557, USA; rooms per person US$105) is a relatively upscale place run by North Americans. It features 10 stone-and-wood cottages with cathedral ceilings and patios. Some share outdoor showers offering ocean views. There's a restaurant, and tours are offered. Rates include meals.

Humble Boy Club (☎ 700-0198; 716-346-3800 in the USA mid-April–Nov; e info@humbleboy.com; rooms US$40, suite US$70), run by a New York couple described as 'modern-day hippies,' has four small, basically furnished rooms with ceiling fans and solar-heated showers. There's a simple yet lively bar (with live music Friday) and restaurant serving Jamaican, European, and North American favorites (US$3-5).

Lost Beach Resort (☎ 819-5678, fax 787-4060; ☎ 800-626-5678, fax 734-663-7477 in the USA; 616 Church St, Ann Arbor, MI 48104, USA; w www.lostbeach.com; cabins US$59-109, one-bedroom apartment US$99-149, two-bedroom apartment US$129-199, three-bedroom apartment US$149-209) is a US-owned, modern hotel with exotic hardwood furnishings in 14 spacious one- to three-bedroom suites with air-con, tile floors, and kitchenettes. Two thatch-and-wood beach cabins have loft bedrooms and kitchenettes. It has a large sundeck, a pool, kid's playground, Jacuzzi, and a huge library with pool table. Rates depend on the month.

Shorty's on the Cliff, 400 yards east of Coconut Cottages, offers simple Jamaican fare.

SAVANNA-LA-MAR

With a population of 18,600, Savanna-la-Mar ('the plain by the sea'), the capital city of Westmoreland, is the largest town in western Jamaica. 'Sav,' as it is locally known, offers few attractions.

Sav is virtually a one-street town. Its axis is mile-long Great George St.

Sav was founded around 1730 and grew modestly as a sugar shipping port during the colonial era. It has an unremarkable history, except where Mother Nature is concerned, as numerous hurricanes have swept the town.

Information

Scotiabank (☎ 955-2601) and **National Commercial Bank** (☎ 955-2623) have branches in town. **Western Union** (☎ 926-2454) is represented by D&Y Supermarket. All are along Great George St.

The **post office** (☎ 955-9295) and the **police station** (☎ 918-1865) are both located near the courthouse midway along Great George St.

You can make telephone calls and send faxes from the **Cable & Wireless Jamaica office** (☎ 955-2520; 43 Great George St) and **Direct Telecom** (☎ 918-1377; Shop 4, 60 Beckford St).

Sav-la-Mar Hospital, on the A2 on the northeast side of town, has a 24-hour **emergency service** (☎ 955-2133), and there's a pharmacy on Great George St.

Great George Street

The English colonialists never completed the **Savanna-la-Mar Fort** at the foot of Great George St. Parts of it collapsed into the swamps within a few years of being built. Its innards form a small cove where locals swim.

The most interesting building is the **courthouse**, built in 1925 at the junction of Great George and Rose Sts, where there's a fountain made of cast iron, inscribed with the words, 'Keep the pavements dry.'

St George's Parish Church, opposite, was built in 1905. It's uninspired, but has a stately pipe organ that was dedicated in 1914.

At the north end of town by the roundabout known as Hendon Circle is the very handsome **Manning's School**, built in 1738 after a Westmoreland planter, Thomas Manning.

Places to Stay & Eat

Hendon House (☎ 955-3943; 93 Great George St; rooms with shared bath US$16 & US$22, with private bath US$26), 50 yards north of Hendon Circle, is a 250-year-old, two-story timber house with funky charm. A spiral staircase leads upstairs to 12 basic rooms. They're lofty and spacious, with fans and jalousie windows. The rooms with private bath have decrepit plumbing.

Lochiel Guest House (☎ 955-9394; Smithfield PO, Savanna-la-Mar; rooms US$20-30), on the A2, just a mile east of town, is another old stone-and-timber, two-story

great house that looks delightful from the outside. Inside however, it's gloomy and rundown, though some of its 14 rooms are appealing. All have utility furniture and hot water in private bathrooms. Eight rooms in a modern annex offer better decor. Meals are not served.

J's Jerk Centre (☎ 918-0159; 10 Rose St) is a tiny outdoor place that is recommended. The owner serves jerk chicken (US$3 per quarter pound) and 'festival' (US$2), plus steam fish (US$3).

For patties, pastries, and desserts, check out **Hammond's Pastry** (☎ 955-2870; 18 Great George St), where Russell and Dorna Hammond make the best traditional cocobread around.

Old Fort Club Restaurant (☎ 955-3362; US$1.50-7), in the fort at the foot of Great George St, serves Jamaican staples such as curried goat. It offers a 'fish fry' at 7pm on Saturday.

For Chinese, try the **Flaming Wok** (☎ 955-2235; Dalling St; US$2-14; open 11am-10pm).

Survivor Hut (☎ 955-3920; 23 Lewis St) is an old wooden building where locals play dominoes and enjoy simple Jamaican fare, including breakfast (US$2-6).

You can buy fresh fish and produce from the market at the base of Great George St, but the sanitary conditions aren't up to par.

Getting There & Around

Buses, coasters, and route taxis operate frequently along the A2/B8 between Montego Bay (buses/coasters and route taxis US$1.50/3) and Negril (US$1/2). Public vehicles also depart on a regular basis from the Beckford St transportation center in Kingston (three hours; US$1.50/8).

Island Taxi (☎ 955-9722; 126 Great George St) offers 24-hour service.

FROME

Frome lies at the heart of Jamaica's foremost sugar estate, in the center of a rich alluvial plain. The area is dominated by a **sugar-processing factory** (☎ 955-2604, 955-2641), on the B9 north of Savanna-la-Mar and south of the town of Grange Hill. Constructed in 1938, the factory became the setting for a violent nationwide labor dispute. During the Depression of the 1930s, many small factories were bought out by the West Indies Sugar Company. Unemployed workers from all over the island converged seeking work. Although workers were promised a dollar a day, the men who were hired received only 15 cents a day and women only 10 cents. Workers went on strike for higher pay, passions ran high, and violence erupted. When the crowds rioted and set fire to the cane fields, the police responded by firing into the crowd, killing four people. The whole island exploded in violent clashes. The situation was defused when Alexander Busta-mante mediated the dispute. His efforts gave rise to the island's first mass labor unions and the first organized political party, under his leadership (also see Birth of Modern Politics in the Facts about Jamaica chapter).

A **monument** at a crossroads north of the factory gates reads:

To labour leader Alexander Bustamante and the Workers for their courageous fight in 1938. On behalf of the Working People of Jamaica.

Free tours of the factory can be arranged by reservation. No high heels or sandals are allowed.

Frome also boasts two attractive churches, including **St Barnabas Anglican Church** in Teutonic style.

ROARING RIVER & BLUE HOLE

Nature lovers and anyone seeking an offbeat experience should spend an hour or two at Roaring River, a natural beauty spot where mineral waters gush up from the ground in a meadow full of water hy-acinths and water lilies. A stone aqueduct takes off some of the water, which runs turquoise-jade. Steps lead up a cliff face gashed by the mouth of a subterranean passage lit by electric lanterns (you can enter the caves only with guides from the cooperative, who have keys to the cave gate). Inside, a path with handrails leads down to chambers full of stalagmites and

stalactites. Take your swimming gear to sit in the mineral spring that percolates up inside the cave, or in the 'bottomless' blue hole outside the cave.

A mento band plays inside the cave. Harmless fruit bats roost in the recesses.

A guided tour costs US$10 for adults (with lunch US$15), US$5 for children. The guides are registered in a coopera-tive: the **Roaring River Citizens' Associa-tion** (☎ 995-2094, 979-7987 in Montego Bay, fax 952-2868) in the landscaped com-pound – Freedom Village – as you enter the hamlet. There's secure parking, plus a reception lounge, changing rooms, play-ground, and crafts shops. A restaurant serves cheap Jamaican fare, as does **Chill Out View,** atop a hill overlooking the bur-bling spring.

Warning: Unregistered touts may try to stop you as you approach Roaring River. They'll try to get you to hire one of them as a guide and will tell you that you can't drive up to the Blue Hole without a guide. It's bull! There have been several reports of heavy-handed extortion in which tourists have been threatened by these con artists.

Blue Hole Ital Gardens

The lane continues beyond Roaring River for about a mile uphill through the village to Blue Hole Ital Gardens (☎ 918-1341, 955-8823; e bluehole68@hotmail.com; ad-mission US$6), a beautiful sinkhole sur-rounded by a landscaped garden full of ginger torch and heliconia on the private property of a Rasta called Esau. Entry is overpriced, but grants a chance for a cool dip with the fish in the turquoise waters. The source of the Roaring River is about 400 yards farther up the road, where the water foams up from beneath a matting of foliage.

This is also a quintessential counter-culture lifestyle retreat that offers two very rustic but charming **cottages** (US$40-80) amid effusive gardens at the edge of the tumbling brook (the 'waterhouse' cabin sits *over* the stream). Bamboo-enclosed toilets and showers are alfresco. You can also rent 'Esau's Mountain Retreat,' with fully-

NEGRIL & WEST COAST

equipped kitchen, a separate cabin in the hills. You can also **camp** (US$10).

Also here is **Lovers Café**, which is known for its salads (US$3), a veggie dinner (US$5), grilled fish (US$7.50), and I-tal dishes, washed down by fruit juices (US$3) and herb teas.

Getting There & Away

Roaring River is at Shrewsbury Estate, about a mile north of the main crossroads in Petersfield (5 miles northeast of Savanna-la-Mar). You can catch a bus in Savanna-la-Mar as far as Petersfield. From there it's a hot walk or rough ride down the potholed road through the cane fields. Route taxis

and coasters also run to Roaring River from Petersfield (US$0.50).

Organized tours to Roaring River are offered by companies in Montego Bay and Negril.

FERRIS CROSS

Ferris Cross is a major crossroads hamlet on the A2, 5 miles east of Savanna-la-Mar. Here, the A2 turns southeast and follows the coast to Black River and the south coast. Another road – the B8 – leads northeast to Galloway (3 miles), where it begins a steep climb to Whithorn and Montego Bay.

South Coast & Central Highlands

For marketing purposes, the Jamaica Tourist Board combines the coastal lowlands of St Elizabeth parish with the central highlands of Manchester parish and refers to them jointly as the 'South Coast.'

The coastal flatlands are replete with natural attractions, such as the Great Morass, Bamboo Avenue, and YS Falls. Along the shore, however, there are few picture-postcard beaches, although a spotlight is increasingly shining on the fishing community of Treasure Beach.

The coastal lifestyle is as yet virtually unsullied by tourism and has a unique lazy calm based on a traditional life that keeps locals rooted and hopeful. Its people are mellower than elsewhere in Jamaica: everyone wishes you a safe journey, fewer people ask you for money, and the ones who do are more inclined to offer thanks.

Historically, as well, the people here have been somewhat different from the rest of Jamaicans, both in their attitudes and bloodlines. Miskito Indians from Central America were brought to Jamaica to help track Maroons during the 18th century and eventually were given land grants in St Elizabeth. The Miskitos, plus 19th-century Scottish castaways and German settlers, are partly responsible for the high percentage of mixed-race peoples around Treasure Beach.

Jamaica's cool central highlands – rising northeast of St Elizabeth – were popular from the 19th century through the mid-1900s as a vacation retreat, when the towns of Christiana and Mandeville became social centers for wealthy Jamaicans and Europeans. Parts of England or Germany come to mind, with rolling hills, bucolic valleys grazed by cattle in fields fringed by hedgerows and stone walls, and intensively farmed mountain slopes where clouds sift through alpine forests of pine and oak.

In the 18th century, the uplands became an important center for coffee cultivation. Sugar estates were absent, and the harsh plantation system never took hold. Following

Highlights

- Black River Great Morass, teeming with wildlife and accessible by boat
- YS Falls for a refreshing dip among splendid scenery
- Lonesome, laid-back, offbeat Treasure Beach
- Funky Alligator Pond, where fishing is still the way of life and tourists are rare
- Appleton Rum Estate for a peek into the making of Jamaica's premier rums
- Mandeville, the most pleasant town on the island, just perfect for a highland escape

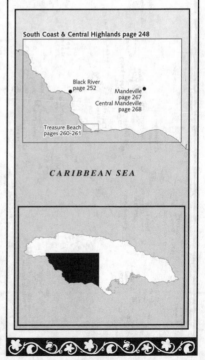

South Coast & Central Highlands page 248

Black River page 252

Mandeville page 267
Central Mandeville page 268

Treasure Beach pages 260-261

CARIBBEAN SEA

SOUTH COAST & CENTRAL HIGHLANDS

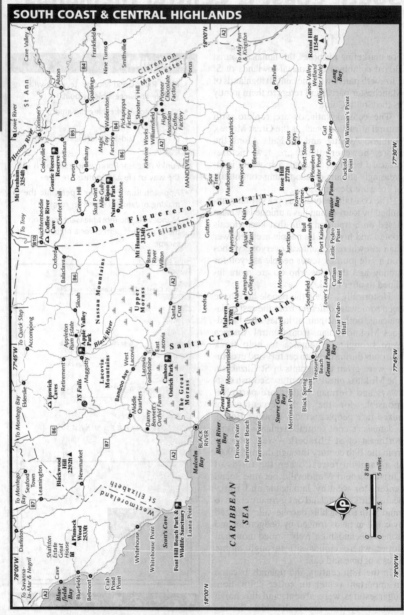

emancipation, newly freed slaves settled as independent farmers and continued to grow coffee. In later years, citrus farms became important, and cattle now grow fat on the lush pastures. St Elizabeth – Jamaica's breadbasket – is an important center of market gardening: melons, peppers, scallions, tobacco, and corn grown here supply the rest of Jamaica. Bauxite is also mined near Mandeville and Santa Cruz, bringing further, much-evident prosperity to the region.

Good resources for information on the region covered in this chapter include W www.jamaica-southcoast.com and W www.southcoast-jamaica.com.

Geography & Climate

The western plains, centered on Black River, are known for the Great Morass, a swampy marsh and forest. Farther east, the plains are lush with cattle pastures, market gardens, and to a lesser degree, sugarcane fields.

Dividing the plains north to south are the Santa Cruz Mountains, a steep-faced chain that slopes to the sea and drops 1700 feet at Lover's Leap. The plains are hemmed in to the west by a range of hills called Surinam Quarters, whose scarp faces fall sharply to the coast; to the north by the Nassau Mountains and Cockpit Country; and to the east by the Don Figuerero Mountains, a wedge-shaped upland plateau dominating Manchester parish. The base of the west-facing escarpment of the Don Figuereros forms the boundary between St Elizabeth and Manchester parishes. Northeast of the Don Figuereros, the Mocho Mountains rise to Christiana and crest at Mt Denham (3254 feet).

The area has distinct climates associated with the temperate uplands and the warmer plains. The latter have a relatively dry, balmy climate, while the highlands are moist and refreshingly springlike.

Whitehouse & Environs

The strip of narrow coast of southeast Westmoreland parish is shadowed by the steep slopes of Surinam Quarters. The few lonesome beaches attract contemplative sorts who like to slumber in hammocks away from the rest of the world. But the area is awakening from its Rip Van Winkle slumber. Plans are moving ahead for two major resort developments that have many local residents concerned about the disruption of their bucolic ways.

BLUEFIELDS

This sleepy fishing village, 12 miles southeast of Savanna-la-Mar, has a long sliver of beach popular with locals on weekends. Colorful fishing boats are drawn up on poles and nets hung out to dry like laundry. You can even see fishing boats and pirogues being carved from cotton trees in the traditional manner. Booby birds, frigate birds, and pelicans roost in the mangroves.

Bluefields Bay provided a safe anchorage for Spanish explorers, British naval squadrons, and pirates, including Henry Morgan, who in 1670 set out from Bluefields Bay to sack Panama City.

Surinam Quarters, inland from Bluefields, is named for the colonists who settled here after the English traded Surinam to the Dutch for New Amsterdam (New York) in 1667. Many Scottish also settled the area after the Battle of Culloden in 1745. You'll see many Scottish place names in the area.

The **police station** (☎ 955-8156) is at the east end of the village. On the A2 nearby, the **Bluefields People's Community Association** (☎ 955-8792, fax 955-8791) is a good resource.

The **Peter Tosh Monument** is a small mausoleum filled with memorabilia in honor of the Belmont-born reggae superstar, who was murdered in 1987. The annual **Peter Tosh Birthday Bash** is held here in mid-October.

Shafston Tours (see Shafston Estate Great House below) offers hikes and offbeat excursions.

Places to Stay & Eat

Shafston Estate Great House (☎ 997-5076; W www.shafston.com; PO Box 19, Bluefields; camping per person US$7.50; rooms single US$15-20, double US$20-70) is a budget traveler's dream. This run-down historic house has a stunning hilltop setting with views down the coast as far east as Negril. Water and toilets are available for campers. It has 10 rooms in the old house, ranging from basic to modest. Thirteen simple yet charming rooms are in a newer block with screened windows and clean, tiled communal unisex showers and bathrooms. A new restaurant offers views as well as seafood, steak, pizza, and pasta (US$2-16). You can relax in hammocks or laze on a new sundeck with pool. Tours are offered. And there's a pool table, darts, and a bar, plus cats and dogs – and their excrement – underfoot. To get there from the A2, take the dirt road opposite Bluefields police station, and then it's a steep 2-mile climb.

Casa Mariner (☎ 955-8487; Belmont District, Bluefields PO; rooms without/with aircon US$25/40), at Cave, 2 miles north of Bluefields, is modest. There are 10 meagerly furnished rooms with private bath and hot water, and three rooms with air-con. Facilities include a large bar with pool tables and a breezy upstairs restaurant.

In Bluefields, **Cool Runnings Villa** (☎ 955-8805; Belmont District, Bluefields PO; rooms US$20-25), half a mile east of the police station, is a Scandinavian-run cottage with two simply furnished air-con rooms for rent. It has a beach bar, and water sports are offered.

In the top-end category, **Horizon** (☎/fax 603-436-4721 in the USA; W www.jamaica escapes.com; Belmont District, Bluefields PO; cottages weekly US$635), in Belmont, is a private walled seaside compound with two utterly charming cottages – Sea Ranch and Rasta Ranch – with separate living/dining rooms, private toilets, and shared hot-water shower in the garden. There's a small beach and jetty, plus sea kayaks.

Braxton and Debbie Moncure run **five deluxe villas** (☎ 202-232-4010, fax 703-549-6517 in the USA; W www.bluefieldsvillas .com; 726 N Washington St, Alexandria, VA 22314, USA). Each villa is fully staffed,

exquisitely furnished, and on the waterfront in Bluefields. Weekly low-season rates for two range from US$2400 to US$3750 (depending on the villa) to US$9000 for 12 people at 'Mullion Cove.' High-season rates are approximately 30% more.

Bluefields Beach Park (☎ 955-8257), along the shore, has stalls selling jerk, roast fish, and natural juices.

WHITEHOUSE
Whitehouse is a fishing village and a great place to sample provincial coastal life. It stretches for about a mile along the A2, parallel to a series of beaches, where motorized boats and pirogues are drawn up. The Whitehouse Fishing Cooperative supplies much of the island with wahoo, tuna, barracuda, bonito, snapper, kingfish, marlin, and lobster taken on the Pedro Banks, about 80 miles out to sea.

Whitehouse is slated to contain the area's first large-scale, all-inclusive resort being built by the Sandals chain.

Activities
You can hire a fishing boat to go **snorkeling** for around US$15 per hour. Better yet, hop aboard with local fishermen for a trip to the fishing banks (typically up to four people for about US$20 per hour). Women should not go unaccompanied.

Oasis Spa (☎ 955-8351, fax 955-8729; Box 18, Bluefields) offers upscale treatments, from a 'coffee scrub' to a 'cucumber wrap for sunburnt skin.'

Places to Stay
Culloden Café (☎ 963-5344; e lyons@cw jamaica.com; Whitehouse PO; cottages US$50), at Little Culloden, a mile northwest of Whitehouse, is highly recommended. Its charming owners have three delightful cottages with exquisite decor (including pastel color schemes), kitchenettes, and porches with hammocks, though bathrooms are tiny. One has a living room. Rates include continental breakfast. It has a beachfront terrace with hammock, and the best restaurant for miles (see Places to Eat & Drink below).

Natania's (☎ 963-5342, fax 963-5724; e jfj@mail.infochan.com; Whitehouse PO; doubles summer US$65), next door to Culloden, is a modestly decorated option run by fundamentalist Christians. A veranda overlooks lush gardens that fall to the rocky shore, where multitiered terraces are built above the coral, with artificial beaches for sunning. Water sports are offered, and there's a large pool and sundeck. The eight meagerly appointed rooms have ceiling fans and wide jalousie windows, sponge mattresses, and measly bathrooms. Wine is served with meals; otherwise no alcohol is allowed.

South Sea View Guest House (☎ 963-5172, fax 963-5763; e info@southseaview.com; Whitehouse PO; rooms US$50-60), at the far southeast end of South Sea Park, is a modern villa with eight air-con rooms, each with private bath, king-size bed, cable TV, and hand-painted tropical murals. There's a swimming pool and a rocky cove good for bathing.

Sandals Whitehouse is a much-troubled project that has been slated to open for a decade or so. Construction of the 360-room resort for singles, couples, and families was still in fitful on-off status at last visit. It is billed to open as Sandals' most elaborate luxury resort, featuring everything from horseback riding and a sports complex to a children's park and an 18-hole golf course. For international contact information, see All-Inclusive Resorts in the Facts for the Visitor chapter.

Places to Eat & Drink

Culloden Café (see Places to Stay above; US$3-16; open 8am-10pm Wed-Mon, closed Tues) is a rare bargain run by Minnesotan Ann Lyons and her fabulous staff. And what food! Typical of daily specials are couscous and vegetable salad, carrot honey-ginger soup, and blackened kingfish. Pizzas are offered on Sunday. Leave room for the key lime pie, and wash it all down with superb homemade limeade.

Culloden Café also has a cozy little TV lounge and bar and the 'largest library in Jamaica' perfect for postprandial pleasure.

This author recommends a Cuban cigar and 12-year-old Scotch malt.

Ruby's 24/7 (☎ 963-5686), on the A2 in Whitehouse, is open 24 hours and serves seafood and Jamaican fare on a shady patio.

Hillfoot Club (US$2.50; open 9pm-4am), on the A2, 100 yards west of Culloden Café, is a none-too-sophisticated go-go club famous as the unlikely setting for a Thursday morning market supplying exotic dancers to other clubs islandwide.

Otherwise, late-night libations are limited to a few simple rum shops.

SCOTT'S COVE

About 5 miles east of Whitehouse, the A2 sweeps around this deep little inlet where dozens of food and beer stalls line the shore. It's a good place to buy fried snapper and *bammy* – a pancake of fried cassava – with onions and peppers for a dollar or two.

Scott's Cove forms the parish boundary between Westmoreland and St Elizabeth.

FONT HILL BEACH PARK & WILDLIFE SANCTUARY

This 3150-acre wildlife reserve and beach park (☎ 818-6088; open 9am-5pm Tues-Sun; adult/child US$3/1), east of Scott's Cove, is owned by the Petroleum Corporation of Jamaica.

The sanctuary comprises scrubby acacia, logwood thickets, and closer to the shore, a maze of interconnected lagoons and swamps with a large population of crocodiles. The birding is fabulous.

Two golden-sand beaches (connected by a trail) are fringed by reef offering great snorkeling and bathing. Dolphins even come into the cove.

There is a restaurant, gift store, bar, changing rooms, picnic booths, volleyball, a boardwalk, interpretive center, and marina.

Free guided walks are offered (tips are appreciated). Ornithologist Peter Marra leads special bird trips; make reservations via Robert Sutton at **Marshall's Pen** (☎ 904-5454); see Mandeville later in this chapter.

Black River & Environs

BLACK RIVER

Peaceful and picturesque, the town of Black River (population 3900), on the west bank of the mouth of the Black River, is a far cry from the heady days of the 18th and 19th centuries, when it prospered from the export of logwood, from which a Prussian-blue dye was extracted.

Early prosperity brought electric power to Black River in 1893, when it was installed in a house called Waterloo, the first such installation in the country. Back then, the town had a racetrack and an active gambling life, and a mineral spa at the west end of town was popular with the well-to-do.

You can catch buses, coasters, and route taxis to Black River from most major towns. Public vehicles arrive and depart Black River from behind the market, just west of the river. Taxis arrive and depart from a lot at the junction of Main and North Sts.

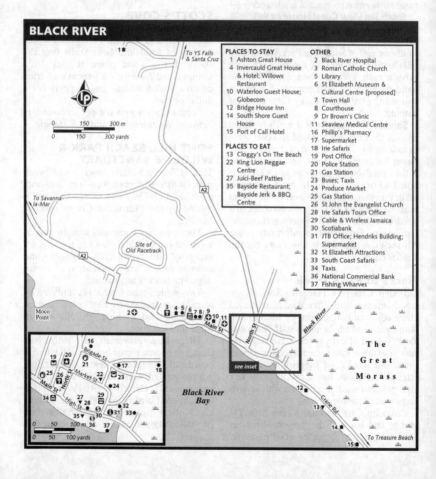

BLACK RIVER

PLACES TO STAY
1 Ashton Great House
4 Invercauld Great House & Hotel; Willows Restaurant
10 Waterloo Guest House; Globecom
12 Bridge House Inn
14 South Shore Guest House
15 Port of Call Hotel

PLACES TO EAT
13 Cloggy's On The Beach
22 King Lion Reggae Centre
27 Juici-Beef Patties
35 Bayside Restaurant; Bayside Jerk & BBQ Centre

OTHER
2 Black River Hospital
3 Roman Catholic Church
5 Library
6 St Elizabeth Museum & Cultural Centre [proposed]
7 Town Hall
8 Courthouse
9 Dr Brown's Clinic
11 Seaview Medical Centre
16 Phillip's Pharmacy
17 Supermarket
18 Irie Safaris
19 Post Office
20 Police Station
21 Gas Station
23 Buses; Taxis
24 Produce Market
25 Gas Station
26 St John the Evangelist Church
28 Irie Safaris Tours Office
29 Cable & Wireless Jamaica
30 Scotiabank
31 JTB Office; Hendriks Building; Supermarket
32 St Elizabeth Attractions
33 South Coast Safaris
34 Taxis
36 National Commercial Bank
37 Fishing Wharves

Information

The **JTB office** (☎ 965-2074, fax 965-2076; 2 High St) is on the upper floor of the Hendricks Building.

Scotiabank (☎ 965-2251; 6 High St) and **National Commercial Bank** (☎ 965-9027; 9 High St) face each other on the main street.

The **post office** (☎ 965-2250) is immediately west of the **police station** (☎ 965-2232 or 119) on North St.

You can make international calls at the **Cable & Wireless Jamaica office** (☎ 965-9915, 888-965-9700; 3 North St) and **Globecom** (☎ 965-9260; e bellsouth@cwjamaica.com; 44 High St), at the Waterloo Guest House, which also offers email and Internet services (US$2.50 for 30 minutes).

Black River Hospital (☎ 965-2212; 45 Main St) is a half mile west of town. Dr John Brown has a **clinic** (☎ 965-2305; 48 Main St), and **Seaview Medical Centre** (☎ 965-9173; open 24 hrs) is 100 yards farther east. **Phillip's Pharmacy** (☎ 965-2984; Shop 2, Brigade St) is well-stocked.

Things to See & Do

High St is lined with colonnaded, Georgian timber houses with gingerbread trim. At the east end is the **Hendricks Building** (2 High St), dating from 1813. Immediately east is an old **iron bridge**, a good spot for watching crocodiles waiting for tidbits thrown by tourists from the riverside berths. Trawlers lie at anchor immediately south of the bridge, and here you can watch fish being hauled ashore onto the wharfs.

Historic structures worth checking out include the yellow-brick **Parish Church of St John the Evangelist**, built in 1837 at the junction of Main and North Sts. Two blocks west are the porticoed **courthouse** and the **town hall**, with lofty pillars, and beyond that a simple **Roman Catholic church**.

Two of the most impressive buildings are the **Invercauld Great House & Hotel** and the **Waterloo Guest House**, both west on Main St and splendid examples of the Jamaican vernacular style, with shady wooden verandas and gingerbread trim (see Places to Stay below).

A **St Elizabeth Museum & Cultural Centre** was planned, to be housed in a restored colonial structure (still derelict at last visit) catercorner to the library.

Places to Stay

Waterloo Guest House (☎ 965-2278, fax 965-2072; 44 High St; old-house rooms US$22, modern complex US$44) is a rickety Georgian edifice offering offbeat charm. There are five meagerly furnished rooms with fans in the old house, plus 16 carpeted, more stylish air-con rooms with cable TV and telephone in a modern annex. All have private bath with shower and hot water.

Bridge House Inn (☎ 965-2361; 14 Crane Rd; rooms US$22-25), east of town, has 14 rooms with fans, plus private bath with hot water; some have air-con. They're clean and comfy but can get hot. It has a bar and TV lounge and a restaurant.

South Shore Guest House (☎ 965-2172; 33 Crane Rd; camping US$10; rooms US$25, with TV & hot water US$35) is a 12-bedroom hotel with a breezy outdoor bar and restaurant. Rooms are spacious, though basic, with utility furniture, fans, and large bathrooms, plus verandas fronting a narrow beach. It permits camping under shade trees on the lawn.

Port of Call Hotel (☎/fax 965-2410; 136 Crane Rd; rooms downstairs/upstairs US$29/34) has 19 rooms, a pool and Jacuzzi, and a restaurant and bar. It looks appealing from the outside, but the interior is disappointing, with meager utility furnishings and a restaurant resembling a military mess hall. Most rooms have a TV and telephone. Those upstairs have air-con. The hotel – which was once the town brothel – offers airport transfers. It rents bicycles.

Ashton Great House (☎/fax 965-2036; e theashton@cwjamaica.com; PO Box 104, Luana, Black River; rooms single US$38, double US$45) has a magnificent setting on a hill beside the A2, about 2 miles north of town. Spacious albeit modestly appointed rooms have telephones and private bath with hot water. A refurbishment was semi-complete at last visit. The restaurant offers somewhat elegant dining.

Invercauld Great House & Hotel (☎ 965-2750, fax 965-2751; e info@invercauld .com.jm; PO Box 12, Black River; rooms US$56-68, suites US$85) includes an impressive centenarian house with gable roofs, bay windows, valances, and intricate fretwork. It has 20 rooms – varying in size and mood – furnished with period antiques and replicas. More modern units feature 32 air-con rooms and suites with private baths and balconies. The hotel has an airy dining room, pool, tennis court, and gift shop. Tours are offered.

Places to Eat

There are plenty of stalls by the market and bus station selling I-tal food. The best is **King Lion Reggae Centre** (☎ 965-9466; Market St), serving health foods and natural juices for under US$3.

Willows Restaurant (US$5-24; open 8am-10pm) at the Invercauld Great House & Hotel, is the fanciest place around. It serves Jamaican and continental favorites in elegant surrounds.

Bridge House Inn (entrées from US$8; open 8am-10pm) serves seafood and Jamaican dishes such as curried goat (a reader complained 'yeuch!'), washed down with health drinks made of beetroot juice and Irish moss.

Bayside Restaurant (17 High St; US$3-12) is a self-proclaimed 'pastry and pub' popular with locals and serving an eclectic menu of Jamaican and continental fare, plus pastries. **Bayside Jerk & BBQ Centre** is at the rear, overhanging the sea.

Waterloo Guest House (see Places to Stay above) has a modest restaurant with an inexpensive Jamaican menu, plus an earthy bar serving ice-cream sodas (US$2.50) and milk shakes (US$1.50).

Riverside Dock Restaurant (☎ 965-9489; open 10am-10pm Mon-Sat, 1pm-9pm Sun) is a Chinese restaurant offering excellent Asian cuisine, including sushi (US$7) and other Japanese fare on weekends. It's open to the river. The spring rolls (US$2.50) are a meal in themselves. Service can be slow.

Cloggy's on the Beach, on Crane Rd, is a simple beachside seafood eatery serving

shrimp (US$11), lobster (US$10.50), and steamed and stewed fish. **Juici Beef Patties** (High St) is a good place to pick up quick snacks.

There's a **supermarket** in the Hendricks Building, and another one 100 yards north. You can buy fruits, vegetables, and meats at the open-air **produce market** on Market St, but hygiene is questionable.

THE GREAT MORASS

This 125-sq-mile wetland extends inland from the mouth of the Black River. It is separated by the narrow Lacovia Gorge into the Lower Morass and Upper Morass, and fed by Jamaica's longest river, navigable for about 12 miles upriver. Beyond the confluence of the YS, Middle Quarters, and Black Rivers, the mangroves broadens into marshy meadows of tall sedges and reeds.

The waters are stained by tannins from decomposed vegetation in the Great Morass, a complex ecosystem and a vital preserve for more than a hundred bird species, including cinnamon-colored jacanas, egrets, whistling ducks, water hens, and seven species of herons. The Morass also forms Jamaica's most significant refuge for crocodiles. About 300 live in the swamps.

Feisty game fish are plentiful, including snook and tarpon. On rare occasions, endangered manatees may even be seen near the river estuary.

Locals take to the waters in dugout canoes, tending funnel-shaped shrimp pots made of bamboo in the traditional manner of their West African forebears.

Boat Tours

A number of places in Black River offer Great Morass tours. **South Coast Safaris** (☎ 965-2513, fax 962-9272; e jcsafari@ hotmail.com; PO Box 129, Mandeville), on the east side of the bridge, offers 90-minute journeys aboard the *Safari Queen* at 9am, 11am, 2pm, and 4pm daily. Trips cost US$15 per person, or US$31 including buffet lunch and a visit to YS Falls. The trips leave from the old warehouse on the east bank of the river.

Similar tours at similar prices are offered by **St Elizabeth Attractions** (☎ 965-2374, 965-2229), behind the Hendricks Building, at 9am, 11am, 2pm, and 3:30pm; and **Irie Safaris** (☎ 965-2221, fax 965-2466; office at 12 High St), wharfside from a jetty just north of the bus station, at 90-minute intervals from 9am to 4:30pm daily.

You can also hire a guide to take you upriver in his canoe or boat for about US$10-20 roundtrip. Ask near the bridge in town.

Midday tours are best for spotting crocodiles; early and later tours are better for birding. Take a shade hat and some mosquito repellent.

What a Croc!

Saltwater crocodiles, once common around virtually the entire coast of Jamaica, are now relegated to a few areas along the island's south coast, most notably the Great Morass. They were once so numerous that one of the earliest laws in Jamaica proclaimed that an 'alligator' should be on the Coat of Arms. Ruthless hunting has greatly reduced their numbers. They have been protected since 1971.

The American crocodile – called an 'alligator' in Jamaica – can grow to 12 feet. Nonetheless, it is relatively shy and eats mostly fish, utilizing conical teeth well-adapted for capturing slippery prey. It goes long periods without eating and can survive on 10lb of food a week.

Early morning is a good time to see crocodiles, when they are sunning on the banks to restore heat lost at night. A legacy of the dinosaur period, the crocodile maintains a body temperature of 77°F by alternating between shade, water, and sun. It hunts at night.

When submerged, its beady eyes watch above the water.

The animal can be seen in the Great Morass, Alligator Hole (Canoe Valley), Font Hill Reserve, and to a lesser degree, Negril.

MIDDLE QUARTERS

This small village on the A2, 8 miles north of Black River, is renowned for its women higglers who stand at the roadside selling delicious pepper shrimps – pronounced 'swimp' locally – cooked at roadside grills. The shrimp (actually, they're crayfish) are caught in traps made in centuries-old African tradition from split bamboo. US$2 will buy a bagful. Careful! They're spicy.

Danny Bennett's Orchid Farm (☎ 965-2229), about 2 miles south of Middle Quarters, shows orchids under shade awnings. It's not open as a tourist entity, but visitors are welcome.

YS FALLS

This series of eight cascades (☎ 634-2454; ℮ ysfalls@cwjamaica.com; open 9:30am-3:30pm Tues-Sun; closed last 2 weeks Oct; adult/child US$10/6) fall 120 feet, separated by cool pools perfect for swimming. They're hemmed in by limestone cliffs and surrounded by towering forest.

A tractor-drawn jitney takes visitors to the cascades, where you'll find picnic grounds and a tree house, plus a rope-swing over the pools. Be careful! The eddies are strong, especially after rains, when the falls are torrential. A stone staircase and pathway follow the cascades upriver. There are no lockers, however, so you'll need to keep an eye on your stuff while you bathe.

A natural swimming pool was being added at last visit.

Admission includes a guide. There's a gift store, and **Mikey's Grill** serving fish and chicken dishes, plus burgers (US$1-4).

The falls are on the YS Estate, 3½ miles north of the A2 (the turnoff is a mile east of Middle Quarters). The entrance is just north of the junction of the B6 toward Maggotty.

St Elizabeth Attractions (☎ 997-6055) and **South Coast Safaris** (☎ 965-2513) operate tours to YS Falls every half-hour from 9am to 3:30pm from Black River.

Buses travel via YS Falls from the Shakespeare Plaza in Maggotty. On the A2, buses, coasters, and route taxis will drop you at the junction to YS Falls, from where you can walk (it's about 2 miles) or catch an Ipswich-bound route taxi.

IPSWICH CAVES

These limestone caverns, about 5 miles north of YS Falls, are full of stalactites and stalagmites. The cave entrance is at Ipswich, an almost derelict hamlet on the old railway line between Montego Bay and Kingston. You can hire a guide to lead you into the stygian chambers for a small fee.

The turnoff is off the B6, about 2 miles north of YS Falls. You'll be glad for a 4WD.

BAMBOO AVENUE

This photogenic archway of towering bamboo has been made famous on tourist-board posters. The 2½-mile-long tunnel shades the A2 between Middle Quarters and Lacovia. Bamboo Avenue was planted by the owners of Holland Estate and is maintained by staff from the Hope Garden in Kingston.

In the fall, the 5km **Holland Bamboo Run** (☎ 929-9200) goes from Bamboo Avenue to Santa Cruz.

LACOVIA

This sprawling village extends for 2 miles east of Bamboo Avenue, and is divided into West Lacovia, Lacovia Tombstone, and East Lacovia.

The only site of interest is the two side-by-side **tombstones** in the center of the junction in front of the Texaco gas station at Lacovia Tombstone. An unlikely legend says that the two young men who lie buried here killed each other in a tavern duel in 1738.

Carlyn Resorts (☎ 607-4826; e danpete@hotmail.com; Lacovia PO; rooms US$15-20) is a wood-and-stone, two-story structure in East Lacovia with five rooms (four new rooms were being added at last visit). They're small and basic but clean, and have private bath (no hot water) and fans. There's a restaurant.

CASHOO OSTRICH PARK

This park (☎ 966-2222, fax 634-0954; e mpvet@cwjamaica.com; PO Box 284; open 10am-4:30pm only during school and public holidays; adult/child US$6/3.50), set on 100 acres of farmland about 2 miles south of East Lacovia, has about two dozen African ostriches. Your guide will indulge you with trivia: ostriches weigh up to 350lb, produce eggs weighing 5lb, can run up to 50mph, and can cover 20 feet in one stride.

The facility includes a large fruit orchard and herb garden, plus a petting zoo with an emu, donkeys, hens, ducks, geese, and swans. There's a kids' playground, bumper cars, swimming pool, badminton court, sand volleyball, and a bar. You can saddle up for horseback rides (US$2).

SANTA CRUZ

Santa Cruz (population 5500) is a bustling market town, and the most important commercial center in southwest Jamaica. During the past few decades it has grown modestly wealthy on revenues from the local bauxite industry. Before that, Santa Cruz was a market center for horses and mules bred locally for the British army. A livestock market is still held on Saturday. Otherwise the town has zero attractions.

Banks include **Scotiabank** (☎ 966-2230; 77 Main St) and **National Commercial Bank** (☎ 966-2204; 7 Coke Dr). **Dr Oliver Myers** (☎ 966-2106; 23 Coke Dr) has a clinic near the **police station** (☎ 966-2289), 200 yards south of the town center on the road to Malvern.

Donbar Guest House (☎ 966-9382; Trevmar Park; Santa Cruz PO; rooms US$32) is a beautiful home in secluded gardens; it's signed at the west end of town. It has five rooms cooled by fans. Some share a bathroom with cold water only. The homey lounge is a surrealistic zoo of gaily painted ceramic animals. Meals can be prepared to order.

Chariots Hotel (☎ 966-2334, 966-3860, fax 966-4880; e pooh@cwjamaica.com; Leeds PO, Santa Cruz; rooms from US$36, suites US$100), at Leeds, 4 miles south of town at the base of the Santa Cruz Mountains on the road to Malvern, is modern and spacious. It has 20 modest rooms, some with air-con, and suites with king-size beds.

Young residents of the picturesque town of Black River

The village of Middle Quarters is renowned for its delicious pepper shrimps cooked at roadside grills.

Fiery sunset skies over Kingston

Boats moored at Port Royal in Kingston

Roadside grill offering roasted corn and other snacks, Kingston

Hind's Restaurant & Bakery (☎ 966-2234; Santa Cruz Plaza, Main St; US$0.50-6) sells baked goods and is a clean, simple place to enjoy Jamaican fare, such as brown stew and curried goat.

Juici Beef Patties (Shop 30, Beadles Plaza, Main St) sells veggie and beef patties for US$0.40. **Fruity's** (Shop 27, Philip's Plaza, Main St) serves delicious ice cream cones.

Club Classique Disco & Lounge (Ledgister & Sons Plaza; open 9pm-3am Wed-Sun) has theme nights. Wednesday is dancehall night, drawing Jamaicans from afar.

Santa Cruz is a main stop for buses, coasters, and route taxis going between Kingston, Mandeville, and Black River. They arrive and depart from the transportation center on the A2, at the east end of Santa Cruz.

GUTTERS & SPUR TREE HILL
Gutters, 10 miles east of Santa Cruz, sits astride the border of St Elizabeth and Manchester parishes at the foot of **Spur Tree Hill** – a long, steep, switchback climb up the Don Figuerero Mountains to Mandeville.

At the top of the hill you can look out over the Essex Valley and the Santa Cruz Mountains. The valley floor is dominated by the Alpart alumina factory at Nain, 5 miles to the southeast, and aglitter at night.

You can admire the view midway up the hill at any of several restaurants.

Nassau Mountains & Cockpit Country (South)

The plains of St Elizabeth are bordered to the north by this low, narrow range of deeply forested hills that merge into the rugged Cockpit Country. Few roads penetrate the hills, where the sparse population is mostly involved in subsistence farming.

Between the Nassau Mountains and Cockpit Country is the wide Siloah Valley, carpeted with sugarcane.

The Cockpit Country is easily accessed from the south via the hamlet of Troy.

See Cockpit Country (North) in the Montego Bay & Northwest Coast chapter for more details, including trails and information on hiring guides.

MAGGOTTY
This regional center, 7 miles north of Lacovia, is laid out on a bend of the Black River at the western end of the Siloah Valley. The upper Black River has been used for canoeing and raft trips offering Class III rapids deep in the Black River Gorge, south of town. You can hike through the gorge, which features a series of 28 roaring cascades with intermittent pools good for swimming. It's an hour's relatively easy trek to the bottom, but the return journey is a stiff hike. No commercial operators were offering trips at last visit, but you can go it alone if you have your own watercraft.

Public vehicles arrive and depart from opposite Shakespeare Plaza, at the north end of Maggotty, connecting to Mandeville and Black River.

Apple Valley Park
This 418-acre family nature park (☎ 963-9508, fax 963-9561; Maggotty PO; adult/child weekends US$6/3.50, weekdays US$4.50/2.50; open 10am-5pm Tues, Thur-Sun), on the south side of Maggotty, surrounds an 18th-century great house. The park has two small lakes and offers fishing and a variety of touristy activities that appeal to Jamaicans. There are paddleboat rides and go-karts, plus canoeing on the Black River. Much of the park is a forest reserve good for birding. The owners also operate a tractor-pulled jitney from the old railway station in Maggotty.

Cycling Tours & Rentals
Manfred's Jamaican Mountain Bike Tours (☎ 705-745-8210 in Canada; e manfreds@ peterboro.net) offers a weeklong tour of the south coast (but based at Apple Valley) with daily cycling excursions geared to moderate riders. A support vehicle is provided. Trips

are offered in midwinter only and cost C$1150 or US$795 excluding airfare but including transfers and accommodations. You can rent a bike for US$25 per day.

Places to Stay & Eat

Apple Valley Park (camping per person US$4.50, bunks US$10, cabin doubles US$18) has camping sites and rustic cabins. Patrick and Lucille Lee, the Chinese-Jamaican couple who run Apple Valley, also have bunks and private rooms in their 18th-century, red-roofed great house south of town. It has five bedrooms and four bathrooms, plus a lounge. Guests have kitchen privileges at the guest house, but there is also an open-air restaurant serving traditional Jamaican dishes (US$2-8). If you can catch carp, silver perch, or red snapper yourself, Lucille will cook it for you (US$2 per pound). Apple Valley Park is reached from behind the police station.

Poinciana Guest House (☎ 963-9676; Maggotty PO; rooms US$17-22), 100 yards south of Apple Valley Park, is a delightful old house on the hill behind the post office. It has six modestly furnished rooms with private bath. There's hot water (when the heater works), and a homey TV lounge. Six more rooms are in an annex. Meals are prepared. Ask at the Happy Time Restaurant.

The air-conditioned **Valley Restaurant** (☎ 963-9508), opposite Apple Valley Park, is open only on weekends (11am to 9pm) or by reservation on weekdays. It offers Jamaican dishes, including vegetarian options. Set breakfasts are US$3 and dinners are US$6.

ACCOMPONG

This lonesome, end-of-the-road village clinging to a hillside on the southwest side of the Cockpit Country is the sole remaining village in western Jamaica inhabited by descendants of the Maroons. It touts itself for that reason, but is also a base for exploring the region of Cockpit Country known as Me No Sen You No Come.

The village still enjoys aspects of quasi-autonomy, and is headed by a 'Colonel' (currently Sydney Peddie) elected by secret ballot for a period of five years. He appoints a council, which he oversees. The inhabitants refuse to pay government taxes, which might explain the dire state of the road!

George Higgins, a local craftsman, still makes goombay drums.

A **public telephone** (☎ 997-9101) opposite Peyton Place Pub serves the whole village. You can buy phone cards at the pub.

The traditional **Accompong Maroon Festival** is held each January 6. For information, call Maroon Attraction Tours (see Getting There & Away later in this section).

Things to See & Do

Accompong is centered on the tiny 'Parade Ground,' where a Presbyterian church looks over a small monument honoring Cudjoe, the Maroon leader (the statue next to it is that of Leonard Parkinson, another Maroon freedom fighter). The **Accompong Community Centre & Museum** is opposite the monument and contains a motley miscellany of goombay drums, a musket, a sword, baskets and other artifacts from the Maroon era. Entry is included only as part of a community tour (US$10).

Three tours are offered, including one to the **Peace Caves** (US$40), where Cudjoe signed the 1739 peace treaty with the British. The cave entrance is almost an hour's hike from Accompong.

Places to Stay & Eat

Peyton Place Pub (Accompong PO; rooms US$12) is a bar and grocery store offering three small, simple, but clean rooms that share a small shower and toilet. They're in the basement and are cool and have windows. The bar serves basic fare for a few dollars and is a colorful place to sup with locals. It features the **Night Rider Disco**, with go-go dancers.

Mystic Pass Villas (no ☎ ; single US$50, double US$60), nearby, has simply furnished, African-style, conical thatched cottages with flush toilets and outside shower.

Getting There & Away

Route taxis run from Shakespeare Plaza in Maggotty (US$1.50).

The route from Maggotty is well signed if driving, but the road is horribly potholed.

Maroon Attraction Tours (☎ 952-4546, fax 979-0308; 32 Church St, Montego Bay) offers excursions from MoBay for US$50, Tuesday, Thursday, and Saturday.

APPLETON RUM ESTATE

The Appleton sugar estate and rum factory (☎ 963-9215, fax 963-9218; w www.appleton rum.com; Siloah PO; closed Sun), a mile northeast of Maggotty, enjoys a magnificent setting in the midst of the Siloah Valley. The yeasty smell of molasses hangs over the cane fields, luring you toward the largest and oldest distillery in Jamaica. The factory has been blending the famous Appleton brand of rums since 1749. It is owned by J Wray & Nephew, Jamaica's largest rum producer.

There's a well-stocked gift store, and a snack bar serves food from 9am to 5pm.

Visitors view a video before setting out on a guided tour of the distillery, ending with a rum-tasting in the 'John Wray Tavern.' Factory tours cost US$12, including rum tasting. A scale model of the factory shows the entire operation. Lunch with coffee costs US$6.

A motor-coach excursion, the **Appleton Estate Rum Tour**, departs from MoBay daily (US$65), and from Ocho Rios (US$65) and Runaway Bay (US$60) on Tuesday and Wednesday. Contact **Caribic Vacations** (☎ 953-9878 in Montego Bay, 957-3309 in Negril, 974-9106 in Ocho Rios) or **Jamaica Estate Tours Ltd** at the Appleton Rum Estate itself.

QUICK STEP

This remote mountain hamlet, 8 miles north of Siloah, offers magnificent views over the portion of the Cockpit Country known as the District of Look Behind. It's eerie and extremely foreboding: a chaos of honeycombed limestone cliffs hewn into bizarre shapes and cockpits (with deep forested bowls up to 500 feet across).

North of Quick Step, the road peters out. Hiking trails lead into the heart of the Cockpits, but you are well advised to hire a guide (see Albert Town in the Montego Bay

Maroon Heritage Theme Park

In 2002, the Jamaican government announced its intent to create this theme park as a 'millennium project' inspired by the creation of Highway 2000 (see the boxed text 'Highway 2000' in the Getting Around chapter).

The planned attraction will include an Eco-Park & Aerial Tram, which will feature four-seat cages suspended on steel overhead cables that take visitors through the forest canopy. There will also be a Maroon Museum & Heritage Yards, with various venues around Accompong, which will include a Middle Passage Museum at Cudjoe's Lookout; a Heritage Museum and Research Centre; a Kumina Yard with drumming and similar performances; and recreational activities such as hot-air ballooning.

& Northwest Coast chapter). One trail leads to Windsor Cave, a full day's hike. It's easy to get lost and this is no place for that. *Don't attempt it alone!*

BALACLAVA

Balaclava sits atop a ridge at the east end of the Siloah Valley. If you're climbing uphill from the west, it's worth resting at the ridge crest to take in the view of the valley laid out below, smothered in sugarcane as flat and green as a billiard table.

An attractive Anglican church and the disused railway station are about the only buildings of interest.

Beware of the dangerous railway crossing hidden atop the hill on the west side of town.

TROY & AROUND

Two miles northeast of Balaclava, the B6 turns southeast for Mandeville; another road (the B10) leads north and climbs to Troy on the border with Trelawny parish. The latter is a spectacular drive as you climb up through a series of dramatic gorges, with the road clinging to the sheer face of the Cockpits.

Troy is the southeastern gateway to the Cockpit Country. It sits in a valley bottom and is surrounded by sugarcane fields. It is also a center of yam cultivation, which grow on tall runners. **St Silas church** is worth a look.

Auchtembeddie, 3 miles south of Troy, is a choice spot for spelunkers, who head for **Coffee River Cave**. It is totally undeveloped for tourism, but local guides will escort you for a negotiated fee.

A dirt road leads 2 miles north from Troy to Tyre, a hamlet on the edge of the Cockpits. Beyond Tyre, the road fades into a bush-enshrouded trail. From here you can hike to Windsor (about 15 miles); see Cockpit Country (North) in the Montego Bay & Northwest Coast chapter. Don't attempt it alone, as there are several forks and it is easy to get lost.

To hire a guide, contact the **Southern Trelawny Environmental Agency** (see Albert Town in the Montego Bay & Northwest Coast chapter) in Albert Town, 11 miles northeast of Troy.

Treasure Beach & Environs

The coastal strip southeast of Black River is sheltered from rains for most of the year by the Santa Cruz Mountains, so there is none of the lush greenery of the north coast. Instead, you'll find acacia trees and cactus towering up to 30 feet.

The region is unsullied by tourism. It's possible here to slip into the kind of lazy, no-frills tropical lifestyle almost impossible to achieve elsewhere on the island's coast.

TREASURE BEACH
Treasure Beach is the generic name given to four coves – Billy's Bay, Frenchman's Bay,

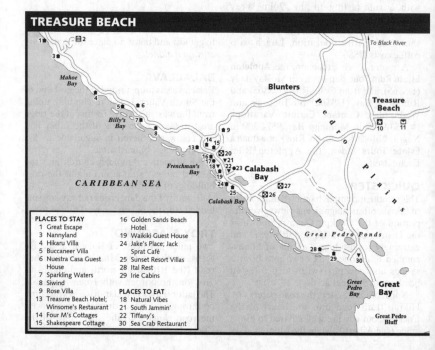

TREASURE BEACH

To Black River

Mahoe Bay

Blunters

Treasure Beach

Billy's Bay

Frenchman's Bay

CARIBBEAN SEA

Calabash Bay

Calabash Bay

Great Pedro Ponds

Great Pedro Bay

Great Bay

Great Pedro Bluff

PLACES TO STAY	
1 Great Escape	16 Golden Sands Beach Hotel
3 Nannyland	19 Waikiki Guest House
4 Hikaru Villa	24 Jake's Place; Jack Sprat Café
5 Buccaneer Villa	25 Sunset Resort Villas
6 Nuestra Casa Guest House	28 Ital Rest
7 Sparkling Waters	29 Irie Cabins
8 Siwind	
9 Rose Villa	**PLACES TO EAT**
13 Treasure Beach Hotel; Winsome's Restaurant	18 Natural Vibes
14 Four M's Cottages	21 South Jammin'
15 Shakespeare Cottage	22 Tiffany's
	30 Sea Crab Restaurant

Calabash Bay, and Great Pedro Bay – with rocky headlands separating lonesome, coral-colored sand beaches. Calabash Bay is backed by the Great Pedro Ponds, which are good spots for birding.

You won't find a more authentically charming and relaxing place in Jamaica. The sense of remoteness, easy pace, and graciousness of the local farmers and fisher folk attract foreign travelers seeking an away-from-it-all, cares-to-the-wind lifestyle. Many have settled – much to local pride.

Water sports haven't yet caught on, although the waves are good for body-surfing (beware of a sometimes vicious undertow). You may even see marine turtles coming ashore to lay eggs (many local fishermen still catch them illegally for their meat and shells).

Developers are buying up land, and it can be only a matter of time before the first major resorts appear. A citizens' committee meets monthly to regulate impending development. Amenities are limited.

It's said that Scottish sailors were shipwrecked near Treasure Beach in the 19th century, accounting for the preponderance of fair hair, green eyes, and reddish skin.

Unless otherwise noted, the address for all entities in this section is 'Great Bay District, Calabash Bay PA, Treasure Beach, St Elizabeth.'

Information

Jake's Place (see Places to Stay later in this section) is an unofficial tourist information source. On the Internet, a good starting point is **W** www.treasurebeach.net. **Global Travel** (☎ 965-0547), a travel agency, is in Treasure Beach Shopping Complex.

The nearest bank is in Southfield, 10 miles east of Treasure Beach. The **post office** is on a hillside beside the **police station** (☎ 965-0163), betwixt Calabash Bay and Pedro Cross.

Island Treasures (☎ 965-0748; **e** treasurebeach@cwjamaica.com), in Kingfisher Plaza, offers Internet service (US$2.50 for 15 minutes; US$6.50 per hour), as does **Lennon Wood Music & Things** (☎ 965-0476), in Treasure Beach Shopping Complex.

For medical problems, Dr Valerie M Elliott is available on call (☎ 607-9074; 7am-10pm Mon, Tues & Fri).

Joshua Lee Stein (☎ 965-0583, 965-0635) offers massages (US$60/hour) at Jake's Place, but he also does the rounds on his tricycle with folding massage table in tow. Also recommended is Shirley Genus' (☎ 426-9723) traditional Jamaican herbal steam bath and massage (US$40-60) at Ital Rest (see Places to Stay later in this section).

Caijan Museum & Art Gallery

This totally offbeat museum (☎ 990-6641; admission free), in the hills a mile west of Billy Bay, is run by Rastafarian 'architect' Brother John Deer in his house – which looks like a Greek troglodyte monastery built into the bare rock wall – and is packed with antiques and an eclectic array of miscellany. A dauntingly steep path to the museum begins at a derelict Ford Prefect beside the road.

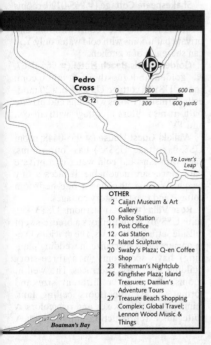

Pedro Cross

| 0 | 300 | 600 m |
| 0 | 300 | 600 yards |

◎ 12

To Lover's Leap

OTHER
2 Caijan Museum & Art Gallery
10 Police Station
11 Post Office
12 Gas Station
17 Island Sculpture
20 Swaby's Plaza; Q-en Coffee Shop
23 Fisherman's Nightclub
26 Kingfisher Plaza; Island Treasures; Damian's Adventure Tours
27 Treasure Beach Shopping Complex; Global Travel; Lennon Wood Music & Things

Boatman's Bay

Treasure Beach Foundation

The Treasure Beach Foundation (Breds; ☎ 965-3000, fax 965-0552; ⓦ www.treasure beach.net/guide/gs/main.html) is dedicated to fostering heritage pride, sports, health, and education among the community. Work includes restoring decrepit housing, sponsorship of a soccer team and a basketball team, and the introduction of a computer lab at the local school.

Donations are welcome.

Organized Tours

At Jake's Place (see Places to Stay later in this section), Jason Henzell arranges boat rides along the coast and into the Great Morass, plus fishing trips and mountain-bike tours (US$30-35 per person), and Julie Kolipulos offers daylong walking tours (US$30).

Dennis Abrahams (☎ 965-3084) and Allan Daley (☎ 965-0552) are fishers who will take you fishing, snorkeling, or on tours of Black River (US$20).

Treasure Tours (☎ 965-0126; ⓔ treasure-tours@cwjamaica.com) offers one-day excursions locally and farther afield.

Damian's Adventure Tours (☎ 965-0224, 965-3101; ⓔ sandybay9@yahoo.com; or contact Jake's Place), in Kingfisher Plaza, offers mountain biking locally, plus hiking and snorkeling.

Special Events

The Treasure Beach Off-Road Triathlon (☎ 965-0635; ⓔ jakes@cwjamaica.com) is held each April and May. The Calabash Literary Festival (☎ 979-8378; ⓔ oz@in fochan.com), a Memorial Day (late May) event, draws leading literary voices from throughout the Caribbean.

In mid-October, the three-day Great Jamaican Canoe Race and Hook 'n' Line Fishing Tournament features the Great Jamaica Canoe Race, a bikini contest, and music and dance. Contact Jake's Place (see Places to Stay below).

A New Year's Eve bonfire party at Fisherman's Beach is an institution.

Places to Stay

Budget Nannyland (☎ 962-0522; camping up to US$15, room US$15, tree house & cabin US$20), at Mahoe Bay, is an offbeat, countercultural kind of place. It has two basically furnished rooms, plus a nice, albeit rustic tree house and a cabin perched at the edge of the cliff, plus a barebones room with private bathroom above the house. Campers have access to outside bathrooms, water, a kitchen, and hammocks slung between trees. Trails lead down to a lonesome red-sand beach with coral tide pools.

Caijan Museum (☎ 990-6641; camping US$10, cottages US$25) rents two stylishly funky cottages at the museum. There's no electricity, but the location and stunning views make amends. You can also camp in the museum grounds. It's best to call between 5pm and 6pm.

Shakespeare Cottage (☎ 965-0120; rooms from US$12), 200 yards east of the Treasure Beach Hotel, has five rooms with fans and private bathrooms with cold water only. You can share use of a kitchen.

Golden Sands Beach Hotel (☎ 965-0167; ⓔ goldensandsguesthouse@yahoo.com; rooms US$30, cottage US$60), has 20 modestly furnished rooms with fans and private bath. It also offers a cottage with air-con and TV.

Waikiki Guest House (☎ 965-0448; room US$30, cottage US$55) has four rooms, each with fans and cold water in a private bath; prices are negotiable. It faces a tiny beach. Waikiki also has a one-bedroom cottage and two two-story cottages.

Rose Villa (☎ 965-3144; rooms US$35-50, suite US$90), inland, enjoys a breeze-swept hillside setting with views. The gracious live-in owners (who specialize in wedding planning) have six rooms in a three-story building with broad terraces. The well-lit rooms – each of a different size and format – have tile floors, ceiling fans, minifridges, safety boxes, and rich colors. A suite has a reproduction antique bed. A caterer will prepare meals on request

(US$10 premium per room). A garden library was to be built at last visit.

Mid-Range **Four M's Cottages** (☎ 965-0131; e fourmscottage@hotmail.com; PO Box 4, Mountainside, St Elizabeth; camping US$10, singles/doubles US$30/40; about 400 yards from the beach, has camping beneath shade trees, and a modern house has six rooms of varying size. Windows are screened, and there are mosquito nets over some beds. Rooms can get hot, although they have fans (but no air-con). Each has a private bath with hot water. The live-in owners grant guests kitchen privileges. No credit cards are accepted.

Irie Cabins (☎ 965-3231; cabins summer/winter US$25/30) has three simple thatched wooden cabins amid lawns about 400 yards inland from Great Bay. They have bare-bones furnishings and share an outside toilet and shower.

Next door, **Ital Rest** (☎ 965-0126, 421-8909; per tent summer/winter US$10/15, room US$30/40, cabins US$50/70) is an atmospheric out-of-the-way place with two exquisite, if rustic and clean, all-wood thatched cabins with showers, toilets, and solar electricity. An upstairs room in the house has a sundeck. Kitchen facilities are shared. There's a small thatched bar, a fantastic herbal steam bath, and camping spots beneath shade trees (plus outdoor showers and toilets); tents and foam mattresses can be rented (US$3).

Nuestra Casa Guest House (☎ 965-0152; doubles per night US$40) is a highly recommended B&B at Billy's Bay. This gem is run by Lillian Brooks, a delightful English lady, and her son Roger, a burly chap with a giant-size humor. A wide veranda has rockers, and a rooftop sundeck is shaded by umbrellas. The reclusive three-bedroom house is tastefully decorated. Two rooms share a bathroom; a third has its own. All have lofty wooden ceilings. It's a tremendous bargain at these rates, which go down for longer stays. Breakfasts (English or Jamaican) are US$5.

Siwind (☎/fax 965-0582; PO Box 40, Treasure Beach; rooms winter US$75), near Nuestra Casa, on a headland overlooking a pocket-size beach between Frenchman's and Billy's Bays, is a five-bedroom house. Each room has a private bath with hot water. Meals are cooked to order.

Great Escape (☎ 800-641-7751; e great escape@jamaicavilla.com; 70847 Claire Dr, Union, MI 49130, USA; per week summer US$1200-3370, winter US$1500-4270), about 1 mile west of Mahoe Bay, is a contemporary three-bedroom, fully-staffed villa on ten acres, with swimming pool and shaded sundeck over the ocean. Rooms have CDs, and a lounge has an entertainment system. A cook prepares meals. A one-week minimum applies. Rates include airport transfers.

Top End **Hikaru Villa** (☎ 800-526-2432, ☎/fax 860-247-0759 in the USA; e DonO Noel@cs.com; c/o the Noels, 141 Ridgefield St, Hartford, CT 06112, USA; villa per week summer/winter from US$1225/1495) is a fully staffed, four-bedroom beachfront villa with private tennis court, croquet lawn, and a sun terrace with 50-foot lap pool. Rates are for up to four people (more for additional people). The owners offer a money-back 'no rain guarantee' in summer.

Sparkling Waters (☎ 927-8020; e reserva tions@sparklingwatersvilla.com; 5 Marescaux Rd, Kingston 5; guest house/villa per week US$1500/1800) has an exquisitely furnished, beach-facing, two-bedroom guest house with TV and VCR, and patio. A similarly appointed two-bedroom villa has a cathedral lounge. There's an outside Jacuzzi and pool.

Treasure Beach Hotel (☎ 965-0110, fax 965-2544; ☎ 800-742-4276 in North America; e treasurebhotel@cwjamaica.com; PO Box 5, Black River; superior singles/doubles summer US$80/90, winter US$90/100; deluxe singles or doubles summer/winter US$103/130) is a rambling property nestled on a hillside overlooking the beach. The 36 air-con rooms include 16 spacious, deluxe oceanfront suites with king-size four-poster beds, cable TVs, tile floors, and patios. A lounge has a TV. There are two swimming pools, a whirlpool, and a volleyball court; sailing and snorkeling are offered. The hotel also has an all-inclusive plan.

Sunset Resort Villas (☎ 965-0143, fax 965-0555; ☎ 800-786-8452 in North America; e srv@sunsetresort.com; rooms US$80-165, villa US$230-935) takes up five acres on Calabash Bay and has ten rooms with aircon and modern furnishings, plus a spacious and elegant three-bedroom, nine-room villa. They share a pool and a basketball court.

Jake's Place (☎ 965-3000, fax 956-0552; ☎ 800-688-7678, 305-531-8800 in North America; ☎ 020-7440-4360 in the UK; w www.jakesjamaica.com; rooms US$95-195, cottages US$225-295) wins the award for the 'chicest shack' between Negril and Kingston. Eclectic and endearing are understatements for this rustic, rainbow-colored retreat run by Sally and Jason Henzell. The place is totally offbeat, yet draws an international A-list of famous names. Local kids and fishermen wander in and out as if they own the place, adding to Jake's unique charm.

There are 13 single rooms (many perched over the sea), four two-bedroom cottages, a three-bedroom villa (rooms can be rented separately) like a mini-Moroccan *ksar*, and a one-up/one-down house – 'Seahorses' – featuring an exterior spiral staircase, terra-cotta tile floors, tile and glass-brick walk-in showers, and exquisite handmade beds. The decor follows Greek and Moslem motifs, with onion-dome curves, bloodred floors, and walls and rough-hewn doors inset with colored bottles and glass beads. Many beds are metal frame antiques. The exquisite pool – lamplit at night – is shaded by a spreading tree.

Jake's has two restaurants. Local mento bands perform; moonlight poetry readings are hosted; and Jason arranges tours and activities (see Organized Tours & Fishing earlier in this section).

Jake's Place handles reservations for a number of exquisite cottages and villas, including **Buccaneer Villa** (c/o Jake's; or ☎ 800-338-1506, 703-765-5449 in the USA; w www.treasurebeach.com; weekly US$2400-3000), designed and tastefully appointed in New Mexican style.

Other villas are featured at the website w www.treasurebeach.net.

Places to Eat

Jake's Place (open 7:30am-10:30pm) is the most atmospheric place – an open-sided wooden restaurant with low lighting and hip music. You can also dine poolside on the patio out back. The menu varies daily, but typical dishes include pumpkin soup (US$2), baked lamb (US$13), stuffed crab (US$7), and chocolate cake (US$2.50). Filling lunches include vegetarian treats such as lima-bean soup (US$3).

Also at Jake's Place, **Jack Sprat Café** (open 7am-midnight), a barefoot and buttoned-down beachside eatery, is open for breakfast, lunch and dinner and offers a simple menu of sandwiches, salads, smoked marlin, and lobster, plus superb pizzas at night (US$3-8).

South Jammin' (☎ 965-0136; open 8:30am-10pm) is a good spot for breakfast of an omelette with toast and fruit salad (US$3.50) or banana pancakes (US$2). Its lunch and dinner menu (US$6-14) includes steamed fish, pepper steak, curried goat, and lasagna. It offers shady patio or indoor dining.

Tiffany's (☎ 965-0300; US$4-12; open noon-10pm), nearby, is elegant and romantic. The eclectic menu includes burgers, T-bone steaks, curried goat, and salads. You feel totally out of place being served by waiters all dressed up as if the place were in Paris.

Natural Vibes (no ☎), 50 yards west of South Jammin', offers such fare as chicken chop suey (US$3.50) and beef stew (US$3).

Winsome's Restaurant (dishes US$7-20), at Treasure Beach Hotel, is a pleasant alternative. It serves Jamaican and continental dishes.

At Great Pedro Bay, **Sea Crab Restaurant** (☎ 965-3456; open 8am-9pm) is a popular and simple eatery serving oxtail (US$4), vegetarian dishes, and tasty seafood for less than US$5.

Q-en Coffee Shop (☎ 812-9505), in Swaby's Plaza, is a small grocery store.

Entertainment

Treasure Beach is a sleepy place at night. **Fisherman's Nightclub** (up a dirt road behind Tiffany's) is the domain of local youth (mostly male) skanking to sounds from a selector (DJ); there's also a pool hall and bar at the back. **South Jammin'**, also called Lisa's Place, draws locals for darts, billiards and dominoes. **Jake's Place** is the place to be for its infamous cocktail hour poolside, and for its weekly beach bonfires. The café here hosts small concerts, poetry readings, and once-weekly outdoor movies, and it has happy hour from 5:30pm to 6:30pm, when a friendly Rasta called 'Fabulous' acts as sound selector.

Shopping

One of the best craft stores is on the front lawn at **Jake's Place** (see Places to Stay earlier in this section).

Island Treasures (☎ 965-0748; e treasure beach@cwjamaica.com), in Kingfisher Plaza, is also well stocked and sells a wide range of gifts, including batiks, swimwear, sandals, coffee, and arts and crafts.

At **Island Sculpture** (☎ 831-6612), opposite Swaby's Plaza, a local called 'LT' crafts precious lignum vitae into abstract animal and mystical forms.

Lennon Wood Music & Things (☎ 965-0476), in Treasure Beach Shopping Complex, sells music CDs.

Getting There & Around

There is no direct service to Treasure Beach from Montego Bay, Negril, or Kingston. Take a coaster or route taxi to Black River (US$3), then connect to Treasure Beach (US$1.75).

Jake's Place arranges transfers from MoBay for US$75 (up to four people), car and motorcycle rental, and transfers by taxi.

MALVERN

This hamlet straddles the Santa Cruz Mountains at a refreshing 2400 feet, a looping 15-mile drive northeast from Treasure Beach. Years ago, Malvern was favored as a summer resort for its temperate climate. Today Malvern serves as an agricultural and educational center.

Malvern is dominated by the cream-colored **Hampton College** (a girls school founded in 1858), about a mile south of Malvern Square, the village center. **Munro College** (a boys school founded in 1856) is 4 miles farther south.

Potsdam Hotel (☎ 361-4485; e crieffe@ cwjamaica.com; Malvern PO, or c/o 10 Crieffe Rd, Kingston), on the main road beside Munro College, was preparing to open at last visit and will offer 16 modestly appointed rooms with views.

LOVER'S LEAP

You need a head for heights to stand by the cliff at Lover's Leap (☎ 965-6634; admission US$3; open 9am-6pm Mon-Thur, 9am-7pm Fri-Sun), a mile southeast of Southfield, where the Santa Cruz Mountains plunge over 1700 feet into the ocean. The headland is tipped by a red-and-white-hooped **lighthouse**.

Far below, waves crash ashore on jagged rocks and wash onto **Cutlass Beach**. You can hike with a guide (US$14 per group): it's a stiff one-hour down. With luck you may see wild mountain goats.

Lover's Leap is named for two young slaves who supposedly committed suicide here. According to legend, the woman was lusted after by her owner, who arranged for her lover to be sold to another estate. When the couple heard of the plot, they fled and were eventually cornered at the cliffs, where they chose to plunge to their deaths.

There's a children's play area, souvenir shop, and small restaurant atop the cliff.

ALLIGATOR POND

Alligator Pond, hidden at the foot of a valley between two steep spurs of the Santa Cruz and Don Figuerero Mountains, is about as far from packaged tourism as you can get. Although Kingstonians crowd in on weekends, this large fishing village remains undiscovered by foreign travelers and offers a genuine, offbeat Jamaican experience.

The hamlet is set behind a deep-blue bay backed by dunes. The main street is smothered in wind-blown sand. Each morning local women gather on the dark-sand beach to haggle over the catch delivered by fishermen, whose colorful old pirogues line the long shore. Local youths surf wooden planks.

The **Sandy Cays**, about 20 miles offshore, are lined with white-sand beaches. The snorkeling and scuba diving are good at

Alligator Reef, about a 20-minute boat ride from shore.

Venus Sunset Lounge & Accommodation (☎ 965-4508; Alligator Pond PA; rooms US$22), a mile east of Alligator Pond, has four simply furnished rooms with fans, shared bath, and cold water. It sits amid lawns and has a thatched bar and basic restaurant overlooking a tiny beach.

Little Ochie Pub (☎ 965-4444; open 7am until last guest leaves) has tremendous atmosphere, with thatched tables and chairs on the beach, including some built into thatch-roof old boats raised on stilts. Specialties include curried conch (US$6), roast fish (US$5), and lobster (US$8.50) prepared seven different ways, plus aphrodisiac tonics such as 'Stallion Punch.'

Coasters and route taxis operate between Alligator Pond and the Beckford St transportation center in Kingston (about US$5), and from Mandeville via Gutters (about US$2).

LONG BAY

Long Bay, east of Alligator Pond, is a near-pristine spot. Virtually the entire 15-mile shoreline, which is hemmed in by mountains, is composed of mangroves and reeds that make up the Long Bay Morass – a nirvana for birders. There are crocodiles, too. And the swamp is a last refuge for endangered manatees.

With boardwalks and an interpretive center, this could be an ecotourist mecca. The area begs for national park status to head off the developers. Alas, no progress had been made at last visit. The cattle that have invaded the wetlands have introduced exotic species of flora. And locals continue to kill marine turtles that come ashore to lay eggs.

The area is uninhabited, with the exception of a meager facility at **Gut River**, 6 miles east of Alligator Pond. Here, a mineral spring emerges from a deep cleft and feeds a pond where the occasional flash reveals mullet and big crabs 20 feet down. The pool grows shallower toward its mouth, where the water is trapped behind a sand spit that hides a lonesome red-sand beach. On Sunday, Jamaicans crowd in for a 'Bashment

on the Beach,' with ear-splitting reggae. When they leave, garbage is strewn everywhere, and nobody bothers to clean it up.

God's Well is a sinkhole that drops to a cave at about 158 feet. Scuba divers occasionally test the waters (God's Well is for experienced divers only – the first diver to tackle it died). Believe it or not, divers have even been known to swim the 'Suicide Run,' a 2-mile swim to the ocean through the seemingly impenetrable swamps. Yes, the chance of bumping into a crocodile is very real, but locals advise: 'Dem alligators no problem, mon…Dem coward. 'Im see you come close, mon, 'im swim fast, fast can go!'

Long Bay extends to Alligator Hole, also known as Canoe Valley Wetlands (see the Kingston & Southern Plains chapter), where you can swim with manatees.

A taxi from Alligator Pond costs about US$8 roundtrip. A coaster travels to Gut River from Mandeville on weekends.

Mandeville

The town of Mandeville (population 43,500), the most prosperous and pleasant on the island, spreads across a rolling plateau on the eastern flank of the Don Figuerero Mountains. The town has a strong English feel that has attracted a large number of English retirees, alongside North Americans who arrived with the bauxite industry.

HISTORY

Mandeville, established only in 1816, began life as a haven for colonial planters escaping the heat of the plains. In the 19th century, the city prospered as a holiday retreat for wealthy Kingstonians and planters, and attracted English retirees from other colonial quarters. Many early expats established the area as a center for dairy farming and citrus and pimento production. Jamaica's unique, seedless citrus fruit, the ortanique, was first produced here in the 1920s and is grown in large quantities.

Alcan, the North American bauxite company, opened operations here in 1940 (in 2000 it sold its operations to a Swiss company, Glencore). Relatively high wage levels lured educated Jamaicans, bringing a middle-class savoir faire to the town.

ORIENTATION

Mandeville is spread across rolling hills in a maze of wriggly streets. At its heart is an historic village green, called Cecil Charlton Park, after a former mayor. The 'green' is ringed by Park Crescent, from which roads radiate out like spokes on a wheel: Manchester Rd leads southeast, Ward Ave leads west, and Main St leads north.

Main St is the main artery and runs north to Caledonia Rd; at the T-junction, Caledonia Rd leads east to Williamsfield; westward it runs back into town parallel to Main St, and continues south as Perth Rd.

The Winston Jones Hwy (A2) skirts the town to the north and west before dropping eastward to Williamsfield and westward to St Elizabeth parish.

INFORMATION

The JTB does not have an office. The best information source is the **Visitor Information Service** (☎ 962-3725) at the Astra

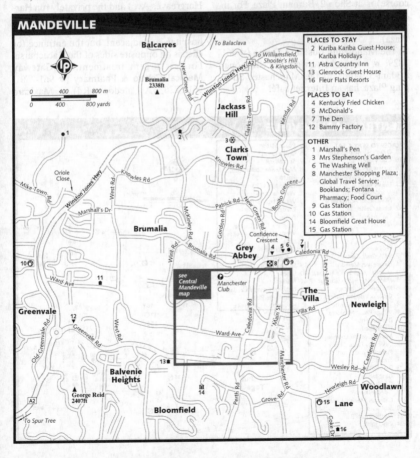

MANDEVILLE

Scale: 0 – 400 – 800 m / 0 – 400 – 800 yards

PLACES TO STAY
2 Kariba Kariba Guest House;
   Kariba Holidays
11 Astra Country Inn
13 Glenrock Guest House
16 Fleur Flats Resorts

PLACES TO EAT
4 Kentucky Fried Chicken
5 McDonald's
7 The Den
12 Bammy Factory

OTHER
1 Marshall's Pen
3 Mrs Stephenson's Garden
6 The Washing Well
8 Manchester Shopping Plaza;
   Global Travel Service;
   Booklands; Fontana
   Pharmacy; Food Court
9 Gas Station
10 Gas Station
14 Bloomfield Great House
15 Gas Station

Country Inn. On the Internet, a good starting point is **w** www.go-mandeville.com.

Scotiabank (☎ 962-1083; cnr Ward Ave & Caledonia Rd; Park Crescent) and the **CIBC** (☎ 962-1480; Park Crescent) have branches, as does **National Commercial Bank** (NCB; ☎ 962-2161; Mandeville Plaza), which has another branch adjacent to the Manchester Shopping Plaza (☎ 962-8600). To receive or send money by remittance, contact **Western Union** (☎ 962-1037) in the Brumalia Town Centre.

The **post office** (☎ 962-2339) is on South Racecourse. **FedEx** (☎ 625-3762; 8 N Racecourse) is at Shop 2, Barnam Plaza. For international calls go to the **Cable & Wireless office** (☎ 888-962-9700; Shop 16, Leaders Plaza).

The **Mandeville Business Centre** (☎ 961-1829; **w** www.wwt@cwjamaica.com; open 8:30am-5:30pm), in the Manchester Shopping Plaza, has an Internet café.

For travel deals try **Sterling Travel** (☎ 962-2203) in Caledonia Plaza; or **Global Travel Service** (☎ 962-2630; 18 Caledonia Rd) in the Manchester Shopping Plaza.

The best bookshop is **Booklands** (☎ 962-9051), in Manchester Shopping Plaza. The **Manchester Parish Library** (☎ 962-2972) is at 34 Hargreaves Ave.

For laundry service, try the **Washing Well** (☎ 961-6111; Shop 18, Caledonia Court; open 7am-6:45pm Mon-Sat, 11am-3pm Sun) or **Mandeville Fabricare** (☎ 962-2471; 30 Hargreaves Ave).

Mandeville Hospital (☎ 962-2067; 32 Hargreaves Ave) and the privately run **Hargreaves Memorial Hospital** (☎ 962-2040; Caledonia Rd) have emergency centers; the hospitals are adjacent, but the entrance for each is on opposite sides of the Racecourse. For less urgent treatment, try **Gateway Medical Centre & Pharmacy** (☎ 961-2501, 961-3726; 3A Caledonia Rd), or **Maxicare**

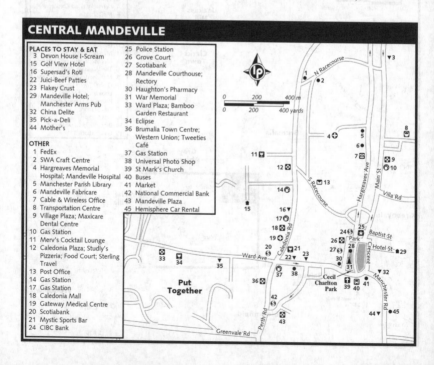

CENTRAL MANDEVILLE

PLACES TO STAY & EAT
3 Devon House I-Scream
15 Golf View Hotel
16 Supersad's Roti
22 Juici-Beef Patties
23 Flakey Crust
29 Mandeville Hotel;
   Manchester Arms Pub
32 China Delite
35 Pick-a-Deli
44 Mother's

OTHER
1 FedEx
2 SWA Craft Centre
4 Hargreaves Memorial
   Hospital; Mandeville Hospital
5 Manchester Parish Library
6 Mandeville Fabricare
7 Cable & Wireless Office
8 Transportation Centre
9 Village Plaza; Maxicare
   Dental Centre
10 Gas Station
11 Merv's Cocktail Lounge
12 Caledonia Plaza; Studly's
   Pizzeria; Food Court; Sterling
   Travel
13 Post Office
14 Gas Station
15 Gas Station
18 Caledonia Mall
19 Gateway Medical Centre
20 Scotiabank
21 Mystic Sports Bar
24 CIBC Bank

25 Police Station
26 Grove Court
27 Scotiabank
28 Mandeville Courthouse;
   Rectory
30 Haughton's Pharmacy
31 War Memorial
33 Ward Plaza; Bamboo
   Garden Restaurant
34 Eclipse
36 Brumalia Town Centre;
   Western Union; Tweeties
   Café
37 Gas Station
38 Universal Photo Shop
39 St Mark's Church
40 Buses
41 Market
42 National Commercial Bank
43 Mandeville Plaza
45 Hemisphere Car Rental

Dental Centre (☎ 962-9279; 29 Main St), in Village Plaza.

Pharmacies include the **Fontana Pharmacy** (☎ 962-3129; Manchester Shopping Plaza), and **Haughton's Pharmacy** (☎ 962-2246; 18 W Park Crescent; open 8am-10pm Mon-Sat, 9am-9pm Sun), on the 'green.'

The **police station** (☎ 962-2250 or 119; Park Crescent) is on the north side of the green.

THINGS TO SEE & DO
Cecil Charlton Park

This tiny English-style 'green,' also known as Mandeville Square, lends a charming village feel to the town center. On the north side is the **Mandeville Courthouse**, of cut limestone with a horseshoe staircase and a raised portico supported by Doric columns. The **Rectory**, the oldest home in town, adjoins the courthouse. Both it and the courthouse were completed in 1820.

On the south side is a produce market. A **cenotaph** stands on the south side of the square, commemorating Jamaica's dead from the two world wars.

St Mark's Church, on the south side of Cecil Charlton Park, was also established in 1820. The timber clerestory is impressive, as is the churchyard.

Bloomfield Great House

This immaculate historic home (☎ 962-7130, fax 961-0549; e bloomfield.g.h@cw jamaica.com; 8 Perth Rd) stands atop a hill southwest of the town center. The two-story structure built in traditional Caribbean vernacular fairly gleams after a fine renovation. The house is about 170 years old (the exact date is uncertain) and began life as the center of a coffee estate and, later, a citrus plantation. It's now one of Jamaica's finest art galleries and premier restaurants.

The galleries feature works by many of Jamaica's leading artists, as well as an international repertoire. Five arts-and-crafts studios and stores comprise the arcade downstairs.

The entrance is 200 yards south of Manchester College, on the opposite side of the road at the crossroads.

Huntington Summit

The extravagant Huntington Summit mansion (☎ 962-2274; George's Valley Rd; admission free, donations accepted; open daily by appointment), in May Day, 2 miles southeast of the town center, is the yang to Bloomfield's yin. The octagonal home is of palatial proportion, with wraparound plate-glass windows and artificial cascades tumbling into a swimming pool where waters feed into a pond in the lounge. The ostentatious furnishings reflect the catholic tastes of its owner, Cecil Charlton, a millionaire farmer, politician, and self-promoter who served as Mandeville's mayor during the 1970s and 1980s. He made much of his money as owner of the Charles-Off betting shops, but also served as chairman of the corruption-ridden National Water Commission.

To get here, take Manchester Rd south to the T-junction; turn right onto Newport Rd, then left onto May Day Rd, and left again after a mile onto George's Valley Rd (you can't miss the big green gates on the left).

Marshall's Pen

This impressive stone-and-timber great house (☎ 904-5454; admission US$10), built in 1795, stands among beautifully landscaped gardens in the midst of a former coffee plantation turned cattle-breeding property on the northwest side of town.

The 300-acre property is owned by Robert Sutton, Jamaica's leading ornithologist, and Anne Sutton, an environmental scientist. Robert can trace his ancestry to the first child born to English parents in Jamaica in 1655.

The Suttons' home has wood-paneled rooms brimming with antiques, leather-bound books, artwork, and other museum-quality pieces. You can tour the minimuseum by appointment only.

Marshall's Pen is splendid for birding: more than 100 species have been recorded here, including 25 of the 27 species endemic to Jamaica. It's a treat to don rubber boots and binoculars and set out with the Suttons and their several dogs swarming happily at your heels. Robert is coauthor with Audrey

Downer of *Birds of Jamaica: A Photographic Field Guide*. Visiting at early morning or evening is best.

Take Oriole Close off the Winston Jones Hwy, about 3 miles from the town center (there's a sign for 'Somerset Quarries' at the junction). Turn right after 100 yards onto Mike Town Rd; the estate entrance – an unmarked stone gateway – is about 400 yards farther on the right. Take insect repellent.

Countrystyle Community Tours (see the boxed text 'Community Tourism') offers tours by appointment (US$10 per person).

Mrs Stephenson's Garden

This well-manicured garden (☎ 962-2909, fax 961-1486; 25 New Green Rd; admission US$2) has been planned and planted, and pruned and mulched, by a stalwart who is really an artist. Carmen Stephenson's garden is a riot of color, a drunkenness of scents, difficult to dampen in even the wettest of weather. Keen amateur gardeners descend year-round to 'tut-tut' at the layout or gasp at the collection that includes orchids and ortaniques. Casual visitors are welcome during daylight hours.

ACTIVITIES

For **golf**, check out the Manchester Club (☎ 962-2403; e mosquito_j@hotmail.com), off Brumalia Rd, northwest of the town center, which has a nine-hole golf course laid out in the 1860s. A round costs US$17. Caddies are compulsory (US$13). It also has three night-lit tennis courts and squash courts (both US$5 per hour).

You can learn to **scuba** with Ralph Pearce of Bloomfield Great House (☎ 962-7130); he teaches classes in a heated pool,

with PADI certification dives at Runaway Bay (about US$200).

ORGANIZED TOURS

Kariba Holidays & Leisure Tours (☎ 961-3829, 962-8006, fax 962-5502), at Kariba Kariba Guest House (see Places to Stay later in this section), offers tours locally and farther afield.

Countrystyle Community Tours (see the boxed text 'Community Tourism') has a 'Highlights Tour' of Mandeville (per person US$10 for 30 min, US$40 full day, including lunch). It also offers tours farther afield, and offers specialist guides for US$10 per hour.

SPECIAL EVENTS

The **Manchester Horticultural Society Show** (☎ 962-2909) is held in late May at Mrs Stephenson's Garden.

Manchester Golf Week is held in late July at the Manchester Club (see Activities earlier in this section); contact the Jamaica Golf Association (☎ 975-4287). The **Jamaica Horse Show** is held in July, and **Tennis Week** in August, at the Manchester Club.

PLACES TO STAY
Guest Houses

Glenrock Guest House (☎ 961-3278, fax 961-3279; e glenrock@cwjamaica.com; 3 Greenvale Rd; rooms US$29-34) is a homey place to try if you're not fussy about decor. It has seven carpeted bedrooms with fans and louvered windows, plus private bath with hot water. Free breakfasts are included with longer stays.

Kariba Kariba Guest House (☎ 961-3829, fax 961-7096; e kariba@cwjamaica.com; PO Box 482; rooms US$50), beside the Winston Jones Hwy north of the town center, is a beautiful fieldstone home run by Derek and Hazel O'Connor, a friendly English-Jamaican couple. It has handsome tile and hardwood floors, a large lounge with exquisite detailing, and large rooms with balconies. A swimming pool and spa were planned at last visit, when six upstairs units (including a bridal suite) were being added. Road noise is a factor. It's a great place for families; Derek and Hazel have two children. Rate includes breakfast. Dinner and lunch cost US$5 each.

Marshall's Pen (☎ 904-5454; e asutton@ uwimona.edu.jm; PO Box 58; rooms US$70) has three bedrooms in the main house, plus five self-catering apartments in a converted coffee warehouse. Meals can sometimes be arranged. Note that this is not a hotel or guest house; rooms are made available at the owners' discretion, and only to devout birders or nature lovers.

Hotels

Astra Country Inn (☎ 962-3725, 962-7758, fax 962-1461; 62 Ward Ave; rooms US$45-65, suites US$115), on the western outskirts of town, has 20 homey rooms (some with king-size beds) with options for TVs and telephone, including suites with kitchenettes. Rooms were in the midst of being refurbished at last visit, bringing the property up to par. Facilities include a pool, an English-style pub, and a pleasant dining room serving tasty Jamaican cuisine.

Mandeville Hotel (☎ 962-2460, fax 962-0700; w www.mandevillehotel.com; PO Box 78, Hotel St; rooms US$65, studios US$80, suites US$85-125, apartments US$95-180), at the bottom of Hotel St, in the town center, is the island's oldest hotel, dating to the 1890s. It has 60 rooms of varying standards; all have cable TV and telephone. Rooms to the rear are a bit dowdy. Spacious suites boast four-poster beds. Self-contained units with kitchenettes are also available. The restaurant overlooks a pool. It has a pub.

Fleur Flats Resorts (☎ 962-1053; 416-445-0209 in Canada; 305-252-0873 in the USA; 020-7964-0047 in the UK; 10 Coke Dr, PO Box 485; 1-/2-bedroom apartments US$57/86) offers spacious, fully furnished apartments that sleep four people in comfort. Rooms have TVs and phones. The family-oriented resort is a 20-minute walk from the town center.

Golf View Hotel (☎ 962-4471, fax 962-5640; w www.thegolfviewhotel.com; 5½ Caledonia Rd, PO Box 189; rooms US$50-60, 1-/2-bedroom suites US$75/100) is a rambling, motel-style property surrounding a small pool in a concrete courtyard. Rooms

have contemporary decor, tile floors, fans, cable TVs, louvered windows, and tub showers. Spacious air-con suites have walk-in showers and four-poster beds. Watch your step on the stairs.

PLACES TO EAT
Fast Food

There are a dozen or so fast-food joints around town. A food court to the rear of the Manchester Shopping Plaza features **Indies Pizza** (☎ 961-1676; Shop 47); **Gee's Café** (☎ 962-2606; Shop 42), recommended for its Jamaican breakfasts; and the **Real Things Health Food Store** (☎ 962-5664). Caledonia Plaza has a food court downstairs, as does Grove Court.

Fast-food junkies will find a **Kentucky Fried Chicken** and **McDonald's** on Caledonia Rd, and **Juici-Beef Patties** on Ward Ave is a good place for quick, cheap patties.

Community Tourism

You won't be long in the Mandeville area before you hear about 'community tourism,' an attempt to foster opportunities for locals wishing to participate more fully in Jamaica's tourism industry.

The dynamo behind the movement is Diana McIntyre-Pike, co-owner and manager of the Astra Country Inn and director of Countrystyle Community Tours (☎ 962-7758, 962-3725, fax 962-1461; e countrystyle@ mail.infochan.com; PO Box 60, Mandeville), a company that specializes in providing alternatives to 'sea and sand' vacations. She helped form the Central & South Tourism Committee, which sponsors special-interest tours, community guides, skills training, and assistance with tourism development at the local level. McIntyre-Pike also runs the Countrystyle Institute for Sustainable Tourism, offering courses from community guide training to environmental waste management.

'Whatever development takes place, it must complement our lifestyle, not change our way of life,' says McIntyre-Pike.

Jamaican

Manchester Arms Pub & Restaurant (☎ 962-9764; US$8-20; open 6:30am-10pm), at the Mandeville Hotel, has a broad menu of Jamaican and continental dishes. It has a poolside barbecue each Wednesday night.

Astra Country Inn (see Places to Stay) also has a notable restaurant. It grows much of its produce in a private garden. Its natural health breakfast costs US$5. A set meal is offered daily, but lunch and dinner can be made to order (from US$6). Sandwiches and other snacks cost US$2.

You can get a cheap breakfast, as well as fish-and-chips, pizza, and sandwiches, at **Tweeties Café** (☎ 962-3426; 2 Perth Rd) in Brumalia Town Centre.

Pick-a-Deli (☎ 961-4096; 13 Ward Ave; US$3-4; open 7am-6pm Mon-Fri) is a clean eatery that serves curried goat, sweet-and-sour chicken, and other Jamaican fare.

Mother's (Manchester Rd) is a good place to buy cheap patties (US$0.40) and baked goods.

Bloomfield Great House Restaurant & Bar (☎ 962-7130; 8 Perth Rd; open noon-10pm Mon-Sat) is one of Jamaica's preeminent restaurants, exemplifying the best of Caribbean fusion cuisine. The creative menu, which changes regularly, includes fresh pastas (about US$15), such as callaloo fettuccine; Punjab prawns in mango curry with coconut (US$20); and filet mignon (US$30). The lunch menu offers caesar salad, pizza, fish-and-chips, and lighter fare (from US$4). Meals are filling and offer great value. Australian wines are well represented. A Sunday champagne brunch is offered, as are free pick-up and drop-off.

Other Cuisines

The Den (☎ 962-3603; 35 Caledonia Rd; US$2-13; open 10am-midnight Mon-Sat) specializes in Asian dishes, including curries and tandooris. It hosts live jazz on Friday nights.

Other reasonably priced Chinese options include the **Bamboo Garden Restaurant** (☎ 961-4221; 35 Ward Ave; open noon-10pm) in Ward Plaza, and **China Delite** (☎ 962-9560; Manchester Rd; open 10am-10pm).

Supersad's Roti (☎ 625-6293; Caledonia Rd; open 11:30am-10:30pm) is a popular eatery serving Indian fare.

Studly's Pizzeria (☎ 962-0082), in Caledonia Mall, is the main pizza parlor.

Bakeries & Groceries

You can buy one-half of Jamaica's famous 'fish and bammy' at Clem Bloomfield's **Bammy Factory** (☎ 963-8636; 40 Greenvale Rd). **Flakey Crust** (11A Manchester Rd) sells fresh-baked breads, pastries, and patties. **Devon House I-Scream** has an outlet at the north end of Main St.

You can buy fresh produce at the **market** on the south side of Cecil Charlton Park, but hygiene is an issue.

ENTERTAINMENT

Mandeville is relatively devoid of an active nightlife; locals have a humorous phrase to describe the town: 'newlyweds and almost deads.'

Eclipse (☎ 962-2660; 33 Ward Ave; entrance US$4) is the only nightclub of note. It has live music out back and a disco inside. Friday is 'Ladies Nite,' with free entry. There are a few other not-so-hot spots.

Bloomfield Great House has live musical entertainment on Friday nights.

For a beer or cocktail in quiet surroundings, try **Merv's Cocktail Lounge** (☎ 962-0124; 11 Caledonia Ave), behind Caledonia Plaza. **Mystic Sports Bar** (Caledonia Rd) is a livelier alternative.

SHOPPING

SWA Craft Centre (☎ 962-0694; 7 N Racecourse), behind the Manchester Shopping Plaza, trains young adults to make a living from crochet, embroidery, weaving, and so on. Its most appealing item is the famous 'banana patch' Rastafarian doll.

Universal Photo Shop (☎ 625-1284; 4B Manchester Rd), 100 yards west of the town square, sells photographic supplies.

GETTING THERE & AROUND

Timair (☎ 952-2516; www.timair.com) serves Mandeville airstrip, south of town, from MoBay.

Mandeville has direct bus, coaster, and route taxi service from virtually every major town in Jamaica. Most buses, and many coasters and route taxis, depart and arrive from the transportation center, off Main St. Others depart and arrive Mandeville from near the market on the main square.

There is no local bus system. You'll find taxis near the market on Cecil Charlton Park. Otherwise, call **United Taxi Service** (☎ 961-3333), in Manchester Shopping Centre.

Hemisphere Car Rental (☎ 962-1921, fax 962-4131; 51 Manchester Rd) rents cars.

Around Mandeville

WILLIAMSFIELD
This village lies 1000 feet below and northeast of Mandeville at the base of the Winston Jones Hwy (A2). There are several sites of interest in the area.

You can take a free tour of the **High Mountain Coffee Factory** (☎ 963-4211; Winston Jones Hwy), where coffee, herbal teas, and coffee liqueurs are produced by the Jamaica Standard Products Co under three labels: Blue Mountain, High Mountain, and Baronhall Estate. It's adjacent to the old railway station just west of the roundabout. Tours are by appointment. The factory is tiny and the tour not overly interesting, but it has a coffee tasting room and store.

Tours of the **Pioneer Chocolate Factory** (☎ 963-4216; Winston Jones Hwy), 400 yards east of the High Mountain Coffee Factory, were no longer offered at press time. But things can change. With luck, you can watch the seeds from the cocoa bean being processed into chocolate bars. There's a factory outlet on the roadside, next to the Texaco gas station.

The **High Mountain 10K Road Race** (☎ 963-4211), Jamaica's largest bicycle road race, is held here every January.

SHOOTER'S HILL
Shooter's Hill begins 2 miles northwest of Williamsfield and climbs steadily and steeply almost 1400 feet to Christiana. A lookout point midway offers splendid views. On the west side of the road, atop a hillock, is the Moravian-built **Mizpah Church**, topped by a four-faced German clock.

Kirkvine Works, an alumina processing plant on the B4 at the base of Shooter's Hill, is owned and operated by Windalco (West Indies Aluminium Company). You can arrange free weekday factory tours through the Astra Country Inn or Mandeville Hotel (see Mandeville earlier in this chapter), or through Mr J Neil at the Kirkvine Works office (☎ 961-7503, 962-3141). A day's notice is usually required. There's a strict dress code: long pants are required, and feet must be covered (no sandals).

The **Pickapeppa Factory** (☎ 962-2928, 962-2809; adult/child US$9/3), on the B6 at the foot of Shooter's Hill, offers 30-minute tours by appointment. The factory produces Jamaica's sinus-searing world-famous sauce (similar to England's Worcestershire sauce). There's not much to see, other than workers stirring giant pots of simmering scallions and other vegetables.

The workshop at the **Magic Toy Factory** (☎ 603-1495; Walderston PO; open 9am-5pm Mon-Fri), in Walderston on the B5 near the top of the hill, lets you watch as they make handmade toys and puzzles, refrigerator magnets, exquisite wall plaques, and a miscellany of other creative pieces jigsawed from wood, then hand-painted in Caribbean colors; all can be purchased here.

MILE GULLY & ENVIRONS
This village sprawls along a valley that runs northwest from Mandeville in the lee of the forested north face of the Don Figuerero Mountains. The B6 leads northwest from Shooter's Hill, winding, dipping, and rising past lime-green pastures dotted with guango and silk-cotton trees and criss-crossed with stone walls and hedgerows.

The valley is pitted with caves, including **Oxford Caves**, near Mile Gully.

About a mile west of Mile Gully, at **Skull Point**, is a venerable blue-and-white 19th-century police station and courthouse at the junction for Bethany.

The Bethany road climbs sharply and delivers you at the **Bethany Moravian Church** – a simple gray stone building dating to 1835, dramatically perched four-square midway up the hill with fantastic valley views. The church is rather dour close up, but the simple interior boasts a resplendent organ.

Another beautiful church – **St Simon's Anglican Church** – sits on a hillside amid meadows at Comfort Hall, 4 miles west of Mile Gully, with huge spreading trees festooned with old man's beard.

To the south of the B6, perched atop the Don Figuerero Mountains, at Maidstone, is **Nazareth Moravian Church**. Maidstone was one of the best-planned post-emancipation 'free villages,' founded in 1840.

The annual **Emancipation Day Fair** (contact Mr Garth Smith, ☎ 770-7152) is celebrated at Maidstone on August 1, with mento bands, Jonkanoo celebrations, and maypole and quadrille dancing.

Ripon Nature Park

Ripon estate (admission US$2.50), dating to 1730, in Mile Gully, produces citrus, flowers, coffee, and cocoa and is being developed into a bird sanctuary, wild garden, and eco-park by Derek O'Connor, owner of **Kariba Holidays & Leisure Tours** (☎ 962-8006) in Mandeville. The 12-acre garden has more than 500 endemic species, including orchids. A palm-lined driveway leads to the vast and varied garden, accessible by trails and open for picnics. Fruit trees include giant plums. The hillsides are carpeted in ferns and creeping jew, and feature benches for quiet contemplation. A hummingbird and butterfly garden were being laid out at last visit.

Interpretative signs were to be added, and a pool and spa, plus fish pond and children's play park were planned. Horseback riding is offered.

Getting There & Away

Coasters and route taxis operate on the B6 between Mandeville and Maggotty via Mile Gully.

If you're driving from Mandeville, the B6 continues west about 5 miles to Green Hill and a T-junction marked 'St Paul's 5 miles'

Jonkanoo

Jonkanoo is a traditional Christmas celebration in which revelers parade through the streets dressed in masquerade. It was once the major celebration on the slave calendar.

The festivity, which originated among West Indian secret societies, evolved on the plantations and gradually adopted European elements, such as Morris dancing, polka, and reel. The all-male cast of masqueraders hid their identity: some dressed as demons, others wore papier-mâché horse heads, and many were on stilts. The elaborate carnival was accompanied by musicians with drums, fifes, flutes, and rattles.

Following emancipation, the Church and state suppressed Jonkanoo as a vulgar pagan rite. Efforts are being made to revive it as an important part of Jamaican culture.

Costumed spectators are expected to offer donations, food, and drink to participants.

(to the left) and 'Balaclava 6½ miles' (to the right). One mile north (to the right) of the junction, en route to Balaclava, is a *very dangerous* spot: you'll climb a short hill that tempts you to accelerate. Unfortunately there's an unmarked railway crossing atop the crest and a hairpin bend *immediately* after. Drive slowly!

Christiana & Environs

Around Christiana, you'd be forgiven for imagining yourself in the Pyrenees or the highlands of Costa Rica. The air is crisp, clouds drift through the vales, and pine trees add to the alpine setting.

The area is an important center for Irish potatoes. Cacao, yams, and coffee production are also important, and during picking season you can watch women with baskets moving among the rows, plucking cherry-red coffee berries.

CHRISTIANA

Lying about 10 miles north of Mandeville at an elevation of 3000 feet, the town of Christiana is the heart of a richly farmed agricultural region of gently undulating hills and shallow vales.

The area was settled by German farmers during the 18th and 19th centuries. Moravian missionaries were also active during that era, and a **Moravian church** commands the northern end of sinuous Main St. During the 19th century, Christiana became a hill-town resort popular with European dignitaries and Kingstonians escaping the heat of the plains.

Christiana is a fairly sleepy place (farmers go to bed early and get up around 4am or 5am), but on Thursday when the higglers come to sell their produce, the roads are so thick you can hardly drive through town. If you're in Christiana on a Thursday, stay through the evening for Higgler's Night.

Christiana is well served by public transport from Kingston and Mandeville. A bus and coasters also operate from Montego Bay and Ocho Rios via Albert Town.

Information

Scotiabank (☎ 964-2223) and **National Commercial Bank** (☎ 964-2466) have branches on Main St.

The **post office** (☎ 964-2279) is at the north end of Main St, next to the **police station** (☎ 964-2250).

Dr Glen Norman Day's clinic (☎ 964-2361; open 9am-3pm Mon, Tues, Thur & Sat) is in Christiana Plaza, off Main St. The government-run **Christiana Health Centre** (☎ 964-2749) is toward the south end of Main St. The **Christiana Pharmacy** (☎ 964-2424; Main St) is well-stocked.

Christiana Bottom

This beautiful riverside spot, in a valley bottom 800 feet below the town, has a waterfall plus picnic spots framed by bamboo. Two sinkholes full of crystal-clear water offer refreshing dips. You can hike from the center of town, though the going at the lower reaches can be muddy and slippery. Take the road that leads east from the National Commercial Bank; it's 2 miles from here. Take the first left and then the second left.

Gourie Forest Reserve

This forest reserve of pines, mahogany, and mahoe growing atop and betwixt dramatic cockpits is 2 miles northwest of town, near Coleyville. The park is laced with hiking trails. Gourie is most noteworthy for having Jamaica's longest cave system. Two **spelunking** routes have been explored. One of the routes is easy; the other is difficult and made more so by the presence of an icy river. Rubber-soled shoes are required and a guide is essential.

The Forestry Dept (☎ 964-2065; Main St) rents two basic wooden **cottages**; you can get the keys from the caretaker at the reserve. The huts were closed for an upgrade at last visit.

To get to Gourie, turn uphill (southwest) at the radio tower immediately south of the junction that leads west for Coleyville and Troy. Immediately, take the left at a Y-fork, then right at the next Y-fork and follow the green wire fence.

Organized Tours

Villa Bella Tours (☎ 964-2243), in the Hotel Villa Bella, offers excursions to the Oxford and Gourie Caves (US$30 for three hours), Lorimar Coffee Estate, and the Moravian churches, plus bird-watching trips to Cockpit Country.

Special Events

On Christmas Eve the streets have traditionally been closed and farming families have poured in for a centuries-old Jonkanoo celebration called **Grand Market Night**, with men on stilts and general festivity in the streets. Alas, the festivities didn't occur in either 2000 or 2001. Call Sherryl McDowell or Audrey Brown at Hotel Villa Bella (see below) for updates.

Places to Stay & Eat

Hotel Villa Bella (☎ 964-2243, fax 962-2765; Ⓦ www.jamaica-southcoast.com; PO Box 473; rooms US$60-80) is a charming and cozy old country inn perched on a hill at

Sedburgh, at the south end of town. This former grande dame retains its original mahogany floors (now somewhat squeaky) and 1940s furniture. The 15 recently renovated, exquisitely decorated rooms have cable TV and deep bathtub-showers. Rooms in the annex are smaller. Gracious and efficient service recalls the days when Christiana was a center for 'old-style tourism.' Facilities include a reading room and TV lounge.

The hotel also offers one of the best and most reasonably priced dining experiences on the island. The superb menu merges Jamaican, Japanese, and Chinese cuisines. Typical dishes include chicken teriyaki (US$10), Chinese-style poached fish in ginger and soy sauce (US$12), and *sole Villa Bella* (simmered in coconut milk, lemon grass, and spices; US$15). Eat on the veranda or the garden terrace, where you can sip homemade ginger beer and admire the flower-filled, 6-acre garden. Afternoon tea is at 4:30pm. And the ackee breakfast is unsurpassed!

Main St has numerous undistinguished restaurants and pastry shops.

Akete Vegetarian Restaurant (Main St; US$2-10) is recommended for I-tal food.

SPALDINGS

Spaldings is a small, often mist-shrouded town at about 3000 feet elevation on the crest of the central highlands, about 3 miles east of Christiana. The hills are planted in market gardens. Ginger and yams are important local crops.

Spaldings is the site of **Knox College**, a highly rated coed religious school founded in 1940 by a progressive educator, Rev Lewis Davidson, who believed that a school should serve to benefit its local community. Hence, the school has its own print works, farm, and even a meat-processing plant.

The B4 continues east, dropping into the Rio Minho Valley (see the Kingston & Southern Plains chapter).

Glencoe B&B (☎ 964-2286; rooms single/double US$40/60) is a delightful piece of Old England at Nash Farm, a mile southwest of Spaldings. The two-story farmhouse has four quaint little upstairs bedrooms with mahogany floors, antiques, and private bathrooms with hot water. An enclosed veranda forms a wraparound lounge with a TV and a small library. Rates include breakfast.

Kingston & Southern Plains

'Kingston' usually refers to the city-parish of Kingston – the nation's capital – and the surrounding parish of St Andrew, which are jointly administered and known as the 'Corporate Area.' Together they cover 191 sq miles, although the metropolitan area measures only 45 sq miles. The city is usually divided into two areas: Uptown and Downtown. The city proper is enfolded by a meniscus of hills, including the Hellshire Hills and Jack's Hill, and the outlying regions of metropolitan Kingston, including Port Royal and outlying areas of St Andrew.

Westward, Kingston seeps onto the plains of St Catherine parish. In colonial days, this and neighboring Clarendon parish were the wealthiest on the island (sugar remains the mainstay of the area). These southern plains are the least known and least visited part of the island, despite historic importance as the locus of the island's first capital – St Jago de la Vega – established by the Spanish and today called Spanish Town, boasting important colonial structures.

Kingston

Dramatically situated between ocean and mountains, Kingston need not be the daunting beginning to a Jamaican vacation so many foreigners assume. While it's true that Jamaica's lively, engaging, teeming, unrepentantly in-your-face capital (population 713,000) is plagued by intractable problems, Kingston's negative image belies its many appealing facets.

The city's history is intriguing. High culture is well developed, boasting attractions that merit a visit, including the National Gallery – a first-rate art museum. And the nightlife is the most cosmopolitan and colorful on the island, with everything from jazz and lively theater to reggae concerts. The city's yearly calendar is replete with festivals and sporting and other events. And there are top-notch hotels and restaurants.

Highlights

- Bob Marley Museum, a fascinating glimpse into the life of Jamaica's most revered contemporary hero

- The Parade, a pulsing marketplace at the heart of Kingston

- Peaceful Lime Cay, a sun-drenched haven from the hustle and bustle

- Historic Port Royal, a disheveled trove of colonial structures with the promise of a glittering restoration

- Hellshire Beaches, a funky fishing village alive on weekends with the Kingston picnic-and-party crowd

SOUTHERN PLAINS

Kingston & Southern Plains page 278

Uptown Kingston pages 294-295
Downtown Kingston pages 286-287
Spanish Town page 318
Port Royal page 309
Kingston & Environs pages 280-281

CARIBBEAN SEA

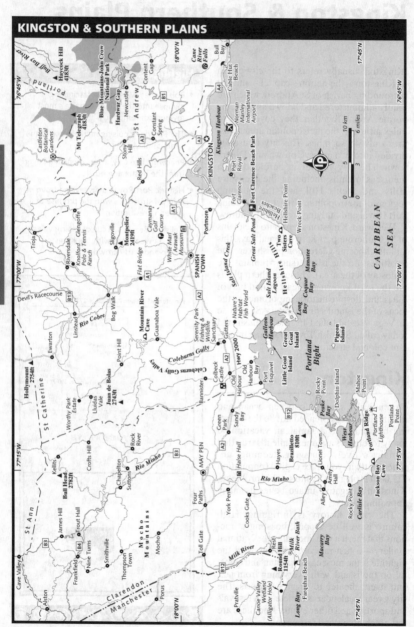

KINGSTON & SOUTHERN PLAINS

SOUTHERN PLAINS

Kingston has a huge middle class and vast acres of well-maintained streets lined with modern houses. It is also a city divided, with hovels and highrises side by side. By day, downtown is dominated by city business – the country's financial institutions are here, as are most of the notable historic buildings. By night, city life is dominated by the urban underclass living in 'yards' (tenements) and urban ghettos where extreme violence rules and the night is riven by the staccato of gunfire.

Clamorous Kingston is definitely a third-world city. Goats run free everywhere, browsing the garbage-filled gutters totally oblivious to your approach by car until the moment you're about to pass them, when the kamikaze herd is sure to dash across your path.

The vast shantytowns that push at the city's margins are for the most part hidden from tourist view, as is the controlled anarchy of the inner-city ghettos. Still, in even the more exclusive areas, makeshift homes of corrugated cardboard litter the spare plots of ground.

At times its culture can be downright intimidating. Seething tensions simmer below the surface and often boil over, making for international headlines that have tended to keep visitors at bay. But this chaotic and vibrant city is the heartbeat of Jamaica and its center of commerce and culture, hustling and bustling with energy.

HISTORY

On May 10, 1655, an English fleet bearing 7000 men sailed into Kingston Harbour and, after desultory resistance from the Spanish defenders at Passage Fort, captured Jamaica for Oliver Cromwell. For several decades the site of the future city was used for rearing pigs. When an earthquake leveled Port Royal in 1692, survivors struggled across the bay and pitched camp with the swine. A town plan was drawn up on a grid pattern, centered on an open square.

Though devastated repeatedly by earthquakes and hurricanes, the port city prospered throughout the 18th century, becoming one of the most important trading centers in the western hemisphere and an important transshipment point for slaves destined for the Spanish colonies.

As the city expanded, the wealthier merchants moved to the cooler heights of Liguanea, where they built more expansive homes. Many built lookout towers atop their homes to check on the movement of ships in and out of the harbor. In 1755, Governor Admiral Charles Knowles bowed to political pressure and transferred his government's offices to Kingston. His successor revoked the act, however, and it wasn't until 1872 that the capital was officially transferred.

The 1907 earthquake leveled much of the city.

In the 1960s, the Urban Development Corporation reclaimed the waterfront, and several historic landmarks, including Victoria Market, were razed to make way for a complex of gleaming new structures, including the Bank of Jamaica and the Jamaica Conference Centre. A modern freight shipping facility – Port Bustamante – was also developed on reclaimed lands to the west.

About the same time, Kingston's nascent music industry was beginning to gather steam, lending international stature and fame to the city. This, in turn, fostered the growth of New Kingston, an uptown area of multistory office blocks, banks, restaurants, shops, and hotels developed in the 1960s on the site of the Knutsford Park racecourse.

A City in Decline

The boom years of the 1960s lured the rural poor, swelling the slums and shantytowns that had arisen in the preceding years. Unemployment soared, and with it, crime. The fractious 1970s spawned politically sponsored criminal enterprises whose trigger-happy networks still plague the city. Commerce began to leave downtown for New Kingston. And the middle class began to edge away as well.

That exodus began a period of decline from which the downtown has yet to recover. Many of the once-vibrant inner-city 'yards' decayed into slums littered with burnt-out cars and scarred with bullet-pocked, barbed wire–topped walls. Slum areas such as the PNP-affiliated Back-A-Wall district were brutally bulldozed (or firebombed) so that politicians such as Edward Seaga (the JLP's then-Minister of Welfare and Development) could build housing projects for their supporters.

A redevelopment project in the 1980s was aimed at the depressed areas south and west of the Parade, but exploring today you have to wonder what exactly the Kingston Restoration Company did with its US$30 million…much of which disappeared as kickbacks to 'dons.'

Kingston's Comeback?

Despite ongoing inner-city strife, hoteliers and the JTB are pushing to dispel the city's negative image and to resurrect its tourist industry. They have long talked-up plans to bring cruise ships and tourists back to Kingston. Development of a free port has been proposed, as has a restoration of the historic downtown and Port Royal, which one day ('soon come') may be restored and turned into the Williamsburg of the Caribbean. Meanwhile, efforts to beautify uptown include the laying out of **Emancipation Park**, a landscaped green swath due for completion in 2003.

ORIENTATION

The city overlooks the seventh largest natural harbor in the world, with the waterfront on its southern border. It spreads out in a fan shape from the harbor and rises gently toward the foothills and spur ridges of the Blue Mountains.

A wooded, steep-faced ridge – Long Mountain – rises to the east, with Dallas Mountain, a spur of the Blue Mountains, rising farther east, parallel and higher. The city is hemmed in to the northeast by Jack's Hill, to the north by Stony Hill, and to the northwest by Red Hills.

Downtown

The historic area just north of the waterfront forms the city center. Ocean Blvd, Port Royal St, and Harbour St parallel the waterfront. King St, the main thoroughfare, leads north from the waterfront to the

KINGSTON & ENVIRONS

PLACES TO STAY & EAT
1 Stony Hill Hotel
5 Abahati Hotel
8 Maya Lodge
10 Blue Mountain Inn
11 Hotel Lori
12 Olympia Crown Hotel
29 Rodney Arms
30 Jewels
31 Seahorse Rider Inn
32 La Roose
33 Casablanca
40 World Meditation Centre
44 Hellshire Beach Club

27 Port Henderson Plaza
28 Cactus Disco
34 Links Pon de Beach
35 Fort Augusta (Prison)
36 Bellevue Hospital
37 Rockfort
38 Fort Nugent
39 Apostles Battery
41 Royal Jamaica Yacht Club
42 Harbour View Shopping Centre; Harbour View Drive-In Cinema
43 Halle J Watersports

OTHER
2 Texaco Gas Station
3 Manor Hill Plaza; Patoo
4 US Embassy
6 Grosvenor Gallery
7 Post Office
9 Produce Market
13 University of Technology; Sculpture Park
14 Transportation Centre; Papine Market
15 University Hospital
16 Gas Station
17 Childcare Medical Centre
18 Jamworld Entertainment Complex
19 Tuff Gong Recording Studios
20 Trench Town Craft Producers
21 Trench Town Culture Yard
22 Mico Teachers College
23 Wolmer's School
24 Up Park Camp; Jamaica Defence Force Museum
25 Gun Court
26 Alpha Boys School

Ferry

A1

To Spanish Town

Waterford Rd

Caymanas Park Racetrack

Passage Fort Dr

16 Passage Fort

17 PORTMORE

Dawkins Dr

18

Dawkins Lagoon

Portmore Parkway

Augusta Dr

33

30

31

27 Naggo Head Dr

28

29 Forum

BRAETON NEWTOWN

PORT HENDERSON

39
40

Salt Island Creek

Rodney's Lookout

Green Bay

Fort Clarence

Great Salt Pond

Fort Clarence Beach Park

43

Fisherman's Beach

Bush Reef

Helshire Hills

Helshire Beaches

44

Two Sisters Cave

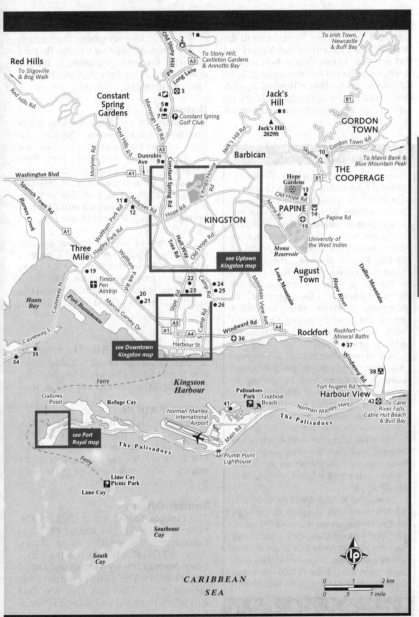

Parade, surrounding a bustling square at the heart of the historic district.

From here, E Queen St runs east to the Norman Manley International Airport and Port Royal. W Queen St runs west for four blocks, then tilts and becomes Spanish Town Rd, which cuts northwest (toward Spanish Town) through Tivoli Gardens and the industrial estates of southwest Kingston, an altogether depressing drive lined with slums and shantytowns.

A dual carriageway east of the junction of Port Royal St and South Camp Rd runs past the General Penitentiary, linking downtown with the Palisadoes and Norman Manley International Airport.

Uptown

Marescaux Rd and Slipe Rd lead north from downtown to 'uptown.' The two roads meet at Cross Roads, a major junction that is the unofficial boundary with New Kingston, immediately to the north. Knutsford Blvd, the main north-to-south artery, bisects New Kingston. Half Way Tree Rd leads northwest, turning into Constant Spring Rd, which leads to Manor Park and Stony Hill.

Northeast of New Kingston lies the middle-class residential area of Liguanea, up Hope Rd from Half Way Tree Rd. Hope Rd ascends gradually past Mona Heights to Papine, the gateway to the Blue Mountains and the University of West Indies campus at Mona.

Maps

You can obtain copies of the JTB's *Discover Jamaica* map from the JTB headquarters (see Tourist Offices below). It features a detailed 1:34,000 scale street map of Kingston.

INFORMATION

Note that while the text here provides information on the main branches for traveler services, such as banks, post offices, telephone centers, and others, refer to the maps for additional locations in the main neighborhoods.

Tourist Offices

The **Jamaica Tourist Board** (JTB; ☎ 929-9200, fax 929-9375; 64 Knutsford Blvd) headquarters has a small research library. Another JTB office is located in the arrival hall at **Norman Manley International Airport** (☎ 924-8024). The **Jamaica Information Service** (☎ 926-3740; 58A Half Way Tree Rd) offers statistical and general information on the island.

SOUTHERN PLAINS

Life on the Edge

Shantytowns sprawl at the edge of Kingston. Endemic rural poverty continues to encourage an enormous pool of starry-eyed youths to seek a better life in the city. For most, the illusion ends in dwellings made of packing cases, fish barrels, tin, and cardboard. To deter squatters, the government has refused to supply public amenities, giving rise to illegal and unsanitary pit latrines.

The lack of basic amenities has not deterred migration from the countryside. Tuberculosis, associated with overcrowded rooms, and typhoid (resulting from inadequate sewage facilities and contaminated drinking water) prevail.

A great percentage of Kingston's *lumpenproletariat* live by pimping, prostitution, and violent crime. Others adapt by 'scuffling' or scraping a living through begging, making handicrafts, and selling the scraps gleaned from garbage dumps such as the 'dungle' on the foreshore in West Kingston.

Life is not altogether dour. As individuals improve their condition, they move on or build more permanent structures that in time become integrated into the city's utilities infrastructure.

Monsignor Richard Albert (☎ 905-1575; 62 Shortwood Rd, Kingston 8) lives like Mother Theresa among the poor of Kingston. His '1000 A Month Club' is a foundation that sponsors inner-city projects and seeks to help shantytown dwellers improve their lives (supporters join the club for J$1000 – less than US$30 – a month).

Foreign Embassies & Consulates
More than 40 countries have diplomatic missions in Kingston. Some are listed in the Facts for the Visitor chapter. Others you'll find in the telephone directories.

Money
Uptown, you'll find more than a dozen banks along Knutsford Blvd, and dozens more elsewhere. Most have foreign-exchange counters as well as 24-hour ATMs. Banking hours are 9am to 2pm Monday to Thursday, and 9am to noon and 3pm to 5pm Friday. Downtown, **Scotiabank** (☎ 922-1000; cnr Duke & Port Royal Sts) has its main foreign-exchange center immediately east of the Jamaica Conference Centre; and **National Commercial Bank** (☎ 922-3940; 77 King St) has a centralized foreign exchange department. See the yellow pages in the telephone directory for bank branches throughout Kingston. For wire remittances, **Western Union** (☎ 926-2454, 888-991-2056; 7 Hillcrest Ave) has about 20 agencies throughout Kingston.

Post & Communications
The main **post office** (☎ 922-2120; 13 King St; open 8am-5pm Mon-Thur, 9am-4pm Fri, 8am-1pm Sat) gets crowded. A better option is the **New Kingston Post Office** (☎ 926-6803; 115 Hope Rd). Other branches are located throughout the city (see the blue pages in the telephone directory). **Federal Express** (☎ 960-9192; 75 Knutsford Blvd; 8:30am-5pm Mon-Fri) and **DHL** (☎ 922-7333; 19 Haining Rd, Kingston 5) have offices throughout Kingston.

You can make international calls and send faxes from most hotels. There are plenty of public call boxes, including at the **Cable & Wireless Jamaica** headquarters, uptown, at the junction of Oxford St and Half Way Tree Rd, and downtown (☎ 922-6031, 888-967-9700; 15 North St) at the corner of Duke St.

Most upscale hotels catering to business travelers provide in-room dial-up Internet access and have business centers offering Internet service. **Innovative Superstore** (☎ 978-3512; 106 Hope Rd), located in the Sovereign Centre, offers email and Internet access for US$2.50 per 30 minutes. **Emoquad Internet Services** (☎ 908-0228; 48 Lords Rd, Kingston 6) also offers Internet access.

Internet Resources
A good starting point on the web is W www.go-kingston.com. Also take a look at W www.go-portmore.com.

Travel Agencies
Two reputable companies are **Grace Kennedy Travel** (☎ 929-6290, fax 968-8418; 1 St Lucia Crescent), and **Praise Travel** (☎ 929-0215; 9 Cecelio Ave), at the junction with Half Way Tree Rd.

Bookstores & Libraries
The following city bookstores are relatively well stocked: **Bookland** (☎ 926-4035; 53 Knutsford Blvd), **The Bookshop** (☎ 920-0568; Knutsford Blvd), **Sangsters Sovereign Centre** (☎ 978-3518; Shop 20, 106 Hope Rd), and **Sangsters** (☎ 967-1930; 33 King St).

The **Jamaica Library Service** (☎ 926-3315; Tom Redcam Ave; open 9am-6pm Mon-Fri, 9am-5pm Sat) is headquartered in the St Andrew Parish Library on a tree-lined avenue. The **National Library of Jamaica** (☎ 922-5533; 12 East St), in the Institute of Jamaica, incorporates the Caribbean's largest repository of audiovisual aids, books, maps, charts, paintings, and documents on West Indian history. The library is open 9am to 6pm Monday to Friday and 9am to 5pm Saturday. The **Jamaican National Heritage Trust** (☎ 922-1287; e jnht@wtjam.net; Headquarters House, 79 Duke St) maintains archives on the island's architectural history.

Universities
'You-wee,' as Jamaicans call the **University of the West Indies** (UWI; ☎ 927-1660; e helpdesk@uwimona.edu.jm), has its campus in northeast Kingston, southeast of Mona Heights (see University of the West Indies later in this chapter). The **University of Technology** (☎ 927-1680; 237 Old Hope Rd) is nearby, in Papine.

Cultural Centers

The **British Council** (☎ 929-6915; 28 Trafalgar Rd) promotes everything British and hosts soirées and cultural events.

Contact the **Jamaica Cultural Development Commission** (☎ 926-5726; 3 Phoenix Ave) for a list of other cultural centers.

Laundry

Among the few self-service laundries are **Speedy's Laundromat** (☎ 924-5846; 108 Red Hills Rd), in Constant Spring Gardens, and **Quick Wash Coin Laundry** (☎ 920-2713; 1 Union Sq). See the yellow pages in the telephone directory for dry-cleaning and other laundry services.

Toilets

You'll find restrooms in the Kingston Mall (US$0.35), near the harbor, and at Nelson Mandela Park at Half Way Tree. They're unsavory places, best avoided.

Luggage Storage

There are no rental lockers at the Norman Manley International Airport, or anywhere else for that matter. Theft is too great a problem. Most hotels permit guests to store luggage with the concierge for up to a week or so at no extra charge.

Medical Services

St John's Ambulance (☎ 926-7656; 2E Camp Rd) offers free ambulance services in Kingston. Private services include **Ambucare Ambulance Service** (☎ 978-2327; 202 Mountain View Ave).

See Ambulances under Health in the Facts for the Visitor chapter for information on air ambulance service.

Private hospitals include the following:

Andrews Memorial Hospital (☎ 926-7401), Hope Rd

Medical Associates Hospital (☎ 926-1400), 18 Tangerine Place

Nuttall Memorial Hospital (☎ 926-2139), 5 Caledonia Ave

Oxford Medical Centre (☎ 926-1525), 22N Old Hope Rd

The following public hospitals all have emergency departments:

Bellevue Hospital (☎ 928-1380), 6½ Windward Rd, Kingston 2

Kingston Public Hospital (☎ 922-0210), North St

University Hospital of the West Indies (☎ 927-1620), UWI campus, Mona

Gynae Associates (☎ 929-5038; 23 Tangerine Place, Kingston 10) specializes in women's medicine. The **Woman's Centre of Jamaica** (☎/fax 926-5768; 42 Trafalgar Rd) has 24-hour counseling for women.

Bustamante Hospital for Children (☎ 926-5721; Arthur Wint Dr, Kingston 5), and **Childcare Medical Centre** (☎ 988-5086; 6 Portmore Dr, Portmore), west of Kingston, specialize in child medicine.

There are dozens of pharmacies in town. Uptown, try **Moodies Pharmacy** (☎ 926-4174; 30 Dominica Dr) in the New Kingston Shopping Centre. Downtown, try **Harport Pharmacy** (☎ 922-7720; 144 Harbour St).

Emergency

The police maintain a **hot line** (☎ 927-7778) and a **tourism liaison** (☎ 922-9321; 79 Duke St). A complete listing of police departments and branches is given in the 'Emergency Numbers' page at the front of the Jamaican telephone directory.

Dangers & Annoyances

The island averages three murders per day, and 75% of these occur in Kingston. Most are drug-related or politically inspired murders in the ghettoes, but the level of general violence and crime has escalated frighteningly throughout the city in recent years.

Avoid Kingston entirely during periods of tension, when localized violence can spontaneously erupt. If you're in town when street violence erupts, definitely avoid downtown, and adhere to any curfews that police may impose.

Stick to the main streets – if in doubt ask your hotel concierge or manager to point out trouble areas. New Kingston and upscale residential areas such as Liguanea and Mona are generally safe for walking, as are most main roads and downtown (though it's certainly *not* an area to be wandering around alone at night). Avoid West Kingston (especially Trench Town, Jones Town, Greenwich Town, and Tivoli), particularly west of the Parade, downtown. The US Embassy also advises caution when traveling to and from Kingston's Norman Manley International Airport via Mountain View and Windward Roads, especially after dark.

Foreigners, especially white tourists, stand out from the crowd. Fortunately, visitors to Kingston are not hassled to anywhere near the degree they are in the north coast resorts. Still, don't loiter! Constant alertness is called for.

And avoid Kingston's buses, which have been the settings for crime.

DOWNTOWN WALKING TOUR
The Waterfront

For several blocks, the waterfront is paralleled by Ocean Blvd, a breeze-swept, 400-yard-long harborfront boulevard.

Start at the **Bank of Jamaica**, the national mint and treasury on Nethersole Place at the east end of Ocean Blvd; it's fronted by a tall concrete statue of Noel 'Crab' Nethersole (minister of finance from 1955 to 1969). Inside you'll find a small **Museum of Coins and Notes** (☎ 922-0750; open 9am-4pm Mon-Fri; admission free) displaying Jamaican currency through the centuries.

Go west half a block along Nethersole Place to get to the **Jamaica Conference Centre** (☎ 922-9160, fax 922-7816; 14-20 Duke St), built in 1982 as the venue for meetings of the United Nations' International Seabed Authority. It's worth popping inside for a free guided tour, not least to admire the intriguing wicker-basket and bamboo ceilings and walls. The names of those who worked on the construction of the center are engraved on a mosaic of metal tiles on the facade outside the main entrance. It reads, 'One one coco full basket,' which roughly translates as 'Everyone's contribution makes something complete.'

Turn onto Ocean Blvd and head west past the *Negro Aroused* statue at the foot of King St (actually, this is a replica; the original is in the National Gallery). This bronze statue depicting a crouched black man breaking free from bondage is the work of Jamaica's foremost sculptor, the late Edna Manley.

Turn right (north) on Orange St to get to the National Gallery.

National Gallery This gallery (☎ 922-1561; 12 Ocean Blvd; admission 'by contribution,' US$0.75 minimum; open 10am-4:30pm Tues-Thur, till 4pm Fri, till 3pm Sat & Sun), in the Roy West Building, displays works encompassing international notables from the English Bloomsbury set to contemporary Cuban painters. Above all, the gallery, part of the Institute of Jamaica, displays Jamaican works from the 1920s to the present. It boasts particularly good collections by John Dunkley and Edna Manley, represented downstairs in the AD Scott Collection. Note, too, the bronze statue of Bob Marley by Christopher Gonzalez in the foyer; it was intended for Celebrity Park but was considered uncomplimentary by Marley fans. You be the judge.

The 10 rooms in the permanent gallery are arranged by decade. The Jamaican School is represented by the works of Dunkley and Manley. One whole room is dedicated to the intuitive works of Mallica 'Kapo' Reynolds. All the big names in the Jamaican artistic pantheon are represented: from Gloria Escoffrey and Barrington Watson to the abstracts of Carl Abrahams melding into the surrealistic art of Colin Garland and the ethereal works of the gallery's former curator David Boxer. (Also see Arts in the Facts about Jamaica chapter.)

Guides are free, but tips are welcome.

An Annual National Exhibition is held December through the spring as a showcase for the best of recent Jamaican art.

The meagerly furnished **African Caribbean Institute** (☎ 922-4793; Orange St; open 9am-3:30pm Mon-Fri), in the building to the north of the gallery, houses a motley museum dedicated to Afro-Caribbean culture.

DOWNTOWN KINGSTON

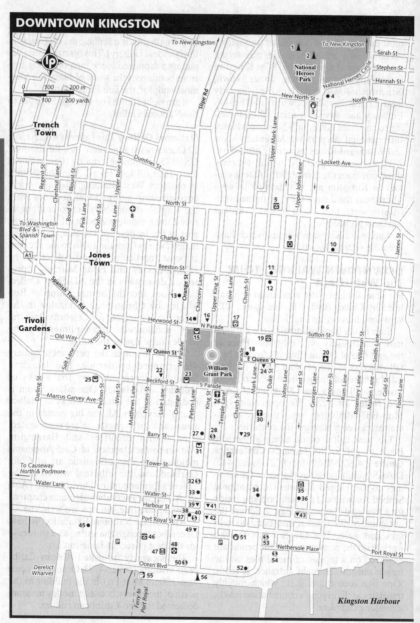

SOUTHERN PLAINS

To New Kingston

To New Kingston

National Heroes Park

Sarah St
Stephen St
Hannah St

New North St

North Ave

Lockett Ave

Trench Town

Slipe Rd

Upper Mark Lane

Upper Johns Lane

North St

James St

To Washington Blvd & Spanish Town

Charles St

Jones Town

Beeston St

Chancery Lane
Upper King St
Love Lane
Church St

Spanish Town Rd

Heywood St

N Parade

Sutton St

Wildman St
Smith Lane

Tivoli Gardens

Old Way

Young St
Salt Lane

W Queen St

W Parade

E Parade

William Grant Park

E Queen St

Duke St

Johns Lane

East St

Georges Lane

Hanover St

Rum Lane

Rosemary Lane

Maiden Lane

Gold St

Foster Lane

S Parade

Beckford St

Marcus Garvey Ave

Matthews Lane
Princess St
Luke Lane
Orange St
Peters Lane
King St
Temple Lane
Church St

Mark Lane

Barry St

To Causeway North & Portmore

Water Lane

Tower St

Water St

Harbour St

Port Royal St

Port Royal St

Derelict Wharves

Nethersole Place

Ocean Blvd

Ferry to Port Royal

Kingston Harbour

0   100   200 m
0   100   200 yards

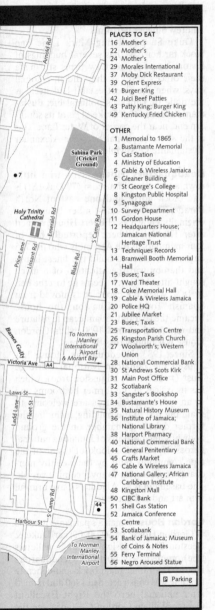

The Parade & Around

King St is the main thoroughfare leading from Victoria Pier to the Parade. It retains many beautiful old buildings with wide sidewalks shaded by columned verandas. Note the decorative carvings and long Corinthian columns at the **National Commercial Bank** building at the corner of King and Harbour Sts.

Half a mile up King St you reach the **Parade**, the streets surrounding William Grant Park at the bustling heart of the downtown mayhem. The gleaming white edifice facing the park's southeast corner is **Kingston Parish Church**, today serving a much reduced congregation of true Kingstonians – those 'born under the clock' (within earshot of its bell). The original church was destroyed in the 1907 earthquake and was replaced (in concrete) by the existing building. Note the tomb dating to 1699, the year the original church was built. Admiral Benbow, the commander of the Royal Navy in the West Indies at the turn of the 18th century, lies beneath a tombstone near the High Altar. Marble plaques commemorate soldiers of the West Indian regiments who died of fever or other hardships during colonial wars.

The **South Parade**, packed with street vendors' stalls, is known as 'Ben Dung Plaza' because passersby have to bend down to buy from street hawkers whose goods are displayed on the ground. The place is clamorous, and stores blast reggae music loud enough to drive away even the most determined visitor (locals seem inured).

Betwixt North and South Parade is **William Grant Park**, which originally hosted a fortress erected in 1694 with guns pointing down King St toward the harbor. The fort was torn down and a garden, Victoria Park, laid out in 1870, with a life-size statue of the queen at its center. She has since been replaced by a bust of Sir Alexander Bustamante; Her Majesty's statue is now a few steps away on the east side of the park. The park was renamed in 1977 to honor black nationalist and labor leader Sir William Grant (1894-1977), who preached his Garveyite message of African redemption here.

At the center of the park is a four-tiered whimsical fountain.

Head west along W Queen St. Stretching three blocks from the Parade is the **Jubilee Market**, a cacophanous hive of vendors' stalls. This writer has always experienced hospitality, but the market borders on Trench Town, within which some archly antiwhite feelings are harbored (see the boxed text 'The Yards' later in this chapter).

Barracks once stood on North Parade, and public hangings took place here in colonial days.

At the northwest corner of the park, the structure with a pink, turreted facade is **Bramwell Booth Memorial Hall**, the headquarters of the Salvation Army, built in 1933.

The impressive sky-blue facade with white trim at the park's northeast corner belongs to the **Ward Theater** (☎ 922-0453), home to the Little Theater Company, and dates from 1907. The doors are usually open and visitors are welcome to nose around.

Coke Memorial Hall faces the eastern side of William Grant Park. This crenelated building has an austere red-brick facade in the dour Methodist tradition. The structure, named after Dr Thomas Coke, founder of the Methodist Missions in the West Indies, dates to 1840, but was remodeled in 1907 after sustaining severe damage in the earthquake. Coke was one of many Methodist missionaries dedicated to the fight to abolish slavery and, like his cohorts, faced the ire of the colonial authorities. Today the building gets little use, but the caretaker is usually around with the key to let you inside for a peek.

Duke Street & Around

From the park's southeast corner, Laws St heads east one block to Mark Lane, leading one block south to **St Andrew Scots Kirk** (☎ 922-1818; 43A Church St). The octagonal Georgian brick structure serves the United Church of Jamaica and Grand Cayman. It was built from 1813 to 1819 by a group of prominent Scottish merchants and is surrounded by a gallery supported by Corinthian pillars. Note the white-on-blue St Andrew cross in the stained-glass window.

You'll be amply rewarded if you visit during a service, when its acclaimed choir, the St Andrew Singers, performs.

Duke St, paralleling Mark Lane one block farther east, has several buildings of historic importance. Law firms still have their offices here, as they did in colonial days, when the street established itself as the node of Jamaica's political life. **Bustamante's House** (1A Duke St) is at its southern end, near the corner of Water Lane. This is the site of national hero Sir Alexander Bustamante's erstwhile office.

Headquarters House This trim little townhouse-turned-museum (79 Duke St) is one block north and one east of North Parade. The brick-and-timber house was originally known as Hibbert House, named after Thomas Hibbert, reportedly one of four members of the Assembly who in 1755 engaged in a bet to build the finest house and thereby win the attention of a much sought-after beauty. It seems he lost the bet. In 1872, when the capital was moved from Spanish Town to Kingston, the house became the seat of the Jamaican legislature and remained so until 1960, when Gordon House was built across the street.

Since 1983, Headquarters House has housed the **Jamaican National Heritage Trust** (☎ 922-1287; admission free), which has its offices in the former bedrooms and in an extension. Visitors are welcome to roam the rest of the building, including the former debating chamber on the ground floor, holding portraits of Jamaica's national heroes. Upstairs is a lookout tower of the type commonly built by the wealthy merchants of yesteryear to spy incoming vessels. The basement is an Aladdin's Cave brimful with art and offbeat relics.

Gordon House Jamaica's parliament meets at Gordon House (☎ 922-0200; cnr Duke & Beeston Sts; admission to public galleries free), immediately north of Headquarters House. The rather plain brick-and-concrete building was constructed in 1960 and named after national hero the Right Excellent George William Gordon (1820-65); see the

Rastafarian iconography, Kingston

Colors of Kingston

Kingston resident with traditional Rasta 'dreads'

Craighton Estate, Blue Mountains

Lush, green hillsides of the Blue Mountains

One of the Blue Mountains' many hidden waterfalls, St Andrew Parish

boxed text 'Jamaica's National Heroes' later in this chapter.

You can visit Gordon House by prior arrangement to watch how the Jamaican parliament conducts business. The legislature has a single chamber, where the House of Representatives and the Senate meet at different times: the former at 2pm on Tuesday (and sometimes, in pressing business, on Wednesday at the same hour), and the latter at 11am on Friday. When the legislature is not in session, the marshal sometimes lets visitors in at his discretion.

Jewish Synagogue Jamaica's only synagogue, the United Congregation of the Israelites, sits on the corner of Duke and Charles Sts. The attractive whitewashed building was built in 1912 (its predecessor was toppled by the 1907 earthquake).

The place is worth a visit for its fine mahogany staircase and gallery. Sand muffles your footsteps as you roam – a memento laid to remember the days of the Inquisition, when Jews fleeing persecution in Spain were forced to practice their faith in Jamaica in secret. The synagogue is usually locked, though the caretaker is often around on weekdays to open up on request for a small donation.

East Street & Around
East St runs parallel to Duke St and is two blocks east, sloping south (one-way for traffic) from National Heroes Park to Ocean Blvd.

Institute of Jamaica Toward the southern end of East St, the Institute of Jamaica (☎ 922-0620, fax 922-1147; **w** www.instituteofjamaica.org.jm; 10-16 East St; open 9:30am-4:30pm Mon-Thur, 9:30am-3:30pm Fri) is the nation's small-scale equivalent of the British Museum or Smithsonian. The institute hosts permanent and visiting exhibitions, and features a lecture hall, plus the **National Library** with Jamaican newspapers and texts dating back more than two centuries.

Also here is a **Natural History Museum** (admission J$20 per person), accessed by a separate entrance around the corner on

Tower St. The dowdy collection offers an array of stuffed birds and an herbarium, rounded out by an eclectic miscellany playing a historical note.

Other Downtown Sites The huge building near the junction of North and East Sts is the **Gleaner Building**, home to Jamaica's leading newspaper. Seven blocks east, the imposing **Holy Trinity Cathedral**, at East St and Emerald Rd, is the center of Roman Catholicism on the island. Admiring its dome and four minarets, visitors can immediately see the Spanish Moorish influence and understand why the Cathedral has been described as a 'reinforced concrete version of St Sophia,' the famous church in Istanbul. Its pipe organ is said to be unmatched in the Caribbean.

A Jesuit boy's school, **St George's College**, stands next door.

National Heroes Park & Around
The 74-acre oval-shaped **National Heroes Park**, at the north end of East St, was formerly the Kingston Racecourse. Today it is a forlorn, barren wasteland grazed by goats. At the park's southern end, **National Heroes Circle** contains a group of statues and memorials, most in dreary realism style. The tomb of

---

The Alpha Boys School

Many of Jamaica's top musicians have been graduates of Kingston's Alpha Boys School (☎ 930-2199, fax 928-2576; **e** suefrsm@yahoo.com; 26 South Camp Rd), opposite Sabina Park cricket ground. The Catholic school was founded in 1880 for delinquent boys and is run by the no-nonsense Sisters of Mercy. It is highly regarded for the quality of its musical tuition and the discipline and sense of self-esteem it instills in the disadvantaged youth. A recent graduate is Yellowman, the 1980s ragga sensation…though the nuns are probably feverishly crossing themselves at the words that pour out of his mouth!

Sir Alexander Bustamante is a flat marble slab beneath an arch. More interesting is the Memorial to 1865, commemorating the Morant Bay Rebellion with a rock on a pedestal flanked by bronze busts of Abraham Lincoln and a black slave with a sword.

Marcus Garvey is also buried here, as is ex-Premier Norman Manley, whose body was flown from England in 1964 and reinterred with state honors. The Manley Monument, honoring his son Michael, was dedicated here in March 2002.

Note the bust of General Antonio Maceo, the Cuban nationalist hero who was given refuge in Jamaica following the failure of the Cuban War of Independence. The Simón Bolívar Monument, dedicated to the liberator of South America, stands in bronze outside the park, in front of the Ministry of Education (2 National Heroes Circle).

Wolmer's School A venerable educational establishment, Wolmer's School (☎ 922-5316; 10 Connolley Ave) was founded in

Jamaica's National Heroes

Jamaica has its equivalent of George Washington and Joan of Arc – individuals who, by force of character, spirit, and example, have been deemed worthy of special status as national heroes, earning the honorific title, 'the Right Excellent.'

Jamaica has seven national heroes:

Paul Bogle (unknown-1865) was an independent smallhold farmer and a Baptist preacher. As a champion of the underclass, he led the march on Morant Bay in 1865 that spun out of control and became the Morant Bay Rebellion. A bounty was placed on Bogle's head. He was captured by the Maroons and executed by the British.

Alexander Bustamante (1884-1977), a firebrand trade unionist and founder of the Jamaica Labour Party, championed independence and became the independent nation's first prime minister, 1962-67.

Marcus Garvey (1887-1940) is considered the father of 'black power' and was named Jamaica's first national hero in 1980. He was born in St Ann's Bay, and in his youth became involved in movements to improve the lot of black people. He traveled abroad widely before founding the Universal Negro Improvement Association and devoting his life to the cause of black nationalism. (See the boxed text 'One God, One Aim, One Destiny' in the Ocho Rios & North Coast chapter.)

George William Gordon (1820-65), a mixed-race lawyer, assemblyman, and post-emancipation nationalist, was self-educated and rose to become a successful landowner and businessman and a powerful advocate of nationalism. He was elected to the Assembly, where he was despised for championing the rights of the poor. Following the Morant Bay Rebellion, political opponents seized the opportunity to brand Gordon responsible. He was arrested, summarily tried, and executed the same day.

Norman Manley (1893-1969) was a lawyer who founded the People's National Party, fought for political autonomy for Jamaica, and became the self-governing island's first prime minister (1959-62), prior to independence.

Nanny (dates unknown) was a legendary leader of the Windward Maroons in the 18th century. She was born and raised in the mountains (like most Maroons, she was of Ashanti origin) and was never enslaved. Nanny rose to become the spiritual leader of the Maroons; folklore attributes her with magical powers.

Sam 'Daddy' Sharpe (1801-32), a town slave named for his owner, was a deacon at the Burchell Baptist Church in Montego Bay. He was hanged by British authorities for his role in leading the 1831 slave rebellion that engulfed the western parishes. (See the boxed text 'Preaching Resistance' in the Montego Bay & Northwest Coast chapter.)

1729 at the bequest of a Swiss-German goldsmith. It has produced many notable figures.

Mico Teachers College The intriguing wooden colonial structures north of Wolmer's School house one of the oldest teacher-training colleges in the world: Mico Teachers College (☎ 929-5260; 1 Marescaux Rd). The college was originally established by the Lady Mico Charity as a primary school in 1834 to educate ex-slaves following emancipation. The impressive main building dates from 1909. Many distinguished Jamaicans were trained here.

Up Park Camp 'The Camp,' midway down Camp Rd (which runs parallel to Marescaux Rd) is the headquarters of the Jamaica Defense Force.

The **Jamaica Defense Force Museum** (☎ 926-8121; open 10am-5pm Mon-Fri by appointment), also called the Military Museum, in front of Up Park Camp, displays uniforms, weapons, and medals of the West Indies Regiment and the Jamaica Infantry Militia that existed between 1602 and 1906.

Immediately south of Up Park Camp is the Gun Court, whose tall barbed-wire fences and guard towers have a conspicuous purpose: to keep dangerous criminals in.

Trench Town Culture Yard & Village

The **Trench Town Development Association** (☎ 757-6739; PO Box 118, Kingston 5), which opened in February 1999 in the presence of England's Prince Charles, has transformed Bob Marley's former home – the 'yard,' which began life as a much-prized housing project erected by the British in the 1930s – into a community-based heritage site featuring the **Trench Town Museum** (☎ 948-1455; 6-10 Lower First St; entrance US$10 to the yard and museum). At last visit, the museum was meagerly stocked with Wailers memorabilia, including Bob Marley's first guitar, an old toilet, pots, and nyahbinghi drums. Eclectic sculptures represent 'intuitive knowing.' That rusted out carcass of a VW bus belonged to Bob Marley & the Wailers in the 1960s.

The guided-tour spiel is like a conversation from *Alice's Adventures in Wonderland,* not least when your guide begins to interpret the natural mystic stones.

At last visit, a restaurant and live lunch-hour concerts were planned.

Trench Town Craft Producers (☎ 792-7053, 367-4222), immediately west of the museum, makes clothes, bags, and batiks, etc. It has a store on-site.

Marley's former home (19 Second St) is in a depressing slum 'yard,' nearby.

The Culture Yard, which is one block off Marcus Garvey Drive, welcomes visitors. But don't go wandering elsewhere around Trench Town on your own. Instead, to visit, contact **Easy Tours** (☎ 989-5597; e nice tours@yahoo.com) or the Trench Town Development Association.

UPTOWN HALF WAY TREE

This important neighborhood, road junction, and major bus terminal is named for a venerable silk cotton (kapok) tree that stood here until the 1870s and whose shaded base became the site of both a tavern and market. Today the spot is marked by a clock tower erected in 1813 as a memorial to King Edward VII, whose bust sits on the south side of the tower at the junction of Hope, Hagley Park, Constant Spring, and Half Way Tree Rds.

Visitors should avoid lingering in and around Nelson Mandela Park, a small landscaped park on the northeast side of Half Way Tree.

St Andrew Parish Church This brick church (☎ 968-9366; cnr Hagley Park & Eastwood Park Rds; services 6:30am & 7:30am Sun, 9am Tues & Fri, 6:30am Wed) is popularly known as 'Half Way Tree Church.' The foundations of the existing church were laid in 1692. The exterior is austere and unremarkable, but the stained-glass windows and organ are worth a peek.

Hope Road

Most of the sites of interest in Uptown are located along this road, which runs from

SOUTHERN PLAINS

Half Way Tree to Papine, at the foothills of the Blue Mountains.

Devon House This house (☎ 929-7029; 26 Hope Rd; open 9:30am-5pm Tues-Sat; admission US$5) nestles in landscaped grounds on the west side of Hope Rd at its junction with Waterloo Rd. The beautiful ochre-and-white house was built in 1881 by George Stiebel, a Jamaican wheelwright who hit pay dirt in the gold mines of Venezuela. The millionaire rose to become the first black custos of St Andrew. The government bought and restored the building in 1967 to house the National Gallery of Jamaica, which has since moved to its present location downtown.

Antique lovers will find a visit worthwhile. Note the trompe l'oeil of palms in the entrance foyer. Stiebel even incorporated a gameroom with whist and cribbage tables, a sewing room, and a gambling room discreetly tucked away in the attic.

The tree-shaded lawns attract couples on weekends. The former carriage house and

courtyard are home to two of Jamaica's more famous restaurants (see Places to Eat later in this section). Admission includes a guided tour.

Jamaica House Half a mile farther up Hope Road on the left is a one-story structure faced by a columned portico and fronted by expansive lawns. Initially built in 1960 as the residence of the prime minister, the building today houses the prime minister's office. You are restricted to peering through the fence.

King's House Hidden amid trees behind Jamaica House is the official residence of the governor-general. It lies at the end of a driveway that begins at the junction of E King's House Rd and Hope Rd.

King's House (☎ 927-6424; open by appointment 9am-5pm Mon-Sat; admission free) was initially the home of the Lord Bishop of Jamaica. The original house was badly damaged in the 1907 earthquake.

The Yards

The ghetto areas of West Kingston are true urban jungles where robbery and murder are 'legitimate' employment. Acre upon acre of these festering tenements spread out west from the Parade, where much of the city's population growth in recent decades has been concentrated. These areas include Trench Town, Jones Town, and sterile housing projects – or 'yards' – such as Majesty Pen and Tivoli Gardens, which were conceived as 'model communities' by ex-Premier Edward Seaga while (ironically) he was Minister of Welfare and Development in the 1960s.

The region was once a calm residential zone. Alas, during the strife of the 1970s, the middle classes debunked and moved to the safety of the suburbs. The poor masses filled the void, and conditions rapidly deteriorated, drawing hoodlums, cutthroats, and other predatory elements, called 'yardies.' The situation was exacerbated by politicians such as Seaga, who shamelessly curried votes by patronizing the 'dons' who lorded over violent gangs or 'posses.' They even provided arms to the gangs and inspired them to intimidate constituents who supported political opponents.

It's easy to tell which party rules behind the stockades. Up-front, no-nonsense wall murals act as territorial markers that tell the tale of a city at war with itself.

The ghettoes are no-go zones for out-of-towners (even people from neighboring areas dare not enter the 'opposition's' turf).

The People's Action for Community Transformation (☎ 920-0334, fax 960-7208; ℮ pactsec@ cwjamaica.com; 2-6 Grenada Crescent, Kingston 5) is a coalition of 26 community-based nongovernmental organizations (NGOs) that work to improve life and community relationships in Kingston's inner city. The organization welcomes donations and will be happy to recommend guides.

Today's visitors explore the remake, built in 1909 to a new design in reinforced concrete. The dining room contains two particularly impressive full-length portraits of King George III and Queen Charlotte by Sir Joshua Reynolds.

The governess hosts free afternoon teas as part of the Meet the People program. Contact the JTB (☎ 929-9200) for information and reservations.

Bob Marley Museum The most-visited site in Kingston is the reggae superstar's former home (☎ 927-9152, fax 978-4906; e marley foundation@cwjamaica.com; 56 Hope Rd; open 9:30am-4pm Mon-Sat; adult/student/child US$10/9/5). An Ethiopian flag flutters above the gate of the red-brick manse that Marley turned into his Tuff Gong Recording Studios (the studios are now in southwest Kingston; see Farther Afield later).

Dominating the forecourt is a gaily colored statue of the musical legend. Some of the guides are deathly solemn, but the hour-long tour provides fascinating insights into Bob Marley's life.

His gold and platinum records (*Exodus,* 1977; *Uprising,* 1980; and *Legend,* 1984) are there on the walls, alongside Rastafarian religious cloaks, Marley's favorite denim stage shirt, and the Order of Merit presented by the Jamaican government. One room upstairs is decorated with media clippings about the superstar. Another contains a replica of Marley's original record shop, Wail'n Soul'm. And his simple bedroom has been retained as it was, with his star-shaped guitar by his bedside.

The former recording studio out back is now an exhibition hall and theater, where the tour closes with a fascinating film of his final days.

No cameras or tape recorders are permitted inside.

Vale Royal
The prime minister's official residence is at the apex of Lady Musgrave and Montrose Rds (south of Hope Rd). The beautiful house was constructed in 1694, when it was known as Prospect Pen and owned by Sir Simon

Taylor, said to have been the richest man in Jamaica. The government bought it in 1928.

The lookout tower on the roof was a common feature of the day, when merchants used spyglasses to keep watch on the movement of ships in Kingston Harbour.

National Stadium & Celebrity Park
The National Stadium (☎ 929-4970; Arthur Wint Dr), built in 1962 when Jamaica hosted the Commonwealth Games, is the venue for most of Jamaica's sporting events of importance. There's a so-called Celebrity Park on the north side of the stadium, although the only statue at present is the famous one of Bob Marley holding his guitar.

FARTHER AFIELD
Hope Gardens
These 45-acre gardens (☎ 927-1257, fax 977-4853; open 6am-6pm daily, till 7pm May-Aug; admission free), at the uppermost end of Old Hope Rd, date back to 1881, when the government established an experimental garden on the site of the former Hope Estate. Part of the Hope Aqueduct, built in 1758 to supply the estate, is still in use. The Ministry of Agriculture, which administers the gardens, maintains a research station and nursery, although the gardens have been in steady decline for some decades and are now in a very sad state.

Among the attractions are cycads, or 'sago palms,' from the antediluvian era. There's a sunken garden, forest garden, orchid house, greenhouses, a small aquarium, ornamental ponds, and a maze. The aviary is a good site for bird-watching.

A small and frankly pathetic zoo (☎ 927-1085; open 10am-5pm daily; admission US$0.50) has a motley display that includes monkeys, lions, and tropical birds.

University of the West Indies
Kingston's UWI campus (☎ 927-1660, fax 977-6669; e helpdesk@uwimona.edu.jm; Mona Campus, Kingston 7), in Papine, is built on the grounds of the former Mona sugar estate. The old aqueduct that bisects the campus once brought water from the Hope

UPTOWN KINGSTON

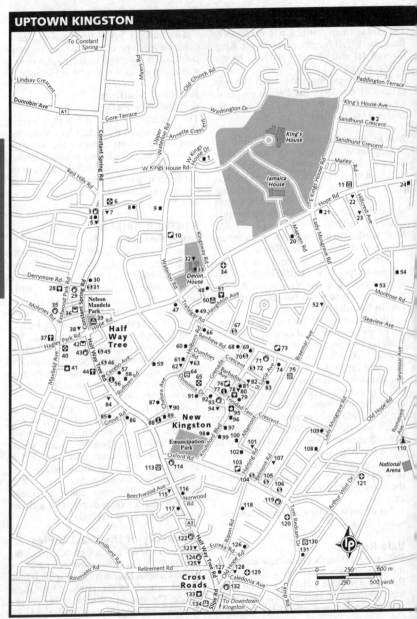

To Constant Spring

Lindsay Crescent

Dunrobin Ave A1

Gore Terrace

Old Church Rd

Myers Rd

Washington Dr

Paddington Terrace

King's House Ave

Sandhurst Crescent

●2

Upper Waterloo Rd

Annette Crescent

Sandhurst Crescent

King's House

Marley Rd

11 🏛

24●

W Kings House Dr

●1

W Kings House Rd

Jamaica House

E Kings House Rd

Hope Rd

22▼
23▼

Hillcrest Ave

Red Hills Rd

Constant Spring Rd

❇6

3●
4▼
5▼

8●

9■

●21

●10

Maeven Rd

20●

●54

●53

Montrose Rd

Kingsway Rd

32▼
33

Lady Musgrave Rd

Devon House

✚
34

Derrymore Rd

28▼

●30
●31

Waterloo Rd

48●
50□

51●

52▼

Eastwood Park

29

Nelson Mandela Park

Taughton Ave

Seaview Ave

Molynes Rd

35

●47

49●

Hagley Park Rd

37🏠

38▼

39

Half Way Tree

Hope Rd

Trafalgar Rd

●66

Renfrew Rd

67●

Braemar Ave

🅿73

68● 69●

70●

71●

72▼

74●

75●

Maxfield Ave

42
40

43●

45

46

Cecelio Ave

●59

60●

Holborn Rd

Dumfries Rd

61●
62▼

63▼

Grenada Crescent

Barbados Ave

St Lucia Ave

76□

82▼

83●

Ruthven Rd

57
58

56

64□
65□

Dominica Dr

77□
78▼

79
80

81●

84▼

87●

91□

92□
90▼
93

94▼

95✚
96

Altamont Crescent

85● 86●

88□
89

Chelsea Ave

Grove Rd

New Kingston

97●

98●

99 100●

Lady Musgrave Rd

109●

Emancipation Park

Knutsford Blvd

101●

102■

108■

Old Hope Rd

Oxford Rd

103●

Hainult Rd

104●

105●

Belmont Rd

106●

107●

110

Seymour Ave

Roosevelt

National Arena

113📷

114

Beechwood Ave

116▼
115▼

Norwood Rd

117●

118●

119●

120●

Tom Redcam Dr

121

Arthur Wint Dr

Lyndhurst Rd

A3

Rousseau Rd

122●
123▼

124▼
125▼

Half Way Tree Rd

Eureka Rd

126●

Ripon Rd

127●
128●

129●

130●

131●

Retirement Rd

Cross Roads

132●

Old Hope Rd

Caledonia Ave

Camp Rd

133❇

134

Slipe Rd

To Downtown Kingston

0   250   500 m

0   250   500 yards

UPTOWN KINGSTON

SOUTHERN PLAINS

PLACES TO EAT
5 McDonald's
7 Taco Bell
16 Juici Beef Patties
19 McDonald's
22 Sugardaddies
23 Portofino's; Western Union
32 Norma's on the Terrace; Devon House I-Scream; Wassi Art Pottery
33 Grog Shoppe; Devonshire
38 Tastee Patties
52 Red Bones Blues Café
62 Akbar; Thai Gardens
63 Indies Sports Bar & Grill
80 Burger King; Pizza Hut; Bullseye Steakhouse & Salad Bar
82 The Coffee Mill of Jamaica
84 McDonald's
90 Chelsea Jerk Centre & Lounge
94 KFC
101 Heather's Garden Restaurant
107 Carlos' Café
115 King's I-tal Vegetarian Restaurant
123 Burger King
125 KFC
128 Doreen's Restaurant

OTHER
3 Gas Station
4 Pablo's Café
6 King's Plaza
8 Wally's Ceramics
10 German Embassy
11 Bob Marley Museum; Queen of Sheba Restaurant
12 Contemporary Art Centre
13 Sovereign Centre; Jade Garden; Mirage; Palace Cineplex; Artisan
14 Mijan Caribbean Clothing
15 Gas Station
17 Scotiabank
18 National Commercial Bank
25 Post Office
26 Gas Station
27 Photo Express
28 Countryside Club
29 Gas Station
30 Photo Express
31 Scotiabank
34 Andrews Memorial Hospital
35 Gas Station
36 Transport Centre
37 St Andrews Parish Church
39 Taxis
40 Half-Way Tree Plaza
41 Police Station
42 Post Office
43 Gas Station
44 Holy Cross RC Church
45 CIBC Bank
46 Scotiabank
47 YMCA
48 Jamaica Cultural Development Commission

PLACES TO STAY
1 Mayfair Hotel
2 Sandhurst
9 Terra Nova All-Suite Hotel; El Dorado Room
20 Shirley Retreat House
21 Medallion Hall Hotel
24 Christar Villas
54 Valerie Dean's Guest House
58 Four Seasons
59 Knutsford Court Hotel
60 Holborn Manor Guest House
61 Indies Hotel
89 New Chelsea Hotel & Amusement Centre
96 Hilton Hotel; Jonkanoo Lounge; Island Car Rentals
97 Courtleigh Hotel & Suites; Sparkles; Alexanders; JUTA
99 Jamaica Pegasus; Pavilion; Pegasus Café; Polo Lounge; Derby Gaming Room
100 Altamont Court
102 Sunset Inn Apartment Hotel
108 Central Court Hotel
111 Crieffe Court
112 Alhambra Inn

49 Women's Centre of Jamaica
50 Limo Taxi Tours
51 Entourage
53 Vale Royal (Prime Minister's Residence)
55 Police Station
56 Jamaica Information Service
57 Praise Travel Service
64 Centerstage Drive-In Theater
65 Lychee Garden; New Kingston Shopping Centre; Moodies Pharmacy
66 JAMPRO
67 National Commercial Bank
68 Island Car Rentals
69 The Bookshop
70 National Commercial Bank
71 Gas Station
72 CIBC Bank
73 British Embassy; British Council
74 Grace Kennedy Travel
75 Emoquad Internet Service
76 Canadian Embassy; DHL
77 Jamaica Tourist Board HQ
78 JamRock Sports Bar & Grill; JamRock Express; Asylum; Halftime Sports Bar; Haphazard Gaming Lounge; Panda Village
79 FedEx
81 Bookland
83 Air Jamaica
85 Caesar's
86 Bolivar Art Gallery
87 Chelsea Galleries
88 Jamaica Information Service
91 BWIA International Airways
92 Platinum
93 Gas Station
95 Police
98 Putt 'n' Play
103 US Embassy; Mutual Life Centre; Mutual Life Gallery
104 National Commercial Bank
105 Scotiabank
106 National Commercial Bank
109 Spartan Health Club; Café Spartan
110 Celebrity Park; Bob Marley Statue
113 Cable & Wireless Jamaica
114 Gas Station
116 FedEx
117 Gemini Club
118 Palaise Royale
119 Gas Station
120 Oxford Medical Centre
121 Bustamante Hospital for Children
122 Gas Station
124 Gas Station
126 DHL
127 Quick Wash Coin Laundry
129 Nuttall Memorial Hospital
130 Little Theater
131 St Andrew Parish Library
132 Gas Station
133 Police Station
134 Carib 5 Cinema

Barbican
Dewsbury Ave
Gloucester Ave
Charlemont Ave
Durham Ave
Liguanea
Mona Heights
To University of the West Indies
Beverly Hills
National Stadium
Statue Dr
Crieffe Rd
Stadium Blvd
To Hope Botanical Gardens, Hwy B1 & Papine

River to turn the old sugarworks, which still stand at the northern end of the campus' circular street, Ring Rd.

Another legacy from plantation days is the chapel of limestone that stands foursquare near the campus entrance.

Two of Jamaica's most famous artworks can be found on the outside walls of the Assembly Hall and the Caribbean Institute of Mass Communications. The walls' elaborate murals are the work of Belgian artist Claude Rahir. Also of note is the metal bird by famous Jamaican sculptor Ronald Moody on the inner Ring Rd, opposite the Institute of Social and Economic Research. It represents *savacou*, a mythical Carib Indian bird of war.

The **Norman Manley Law School** contains a room dedicated to the ex-premier, replete with some of his office furniture and personal memorabilia.

University of Technology Sculpture Park

This sculpture garden, on the grounds of the University of Technology (☎ 927-1680; 237 Old Hope Rd), just north of the UWI campus, was unveiled in 2000 featuring nine sculptures by acclaimed Caribbean artists such as Christopher Gonzalez. Notable figures include Laura Facey's sculpture of a woman's torso stretched in a yoga position, and Basil Watson's *The Compass,* depicting humanity shaping the environment with the use of technology.

Tuff Gong Recording Studios

Bob Marley's son Ziggy Marley runs the studios (☎ 923-9380, 923-5814, fax 923-4657; e tuffgong@cwjamaica.com; w www.bobmarley-foundation.com; 220 Marcus Garvey Dr) in southwest Kingston. Drop-in visitors are welcome. Free tours are hosted. A gift store sells CDs and singles, plus T-shirts, tapes, crafts, and a miscellany of Marley mementos, with discs spun by a colorful 'selector,' Selvyn.

Castleton Gardens

These gardens (☎ 927-1257; open 7am-5pm daily, till 6pm in summer; admission free),

straddling the A3, 17 miles north of Half Way Tree, are spread over 30 acres on the banks of the Wag Water River. Many exotic species introduced to Jamaica were first planted here.

The gardens, which rise up the hillside on the west side of the road, date back to 1860, when 400 specimens from Kew Gardens in London were transplanted on the former sugar plantation owned by Lord Castleton. More than 1000 species of natives and exotics are displayed.

There's a picnic area with cafeteria and toilets. The guides are unpaid (they're not allowed to charge), but tips are welcome.

ACTIVITIES

Constant Spring Golf Club (☎ 924-1610; Oliver Rd) has a 6196-yard, par-70 course and boasts a swimming pool, bar, and tennis, squash, and badminton courts. Visitors can use the club facilities for US$25 daily. **Caymanas Golf & Country Club** (☎ 922-3386, fax 922-3394; e play@caymanasgolfclub.com; PO Box 61, Spanish Town), 6 miles west of Kingston in the hills north of Spanish Town Rd, is a 6844-yard, par-70, 18-hole course (US$50 green fees). Facilities include a pool, gym, squash and tennis courts, jogging trails, horseback riding, and a restaurant.

Putt 'n' Play Mini-Golf Park (☎ 906-4814; 78 Knutsford Blvd; open 5pm-11pm Mon-Thur, 5pm-midnight Fri, 11am-midnight Sat & Sun; adults/children & seniors US$6/3), next to the Liguanea Golf Club, is an 18-hole miniature golf course complete with miniature waterfalls, meandering streams, ponds, sand traps, and natural obstacles.

A favorite spot for runners and walkers is the **Palisadoes**, where you can run along the beach or the main road (see The Palisadoes later in this chapter). If you're into social running, contact the **Hash House Harriers** (☎ 927-3261; e hashpage@jah3.virtual ave.net), a social group that has 'Hare and Hounds' runs on a regular basis.

The **National Stadium** (☎ 929-4970; c/o Institute of Sports, Arthur Wint Dr) has a public Olympic-size swimming pool (admission US$1). The **YMCA** (☎ 926-0801, fax 929-9387; e kymca@cwjamaica.com; 21 Hope Road, Kingston 10), at the corner of Hope &

Trafalgar Rds, has a swimming pool. The best gym is **Spartan Health Club** (☎ 927-7575; 9 Lady Musgrave Rd; nonmembers US$15) in uptown Kingston.

ORGANIZED TOURS

JUTA (☎ 926-1537; 85 Knutsford Blvd, Kingston 5) and **Galaxy Tours** (☎ 931-0428, fax 925-6975; 75 Red Hills Rd) offer specialty city tours. **Island Car Rentals** (☎ 926-8861, 929-5875, fax 929-6787) offers chauffeured city tours. Other companies offering area tours include **Gemini Tours** (☎ 968-2473; 2 Eastwood Ave, Kingston 10) and **Infinity Tours** (☎ 967-2399; 40 Duke St, Kingston 5).

SPECIAL EVENTS
Carnival

Kingston's weeklong carnival (☎ 923-9138; W www.jamaicacarnival.com), held over Easter in March or April, is the highlight of the year, albeit lackluster compared to the carnivals of Trinidad or Brazil. It's a big blowout for the Jamaican masses, when costumed revelers take to the streets in droves. There's reggae and calypso, of course, but soca is king. The fun turns salacious – the dance style is called 'dry-shagging' – and not a little promiscuity is obvious.

Two carnival camps command the scene: Jamaica Carnival and Bacchanal Jamaica, both of which put on their own gigs.

A highlight is **J'Ouvert**, which begins late at night and continues past dawn. Take some grungy clothes, as the revelers like to throw paint over folks. Carnival ends with the **Road March**, when the two camps parade through the streets in carnival costume.

Carnival is preceded by the **John Greaves Beach Party**, with free booze and music.

Other Events

Other major happenings that take place in Kingston include the following:

January

National Exhibition Goes all month (see December listings)

Jamaica School of Dance Concert Season (☎ 926-6129, 922-5988) Features creative, Caribbean-themed dancing at the Little Theater

LTM Pantomime Runs through April (see December listings)

February

Bob Marley Birthday Bash (☎ 927-9152) Brings reggae fans to the Bob Marley Museum in early February

UWI Carnival (☎ 927-1660) Lasts a week and is staged by university students from throughout the Caribbean

Shell/Sandals Limited Overs Cricket Competition Brings together the national teams of Jamaica, Barbados, and Trinidad and Tobago at Sabina Park

Carib Cement International Marathon (☎ 928-6231) Attracts top national and international athletes

March

JAMI (Jamaica Music Industry) Awards (☎ 960-1320) Features guest performers from reggae to classical

Miss Universe Jamaica Beauty Pageant Determines who represents the island in the Miss Universe contest

April

Cariflora Festival (☎ 754-7201, W www.cariflora festival.com) Jamaica's equivalent to the Chelsea Flower Show

Cable & Wireless Test Cricket Features the West Indies team in an international cricket match at Sabina Park

Devon House Craft Fair (☎ 929-7029) Lays out arts-and-crafts displays, in addition to Jamaican foods

May

Jamaica Horticultural Society Show (contact JTB offices) Held in the National Arena

All-Jamaica Tennis Championships (☎ 929-5878) Hosted late May through mid-July at the Eric Bell Tennis Complex

July

National Dance Theater Company's Season of Dance (☎ 926-6129) Offers a summerlong season of performances

August

Independence Day Festival & Street Parade (☎ 926-5726) Features music festivals and a traditional Jonkanoo street parade, live music, and modern dances

September

Miss Jamaica World Beauty Pageant (☎ 927-7575) The winner of this gala crowning pageant represents Jamaica in the Miss World contest.

October

Shell/Sandals Cricket Competition (☎ 967-0322) Held at Sabina Park, features regional teams

Caribbean Heritagefest (☎ 926-5726) A two-day event in mid-October at the Jamworld Entertainment Complex, Portmore, outside Kingston. It features food and crafts fairs, folk theater, traditional dance and drumming, and musical performances.

December

Devon House Christmas Fair (☎ 929-7029) Promotes a colorful display of arts, crafts, and culinary delights

LTM Pantomime (☎ 926-6129) A witty satire with a gala opening on Boxing Day (December 26) at the Ward Theater, running through January; it continues through April at the Little Theater.

National Exhibition (☎ 922-1561) Jamaica's finest artists showcase their work December to February at the National Gallery.

PLACES TO STAY

Most hotels are located in uptown Kingston, and the classier hotels, catering predominantly to business travelers, are all in the neighborhood of New Kingston. In addition, several fine hotels are perched in the cooler hills overlooking the city. Pickings are virtually nonexistent downtown; there are a few guest houses on the edge of downtown, but expect them to be hovels.

Kingston hotel rates are usually the same year-round. All rates quoted are for nonresidents (most hotels offer lower rates for Jamaican citizens).

Places to Stay – Budget

Uptown New Chelsea Hotel & Amusement Centre (☎ 926-5803, fax 929-4746; 5 Chelsea Ave; rooms US$25-40) is a basic option. Older rooms are dark; modern rooms in an annex are slightly better. All feature air-con, hot water, and cable TV. A fifth night is free. It has a pool hall and amusement center, plus disco and rooftop bar.

Central Court Hotel (☎ 926-6040; 47 Old Hope Rd, Kingston 5; rooms single/double US$27/33), near the junction of Old Hope and Lady Musgrave Rds, is a bare-bones option with 34 clean, carpeted rooms and suites with fans, TV, and telephone, plus hot water. Some have air-con (US$4.50 extra). It has a seafood restaurant.

A reader recommends **Valerie Dean's Guest House** (☎ 978-4859; 5 Upper Montrose Rd, Kingston 6; rooms US$30-35), near the Bob Marley Museum. It has eight rooms, including studio apartments, in a handsome home. The landlady 'receives you with warmth.'

Farther Afield You can camp on the riverbank at **Castleton Gardens** (☎ 927-1257) for US$2. There's water. A lively little jerk center is about 100 yards north of the gardens.

Maya Lodge (☎ 702-0314; Peters Rock Rd, Jack's Hill PO; camping per person US$10, cabins US$23, rooms with shared bath US$35), at Jack's Hill, is hidden in a trough below Skyline Drive. It was once an institution among budget travelers seeking 'alternative' bare-bones accommodations. After Peter Bentley, the original owner, left, prices soared and at last visit the place was in poor repair and unattended. Fifteen campsites are cut into the steep hillside amid tall grass and bamboo; you need to bring your own tents and equipment. Wooden cabins sleep up to four people but have neither electricity nor hot water. There are also double rooms, most with shared bath; one room has a private bath. Campers can cook outside for US$3 per use. Sometimes there is only meager fare available at the café, but you can bring your own food. If the place is empty, check with Valerie Phipps at the grocery store outside the entrance. She cooks simple meals. Maya is a resource and starting point for hikers heading into the Blue Mountains. Guided hikes are offered.

Hotel Lori (☎ 923-4647, fax 937-5516; @ hotellorija@hotmail.com; 111 Waltham Park Rd, Kingston 10; rooms with fans US$18, with air-con US$33), formerly

Artland Guest House, on the corner of Molynes Rd west of uptown, offers 28 modestly furnished rooms in two buildings; the more expensive rooms have air-con and cable TV, and all rooms have private bath (cold water only). There's a lounge plus small bar and restaurant. It also operates as a short-time 'love' motel.

Places to Stay – Mid-Range
Uptown Holborn Manor Guest House (☎ 926-0296; 3 Holborn Rd; rooms US$55) has 12 rooms with fans, TV, and phones but modest, dowdy furnishings and cold water only. Rates include breakfast. You'll pay US$5 less without TV, and there's a TV lounge where you can sink into crimson, crushed-velvet sofas.

Indies Hotel (☎ 926-2952, fax 926-2879; e indies@discoverjamaica.com; 5 Holborn Rd, Kingston 10; singles US$35-55, doubles US$57-61), next door to Holborn Manor, also has utility furniture, plus carpets and bright floral spreads, in its 15 spacious rooms (most with air-con; all with TV and telephone) – and there's hot water. A bar and restaurant is in the courtyard. Take an upstairs room for sunlight.

Mayfair Hotel (☎ 926-1610, fax 926-7741; e mayfair@in-site.com; 4 W Kings House Close, Kingston 10; standard rooms US$61, superior US$72, suites US$90-127), north of Devon House, is a popular option with locals. The columned portico entrance hints at grandeur within, but the 32 air-con rooms in eight individual houses are fairly basic, with utility furniture, TV, and telephone, though all are clean and well lit. Its best feature is the views toward the Blue Mountains. A buffet is hosted poolside on Wednesday and Saturday nights.

Sandhurst (☎ 927-8244; 70 Sandhurst Crescent, Kingston 6; singles US$40, doubles US$45-50, doubles with air-con US$55), in a quiet residential neighborhood in Liguanea, is a favorite option in this price bracket. It verges on the eccentric. The 43 spotlessly kept pale-blue rooms with their black-and-white tile floors, utility furniture, and plastic flowers conjure images of Miami in the

1960s. The rooms are somewhat gloomy and stuffy. Some have TV and telephone and private veranda. A dining terrace has views toward the Blue Mountains.

Shirley Retreat House (☎ 927-9208, 946-2678; 7 Maeven Rd, Kingston 10; singles/doubles US$45/55) is operated by the United Church of Jamaica and has four simply furnished, well-lit rooms with hardwood floors, pleasant fabrics, fans, and private bath with hot water. There's a TV in the lounge (two rooms have small TVs, and one has air-con). Rates include continental breakfast. Meals are cooked on request.

Medallion Hall Hotel (☎ 927-4081, fax 978-2060; e medallionhall@cwjamaica.com; 53 Hope Rd, Kingston 8; rooms US$65, suites US$78) is a well-run and atmospheric option close to the Bob Marley Museum. It has 14 rooms with adequate furnishing and private bath. Hardwoods abound. There's a modest restaurant and English pub.

Sunset Inn Apartment Hotel (☎ 929-7283, fax 968-5185; e sunsetinn@mindspring.com; 1A Altamont Crescent, Kingston 5; studios US$58-67, rooms US$62-75) offers an advantageous location in the heart of New Kingston. Alas, the 11 rooms are dowdy with little light, though large bathrooms make amends. The studios are small, and don't have a kitchenette; the one-bedroom units have kitchenettes. All have TVs, telephones, and fans. Take an upperstory room to catch the breeze.

Altamont Court (☎ 929-5931, fax 929-2118; e altamont@n5.com.jm; 1 Altamont Crescent, Kingston 5; rooms US$95, suites US$120) is an attractive alternative with lush foliage and 55 modern, clean, one-bedroom studios, as well as suites, each with air-con, telephone, cable TV, safe, and contemporary furnishings. Facilities include an attractive restaurant and a small pool with bar.

Knutsford Court Hotel (☎ 926-1207, fax 926-8443; 11 Ruthven Rd, Kingston 10), formerly Sutton Place Hotel, was in the midst of a total remake at last visit, when the previously soulless, 160-room property was being upgraded to target value-conscious business and leisure travelers.

SOUTHERN PLAINS

Crieffe Court (☎ 927-8033, fax 978-8382; 10 Crieffe Rd; e crieffe@cwjamaica.com; rooms/studios US$44/45) is a well-kept hotel run by a super friendly and helpful man named Ron. There's nothing inspirational in the basic decor, but the 20-room hotel is spotless and the rooms are spacious, if dark. Ron also has studios with kitchens. All rooms have fans, TV, and hot water; upstairs rooms have a balcony. All have double beds. Potted plants abound, and the small restaurant has a tree growing through the floor.

Farther Afield Abahati Hotel (☎/fax 924-2082; 7 Grosvenor Terrace, Kingston 8; rooms US$30-50), in a reclusive upscale neighborhood in Constant Spring, at the base of Stony Hill, offers a cool location at 600 feet elevation. The 12 rooms are carpeted and clean, with lots of light but tired furniture. Some have air-con. Spacious gardens and a pool offer a chance to relax. The hotel's highlight is a pleasing restaurant, Pearl's Café.

Olympia Crown Hotel (☎ 923-5269, fax 901-6688; 53 Molynes Rd, Kingston 10; rooms with fan US$49, with air-con US$56), 100 yards east of the Four Roads junction in northwest Kingston, is for fitness devotees. This modern, motel-style property has 90 rooms. There's a large-screen TV in the lobby, plus a fully equipped fitness center with steam room and massage, tennis courts, and even a jogging track and the Colors lounge, hosting jazz.

Stony Hill Hotel (☎ 942-2357; PO Box 111, Kingston 8; rooms US$60-70) is a rambling, slate-roofed hotel, in the hills 5 miles north of Half Way Tree on the A3, boasting fabulous views over Kingston. A Model-T Ford stands in the forecourt. This Old-World charmer has 35 rooms, all with private bath with hot water, large windows with views, and an intriguing blend of homey 1960s decor and modern art. Some rooms have air-con and cable TV. Potted plants abound. The modestly elegant restaurant is open to nonguests. There's a pool, plus a bar that's a 1950s time warp; a spa was planned at last visit. The turnoff is on a dangerous hairpin bend by the Texaco gas station.

Places to Stay – Top End

Uptown Christar Villas (☎ 978-3933, fax 978-8068; w www.christarvillashotel.com; 99a Hope Rd, Kingston 6; standard rooms US$93, studios US$117, 2-bedroom suites US$163-175), just east of the Bob Marley Museum, is the pick of the self-catering options. You can choose from modern, pleasantly furnished studio apartments and one- and two-bedroom suites with satellite TVs but no phones, and full kitchen and comfy beds. Rates include tax and free airport transfer. Upper-story suites tend to get hot. You can cool off in the pool, and there's a self-service laundry, a restaurant, and a gym.

Alhambra Inn (☎ 978-9072, fax 978-4338; e alhambra@cwjamaica.com; 1 Tucker Ave; singles/doubles US$75/85), across from the National Stadium, is an attractive, two-story property with 20 air-con rooms in Spanish style. It's designed to lure convention business and offers gracious furnishings, cable TV, telephones, and spacious bathrooms. Upstairs rooms have lofty ceilings and king-size beds. Rates include taxes. Facilities include a restaurant, two bars, and a pool in the courtyard.

Four Seasons (☎ 926-8805, 800-526-2422, fax 929-5964; w www.hotelfourseasonsja .com; 18 Ruthven Rd, Kingston 10; standard rooms US$80, deluxe US$90), a venerable English-style, German-run place, exudes an aged European ambience with its mahogany wall panels and doors, gilt chandeliers, and French curtains. The hotel has 76 air-con rooms, all with TV, telephone, and private bath. Rooms in the original house, though modest, are spacious, lofty, airy, and light. Some have half-canopy beds and mahogany furniture. Rooms in the garden units and a 40-room annex centered on a swimming pool and bar to the rear offer a more amenable, resort-style feel, plus direct-dial phone, and in-room safe. Business discounts are offered for longer stays.

Hilton Hotel (☎ 926-5430, fax 929-7439; ☎ 800-445-8667 in North America; 0845-7581-595 in the UK; w www.hilton.com; 77 Knutsford Blvd, Kingston 5; rooms US$130-195, suites US$255-290) is strongly oriented toward the business traveler, and boasts contemporary architecture and furnishings and a full complement of facilities. It has 303 rooms, including 13 suites. The spacious rooms are elegantly furnished and have a small work desk, direct-dial telephones, satellite TV, and Internet access. Other features include a fitness center, boutique, two tennis courts, a cyber center, and the Jonkanoo Lounge for night owls.

Courtleigh Hotel & Suites (☎ 929-9000, fax 926-7744; ℮ courtleigh@cwjamaica.com; 85 Knutsford Blvd; deluxe rooms single/double US$115/125, 1-bedroom suites US$190/200, penthouses $135-400/145-420), adjoining the Hilton, is a splendid contemporary option with deluxe rooms and one-bedroom suites featuring four-poster beds and tasteful mahogany furnishings, plus cable TV, direct-dial telephone, hair dryer, work desk, and in-room data port for Internet access. The building and 40 rooms are handicap accessible. Suites have kitchenettes. There's a state-of-the-art business center, a respected restaurant, and the Sparkles bar, plus a pool with bar, a small gym, and a coin-operated laundry. Rates include continental breakfast.

Terra Nova All-Suite Hotel (☎ 926-2211, 926-9334, fax 754-9389; ☎ 800-526-2422 in North America; ℮ terranova@cwjamaica .com; 17 Waterloo Rd, Kingston 10; single or double US$165, extra person US$25) is an intimate, all-suite hotel with among the most beautiful and sophisticated rooms in town. It recently reopened with a new look after a complete renovation in 2001. Though the colonial mansion was built in 1924, the 35 spacious junior suites in three two-story wings have a contemporary feel, with tropically vibrant fabrics. King-size beds and cable TV are standard, as is high-speed Internet access. And thumbs up for the marble bathrooms. Facilities include a 24-hour business center and fitness center. The El Dorado dining room (see Places to Eat later in this section) is supremely elegant, plus there's a patio restaurant and La Fresca poolside bar and grill. Rates include taxes and service charge and breakfast.

Jamaica Pegasus (☎ 926-3690, fax 929-5855; ☎ 800-543-4300 in North America;

0800-317006 in the UK; 02-262-4940 in Australia; ℮ jmpegasus@cwjamaica.com; 81 Knutsford Blvd; singles/doubles US$180/190, Knutsford Club US$15 extra, suites US$275-570), a 17-story property, formerly Le Meridien Jamaica Pegasus, has 300 air-con rooms, including 13 suites and three luxury suites. It even has 'female business traveler rooms' and nonsmoking floors. It also offers a panoply of facilities and a selection of restaurants, including the elegant Pavilion for international dishes. It has a slight edge over the Hilton with its full-service business center and the Knutsford Club – a more exclusive enclave of rooms and suites catering to businessfolk – although at last visit many room fixtures were broken.

PLACES TO EAT

There are dozens of **McDonald's** and **KFC** outlets, and Jamaican equivalents, around town. The major shopping centers have fast-food restaurants. Some, such as **Sovereign Centre** (106 Hope Rd), have food courts – whole floors dedicated to fast-food outlets. Most major shopping malls will also have supermarkets.

For produce, head to **Papine Market** at the top end of Hope Rd, or to the market north of uptown on Constant Spring Rd.

The **Coffee Mill of Jamaica** (☎ 924-8951; 17 Barbados Ave) is recommended for excellent cappuccinos, espressos, etc.

Devon House I-Scream (☎ 929-7086; open 10am-10pm Mon-Sat, 11am-10pm Sun & holidays), behind Devon House, sells excellent ice cream.

Jamaican

Lots of places sell patties for less than US$1. **Patty King** (cnr Harbour & East Sts) and **Juici-Beef Patties** (cnr Harbour & King Sts; cnr Hope Rd & Wiltshire Ave) charge about US$0.50 for patties. **Mother's** also has several outlets downtown and also sells meat patties and burgers. Uptown, try **Tastee Patties** (☎ 926-2834; cnr Constant Spring & Hagley Park Rds).

Moby Dick Restaurant (☎ 922-4468; 43 Port Royal St; open 10am-6pm Mon-Sat), downtown, is the best option. It's clean and friendly and serves real Jamaican fare, including curry dishes.

Chelsea Jerk Centre & Lounge (☎ 926-6322; 7 Chelsea Ave; open 11am-midnight), 100 yards east of Half Way Tree Rd, is *the* place for jerk. Mouth-searing jerk pork and chicken dishes cost US$3-12.

Doreen's Restaurant (cnr Old Hope Rd & Caledonia Ave; US$1.50-9; open 7:30am-10pm) is popular with the impecunious seeking filling Jamaican fare.

Sugardaddies (☎ 925-7267; cnr Hope Rd & Hillcrest Ave; US$1.50-9; open 10am-10pm) has lively tropical decor and serves inexpensive, unpretentious 'Caribbean soul food.'

Grog Shoppe (☎ 968-2098; 26 Hope Rd; from US$6; open noon-midnight Mon-Fri, 10am-2pm Sun), on the grounds of Devon House, serves ackee crepes, baked crab backs, roast suckling pig with rice and peas, as well as more recherché nouvelle Jamaican dishes. It's known for its Sunday brunch (US$17).

Alexanders (☎ 929-9000; entrées from US$12; open noon-3pm & 6pm-10:30pm daily), in the Courtleigh Hotel & Suites, combines classy ambience with flavorful international and Jamaican cuisine.

Boon Hall Oasis (☎ 942-3064; meals served 3pm & 6pm-9pm, afternoon tea 3pm-6pm), farther north at Stony Hill, is popular for its traditional Jamaican buffet. A calypso band plays during Sunday buffet brunch (US$20; 11am-3pm).

Nouvelle Jamaican At Devon House, **Norma's on the Terrace** (☎ 968-5488; 26 Hope Rd; entrées US$12-23; open 11am-10pm Mon-Sat) fuses Jamaican with international influences into such dishes as red pea bisque with rum (US$4.50), and jerk smoked pork chops in guava sauce with rum-soaked raisins and fruit flambé (US$16.50). It also has creative salads and killer garlic bread and desserts (the English trifle is excellent). The candlelit terrace setting is romantic. Reservations are recommended. It's closed on public holidays.

Red Bones Blues Café (☎ 978-8262; 21 Braemar Ave; US$20-40; open 11am-1am Mon-Fri, 7pm-1am Sat), *the* in-spot in town,

is recommended for its warm and lively ambience and imaginative cuisine, such as drunken codfish in avocado halves, and chicken stuffed with cream cheese and herbs in white wine sauce (US$19). Opt for patio dining or the handsome bar.

I-tal & Health Food

Morales International (☎ 777-2158; 46 Church St; open 8:30am-7pm), downtown, serves pepperpot soup (US$1), roast fish (US$3), carrot cake, and natural juices (US$1-2).

Queen of Sheba Restaurant (open 9am-5pm), in the forecourt of the Bob Marley Museum on Hope Rd, serves I-tal stew (US$5), broad bean stew (US$5), curried fish (US$6.50), and fruit juices at the 'Jus Juice' bar.

King's I-tal Vegetarian Restaurant (☎ 929-1921; 41 Half Way Tree Rd; US$1-10) is popular with reggae stars. It serves ackee stew, and even tofu, as well as veggie patties and natural juices.

Café Spartan (☎ 927-7575; 9 Lady Musgrave Rd; US$2-7.50), in the Spartan Health Club, offers pumpkin soup, stew peas, chicken and pineapple salad, and tuna salads.

Continental

El Dorado Room (☎ 926-2211; US$4-25; open noon-2:30pm & 7pm-11pm), in the Terra Nova All-Suite Hotel, is a regal venue. The European menu has hints of the Caribbean as well as steadfast Jamaican favorites such as pepperpot soup and grilled snapper. Bring a sweater against the frigid air-conditioning. The hotel also has a less-expensive outdoor restaurant that serves continental fare. There's a daily salad bar. A seafood buffet is offered for Wednesday lunch and dinner. A Jamaican buffet lunch is offered weekdays, and a Sunday brunch buffet (US$21) draws the Jamaican middle class. Afternoon tea is offered 3pm-6pm (US$16.50).

Portofino's (☎ 927-8078; 7 Hillcrest Ave; open 11am-11pm Tues-Sun) is where the cognoscenti head for Italian meals. Minestrone (US$4.50), mussels (US$13), pastas (US$8.50-18), veal, and seafood dishes are served alfresco under a spreading lignum vitae tree and indoor in elegant surroundings.

Pegasus Café, in the Jamaica Pegasus hotel, has a daily brunch special (US$19) and serves excellent espresso coffees, and the **Mayfair Hotel** has a traditional Sunday brunch.

Asian

The **Orient Express** (☎ 967-2198; 135 Harbour St; US$2-12; open 10:30am-3:45pm Mon-Fri, 10:30am-2pm Sat) is the best option downtown. It has the usual full-range Chinese menu.

Lychee Garden (☎ 929-8619; 30 Dominica Dr), upstairs in the uptown New Kingston Shopping Mall, is a popular, inexpensive eatery; the lunch special is US$3.

Similarly, **Panda Village** (☎ 926-8639; cnr Knutsford Blvd & Trinidad Terrace; open 11am-10pm Mon-Sat) has cheap lunch specials and a wide-ranging menu.

Jade Garden (☎ 978-3476; 106 Hope Rd; open noon-10pm), in the Sovereign Centre, specializes in dim sum; it has a Sunday dim-sum brunch for US$14.50. Don't expect to eat for much less than US$25 a head.

Akbar (☎ 926-3480; e akbar@colis.com; 11 Holborn Rd; appetizers US$1-12, entrées US$8-24; open noon-4pm & 6pm-11pm daily) is recommended for its evocative Mughal decor and reasonably priced menu that includes tandooris and vegetarian dishes. The Indian food is excellent. It offers a buffet lunch special (US$15). Reservations are recommended.

Thai Gardens is a Thai restaurant in the patio attached to Akbar. Its extensive menu includes pad thai (US$11-20) and curries (US$8-22).

Other Cuisines

Carlos' Café (☎ 926-4186; 22 Belmont Rd; open 11am-2am) is a trendy bar that serves stuffed crab, pastas, surf-n-turf, and – on Monday – real Alaskan king crab.

JamRock Express (☎ 754-4032; 69 Knutsford Blvd; open 10am-midnight), next to the JamRock Sports Bar & Grill, offers the widest menu. This food-to-go outlet rounds out its salads, sandwiches, and the like with croissants, bagels, and great desserts.

The **Indies Sports Bar & Grill** (☎ 920-5913; 8 Holborn Rd; open 7am-10pm), opposite the Indies Hotel, has pizzas (US$5-12), burgers (US$2), fish-and-chips, and Jamaican dishes. You can choose to dine outside or in the air-conditioned lounge, which resembles a traditional English pub.

Heather's Garden Restaurant (☎ 926-2826, 960-7739; 9 Haining Rd; 10am-11:30pm Mon-Sat) is also known for its tasty, moderately priced fare ranging from Jamaican crab backs (US$5) and buffalo chicken wings (US$4.50) to cottage pie (US$6), charbroiled lamb chops (US$11), kebobs, and seafood.

Bullseye Steakhouse & Salad Bar (☎ 960-8724; 57 Knutsford Blvd; US$4-14) has a salad bar and serves burgers, steaks, and fish-and-chips.

ENTERTAINMENT

Secure Any Tickets (☎ 967-2213; 25 Sutton St, Kingston 10) is a ticket office for entertainment and sporting events that take place in Kingston.

Bars

JamRock Sports Bar & Grill (☎ 754-4032; 69 Knutsford Blvd) is an in-vogue bar drawing an educated crowd. It has TVs all around and plays world beat music. It has 'happy hour' from 4:30pm to 6:30pm Monday to Saturday.

Halftime Sports Bar (☎ 906-1452; 61 Knutsford Blvd), next door, competes and also has pool tables, large screen TVs, air hockey; there's a cyber café.

Red Bones Blues Café (see Places to Eat above; open 11am-1am Mon-Fri, 7pm-1am Sat) could become your favorite spot in town – a hip bar with a cool ambience, good conversation, and great music.

Carlos' Café (see Places to Eat above) is an open-air bar with lively tropical decor, a pool table, video poker, table football, and occasional cabaret. It hosts karaoke on Friday.

Sparkles, in the Courtleigh Hotel & Suites, and **Polo Lounge**, in the Jamaica Pegasus hotel, have pleasant bars.

Discos & Nightclubs

Asylum (☎ 929-4386; 69 Knutsford Blvd) is *the* happening scene, packing in crowds Tuesday through Sunday. Wednesday draws a more elderly middle-class crowd for '80's music.

Mirage (☎ 978-8557; 106 Hope Rd; admission US$5), in the Sovereign Centre, also draws the crowds Wednesday through Sunday.

Countryside Club (☎ 920-6645; 7 Derrymore Rd), just off Half Way Tree Rd, is contrived but pleasant, with a restaurant and bar, plus dancing to live music, especially Latin sounds on Thursday nights. On Saturday, the Latin scene shifts to the **Jonkanoo Lounge**, in the Hilton Hotel, which along with **Sparkles**, in the Courtleigh Hotel & Suites, attracts an older, more sophisticated crowd. Sparkles swings to a Latin beat on Saturday.

Entourage (☎ 926-0303; e brian@colis.com; 3a Haughton Ave; admission US$5) is a gay and lesbian club.

Dancehall For a *really* Jamaican experience, head to a dancehall club. Dress code for the ladies is as little and as tight as possible, and the more gaudy the better (G-strings or tighter than tight 'batty rider' shorts – hot pants – are de rigueur). Fishnet stockings and colored wigs are highly favored. For guys, string vests, baggy pants, and flashy ornamentation rule the roost. The party usually doesn't peak until the wee hours.

Dance styles vary. At press time, hot new styles included 'The Jerry Springer' (simulating fighting), the wiggly 'Prong,' and the salacious 'Go Go Wine.'

Dancehall venues include **Mirage** on Tuesday, **Cactus Disco** (see Portmore later in this chapter) on Wednesday, and **Asylum** on Thursday.

Stageshows & Sound Systems

Kingston has frequent live stageshows, which are announced in newspapers and on streetside billboards. Top-name artists often perform at the **National Arena** (☎ 929-4970; Arthur Wint Dr), as do international R&B stars such as Whitney Houston and Roberta Flack.

Look for posters by Stone Love, the biggest name in sound-system (street party, or 'bashment') productions. A good source is the **Tuff Gong Studios** (☎ 923-9383, 923-5814; 220 Marcus Garvey Dr).

Fort Clarence Beach Park at Hellshire Beach Recreation Area (see later in this chapter) hosts regular bashments.

Live Music

Live jazz is hosted in the basement of the **Mutual Life Centre** (☎ 926-9024; 2 Oxford Rd) every last Wednesday evening of the month, and the **Polo Lounge** in the Jamaica Pegasus hotel has live jazz on Tuesday night.

Grog Shoppe (☎ 968-2098; 26 Hope Rd), on the grounds of Devon House, hosts jazz at 7pm on the middle Tuesday of each month (US$7.50), and it has musical events on other nights; the **Devonshire**, adjacent, is open for live music Thursday through Saturday.

Terra Nova All-Suite Hotel (☎ 926-2211; 17 Waterloo Rd) has calypso poolside on Sunday afternoons.

Boon Hall Oasis (☎ 942-3064; 4 River Rd, Stony Hill; open 9am-5pm Mon-Sat, also 6pm-midnight Fri), north on the A3 in Stony Hill, hosts a 'Friday Evening Jam' featuring jazz.

Theater

Little Theatre (☎ 926-6129; 4 Tom Redcam Dr) puts on plays, folk concerts, and modern dance throughout the year. The main season is July through August, and a 'miniseason' is held each December.

Ward Theatre (☎ 922-0453; admission US$3-8), on North Parade, is home to both the Little Theater's annual pantomime (see Pantomime under Arts in the Facts about Jamaica chapter) and the **National Dance Theater Company**, known for its rich repertory that combines Caribbean, African, and Western dance styles. The **Jamaica Folk Singers** and other companies also perform here.

Look for performances by the **University Singers** (☎ 702-3518), who are justly acclaimed for their repertoire of Caribbean folk and popular music, choral performances, madrigals, jazz, African songs, and pantomime; and don't miss the **Cari-Folk Singers**, who are dedicated to preserving the Jamaican folk genre.

Go-Go Clubs

The two top spots are **Platinum** (☎ 908-1143; 10 Dominica Dr, Kingston 5; open 10pm-4am Mon-Sat; admission US$10), which draws a middle-class crowd lured by predominantly Russian and Eastern European dancers; and **Caesar's** (☎ 929-6374; 5 Balmoral Ave; open 8pm-5am Wed-Sun; admission US$6.50), with local dancers a notch above the competition.

The less salubrious **Gemini Club** (☎ 920-0013; Half Way Tree Rd), **Pablo's Café** (☎ 908-3337; 32 Eastwood Park Rd; admission US$2.50), and slightly more upscale **Palaise Royale** (☎ 929-1113; 14 Ripon Rd; admission US$5) are alternatives.

Other Venues

The five-screen **Carib 5 Cinema** (☎ 926-6106; cnr Slipe & Half Way Tree Rds) and **Palace Cineplex 1 & 2** (☎ 978-3522; 106 Hope Rd), in the Sovereign Centre, show first-run Hollywood movies.

The **Derby Gaming Room**, at the Jamaica Pegasus hotel, has video slots, as does **Haphazard Gaming Lounge** (☎ 906-1452; 61 Knutsford Blvd).

SPECTATOR SPORTS

Sabina Park (☎ 967-0322; South Camp Rd) is *the* place for cricket! See Special Events earlier in this chapter.

For track-and-field enthusiasts, **National Stadium** (☎ 929-4970; Arthur Wint Dr) hosts sporting events. Kingston hosts the annual **Carib Cement International Marathon** (☎ 928-6231) each February.

For information on horse racing, see Portmore later in this chapter.

SHOPPING

Several modern shopping malls are concentrated on Constant Spring and Hope Rds. Two of the largest are **Sovereign Centre** (106 Hope Rd) and **New Kingston Shopping Mall** (Dominica Dr).

Crafts Stalls & Art Galleries

The waterfront **Crafts Market** (Pechon & Port Royal Sts; open Mon-Sat), in an old iron building, has dozens of stalls selling wickerwork, carvings, batiks, straw hats, and other crafts. Watch your wallet!

Wassi Art Pottery (☎ 906-5016; 26 Hope Rd), at Devon House, sells marvelous vases, planters, plates, bowls, etc, each hand-painted and signed by the artist.

Wally's Ceramics (☎ 926-4898; 9 Merrick Ave) also sells quality ceramics.

Bolivar Art Gallery (☎ 926-8799; 1D Grove Rd) has works by Jamaica's leading artists, but also offers fine books, antiques, and maps.

Also selling the best of Jamaican creative talent is **Artisan** (☎ 978-3514; 106 Hope Rd) in the Sovereign Centre, and **Patoo** (☎ 924-1552; 184 Constant Spring Rd) in the Manor Hill Plaza. The latter is a casbah of local treasures (Tortuga puddings laced with rum, Busha Brown sauces, potpourri baskets, ceramic tableware, decorative ornaments, and batik sarongs).

Chelsea Galleries (☎ 929-0045; 12 Chelsea Ave), in the Island Life Centre, displays works by Jamaica's leading artists, as do **Contemporary Art Centre** (☎ 927-9958; 1 Liguanea Ave); **Gallery Pegasus** (☎ 926-3690), in the basement of the Jamaica Pegasus hotel; **Grosvenor Gallery** (☎ 924-6684; 1 Grosvenor Terrace); and **Mutual Life Gallery** (☎ 929-4302; 2 Oxford Rd), in the Mutual Life Centre.

Flea Markets

Local markets include **Papine Market** on weekends at the top end of Old Hope Rd, or the crowded **Jubilee Market**, on W Queen St west of the Parade. *Don't* go wandering any farther west downtown without a guide who's respected locally. Leave valuables and all but a minimum of money in your hotel safe. And be alert. This is a *real* Jamaican experience!

Other

Mijan Caribbean Clothing (☎ 977-5133; 20 Barbican Rd) sells quality Jamaican designs.

Downtown, **Techniques Records** (☎ 967-4367; 99 Orange St), north of the Parade, is

SOUTHERN PLAINS

a good place for reggae cassettes or CDs, and **Tuff Gong Recording Studios** (☎ 923-9383; Marcus Garvey Dr) has a superb reggae selection.

Photo Express (☎ 977-2679; 130 Old Hope Rd, Kingston 6) is fully stocked with film and photography equipment.

GETTING THERE & AWAY
Air

Norman Manley International Airport handles international flights. Domestic flights depart and land at Tinson Pen Airport. For information on Norman Manley, see the Getting There & Away chapter. For more on Tinson Pen, see the Getting Around chapter.

For international airlines with offices in Kingston and at Norman Manley International Airport, see the Getting There & Away chapter.

Air Jamaica (☎ 923-8680 in Kingston, 888-359-2475 islandwide; St Lucia Ave; open 8:30am-4:30pm weekdays) has its headquarters uptown. At press time, Air Jamaica Express had five flights daily to/from MoBay and Tinson Pen, and 10 flights to/from Norman Manley International Airport. Flights between Kingston and Negril, Ocho Rios, and Port Antonio connect through MoBay.

Airspeed Express (☎ 923-0486); **Tropical Airlines** (☎ 920-3770); **Jamaica Air Link** (☎ 923-0486); and **Aero Express** (☎ 937-5011) all offer charter service to MoBay, Negril, and Port Antonio.

Public Transportation

Buses, coasters, and route taxis run between Kingston and every point on the island. They arrive and depart from the terminal at Beckford and Pechon Sts, five blocks west of the Parade, downtown. The terminal adjoins Trench Town, and travelers should exercise caution when passing through. It should be avoided entirely during times of strife. (See the Getting Around chapter for information about Jamaica's bus system.)

Buses to Ocho Rios (four daily) and Port Antonio (four daily) cost about US$1.75; those to Montego Bay (four daily) cost about

US$3.50. Coasters run more frequently (to Montego Bay, US$10; to Ocho Rios, US$7).

GETTING AROUND
To/From the Airports

Norman Manley International Airport is midway along the Palisadoes, about 17 miles southeast of downtown Kingston. The bus stop is opposite the police station. Bus No 98 operates about every 30 minutes between the airport and the west side of the Parade (US$0.75). Route taxis also operate between the airport and West Parade (US$1.75).

A taxi (JUTA; ☎ 927-4534, 926-1537; 85 Knutsford Blvd, Kingston 5) between the airport and New Kingston will cost about US$20.

From Tinson Pen Airport on Marcus Garvey Drive a taxi costs about US$8 to New Kingston, and a bus to the Parade downtown is about US$0.25.

Limo Taxi Tours (☎ 968-3775, fax 944-3147; 3A Haughton Ave, Kingston 10) and **Island Car Rentals** (see Car Rental below) offer chauffeured transfers.

Public Transportation

The major downtown terminus for service within the city is the North and South Parade. At last visit, buses, coasters, and route taxis also departed and arrived at Half Way Tree and at Papine. However, a new uptown transportation station was scheduled to be built on the northwest side of the Half Way Tree junction. See the Getting Around chapter for general information on all the public transportation options.

The **Transport Authority** (☎ 926-5328; e transauth@infochan.org; w www.transport-authority.com; 119 Maxfield Ave, Kingston 10) has overall authority.

The mega-problems that have traditionally plagued Kingston's bus system have been alleviated in recent years, and the system is much improved. It is operated by the **Jamaica Urban Transport Co Ltd** (JUTC; ☎ 749-3196; Michael Manley Blvd, Twickenham Park), which replaced the problem-riddled franchise system previously operated so badly by KMTR and the National Transport Co-op Society (NTCS). KMTR and NTCS still operate bus service to/from Portmore and the outlying hill areas under sub-lease.

Most buses are now modern Mercedes-Benz and Volvo buses, including buses for the disabled.

Fares are determined by a six-stage system according to distance; they range from J$10 to J$25 (less than US$1, regardless). Eventually, plans call for replacing the cash system with a 'smartcard' that operates on the same basis as a telephone card.

Buses stop only at official stops and operate from 5am to 10pm. At last visit, the Transport Authority was preparing to add bus schedules to its website. For a current schedule, you can telephone the JUTC at ☎ 888-588-2287.

Taxis are numerous in Kingston except when it rains, when demand skyrockets. Use licensed cabs only (they have red PPV license plates). Taxis wait outside most major hotels. Taxis are listed in the yellow pages. Fares from New Kingston to downtown are about US$5.

Car Rental

Most car-rental companies offer free airport shuttles. Jamaica's largest and most reputable company, **Island Car Rentals** (☎ 926-5991, 888-991-4255, fax 929-6987; ☎ 800-892-4581 in North America; **W** www.islandcarrentals.com; 17 Antigua Ave & 77 Knutsford Blvd) has its main office near the top of Knutsford Blvd in New Kingston, plus an outlet at the Hilton Hotel.

See Rental Companies under Car Rental in the Getting Around chapter for other companies with offices in Kingston and at the Norman Manley International Airport.

East of Kingston

Kingston is hemmed in to the east by Long Mountain, which forms a narrow bottleneck for the A4, the only road east out of town. Beyond Long Mountain lies a narrow coastal plain. About 4 miles east of downtown, at Harbour View, a road to the right at the traffic circle (roundabout) leads along the Palisadoes to the Norman Manley International Airport and Port Royal.

ROCKFORT MINERAL BATHS

These baths are 3 miles east of downtown Kingston. Rockfort (☎ 938-6551, fax 928-6096; Rockport PO, Kingston 2; open 7am-5:30pm Mon-Fri, 8am-6pm Sat & Sun; public pool adult/child US$2/1.20; private pools from US$15) has one large public pool and 11 private pools of varying sizes, all with whirlpools and wheelchair access. The slightly saline and moderately radioactive water rises from a cold spring. One hour is the maximum allowed. There's a cafeteria and juice bar, plus changing rooms and lockers. Adjacent to the baths is an English fort – Rockfort – with cannons. The remains of another fort – **Fort Nugent** – stand on the hillside about 1 mile east of Rockfort.

Bus No 99B operates from the Parade and Half Way Tree and travels along Windward Rd (US$0.25). You can also take the No 98, which departs from the Parade and passes Rockfort en route to Port Royal.

THE PALISADOES

The Palisadoes is a narrow, 10-mile-long spit that forms a natural breakwater protecting Kingston Harbour. It extends due west from

SOUTHERN PLAINS

Windward Rd. At the western end, reached via Norman Manley Hwy, lies the historic city of Port Royal, set on a former cay that the Spanish called Cayode Carena, where they careened their ships. The spit earned its name for the defensive palisade that was built across the spit to defend Port Royal from a land-based attack. The Palisadoes is fringed on its harbor side by mangroves that shelter crocodiles and colonies of pelicans and frigate birds.

Note that the US Embassy advises travelers to exercise caution when traveling to and from Norman Manley International Airport via Mountain View and Windward Rds, especially after dark.

Plumb Point Lighthouse

The 70-foot-tall, stone-and-cast-iron lighthouse lies midway along the Palisadoes at its elbow. It was built in 1853 and still functions. Despite the lighthouse's presence, in 1997 a freighter ran aground nearby on the windward side of the spit. It is still rusting away.

Royal Jamaica Yacht Club

This club (☎ 924-8685) and marina is open to bona fide members of international yacht clubs only. Berthing costs US$1.30-3.70 per foot, depending on location. It has a swimming pool and sundeck, nice restaurant, and a patio bar. You can also rent sailboats, yachts, and cruisers.

PORT ROYAL

Port Royal is a dilapidated, ramshackle place of tropical lassitude, replete with important historical buildings collapsing to dust. Today's funky fishing hamlet was once the pirate capital of the Caribbean. Later, it was the hub of British naval power in the West Indies, but the remains give little hint of the town's former glory. Its inhabitants today mostly make a living from fishing.

Locals show their birthright as descendants of pirates and slaves in their ruddy complexion and Caucasian features.

Local developers have long touted the city as a possible marine archaeological attraction. While much lip service has been devoted to restoring Port Royal, at last visit

the much-hyped restoration – including an 80-acre theme park, cruise ship pier, entertainment center and arcade, Jamaica music museum, and sound and light show reenactments (including townsfolk in period costumes) to bring the past alive – was no nearer getting off the ground. Still, there seemed hope that work might begin on the naval museum and chapel, intended to house the Admiral Edward Vernon Collection of historical documents, photographs, and artifacts relating to local naval history.

Most tourist sites are open 9am to 4pm weekdays and 10am to 5pm weekends.

History

The English settled the isolated cay in 1656. They called it 'Cagway' or 'The Point' and built Fort Cromwell (renamed Fort Charles after the Restoration in 1660). Within two years General William Brayne was able to report that 'there is the faire beginning of a town upon the poynt of this harbor.'

Era of the Buccaneers At the time, England was sponsoring freelance pirates in their raids against Spanish ships and possessions. Almost as soon as the English had captured Jamaica, buccaneers – organized as the Confederacy of the Brethren of the Coast – established their base at Port Royal. They were alternately welcomed and discouraged by the authorities according to the dictates of England's foreign policy. (See the Rise of the Buccaneers under History in the Facts about Jamaica chapter.)

The lawless buccaneers were big spenders who disposed of their loot 'in all manner of debauchery with strumpet and wine.' The wealth flowing into Port Royal attracted merchants, rum traders, vintners, prostitutes, and others seeking a share of the profits. Townsfolk even invested in the expeditions in exchange for a share of the booty (by tradition, the governor, who then lived at Port Royal, was the first person allowed to step aboard when the ships dropped anchor; he claimed one-tenth of the booty).

The clergy called it 'the wickedest city on earth' and proclaimed that damnation would follow.

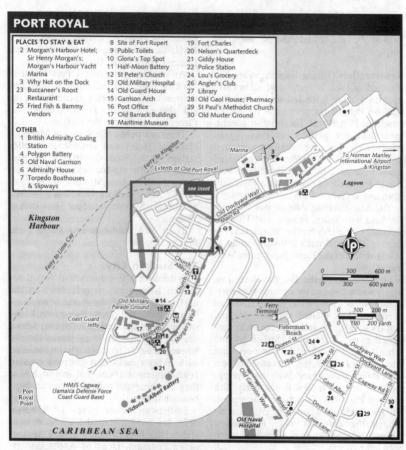

PORT ROYAL

PLACES TO STAY & EAT
2 Morgan's Harbour Hotel;
  Sir Henry Morgan's;
  Morgan's Harbour Yacht
  Marina
3 Why Not on the Dock
23 Buccaneer's Roost
   Restaurant
25 Fried Fish & Bammy
   Vendors

OTHER
1 British Admiralty Coaling
  Station
4 Polygon Battery
5 Old Naval Garrison
6 Admiralty House
7 Torpedo Boathouses
  & Slipways

8 Site of Fort Rupert
9 Public Toilets
10 Gloria's Top Spot
11 Half-Moon Battery
12 St Peter's Church
13 Old Military Hospital
14 Old Guard House
15 Garrison Arch
16 Post Office
17 Old Barrack Buildings
18 Maritime Museum

19 Fort Charles
20 Nelson's Quarterdeck
21 Giddy House
22 Police Station
24 Lou's Grocery
26 Angler's Club
27 Library
28 Old Gaol House; Pharmacy
29 St Paul's Methodist Church
30 Old Muster Ground

SOUTHERN PLAINS

By 1682 Port Royal was a town of 8000 people, with 800 houses 'as dear-rented as if they stood in well-traded streets in London.' There were fortresses all around, plus two prisons and, ironically given the number of brothels and alehouses, two Anglican churches, a Presbyterian church, a Roman Catholic chapel, a Jewish synagogue, and a Quaker meeting house.

Earthquake & Destruction At noon on Tuesday, June 7, 1692, a great earthquake convulsed the island, and the doomsayers were vindicated: Port Royal was destroyed.

The wharves and streets nearest the water's edge keeled over like stricken ships. Fort Carlisle, Fort James, Fort Rupert, and Fort Walker sank beneath the waves. Nine-tenths of the town disappeared underwater, where it remains. The massive quake was followed by a huge tidal wave that washed one ship, the *Swan,* into the center of the town, where it rested on the rooftops, providing shelter for those fortunate enough to scramble aboard. More than 2000 people died, many having fallen into great fissures before being 'squeezed to pulp' when a second tremor closed the gaping holes like pincer jaws. Many of the survivors were claimed by the pestilence that followed, caused by the hundreds of unburied corpses.

Resurrection Official English policy had changed, and sea-rovers who would not give up piracy were hounded and hanged at Gallows Point, a promontory at the harbor mouth of Port Royal. The English government had not written off Port Royal, however. The defensive works were repaired in time to repel a French invasion mounted against Jamaica in 1694. Gradually Port Royal regained its stature as a merchant town and as center of the turtling industry.

The near-constant state of war between England and Spain, France, and Holland throughout the 18th century marked the beginning of Port Royal's 250-year tenure as headquarters of the Royal Navy in the West Indies.

Six forts protected the naval station, which was supported by a prosperous merchant town of 2000 buildings. The advent of peace in 1815 spelled the end of Port Royal's naval glory, and a fire that year consumed much of the town. Struck by one calamity after another, the old port sank into decline. In 1838, Jamaica ceased to be a separate naval command. With the development of steam warships in the early 20th century, Port Royal's demise was sealed. The naval dockyard closed in 1905, and although the defenses were maintained through both world wars, they have since been left to decay.

Orientation & Information

Approaching the town, Norman Manley Hwy runs beside a long brick wall enclosing the old British Admiralty Coaling Station, former Admiralty House, naval garrison quarters, and naval dockyard. You enter town through a breach in the old town wall to the main square, or Muster Ground, overlooked by the Half-Moon Battery on the left. A parapetted town wall of cut limestone blocks (popularly known as Morgan's Wall) leads along Tower St, past the old military hospital, and from thence passing

beneath Garrison Arch to Nelson Square, the old parade ground once known as Chocolata Hole. At the tip of the spit is HMJS *Cagway,* headquarters of the Jamaica Defense Force Coast Guard.

An excellent map called 'Port Royal: A Walking Tour' is included in *Port Royal* by Clinton V Black, which you can buy in the gift store of Morgan's Harbour Hotel (see Places to Stay later in this section).

There are public telephones at Morgan's Harbour Hotel and outside the **police station** (☎ 967-8068; Queen St). The **post office** is in the old barracks near the fort (open 8am to 4pm Monday to Friday). There's also a well-stocked **library** (☎ 967-8391; Broad St; open 9am-5pm Mon, Tues, & Thur-Sat).

There are **public toilets** on the old Muster Ground.

The Sunken City

Two-thirds of 17th-century Port Royal lies hidden from view, 30 feet deep in the harbor offshore of the naval hospital. A beacon about 100 yards offshore marks the site of one of the sunken forts: Fort James. Legend says that the buoy marks the site where St Paul's Church (not to be confused with today's methodist church) sank in 1692 (fishermen claim that in rough seas they can hear the tolling of church bells beneath the sea).

Underwater 'excavations' (☎ 979-845-6398, fax 845-6399 in the USA; ⓦ naut arch.tamu.edu/portroyal; Nautical Archaeology Program, Dept of Anthropology, Texas A&M University, College Station, TX 77843-4352, USA) have been ongoing since 1959.

Old Naval Hospital

The dilapidated hospital sits at the northwest side of town. It was built in 1742 atop a part of the old city that sank in the earthquake. Fire later destroyed the original. The existing 380-foot-long structure is remarkable for its prefabricated cast-iron framework designed to withstand both earthquake and hurricane. The structure dates back to 1819 and remained in use until 1905.

The Archaeological and Historical Museum, once housed here, is no longer.

Fort Charles

Jamaica's latitude and longitude are measured from the flagstaff of Fort Charles (☎ 967-8438; open 9am-5pm, closed Good Friday, Christmas Day, and New Year's Day; admission US$2.50), a weathered redoubt originally laid in 1655. It alone withstood the 1692 earthquake (the other five forts in Port Royal sank into the sea). Being 'not shook down but much shattered,' it was rebuilt of red brick in 1699 and added to several times over the years. It was originally washed by the sea on three sides, but silt gradually built up and it is now firmly landlocked.

At its peak, 104 guns protected the fort. Many cannons still point out from their embrasures.

The marvelous **Maritime Museum** stands in the courtyard and contains a miscellany of nautica from the heyday of the Royal Navy, plus a fabulous model of the *Jamaica Producer* cargo ship. Nelson lived in the small 'cockpit' while stationed here, and his quarters are replicated. A plaque on the wall of the King's Battery, to the right of the main entrance, commemorates his time here.

A small hut, the **Giddy House,** sits alone amid scrub-covered, wind-blown sand 100 yards to the southwest of Fort Charles. The red-brick structure was built in 1888 to house the artillery store. The 1907 earthquake, however, briefly turned the spit to quicksand and one end of the building sank, leaving the store at a lop-sided angle. It is known as the Giddy House because it produces a sense of disorientation to people who enter.

Next to the Giddy House is a massive gun emplacement and equally mammoth cannon – part of the easternmost casement of the **Victoria & Albert Battery** that lined the shore, linked by tunnels. The cannon keeled over in the 1907 earthquake.

There's a snack bar in the old artillery store.

Old Gaol House

The only fully restored historical structure in town is the sturdy Old Gaol House, made of cut stone on Gaol Alley. It predates the 1692 earthquake, when it served as a women's jail. Today it houses a pharmacy.

St Peter's Church

Built in 1725 of red brick, this church is handsome within, despite its faux-brick facade of cement. Note the floor paved with original black-and-white tiles, and the beautifully decorated wooden organ loft built in 1743 and shipped to England in 1996 for restoration. The place is replete with memorial plaques. The communion plate kept in the vestry is said to have been donated by Henry Morgan, though experts date it to later times.

Most intriguing is a churchyard tomb of Lewis Galdye, a Frenchman who, according to his tombstone:

> …was swallowed up in the Great Earthquake in the Year 1692 & By the Providence of God was by another Shock thrown into the Sea & Miraculously saved by swimming until a Boat took him up.

Naval Dockyard

The old naval dockyard lies to the east of Morgan's Harbour Hotel (see Places to Stay & Eat later in this section). Its perimeter walls still stand, as does the Polygon Battery and torpedo slipways, though most of the buildings within are gone. The old coaling station lies immediately to the east. Most of the famous ships of the Royal Navy from the 18th century to the age of steam berthed here.

Naval Cemetery

Half a mile east of the dockyard, also enclosed by a brick wall, is the intriguing naval cemetery, where sailors lie buried beneath shady palms. Alas, the cemetery's most ancient quarter, which contained the grave of the famous buccaneer Sir Henry Morgan, sank beneath the sea in 1692.

Activities

The harbor and adjacent waters have abundant coral reefs, such as the **Water's Edge** and **Southeast Cay Wall**, where you can swim with nurse sharks, turtles, and dolphins, and where you can explore wrecks such as the *Texas,* a warship covered in black coral. The highlight, however, is the Sunken City. At press time, diving the Sunken City was by permit only, accompanied by a coast guard diver. To verify the status of regulations, call the **Jamaican National Heritage Trust** (see Bookstores & Libraries under Kingston earlier in this chapter), which issues permits and can make arrangements.

The scuba facility at Morgan's Harbor Hotel had ceased to function at last visit. For scuba trips, try Halle J Watersports at the Hellshire Beach Recreation Area (see later in this chapter).

Morgan's Harbour Yacht Marina (VHF channel 68; radio call 'Morgan's Harbour') is a full-service facility that rents boats and yachts and offers deep-sea fishing. Deep-sea fishing trips (per hour US$120) are also offered from **Why Not On The Dock** (☎ 967-8448), nearby, as are boat trips to Lime Cay (per person US$7).

Dade's Jet Ski Rental (☎ 789-3008), at Why Not On The Dock, offers trips to the mangrove swamps in Kingston Harbour (US$10), where crocodiles still inhabit the inner sanctums; the mangroves are also a nesting site for frigate birds and pelicans.

Organized Tours
Tour operators in Kingston offer guided tours (about US$30). See Organized Tours under Kingston earlier in this chapter.

Harbour Cruises Ltd (☎ 926-6122; 13 Queens Way, Kingston 10; cruise US$55) offers a cruise from Kingston to Port Royal each last Saturday of the month, with cocktails and a buffet dinner at Morgan's Harbour Hotel.

Places to Stay & Eat
Morgan's Harbour Hotel (☎ 967-8030, fax 967-8073; ☎ 800-852-1149 in the USA; ☎ 020-7930-8600, fax 7930-9232 in the UK; e mharbour@kasnet.com; Port Royal PO; singles/doubles from US$130/150) is an atmospheric though overpriced hotel within the grounds of the old naval dockyard. It has 63 spacious air-con rooms with terracotta tile floors and French doors opening

onto balconies. Cable TV is standard, as are firm king-size beds. Facilities include a swimming pool, gift store, restaurant, and a handsome outside bar. Alas, standards have seriously declined in recent years. Rates include taxes and airport transfers.

Buccaneer's Roost Restaurant (☎ 967-8053; Queen St), a down-to-earth eatery serving seafood for under US$4, is popular with Kingstonians, who spill out onto the street on weekends.

Sir Henry Morgan's (meals US$5.50-34), in Morgan's Harbour Hotel, is popular with the Kingstonian middle class for Sunday brunch. The dinner menu is heavy on seafood and includes grilled lobster, jerk pork, and Jamaican specialties, plus salads and sandwiches. A reader complained about food quality and service.

Why Not On The Dock (☎ 967-8448; open noon-8pm Mon-Fri, 9am-1am Sat & Sun) serves sandwiches and inexpensive cooked meals only on Friday and Sunday.

Vendors sell fried fish and bammy on the main square. Washed down with a beer, your lunch should cost less than US$3. And **Lou's Grocery** (High St) has a minimal stock of groceries.

Entertainment
Gloria's Top Spot (☎ 967-8220; 15 Foreshore Rd), 100 yards east of the muster ground, is *the* place to be on a Saturday night, when local men of all ages – from youths in the latest hip-hop fashion to geezers in yesterday's duds – filter in and warm up at the bar to await the arrival of the women – from young and attired in spandex 'batty riders' to grannies in more conservative garb. By midnight, everyone is dancing to ska, twist, and disco music. Eventually the 'wining' turns truly salacious...with couples simulating copulation to the whistles and cheers of the crowd.

Angler's Club (☎ 967-8101; 40 New St), alias Fisherman's Tavern, is a funky watering hole drawing locals who wash in and out, overindulge in white rum, and pick fights while bartenders boogie at the bar. 'There are a few scalawags, but mostly it's harmless stuff,' one bartender said. It has tremendous character on Friday nights when a mountain of speakers is built 20 feet high in the square and ska music reverberates across the harbor.

Morgan's Harbour Hotel (see Places to Stay & Eat above) sometimes has live bands and dancing, and it offers karaoke on Friday nights

Getting There & Away
Bus No 98 runs from the Parade in downtown Kingston several times daily (US$0.60).

A route taxi from the Parade in Kingston costs about US$0.75; a licensed taxi costs about US$35 one-way. Morgan's Harbour Hotel offers free airport transfers to guests. Otherwise, it's about US$15 for the five-minute taxi ride.

A ferry sails from the waterfront at the foot of Princess St, on Ocean Blvd, in Kingston. It's a 30-minute journey and costs US$0.50 one-way. The ferry departs from Kingston at 10am, 12:30pm, and 5pm Monday to Friday, and at 10am, 12:30pm, 2pm, 4pm, and 6pm Saturday and Sunday; it departs Port Royal for Kingston 30 minutes later.

LIME CAY & ENVIRONS
Lime Cay is one of half a dozen or so uninhabited, sand-rimmed coral cays sprinkled about 2 miles offshore from Port Royal. It's the perfect spot for sunbathing and snorkeling. Kingstonians flock on weekends for picnics.

Maiden Cay is a smaller, shadeless option nearby; it's popular with nudists.

En route to Lime Cay, you'll pass what little remains of **Rackham's Cay** (it's rapidly disappearing beneath the waves); it was named for the infamous Jack Rackham, one of scores of pirates hung here in metal casings after execution. Nearby is **Gun Cay**, named for the cannons that can still be seen, legacies of a British fortification.

You can rent motorized boats (called 'canoes') from fishermen in Port Royal for about US$15 roundtrip and from Why Not On The Dock (per person US$7, 4-person minimum). Morgan's Harbour Yacht Marina

offers customers a two-hour tour of the cays (US$10), plus a one-hour tour of both Lime Cay and the harbor mangroves (US$10). See the Port Royal section, above, for contact information.

BULL BAY
Bull Bay is a small town (with a reputation for anarchy) 9 miles east of downtown Kingston.

Beyond Bull Bay, the main road climbs the scrub-covered hill before making a hairpin descent to Grants Pen and St Thomas parish (see the Blue Mountains & Southeast Coast chapter). Near the summit you'll pass a **monument to Three Finger Jack**, one of Jamaica's most legendary folk heroes. The marker was erected by the National Heritage Trust to recall the deeds of Jack Mansong, who in 1780 and 1781 often single-handedly waged a war of terror against the English soldiers and planters who held the slave territory. Strong, brave, and skilled with machete and musket, his bold exploits were equalled only by his chivalry.

Surfers acclaim the waves that come ashore at **Cable Hut Beach**, about 1 mile west of Bull Bay.

Cane River Falls, 2 miles west of Bull Bay, are a popular bathing spot for locals; the turnoff from the A4 is at Seven Mile, 2 miles east of the Harbour View roundabout. Bob Marley immortalized the place in song: 'Up to Cane River to wash my dread. Upon a rock, I rest my head.'

Unless you are heading for the Black Sovereign Ethiopian Embassy, the only place to stay is at Cable Hut Beach, where a Rasta named Billy 'Mystic' Wilmot runs **Jamnesia Surf Camp** (☎ 750-0103; ⓔ jasurfas@hotmail.com; PO Box 167, Kingston 2; rooms single/double US$25/35; camping per person US$6, with camp-provided tent US$15). It has simple rooms, plus camping, with shared kitchen facilities and bathrooms. You can pitch your own tent, or use a camp-provided tent, which comes with sleeping mat, pillow, linen, night lamp, and flashlight. Six-night packages are offered (US$250-410).

To get to Bull Bay from Kingston, take a coaster or route taxi from the Parade, or take the No 97 bus from Half Way Tree or the Parade (US$0.30).

Black Sovereign Ethiopian Embassy

This makeshift camp (Ethiopia Africa Black International Congress; 10 Miles, Bull Bay PO, St Andrew), painted in the Rasta colors of red, gold, and green, is the home of the Bobo Ashantis ('Bobbaheads') and sits on the Queensbury Ridge above Bull Bay. About 100 fundamentalist Rastafarians live here and make a living from farming or their skills on the street. The government considers them squatters.

The commune ('Dis not Jamaica, mon. Dis is Jah-mekya **God made her**') originated in 1958, when it was founded by the Right Honorable Prince Emmanuel Charles Edward, revered by his gaily robed followers as a black Christ. Male elders are referred to as 'my lord.' Women are addressed as 'honorable empress.' Everyone greets their fellows in passing with the term, 'Blessed!'

Guests are welcome as long as they respect 'manners and principles.' When you arrive, you are led to a room festooned with portraits of Haile Selassie. Here you're greeted by the head priest, who will give you a spiel rich in clever metaphor that offers a fascinating insight into Rastafarian philosophy, including Rasta interpretations of history and politics. You're requested to empty your pockets and turn to give praise to Haile Selassie, an act that you may be asked to repeat each time someone enters and bows to pray to this unlikely god. Your hosts can get quite upset if you don't do this. Of course, you'll be hit up to pay a donation for your visit, and for sundry extras!

You are welcome to stay overnight or as long as you wish in simply furnished rooms, but you must contribute 'something' and 'come to salvation' through performing duties on 'campus.' Cameras are welcome. Women can only enter if they've been 'free' from the beginning of their menstrual cycle for 21 days.

It's a little more than half a mile uphill from the bridge on the A4, 20 yards east of the Red Lion Pub. You'll need 4WD.

Writer Chris Salewicz warns that many among the community are ex-criminals, and that the area is dangerous. You should present yourself at the Bull Bay police station (on the A4) for an escort up the hill.

West of Kingston

The A1 – Nelson Mandela Hwy – runs west out of town past Spanish Town, then as the ruler-straight A2 to Old Harbour and May Pen. The highway is dangerously fast and notorious for fatal accidents. Use caution!

In 2002, ground was broken on Hwy 2000, the nation's first tollway, which will parallel the A2.

PORTLAND BIGHT PROTECTED AREA

This 754-sq-mile region (PBPA), created in 1999, is Jamaica's largest protected area and includes 81 sq miles of dry limestone forest and 32 sq miles of wetlands, as well as precious coral reefs (two-thirds of the protected area lies offshore). Its convoluted boundaries extend westward from Kingston Harbour across St Catherine and Clarendon parishes as far as Canoe Valley Wetland (see later in this chapter), on the border with Manchester parish.

This vital habitat for birds, iguanas, crocodiles, manatees, marine turtles, fish, and 50,000 human beings is managed by the **Caribbean Coastal Management Foundation** (CCAM; ☎ 986-3344, fax 986-3956; ℮ pespeut@infochan.com; PO Box 33, Lionel Town, Clarendon) and **Natural Resources Conservation Authority** (NRCA; ☎ 754-7546; ℮ publiced@nrca.org; 10 Caledonia Ave, Kingston 5).

The CCAM is sponsoring community tourism, using local fishers to lead guided boat tours and hikes. An Eco-Heritage Trail beginning at the Hellshire beaches and ending at Canoe Valley Wetland (see later in this chapter) was in development at last visit. Eventually the trail will feature educational signs and an accompanying guidebook. A visitor center was slated as part of a Biodiversity Conservation Centre and botanical garden (with trails) in the Hellshire Hills, where native and endemic plants will be propagated. And tours throughout the region are planned. *Soon come!*

PORTMORE

Portmore (population 90,000) is a sprawling residential suburb that stretches for miles across the plains west of Kingston. Shopping malls, entertainment centers, and fast-food joints add color to an otherwise drab environment. It is linked to the capital by the Portmore-Kingston Causeway.

Augusta Drive runs along the breeze-blown harbor shoreline parallel to **Port Henderson Beach** – the thin strip of sand is disgustingly littered. At its eastern end is **Fort August**, dating from 1740. The original fort was destroyed when lightning struck the magazine holding 3000 barrels of gunpowder, killing 300 people. The huge crater was filled in and the fort rebuilt. Much decayed, the fort is now a prison.

For updates on the area, visit **w** www.goportmore.com.

Port Henderson

At the west end of the beach (at the southeast corner of Portmore) is a funky fishing hamlet backed by some fine examples of 18th- and 19th-century architecture, notably **Rodney Arms**, a restaurant and pub housed in a beautifully restored Georgian limestone building that was once the Old Water Police Station, where pirates and miscreant marines were detained. It is named after Admiral George Rodney, who commanded the naval station at Port Henderson.

About 200 yards uphill from the Rodney Arms is the ruins of a semicircular gun emplacement replete with cannon, and an old fort and battery – the **Apostles Battery**. It is worth the visit for the views across the harbor, especially at sunset, when Kingston glistens like hammered gold.

Continue along the potholed road for a half mile uphill, and you'll reach **Fort Clarence**, the headquarters of the Jamaica Defense Force (JDF). Signs read, 'Restricted Area: No Unauthorized Person Allowed Beyond this Point.'

Horse Racing

Caymanas Park (☎ 939-0848, 988-7258; Caymanas Dr; admission US$0.35-1.10), in Portmore, has racing each Wednesday and Saturday, plus public holidays.

Places to Stay

World Meditation Centre (camping US$5), directly below the Apostles Battery, lets you pitch a tent here, courtesy of Lanceford Haughton, the Rasta squatter-'owner.' Bring your own food and water. The breezy campsites sit on little terraces on the rocky shore over the water, with cactus all around. It's a fantastic setting, with views across the harbor.

Augusta Drive is lined with hotels that also operate as 'short-time' motels, renting rooms for coital convenience (a four-hour minimum usually applies). The best of the bunch include:

Casablanca (☎ 939-6750; rooms US$51-55) is a modern, castlelike structure with 36 air-con rooms with cable TV and telephone. It has a restaurant and bar. Rates include complimentary breakfast.

La Roose (☎ 998-4654; rooms/suites US$22/33) offers nine clean yet modestly furnished rooms with fans, as well as air-con suites. All have private bath with hot water; some have TV and telephone. Its fairly elegant restaurant specializes in seafood, and there's a handsome English-style pub.

Appropriately named **Jewels** (☎ 988-6785; PO Box 3, Port Henderson; rooms with fan/air-conditioning US$40/45-60) is a gleaming-white hotel, 400 yards west of La Roose, with 25 rooms aired by the breezes that channel down the corridors. Rooms are nicely if simply decorated with bright tropical fabrics; upstairs rooms have lofty wooden ceilings.

Seahorse Rider Inn (☎ 704-6245, fax 939-5652; **e** seahorse@cybervale.com; rooms US$45-49, deluxe US$50-55) was near completion at last visit and offers pleasant-enough rooms with ceiling fan, air-con, and cable TV. A junior suite has a king-size bed and Jacuzzi.

Places to Eat

Rodney Arms (☎ 988-1063; Old Water Police Station, Port Henderson Rd; open 4pm-11:30pm Mon-Fri, 10am-midnight Sat & Sun) offers crab, a seafood platter, garlic shrimp, and other seafood dishes. Prices range from US$12 for steamed fish to US$23 for curried garlic lobster. Its outdoor **Rathid Oyster Bar**, adjoining, was not operating at last visit but was used as an outside dining terrace.

Links Pon Di Beach, a beach park at the east end of Port Henderson Beach, serves snack foods and Jamaican fare.

Entertainment

Cactus Disco (☎ 998-5375), upstairs at the Portmore Plaza, is one of the Kingston area's better nightclubs. This hot spot features an oldies party on Sunday.

Rodney Arms has live bands on Friday and Saturday.

Getting There & Away

Portmore and Port Henderson are reached via the Causeway, which begins in Kingston at the southern end of Hagley Park Rd (at its junction with Marcus Garvey Dr). No eastbound traffic *into* Kingston is allowed along the Causeway between 4:30pm and 7pm; no westbound traffic is allowed between 6:30am and 9am.

Buses to Portmore (US$0.40) operate from Half Way Tree, the Parade, and Three Mile (at the junction of Hagley Park and Spanish Town Rds). Alternately, take a coaster or route taxi from the Parade.

HELLSHIRE HILLS

This area is a 100-sq-mile, totally uninhabited upland region due south of Portmore. The hills are enveloped on three sides by the Caribbean and covered in knife-sharp limestone and inhospitably thick and thorny scrub and cactus, what's known as 'dry limestone forest.'

The Hellshires are an important habitat for migrant birds and a last refuge for endangered species such as the yellow snake, the Mabuya maboua skink, the coney or Jamaican *hutia*, and the Jamaican iguana. The endemic iguana *Cyclura collei* is Jamaica's largest land animal, sometimes growing over 6 feet long. Once common throughout the southern scrublands and tropical dry forests, it has suffered over the past two centuries from forest degradation and the predation of mongooses, feral pigs, cats, and dogs. Less than 100 individual iguanas cling to life within sight of the nation's capital.

Despite the area's legal protection, slash-and-burn agriculture, squatting, wild-pig hunters, and other destructive uses occur in the forest without control. And the area is threatened by encroaching urbanization.

Hiking

The Hellshires are perfect for hiking – if you can rough it. There are no facilities. Hire a guide familiar with the area, take plenty of water, and stay on the trails; the limestone terrain is pitted with scrub-covered sinkholes and it is all too easy to break a leg or worse. Don't underestimate this environment!

At last visit, the CCAM (see Portland Bight Protected Area, earlier in this chapter) was developing trails for day and overnight guided hikes, and a rustic campsite was planned.

Jamaican Iguana Research & Conservation Group (☎ 927-1202, 927-1660; e help desk@uwimona.edu.jm; c/o Dr Peter Vogel, Dept of Zoology, University of the West Indies, Kingston 7) has a one-day 'Iguana Project' trip.

HELLSHIRE BEACH RECREATION AREA

White-sand beaches (owned and operated by the Urban Development Council) fringe the eastern Hellshire Hills and are reached via a road that leads south from Portmore via Braeton Newtown to Hellshire Point, 8 miles south of Braeton.

The road meets the coast at **Great Salt Pond**, a circular bay lined with briny mangrove swamps where snook, mullet, stingrays, and crocodiles ('alligators') can be seen.

At the southeasternmost point of Great Salt Pond is **Fort Clarence Beach Park** (☎ 968-4409; adult/child US$3/1.50; open 10am-6pm Fri-Tues), popular with Kingstonians on weekends. It hosts beauty contests and live reggae concerts ('bashments'). It has showers and toilets plus secure parking. A restaurant and bar are open weekends only.

A road to the left of the second, more southerly roundabout leads east to the main beach, called **Fisherman's Beach**, which is the setting of a funky fishermen's and Rasta 'village' with dozens of gaily painted huts and stalls selling beer, jerk, and fried fish and 'festival' (fried biscuit or dumpling). The place gets crowded on weekends. In the morning fishing pirogues come in with their catch. On any day of the week, though, it's a fascinating visit, a slice of the 'real' Jamaica up close. Toilets and changing rooms were being installed at last visit.

Halle J Watersports (☎ 998-9422, 770-1355) offers sightseeing and scuba trips to Lime Cay and Port Royal, and offers water-skiing, snorkeling, and horseback riding and rents Jet Skis and inflatable sea bikes. Some of the best reef development for scuba diving in Jamaica is in this area, with small cays separated by clear blue water no deeper than 50 feet, surrounded by an outer reef with a drop-off point at 80 feet. The **Southeast Cay Wall** is a drift dive. Nurse sharks are common, as are encounters with dolphins. For a true blue-water dive, head out to **Windward Edge**, about 7 miles south of Kingston Harbour.

From Fisherman's Beach, the road winds south along a dramatic, virtually uninhabited shore. After 2 miles you'll reach **Two Sisters Cave** and **Arawak Museum**, a single site still closed at last visit but touted for restoration by the CCAM. A sign nearby warns that bathing is prohibited due to 'bacterial contamination.'

Hellshire Beach Club (☎ 989-8306; 1A St George's Cliff, Portmore; rooms US$30-35) is a modern, handsome, two-story complex with 60 air-con rooms, all with TV and private bath and shower. It has a pool, bar, and restaurant. It's popular with beach-goers making out…hence the mirrored ceilings.

From Kingston, buses operate to Hellshire Beaches from Half Way Tree and the Parade (US$0.40; 30min). Coasters and route taxis (US$1) run from the Parade.

Spanish Town

The island's second-largest urban center (population 130,000) and the capital of St Catherine parish, boasts a wealth of historic buildings, most in a sad state of repair. Vandalism, demolition, fires, hurricanes, and time have taken their toll on a city that was the capital of Jamaica between the years 1534 and 1872.

HISTORY

After the settlement at Sevilla la Nueva failed in 1534, the Spanish established a new capital at Villa de la Vega – 'the town on the plain' – atop foundations that had been laid down earlier by Christopher Columbus' son, Diego. The town grew modestly as the administrative capital, helped along by a silk-spinning industry. However, Villa de la Vega (later renamed St Jago de la Vega) languished, and at its peak had a population of only about 500 people.

The town was poorly defended and was ransacked several times by English pirates. Eventually, in 1655, an English invasion fleet landed and captured the city. The English destroyed much of the town, then they renamed it 'Spanish Town' and made it *their* capital.

For the next 217 years, the town prospered as Jamaica's administrative capital. The menacing Victorian prison and gallows were here. So, too, a slave market, Jewish synagogues, and theaters. Taverns served planters, their families, and entourages, who flocked to Spanish Town from all over the island during the 'dead season' (October to December) on the sugar estates, when the legislature was also in session.

Eventually Spanish Town was outpaced by Kingston, the mercantile capital, and decline set in. When novelist Anthony Trollope called on the governor in the 1850s, he described Spanish Town as 'stricken with

SOUTHERN PLAINS

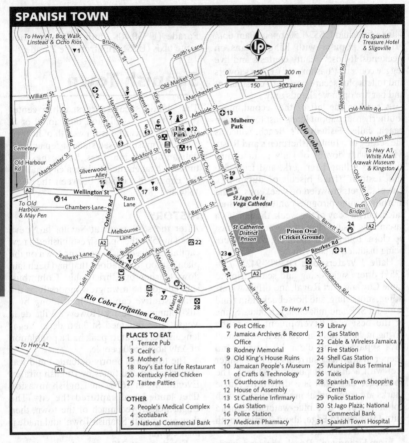

SPANISH TOWN

PLACES TO EAT
1 Terrace Pub
3 Cecil's
15 Mother's
18 Roy's Eat for Life Restaurant
20 Kentucky Fried Chicken
27 Tastee Patties

OTHER
2 People's Medical Complex
4 Scotiabank
5 National Commercial Bank
6 Post Office
7 Jamaica Archives & Record Office
8 Rodney Memorial
9 Old King's House Ruins
10 Jamaican People's Museum of Crafts & Technology
11 Courthouse Ruins
12 House of Assembly
13 St Catherine Infirmary
14 Gas Station
16 Police Station
17 Medicare Pharmacy
19 Library
21 Gas Station
22 Cable & Wireless Jamaica
23 Fire Station
24 Shell Gas Station
25 Municipal Bus Terminal
26 Taxis
28 Spanish Town Shopping Centre
29 Police Station
30 St Jago Plaza; National Commercial Bank
31 Spanish Town Hospital

eternal death.' Kingston was officially named the capital in 1872, and Spanish Town sank into a century of sloth.

The past decade has seen the establishment of light industrial factories on the outskirts of town, lending a certain commercial vitality.

ORIENTATION

The town sits on the west bank of the Rio Cobre. At its center is the Georgian square, the Park (formerly called the Parade), between King and White Church Sts and Adelaide and Constitution Sts. The Spanish

laid out the town on a quadrangular grid around the plaza (although it is easy to become confused and lose your sense of direction in the tight, convoluted one-way system).

From Kingston, you approach along Bourkes Rd, a major commercial street connecting to the Nelson Mandela Hwy linking Spanish Town with May Pen to the west (the A2) and with Kingston to the east (the A1). Barrett St leads northwest from Bourkes Rd to White Church St, which leads past St Jago de la Vega Cathedral and connects to the Park.

INFORMATION

There is no tourist information office.

Banks include **Scotiabank** (☎ 984-3024; 27 Adelaide St) and **National Commercial Bank** (☎ 984-3017; 14 Nugent St), which has a couple of branches, including one at St Jago Plaza.

The **post office** (☎ 984-2409) is at the corner of King and Adelaide Sts. You can make international calls and send faxes from **Cable & Wireless Jamaica** (☎ 984-7010) in the Spanish Town Shopping Centre and on Condrans Ave.

The **public library** (☎ 984-2356; 1 Red Church St) is opposite the cathedral.

Spanish Town Hospital (Bourkes Rd) has a 24-hour **emergency department** (☎ 984-3031), as does **St Catherine Infirmary** (☎ 984-3600; 13 Monk St). For other treatment, try **People's Medical Complex** (☎ 984-6941; 55 Young St). Pharmacies include the **Spanish Town Pharmacy** (☎ 984-1314; 17 Bourkes Rd) in the Spanish Town Shopping Centre, and **Medicare Pharmacy** (☎ 984-2624; 10 Wellington St).

There are two **police stations** (☎ 984-2775, 984-1683; cnr Oxford Rd & Wellington St; 3 Bourkes Rd).

Spanish Town is a hard-edged city; as in Kingston, political gangs hold sway over parts of the city. You should be cautious, especially of petty theft. Avoid exploring away from main downtown streets. And avoid driving near the market (at the western end of Adelaide St), where whole streets are blocked by stalls and piles of rotting, stinking garbage – a stomach-turning sight – and the higglers are surly toward vehicles and foreigners.

WALKING TOUR

Begin at the town square, at the junction of King St and Constitution St.

The Park

Spanish Town's finest old buildings enfold the Park, the town square established by the Spanish as the center of Jamaica's capital city in 1534. Dominating the square on the north side is the elaborate **Rodney Memorial**, built in honor of Admiral George Rodney, who crowned his four-year service as Commander in Chief of the West Indian Naval Station in 1782, when he saved Jamaica from a combined French and Spanish invasion fleet at the Battle of the Saints. He stands within a cupola temple, with sculpted panel reliefs showing the battle scenes. The monument is fronted by two brass cannons from the French flagship.

The building behind the memorial is the **Jamaica Archives & Record Office** (☎ 984-2581), with national documents dating back centuries. It contains the **Clinton Black Reading Room** (open 9am-4:30pm Mon-Thur, 1pm-3:30pm Fri).

On the eastern side of the plaza is the red-brick **House of Assembly**, erected in 1762 and today housing the offices of the St Catherine Parish Council. It has a beautiful wooden upper story with a pillar-lined balcony. The Assembly and Supreme Court sat here in colonial days, when it was the setting for violent squabbles among feuding parliamentarians.

Moving to the south side of the square, you pass the fenced-off **Courthouse Ruins**, destroyed in 1986 by fire. The Georgian building dates from 1819, when it was used as a chapel and armory, with the town hall upstairs.

Finally, on the west side of the plaza is the porticoed Georgian red-brick facade of the ruins of the **Old King's House**, a once-grandiose building erected in 1762 as the official residence of Jamaica's governors. The building was destroyed by fire in 1925, leaving only the restored facade. Today the stables, to the rear, house the **Jamaican People's Museum of Crafts & Technology** (☎ 907-0322; open 9:30am-4:30pm Mon-Sat; adult/child US$2/1). A reconstructed smith's shop and an eclectic array of artifacts – from carpenter's tools to Indian corn grinders – provide an entry point to early Jamaican culture. A model shows how Old King's House once looked.

St Jago de la Vega Cathedral

From the square, take White Church St south for three blocks to St Jago de la Vega Cathedral, the oldest Anglican cathedral in the former British colonies. It's also one of the prettiest churches in Jamaica, boasting wooden fluted pillars, an impressive beamed ceiling, a magnificent stained-glass window behind the altar, and a large organ dating to 1849. The church stands on the site of one of the first Spanish cathedrals in the New World: the Franciscan Chapel of the Red Cross, built in 1525. English soldiers destroyed the Catholic church and used the original materials to build their cathedral. The current structure dates from 1714. Note the handsome octagonal steeple with faux-Corinthian columns, and the negroid gargoyles, considered unique in the world, above the south window.

Many leading personalities are buried within its precincts. The oldest tomb dates to 1662 and is inset in the black-and-white transept aisle laid by the Spanish.

Exiting the church, walk southeast along Barrett St.

St Catherine District Prison

Walking southeast along Barrett St from the church, you'll pass behind the St Catherine District Prison. Hangings have been carried out here since 1714. Today, many prisoners are on death row in narrow cells that date back almost three centuries. Conditions in the prison – Jamaica's largest – were condemned in 1994 by the United Nations Human Rights Committee, and a British Member of Parliament described a recent visit as 'like something out of a nightmare.'

Iron Bridge

At the bottom of Barrett St, turn left onto Bourkes Rd and follow it east to the narrow Iron Bridge spanning the Rio Cobre. The span was made of cast iron prefabricated at Colebrookdale, England, and was erected in 1801 on a cut-stone foundation that dates to 1675. The only surviving bridge of its kind in the Americas, it is still used by pedestrians, if barely. A portion of the neglected structure finally collapsed in 2001.

WHITE MARL ARAWAK MUSEUM

Contemporary Jamaican culture owes much to the influence of the Arawaks, whose history is on display at this meager museum atop a large pre-Columbian settlement. Archaeological research has been ongoing here since the 1940s. Hunting and agricultural implements, jewelry, and carvings are featured. A reconstructed Arawak village is up the hill behind the museum, which was closed at last visit. For a status update, contact the **Jamaica National Heritage Trust** (see Bookshops & Libraries under Kingston earlier in this chapter).

The museum is 200 yards north of the A1, about 2 miles east of Spanish Town.

PLACES TO STAY & EAT

The motel-style **Spanish Treasure Hotel** (☎ 984-2474; PO Box 694; Sligoville Rd; rooms with fan/air-con/TV US$31/33/45), 1½ miles northeast of town, has 60 basic but clean rooms. Rooms are also rented by 'short-time' guests seeking a place of coital convenience. It has a pool and Jacuzzi, a restaurant and bar, and the glitzy Spanish Treasure Nightclub (admission US$3), which opens onto the pool at night. It can get noisy when the disco is going.

Cecil's (☎ 984-1927; 35 Martin St), near the corner of Old Market St, is one of the nicer places to eat. It serves brown stew, callaloo, oxtail, curried goat, and steam fish for under US$5.

Roy's Eat For Life Restaurant (☎ 984-0551; 12 Wellington St) is a vegetarian restaurant and health-food store selling I-tal foods and juices.

Mother's (☎ 984-5547; cnr Wellington & Oxford Rds) is a good bet for patties and baked goods, as is **Tastee Patties** (☎ 984-5019; 1 Bourkes Rd). There's a **Kentucky Fried Chicken** (cnr Bourkes Rd & Condrans Ave).

Shopper's Fair Supermarket (☎ 907-0907) is a food court in St Jago Plaza.

Terrace Pub (☎ 907-5216; Young St) is a nightspot with a shaded patio hosting live music and a pool table. It serves snacks and simple Jamaican fare.

GETTING THERE & AWAY

In Kingston, buses depart frequently for Spanish Town from both the Parade and Half Way Tree (about US$0.50). In Spanish

Town, buses, coasters, and route taxis leave from the **Municipal Bus Terminal** on Bourkes Rd.

A taxi ride between Kingston and Spanish Town will cost about US$15. Taxis depart from outside the transportation center on Bourkes Rd.

Around Spanish Town

BOG WALK GORGE

About 7 miles north of Spanish Town the A1 cuts through a great limestone canyon – Bog Walk Gorge – carved by the slow-moving Rio Cobre. You drop into the gorge and cross the river via the Flat Bridge, an 18th-century stone bridge.

Every rainy season, landslides block the road, disrupting traffic and adding to the damming effect of the narrow gorge. Flat Bridge is frequently under water after heavy rains; the high-water mark of August 16, 1933, is shown on the rock face, when the river rose 25 feet above the bridge!

SLIGOVILLE

This small village sits on the upper story of Montpelier Mountain (2419 feet), 5 miles east of Bog Walk at a junction with roads for Kingston (via Red Hills) and Spanish Town.

During the colonial era the area was a popular summer retreat for white society, and the second Marquis of Sligo, pro-emancipation governor of Jamaica from 1834 to 1836, had a home here. The house, **Highgate Park** (☎ 749-1845; e sligoville1@ hotmail.com), was recently restored by the National Heritage Trust with the help of US Peace Corps volunteers, and today it serves as an environmental center. It also runs a hostel with bunk beds (US$20) and private rooms with baths (US$30).

LINSTEAD

An important market town in the mid-19th century, Linstead has retained its role as a regional market center and is celebrated in the popular song 'Linstead Market,' which

tells of a woman with fruit still unsold in her basket at evening time and her children hungry at home. Everyone who passes by feels her produce for ripeness, then goes away without buying even a quattie-worth:

> Carry em ackee go a Linstead market,
> Not a quattie worth sell.
> Lord, what a night, not a bite
> What a Saturday night,
> Everybody come feel-up, feel-up
> Not a quattie worth sell…

On Saturday, higglers still descend on the town from far and wide, and the streets are packed with women selling their yams, corn, tomatoes, and other produce.

The compact and bustling little town is centered on an old clock tower. Otherwise, the town – which has a confusing system of one-way streets – has no tourist appeal.

At Riversdale, in the Rio d'Oro valley about 10 miles east of Linstead, **Knolford Polo & Tennis Ranch** (☎ 929-8304, fax 929-7139; e knolford@yahoo.com; 12 Trinidad Terrace, Kingston 5; rooms polo player US$300, nonplayer US$150) has 15 modest yet pleasantly furnished rooms, plus a bar and restaurant; rates are all-inclusive. There's a regulation polo field, swimming pool, tennis courts, and eco-trails. The easiest way to get here is to take the B2 from Bog Walk.

EWARTON

Ewarton, on the A1, 7 miles north of Linstead, owes its relative prosperity to the **Ewarton Works** (☎ 985-2301). You may be able to get a factory tour by calling ahead of time.

North of Ewarton, the road begins its steep ascent over Mt Diablo to St Ann parish.

GUTTERS

This roadside hamlet, on the A2 about 5 miles west of Spanish Town, was scheduled to become a major junction on Highway 2000 (see the boxed text 'Highway 2000' in the Getting Around chapter), with the branch tollway to Ocho Rios situated here.

Serenity Park Fishing & Wildlife Sanctuary

Jamaica's 'wildlife safari park' (☎ 708-5515, fax 708-5522; open 10am-6pm Thur-Sun; adult/child US$6/2.50) is a 35-acre facility boasting a menagerie from around the globe: a spider monkey, dozens of snake species, llamas, a buffalo, wallabies, pheasants, and ostriches. It features birds from throughout the Americas, including macaws and a large selection of smaller parrots. There's a kids' petting zoo, and pony rides are offered.

The entrance fee includes fishing (including bait and rods) in breeding ponds stocked with tilapia. Paddleboats are available (per boat US$4.50), as is horseback riding (US$2). There's a Jerk Centre and a restaurant.

Deafening piped-in music detracts from the, er, serenity?

Fishing

The road south from Gutters runs 10 miles through cane fields to Bushy Park in the flatlands at the base of the Hellshire Hills, where **Nature's Habitat Fish World** (☎ 969-2285) and **Little's Hobby Hut** (☎ 995-8500) have a series of man-made lagoons stocked with tilapia. Both sites are popular with Jamaican families who come down to fish with scoop nets for their supper.

OLD HARBOUR

This otherwise nondescript town is famous for its iron clock tower in the town square. The Victorian tower is marvelously preserved, as is the clock, which was installed shortly after the English invasion in 1655 and, amazingly, still keeps good time. Other points of interest are the Church of St Dorothy, one of the oldest on the island. The **Bodles Agricultural Station** (☎ 983-2267) is famous for research in breeding hardy cattle strains. It offers tours by appointment.

The ruins of the Colbeck Castle great house stand amid scrubby grounds 1½ miles northwest of Old Harbour; to reach them, follow the road north from the clock tower.

OLD HARBOUR BAY

This large fishing village, facing Portland Bight (see below), 2 miles south of Old

Harbour, is the site of the south coast's largest fish market. Fishermen land their catch midmorning, and it makes a photogenic sight with the nets laid out and the colorful pirogues drawn up on the otherwise ugly shore. The village is a squalid place of tin and wood shacks and is prone to flooding in the rainy season.

The **Cockpit Salt Marsh**, an estuary near the mouth of the Bowers River, is good for birding and spotting crocodiles. The CCAM (see Portland Bight Protected Area, earlier in this chapter) offers nature trips by rowboat. Similar trips are offered to Salt Island & Black Creeks, which are navigable for several miles, and in combination with the Goat Islands (see Portland Bight below).

You can catch a bus from Old Harbour. A bus also runs daily from the Parade in Kingston.

PORTLAND BIGHT

This deep bay is pocked with islands that await development for ecotourism. At last visit, the CCAM (see Portland Bight Protected Area, earlier in this chapter) was developing such plans, which would include creation of three 'recreation areas': one for Pigeon Island; one for the Pelican Cays (Big and Little) and Tern Cay; and one for the Goat Islands (Great and Little), rimmed with nice beaches and a refuge for the Jamaican iguana, coney, and Jamaican boa.

Plans for Goat Island Recreation Area call for development of the Great Goat Island National Nature Reserve with hiking trails, a reconstructed Taino village, and a museum on the WWII US Naval Air Base on the larger island. A ranger station was planned.

COLEBURNS GULLY

This off-the-beaten-track valley extends northwest from Spanish Town into the central highlands. The road via Guanaboa Vale leads north 5 miles to **Mountain River Cave**, a National Trust site of archaeological import, 2 miles above Guanaboa. Guides will lead you down 1 mile and across the river, where the cave entrance is barred by a grill gate; the steep track is sweaty going, but there's a good spot for swimming in a small river with waterfall. Inside, you'll discover Arawak petroglyphs painted in black on the walls and ceiling. Many date back up to 1300 years. However, this is not Lascaux!

Contact Lloyd Wright at the Jamaica National Heritage Trust (☎ 922-1287; e jnht@wtjam.net; 79 Duke St, Kingston) to arrange guided tours.

At the top of the valley is the village of **Lluidas Vale**, set in a beautiful green trough filled with cane fields. A roadside monument commemorates Juan Lubolo, a former slave turned guerrilla leader in the 17th century. The Juan de Bolas Mountains, which reach 2743 feet, are named after him.

May Pen & Environs

The A2 continues westward from May Pen across the flatlands of the Clarendon Plains to Toll Gate, marking the beginning of a 2000-foot, 9-mile ascent of Melrose Hill, which deposits you near Mandeville (see the South Coast & Central Highlands chapter).

The B12 runs south from Toll Gate to several sites of modest interest.

MAY PEN

The capital city (population 49,200) of Clarendon parish, 36 miles west of Kingston, has a strategic location midway between Spanish Town and Mandeville. It's bypassed by the A2 (Sir Alexander Bustamante Hwy), which runs about 1 mile south of town. The town center teems, especially on Friday and Saturday when the market is held south of the main square. Be prepared for terrible congestion, honking horns, and pushy drivers who add to the general mayhem.

An annual **Denbigh Agricultural Show** is held on the Denbigh Showground, 2 miles west of town, during Independence weekend each August. For information, contact the **Jamaica Agricultural Society** (☎ 922-0610, 967-4094, fax 922-0613; 67 Church St, Kingston).

There's nothing of interest to see or do once you've seen Halse Hall.

Information
National Commercial Bank (☎ 986-2343; 41 Main St), **Scotiabank** (☎ 986-2212; 36 Main St), and **CIBC** (☎ 986-2578; 50 Main St) have branches.

The **post office** (☎ 986-2443) is 100 yards northeast of the square. You can make international calls and send faxes from the **Cable & Wireless office** (☎ 986-2342; Fernleigh Ave) at the west end of town.

May Pen Hospital (☎ 986-2528; Muirhead Ave) is 2 miles west of the town center. **May Pen Medical Centre** (☎ 986-2717; 10 Manchester Ave) can assist with routine diagnosis and prescriptions.

The local **police station** (☎ 986-2208; Main St) is 100 yards west of the main square.

Halse Hall
This handsome great house (☎ 986-2561), on the B12, 3 miles south of May Pen, is situated on a hillock surrounded by pastures. After the English invasion in 1655, the land was granted to Major Thomas Halse, who built the house on an old Spanish foundation. For a time it was occupied by Sir Hans Sloane, the famous doctor and botanist whose collection of Jamaican flora and fauna formed the nucleus of what later became the British Museum of Natural History in London.

It is owned by Alcoa Minerals, which uses it for conferences and social functions. Tours can be arranged by appointment (ask for Mrs Chambers).

Places to Stay & Eat
Versalles Hotel (☎ 986-2775, fax 986-2709; e info@hotelversallesjamaica.com; 42 Longbridge Ave; basic singles or doubles US$36, standard rooms US$59-74, suites US$89-112), a mile southwest of town, has the only accommodations of any worth. This expansive, modern hotel sports lush lawns nibbled by Shetland ponies. It has 32 modestly furnished rooms with telephone and private bath. Sixteen suites have air-con. There's a lap pool, restaurant, and business center. In

addition, **Versalles Disco** (admission US$4; open Thur-Sun) has dancing, and the hotel operates the **Versalles Queen**, a party cruise ship. Theme cruises include karaoke on Thursday, Latin music on Saturday, and oldies on Sunday.

Hot Pot (☎ 986-2586; 18A Manchester Ave) is the place for inexpensive Jamaican fare.

There are plenty of fast-food joints and simple restaurants on Main St.

Getting There & Around

The new transportation center is on Main St, 200 yards southeast of the main square. You can catch buses, coasters and route taxis here to Christiana, Spanish Town, Kingston, Ocho Rios, Mandeville, Negril, Milk River, and most other destinations in the region.

LIONEL TOWN

Lionel Town is a busy market town, 13 miles south of May Pen. It's totally off the beaten path in the midst of sugarcane fields of the West Indies Sugar Company (a subsidiary of Tate & Lyle Ltd). You'll know you've arrived because of strong odors from the **Moneymusk Sugar Factory**, a mile west of town.

Near Moneymusk, just east of the hamlet of Alley, is the hamlet of **Amity Hall**, boasting a notable Anglican church – St Peter's – with bleached gravestones shaded by giant silk-cotton trees. Guided bird-watching tours were planned at last visit; contact the CCAM (see Portland Bight Protected Area earlier in this chapter).

Beaches & Nature Attractions

Much of the shore east and south of Lionel Town is fringed by sand and precious mangrove forest – the habitat of crocodiles and prolific birdlife. Most of the beaches lack for beauty, however, and are the province of fishers and of May Pen residents seeking any old patch of sand on weekends. Some, such as the village and beach of **Rocky Point**, are deplorably littered!

The CCAM (see Portland Bight Protected Area earlier in this chapter) has plans to develop Peake Bay – 8 miles east of

Lionel Town – and the dry forest that backs it as Peake Bay Recreation Area, which will include the mangrove swamp of West Harbour, south of Peake Bay and accessed from Barmouth Beach in Portland Cottage. Boat tours were being planned.

Plans call for an old sugar warehouse at Salt River, 10 miles east of Lionel Town, to become a history and environmental museum.

Jackson Beach Recreation Area, with coral-colored sand, about 8 miles south of Lionel Town, was also being developed, and at last visit the CCAM was contemplating establishing an educational booth on the beach.

Portland Ridge The southernmost extension of Jamaica is a rugged, upland, scrub-covered ridge rimmed by mangrove swamps and offshore coral reefs. It's totally away from the tourist path and difficult to access. Adventurous travelers will find it good for lonesome hiking and for spelunking. **Jackson Bay Cave** has about 12,000 feet of passageways, underground lakes, and stygian chambers festooned with rock formations.

MILK RIVER BATH

This well-known spa (☎ 902-6902, fax 902-4974; open 7am-9pm daily; adult/child per bath US$25/12.50), 14 miles southwest of May Pen, is fed from a saline mineral hot spring that bubbles up at the foot of Round Hill, 2 miles from the ocean. The waters are a near-constant 92°F. An immersion is said to cure an array of ailments ranging from gout and lumbago to rheumatism and nervous conditions.

The spa, which is attached to the Milk River Mineral Bath Hotel, is owned by the government. The six timeworn public mineral baths and three private baths are cracked and chipped, though clean.

These are the most radioactive waters in the world (50 times more so than Vichy in France and three times those of Karlsbad in Austria). Hence, bathers are limited to only 15 minutes, though you are allowed three baths a day. Imbibing the waters is also recommended by the spa staff as a stirring tonic. Kingstonians flock on weekends seeking treatments. Massages are offered (US$25 per hour).

In 2002, the government announced plans to develop 35 acres with a new 136-room resort.

About 200 yards north of the spa is the **Milk River Spa Mineral Pool** (c/o Ministry of Tourism; ☎ 920-4929; open to the public 10am-6pm Sat, Sun & holidays), an open-air swimming pool.

Beyond Milk River Bath, a dirt road lined with tall cacti leads 1½ miles to **Farquhar Beach**, a funky fishing village at the river mouth. You can watch fishermen tending their nets and pirogues, and you can hire a boat and guide to take you to the mouth of the Alligator Hole River in search of crocodiles and elusive, endangered manatees.

A bus operates from May Pen three times daily.

Places to Stay & Eat

Milk River Mineral Bath Hotel (☎ 924-9544, 1-995-4099 cell, fax 986-4962; Milk River PO, Clarendon; doubles without/with bath US$33/40) is a rambling, homey, white-porched hotel with shady verandas, louvered windows, etched wooden motifs above the doors, well-worn pine floors, and 20 modestly furnished, pleasant rooms. Guests are not charged for using the mineral spa. Meals are served in a cozy dining room, where the menu includes Jamaican favorites such as mutton stew and stewed fish. Breakfasts include a health-food special for US$5.

Diana's Seafood Bar, at Farquhar Beach, is a sky-blue shack serving steam fish (US$4) and basic Jamaican fare. Diana, a pleasant young lady, also has **Diana's Guest House**; its one room has a double bed and an outside bathroom and toilet, but no electricity (it's lit by a kerosene lamp). Rates are negotiable.

CANOE VALLEY WETLAND

This government-owned wildlife reserve (☎ 385-0492, 377-8264; admission free), also known as Alligator Hole, is famous for its family of three manatees (all females) that inhabits the diamond-clear water, in which crocodiles (called 'alligators' locally) also hover. They live amid dense, three-foot-tall reeds in jade-blue pools fed by waters that emerge at the base of limestone cliffs. Herons, grebes, jacanas, gallinules, and other waterfowl are abundant.

You are permitted to swim.

There's a small visitor center. You can take an hour-long trip by canoe with a guide. Tip the guides.

The turnoff is signed a mile north of Milk River Bath on the B12.

Blue Mountains & Southeast Coast

If you tire of reggae and beach-bumming and want to cool off in fern-festooned forests, head to the Blue Mountains at Jamaica's eastern end.

Highlights

- A meal, spa treatment, or night of romance at Strawberry Hill

- The trail to Blue Mountain Peak, for the greatest high in Jamaica

- Old Tavern Estate, for the best coffee in the world

- Morant Point Lighthouse – getting there is half the fun

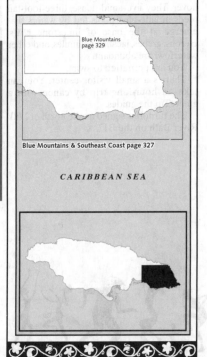

Blue Mountains page 329

Blue Mountains & Southeast Coast page 327

CARIBBEAN SEA

The Blue Mountains rise northeast of Kingston and soar upwards in green pleats to a knife-edged backbone that extends west-northwest and east-southeast for 30 miles. The chain is flanked to the east by the lower John Crow Mountains; to the west are the less distinct Port Royal Mountains. Travelers are drawn by the area's fabulous hiking, colorful, well-watered gardens, and scenic beauty.

The parish of St Thomas, east of Kingston, lies in the shadow of the Blue Mountains. This southeast corner of the country is one of the island's least scenically attractive areas and has limited appeal to foreigners.

Blue Mountains

The Blue Mountains dominate the eastern parishes of St Andrew, St Thomas, Portland, and St Mary, rising swiftly from the coast to a series of rounded peaks culminating in Blue Mountain Peak (7402 feet), the highest point in Jamaica.

The ranges east of Blue Mountain Peak (and the upper northern slopes) are virtually uninhabited. Wild indeed!

Dirt roads link hamlet with hamlet, luring you off the tourist path to appreciate life in the mountains. Many roads are rutted, rain-washed tracks full of holes and huge rocks. Often they deteriorate into muddy stairways that your car negotiates with wheezing difficulty. Fancy clutch skills are called for, and 4WD is essential.

Fill up on gas in Kingston, as there are no gas stations in the Blue Mountains; the nearest is at Papine.

ORIENTATION

From Kingston, simply follow Hope Rd uphill to Papine, a market square and bus station, where Gordon Town Rd leads into the mountains. At the Cooperage, the B1 (Mammee River Rd) forks left steeply

BLUE MOUNTAINS & SOUTHEAST COAST

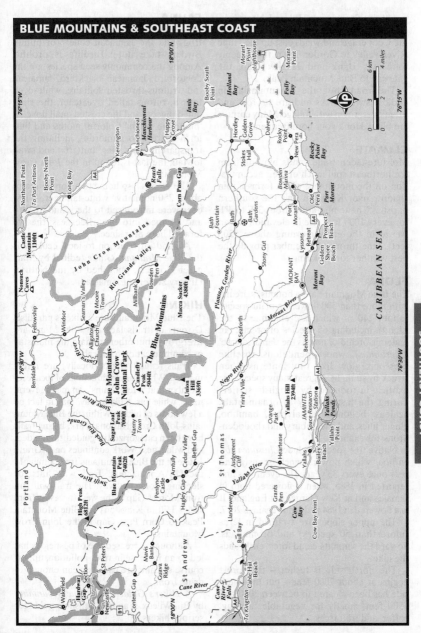

SOUTHEAST COAST

uphill for Strawberry Hill and Newcastle. Gordon Town Rd continues straight from the Cooperage and winds east up the Hope River Valley to Gordon Town, then steeply to Mavis Bank and Hagley Gap, the gateway to Blue Mountain Peak.

The roads hug the mountainside in endless switchbacks and are narrow and often overgrown with foliage. Many corners are blind. Honk your horn frequently.

CLIMATE

Moisture-laden trade winds blowing from the northeast spill much of their accumulation on the mountains, which forms a rain shadow over Kingston and the southern parishes. The temperature drops 3°F to 4°F for every 1000-foot rise in elevation (it can freeze in the early morning above 5500 feet). June through September provide the best weather for exploring.

FLORA

The Blue Mountains are a botanist's dream, with more than 500 flowering plant species (about 240 of which are endemic to the island), including 65 species of orchid. An endemic orchid of note is the 'Jamaica rose' *(Merianias)*, whose pendulous, roselike blossoms glow like tiny lanterns when struck by sunlight. A great many species are exotics introduced by English settlers during the last century as ornamentals: azaleas, begonias, eucalyptus, bamboo, ginger lilies, and cheesebury and rhododendrons, for example.

Native tree species include *Chusquea abietifolia,* which flowers synchronously and only once every 33 years. The event was first reported in 1885, when it flowered both in Jamaica and at Kew Gardens in England. It last flowered in 1984 and is due again in 2017.

The upper slopes are swathed in ferns (more than 50 species) and bromeliads. Toward the summits, cloud forest enshrouds the hiker.

The north side is lusher – the forest begins at about 2000 feet – but the south side has been cleared to between 3000 and 4500 feet, mostly for vegetable farming, coffee, and fruit trees.

FAUNA

The mountains are home to eight species of frogs and the Jamaican coney (or hutia). Birders take note: Birdlife is prolific. Among the commonly seen species are the doctorbird, Jamaican blackbird, Jamaican tody, rufous-throated solitaire, white-eyed thrush, rufous-tailed flycatcher, the ringtailed pigeon, and the crested quail dove, or 'mountain witch.' Colorful moths and butterflies are also numerous, including the transparent 'glass wing' butterfly and swallowtail; the last is found in the John Crow Mountains.

The area is also home to a population of about 250 nonnative white-tail deer. A few deer were introduced to the island in 1980 and escaped into the wilderness; they've foraged here ever since.

A good introduction to local ecology is the *Blue Mountain Guide* (edited by Margaret Hodges), published by the Natural History Society of Jamaica.

HIKING

The Blue Mountains are a hiker's paradise. Dozens of trails lace the hills. Many are overgrown, but others remain the mainstay of communication for locals.

Trails (called 'tracks' locally) are rarely marked. When asking directions of locals, remember that 'a few chains' can mean several miles, while 'jus' a likkle way' may in fact be a few hours of hiking. Within the Blue Mountains-John Crow National Park, hiking trails have been categorized as guided, nonguided, and wilderness. Work continues on a 'Grand Ridge of the Blue Mountains Trail,' similar to the US Appalachian Trail, with huts for sleeping along the way. The trail will run from Morces Gap in the west (access is from Jack's Hill in Kingston) via Blue Mountain Peak to Corn Puss Gap in the John Crow Mountains.

Although increased use of pesticides has led to an increase in river pollution, upper-course streams are usually clean enough to drink from.

A Hiker's Guide to the Blue Mountains, by Bill Wilcox, is an indispensable guide for serious hikers.

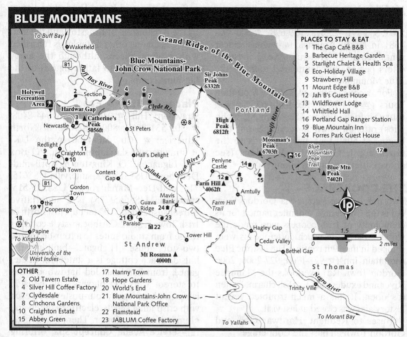

BLUE MOUNTAINS

To Buff Bay
Wakefield
Grand Ridge of the Blue Mountains
B1
Buff Bay River
Blue Mountains-
John Crow National Park
Sir Johns
Peak
6332ft
Holywell
Recreation
Area
Section
Hardwar Gap
Clyde River
Portland
Swift River
Newcastle
Catherine's
Peak
5056ft
St Peters
High
Peak
6812ft
Mossman's
Peak
6703ft
Blue
Mountain
Peak
Trail
Blue Mtn
Peak
7402ft
Redlight
Craighton
Hall's Delight
Penlyne
Castle
Farm Hill
4062ft
Arntully
Irish Town
Content
Gap
Yallahs River
Green River
B1
Gordon
Town
Farm Hill
Trail
the
Cooperage
Guava
Ridge
Mavis
Bank
Hagley Gap
Paraiso
Papine
Tower Hill
Cedar Valley
To Kingston
St Andrew
University of the
West Indies
Mt Rosanna
4000ft
Bethel Gap
St Thomas
Trinity Ville
Negro River
To Yallahs
To Morant Bay

PLACES TO STAY & EAT
1 The Gap Café B&B
3 Barbecue Heritage Garden
5 Starlight Chalet & Health Spa
6 Eco-Holiday Village
9 Strawberry Hill
11 Mount Edge B&B
12 Jah B's Guest House
13 Wildflower Lodge
14 Whitfield Hall
16 Portland Gap Ranger Station
19 Blue Mountain Inn
24 Forres Park Guest House

OTHER
2 Old Tavern Estate
4 Silver Hill Coffee Factory
7 Clydesdale
8 Cinchona Gardens
10 Craighton Estate
15 Abbey Green
17 Nanny Town
18 Hope Gardens
20 World's End
21 Blue Mountains-John Crow
  National Park Office
22 Flamstead
23 JABLUM Coffee Factory

0   1.5   3 km
0   1   2 miles

See the Blue Mountains-John Crow National Park section, later in this chapter, for details on the park.

Guides & Organized Hikes

Guides can be hired from most hotels in the area for about US$25 for a half day, US$35 for a full day. Freelance guides hire themselves out at Penlyne Castle, Hagley Gap, and Mavis Bank (see all later in this chapter). On overnight trips, you're expected to buy the guide's food and pay for his accommodations.

In addition to others, the following offer guided hikes:

Destinations (☎ 702-0314, 702-0112), Maya Lodge, Peter's Rock Rd, Jack's Hill PO

Sun Ventures (☎ 960-6685, fax 920-8348; W www.sunventuretours.com), 30 Balmoral Ave, Kingston 10

Strawberry Hill (☎ 944-8400, fax 944-8408; e lyndaleeburks@yahoo.com)

Maps

If you hike alone, buy the Survey Dept 1:50,000 or 1:12,500 Ordnance Survey topographic map series, available from the Survey Dept (☎ 922-6630; 23½ Charles St, PO Box 493, Kingston). Four different sheets – numbers 13, 14, 18, and 19 – cover the area around Blue Mountain Peak; you may need to buy all four (US$5 each). Also see Maps in the Facts for the Visitor chapter.

ORGANIZED TOURS

Safari Tours Jamaica (☎/fax 972-2639; W www.jamaica-irie.com/safari; Arawak PO, Mammee Bay) offers daylong 'jeep safaris' into the Blue Mountains. It also has a two-day mule ride and a trekking tour. **Barrett Adventures** (☎ 382-6384, fax 979-8845; e carolyn@barrettadventures.com; Rose Hall, Little River PO) offers customized tours by minivan. **Go Active Vacations** (☎ 944-8151; e jamaicaEU@cwjamaica.com;

Mt Edge, Newcastle) offers adventure tours and excursions. **Island Car Rentals** (☎ 926-5991, 888-991-4255, fax 929-6987; ☎ 800-892-4581 in North America; W www.islandcarrentals.com; 17 Antigua Ave, Kingston) offers personally chauffeured tours of the Blue Mountains.

For cycling enthusiasts, **Blue Mountain Tours** (☎ 974-7075, fax 974-0635; e bmtours@infochan.com; 152 Main St, Ocho Rios) offers a downhill bicycling tour that begins at 5060 feet and descends to the north coast. Go Active Vacations (see above) offers mountain biking.

THE COOPERAGE

Two miles above Papine via Gordon Town Rd is the Cooperage, a hamlet named for its community of Irish coopers who made the wooden barrels in which coffee beans were shipped in the 19th century. The historic **Blue Mountain Inn** (☎ 927-1700, 927-2606; 2606 Gordon Town Rd) overlooks the Mammee River and exudes olde English charm…when it's open. It has a much-troubled recent history and was closed at last visit.

Buses to Redlight, Hardwar Gap, and Gordon Town all pass the Cooperage.

IRISH TOWN

Mammee River Rd (the B1) climbs to Irish Town, a small hamlet where the coopers lived during the 19th century. Potatoes are still an important crop, reflecting the Irish influence. Farther uphill is **Redlight**, a hamlet apparently named for the fact that it served as a brothel for soldiers from the Newcastle barracks.

In an emergency, call the **police station** (☎ 944-8242).

To get to Irish Town, you can take a bus (US$0.30) or route taxi (about US$1) from Papine.

Craighton Estate

Craighton Estate (☎ 929-8490 or 944-8224, fax 944-8653; open 8am-4pm Mon-Fri, by appointment Sat & Sun; guided tour adult/child over 12 US$15/7.50), 6½ miles above the Cooperage, is a coffee plantation and garden owned by Ueshima, the largest

coffee company in Japan. The restored great house, built in 1805 and formerly occupied by the Archbishop of Kingston and the Earl of Elgin, among other notables, is furnished with original pieces, although the entry lobby is dedicated to father figures of the Ueshima company.

Places to Stay & Eat

Strawberry Hill (☎ 944-8400, fax 944-8408; ☎ 305-531-8800, 800-688-7678 in North America; ☎ 020-7440-4360 in the UK; e strawberry@islandoutpost.com; PO Box 590, Liguanea PO, Kingston 6; April–mid-Dec rooms US$315-475, suite/villa US$615/715; mid-Dec–March rooms US$325-515, suite/villa US$665/775) is a superlative retreat suspended 3100 feet up, just north of Irish Town. The 12 Caribbean-style cottages range from studio suites to a four-bedroom, two-story house – Highgate – built into the hillside. Each cottage is a statement in elegance, from hand-molded hardwood sofas to stereos with CD players, chic bedside lamps, and mahogany four-poster beds, each with crisp linen sheets, electric blanket, and plump down comforter. There's a deluxe, full-service **Aveda Concept Spa,** offering essential-oil treatments, steams, and massages, plus a pool, and exquisite garden. Breakfast is included in the rates, as are transfers. Birding and hiking tours are offered. No children are allowed.

Many Kingstonians make the tortuous drive to Strawberry Hill for some of the finest nouvelle Jamaican cuisine on the island. Among the savory dishes are curried pumpkin soup (US$4), curried walnut loaf with tomato mint sauce (US$22), curried jumbo shrimps with ginger chips and sweet plantain (US$30), and jerk lamb loin with roasted garlic (US$22). Reservations are advised.

Strawberry Hill also hosts a calendar of special events throughout the year.

NEWCASTLE

Newcastle hangs invitingly on the mountainside high above Irish Town. The road climbs to 4000 feet where, 13 miles from Kingston, you suddenly emerge on a wide parade ground guarded by a small cannon. The military encampment clambers up the slope above the square. Newcastle was founded in 1841 as a training site and convalescent center for British soldiers. Since 1962, the camp has been used by the Jamaica Defense Force.

With good fortune you may even arrive to watch recruits being drilled. Note the insignia (which date back to 1884) on the whitewashed stone wall, commemorating those regiments stationed at Newcastle. Visitors are allowed only around the canteen, shop, roadways, and parade ground.

Two miles above Newcastle you reach Hardwar Gap, at the crest of the Grand Ridge.

Hiking

A path marked **Woodcutter's Gap** begins from the road above the parade ground and links with the Fairy Glade Trail (see Holywell Recreation Area later in this chapter). The Green Hills Trail, Fern Walk Trail, and Woodcutter's Trail also begin north of Newcastle.

The camp store – the **Tuck Shop** – sells groceries and is a good place to provision for hiking.

Places to Stay & Eat

Mount Edge B&B (☎ 944-8151, 1-770-6849 cellular; @ jamaicaeu@kasnet.com, or mfo x80@yahoo.co.uk; Newcastle PO; double per week US$120-250, per month US$250-500) is a good budget option, especially for longer stays. The all-wood house has three rooms, including one with a four-poster king-size bed. A basic bamboo 'camper's' room (US$8-10) and outside shower/toilet were being added at last visit. The spacious, no-frills lounge has a kitchen and wide glass windows on all sides. Meal packages are offered. The place is an official bird-watching station.

Barbecue Heritage Garden (☎ 978-4438, 960-8627; Newcastle PO; cottage US$45), 400 yards east of Newcastle parade ground, is a simple yet exquisite two-bedroom, one-bathroom wooden cottage (with live-in caretakers) set in a circa-1750 coffee estate with views toward Kingston. The bathroom has a

claw-foot tub and hot water, and there's a kitchen and a TV lounge with sofa bed and telephone. The old coffee-drying barbecues are now laid out as gardens.

The Gap Café Bed & Breakfast (☎ 997-3032; 1-919-1846 cellular, 923-7078, fax 923-5617; c/o 156 Spanish Town Rd, Kingston 11; single or double US$80), on the hillside at 4200 feet at Hardwar Gap, just below the entrance to Holywell Recreation Area, has a cozy Hansel-and-Gretel-style, one-bedroom, self-catering cottage with a veranda. Rates include breakfast. Walkways lead through beautiful gardens.

The **Café** (open 10am-5pm Mon-Fri, 10am-6pm Sat & Sun; closed Good Friday) is a fabulous place to rest and take in the vistas over a soda or cappuccino. It offers dining either indoors or alfresco on a wooden terrace. A 'Jamaican special' breakfast costs US$12. Afternoon tea is also served (US$2). And the eclectic lunch menu includes curried Caribbean shrimp, shepherd's pie, sandwiches, and delicious pastries. A cup of Blue Mountain coffee costs a steep US$3.50! Dinner is by reservation only. Bring mosquito repellent.

Full Moon Frolics (US$5) are hosted at the Gap Café, drawing locals for music, dance, and fine dining.

BLUE MOUNTAINS-JOHN CROW NATIONAL PARK

The Blue Mountains-John Crow National Park protects 193,260 acres and is managed by the Natural Resources Conservation Authority (NRCA). The park includes the forest reserves of the Blue and John Crow Mountain Ranges and spans the parishes of St Andrew, St Thomas, Portland, and St Mary. Ecotourism is being promoted, and locals are being trained as guides.

Buses (US$0.30) operate twice daily between Papine and Buff Bay (on the north coast) via Newcastle, Hardwar Gap, and Section. Route taxis cost about US$0.75.

Camping is not permitted except at designated sites listed below; further campsites are planned. Camping 'wild' is not advised.

Also see Hiking, earlier in this chapter, and Blue Mountain Peak, later in this chapter.

Information

There are ranger stations at Holywell and Portland Gap, and at Millbank in the Upper Rio Grande Valley (see the Port Antonio & Northeast Coast chapter). The **Blue Mountains-John Crow National Park Office** (☎ 977-8044; Guava Ridge; open 10am-4pm Mon-Fri) is west of Mavis Bank, St Andrew parish. Entry to the park is free, except for Holywell Recreation Area (see below). For more information, contact the **Jamaica Conservation & Development Trust** (☎ 960-2848, fax 960-2850; ⓔ jcdt@kasnet.com; 95 Dumbarton Ave, Kingston 10), or the **NRCA** (☎ 923-5125; 53 Molynes Rd, Kingston 10).

Holywell Recreation Area

Holywell Recreation Area (adult/child US$4.50/1.50), spanning Hardwar Gap, protects 300 acres of this remnant woodland, lush with dozens of fern species, epiphytes, impatiens, violets, nasturtiums, and wild strawberries and raspberries. The mist-shrouded uppermost slopes are densely forested with rare primary montane forest. Pine trees dominate. The birding is fabulous. A ranger station is a short distance beyond the entrance. An orientation center hosts occasional live entertainment, such as traditional music and dance, plus outdoor games, storytelling and a treasure hunt for the kids (contact the national park office, above, for information). The park has viewpoints and picnic spots.

Hiking trails lead off in all directions through the ferny dells, cloud forest, and elfin woodland. The **Fairy Glade Trail** is a four-hour scramble to the summit of Mt Horeb (4037 feet). The 1.2-km-long **Oatley Mountain Trail**, which requires a guide (US$9), has educational signs leading to a river good for bathing. Another trail leads down to Peter's Rock and Jack's Hill.

Camping (per person US$2.50) is allowed. There are water faucets and toilets. You can rent rustic **cabins** (2-bed cabin US$55, 4-bed cabin US$78) with twin beds (reportedly damp) and a basic kitchen; bring your own bedding and food (there's a gas ring and fridge). Advance reservations are essential via the Blue Mountains-John Crow National Park Office or Jamaica Conservation & Development Trust (for both, see Information earlier). Holiday and weekend stays should be booked several weeks in advance. There's a security guard.

SECTION

Heading north from Holywell, the road drops steeply toward the hamlet of Section and then curls its way down to Buff Bay, 18 miles north. As soon as you crest the ridge, the vegetation on the north-facing slope is noticeably lusher. You'll pass several cottages with colorful gardens.

A turnoff to the right at Section leads a mile to the ridge crest, where the main road loops south and drops to Content Gap, eventually linking up with the road from Gordon Town to Mavis Bank. A steep and muddy dirt road to the left drops to the simple **Silver Hill Coffee Factory**, where tours are offered; 4WD is recommended.

Old Tavern Estate

A mile south of Section is a small, anonymous cottage (☎/fax 924-2785; Ⓦ www.exportjamaica.org/oldtavern; PO Box 131, Kingston 8; closed Fri) that you would surely pass by if you didn't know that its occupants, Alex and Dorothy Twyman, produce the best of the best of Blue Mountain coffee (their coffee was named 'Best in the Caribbean' in 1998). The Twymans welcome visitors by prior arrangement, except Friday.

Although the Twymans' coffee is acclaimed as the best on the island, until recently they weren't allowed to sell an ounce due to Kafkaesque government regulations. Mr Twyman stopped selling his beans to the coffee board in 1982 and began storing his unroasted beans at a warehouse. Finally, in 1997, the Twymans were begrudgingly granted an exclusive license to grow, process, roast, and sell a 'single estate coffee' under an estate label – the *only* estate on the island so permitted.

See the boxed text 'Hallowed Grounds' in the Facts about Jamaica chapter for more details on the politics of Blue Mountain coffee.

Visitors can sample the coffee and home-made mead, honey, and coffee liqueur.

You can order Twyman's estate-roasted coffee in North America from **23 Degrees North** (☎ 888-228-6759; ℮ 23degreesnorth@fintrac.com).

Strawberry Hill (see Irish Town earlier in this chapter) and Barrett Adventures (see Organized Tours earlier in this chapter) both run tours to Old Tavern Estate.

Places to Stay & Eat

Starlight Chalet & Health Spa (☎ 968-3116, fax 906-3075; ℮ chalet@cwjamaica.com; c/o 21 Ballater Ave, Kingston 10; single US$59, double US$66, suites US$132-197), in the lee of the mountain divide at the turnoff for the Silver Hill Coffee Factory, is a recent addition set amid a flower-filled hillside garden offering dramatic alpine vistas. This modern, three-story plantation-style hotel has carpeted, modestly furnished rooms and oversize two- and three-bedroom suites. There's a small bar and restaurant where filling homey meals are served by gracious staff. The no-frills spa has a sauna and massage rooms, and offers full treatments (US$45-75). Nature walks and special-interest excursions are offered, as are yoga programs. It makes a fantastic base for hiking and birding.

CLYDESDALE

Clydesdale is a derelict old coffee plantation and a popular spot for budget accommodations. The much-battered waterwheel and coffee mill machinery are partially intact. It has picnic spots and a small waterfall where you can skinny-dip. The **Morces Gap Trail** begins here.

From Section, take the horrendously potholed 'main' road to Guava Ridge; the turnoff for Clydesdale is just above the hamlet of St Peters. Then you cross over the Chestervale Bridge above the Brook's River and immediately reach a **Y**-fork. Take the left, steeply uphill road for Clydesdale and Cinchona Gardens. It's a terribly rocky drive, suited for a 4WD only.

Clydesdale (☎ 924-2667 reservations; Forestry Dept, 173 Constant Spring Rd,

Kingston; camping and dormitory US$5; cabins US$10) has a *very* basic dormitory and cabins. You must pick up your cabin reservations in advance in Kingston. Bring your own food. You can also camp; water, toilets, and basic kitchen facilities are available.

Eco-Holiday Village (☎ 968-8445, 929-6163 in Kingston; c/o 12 Brentford Rd, Kingston 5; camping per tent US$1.50, dorm beds US$5.50, rooms single/double US$13/22, self-contained flat US$66) lets you camp amid breeze-swept pastures surrounded by pine forest. Campers can bring food (but can't use the kitchen) and a cook will prepare meals, which are also prepared on request (US$2.50 for three meals). There are also 560 bunk beds in dormitories, plus self-contained flats and cabins with kitchens, including some with private bath and hot water. There is a laundry service. The village is popular with police, youth, and church groups. There's volleyball, netball, and soccer fields, plus a bar and 'tuck shop' (snack bar). The turnoff is 500 yards above the turnoff for Clydesdale after you cross the Chestervale Bridge.

CINCHONA GARDENS

Cinchona (☎ 927-1257, fax 977-4853; admission free, but a tip to caretaker-guide expected), at about 4500 feet, is one of the most spectacularly situated gardens in the world, with fabulous views north to the peaks and down the valleys of the Clyde, Green, and Yallahs Rivers. It was founded in 1868 when Assam tea and cinchona (an Andean plant) were planted – the latter for quinine, which is extracted from the bark, to fight malaria. The grounds were later turned into a garden to supply Kingston with flowers. In 1903 the Jamaican government leased Cinchona to the New York Botanical Garden and, later, to the Smithsonian Institute.

A dilapidated old house chock-full of weathered antiques sits atop the 6-acre gardens, fronted by lawns and exquisite floral beds. The **Panorama Walk** begins to the east of the gardens, leading through a glade of towering bamboo and opening to staggering views. Half a dozen other tracks snake off into the nether reaches of the mountains.

You can **camp** here for US$5; reserve in person at the Forestry Dept in Kingston (see Clydesdale above).

Finding Cinchona is difficult without a guide. From Clydesdale, continue uphill along the muddy dirt track for about 2 miles. There are several unmarked junctions; you'll undoubtedly take some wrong turns and need to backtrack. Ask at every opportunity. Don't underestimate the awful road conditions, with ruts deep enough to hang up your chassis and leave your wheels spinning in thin air. *A 4WD with low-gear option is absolutely essential.*

Far easier is a more direct and populated route via Mavis Bank; you'll still need to ask directions.

Strawberry Hill (see Irish Town earlier in this chapter) and Barnett Adventures (see Organized Tours earlier in this chapter) offer excursions to Cinchona Gardens.

GORDON TOWN

Gordon Town, at 1200 feet, is a hamlet centered on a wide square with a **police station** (☎ 927-2805), post office, and tiny courthouse. It began life as a staging post for Newcastle in the days before the Mammee River Rd was cut from the Cooperage. To reach Cinchona, Mavis Bank, and the trail to Blue Mountain Peak, turn right at the square and cross the narrow bridge.

The **Gordon Town Trail** begins in Gordon Town and follows the Hope River Valley via Mt Industry and Redlight. Another 13-mile trail leads from Gordon Town to Sugar Loaf (7000 feet), Content Gap, Top Mountain, and Cinchona. A third 10-mile track leads via Flamstead and Orchard to Mavis Bank.

Three miles east of Gordon Town on the road to Guava Ridge, **World's End** is a pretty roadside cottage that clings to the mountainside at 2500 feet. Despite its Hansel-and-Gretel appearance and outside walls painted with murals, World's End was until recently a factory that produced Sangster's world-famous rums and liqueurs, sold in reproduction ceramic bottles. Alas, the company has suffered economic difficulties and at last visit the facility had closed.

There is nowhere to stay, and eating options are relegated to a few simple rum shops and stalls.

Buses and coasters operate from the Parade, Half Way Tree, and Papine in Kingston (US$0.30).

GUAVA RIDGE

Guava Ridge is the site of a ridgecrest junction for Content Gap and the Silver Hill Coffee Factory (to the left), with Mavis Bank and Blue Mountain Peak straight ahead.

A road to the right, signed for 'Bellevue House' 50 yards east of Guava Ridge, leads 4 miles through forests of pine and eucalyptus to the coffee plantation of **Flamstead** (Flamstead Heritage Society; ☎ 960-0204; ⓔ peterking@flamstead.com; 11A Waterloo Rd, Kingston; visits by prior appointment). This is the former great house of Governor Edward Eyre (see History in the Facts about Jamaica chapter) and a lookout from which Horatio Nelson and other British naval officers once surveyed the Port Royal base. The view over the Palisadoes and Kingston Harbour is fabulous. Flamstead great house was in the process of restoration at last visit.

MAVIS BANK

Mavis Bank, a one-hour drive from Kingston, is a tidy little village in the midst of coffee country.

In the village center you'll find **People's Cooperative Bank** (☎ 977-8010; open 9am-3pm Mon-Fri), which represents Western Union; the **police station** (☎ 977-8004); the post office; and a public telephone.

A bus runs twice daily from Papine via Gordon Town (US$0.75). Route taxis operate more frequently (US$1.50). A tourist taxi from Kingston costs about US$15.

The **JABLUM** Coffee Factory (☎ 977-8005, fax 977-8014; ⓔ jablum@wtjam.net, or contact@bluemountaincoffeeinc.com; open 9:30am-11:30am & 12:30pm-3:30pm Mon-Fri), half a mile west of Mavis Bank, is owned by Keble Munn, former Minister of Agriculture and a descendant of national hero George William Gordon. There's a small 'museum' with historical artifacts and photos of Keble Munn through the ages (there he is in 1923, at three years old, raking coffee in knee-breeches). Ask chief 'cupper,' Norman Grant, to demonstrate 'cupping' (tasting), the technique to identify quality coffee. You can tour the factory by appointment (US$8) to see the coffee beans drying (in season) and being processed. For more on Blue Mountain coffee, see the boxed text 'Hallowed Grounds' in the Facts about Jamaica chapter.

Farm Hill Trail begins at Churchyard Rd and leads steeply uphill for 5 miles to Penlyne Castle and thence to Blue Mountain Peak; see Blue Mountain Peak later in this chapter. **Climb Every Mountain** (☎ 977-8541, ask for Miss Campbell), near the police station, offers guided hikes and guides, and rents tents and camping equipment.

Forres Park Guest House & Farm (☎ 977-8141, 927-5957 in Kingston, fax 978-6942; **w** www.forrespark.com; Mavis Bank PO; cabins US$60, rooms US$70), as you enter the village, is a working coffee farm with an enviable hillside setting amid lush gardens and tiers of coffee bushes flowing downhill like folds of green silk; tours are offered. It rents six rooms (with balconies) in the main lodge and three basic wooden cottages with red concrete floors and pine furniture. Meals are cooked by request. You can rent mountain bikes. Birding tours are offered by appointment, as are guided hikes to Blue Mountain Peak.

HAGLEY GAP & PENLYNE CASTLE
The ramshackle village of Hagley Gap sits abreast a hill east of Mavis Bank and is the gateway to the Blue Mountain Peak. The road forks in the village, where a horrendously denuded dirt road for Penlyne Castle begins a precipitous ascent.

Penlyne Castle is the base for 7-mile hikes to Blue Mountain Peak. Most hikers stay overnight at one of three simple lodges near Penlyne Castle before tackling the hike in the wee hours.

Bring warm clothing. One minute you're in sun-kissed mountains. The next, clouds swirl in and the temperature plunges.

Places to Stay & Eat
You can camp at **Abbey Green** (no ☎; US$5), but you'll need to be self-sufficient, including water. **In-Tents Camping Site** (☎ 929-5395), 100 yards before you reach Wildflower Lodge, also has camping under shade trees. You can rent camping gear.

Wildflower Lodge (☎ 929-5395; c/o Eric Leiba, 10 Ellesmere Rd, Kingston 10; rooms with/without bath US$33/13, cottage US$55), 400 yards east of the ridge crest at Penlyne Castle, is a hardwood structure with 36 bunks in basic rooms with communal bathrooms with solar-heated water, plus three more-appealing private rooms with private bath downstairs. A two-bedroom cottage at the bottom of the garden sleeps up to six. An atmospheric dining room has hammocks on the veranda and faces southeast down the mountain. Breakfasts cost about US$5; lunch and dinner cost US$6.50. You have use of a large but basic kitchen. The lodge offers horseback rides and guides for the climb. Readers report that management can be unresponsive to problems.

Whitfield Hall (☎ 927-0986; c/o John Algrove, 8 Almond Crescent, Kingston 6; camping US$6; bunks per adult/child/Peace Corps volunteer & student US$15/7/9), about 400 yards uphill from Wildflower, nestled amid pine trees, is a more basic option with bunks for up to 40 people. The dark, gloomy lounge has a huge fireplace (there's a US$5 firewood charge) and smoke-stained ceiling. An old grandfather clock stands like a silent sentinel. Gas lamps provide illumination. Guests share two basic bathrooms with toilets and tubs (cold water only), plus a small kitchen. If the hostel is full, camping is allowed on a wide lawn beneath eucalyptus. There are picnic tables, benches, and a barbecue pit, as well as water and toilets. Locals will cook on request. You can hire guides (US$33 to the peak).

A friendly Rasta, Jah B, has a basic but cozy wooden **guest house** (☎ 977-8161; per person US$12), on the left 400 yards below Wildflower Lodge. It has three rooms with four bunks apiece, plus a shared shower and flush toilet. Jah B cooks I-tal meals (about US$5) amid a cloud of ganja smoke and a

SOUTHEAST COAST

nonstop volley of friendly banter. He offers transfers from Kingston in his beat-up Land Rover and will guide you up Blue Mountain Peak for US$40.

Getting There & Away
A bus (US$0.40) and route taxi (US$1.50) from the Parade and Papine in Kingston run to Hagley Gap via Bull Bay and Cedar Valley.

If driving, continue through Mavis Bank to Mahogany Valle and cross the Yallahs River.

Penlyne Castle is reached via a 3-mile dirt road that ascends precipitously from Hagley Gap. Only 4WD vehicles with low-gear option can make the journey, which is dauntingly narrow and rugged. Land Rovers can be rented in Hagley Gap (about US$20).

Most hotels (including Whitfield Hall and Wildflower Lodge) in the Blue Mountains offer 4WD transfers to Penlyne Castle from Mavis Bank (from US$20 per vehicle) or Kingston (from US$40). The Wildflower and Whitfield transfers are untrustworthy in late evening, when drivers often don't show up (or refuse to continue), stranding people in Mavis Bank. Be sure to arrange a transfer for no later than midafternoon.

BLUE MOUNTAIN PEAK
It's a 3000-foot ascent from Penlyne Castle to the summit of Blue Mountain Peak (7402 feet) – a three- or four-hour hike one-way. It's not a serious challenge, but you need to be reasonably fit.

Don't litter, and *stay on the path!*

Most hikers set off from Penlyne Castle in the wee hours to reach the peak for sunrise. Your guide will rouse you at about 2am. Fortified with a breakfast of coffee and cereal, you set out single file in the pitch black along the 7½-mile trail (you'll need a flashlight and a spare set of batteries – just in case). Midway, at Portland Gap, there's a **ranger station** and cabin (see Places to Stay, below).

As you hike, reggae music can be heard far, far below, competing with the chirps of crickets and katydids singing to attract mates. Myriad blinkies and peeny-wallies will be doing the same, signaling, with their phosphorescent semaphore.

You should arrive at the peak around 5:30am, while it is still dark. Your stage is gradually revealed: a flat-topped hump, marked by a scaffolding pyramid and trig point (in the cloud it is easy to mistake the *real* summit for a smaller hump to the left of the hut near the summit).

From the peak (which casts a distinct shadow over the land below), Cuba can be seen hovering on the horizon, 90 miles away. After a brief celebratory drink and snacks, you'll set off back down the mountain, arriving at Whitfield or Wildflower in time for brunch.

By setting out for the summit a few hours later, say 5am, you may still make the top before the mists roll in, and you will have the benefit of enjoying the changing vegetation and unraveling scenery with greater anticipation for what lies ahead (and above). You pass through several distinct ecosystems, including an area of bamboo and primordial giant tree ferns. Farther up is cloud forest, dripping with filaments of hanging lichens and festooned with epiphytes and moss. Near the top is stunted dwarf or elfin forest, with trees such as hirsute soapwood and rodwood no more than 8 feet high – an adaptation to the extreme cold.

Don't hike without a guide at night. Numerous spur trails lead off the main trails and it is easy to get lost. These mountains are not kind to those who lose their way.

What to Bring
Although hiking boots or tough walking shoes are best, sneakers ('buggas' or 'puss boots') will suffice, though your feet will likely get wet. At the top it can be icy with the wind blowing, and temperatures can approach freezing before sunrise, so wear plenty of layers. Rain gear is also essential, as weather can change rapidly. Clouds usually begin to form in early morning, followed by a cold breeze.

Guides & Organized Hikes
Guides (around US$20 per half day or US$30 for a full day) can be hired locally at Hagley Gap, Penlyne Castle, or from most local hotels (see Mavis Bank, Section, Irish

Town, and others earlier in this chapter). For organized hikes, see Hiking and Organized Tours earlier in this chapter.

Places to Stay

A funky cabin (little more than a lean-to) 40 feet below the summit can be rented for US$2.50 from the Forestry Service (☎ 924-2667; 173 Constant Spring Rd, Kingston), which also maintains a more substantial, dimly lit cabin halfway up the trail at Portland Gap (2½ miles above Abbey Green). You can camp (US$5) outside, where there's a cooking area and water from a pipe. Again, this is by Forestry Service reservation only. The terribly run-down hut has a fireplace, but holes in the roof can douse the fire (a waterproof cover for your sleeping bag is a good idea).

Southeast Coast

Jamaica's southeast corner is the island's ugly duckling and one shunned by most tourists. Its narrow scrub-covered coastal plain has only unappetizing gray-sand beaches, and only a limited tourist infrastructure exists. Life revolves mostly around small fishing villages where the work is still performed by canoe and net. Surfers, however, rave about more than a dozen prime surf spots. (For specifics, contact the Surfing Association of Jamaica; see Surfing in the Facts for the Visitor chapter.)

YALLAHS & ENVIRONS

East of Bull Bay and the parish boundary between St Andrew and St Thomas, the A4 from Kingston makes a hairpin descent to Grants Pen, then winds through scrub-covered country until it reaches the coast at Yallahs, 10 miles east of Bull Bay. Past Yallahs Ponds, a series of long, dark-gray beaches, with colorful pirogues drawn up, extends eastward to Morant Bay.

The wide gully of the Yallahs River, 2 miles west of town, begins 4500 feet up in the Blue Mountains. The boulders along the lower riverbed attest to the power and threat of flash floods.

Yallahs River Valley

A road leads north from Yallahs through this rugged valley. About 3 miles north of town, you cross the river near Heartease, where it is said you can witness Revivalist spirit-cult meetings occasionally held on the eastern riverbank near the old bridge.

At the village of Llandewey, 7 miles northwest of Yallahs, you gain a fine view of Judgement Cliff, a sheer cliff that looms up 1000 feet, the result of a 1692 earthquake that caused the mountainside to collapse.

The deteriorating road claws its way up into the Blue Mountains, ascending sharply beyond the hamlet of Bethel Gap to Hagley Gap and Mavis Bank; you'll need a 4WD.

Orange Park This 400-year-old great house, at 1500 feet elevation above Yallahs, is today the gracious home of world-renowned artist Barrington Watson (☎ 371-5805; ⅏ www.barringtonwatson.com) and his collection of handcrafted furniture, art, and antiques. The lush grounds, comprising 14 acres of a former coffee plantation, still have its aqueducts and coffee-drying beds, and remains of a windmill. At last visit, a museum of Jamaican and Caribbean art was planned, along with an arts center with exhibition space, studios, performing arts, and classes by artists in residence.

Visits (free) to Orange Park can be arranged by appointment.

Yallahs Ponds

Two large lakes east of Yallahs, the Yallahs Ponds, are enclosed by a narrow, bow-shaped, 4-mile-long sandspit. The ponds are exceedingly briny due to evaporation. Algae flourish and often turn the ponds a deep pink, accompanied by a powerful smell of hydrogen sulfide ('bad egg gas').

You can still see the remains of an old stone signal tower built on the sandspit in the 1770s by the English to communicate with Port Royal. It is listed as a national monument.

On the hillside just beyond Yallahs Ponds is the JAMINTEL space research station, linking Jamaica to the international satellite network.

SOUTHEAST COAST

MORANT BAY

Morant Bay (population 9900), the only town of importance along the south coast, squats on a hill behind the coast road. Most of the town's early colonial-era buildings were burned in the Morant Bay Rebellion of 1865, led by the town's national hero, Paul Bogle (see History in the Facts about Jamaica chapter), but a couple of gems remain. A high-tech industrial center was being built on the outskirts at last visit.

October 11 is **Paul Bogle Day**, when a party is held in the town square and a 6-mile road race sets out from Stony Gut.

Buses and coasters arrive and depart from beside the Shell gas station on the A4 at the west end of town.

Information

There's a **National Commercial Bank** (☎ 982-1217; 39 Queen St), opposite the Texaco gas station, and a **Scotiabank** (☎ 982-1577; 23 Queen St) nearby.

There's a **post office** (☎ 982-2294; Queen St), and you can make international calls and send and receive faxes at the **Cable & Wireless Jamaica office** (☎ 982-2200; 2 Church St).

The **police station** (☎ 982-2233; 7 South St) is next to the old courthouse.

Things to See

The **Paul Bogle statue** stands in front of the courthouse. The work, by noted sculptor Edna Manley, depicts Bogle standing grimly, hands clasped over the hilt of a machete. The **courthouse** was rebuilt in limestone and red brick after being destroyed in the 1865 rebellion.

Catercorner to the courthouse is a handsome, ochre-colored **Anglican church** dating to 1881.

The **Stony Gut Monument**, commemorating Bogle, stands opposite his **chapel**, 9 miles inland at the village of Stony Gut.

Places to Stay & Eat

Morant Villas (☎ 982-2422, fax 982-1937; 1 Wharf Rd; rooms US$33-45, studios/suites US$40/55) sits amid lawns and tall palms atop a bluff on the coast road just east of

town. It has 22 simple yet clean rooms with fans and private bath with hot water. There are also 10 studios with kitchens, plus suites. A restaurant and bar serves seafood for US$6 to $12.

RETREAT

Retreat is a small beachside residential community about 3 miles east of Morant Bay that draws Kingstonians on weekends. It sits between two of the few pleasant beaches along Jamaica's southern coast. The aptly named **Golden Shore Beach** is hidden from view from the road. Watch for the hand-painted sign. Farther east is **Prospect Beach**, a 'public bathing beach.'

Golden Shore Beach Resort (☎/fax 982-9657; ℮ goldenshorehotel@hotmail.com; Lot 288B Windward Dr, Lyssons; downstairs rooms without/with TV US$38/42, upstairs US$47), at Golden Shore Beach, has 17 rooms in three categories in a condo-style unit amid landscaped grounds. They're clean and boast refreshing, contemporary furnishings. The resort's gracious restaurant opens onto lawns fronting a beach.

Whispering Bamboo Cove (☎ 982-2912, fax 734-1049; 105 Crystal Dr, Retreat; rooms US$53-88, cottage US$90) is a contemporary villa-style hotel with 10 rooms that are airy, spacious, and tastefully furnished with tropical fabrics and antique reproductions.

BATH

This village, 6 miles north of Port Morant, lies on the bank of the Garden River, amidst sugarcane and banana plantations. The town owes its existence to the discovery of hot mineral springs in the hills behind the present town in the late 17th century. A spa was developed, and socialites flocked. Today, it's relative poverty attests to the pitiful wages paid to plantation workers.

The one-street hamlet has a post office, **police station** (☎ 982-2115), and a Shell gas station.

A bus (US$0.50) runs daily from the Parade in Kingston, as do coasters and route taxis (US$2.50).

Bath Garden

At the east end of town is an old limestone church shaded by royal palms that flank the entrance to a horticultural garden established by the government in 1779. Many of the exotics introduced to Jamaica were first planted here: bougainvillea, cinnamon, mango, jackfruit, jacaranda. Most famous is the breadfruit, brought from the South Pacific by Capt William Bligh aboard HMS *Providence*. The garden has seen better days, but at least there's no admission charge.

Bath Fountain

Local legend says that in the 1690s a runaway slave discovered hot mineral springs that cured the injuries he had received while escaping. He was so impressed by the miracle that he returned to tell his master. In 1699 the government bought the spring and an adjoining 1130 acres, created the Bath of St Thomas the Apostle, then formed a corporation to administer mineral baths for the sick and infirm. The waters have therapeutic value for treating skin ailments and rheumatic problems.

Two springs issue from beneath the bath house (open 8am-9:30pm Tues-Sun; adult/child US$5/3 for 20 min). The water can be scorching (it varies from 115°F to 128°F). You soak in a deep, ceramic-tile pool. The homey spa also offers a variety of massages. Arrive early on weekends, before the crowds from Kingston arrive. To get there, turn up the road opposite the church and follow the road 2 miles uphill.

Pay no attention to the touts attempting to 'guide' you to the springs, offer 'massage' (to females only), or sell you dead swallowtail butterflies.

Hiking

A trail, for experienced hikers only, leads from Bath Fountain up over Cuna Cuna Gap to the Rio Grande Valley. Obtain Sheet 19 (showing St Thomas parish) and Sheet 14 (Portland parish) of the Ordnance Survey 1:12,500 map series from the Survey Dept at 23½ Charles St, Kingston.

Places to Stay & Eat

Bath Fountain Hotel & Spa (☎ 703-4345; Bath PO; rooms with/without bath US$40/30, deluxe rooms US$50) is your only option. It's a recently renovated, pink colonial hotel that dates to 1747 and contains the spa baths on the ground floor. The clinically white bedrooms are modestly furnished. It has a small **restaurant** serving breakfast (US$2.50-5) and lunch and dinner (US$7.50-11), plus sandwiches.

GOLDEN GROVE

Golden Grove, 6 miles east of Port Morant (and 7 miles east of Bath), is a desperately poor hamlet of corrugated-tin and wood huts on stilts, dominated by the plantations of Tropicana Sugar Estates, east of the road, and the banana plantations of Fyffes to the west.

On the A4 west of Golden Grove, a side road loops eastward via Old Pera and New Pera, eventually depositing you at **Rocky Point Beach,** where fishing pirogues are drawn up. Locals pour in on any weekend to splash in the shallows and jive to ear-shattering reggae and rap.

MORANT POINT

Golden Grove is gateway to a large peninsula – Morant Point – that juts into the Caribbean Sea.

The 100-foot-tall, red-and-white-striped **Morant Point Lighthouse** (admission free) marks Morant Point, the easternmost tip of Jamaica. Ask the lighthouse-keeper to show you the way to the top. The powerful view and the windy silence make for a profound experience as you look out over rippling sugarcane fields toward the cloud-haunted Blue Mountains.

The lighthouse is best reached by car from the gas station on the A4 in Golden Grove. It's a labyrinthine course, however, and you'll need a guide to lead you; ask at the gas station. A 4WD is recommended.

SOUTHEAST COAST

Language

UNDERSTANDING PATOIS

When Jamaicans speak patois, the discussion may be incomprehensible to visitors. It might sound like a chaotic babble without rules. But there are rules. They're just different from those of traditional English grammar.

Some words are unexpectedly present, for example, where others are unexpectedly missing. New words are invented and slip into general parlance as quickly as others fall from grace. And vowel sounds go sliding off into diphthongs. Like Yorkshire folk, Jamaicans often drop their 'h's (thus, ''ouse' instead of 'house') and add them in unexpected places (for example, 'hemphasize'). Jamaicans usually drop the 'h' from 'th' as well: hence, 't'ree' for 'three,' and 't'anks' for 'thanks.' 'The' is usually pronounced as 'de' and 'them' as 'dem.' They also sometimes drop the 'w,' as in 'ooman' (woman).

Jamaicans also often use transliteration, as in 'flim' for 'film,' and 'cerfiticket' for 'certificate.' They rearrange syllables and give them their own inflections. In patois, the word 'up' is used to intensify meaning: thus, cars 'mash up.' Patois words are usually spelled phonetically.

In order to express the mood of the moment, 'Jamaica talk' infuses words with intonation, repetition, gesture, imagery, and drama. It is not a static, written language, but an oral, vital thing that infuses life into inanimate objects. Thus, one does not forget to mail a letter; instead, 'dat letter jus' fly out of mi mind.' And a waiter does not simply drop a tray full of crockery; 'dat wurtless t'ing jump right out of mi hands.' Among a people that superstitiously believes in *duppies* (ghosts), such reasoning permits individuals to disclaim responsibility for their actions.

Such animate imagery, a carryover of West African proverbs, infuses Jamaica talk with life and is used to crystallize sayings based on the wisdom of experience, often using living creatures as teachers. In the context of a society torn from its roots and oppressed, the islanders have evolved countless sayings that express simple warnings about behavior and interpersonal relationships. Thus, 'Every day you goad donkey, 'im will kick you one day.' Or, 'When you go to donkey's house, doan't talk about ears.' And, 'If you play with puppy, 'im lick your mouth.'

Jamaican patois is liberally laced with sexual innuendo and slang, often of an extremely sexist nature, as personified by the 'slackness' of modern DJ culture. Cuss words abound, especially the word 'rass,' an impolite term that originally meant 'backside' or 'arse' but whose meaning now varies according to circumstance. It's a word visitors to Jamaica should know, as it's one of the most commonly used (and misunderstood) words. Generally it is a term of abuse, as in ''Im a no good rass!' (mild), or when used with the most offensive (yet common) Jamaican derogatory term, ''Im a rass blood claat' (a menstrual pad). It can also be used as an endearment ('Hey, rass, gi mi smallers') or in a similar vein to describe a superlative ('Dat gal pretty to rass, mon!').

Patois is not gender specific. Everyone and everything is simply ''im' or 'dem.' Possessive pronouns such as 'my' and 'mine' are often replaced with 'a fi,' which can also be an intensifier, as in 'A fi mi bike' ('It's *my* bike'). And plurals are often either ignored (as in 'five finger') or signified by the word 'dem,' as in 'De byah dem go to school' ('The boys have gone to school'). Note how the present tense is used to convey a past action.

And since you'll not be able to walk far without being asked for money, it helps to know enough patois to comprehend what you're hearing. Expect to hear 'Gi mi a smallers no bass' ('Give me some money now boss'); 'bass' means boss and is often used to address persons in authority or those able to dispense favors.

There are several Jamaican pocket guides to understanding patois, including

Memba de Culcha: Chief Words, Phrases, Proverbs & Riddles in Jamaican Dialect by Cecily Reece-Daly.

Colonial Carryovers

Many words in the Jamaican lexicon are carryovers from early English colonial days – true Shakespearean English. The language is imbued with terms otherwise considered archaic. One of the most obvious is 'chain,' the old English measurement (22 yards), which is still used liberally, though rarely accurately. Similarly, you may be served a drink in a 'goblet.'

A few terms derive from slave days. Thus visitors can expect to be called 'massa' (master) or 'mistress.' The term 'pickaninny' is still used for children, despite the racist overtones associated with it in Western culture; for example, the bus conductor might say 'pickney stan' up an gi big people seat.'

African Heritage

Scores of words have been passed down from Africa, mostly from the Ashanti, Cormorante, and Congolese languages. Thus, a Jamaican may refer to a fool as a 'bo-bo.' A commonly used word is 'nyam,' which means 'to eat.'

Sayings & Proverbs

Jamaicans use plenty of metaphors and proverbs. They will tell you 'Cockroach no business in a fowlyard' ('Mind your own business'). If a Jamaican tells you, 'De higher monkey climb, de more 'im expose,' he or she is telling you that your boasting is transparent and that you're acting pretentiously, exposing more than you should.

Some phrases you'll hear may not mean what they suggest. 'Soon come,' for example, is a common refrain, but don't hold your breath! The phrase *really* means the subject will arrive eventually – almost the opposite of what you would expect. Likewise, 'jus' up de road' or 'jus' a likkle distance' can mean miles or the other side of town.

The most common greeting is 'Everyt'ing cool, mon?' or 'Everyt'ing irie?'

'Jamaica Talk'

A good preparatory source is the movie *Dancehall Queen,* with dialogue in thick, at times impenetrable, Jamaican dialect. Here's a sampling of words you'll be sure to hear while strolling through the streets.

ago – to be intent on doing something, as in 'me ago duntown'

agony – a sexual act, or a style of dancing that suggests it

almshouse – anything negative

arms house – a violent posture, common during sound-system clashes

atops – Red Stripe beer

Babylon – the establishment, white society

bakra – a slave owner, white man

baldhead – a non-Rasta; person of unsound viewpoint

bandulu – a hustler, criminal, or the act of being swindled

bangarang – a commotion, sometimes associated with rival, deafening sound-system noise

bankra – a basket

bashment – a large dance or party; anything fabulous

batty – a bottom or rear end, as in 'Yu batty too big, mon!' (as heard from a woman who doesn't give a damn for a propositioner's looks)

batty boy – a gay man

batty riders – tight lycra hot pants for showing off one's *batty,* favored by *dancehall queens*

bawl – to call out, especially in anguish

beenie – small

big up – to inflate or promote oneself, as in 'Big up yo chest, mon!'

blood – a respectful greeting, as in 'Wh'appen blood?' Also a swear word, most often used with *claat* (see Understanding Patois, earlier)

bly – a chance or opportunity; sometimes a feeble excuse

Bobo dread – a Rastafarian follower of Prince Emanuel Edwards

bomba – commonly used abusive term, usually allied with *clawt,* as in 'Get de bomba-clawt car out mi way!'

boonoonoonoos – fabulous, greatest; street or beach party

boops – a man who keeps a woman in idle splendor. (Men, watch out if a woman tells you, 'Mi wan' you fi mi boops.')

brawta – additional

breadkind – any starchy vegetable used as a side dish in lieu of bread

bredda – a friend, usually male

bredren – male friends

brownings – brown-skinned women; also a 'well-heeled' woman showing off her status

buck – to meet someone

bumper – a rear end or backside

burn – to smoke ganja

busha – an overseer of a slave plantation

byah – a boy

carry go bring come – to spread gossip

chalice – a Rastafarian's holy ganja pipe (also known as a *cutchie*)

charged – stoned or drunk

check – to appreciate, especially a point of view or a person's physical attraction; also to pay a visit

chillum – a pipe for smoking ganja

cho – an expression to signify that the speaker is becoming annoyed

chronic – particularly potent ganja

claat, clawt – one of the strongest and most frequently heard Jamaican expletives (see Understanding Patois earlier)

coolie – someone from India

cool runnings – no problem

cool yu foot – slow down, relax

copasetic – cool, *irie*

cork – full

cotch – to relax, rest; also means to brace or support something, as well as a place to sleep

cris – from the word 'crisp,' meaning attractive or top-notch; "Im a cris, cris t'ing!" ('He's handsome!')

cris-biscuit – anything *cris* or excellent

crub – to dance salaciously, as in 'wining'

culture – used to signify that something is Rastafarian

cuss-cuss – an argument

cutchie – ganja pipes

dally – the opposite of to linger; to go

dawta – a respectful term for a young woman

de – the

degeh – measly or pathetically small, usually used in a derogatory sense

deh-deh – to be someplace, as in 'Mi deh-deh!' ('I'm here!')

deportees – used cars, imported from Japan

dibby-dibby – pathetic, especially a competitor's weak sound system

do – please, as in 'Do, me a beg yu'

don – a male authority figure

downpresser – a Rastafarian term for an oppressor

dread – a Rastafarian; also refers to a terrible situation

dunzer – money; also known as *smallers*

duppy – a ghost

facety – cheeky, impertinent, as in 'Yu facety to rass, gal!' ('You're rude, girl!')

fiyah – a Rastafarian greeting

flex – how one behaves; to party wildly

ganga-lee – a gangster

ganja – marijuana; also known as 'de 'oly 'erb,' 'wisdom weed,' 'colly weed,' *kaya, sensie,* and *tampie*

ginnal – a swindler or con artist

gorgon – a person to be feared

gow – an empty boast

gravilishas – greedy

grind – see *flex*

guidance – a Rastafarian parting term, meaning 'May God be with you'

guinep – a small green fruit, often sold by the bunch at the roadside

gwan – go away

gyal – a woman

heartical or 'eartical – an esteemed person, someone with integrity; authentic

herb or 'erb – marijuana (see *ganja*)

higger or 'iggler – a market vendor, usually female; also a person who bargains

him or 'im – any singular pronoun: he, she, him, her, it

hottie-bottie or 'ottie-bottie – an attractive woman

Idren – brethren, used by Rastafarians to mean friends

irie – alright, groovy; used to indicate that all is well; also a greeting ('Everyt'ing irie?')
iron bird – an airplane
I-tal – natural foods, health food, purity
iyah – a greeting

Jah – God; an Old Testament name, popular with Rastafarians
Jamdung – Jamaica (also known as Jah-Mek-Ya, as in 'God's work')
janga – shrimp, crayfish
Joe Gring – a man with whom a woman has an affair while her husband or boyfriend is away
jook – to pierce or stab

kaya – marijuana (see *ganja*)
kingman – a husband
kiss me neck – to express surprise
kiss mi – not an invitation, but a common profane exclamation, as in 'Kiss mi rass!'

labba labba – talk
labrish – gossip
leggo beast – rowdy person
let off – to give
level vibes – no problem
lick – to smoke; to be in vogue; to strike a blow
lick shot – a gun fired at a dancehall to express appreciation
lion – upright, usually describes a righteous Rastafarian
lovers rock – romantic reggae

maarga – thin (from meager), as in 'Da boy deh maaga' ('That man there is skinny')
mantel – good-looking man, usually one who's promiscuous
market mammie – a higgler
mash up – to have an accident
massah – mister; derived from 'master' of slavery days and now used for any male, particularly one in authority
massive – a noun used to describe a crowd
matey – girlfriend who is one of several sexual partners
men – used in the singular for a gay man
mule – childless woman
myal – white magic, used to do good, that incorporates use of herbal medicines and control of *duppies*

naa – won't, as in 'Mi naa go dung deh' ('I won't go down there')
natty – dreadlocks; also 'natty dread'; also used for a Rastafarian
nuff – plentiful; also used as a greeting with 'respect,' as in 'Nuff respect!'

obeah – illegal black magic that incorporates use of herbal medicines as well as witchcraft
one love – parting expression meaning unity

peeny-wally – a type of insect that flashes phosphorescent
pickney – child or children, shortened version of 'pickaninny'
pollution – people who are living in spiritual darkness
posse – a group of young adults who form a clique
prentice – a young man
punny printers – extremely tight *batty riders*

queen – a respectful term for a woman, usually a Rastafarian woman

ragamuffin – a no-good person
ramp – to annoy someone or interfere, as in 'De gyal ramp wid me!'
rass – a backside; also one of the most violent cuss words (also see Understanding Patois earlier)
reach – to arrive, as in 'De bus not reach yet, mon!'
reality – ghetto reality or a hard life
reason – to debate or discuss
red-eye – an envious or greedy person
renk – foul-smelling; extreme rudeness
respect – commonly used greeting and farewell
rhaatid – like *rass,* but a gentler and more commonly used expletive; its meaning depends on intonation and facial expression, but usually expresses surprise
riddim – Jamaica's reggae has it
risto – a member of the elite (derives from aristocrat)
roots – coming from the people or communal experience
roughneck – a scoundrel or ragamuffin
rude boy – a ghetto criminal or vandal

runnings – whatever is happening; also means crafty business schemes

rush – to be the focus of things

samfi-man – a con man

satta – an invitation to sit, usually to meditate

sensie – marijuana (see *ganja*)

sipple – slippery

skank – to con; also an early 1970s dance move

sketel – a beautiful and promiscuous woman, one with many boyfriends

skin-out – to abandon whatever one is doing to have sex, usually at a stageshow

skylark – to dawdle or idle

slack – sexually explicit lyrics

smaddy – somebody

smallers – money; also known as *dunzer*

soke – to fool around, as in 'No soke wi' mi' ('Don't mess with me')

stageshow – a live music event

stoosh – airs of superiority, condescending behavior

structure – one's body, as in 'A fi mi structure!' ('It's my body!')

sufferer or suffrah – a poor but righteous person

swimp – shrimp

talawah – small but powerful, as in 'De byah likkle but 'im talawah'

tampie – marijuana (see *ganja)*

tea – any hot drink

ting – a thing or woman, as in 'A mi ting, she' ('That's my girlfriend'); also used for genitals (male or female)

trace – to cuss someone

trash – to dress up, to be well turned-out

wine – a sensuous dance movement

wolf – a Rastafarian imposter

work – sex

yard – a Jamaican's home

yardie – a gangster-type from the ghettoes, used by Jamaicans to mean anyone from Jamaica

yush – a greeting used by *rude boys*

Glossary

The following are common nouns and other terms used in this book.

abeng – goat horn

ackee – a tropical fruit popular as a breakfast dish

all-inclusive resort – a resort-hotel where all activities, meals, beverages, entertainment, etc, are included in the room rate

Antilles – the Caribbean islands

Arawak – the indigenous pre-Columbian inhabitants of Jamaica

balm – folk medicine

bammy – pancake-shaped cassava bread

bongo – a small drum; someone with strong African roots

calabash – a gourd whose hardened shell serves as a vessel for holding liquid

callaloo – a spinachlike vegetable

Carib – a warlike indigenous pre-Columbian people

cassava – a root crop used as a *breadkind*

cay – a coral isle

charcoal-burners – people who eke a meager living burning mangrove to make charcoal

cimaroon – a Spanish term for escaped slave

cockpits – limestone hillocks separated by canyons

custos – the colonial-era representative of the Crown at parish level

dancehall – a type of reggae, popularized through the 1980s, in which DJs perform over prerecorded music; place where dancehall is performed (usually an open space)

dancehall queen – a female habitué of dancehall clubs

DEA – US Drug Enforcement Agency

dreadlocks – uncut, uncombed hair, as worn by Rastafarians

dub – a remixed version of a recording with the vocal removed

endemic – native, or regularly found here (usually refers to species of flora and fauna)

festival – a fried biscuit or dumpling
free colored – the offspring of white slave owner and black slave; accorded some special rights

General Consumption Tax (GCT) – a charge of between 6.25% and 15% on most hotel bills and some restaurant or store purchases
go-go – exotic dancing; a staple of Jamaican nightlife

JABLUM – Jamaica Blue Mountain coffee processors
Jamintel – Jamaica International Telephone
jerk – meat or fish smoked and seasoned with tongue-lashing sauce
JLP – Jamaica Labour Party
JTB – Jamaica Tourist Board
JUTA – Jamaica Union of Travelers Association

Maroons – the community of escaped slaves who were antagonistic to the British during the colonial period; also their contemporary descendants
mento – the first indigenous Jamaican music
MoBay – slang for Montego Bay

NEPA – Negril Environmental Protection Area
NRCA – Natural Resources Conservation Authority
NWC – National Water Commission
Nyahbinghi – Rastafarian council site; also a type of drum

Ochi – slang for Ocho Rios

PADI – Professional Association of Dive Instructors

parish – one of 14 political districts
patty – thin crusty pastry filled with meat or vegetables, usually spiced
pirogue – a canoe hollowed from a large tree trunk; long wooden fishing boat
plantocracy – the community of plantation owners as a social and political entity
PNP – People's National Party

ragga – the type of digital reggae epitomizing dancehall music since 1985
Rasta, Rastafarian – an adherent of the religious philosophy Rastafarianism, whose main tenets hold that blacks are one of the 12 Lost Tribes of Israel, that Emperor Haile Selassie is divine, and that Selassie will lead Rastafarians to *Zion*
rum shop – a local bar, usually utilized by the working class

Sandals – a large chain of all-inclusive resort hotels
soca – the combination of soul and calypso music
sound system – a mobile disco using giant speakers, such as a *dancehall*
spliff – a joint (marijuana leaves rolled up in paper)
steel band – music group composed of drummers using oil drums
SuperClubs – a large chain of all-inclusive resort hotels

toast – when a DJ talks or sings over a record in a dancehall
TOJ – Telecommunications of Jamaica

Xaymaca – the Arawak term for Jamaica

yabbas – earthenware pots

Zion – the Promised Land (Ethiopia) in the Rastafarian religion

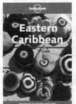

Index

Text

Bold indicates maps.

Boxed Text

MAP LEGEND

ROUTES

City | **Regional**

.... Freeway
.... Toll Freeway
.... Primary Road
.... Secondary Road
.... Tertiary Road
.... Dirt Road

.... Pedestrian Mall
.... Steps
.... Tunnel
.... Trail
.... Walking Tour
.... Path

TRANSPORTATION

.... Train
.... Metro
.... Bus Route
.... Ferry

HYDROGRAPHY

.... River; Creek
.... Canal
.... Lake
.... Spring; Rapids
.... Waterfalls
.... Dry; Salt Lake

BOUNDARIES

.... International
.... State
.... Marine Park
.... Parish
.... Disputed
.... Cliff

ROUTE SHIELDS

A1 Highway

AREAS

.... Beach
.... Building
.... Campus
.... Cemetery
.... Forest
.... Garden; Zoo
.... Golf Course
.... Park
.... Plaza
.... Reservation
.... Sports Field
.... Swamp; Mangrove

POPULATION SYMBOLS

◎ NATIONAL CAPITAL ...... National Capital
◉ PARISH CAPITAL ...... Parish Capital
● **Large City** ...... Large City
● **Medium City** ...... Medium City
● **Small City** ...... Small City
● Town; Village ...... Town; Village

MAP SYMBOLS

■ ...... Place to Stay
▼ ...... Place to Eat
● ...... Point of Interest

.... Airfield
.... Airport
.... Archeological Site; Ruin
.... Bank
.... Baseball Diamond
.... Battlefield
.... Bike Trail
.... Border Crossing
.... Buddhist Temple
.... Bus Station; Terminal
.... Cable Car; Chairlift
.... Campground
.... Castle
.... Cathedral
.... Cave

.... Church
.... Cinema
.... Dive Site
.... Embassy; Consulate
.... Footbridge
.... Gas Station
.... Hospital
.... Information
.... Internet Access
.... Lighthouse
.... Lookout
.... Mine
.... Mission
.... Monument
.... Mountain

.... Museum
.... Observatory
.... Park
.... Parking Area
.... Pass
.... Picnic Area
.... Police Station
.... Pool
.... Post Office
.... Pub; Bar
.... RV Park
.... Shelter
.... Shipwreck
.... Shopping Mall
.... Skiing - Cross Country

.... Skiing - Downhill
.... Stately Home
.... Surfing
.... Synagogue
.... Tao Temple
.... Taxi
.... Telephone
.... Theater
.... Toilet - Public
.... Tomb
.... Trailhead
.... Tram Stop
.... Transportation
.... Volcano
.... Winery

Note: Not all symbols displayed above appear in this book.

LONELY PLANET OFFICES

Australia
Locked Bag 1, Footscray, Victoria 3011
☎ 03 8379 8000 fax 03 8379 8111
email talk2us@lonelyplanet.com.au

USA
150 Linden Street, Oakland, California 94607
☎ 510 893 8555, TOLL FREE 800 275 8555
fax 510 893 8572
email info@lonelyplanet.com

UK
10a Spring Place, London NW5 3BH
☎ 020 7428 4800 fax 020 7428 4828
email go@lonelyplanet.co.uk

France
1 rue du Dahomey, 75011 Paris
☎ 01 55 25 33 00 fax 01 55 25 33 01
email bip@lonelyplanet.fr
www.lonelyplanet.fr

World Wide Web: www.lonelyplanet.com *or* AOL keyword: lp
Lonely Planet Images: lpi@lonelyplanet.com.au